The Colonization of North America 1492-1783

Herbert Eugene Bolton

And

Thomas Maitland Marshall

Alpha Editions

This edition published in 2019

ISBN : 9789353709396

Design and Setting By
Alpha Editions
email - alphaedis@gmail.com

THE COLONIZATION OF
NORTH AMERICA

1492–1783

BY

HERBERT EUGENE BOLTON, Ph. D.

PROFESSOR OF AMERICAN HISTORY IN THE UNIVERSITY OF CALIFORNIA

AND

THOMAS MAITLAND MARSHALL, Ph. D.

PROFESSOR OF HISTORY IN WASHINGTON UNIVERSITY

New York
THE MACMILLAN COMPANY
1936

: Printed in the United States of America :

PREFACE

This book represents an attempt to bring into one account the story of European expansion in North America down to 1783. Text-books written in this country as a rule treat the colonization of the New World as the history, almost solely, of the thirteen English colonies which formed the nucleus of the United States. The authors have essayed to write a book from a different point of view. It has been prepared in response to a clear demand for a text written from the standpoint of North America as a whole, and giving a more adequate treatment of the colonies of nations other than England and of the English colonies other than the thirteen which revolted. This demand is the inevitable result of the growing importance of our American neighbors and of our rapidly growing interest in the affairs of the whole continent, past as well as present.

The book is divided into three main parts: I. The Founding of the Colonies; II. Expansion and International Conflict; III. The Revolt of the English Colonies. The keynote is expansion. The spread of civilization in America has been presented against a broad European background. Not only colonial beginnings but colonial growth has been traced. This method accounts for the development of all geographical sections, and shows the relation of each section to the history of the continent as a whole. When thus presented the early history of Massachusetts, of Georgia, of Arkansas, of Illinois, or of California is no longer merely local history, but is an integral part of the general story. The colonies of the different nations are treated, in so far as practicable, in the chronological order of their development, the desire being to give a correct view of the time sequence in the development of the different regions.

A principal aim of the authors has been to make the book comprehensive. The activities of the Dutch and Swedes on the Atlantic mainland are given a large setting in both Europe and

v

the New World. The account of French expansion in North
America has been extended beyond the conventional presentation
to embrace the West Indies, the founding of Louisiana, and the
advance of the French pioneers across the Mississippi and up its
tributaries, and up the Saskatchewan to the Rocky Mountains.
The story of English expansion embraces not only the thirteen
colonies which revolted, but also the Bermudas, the West Indies,
Hudson Bay, Canada, and the Floridas. The treatment of the
new British possessions between 1763 and 1783 aims to present
in one view the story of the expansion of the whole English
frontier, from Florida to Hudson Bay.

The Spanish colonies of North America, in particular, have
been accorded a more adequate treatment than is usual in text-
books. To writers of United States history the Spaniards have
appeared to be mere explorers. Students of American history in a
larger sense, however, know that Spain transplanted Spanish
civilization and founded vast and populous colonies, represented
to-day by some twenty republics and many millions of people.
The notion, so widely current in this country, that Spain "failed"
as a colonizer, arises from a faulty method. In treating Spain's
part in the New World it has been customary, after recounting
the discovery of America, to proceed at once to territory now
within the United States—Florida, New Mexico, Texas—for-
getting that these regions were to Spain only northern outposts, and omitting the wonderful story of Spanish achievement
farther south. This book being a history of the colonization of
North America, Spain's great colonies in South America, now
powerful nations, fall beyond our geographical limits.

When approached from a new viewpoint many familiar things
appear in a new light. Hitherto, for example, the inter-colonial
wars in North America have been regarded mainly as a struggle
between France and England, and as confined chiefly to the
Canadian border. By following the larger story of European
expansion, however, it becomes plain that there was an Anglo-
Spanish and a Franco-Spanish, as well as a Franco-English
struggle for the continent, not to mention the ambitions and
efforts of Dutch, Swedes, Russians, and Danes. In nearly all the
general inter-colonial wars the Caribbean area and the Carolina-
Florida frontier were scenes of frequent conflicts quite as im-

portant as those waged on the Canadian border. Between France and Spain a border contest endured for more than a century and extended all the way from the Lesser Antilles to the Platte River. The Anglo-French contest ended in 1763; but the Anglo-Spanish conflict, which began in the sixteenth century, endured to the end of the eighteenth and, in the hands of the American offspring of Spain and England, to the middle of the nineteenth century.

Some teachers may for special reasons wish to treat the development of the colonies of a single nation as a continuous movement, or in longer periods, less frequently broken by happenings in the colonies of other nations. This can be done conveniently by grouping the chapters in the desired order. A continuous account of Spanish expansion is given in Chapters II, III, XIII, XVI, and XXI. A connected story of French America is told in Chapters IV, XIV, XV, XX. By omitting these and Chapter IX a continuous narrative of English expansion is obtained.

August, 1920.

103
75
20
_____
800 +
40
50
_____

TABLE OF CONTENTS

THE FOUNDING OF THE COLONIES

THE REVOLT OF THE ENGLISH COLONIES

LIST OF MAPS

xvi   LIST OF MAPS

THE COLONIZATION OF NORTH AMERICA

THE COLONIZATION OF NORTH AMERICA

THE FOUNDING OF THE COLONIES

CHAPTER I

THE BACKGROUND AND THE DISCOVERY

The fifteenth century witnessed the culmination of the Renaissance, the rise of the Turkish Empire, the shifting of the commercial center from the Mediterranean to the Atlantic, the discovery of America and the opening of the Cape route to India. Portugal and Spain started on their careers as great commercial and colonizing nations, the former destined for a time to control the commerce of the Far East, the other to possess more than half of the Americas and to dominate the Pacific.

GROWTH OF GEOGRAPHICAL KNOWLEDGE

Classical ideas of the world.—The discoveries of the century completely transformed the conceptions of geography. Greek and Roman scholars had agreed that there were three continents, Europe, Asia, and Africa, encircled by the ocean. Aristotle, Strabo, and others accepted the theory that the earth was a sphere, but they usually underestimated its size. Ptolemy, the greatest of the ancient geographers, made two fundamental errors, which most of the Arab and Christian scholars accepted. He depicted the Indian Ocean as an inland sea, and greatly extended Africa until it filled the entire southern hemisphere, China and Africa being connected.

Arab theories and Christian scholars.—The Arabs believed that the earth was a disc or ball, which was the center of the universe. The center of the earth's surface they called Arim, meaning the cupola of the earth. At the eastern extremity stood the pillars of Alexander, at the western the pillars of Hercules, while the north and south poles were equally distant from Arim. The Ptolemaic idea of Africa was accepted by most of the Arabs, but many of their later map makers decreased its size, cutting it off in the neighborhood of Cape Bojador on the African coast, and calling the region beyond the "Green Sea of Darkness." Others sketched in a great southern continent below Africa. The "Green Sea of Darkness" was filled with terrors, whirlpools ready to destroy the adventurous mariner, a sea of mist, fog, and vapor, peopled by monsters. If he escaped these as he ventured southward, he would come to a zone of torrid heat where no man could survive. Roger Bacon, the great Christian scientist, accepted the Arabian theories but supplemented them by a study of the classics. He believed that the habitable world was more than half of the whole circuit, an idea which was repeated in the *Imago Mundi* of Pierre d'Ailly, a work which may have influenced Columbus.

Early Asiatic contact with America.—Some scholars believe that the western coast of North America was visited by Asiatics long before the eastern shores were reached by Europeans. In 499 a Buddhist priest returned from a voyage claiming to have been to a country called Fusang, lying far to the east. The location of Fusang has interested numerous students, whose conjectures have been marshalled by Vining to prove that it was Mexico. Some have attributed the remarkable sporadic growth of cypress trees below Monterey, California, to this episode. The trend of opinion accepts ethnographic and linguistic similarities as of greater conclusiveness than recorded Chinese history. Belief in early Japanese contact with America rests on a similar basis.

The Northmen.—The first Europeans to venture far out on the Atlantic were the Northmen, a people but little touched by classical, Arabic, or Christian culture before their great period of expansion. The western sea to them had no terrors. Near the close of the eighth century they appeared in England; in 860 they sighted Iceland and in 874 commenced its colonization. Three years later they discovered Greenland, but it was not until 986 that Eric the Red colonized it. In the year 1000, Lief, the son of Eric, went in quest of a land to the west, of which he had

heard report. The result of the voyage was the discovery of Vin-
land, the exact whereabouts of which has been one of the puzzles
of history, some scholars claiming it to have been Nova Scotia,
others New England. Wherever it may have been, it probably
played no part in the Columbian discovery of America, for though
the settlements in Greenland continued until early in the fifteenth
century, scientists and mariners remained in almost complete
ignorance of the far-off activities of the Northmen.

Mediæval travelers.—During the period of the Crusades,
travel became more and more extensive. Returning crusaders
told of their adventures and of the lands which they had visited.
Pilgrims returning from the East increased the store of geographical knowledge and repeated marvelous tales of Russia, China,
and India, although none of them had first-hand knowledge. But
during the thirteenth century accurate information was obtained.
John de Plano Carpini, a Neapolitan Franciscan, went as a legate
of Pope Innocent IV to the Great Khan in Tartary. His *Book
of the Tartars* is the first reliable account of the empire of the
Great Mogul. A few years later William de Rubruquis was sent
by St. Louis of France to the same court, and returned to tell a
tale of wonders.

Between 1255 and 1265 two Venetians, Nicolo and Matteo
Polo, were trading in southern Russia, and eventually they
visited the court of Kublai Khan in Mongolia, later returning
to Europe. In 1271 they again visited the Far East, this time
accompanied by their nephew, Marco, whose account of their
journeyings is the most famous book of travel. Marco became
an official at the Mongol court and was sent on various missions
which carried him over a large part of China. He also learned
of the wonders of Cipango or Japan. In 1292 the Polos left
China, visited Java, India, and Ceylon, and eventually returned
to Europe. Their travels made known a vast region which had
previously lain almost outside the reckoning of geographers, and
gave to Europeans a fairly accurate as well as a fascinating account of the Far East.

Early maritime activities on the African coast.—While the Polos
were in Asia, mariners were beginning to explore outside the
Pillars of Hercules. In 1270 the Canaries were discovered by
Malocello and a few years later Genoese galleys reached Cape

Nun. In 1341 the Canaries were again visited, this time by an expedition from Lisbon, and in 1370 an Englishman, Robert Machin, who had eloped from Bristol with Anne d'Arfet, was driven from the French coast in a storm and came to Madeira where they both died from exposure. Some of the crew, however, returned to tell the tale. In 1402 a Norman, De Béthencourt, reached the Canaries and several of the islands were soon colonized.

Advance of maritime science.—As sea voyaging progressed, maritime science was also advancing. A large number of coast charts called Portolani were made, which plotted with remarkable accuracy the coast lines of Europe and northern Africa. Over four hundred of these charts are still in existence. Their accuracy was largely due to the use of the compass and astrolabe, which are known to have been invented before 1400.

PORTUGUESE DISCOVERIES

The rise of Portugal.—In the work of geográphical and commercial expansion Portugal now took the lead. The little kingdom, from a small territory to the north of the Douro, had gradually extended its domain to the southward by driving out the Moors. Its commercial importance began by the opening of a trade with England. From 1383 to 1433 Portugal was ruled by John the Great, and during his reign the oversea expansion of the country began.

Henry the Navigator.—The greatness of Portugal was largely due to one of King John's sons, Prince Henry. He was born in 1394 and at an early age became interested in furthering trade with the interior of Africa. In 1410 or 1412 he is said to have sent caravels down the coast. In 1415 he assisted in the capture of the Moorish stronghold of Ceuta, where he gained great military renown. In 1419 he was made governor of Algarve, the southern province of Portugal. He established himself at Sagres, on Cape St. Vincent, where he enlarged the old naval arsenal, built a palace, chapel, study, and observatory, and here it was that he spent the greater portion of his life.

Henry had three main objects: first, to open trade with the

interior of Africa; second, to found a colonial empire; third, to spread the Christian faith. A tale was current that somewhere in Africa lived a Christian king called Prester John, who was cut off from the world by Islam. To find his kingdom and unite with him in the overthrow of the Mohammedans was a natural ambition in a prince who had already assisted in the capture of Ceuta.

Henry gathered about him a group of trained mariners, some of whom were Italians, made a study of geography and navigation, instructed his captains, and sent them out from Lagos to find new markets. Between 1420 and 1430 Cape Blanco was discovered and the first slaves were brought back, this being the beginning of an extensive traffic. Four years later Cape Verde was reached, and in 1455 the Cape Verde Islands were discovered and the coast of Senegal explored. The results of the Portuguese explorations under Prince Henry were incorporated in a map of the world, made by Fra Mauro in the convent of Murano, near Venice.

Discovery of a route to India.—During the sixty years which followed the death of Prince Henry, 1460–1520, the Portuguese completed the exploration of the west coast of Africa, discovered a route to India, explored a considerable part of the eastern coast of North and South America, and founded a colonial empire. In 1486 Bartholomew Diaz passed the Cape of Good Hope and in 1498 Vasco da Gama, spurred on by the discoveries of Columbus, crossed the Indian Ocean to Calicut.

It has been customary to ascribe the diversion of trade from the eastern Mediterranean to the Cape of Good Hope route to the rise of the Turkish Empire, which was supposed to have cut the old lines of communication to the Far East. Recent investigation has shown that such is not the case. As Professor Lybyer says, "They [the Turks] were not active agents in deliberately obstructing the routes. . . . Nor did they make the discovery of new routes imperative. On the contrary they lost by the discovery of a new and superior route." This superiority was due to the fact that the Cape route was an all-water route which did not require the rehandling of goods and expensive caravan transportation. Not the Turk, but cheap freight rates, diverted trade from the Mediterranean to the Cape route.

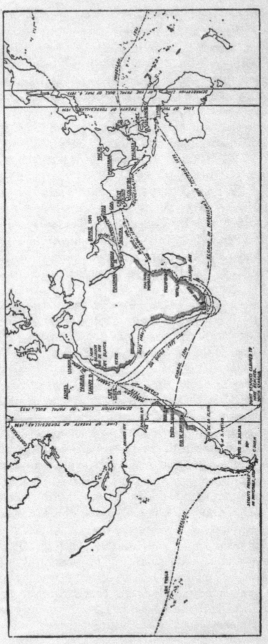

Portuguese Expansion and Magellan's Voyage

COLUMBUS AND THE DISCOVERY OF AMERICA

Early life of Columbus.—Meanwhile America had been discovered by Christopher Columbus, in the service of Spain. Much that was formerly believed to be true concerning the early life of Columbus recent research has proved to be false or to rest upon doubtful evidence. He was born at or near Genoa, probably in 1452, and was the son of a woolen weaver. Little is known of his education, but in some manner he acquired a knowledge of Latin, read the principal geographical works then accessible, and acquired a wide knowledge of navigation. Three books which he studied with care were the *General History and Geography* by Æneas Sylvius, the *Imago Mundi* of Pierre d'Ailly, and the *Travels* of Marco Polo.

He entered the marine service of Portugal, probably lived for a time on the island of Porto Santo, one of the Madeiras, visited the coast of Guinea, and sailed as far north as England. He married Felipa Moniz, a niece of Isabel Moniz, whose husband was Bartholomew Perestrello, who served under Prince Henry. It is probable that a correspondence occurred between Columbus and the Florentine geographer, Toscanelli, who is said to have suggested to the navigator the possibility of reaching the Indies by sailing west and to have sent him a copy of a chart which he had prepared. The Toscanelli map has not come down to us, the so-called reproduction of it being an adaptation of Behaim's globe of 1492. Through these various influences Columbus conceived the plan of seeking new lands in the Atlantic and became convinced of the feasibility of opening a western route to the Indies.

His sojourn in Spain.—After unsuccessfully urging his views in Portugal, in 1484 Columbus went to Spain, where he presented himself at the court and made the acquaintance of many influential persons. He also sent his brother Bartholomew to obtain assistance in western exploration from Henry VII of England. Columbus met with slight encouragement in Spain, and decided to seek French aid, but just as he was making his departure he was recalled, Queen Isabella having been brought to a favorable decision by Fray Juan Pérez, a former confessor, by Luis de Santangel, the treasurer of Aragon, by the Count of Medina-Celi, and by the Marquesa de Moya.

His commission.—Columbus was given a commission authorizing him to explore and trade. It said nothing of a route to the
Indies. The enterprise of discovery was essentially a new one,
and it was natural that the first patent should contain only general provisions. Indeed, the document was so brief and incom-
plete that many supplementary orders had to be issued before
the expedition was ready. In return for services and to provide
a representative of Spanish authority in anticipated discoveries,
Columbus was ennobled and made admiral, viceroy, and governor-general in such lands as he might add to the Castilian realm.
These offices were patterned after well-known institutions then
in use in Spain. The titles were to be hereditary in Columbus's
family. The admiral was to have a tenth of the net profits of
trade and precious metals within his discoveries. By contributing an eighth of the expense of commercial ventures, he was entitled to an additional eighth of the profits from trade. To encourage the expedition all duties on exports were remitted.

Outfitting the expedition.—The story that Isabella pawned her
jewels to equip the expedition is now disproved, the royal share
of the money apparently being loaned to the Castilian treasury
by Luis de Santangel. The total cost of outfitting was probably
somewhat less than $100,000, of which Columbus or his friends
furnished an eighth. Three vessels, the *Santa Maria*, the
Pinta, and the *Niña*, were provided. The number who sailed
is variously estimated at from ninety to one hundred and twenty
men.

The discovery.—In August, 1492, the three vessels sailed from
Palos to the Canaries, those islands then being a possession of
Spain which she had acquired from Portugal in 1479. During
the entire colonial period they were an important factor in navigation, being a place for refitting before the long trans-Atlantic
voyage. The vessels left the Canaries on September 6 and sailed
almost due west. They met with fair weather, but the length
of the voyage caused much complaint, which resulted in a plot
to get rid of Columbus. The Admiral succeeded in quelling the
mutiny, however, and shortly afterward land was sighted.

On the evening of October 11 a light in the distance was twice
seen by the commander, and before morning the moonlight disclosed to the lookout of the *Pinta* a sandy beach. The landfall

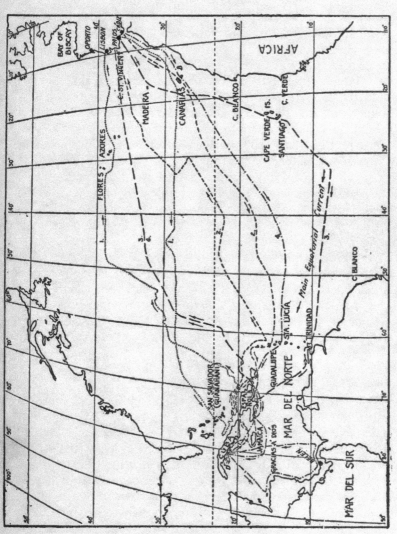

The Four Voyages of Columbus

was a small coral island of the Bahamas, which Columbus named San Salvador and which was probably the one now called Watling's Island. Believing that he had reached the Indies, he called the inhabitants Indians, a name which has clung ever since to American aborigines.

Sojourn in the West Indies.—Through all of his sojourn in the West Indies, Columbus was filled with the idea that he had found the Indies. Hearing of Cuba and believing that it was Cipango, he planned to visit the mainland and go to the city of Guisay, the Quinsai of Marco Polo. From the Bahamas he proceeded to Cuba and explored the eastern third of its northern coast. He despatched an interpreter to the Grand Khan, but instead of a mighty city, an Indian village was discovered. There Europeans first saw the smoking of tobacco. From Cuba the expedition went to Haiti, which Columbus named Española (Little Spain), corrupted in English to Hispaniola, and there the *Santa María* was wrecked.

The return voyage.—Having built a fort on the northern shore of Española not far from its westernmost point, which he named La Navidad (the Nativity) because the neighboring harbor was entered on Christmas day, Columbus left forty-four of the crew with ample provisions, implements, and arms, and began the return voyage on January 4, 1493. Two violent storms were encountered, but both were weathered, and on March 4 the vessels came to anchor in the mouth of the Tagus.

His reception.—In Lisbon the news of the discovery created great excitement. The King of Portugal invited Columbus to court and entertained him royally. On March 13 he sailed for Spain, arriving at Palos two days later. The citizens adjourned business for the day; bells were rung, and at night the streets were illumined with torches. From there he proceeded to Seville and then to the court at Barcelona, where the greatest honors were bestowed upon him. He was allowed to be seated in the presence of the sovereigns, who showed the keenest interest in his specimens of flora and fauna, pearls and golden trinkets, but especially in the Indians whom he had brought from Española. The theory that he had reached the outlying parts of the Indies was readily accepted, and the sovereigns at once prepared to take possession of the newly discovered lands.

The line of Demarcation.—The king of Portugal, jealous of Spain's triumph, is said to have planned to send a fleet across the Atlantic to dispute the Spanish claims. Ferdinand and Isabella hurried a messenger to Rome asking the pope to confirm their rights to the new discoveries. Accordingly, on May 4, 1493, Pope Alexander VI assigned to Spain all lands west of a meridian one hundred leagues west of the Azores and Cape Verde Islands. King John was not satisfied, and a year later, by the treaty of Tordesillas, a division line was fixed at 370 leagues west of Cape Verde Islands. This change gave Portugal title to her later discoveries on the Brazilian coast, though it lessened her possessions in the Orient.

READINGS

GROWTH OF GEOGRAPHICAL KNOWLEDGE

Beazley, C. R., *The Dawn of Modern Geography; Prince Henry the Navigator*, 1–105; Fischer, J., *The Discoveries of the Northmen in America;* Fiske, John, *The Discovery of America*, I, 151–255, 363–381; Hovgaard, W., *The Voyages of the Norsemen to America*, 221–255; Marco Polo, *The Book of Ser Marco Polo the Venetian*, Yule ed.; Olson, J. E., and Bourne, E. G., eds., *The Northmen, Columbus, and Cabot (Original Narratives of Early American History)*, 3–84; Vining, E. J., *An Inglorious Columbus; or evidence that Hwi Shan . . . discovered America in the Fifth Century*; Winsor, Justin, *Narrative and Critical History of America*, I, 1–58; Fossum, A., *The Norse Discovery of America;* Steensby, H. P., *The Norsemen's Route to Wineland;* Larson, L. M., "The Church in North America (Greenland) in the Middle Ages," in *The Catholic Historical Review*, V, 175–194.

PORTUGUESE DISCOVERIES

Beazley, C. R., *Prince Henry the Navigator*, 123–307; Bourne, E. G., "Prince Henry the Navigator," in *Essays in Historical Criticism*, 173–189; Cheyney, E. P., *European Background of American History*, 60–70; Helps, Arthur, *The Spanish Conquest in America*, I, 1–54; Jayne, K. G., *Vasco da Gama and his Successors*, 7–240; Lybyer, A. H., "The Ottoman Turks and the Routes of Oriental Trade," in *The English Historical Review*, XXX, 577–588; Major, R. H., *The Discoveries of Prince Henry the Navigator;* Martins, J. P. O., *The Golden Age of Prince Henry the Navigator*, 66–84, 205–231; Stephens, H. M., *Portugal*, 115–248; Vander Linden, H., "Alexander VI., and the Demarcation of the Maritime and Colonial Dominions of Spain and Portugal," in *American Historical Review*, XXII, 1–20.

COLUMBUS

Biggar, H. P., "The New Columbus," in Am. Hist. Assoc., *Ann. Rpt.*, *1912*, pp. 97–104; Bourne, E. G., *Spain in America*, 8–32; Channing, Edward,

History of the United States, I, 14–25; Hart, A. B., *American History told by Contemporaries*, I, 28–48; Helps, Arthur, *The Spanish Conquest in America*, I, 55–88; Herrera, Antonio, *Historia General;* Las Casas, Bartholomew, *Historia de las Indias;* Major, R. H., *Select Letters of Columbus;* Markham, Clements, *Life of Columbus;* Navarrete, M. F., *Colección de los Viages y Descubrimientos;* Olson, J. E., and Bourne, E. G., eds., *The Northmen, Columbus, and Cabot (Original Narratives)*, 89–383; Peter Martyr, *De Orbe Novo* (F. A. McNutt, trans.); Richman, I. B., *The Spanish Conquerors*, 1–63; Thacher, J. B., *Columbus;* Vignaud, Henry, *Toscanelli and Columbus:* Winsor, Justin, *Columbus.*

CHAPTER II

THE FOUNDING OF NEW SPAIN (1492-1543)

SPAIN DURING THE CONQUEST

The discoveries of Columbus opened to Spain the opportunity to found a great colonial empire in the new world. For this work Spain had been prepared by the welding of the nation which was perfected during the reign of Ferdinand and Isabella.

The Christian reconquest.—In the eighth century the Mohammedan Berbers had overthrown the Visigothic kingdom, the unconquered Christian princes retiring to the mountain regions of the north. Gradually they reconquered the country. By 910 they had established the kingdoms of León and Navarre, and the county of Barcelona. By 1037 León and Castile had united and conquered a wide tract south of the Douro River. Aragon, originally a Frankish country, had also become an independent kingdom. By 1150 almost two-thirds of the peninsula had been conquered; Portugal now extended from the Minho River to the Tagus; Castile occupied the central region, and Aragon had incorporated Barcelona and Catalonia. During the next two centuries the rest of the peninsula, except the small kingdom of Granada, was conquered, and Aragon established her power in the Balearic Isles, Sardinia, and southern Italy. In 1469 Isabella of Castile married Ferdinand of Aragon, thus uniting the two great states. In 1481 they made war upon Granada, completing its conquest in the year of the discovery of America. All of these changes had been chiefly of rulers, the great body of the people remaining of the original Iberian stock.

Lack of unity.—But there was neither unity of speech, customs, nor institutions. There were three main religious groups, Christians, Mohammedans, and Jews. The people were also divided into social classes, nobility, clergy, common people, and slaves. The ranks and privileges of the nobility varied greatly, some having immense estates and almost sovereign powers, others being landless soldiers of fortune. Castile was the land of castles. The nobles were turbulent and warlike. They delighted in chivalry, which probably attained a higher development in Spain than in any other country. Furthermore, there were three great military orders, which had grown in strength during the Moorish wars; these were the Knights of Santiago, of Calatrava, and of Alcántara, at the head of each of which was a grand master. The orders, the landed nobility, and the church owned about one-third of the land and controlled large military forces. The cities were also powerful; they were strongly fortified, regulated their own affairs, and many of them had great fleets and extensive commerce. Life outside of the cities was largely pastoral, wool growing being the principal industry. Both Castile and Aragon contained governing bodies called *Cortes*, to which some of the larger cities sent representatives, but they were of little importance, most of the work of lawmaking being done by the sovereign acting with his Council of State.

Establishment of unity.—To bring the entire country into religious and political unity was the great task of Ferdinand and Isabella. This was accomplished partly through the *Hermandad* and the organization of several royal councils. The *Hermandad*, originally a local police, was organized as a state police; captured offenders were punished before local officers of the crown called *alcaldes*. Turbulent nobles and brigands were made to feel the long arm of the royal power. The nobles were also curbed by transferring the grand masterships of the military orders to the crown and the sovereigns resumed control of many estates which had been granted to churches and nobles. The royal council of twelve had been the principal governing body. Under Ferdinand and Isabella it was divided into three councils, justice, state, and finance. Other councils were added from time to time; among these was the Council of the Inquisition, whose business it was to stamp out heresy. By its efforts unbaptized Jews and Moors were expelled. The rulers also sent royal officers called *corregidores* into the local communities, who gradually extended the powers of the crown at the expense of local government. Thus were laid the foundations of an absolute monarchy, which, in the sixteenth century, became the most influential in Europe.

Charles V.—The prestige of Spain was greatly enhanced in the

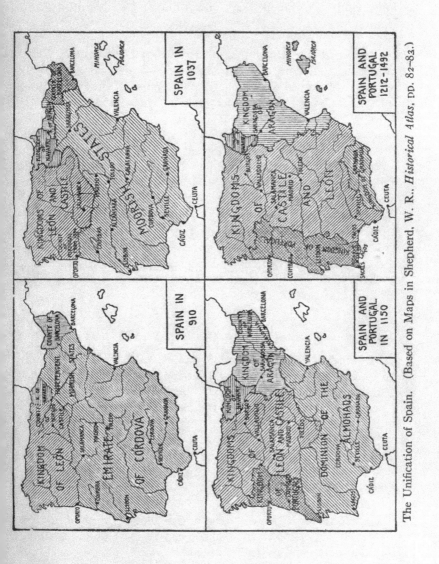

The Unification of Spain. (Based on Maps in Shepherd, W. R. *Historical Atlas*, pp. 82–83.)

sixteenth century by the Emperor Charles V, the grandson of
Ferdinand and Isabella. From his mother he inherited Spain,
Naples, and Sicily, and possessions in the new world and the Far
East; from his father the Netherlands; from his grandfather,
Maximilian I, the Hapsburg inheritance in Germany. By election he became Holy Roman Emperor. The larger part of the
reign was occupied by three great European contests; a series
of struggles with Francis I of France for the control of Italy, the
Reformation in Germany, and the curbing of the westward advance of the Turks. The almost constant wars of the Emperor
kept him away from Spain nearly his entire time, but he used the
centralized system of Ferdinand and Isabella to supply him with
soldiers and money. The constant drain of treasure overtaxed
the resources of Spain, but the rich mines of the new world furnished the surplus for his vast undertakings. The fact that
Charles was successful in retaining his power in Italy, coupled
with his struggle against the Protestants and the Turks, made
him the recognized protector of the Catholic church. His reign,
marked by many sad failures in Europe, witnessed a phenomenal
expansion of Spain's colonies.

THE OCCUPATION OF THE WEST INDIES

The rule of Columbus in the Indies.—When Columbus discovered a new world for Spain, that country was placed in a new
situation, and a settled colonial policy was developed only with
experience. A department of Indian affairs was created at once
and put in charge of Fonseca, a member of the royal council.
A combined interest in commerce, religion, and colonization was
shown in all the arrangements for a second voyage by Columbus,
but commerce was the primary object. At first it was planned
to send a thousand colonists, but so eager were the applicants
that fifteen hundred embarked. The expedition was equipped
at the queen's expense, and most of the colonists were in her pay.

Reaching Española in November, 1493, Columbus found
Navidad destroyed by Indians; he accordingly established a new
settlement, named Isabella, at a point farther east. Leaving his
brother Diego in charge, Columbus explored the southern coast
of Cuba, discovered Jamaica, and circumnavigated Española.

Complaints being made against his administration, in 1495 Columbus returned to Spain to defend himself. Shortly after his departure, gold being found in the southern part of Española, the new town of Santo Domingo was founded there and became the capital. Other men were eager for commercial adventure, and, in response to their demands, in 1495 trade in the Indies was opened to all Spaniards, at their own expense. Columbus regarded this an infringement upon his rights, and on his return to Spain he protested, but to little purpose.

In 1498 Columbus sailed on a third voyage, taking some two hundred colonists. On the way he discovered the mainland of South America near the Orinoco River, and, farther west, valuable pearl fisheries. During his absence a civil war had occurred in Española, and, at the end of two years of trouble with the contending factions, Columbus was sent to Spain in chains by Bobadilla, a royal commissioner, who remained to govern in his place. The charges against Columbus were dismissed, but he was not restored to his rule in the Indies. In 1502 Nicolás de Ovando was sent to replace Bobadilla, taking with him 2500 new colonists.

Spread of settlement in the West Indies.—After 1496 Santo Domingo became the chief town of Española and the seat of Spanish rule in America. In rapid succession posts and mining camps were established in various parts of the island, and by 1513 there were seventeen chartered towns in Española alone. Santo Domingo at that time had a population of fifteen hundred persons. It was some fifteen years after the settlement of Española before the other islands began to be occupied, attention being first given to making cruises along the southern mainland. Ovando began the conquest of the other islands, however, and Diego Columbus, his successor, prosecuted the work with more vigor. In 1508 Ponce de León was sent to conquer Porto Rico, and in 1511 the present city of San Juan was founded. The settlement of Jamaica was begun in 1509 by Esquivel, under orders of Diego Columbus. Several towns were soon established, and a shipyard opened. In 1537 Jamaica became a possession of the family of Columbus, with the title of Marquis till 1557, then of Duke of La Vega. In 1508 Ocampo circumnavigated Cuba and in 1511 Velasquez began the conquest of the island. Santiago

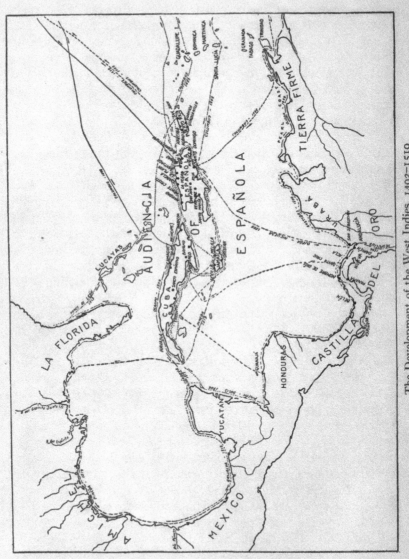

The Development of the West Indies, 1492–1519

was founded in 1514 and Havana a year later. Thus the West Indies became the nursery of Spanish culture and institutions in America.

Gold mining was important in Española for a time, but the mines were soon exhausted. In all the islands cotton, sugar, and cattle raising soon acquired some proportions, but the native population rapidly decreased, negro slaves were expensive, and rich profits attracted the settlers to the mainland; consequently, after the first quarter century the islands declined in prosperity and Porto Rico was for a time actually abandoned.

BEGINNINGS OF COLONIAL ADMINISTRATION AND POLICY

The Casa de Contratación.—For ten years Fonseca remained at the head of American affairs, being in effect colonial minister. In 1503 the Casa de Contratación or House of Trade was established at Seville, to direct commerce, navigation, and all related matters of the Indies. In charge of the Casa was a board of officials, including factors, treasurer, auditor, and notary. They maintained a warehouse for receiving all goods and treasure going to or from the islands. They were required to keep informed of the needs of the Indies, assemble and forward supplies, organize trading expeditions, and instruct and license pilots. Later on a professorship of cosmography was established for the purpose of instructing pilots, who were required to keep diaries of their voyages. This provision resulted in the accumulation of a vast amount of historical and geographical information in the government archives, much of which is still extant.

The Council of the Indies.—Spanish America was a possession of the sovereigns of Castile, as heirs of Queen Isabella, under whose patronage America had been discovered. At first, legislative and political matters relating to the Indies had been considered by the sovereigns in consultation with Fonseca and other personal advisors, but to supervise these matters a new board was gradually formed. In 1517 it was formally organized, among the members being Fonseca and Peter Martyr, the historian. In 1524 the board was reorganized as the Council of the Indies. This body was the supreme legislative and judicial authority, under the king, of Spanish-America. The Casa de Contratación was subordinate to the Council, which likewise supervised all civil and ecclesiastical appointments in the colonies. Usually some of the members of the Council had served in the Indies.

The governors-general and the audiencia.—Ovando ruled in Española until 1509, when Diego Columbus, son of Christopher, after a struggle for his hereditary rights, was made admiral and governor-general of the Indies. Complaint against Diego's administration led to the establishment at Santo Domingo of a superior court with appeals from the decisions of the governor-general. This was the germ of the Audiencia of Santo Domingo, which, for a time, was the administrative head of the greater part of the Indies. By decree of September 14, 1524, the Audiencia was formally established, with a president, four judges, a fiscal, a deputy grand-chancellor, and other officers. ·

The towns.—In the early sixteenth century the colonial towns showed some political activity. In 1507 the municipalities of Española sent delegates to Spain to petition for the rights enjoyed by Spanish towns. The request was granted, and, among other privileges, fourteen towns were granted coats-of-arms. Conventions of delegates from the towns were often held in these early days, to consider common needs and to draw up memorials to the home government. In 1530 Charles V decreed that such conventions should not be held without his consent, and the tendency thereafter was toward stronger absolutism and away from local political life. But there never was a time when the right of petition was not freely exercised, and with great effect on actual administration. In the sixteenth century the towns sometimes elected proctors to represent them before the Council of the Indies. In the seventeenth century they sometimes employed residents of Spain for this purpose.

In the colonial towns, both Spanish and native, there was some degree of self-government. Each Spanish town had its *cabildo* composed of *regidores*. In 1523 the *regidores* were made elective, but the tendency was to secure the office by purchase or inheritance, as was the case in Spain. The functions of the *cabildos* were similar to those of a New England town council, embracing legislation, police matters, care of highways, sanitation, and analogous functions.

Emigration.—The notion sometimes voiced that Spain did not
"colonize" America is unfounded. Emigration to America was
encouraged by subsidies and other means, and in early days large
colonies were sent by government authority. It has been seen,
for example, that on his first three voyages Columbus took over
about 100, 1500, and 200 colonists respectively, and that Ovando
took 2500. During the entire sixteenth century the emigration
to America averaged from 1000 to 2000 persons per year. In
general, emigration was restricted to Spaniards of undoubted
orthodoxy, hence Jews, Moors, and recent converts were excluded. Naturalization was relatively easy, however, and by
means of it many foreigners were admitted. Portuguese, for
example, were numerous in the Indies, especially among the
seamen. Charles V adopted the liberal policy of opening the
Indies to subjects of all parts of his empire, but Philip II returned to the more exclusive practice. Later on, as the trade
monopoly broke down, it became necessary to admit foreign
traders to American ports, but they were required to return
within specified periods.

Married Spaniards emigrating from Spain were urged or even
required to take their families, but the emigration of unmarried
Spanish women was discouraged. Intermarriage of Spaniards
with native women was favored by the authorities, and, as a large
majority of the immigrants were single men, the practice was
common, either with or without formal sanction. An effort to
supply the lack of women by sending white slaves to the islands
failed, and in 1514 marriage with Indian women was approved
by royal order. With the opening of Mexico and Peru the island
colonies were in danger of depopulation. To prevent this from
happening, migration to the mainland was forbidden under heavy
penalties (1525–1526), and the recruiting of new conquering
expeditions in the islands was prohibited. To secure settlers for
Española, in 1529 attractive feudal lordships were offered to
founders of colonies.

Agriculture.—Agriculture in the West Indies was encouraged
by all means available. Duties on imports were remitted for a
term of years. In 1497 the sovereigns ordered a public farm established to provide loans of stock and seed, to be paid back by
colonists within a term of years. Free lands were granted to

settlers, with a reservation of the precious metals to the crown. Special orders were given for mulberry and silkworm culture. These efforts to promote agriculture in the West Indies, however, were made largely nugatory by commercial restrictions and the superior attractions of the mainland.

Indian policy.—Columbus found Española inhabited, it was estimated, by a quarter of a million of Indians, and the other islands similarly populated. He was instructed to treat the natives well and to do all in his power to convert them. The sovereigns frequently repeated these orders, and commanded that the natives be treated as free men and paid for their work. But the shortage of a labor-supply and the relative position of the two races led quickly and almost inevitably to the practical enslavement of the weaker.

Encomiendas.—Following the rebellion of 1495, the subdued natives were put under tribute in the form of specified amounts of products, commutable to labor. In 1497 a practice was begun of allotting lands to Spaniards, the forced labor of the natives going with the land. Complaint being made by priests and seculars that the Indians could neither be made to work, nor be taught or converted without restraint, in 1503 it was ordered that they should be congregated (*congregados*) in permanent villages and put under protectors (*encomenderos*), who were obliged to teach and protect them, and were empowered to exact their labor, though for pay and as free men. This provision contained the essence of the encomienda system, which was designed to protect and civilize the native, as well as to exploit him. But there was always danger that the former aim would yield to the latter, and, contrary to royal will, the condition of the natives fast became one of practical slavery.

Depopulation of the islands.—Moreover, in a very short time the islands became nearly depopulated of natives. Many were slain in the wars of conquest and during rebellions, or died of starvation while in hiding. Perhaps a greater number died of smallpox, measles, and other diseases brought from Europe. The result was that by 1514 the native population of Española was reduced to 14,000. A similar reduction of native population occurred in the other islands as they were successively occupied.

Indian slavery.—Indian slavery was not generally allowed in theory. But the Lesser Antilles, the Bahamas, and Florida were found to be inhabited by hostile cannibals, who were regarded as fair prize for enslavement. As early as 1494 Columbus suggested that permission be given to sell Caribs. In 1498 he took a cargo of six hundred of them to Spain. Soon it became an accepted legal principle that cannibals and rebellious Indians could be enslaved. The idea was encouraged by the lack of Spanish laborers, and by the disappearance of the native population of Española. Slave-hunting was soon extended, therefore, to the coasts of Florida, Pánuco, and other parts of the mainland. The practice was continued, as the frontier advanced, to the eighteenth century when, for example, Apaches of Texas and Pawnees of Kansas were often sold to work on plantations in Louisiana or Cuba.

Las Casas.—Numerous prominent Spaniards in the Indies early opposed encomiendas on moral grounds. Among them the most aggressive was Father Bartolomé de las Casas. He had come to the Indies as a layman, had held an encomienda after becoming a priest, but in 1514 had renounced it. In the following year he went to Spain, secured the appointment of a commission of Geronymite friars to enforce the laws regarding Indians in the islands, and was himself made Protector of the Indians. In 1516 he returned to Española, but, being dissatisfied with the work of the commission, he returned to Spain, where he favored negro slavery as a means of sparing the natives. In 1521 he tried to found a Utopian colony on Tierra Firme, to furnish an humane example, but through unfortunate circumstances it failed completely.

EXPLORATION OF THE MAINLAND COASTS AND THE SEARCH FOR A STRAIT

Voyages toward the South.—The discovery by Columbus (1498) of pearls on the southern mainland, combined with the Portuguese successes in India, gave new incentive to voyages, and within the next few years many thousands of miles of coastline of South and Central America were explored in the interest of trade, discovery, and international rivalry. In 1499 Ojeda explored from near Paramaribo to the Gulf of Maracaibo. In 1500

Pinzón and DeLepe sailed north to the Pearl Coast from points near 8° and 10° south, respectively, and Bastidas made known the coast from the Gulf of Maracaibo to Nombre de Diós, on the Isthmus of Panama. The chain of discoveries was carried in 1502 from the north shore of Honduras to Nombre de Diós by the fourth voyage of Columbus, made primarily in search of a strait through the troublesome lands which he had discovered. In 1504 La Cosa and Vespucius, during a trading voyage on the Gulf of Urabá, ascended the Atrato River two hundred miles by a route which has since been proposed as an interoceanic canal. Meanwhile numerous other voyages were made to the Pearl Coast for commercial purposes. They added little more to geographical knowledge, but led to colonization on the southern mainland.

Portuguese competition.—Spanish efforts to find a passage to the Indian Ocean by going to the southward were stimulated by the Portuguese voyages in the same direction. In 1500 Cabral, on his way to India, took possession for Portugal at a point near 18° south latitude on the Brazilian coast. In the following year a Portuguese expedition, in which Americus Vespucius was pilot, explored the coast from 5° to 32³ south latitude, discovering the La Plata River on the way. It was to this voyage of Vespucius, made in the interest of Portugal, that America owes its name. First applied to South America, it was soon extended to the northern continent. A Portuguese voyage made in 1503 by Jaques, in search of a passage to the East, is said to have reached 52° south.

Establishment of the Portuguese Empire in the East.—Gama's voyage was promptly followed by the founding of Portuguese colonies in the East. The chief actor in this work was Alburquerque, who accompanied an expedition to India in 1503 and became viceroy in 1509, an office which he held until his death in 1515. During his rule the Portuguese established themselves at Goa, which gave them control of the Malabar coast, and at Malacca, from which point they were able to control the trade of the Malay Peninsula and the Spice Islands. Ormuz was captured, making them supreme in the commerce of the Persian Gulf. In succeeding years they acquired Ceylon and established trading settlements in Burma, China, and Japan.

Continued quest for a strait.—These Portuguese successes were an incentive to further Spanish efforts to find the strait. In 1506 Vicente Yáñez Pinzón, accompanied by Juan de Solís, in search of a passage explored the Gulf of Honduras and eastern Yucatan from Guanajá Islands, the western limit of Columbus's voyage, to the Island of Caría. In 1509 Solís, in the service of Spain, reached 42° south, while in search of the desired route. The discovery of the Pacific Ocean by Balboa in 1513 aroused Spain to renewed efforts to find the strait. Exploration was at once undertaken on the southern shores of Panama, and in 1515 Solís again was sent down the Brazilian coast. Reaching the La Plata River, he was killed and eaten by the savages.

Magellan and Elcano.—The solution of the problem of the southern strait was left for Ferdinand Magellan, a Portuguese who had seen service in the Far East. Returning to Portugal, he proposed to the king the opening of a route to the East by going west. His offer being refused, like Columbus he turned to Spain, where his plan found favor. Sailing with five vessels in 1519, he discovered the Straits of Magellan and crossed the Pacific Ocean to the Philippines, where he was killed in 1521. Part of the crew, led by Elcano, continued round the world and reached Spain in September, 1522, after one of the most remarkable voyages in all history.

The mapping of the Gulf coast.—Meanwhile the outlines of the Gulf of Mexico had been made known, and by 1525 the continued search for the strait and efforts to settle on the mainland had carried Spanish explorers nearly the whole length of the North Atlantic coast. In 1508 Ocampo had circumnavigated Cuba. Sailing from Porto Rico in 1513 Juan Ponce de León, who was interested in slave-hunting and exploration, discovered and coasted the Peninsula of Florida.

Four years later Córdova, under a license from Velásquez, governor of Cuba, explored Yucatan, finding signs of large cities and of wealth. The reports aroused new interest in the mainland, and Velásquez sent out Grijalva, who coasted the shore from Yucatan to Pánuco River, securing on the way twenty thousand dollars' worth of gold. To take advantage of Grijalva's discoveries, Velásquez organized another expedition and put it in charge of Hernando Cortés. Garay, governor of Jamaica, also sent out an expedition, under Pineda, with instructions to seek new lands and look for a strait. Sailing north to the mainland in 1519, Pineda completed the mapping of the Gulf by coasting from Florida to Vera Cruz and back. On the way west he discovered the Mississippi River, which he called Río del Espíritu Santo. On the strength of Pineda's discoveries, Garay now secured a patent to the northern Gulf shore, and undertook to colonize the province of Amichel.

The North Atlantic coast.—The exploration of the North Atlantic coast soon followed. In 1513 De León had rounded the Peninsula of Florida. Eight years later Gordillo, sailing from Española in the employ of Ayllón, and Quexos, a slave hunter whom Gordillo met on the way, reached the mainland at 33° 30′, near Cape Fear in a region called Chicora. Ayllón in 1523 secured a patent authorizing him to seek a strait in the north and found a colony. In Ayllón's employ, Quexos in 1525 coasted north perhaps to 40°. In the same year Stephen Gómez, under contract to seek a northern strait, descended the coast from Nova Scotia to Florida. Over the northern part of his route he had been preceded by the English explorer John Cabot (1497). With the return of Gómez the entire Atlantic shore from the Straits of Magellan to Nova Scotia had been explored by expeditions made in the name of Spain.

THE MAYAS AND THE NAHUAS

A Double Movement.—Having subdued the islands and run the eastern coastline, the Spaniards proceeded to take possession of the mainland. To the southward they were attracted by trade, rumors of gold, and the hope of finding a strait leading to the East. To the westward they were drawn by the semi-civilized Nahuas and Mayas, who lived in substantial towns, possessed accumulated wealth, had a stable population used to hard labor, and were worth exploiting. The advance into the interior was a double movement, one proceeding north from a base on the Isthmus of Panama, the other radiating in all directions from the Valley of Mexico.

Two Civilizations.—The Nahuas occupied Mexico south of a line drawn roughly from Tampico through Guadalajara to the Pacific Ocean. The Mayas lived principally in Yucatán and

Guatemala. The Nahuas had acquired much of their culture from the Mayas, and the cultural areas overlapped. These peoples had several features in common. They lived in substantial pueblos, or towns, and practiced agriculture by means of irrigation, raising extensively maize, beans, potatoes, and tobacco. Maguey was a staple crop in the Valley of Mexico and henequén in Yucatán. Mayas and Nahuas both lacked important domestic animals. They were dominated by a powerful priesthood and practiced slavery and human sacrifice.

Maya Characteristics.—Certain features distinguished the two civilizations. The Mayas had imposing architectural structures devoted to religion, notably at Palenque, Uxmal, and Chichén Itza. They had made considerable advance toward written records in the form of ideograms. More than 1500 Maya manuscripts, written on henequén, have been preserved but are as yet in the main undeciphered.

The Nahuas.—The Nahuas had made remarkable progress in astronomical calculations, and their worship was closely connected with the planetary system. The most notable religious monuments were the pyramids which are widely scattered over the country. Some of these, it is believed, are of Maya origin. Calendars of great perfection had been devised, the famous Calendar Stone now preserved in the National Museum at Mexico being one of the rare treasures of archæology. The Nahuas had achieved a more highly developed agriculture than the Mayas, had a stronger military and political organization, and larger and better constructed towns. Of these the most notable was Mexico (Tenochtitlán). It was built in a lake in the center of the great valley of Anáhuac, and had a population of perhaps 60,000 when the Spaniards came.

Nahua History.—The Nahuas had come from the north about the time when the Germanic tribes were overrunning southern Europe. According to their own traditions the first Nahua tribe, the Toltecs, entered the Valley of Mexico in 596 A. D., and were overpowered by the barbarians whom they found there, but civilized them. In succeeding centuries they were followed by other Nahua tribes, whose names are now borne by numerous cities in the Valley of Mexico. Among the late comers were the Aztecs, who, according to tradition, founded their lake-city in 1325 A. D. Their military stronghold was the crag of Chapultepec, where the presidential mansion of Mexico now stands.

The Triple Alliance.—Among the numerous cities or pueblos built by these struggling tribes four emerged into prominence. First Atzcapotzalco, then Tezcuco, then Mexico acquired supremacy. Placing itself at the head of a triple alliance (Mexico, Tezcuco, and Tacuba), Mexico in the fifteenth century engaged in a series of conquests which carried the Aztec power to the Gulf of Mexico, to the Pacific Ocean, and well into the Maya regions of Central America. War became a national impulse, closely identified with the religion of which human sacrifice was a central feature. The "empire" was but a military overlordship, however, and had for its chief objects tribute and human beings for sacrifice.

The hegemony was not secure, nor did it embrace all of the semi-civilized peoples. The Tarascans and other tribes to the west had resisted its power, and shortly before the advent of the Spaniards the Tlascalans to the east had defeated the Aztecs in battle. At the coming of the Europeans the "empire" was losing its hold. The subject peoples were becoming more restless under the burden of tribute; and the ruler, Montezuma II, was a superstitious fatalist. The Spanish conquerors arrived at the opportune moment for success.

THE CONQUEST OF CENTRAL AMERICA

Castilla del Oro.—At the same time that the islands other than Española were being occupied, beginnings of settlement were made in Central America. In 1503 Christopher Columbus had attempted to establish a colony on the Veragua coast, but had failed. After several successful trading voyages had been made, however, two colonies were planned for the southern mainland. Ojeda received a grant called Urabá, east of the Gulf of Darién, and Nicuesa obtained a grant called Veragua, lying west of that Gulf. Ojeda founded a colony at San Sebastián (1509), which was shortly afterward moved to Darién, where Vasco Nuñez de Balboa soon became the leading figure and governor *ad interim* (1511). Nicuesa's colony was founded at Nombre de Diós (1510), but it did not flourish. The Darién region became known as

Nueva Andalucía, and in 1513 the whole southern mainland, excepting Veragua, Honduras and Yucatán, to the west and Paria, to the east, was reorganized into one grand jurisdiction called Castilla del Oro, and made independent of Española.

Balboa.—Hearing of gold and a sea toward the south, Balboa led a band of men in 1513 across the Isthmus of Panamá and discovered the Pacific Ocean. The discovery was an important factor in leading to Magellan's great voyage, already recounted, and it set in motion a wave of explorations both up and down the Pacific coast, and led to the conquest of Peru. Balboa had made enemies, and he fell under the suspicion of the new governor of Castilla del Oro, Pedrarias de Ávila, who arrived at Darién in 1514 with a colony of fifteen hundred persons; but a conciliation occurred, and in 1515 Balboa was made Adelantado of the Island of Coiba, in the South Sea. To explore that water he built vessels on the north coast and had them transported across the Isthmus on the backs of Indians. The vessels proved unseaworthy, and while Balboa was building two more at the Isle of Pearls, he was summoned by Pedrárias, charged with treason, and beheaded (1519).

Exploration on the South Sea.—Balboa was succeeded by Espinosa in charge of the southern coast. He at once began plundering raids westward by land, seeking gold and slaves. The South Sea now became the chief center of interest, and, to provide a better base, in 1519 Pedrárias founded Panamá, moved his capital thither, refounded Nombre de Diós, and opened a road across the Isthmus between the two places.

Rapidly now the conquerors and explorers, under Pedrárias, pushed their way westward, by water and by land. With two of the vessels built by Balboa, in 1519 Espinosa sent an expedition under Castañeda which reached the Gulf of Nicoya, some five hundred miles from Panamá. In 1522 Andrés Niño and Gil González Dâvila fitted out a joint expedition, planning to sail west one thousand leagues, to seek spices, gold, and silver. After sailing one hundred leagues westward, González proceeded west by land, while Niño continued with the fleet. González reached and conquered the country bordering on the Gulf of Nicoya and Lake Nicaragua, places so named from local chieftains. Niño sailed west to Fonseca Bay, thus coasting the entire length of

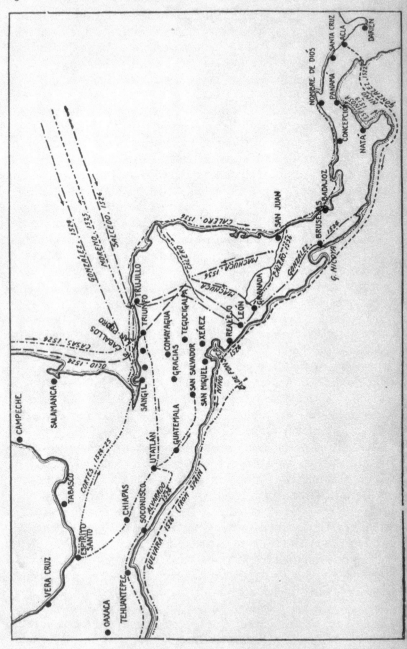

Nicaragua. When the commanders returned to Panamá they reported thirty-two thousand baptisms, and presents in gold and pearls worth more than $112,000.

The Conquest of Costa Rica and Nicaragua.—These profitable explorations stimulated renewed interest, and were followed by conquest and settlement in Costa Rica and Nicaragua. González desired to return at once to occupy the country which he had explored, and, meeting hindrance from Pedrarias, he went to Española to organize another expedition, while awaiting royal consent. Meanwhile Pedrarias set about conquering Nicaragua for himself. With funds borrowed from Francisco Pizarro and others, he equipped a small expedition and sent it under Francisco Hernández de Córdova. One of the commanders was Hernando de Soto, who later became famous in Peru and Florida. Proceeding westward, in 1524 Córdova founded Bruselas, on the Gulf of Nicoya, and parceled out the natives among the settlers. Continuing into Nicaragua, he founded the cities of León and Granada. In the struggle which followed, Bruselas was abandoned and the settlement of Costa Rica proceeded slowly.

González in 1524, having secured royal permission, entered Honduras from the northeast, with an expedition destined for Nicaragua. De Soto, sent against him by Córdova, was easily subdued, but González was defeated by the agents of Cortés, who was now engaged in the conquest of Mexico. In Nicaragua Córdova revolted against Pedrárias and was executed. In 1527 Pedrárias became governor of Nicaragua, where he ruled till 1531. During all these wranglings the Indians were the chief sufferers. They were granted in encomienda, employed as beasts of burden, or branded and sold as slaves in Panamá, Peru, or the West Indies.

Guatemala, San Salvador, and Honduras.—Meanwhile the north-moving conquerors who went out from Panamá had met and struggled in Guatemala, San Salvador, and Honduras with the companions of Cortés, moving southward from Mexico. The history of the conquest of these disputed regions, therefore, becomes a part of the story of the exploits of Cortés and his lieutenants, recounted below.

Exploration of San Juan River.—One of the acts which relieve the bloody story of the career of Pedrarias was the sending in

1529 of an expedition under Estete to find the outlet to Lake Nicaragua. Estete descended the San Juan River until a glimpse was had of the sea, but hostile Indians prevented him from reaching it. It was believed that the lake and river drained a country rich with gold, and explorations continued. In 1536 the San Juan, with tributary branches, was explored by Alonso Carrero and Diego Machuco, under orders from the new governor of Nicaragua. Soon the lake and river became the principal highway from Nicaragua to the Atlantic Ocean, and to the Porto Bello fairs.

The Dukedom of Veragua.—It was a long time after Nicuesa's failure in 1510 before another attempt was made to settle Veragua, one reason being that the region was tenaciously claimed by the heirs of Columbus. In 1535 Alonso Gutiérrez was made governor of Veragua, as agent of the widow of Diego Columbus, but misfortune attended his efforts to found a colony. Shortly afterward (1537) the discoverer's grandson, Luís, was made Duke of Veragua; several attempts to colonize it failed, however, and in 1556 the region was surrendered for a small pension.

Continued struggle in Central America.—These conquests were but the beginning of a long struggle of the Spaniards with the natives in Central America. The first stages of the conquest were over by the middle of the sixteenth century, but many parts of the country were still unconquered at the end of the seventeenth. Some tribes, indeed, are unsubdued and uncivilized to this day.

THE CONQUEST OF THE VALLEY OF MEXICO

The revolt of Cortés.—In the very year of the founding of Panamá Hernando Cortés entered Mexico. The return of the expeditions of Córdova and Grijalva to the Mexican coast had caused excitement in Cuba. Governor Velásquez prepared an expedition to follow them up, and appointed Cortés to lead it. Becoming distrustful of his lieutenant, Velásquez sent messengers to recall him, but Cortés set forth, nevertheless. In defiance of the governor, on February 18, 1519, he left Cuba, a rebel, with eleven vessels, some six hundred men, and sixteen horses. Proceeding to Tabasco and up the coast, he founded Vera Cruz, by whose *cabildo* he was chosen captain-general and *justicia mayor*. and his position was thus given the color of legality. By this act Cortés placed himself under the immediate protection of the king.

The march to Mexico.—On the way and while at Vera Cruz Cortés had learned that the Aztec "empire" was honeycombed with dissension, and that the subject peoples were burdened with tribute and filled with hatred for Montezuma, the native ruler at the city of Mexico. He therefore assumed the rôle of deliverer, and the Indians rallied to his standard. At Cempoalla he connived at a revolt against Montezuma's tax gatherers. Scuttling his ships and thus cutting off all chance for retreat, in August he set out for Mexico. His march was a succession of audacious deeds. At Cempoalla he threw down heathen idols and imprisoned the chiefs. At Tlascala he was attacked by several thousand warriors, but his genius changed them into allies in his train. At Cholula, discovering a conspiracy, he raked the streets with cannon shot and burned the leaders at the stake. In triumph he entered the great pueblo of Tenochtitlan or Mexico. While lodged as a guest of Montezuma in the center of the city, he seized the Aztec ruler and held him prisoner.

The loss and recapture of the city.—In the spring of 1520 Cortés learned that Pánfilo de Narváez had arrived at Vera Cruz with nearly a thousand men, under orders from Velásquez to arrest him. Leaving Pedro de Alvarado in charge, he hastened to the coast, won over most of Narváez's men, and then hurried back to Mexico. During his absence the Aztecs had revolted, through the rashness of Alvarado. Soon after the return of Cortés the natives rose again, killed Montezuma, and replaced him by Cuautehmoc, a more vigorous leader. Cortés now sought safety in flight, but during the night retreat he lost more than half his men. This "unfortunate night" became known as "Noche Triste." But the defeat was only temporary. Raising new allies, Cortés conquered the towns round about Mexico, built a fleet at Tlascala, launched it on Lake Tezcuco, besieged the city, and by a combined attack, by land and water, on August 13, 1521, he recaptured Mexico, the most important native town in all America.

Cortés's contest with Velásquez.—Knowing that Velásquez would oppose him, Cortés, while at Vera Cruz in 1519, had at once sent agents, bearing rich presents, to represent him at the court of Charles V. Then began a three-year contest with the agents of the Cuban governor. The delay was fortunate for Cortés, for in the course of it he won favor by his remarkable feats of conquest. Through the influence of Fonseca, Velásquez secured the appointment of Cristóbal de Tápia, an official of Española, as governor of New Spain, to take charge of the government and investigate Cortés. But Cortés got rid of him as he had disposed of Narváez. Arriving at Vera Cruz in December, 1521, Tápia was met by a council of delegates from the conqueror and practically driven from the country, on the ground that new orders were expected from the king.

Cortés made Governor and Captain-General.—Before this Cortés had sent Avila to the Audiencia of Santo Domingo to obtain its favor. Scarcely had Tapia been ejected when Avila returned with tentative authority for Cortés, subject to royal approval, to continue his conquests and to grant encomiendas. This greatly strengthened Cortés's position. Having succeeded so well in Española, Avila was now sent to Spain. Here he triumphed also, for on October 15, 1522, the emperor approved the acts of Cortés and made him governor and captain-general of New Spain. The victory of Cortés was as complete as the discomfiture of Velásquez and Fonseca.

Mexico rebuilt. Encomiendas granted.—The work of conquest on the mainland was accompanied by the evolution of government and the establishment of Spanish civilization, just as had been the case in the West Indies during the earlier stages of the struggle. Wherever the Spaniards settled, they planted their political, religious, economic, and social institutions. Mexico was rebuilt in 1522 as a Spanish municipality, Pedro de Alvarado, the most notable of Cortés's lieutenants, being made first *alcalde mayor*. In the regions subdued the principal provinces were assigned to the conquerors as encomiendas. Much of the actual work of control was accomplished through native chiefs, who were assigned Spanish offices and held responsible for good order and the collection of tribute. This method was later adopted by the British in India.

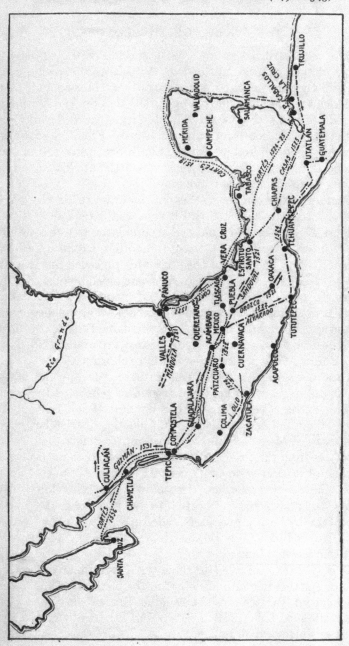

The Development of Southern Mexico, 1519–1543

THE SPREAD OF THE CONQUEST

The semi-civilized tribes.—With the fall of the city the first stage of the conquest had ended. Within the following decade most of the semi-civilized tribes of southern Mexico and Central America were brought under the dominion of Spain. During this period Spanish activities were directed from the Valley of Mexico to the eastward, southward and westward. From the south came rumors of gold and reports of the South Sea, while to the north, among the barbarian tribes, there was little, at this stage of the conquest, to attract the conquerors.

Factors in the conquest.—Several factors explain the marvelous rapidity with which Spanish rule was extended. The conquerors were looking for gold and accumulated treasure; not finding it in one place they hastened to another, led off by any wild tale of riches. The fame of the Spaniards preceded them and paralyzed resistance. They were everywhere aided by great armies of allies, eager to help destroy their hated enemies. Finally, Cortés, himself a genius, was assisted by an able body of lieutenants; in the spread of the conquest Cortés remained the central figure, but the actual work fell mainly to Orozco, Alvarado, Olid, Sandoval, Chico, Avalos, Montejo and other subordinates.

Vera Cruz, Oaxaca, and Tehuantepec.—In the fall of 1520 Sandoval, in search of gold and to punish rebellious Indians, invaded southern Vera Cruz with a handful of soldiers, aided by thirty thousand Indian allies. To hold the district he founded the towns of Medellín and Espíritu Santo. Before the expulsion of Cortés from the city, goldseekers had been sent to Oaxaca and Tehuantepec and were well received, but the "Noche Triste" was followed by a reaction. Orozco was sent, therefore, to subdue Oaxaca, which he reported to be rich in gold. In 1522 an attack by hostile neighbors called Alvarado to Tehuantepec. Gold was found, and as the district bordered on the South Sea, settlements were formed to hold it.

Olid in Michoacán.—The same year, 1522, marks the extension of Spanish rule into Michoacán, the territory of the hitherto independent Tarascans. The cacique Tangaxoan visited Cortés and made submission, and in return Olid was sent to found a settlement at Patzcuaro on Lake Chapala. Before the end of the year part of the settlers moved to the seacoast and settled at Zacatula, in the modern state of Guerrero, where a post had been established.

Colima and Jalisco.—From Michoacán the conquest at once spread north into Colima and Jalisco. Gold being reported in Colima, Avalos and Chico, lieutenants of Olid, entered the country, but were defeated by the natives. Thereupon Olid followed, subdued the mountain region by force, and founded the town of Colima (1524), which became a base for new advances. On his return to Mexico, Olid brought samples of pearls from Colima, and reports of an Amazon Island ten days up the coast, where there were said to be great riches. To investigate these reports, in 1524 Francisco Cortés was sent north. He reached Río de Tololotlán, and secured the allegiance of the "queen" of Jalisco, but found little gold and no Amazon Island.

Amichel and Pánuco.—In 1522 the Huasteca country, to the northeast, came under the control of Cortés. It was three years before this that Pineda, as representative of Garay, governor of Jamaica, had visited the region. Garay applied for a grant of a province called Amichel, extending from Florida to Mexico, and set about colonizing it. In 1520, before the patent was secured, a party of his men met disaster near Pánuco River. Hearing of Garay's operations, in 1522 Cortés led forty thousand allies into the country, subdued it, and founded San Estéban, on Pánuco River. In 1523 Garay led a colony to the same region, but found himself forestalled by Cortés, by whom he was sent to Mexico, where he soon died. The rivalry of the Spaniards encouraged an Indian revolt, but Sandoval, as agent of Cortés, put down the disturbance with extreme cruelty. In 1527 the Pánuco district, under the name of Victoria Garayana was separated from Mexico, Nuño de Guzmán being made governor, while the region called Florida, further north, was assigned to Pánfilo de Narváez. Guzmán's rule of six months was characterized by attempts to extend conquests northward into Narváez's territory, by wars with the Huasteca chieftains, and by constant slave-hunting raids, through which the country was nearly depopulated.

Alvarado in Guatemala and San Salvador.—By this time the conquests of Cortés and his lieutenants had extended into Central America, where they encountered the agents of Pedrarias.

In 1522 embassies from the large cities of Utatlan and Guatemala had visited Cortés and made submission. In the following year Alvarado, with four hundred Spaniards and twenty thousand allies, entered the region and conquered the Quichés and Cakchiquels. This task partially completed, he continued south and extended his conquests into San Salvador (1524).

Olid and Casas in Honduras.—Cortés believed that Honduras was rich, and that a strait lay between it and Guatemala. Moreover, Gil González and the agents of Pedrarias had begun to operate there. Consequently, at the same time that Alvarado went to Guatemala, Olid was despatched to Honduras. Reaching there in 1524 he tried to imitate his master's example by making a conquest for himself. He succeeded in defeating González, as has been seen, but was in turn beheaded by Francisco de las Casas, who was sent by Cortés to overthrow him. During this struggle the city of Trujillo was founded.

The march of Cortés to Honduras.—In doubt as to the wisdom of sending Las Casas after Olid, in October, 1524, Cortés set out for Honduras in person, with about one hundred and forty Spaniards and three hundred Indians in his train, the latter led by three famous Aztec chiefs. In his rear was driven a herd of swine. The route lay through southern Vera Cruz, Tabasco, and Chiapas, to Golfo Dulce, his way being obstructed by vast morasses, swollen streams, and flint-strewn mountains. In a single province fifty bridges had to be constructed in a journey of as many miles. In Chiapas it became necessary to bridge with trees a channel five hundred paces wide. On the way the Aztec chieftains, including the noble Cuauhtemoc, being charged with conspiracy, were hanged, an act which is variously characterized as a "necessary punishment" and a "foul murder." Leaving his cousin, Hernando Saavedra, in command as captain-general in Trujillo, Cortés sent his men home by way of Guatemala and returned by sea to Mexico in May, 1526. After attempting for two years to explore on the South Sea, in 1528 he went to Spain to refute his enemies, chief of whom was Nuño de Guzmán, now president of the recently established Audiencia of Mexico. He returned two years later.

Yucatán.—The conquest of Yucatán was begun in 1527 by Francisco de Montejo, an agent of Cortés. Initial success was followed by native revolts, and it was 1541 before the conquest was made secure. There were frequent rebellions thereafter, but never again united resistance.

Las Casas in Guatemala.—Thus far the conquest had been one of force. But now an example of the power of gentleness was furnished by Father Las Casas, the Dominican friar who had opposed encomiendas so vigorously in Española. About 1532 he entered Nicaragua as a missionary, where he attacked the ill-treatment of the Indians. Being opposed by the governor, in 1536 he went to Guatemala. Shortly before this he had written a treatise to prove that conversion by force was wrong, and that only persuasion should be used. To test his views he was granted sole control for five years of a hostile region known as "the Land of War," and by mild means he and his companions soon converted the district into a land of True Peace (Vera Paz), as it is still called.

Guzmán in Sinaloa.—While Cortés was in Spain Guzmán, fearing his own downfall, and hoping to save himself by offering new provinces to the king, undertook the conquest of northern Jalisco and of Sinaloa. Leaving Mexico in December, 1529, with ten thousand allies, he marched through Michoacán and Jalisco, leaving behind a trail of fire and blood, for which he has ever since been execrated. Part of Sinaloa was explored, and Culiacán was founded as an outpost in 1531. The region subdued by Guzmán was named Nueva Galicia, of which the conqueror became governor and Compostela the capital.

Buffer province of Querétaro.—At the coming of the Spaniards the country north of the valley of Mexico had never been conquered by the Aztecs. The Spaniards, in turn, adopted the policy of entrusting its subjugation to native caciques, treating the region as a buffer Indian state. The leading figure in the conquest was a Christianized Otomí chief, named Nicolás de San Luis. By Charles V he was made a knight of the Order of Santiago and a captain-general in the army. Another Otomí cacique who played a similar though less conspicuous part was Fernando de Tapia. The most notable event in the conquest was the reduction of Querétaro in 1531. For thirty years San Luís served the Spaniards in the control of the Querétaro border.

The Mixton War.—The first half century of expansion toward the north was closed by a widespread native uprising in Nueva Galicia which for a time checked advance in that direction and even caused a contraction of the frontier. Guzmán had left Nueva Galicia in a deplorable condition. After several minor uprisings, the rebellious natives broke forth in 1541, during the absence of Governor Coronado and his army in New Mexico. The Indians refused to pay tribute, killed their encomenderos and the missionaries, destroyed the crops, and took refuge in the *peñoles* or cliffs of Mixton, Nochistlán, Acatic, and other places near Guadalajara. The defence fell to Cristóbal de Oñate, lieutenant governor of Nueva Galicia. Pedro de Alvarado, who chanced to arrive from Guatemala at Navidad with a force of men, led them against Nochistlán and lost his life in the encounter. Viceroy Mendoza at last took the field with four hundred and fifty Spaniards and thirty thousand allies, and crushed the revolt.

EXPLORATIONS IN THE NORTHERN INTERIOR AND ON THE PACIFIC

FLORIDA

De León.—While some conquerors were struggling in Central America, Mexico, and Peru, others were trying to subdue the vast northern region called Florida. In 1514 Juan Ponce de León secured a patent to colonize Florida and Bimini, which he had explored in the previous year. Instead of proceeding to the task, however, he engaged in a war against the Caribs, and it was not until 1521 that he attempted to carry out his project. In that year he led a colony of two hundred men to the Peninsula, landed on the west coast, and tried to establish a settlement. But he was attacked by natives, and driven back to Cuba, mortally wounded.

Ayllón's colony on the Carolina coast.—To carry out his contract to colonize Chicora, in July, 1526, Ayllón sailed from Española with six vessels and a colony of five hundred men and women, Dominican friars, and supplies, prepared to find a new home in Carolina. But the experiment was doomed to be another failure. Landing was first made on the river called the Jordan, perhaps

Cape Fear River. On another stream, perhaps the Peedee, the settlement of San Miguel de Gualdape was begun. But supplies gave out, and at the end of two years Ayllón died (October, 1528). Quarrels ensued, and in midwinter the survivors, only about one hundred and fifty now, returned to Santo Domingo.

Narváez.—At the same time the conquest of Florida was attempted by Panfilo de Narváez, the man who had been sent to Vera Cruz to arrest Cortés. In 1526 he secured a patent to the lands of Ponce de León and Garay. Raising a colony of six hundred persons in Spain, in 1528 he reached Florida, landing near Tampa Bay. Hearing of a rich province called Apalachen (Apalache), he sent his vessels along the coast and himself marched up the peninsula at the head of three hundred men to find the Promised Land. He found the place sought near modern Tallahassee, but it proved to be a squalid Indian village of forty huts. A few weeks having been spent in exploration and warfare, Narváez went to the coast near St. Marks Bay, built a fleet of horse-hide boats, and set out for Pánuco. After passing the mouth of the Mississippi a storm arose, and all were wrecked on the coast of Texas.

Cabeza de Vaca.—In a short time most of the survivors of Narváez's party died of disease, starvation, and exposure, or at the hands of the savages. Having passed nearly six years of slavery among the Indians, Alvar Núñez Cabeza de Vaca, the treasurer of the colony of Florida, with three companions, escaped westward, crossed Texas, Coahuila, Chihuahua, and Sonora, and in 1536 reached Culiacán, the northern outpost of Sinaloa, after a most remarkable journey.

De Soto.—Vaca went to Spain (1537) to apply for the governorship of Florida, but it had already been conferred on Hernando de Soto, who had taken a prominent part in the conquest of both Central America and Peru. In 1539 De Soto reached Florida with a colony of six hundred persons. Landing at Tampa Bay, as Narváez had done, he soon set out to look for a rich province called Cale. This was the beginning of an expedition lasting nearly four years, during which the Spaniards were led on by tales of gold and treasure from one district to another, hoping to repeat the exploits of Cortés and Pizarro. As he passed through the country De Soto imitated those captains by capturing the chiefs, holding them as hostages, and compelling them to provide food and men to carry the baggage. Going to Apalachen he wintered there, meanwhile discovering Pensacola Bay. From Apalachen he went to the Savannah River, thence northwest to the North Carolina Piedmont, south toward Mobile Bay, northwest to the Mississippi near modern Memphis, westward across Arkansas into Oklahoma, thence down the Arkansas River to its mouth, where he died, in May, 1542, being buried in the Mississippi.

Moscoso in Arkansas and Texas.—De Soto's followers, led by Luís de Moscoso, now set out for Pánuco, crossing Arkansas to the Red River, then turning southwest through eastern Texas, perhaps reaching the Brazos River. Giving up the attempt by land, they returned to the Mississippi, built a fleet of boats, descended the river, and skirted the Texas coast, reaching Pánuco in 1543. Thus ended the fourth attempt to colonize Florida.

CÍBOLA AND QUIVIRA

Cortés on the South Sea and in California.—Another line of advance toward the northern interior had been made by way of the Pacific slope. The discovery of the South Sea was followed immediately by exploration along the western coast. Balboa himself had begun that work, before his death in 1519. Espinosa had reached Nicaragua in 1519, and three years later Niño had reached Guatemala. By this time Cortés had also begun operations on the South Sea by building a shipyard at Zacatula, hoping to discover a strait, find rich islands and mainland, reach India by way of the coast, and open communication with the Moluccas. In 1527 he sent three vessels under Saavedra across the Pacific. The operations of a new fleet built by him were hindered by the Audiencia of Mexico, but in 1532 he sent an expedition north under Hurtado de Mendoza, which reached Río Fuerte in northern Sinaloa. In the following year another expedition sent by Cortés under Jiménez discovered Lower California, which was thought to be an island and where pearls were found. The discovery of an island with pearls confirmed the geographical ideas of Cortés, and in 1535 he himself led a colony to La Paz, but within a few months it was abandoned. This was the first of a long series of efforts to colonize California.

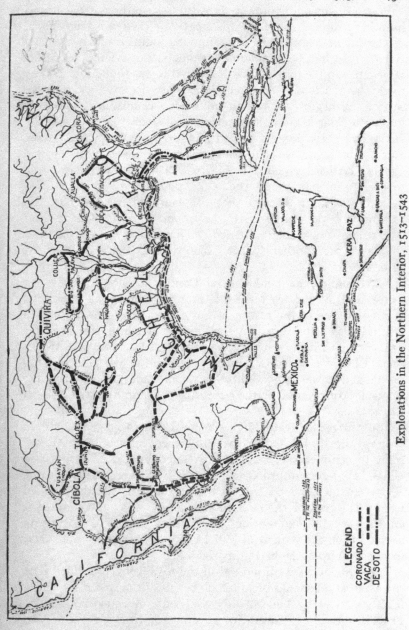

Explorations in the Northern Interior, 1513-1543

LEGEND
CORONADO ---·---·
VACA ---··---··
DE SOTO ---···---···

Friar Marcos discovers Cíbola.—Interest in the north country, both in Spain and America, was greatly quickened by the arrival of Cabeza de Vaca in Mexico after his journey across the continent. He had seen no great wonders, but he had heard of large cities to the north of his path, and it was thought that they might be the famed Seven Cities. The viceroy took into his service the negro Stephen, one of Vaca's companions, and sent him with Friar Marcos, a Franciscan missionary, to reconnoitre. In March, 1539, they set out with guides from Culiacán. Going ahead, Stephen soon sent back reports of Seven Cities, called Cíbola, farther on. Friar Marcos hastened after him, and reached the border of the Zuñi pueblos in western New Mexico, where he learned that Stephen had been killed. Returning to the settlement, he reported that Cíbola was larger and finer than Mexico. This story, of course, was the signal for another "rush," like that to Peru a few years before.

Ulloa rounds the peninsula of California.—Rivalry between Cortés and the viceroy regarding exploration was now keen, and about the time of the return of Fray Marcos, Cortés, hoping to forestall his competitor, sent three vessels north to explore under Francisco de Ulloa. One of the vessels was lost, but with two of them Ulloa succeeded in reaching the head of the Gulf of California, and learned that California was a peninsula. Descending the Gulf he proceeded up the outer coast of California to Cabo del Engaño.

The contest for leadership.—While Ulloa's voyage was still in progress, Cortés hurried to Spain to present his claim of exclusive right to conquer the country discovered by Fray Marcos and Ulloa. He never returned to Mexico. Other contestants arose. The agents of De Soto, who at the time was in Florida, claimed Cíbola as a part of the adelantado's grant. Guzmán claimed it on the basis of explorations in Sinaloa. Pedro de Alvarado claimed it on the ground of a license to explore north and west, for which purpose he had prepared a fleet.

The Coronado expedition.—But the royal council decided that the exploration should be made on behalf of the crown, in whose name the viceroy had already sent out an expedition under Francisco Vásquez Coronado, governor of Nueva Galicia. To coöperate with Coronado by water, Alarcón was sent up the coast from Acapulco with two vessels.

In February, 1540, Coronado left Compostela with some two hundred horsemen, seventy foot soldiers, and nearly one thousand Indian allies and servants. So eager were the volunteers that it was complained that the country would be depopulated. The expedition was equipped at royal expense with a thousand horses, fine trappings, pack-mules, several cannon, and with droves of cattle, sheep, goats, and swine for food. From Culiacán Coronado went ahead with about one hundred picked men and four friars. Following behind their leader, the main army moved up to Corazones, in the Yaqui River valley, where the town of San Gerónimo was founded and left in charge of Melchor Díaz.

Zuñi, Moqui, the Colorado, and the Rio Grande.—In July Coronado reached the Zuñi pueblos, which he conquered with little difficulty. But the country was disappointing and the expedition resulted only in explorations. These, however, were of great importance. At Culiacán Alarcón procured a third vessel, then continued to the head of the Gulf, and ascended the Colorado (1540) eighty-five leagues, perhaps passing the Gila River. Shortly afterward Melchor Díaz went by land from San Gerónimo to the Colorado to communicate with Alarcón, but failed and lost his life. During the journey, however, he crossed the Colorado and went some distance down the Peninsula of California.

Hearing of the Moqui pueblos, to the north of Zuñi, in July Coronado sent Tobar to find them, which he succeeded in doing. Shortly afterward Cárdenas went farther northwest and reached the Grand Canyon of the Colorado. Moving to the Rio Grande, Coronado visited the pueblos in its valley and camped at Tiguex above Isleta. In the course of the winter the Indians revolted and were put down with great severity.

Gran Quivira.—Meanwhile Coronado heard of a rich country northeastward called Gran Quivira, and in April, 1541, he set out to find it. Crossing the mountains and descending the Pecos, he marched out into the limitless buffalo-covered plains, the "Llanos del Cíbola," inhabited by roving Apaches. Near the upper Brazos he turned north, crossed the Texas Panhandle and Oklahoma, and reached Quivira in eastern Kansas. It was probably a settlement of Wichita Indians. Disappointed, and urged by his men, Coronado now returned to Mexico. Three fearless missionaries remained to preach the gospel, and soon achieved the crown of martyrdom. Coronado had made one of the epochal explorations of all history.

The Pueblo Indians of New Mexico.—Coronado found large parts of New Mexico and adjacent regions inhabited by Indians who dwelt in substantial towns (pueblos) and possessed a civilization similar to that of the Aztecs. Their terraced dwellings, which were also fortifications, were built of stone or adobe, and were several stories high. The inhabitants lived a settled life, practiced agriculture by means of irrigation, and raised cotton for clothing. They were constantly beset by the more warlike tribes all about them, and were already declining under their incursions. At the time of the conquest there were some seventy inhabited pueblos, whose population may have been from 30,000 to 60,000. The principal pueblo regions were the upper Rio Grande, the upper Pecos, Ácoma, and the Zuñi and Moqui towns. Remains of prehistoric pueblos occupy a much wider range in the Southwest, and are now the scene of important archæological research.

CALIFORNIA AND THE PHILIPPINES

Alvarado's fleet.—Shortly after Coronado left New Mexico, two important expeditions were despatched by Viceroy Mendoza to explore in the Pacific. Magellan's voyage had been a signal for a bitter conflict between Spain and Portugal in the East, in which Portugal long had the upper hand. After the failures of Loaisa (1525) and Saavedra (1527) Charles V sold Spain's claims on the Moluccas to Portugal, but continued to claim the Philippines. In spite of former disasters to eastern expeditions, both Cortés and Pedro de Alvarado planned discoveries in the South Sea. In 1532 Alvarado made a contract for the purpose, but was led off by the gold "rush" to Peru. In 1538 he obtained a new grant, authorizing him to explore "in the west toward China or the Spice Islands," or toward the north at the "turn of the land to New Spain." Early in 1539 he left Spain with equipment for a fleet, which he transported across Honduras and Guatemala on the backs of natives. On hearing of the discoveries of

Fray Marcos, he hastened north with his fleet, but stopped in Mexico, where he and Mendoza, who had already sent out Coronado, made an agreement, as mutual insurance, to divide the profits of their respective explorations. Before continuing his expedition Alvarado was killed in the Mixton War (1541). This left the fleet in Mendoza's hands, and with it he carried out Alvarado's plans by despatching two expeditions, one up the California coast, the other across the Pacific.

Cabrillo and Ferrelo.—The coast voyage was conducted by Juan Rodríguez Cabrillo, and was especially designed to look for a northern strait. Leaving Navidad in June, 1542, Cabrillo explored the outer coast of the Peninsula, discovered San Diego Bay, reached Northwest Cape (latitude 38°31'), descended to Drake's Bay, and then returned to the Santa Barbara Channel, where he died. Sailing north again in 1543, his pilot, Ferrelo, reached the Oregon coast (42½°), returning thence to Navidad. Cabrillo and Ferrelo had explored the coast for more than twenty-three degrees, but had missed both San Francisco and Monterey bays.

Villalobos.—The other expedition was led by López de Villalobos, who was instructed to explore the Philippines and to reach China, but not to touch at the Moluccas. Sailing in November, 1542, he took possession of the Philippines, but, being forced to leave on account of native hostility, he was captured by the Portuguese. Villalobos died in the Moluccas, where the enterprise went to pieces. The expeditions of Coronado, De Soto, Cabrillo, and Villalobos brought to an end a remarkable half century of Spanish expansion in North America and in the Pacific Ocean.

THE ESTABLISHMENT OF THE VICEROYALTY OF NEW SPAIN

Cortés as administrator.—Cortés was not a mere conqueror. He appointed officers, and issued general ordinances affecting nearly all lines of activity. Encomenderos were required to equip themselves for defense and to promote agriculture. Cortés himself became a great planter, notably at Oaxaca. He introduced agricultural implements, opened a port at Vera Cruz, and established markets in Mexico City. In 1523 the king had forbidden encomiendas, but Cortés made so strong a protest on the grounds of policy and royal interest that the order was withdrawn.

Royal officials arrive.—In 1524 a corps of royal officials arrived to take the places of those appointed by Cortés. Estrada came as treasurer, Salazar as factor, Albórnoz, as contador, and Chirinos as veedor. They came empowered to interfere in the government of Cortés, especially in matters of finance, a policy quite in keeping with the general Spanish practice of setting one officer to watch another.

The powers of Cortés curtailed.—The new officials were not slow to make trouble for Cortés. While he was in Honduras his enemies set about undermining him, both in Mexico and Spain. Salazar and Chirinos usurped authority, persecuted the conqueror's partisans, confiscated his property, and spread reports that he was dead. At last the friends of Cortés rebelled, overthrew the usurpers, Salazar and Chirinos, and sent for Cortés to return from Honduras. In May, 1526, he reached Vera Cruz. Two years of investigation and persecution by other crown officials followed.

In response to complaints in Spain, Luis Ponce de León was sent early in the same year as governor and to hold a *residencia* of Cortés, while the latter's jurisdiction as captain-general was lessened by the appointment of Nuño de Guzmán as governor of Pánuco. Ponce de León died in July, leaving Aguilar as governor. Aguilar died early in 1527 and Estrada became governor. He interfered with Cortés's explorations in the South Sea, and banished him from Mexico City as dangerous, but the breach was soon healed when both were threatened by the usurpations of Guzmán. It was at this time that Cortés, finding his position unbearable, went to Spain for redress and to answer charges.

The first Audiencia of New Spain.—In view of the disturbed conditions in New Spain, in 1528 Charles V created an Audiencia or supreme court for Mexico, and empowered it to investigate the disorders and hold the *residencia* of Cortés. It was composed of four *oidores* and a president. To the latter office was appointed Nuño de Guzmán. He proved to be an extreme partisan against Cortés, and so avaricious that he soon won the hatred of almost everyone except a few favorites. The old friends of Cortés stood by him and he secured the support of Bishop Zumárraga.

Cortés made Marquis of the Valley.—The arrival of Cortés in Spain caused his detractors to slink from sight, and he was conducted to court with almost royal honors. In consideration of his brilliant services, in 1529 he was granted twenty-two towns, with twenty-three thousand vassals, with full civil and criminal jurisdiction and rentals for himself and his heirs. With these honors he was given the titles of Marquis of the Valley of Oaxaca, captain-general of New Spain, and governor of such islands as he might still discover in the South Sea. In 1530 he returned to New Spain, where he was acclaimed by the people, though opposed by the Audiencia.

The second Audiencia.—The abuses of the first Audiencia led to its replacement in 1530 by a new corps of judges, of whom the president was Sebastián Ramírez de Fuenleal. The oidores appointed were Salmerón, Maldonado, Ceynos, and Quiroga. They were especially instructed to hold the *residencias* of their predecessors, restore the estates of Cortés, and consider the abolition of encomiendas. To replace control by encomenderos, local magistrates called *corregidores* were introduced. A few of these functionaries were appointed, but the colonists raised such a cry that little change was accomplished, and the Audiencia confined itself, in this particular, to checking abuses of the encomienda system. Quiroga later became bishop and civilizer of Michoacán, where he is still gratefully remembered.

The viceroyalty established.—The difficulties of government and the spread of conquests made closer centralization necessary, and New Spain was now made a viceroyalty. The first incumbent of the office of viceroy was Antonio de Mendoza, a nobleman of fine character and ability. He arrived in 1535. As viceroy he was president of the Audiencia, governor, and captain-general, personally representing the king in all branches of government.

The Audiencias of Panamá and Guatemala.—Alvarado served as governor and captain-general of Guatemala through appointment by Cortés till 1528, when he was commissioned directly by the emperor. Though frequently absent, he continued in office till his death in 1541. In 1537 Panamá and Veragua were erected into the Audiencia of Panamá, which was later attached to the viceroyalty of Peru, because the commerce of Peru crossed the

Isthmus. Six years later the Audiencia of the Confines of Panamá and Nicaragua was established. After various changes, by 1570 Guatemala became the seat of an Audiencia embracing all of Central America except Panamá, Veragua, and Yucatán.

The New Laws.—Las Casas and others continued to oppose the encomienda system. In 1539 the great missionary returned to Spain to conduct the fight. While there he wrote his celebrated works called *The Destruction of the Indies* and the *Twenty Reasons* why Indians should not be enslaved. His pleadings were not in vain, for in 1542 the Council issued a new Indian code called the *New Laws*, which provided that encomiendas should be abolished on the death of the present holders. But so great was the opposition that in 1545 the vital clauses of the ordinance were repealed. In Peru the attempt to enforce the laws even led to bloodshed.

Mendoza sent to Peru.—Viceroy Mendoza continued to rule for fifteen years. He proved to be a wise, able, and honest administrator, who tried to improve the condition of both the colonists and the helpless natives. He prohibited the use of the Indians as beasts of burden. In 1536 he established the printing press in Mexico, the first book published on the continent appearing in 1537. In that year he founded the college of Santa Cruz de Tlatelalco for the education of noble Indians. He opened roads from Mexico to Oaxaca, Tehuantepec, Acapulco, Michoacán, Colima, Jalisco, and other distant points. In 1550 he was sent to rule in troubled Peru, where the Spaniards were duplicating the brilliant exploits of Cortés and his followers.

READINGS

SPAIN DURING THE CONQUEST

Armstrong, E., *The Emperor Charles V.;* Bourne, E. G., *Spain in America*, Ch. I; Chapman, Charles E., *A History of Spain*, 1-246, especially Chapters X-XXII; Cheyney, E. P., *European Background of American History*, Ch. V; Hume, M. A. S., *Spain, its Greatness and Decay;* Hume, M. A. S., *The Spanish People;* Lane-Poole, S., *The Moors in Spain;* Lowery, W., *Spanish Settlements within the present limits of the United States*, 1513-1565, pp. 79-101; Merriman, R. B., *The Rise of the Spanish Empire;* Prescott, W. H., *Ferdinand and Isabella;* Haring, C. H., *Trade and Navigation between Spain and the Indies in the Time of the Hapsburgs.*

THE WEST INDIES, CENTRAL AMERICA, AND MAGELLAN

Altolaguirre y Davale, D. Angel de, *D. Pedro de Alvarado, Conquistador de Guatemala y Honduras;* *Vasco Nuñez de Balboa;* Bancroft, H. H., *Central America*, I, 183–247, 321–412, 478–511; Bourne, E. G., *Spain in America*, 20–53; 115–132; Fiske, John, *The Discovery of America*, I, 465–512, II, 184–212; Fortier, A., and Ficklen, J. R., *Mexico and Central America*, 1–102; Guardia, R. F., *History of the Discovery and Conquest of Costa Rica:* Guillemand, F. H. H., *Life of Magellan;* Helps, Arthur, *The Spanish Conquest*, I, 89–142, 193–320; Lowery, Woodbury, *Spanish Settlements within the present Limits of the United States*, 102–122; Richman, I. B., *The Spanish Conquerors*, 64–91, 139–154; Wright, I. A., *The early History of Cuba, 1492–1586.*

CORTES AND HIS FOLLOWERS

Bancroft, H. H., *Central America*, I, 522–643; Diaz del Castillo, Bernal, *True History of the Conquest of New Spain;* Fortier and Ficklen, *Mexico and Central America*, 181–238; Helps, Arthur, *Life of Cortés; Life of Las Casas; The Spanish Conquest*, III, 23–67, 164–289; McNutt, F. A., *Cortés and the Conquest of Mexico*, 43–67; *The Letters of Cortés to Charles V;* Prescott, W. H., *The Conquest of Mexico*, Bks. II–IV; Bolton, H. E., *The Spanish Borderlands;* Means, P. A., *History of the Spanish Conquest of Yucatán and of the Itzas.*

EXPLORATIONS TO THE NORTH AND IN THE PACIFIC

Bancroft, H. H., *History of California*, I, 64–81; Bandelier, A. D. F., *The Gilded Man; Journey of Cabeza de Vaca (Trail Makers' Series);* Blair and Robertson, *The Philippine Islands*, I–II; Bolton, H. E., *Spanish Exploration in the Southwest, 1542–1706 (Original Narratives Series)*, 1–39; Bourne, E. G., *Spain in America*, 158–174; *Narratives of the Career of Hernando de Soto (Trail Makers' Series);* Brittain, Alfred, *Discovery and Exploration*, 343–361; Hodge, F. W., and Lewis, T. H., *The Spanish Explorers in the Southern United States, 1528–1543 (Original Narratives Series);* Irving, Theodore, *The Conquest of Florida;* Lowery, Woodbury, *Spanish Settlements within the present Limits of the United States*, 130–350; Richman, I. B., *California under Spain and Mexico*, 3–11; Schafer, Joseph, *Pacific Coast and Alaska*, 3–23; Winship, G. P., *The Coronado Expedition* (Bureau of American Ethnology, *14th Report*, Part I.); *The Journey of Coronado (Trail Makers' Series);* Richman, I. B., *The Spanish Conquerors*, 91–139.

CHAPTER III

THE EXPANSION OF NEW SPAIN (1543-1609)

OLD AND NEW SPAIN UNDER PHILIP II

Philip's inheritance.—Charles V's stormy reign came to a close in 1556, when he abdicated in favor of his son, Philip II, who inherited Spain with its colonies, Naples, Milan, Franche Comté, and the Netherlands. The imperial office and the Hapsburg possessions went to Charles's brother, Ferdinand I.

The Protestant movement.—The Protestant movement, which began in Germany and Switzerland, spread into France, England, Scotland, the Netherlands, and the Scandinavian countries. The Catholic church saw itself in danger of losing the religious supremacy in Europe, and put forth all its power to check it. Its three great agencies in the Counter-Reformation were the Council of Trent, the Jesuits, and Philip II.

The Revolt of the Netherlands.—The Spanish king devoted all his resources to stamping out Protestantism in the Netherlands, France, and England. To the wealthy Dutch burghers Philip was a foreigner; they resented the quartering of his soldiers and they objected to his regent, the duchess of Parma, the king's half sister. The Inquisition had been introduced into the Netherlands by Charles V, and it became more active under his son. In 1566 the Dutch nobles headed a revolt, which was furthered by the Protestant preachers. The Duke of Aiva was sent with an army to suppress it. William of Orange and other leaders fled the country, as did many Flemish weavers. Alva established a special court which became known as the Council of Blood; a reign of terror followed, thousands being executed. William of Orange, known as the Silent, in 1568 collected a small army and began the struggle for independence. After many years of warfare the Protestant provinces in the north gained their autonomy.

The Defeat of the Armada.—In France the Protestant leader, Coligny, attempted to unite both Catholics and Protestants in a national war against Spain. This was frustrated by the Guises. Later, when they intrigued to place Mary Queen of Scots upon the English throne, Philip entered into their designs, but was prevented from giving much assistance by the revolt in the Netherlands. The English retaliated by raiding the Spanish Main. The culmination of the struggle was the defeat of the Spanish Armada, in 1588, which freed England from the danger of invasion. In Spain Philip carried out his policy of expelling the rest of the Moors, the most industrious and enlightened of his subjects, and by rigorously pushing the work of the Inquisition.

Spanish weakness.—The reign of Philip II had witnessed a vast change in Europe. England had become a Protestant country. In France the wars of religion had culminated by Henry IV ascending the throne. In the Netherlands the northern half had risen into an independent state. Portugal had become a Spanish province. In Spain the expulsion of the Moors, the constant drain upon the country to carry on Philip's foreign enterprises, and the commercial losses inflicted by the English, had weakened the country to such an extent that it could no longer be looked upon as preëminent in Europe. Nevertheless, the Spanish colonies continued to develop and expand. The story of that expansion is the subject of this chapter.

Luís de Velasco, second viceroy (1551–1564).—Viceroy Mendoza was succeeded by Luís de Velasco, a member of a noble Castilian family, who took possession in Mexico in 1551 and ruled till 1564. Velasco installed his rule by releasing 160,000 natives from forced labor in the mines. To put down disorder and protect the natives in 1552 he established in Mexico the Tribunal de la Santa Hermandad. A year later the royal University of Mexico was founded, the first in North America. During Velasco's rule the great canal of Huehuetoca for draining the City of Mexico was begun, 6000 Indians being employed in the work. Velasco was an expansionist, and vigorously promoted the colonization of Florida, the Philippines, and Nueva Vizcaya.

Martin Cortés, second Marquis of the Valley.—At the same time with Velasco came Martin Cortés, son of the conqueror, and second Marquis of the Valley of Oaxaca. He possessed city property in Mexico, Oaxaca, Toluca, and Cuernavaca, and his estates were the richest in New Spain. Other encomenderos looked to him as their protector against the royal officials and induced him to conspire for an independent crown. He yielded, but with six others was arrested in 1568. Two of the conspirators were executed, Cortés and the rest being sent to Spain.

Expansion of the frontiers.—Having exploded for the time being some of the notions of great wonders in the far distant interior, the Spanish pioneers fell back on the established frontiers, and by a more gradual and rational process extended them northward, much as the English a century later slowly pushed their settlements from the Atlantic shoreline across the Tidewater and up into the Piedmont.

On the Atlantic seaboard Spanish outposts were advanced from the West Indies into what are now Florida, Georgia, South Carolina, and, momentarily, into Virginia. In Mexico, missions, mines, farms, and stock ranches advanced northward in regular succession or side by side. Between the return of Coronado and the end of the century the frontiers of actual occupation moved forward, roughly speaking, from Guadalajara, Querétaro, and Pánuco, to a line drawn irregularly through the mouth of the Rio Grande westward to the Pacific, with many large spaces, of course, left vacant to be filled in by subsequent advances. The Spanish pioneers, like those of England and France, recorded their home attachments by the place names given their new abodes, and thus the whole northern district of Mexico was comprised within the three provinces of New Galicia, New Vizcaya, and New León. During the same period the Philippine Islands had been occupied as an outpost of Mexico.

The Adelantados.—The latter sixteenth century was still within the age of the *adelantados*, when the development of the Spanish frontiers was left largely to men of means, obligated to bear most of the expense of conquering and peopling the wilderness, in return for wide powers, extravagant titles, and extensive economic privileges. As types of these proprietary conquerors of the period there stand out Ibarra in Nueva Vizcaya, Menéndez in Florida, Legazpi in the Philippines, Carabajal in Nuevo León, and Oñate in New Mexico. The period likewise was still within the age of the *encomienda*, when the right to parcel out the natives was inherent in the privilege of conquest. With the turn of the century the custom practically ceased, a fact which sharply distinguishes Florida and New Mexico from the later frontier Spanish provinces of Texas, California, and Louisiana.

A new spirit.—The age of wanton bloodshed, too, had largely passed. The New Laws, promulgated in 1543, stood for a new spirit, and royal authority had by now become somewhat established on the frontiers. In proportion as the *encomenderos* were discredited for their abuses and as their power over the Indians was checked, a larger and larger place was found on the frontier for the missionaries, to whom passed much of the actual work of subduing and controlling the natives.

THE MINES OF NORTHERN MEXICO

Audiencia and diocese of Nueva Galicia.—In 1544 Compostela became the seat of the new diocese of Nueva Galicia. Four years later the new Audiencia of Nueva Galicia was established there. About 1550 Guadalajara became the seat of both jurisdictions, and the judicial and ecclesiastical capital of all the country to the north and northeast, a position which it long occupied. The Audiencia district was subdivided into *corregimientos*, each under an alcalde, subject to the Audiencia. Within the *corregimientos* were Indian *partidos*, each under a native alcalde, subject to the encomenderos or the missionaries.

The Zacatecas mines.—In spite of the check caused by the Mixton War, northward expansion in Mexico was soon stimulated by the discovery of rich mines, and by the ambitions of the new viceroy. Mines developed in southern Nueva Galicia were soon eclipsed by those of Zacatecas, which were opened in 1548 by Juan de Tolosa, Cristóbal de Oñate, Diego de Ibarra, and Baltasar Treviño. These men soon became the richest in America, and Zacatecas the first mining town in New Spain. The fame of the "diggins" spread, and other parts of the country were for a time nearly depopulated by the rush of miners.

Francisco de Ibarra.—Inspired by the "boom" at Zacatecas, the Audiencia of Nueva Galicia planned to subdue the districts of Sinaloa and Durango. Ginés Vázquez de Mercado, sent for this purpose in 1552, wasted his energies in a fruitless search for a fabled mountain of pure silver, and was defeated by the Indians near Sombrerete. Martin Pérez, sent by the Audiencia to the same district in 1558, came into conflict with Francisco de Ibarra, agent of the viceroy. In 1554 Ibarra began a series of explorations by means of which, in the course of eight years, he and his men opened in northern Zacatecas the mines of San Martín, San Lucas, Sombrerete, Chalchuites, Aviño, Fresnillo, and other places. To make these expeditions, he equipped himself at his own or his uncle's expense with soldiers, horses, Negro slaves, Indian servants, and droves of stock for food. He attracted miners and settlers by furnishing them with outfits and by giving them free use of mineral deposits.

Nueva Vizcaya founded.—In 1558 Velasco planned to send Ibarra northward to pacify a region called Copala, but his departure was delayed by the sending of the De Luna expedition to Florida.. In 1562 Ibarra was made governor and captaingeneral of a new province called Nueva Vizcaya, comprising the unconquered districts beyond Nueva Galicia, to which Zacatecas remained attached. In the following year he founded Nombre de Diós and Durango, the latter of which became and long remained the military capital of all the northern country. In the same year Rodrigo del Río de Losa was sent with soldiers and miners to open the mines of Indé, and of Santa Bárbara and San Juan in southern Chihuahua. The shortage of Indian labor in the mines there resulted by 1580 in slave hunting raids down the Conchos River and across the Rio Grande into modern Texas.

Ibarra on the Pacific slope.—Amid extreme hardships in 1564 Ibarra crossed the mountains to the westward, and conquered Topia, which he had hoped would prove to be "another Mexico." Disappointed in this, he spent two or three years in developing Sinaloa. Beyond Culiacán, on the Río Fuerte (then called Río Sinaloa) he founded the Villa of San Juan. From here with new recruits from Mexico and Guadalajara, in June, 1567, he set out northward. Ascending the Yaqui valley, at Zaguaripa he defeated the very Indians who had destroyed Coronado's town of San Gerónimo. Crossing the sierra eastward, he emerged on the plains at the river and ruined pueblo of Paquimé (Casas Grandes) in northern Chihuahua. Turning back along the eastern slope of the Sierras, he recrossed them, with terrible hardship, into the lower Yaqui valley. Returning to Chiametla, he died about

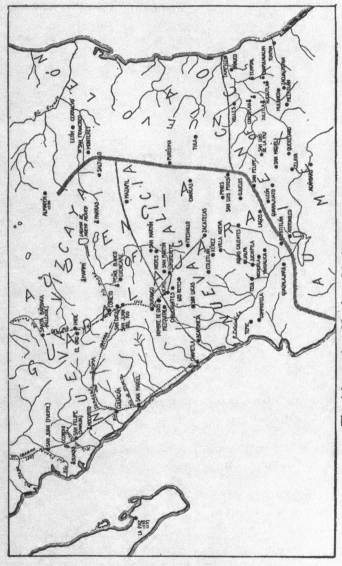

The Advance into Northern Mexico, 1543-1590

1570, after twenty years of exploring, mining, colonizing, and administration. He was one of the ablest of the second generation of colonizers in New Spain.

Development of Nueva Vizcaya.—Shortly after Ibarra left Sinaloa the Indians of San Juan revolted, drove out the encomenderos, and murdered the friars; the settlement was therefore moved to the Petatlán (Sinaloa) River, and named San Felipe. In the last decade of the century a presidio and an Aztec-Tlascaltec colony were founded at San Felipe, and Jesuit missions were planted in the vicinity. East of the mountains, in Durango and southern Chihuahua, mining, stock raising, and agriculture developed side by side. In 1586, for example, Diego de Ibarra branded 33,000 head of cattle, and Rodrigo del Rio, then governor, 42,000 head. Several new mining districts were opened before the end of the century. In 1574 Nueva Galicia and Nueva Vizcaya (including Zacatecas and Sinaloa) had a population of 1500 Spanish families, perhaps 10,000 persons living in some thirty settlements, about half of which were mining camps. Guadalajara had a population of one hundred and fifty families and Culiacán about thirty. The Franciscan missionaries had played an important part in the founding of Nueva Vizcaya. They accompanied or went before the explorers and established themselves at the principal mining camps and towns. In 1590 the custodia of San Francisco de Zacatecas embraced ten monasteries east of the Sierras. In 1591 the Jesuits entered the province.

Querétaro, Guanajuato, and Aguas Calientes.—For twenty years after the battle at Querétaro (1531) the Chichimec border was left practically unsettled, under the control of native leaders. But the need of communication with the Zacatecas veins made its complete subjugation necessary, and Viceroy Velasco undertook the task. In or about 1550 the town of Querétaro was founded, and Silao three years later. The marvelous Guanajuato mines were now opened; in 1554 the city of Santa Fé de Guanajuato was founded; and shortly afterward rich veins were opened at Aguas Calientes. These "strikes" caused "rushes," just as those in Zacatecas had done, but they were offset by others in Durango, where Ibarra was operating. To secure further the roads to the mines, new towns and presidios were established

along the way, and thus San Miguel el Grande (Allende), San
Felipe, Santa María de Lagos, Aguas Calientes, Ojuelos, Porte
zuelos, Jérez, and Celaya came into being. To supplement the
presidios, strong houses (*casas fuertes*) were provided as camping
stations for travelers and silver trains, and parties were equipped
with fortified wagons or movable strong houses.

San Luis Potosí and. Southern Coahuila.—For some time the
region of Charcas, now called San Luis Potosí, was a sort of
No-man's-land between the westward, eastward, and northward
moving columns of frontiersmen. It was the home of the powerful but savage Guachichiles. The definite conquest of the
region, already known to explorers and missionaries, was begun
about 1550 by Francisco de Urdiñola, who operated under
Velasco's orders, and who is said to have reached the vicinity
of Saltillo and Monterey. The settlement of the district soon
followed. Matehuala was founded in 1550, San Gerónimo in 1552,
Charcas in 1564, and the San Pedro mines about 1568. By 1576
San Luis Potosí, the site of rich ores, had become a villa, and
before long was the seat of an *alcaldía mayor*.

Mining developments spread northeastward from Zacatecas
to Mazapil and Saltillo. By 1568 Mazapil was the seat of an
alcaldía mayor, under the Audiencia of Nueva Galicia. In that
year Francisco del Cano, sent by the "very magificent alcalde
mayor," went north and discovered the "Lake of New Mexico,"
perhaps Laguna de Parras. In 1575 Francisco de Urdiñola, son
of the former conqueror, is said to have settled sixty families
at Saltillo, within the jurisdiction of Nueva Vizcaya. As early
as 1582 a Franciscan monastery was established there, and in
1592 Saltillo was created a villa.

The Tlascaltecan colonies.—Querétaro had been the scene of
one interesting experiment in utilizing the natives as agents of
control; in San Luis Potosí another was now tried. As a means
of reducing the great central region, the plan was devised of
planting in it colonies of Tlascaltecan Indians, to defend the
settlers and to teach the rude tribes the elements of civilization.
The Tlascaltecans had proved their loyalty in the days of Cortés,
and this loyalty was insured by their exemption from tribute
and by other privileges. The practice of using them as colonists
in San Luis Potosí seems to have been begun as early as 1580.

In 1591 four hundred families were sent northward, most of them being distributed at various places in modern San Luis Potosi, but eighty families were established at Saltillo in a separate pueblo called San Estéban. Thence in later days little colonies were detached to all parts of Coahuila, Nuevo León, and Texas.

Parras; Urdiñola the Younger.—In 1594 Jesuits from Durango founded the mission of Santa Maria de Parras, and shortly afterward a colony of Spaniards and Tlascaltecans was established there. Of this district Urdiñola the Younger, lieutenant-governor of Nueva Vizcaya, became the magnate. He opened mines, subdued Indians, established immense ranches, and was veritable feudal lord. His principal hacienda was at Patos, but he had others, as at Parras and Bonanza. In 1594 he secured a commission to conquer New Mexico which was subsequently rescinded. A female descendant of his became the wife of the first Marquis of San Miguel de Aguayo, a title created in 1682 and long held by the leading men of the northeastern frontier.

Nuevo León.—A new jurisdiction was now carved out on the Gulf coast. In 1579 Luis de Carabajal, a Portuguese of Jewish extraction, secured a patent naming him governor and captain-general of the Kingdom of Nuevo León, a region extending two hundred leagues north and west from Pánuco, and delimiting Nueva Vizcaya and Nueva Galicia on the north and east. Carabajal's was the first conquistador's patent issued for New Spain based on the general ordinance of 1573 regulating new conquests. He was made governor and alguacil-mayor "for two lives," with a salary of 20,000 pesos and two encomiendas for himself. He had authority to grant encomiendas, and was obligated to make new conquests and settlements. Raising two hundred men in Spain and Mexico, he established headquarters for a time at Pánuco, whence he made exploring, gold hunting, and slave hunting expeditions.

León and Monterey.—Discovering minerals in the Sierra de San Gregorio, near the Rio Grande, in (or by) 1583, Carabajal founded there the city of León (now Cerralvo). Securing other families from Saltillo, in 1584 he founded San Luis, near the later Monterey, and appointed Castaño de Sosa alcalde mayor. Slave hunting expeditions from León proved so profitable that soon two hundred or more adventurers were attracted to the place, for the slaves found ready market at the mines of the interior. When the viceroy checked the abuse, León was gradually abandoned. With another colony from Saltillo, Carabajal founded Nuevo Almadén, near the present Monclova. While thus engaged he was charged with heresy, arrested, and condemned by the Inquisition together with almost his entire family. In 1596 Luis de Montemayor, lieutenant-governor of the province, founded Monterey with families from León and Saltillo. Three years later Montemayor was made governor, directly under the viceroy. In 1603 a Franciscan monastery was founded at Monterey, and became a new missionary center. Conflicts of jurisdiction between Nuevo León and Nueva Vizcaya became chronic and a serious hindrance to prosperity.

THE SETTLEMENT OF THE ATLANTIC SEABOARD

Fray Luís Cancer.—Meanwhile Florida and the Philippines had been conquered and colonized. Shortly after Coronado returned from New Mexico, the Moscoso party reached Pánuco. Viceroy Mendoza, in spite of previous failures, was willing to try his hand in ill-fated Florida, and he offered to equip Moscoso and his men for another attempt, but they declined. Florida had been "running with the blood of Indians," but Fray Luís Cancer, a disciple of Las Casas, offered to try to subdue it by peaceful methods. With a royal license he equipped a vessel at Vera Cruz, and with a few companions went in 1549 to Florida to convert the natives. He was murdered by them, however, and his companions returned.

De Luna and Villafañe.—But Florida was thought to be rich, especially at Coça, in northern Alabama, and new attempts at settlement were made. In 1558 the new viceroy was ordered to colonize Santa Elena, the scene of Ayllón's failure on the Carolina coast, and some other point not specified, the missionary work to be entrusted to the Dominicans. In the following year, therefore, Velasco sent Tristán de Luna, Coronado's second in command, from Vera Cruz with thirteen vessels and 1500 soldiers and colonists. Of the six captains three had been with De Soto, a fact which indicates the continuity of frontier interests.

The expedition landed at Pensacola Bay. Three vessels sent

on to Santa Elena were storm-driven and returned to Vera Cruz. Establishing a garrison at Pensacola (Ichuse), De Luna moved about a thousand colonists inland to Nanipacná on the Alabama River, whence an expedition was sent north to Coça. In 1560 the colony returned to Pensacola, where De Luna was replaced by Villafañe, who had been sent with supplies from Mexico. In the following year Villafañe went with most of his colony to Santa Elena, but failed to make a settlement, and the Pensacola garrison was soon withdrawn. In view of these repeated disasters, in 1561 Philip II declared that for the present no further attempt should be made to colonize Florida.

The French in Florida.—Notwithstanding this decision, there were reasons why Florida should be occupied. The route of the treasure and merchant ships lay through the Bahama channel, and French and English pirates had begun to attack them. To lessen the danger, vessels were ordered to go in company, and as early as 1552 a fleet of war vessels was sent to escort them to Havana. But a port was needed to give aid against the pirates, as well as to provide refuge from the violent storms on the Florida coast. Moreover, the French were operating on the northern Atlantic, and it was feared that they would occupy this region.

This fear was realized in 1562 when Jean Ribaut led a French Huguenot colony to Port Royal, South Carolina. The colony miserably failed, but in 1564 another, led by Laudonnière, settled on St. John's River and built Fort Caroline. Just as Laudonnière was about to abandon the place, Ribaut arrived with a third colony, bearing instructions to fortify a position that would enable him to command the route of the Spanish treasure fleets.

Menéndez de Avilés, and the expulsion of the French.—Philip decided now to eject the French and colonize Florida, and entrusted the task to Menéndez de Avilés, a great naval officer. He was made adelantado of Florida, and promised a private estate twenty-five leagues square, or some 300,000 acres. In return he agreed to take a colony of five hundred persons to Florida, build at least two fortified towns, and expel foreign "settlers and corsairs." In September, 1565, Menéndez reached Florida and founded St. Augustine. Ten days later he marched overland against Fort Caroline, surprised and captured it, and mercilessly

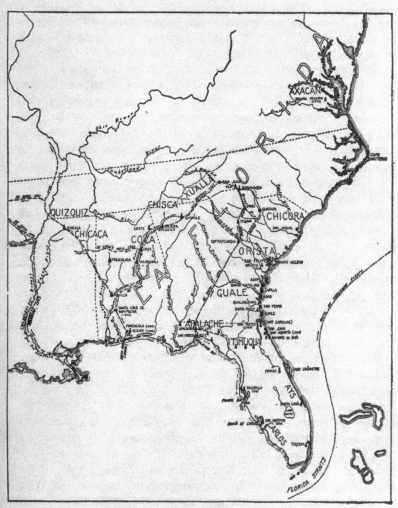

Spanish Florida

slew most of its defenders. On the spot the garrison of San Mateo was established.

Menéndez's relentless deed caused an outburst of indignation in France, and perhaps only Catherine's reliance on Philip in her troubles with the Huguenots prevented war. Vengeance was left to a private individual, Dominique de Gourgues. Getting up an expedition ostensibly to trade, in 1567 he went to Florida, and slew the garrison at San Mateo. The prisoners taken were hanged "not as Spaniards" but "as traitors, robbers, and murderers."

New settlements in Florida.—Menéndez planned great things. He would fortify the Bahama Channel, occupy Santa Elena and Chesapeake Bay, and in the latter seek the northern strait. As a base for expanding toward Pánuco, he would occupy the Bay of Juan Ponce, and he had great hopes of agricultural prosperity.

To carry out these plans, active steps were taken. Before Menéndez returned to Spain in 1567, several new Spanish posts were founded between the point of the peninsula and South Carolina. San Mateo was reoccupied. At Charlotte Bay Menéndez made an alliance with the much-feared Chief Carlos by marrying his sister, and founded there the presidio of San Antonio. Other garrisons were established on the peninsula at Ays, Santa Lucía, Tocobaga, and Tegesta. At Santa Elena, in South Carolina, Menéndez founded the colony of San Felipe, and in Guale (northern Georgia) he founded a presidio.

Explorations in the Alleghanies.—In November, 1566, Menéndez sent Juan Pardo from Santa Elena "to discover and conquer the interior country from there to Mexico," to join the two frontiers. Going northwest, he reached the snow covered Alleghanies in western North Carolina, established two garrisons on the way, and returned. Boyano, left at one of the garrisons, made expeditions into the mountains, and in 1567 marched southwest to Chiaha near Rome, Georgia. Being joined there by Pardo, they set out "in the direction of Zacatecas and the mines of San Martin," in Mexico, but were turned back by Indian hostility. On his way to San Felipe Pardo left two garrisons, which were soon massacred by Indians.

The Jesuit missions in Florida.—In 1566 Menéndez secured three Jesuit missionaries for Florida. Another band arrived in 1568, and went to Santa Elena, Orista, and Guale, where they founded missions. At first they were successful, but in 1570 they were driven out by native opposition. By this time the garrison at Tocobaga had been massacred and those at San Antonio and Tegesta withdrawn on account of Indian hostility.

The Virginia mission.—Father Segura, the Jesuit superior, now transferred his efforts to Chesapeake Bay, whither he went in 1570 with six missionaries. They founded a mission, perhaps on the Rappahannock, but soon all were slain. In 1571 Menéndez went in person to avenge the outrage. Two years later his nephew explored the entire coast from the Florida Keys to Chesapeake Bay. In 1573, the year before his death, Menéndez's grant was extended west to Pánuco.

Franciscans on the Georgia coast.—The martyrdom of Father Segura and his band caused the Jesuits to abandon the field for Mexico, but in 1573 Franciscans began work in the province. Twenty years later (1593) twelve more arrived under Father Juan de Silva. From the central monastery at St. Augustine they set forth and founded island missions all up the Florida and Georgia coast, on Amelia, Cumberland, St. Simon, San Pedro and Ossabua islands. Fray Pedro Chozas made inland explorations, and Father Pareja began his famous work on the Indian languages. Owing to an Indian uprising in 1597 the missions were abandoned for a time, but were soon restored as a check against the English, who now entered Virginia.

FOREIGN INTRUSIONS IN THE ATLANTIC

The Spanish trade monopoly.—The French had been expelled from Florida, and the coast occupied up to Port Royal Sound, but freebooters continued to prey on treasure and merchant vessels. Spain undertook to preserve the trade and wealth of the Indies as an absolute monopoly. All trade must be conducted by Spaniards in Spanish vessels, from specified Spanish ports to specified American ports. This monopoly was objectionable not only to the traders of other nations but to the Spanish colonists as well. To this economic grievance was added the bitter hatred felt by Protestant Frenchmen, Englishmen and Dutchmen for Catholic Spain, whose subjects were regarded as lawful prey.

The merchant fleets.—To prevent the plundering of commerce in the Indies, by French, English, and Dutch, Spain was forced to adopt a system of fleets sailing periodically and protected by convoys of armed galleons. After 1561 it became unlawful for vessels to sail alone to the Indies, except under special circumstances. Two fleets left Spain each year, one for Tierra Firme and Nombre de Diós (later Porto Bello) and the other for Vera Cruz. In the later sixteenth century the Nombre de Diós fleet comprised as many as forty armed galleons, but thereafter the number was much smaller, as foreigners cut into Spanish trade. The Vera Cruz fleet comprised fifteen or twenty merchantmen convoyed by two galleons. At Nombre de Diós goods and treasure from Peru and Chile were taken on. At Vera Cruz were gathered the exports from New Spain, the cargo from the Manila galleon brought overland from Acapulco, and the ten or twelve million dollars of royal revenues from the mines and taxes.

The freebooters.—This arrangement was an improvement, but French, Dutch, and English freebooters hung in the wake of the fleets to plunder any vessel which fell behind the galleons, while smuggling and town-sacking grew in frequency with the growing jealousy and hatred of Spain. The prototype of the English freebooters was John Hawkins, whose fleet was destroyed by the Spaniards at Vera Cruz in 1567. More famous was Francis Drake, who in 1585, during his third marauding expedition, went to the West Indies with twenty-five vessels, captured Santo Domingo, held Cartagena for ransom, and in May, 1586, sacked and burned St. Augustine, Florida. Hawkins and Drake were only two of a score of English freebooters who in the later sixteenth century harried Spanish commerce and plundered the coast towns. In the list are the names of Oxenham, Raleigh, Grenville, Clifford, Knollys, Winter, and Barker. The last exploit of the century was Clifford's capture of San Juan, Porto Rico, in 1598.

The English in the north Atlantic.—The voyages of Frobisher, Davis, and Gilbert in the northern Atlantic between 1576 and 1587, in search of the northwest passage, caused uneasiness for the security of Florida and of the northern strait. Equally disturbing were the efforts of Raleigh and his associates to colonize Roanoke Island and Guiana.

Decline of the West Indies.— The raids of the freebooters, the restrictions placed on commerce, the decline of mining and of the native population, and the superior attractions of Peru, Central America, and Mexico, had greatly reduced the prosperity of the West Indies. In 1574 Española had ten towns with 1000 Spanish families, and 12,000 negro slaves. The native population had dwindled to two villages. Santo Domingo, seat of the Audiencia and of the archdiocese, had seven hundred families. Cuba was less prosperous than Española, and population was still declining. The island had eight Spanish towns with a total population of some three hundred families and about an equal number of Indians. Santiago, once with a population of one thousand families, now had thirty. Havana, somewhat larger, was the residence of governor and bishop. Jamaica had three Spanish settlements and no Indians. Porto Rico, with three Spanish towns, had a population of some two hundred and eighty families, of whom two hundred lived at San Juan. The principal industries in all of the islands were sugar and cattle raising. There being no Indians in the West Indies now, there were no encomiendas.

THE PHILIPPINES AND CALIFORNIA

A new attempt in the East.—At the same time that Menéndez was establishing the province of Florida, the right wing of the Indies, Legazpi was conquering the Philippines, the left wing. The principal result of the Villalobos expedition (1542) had been to give the name of the Philippines to the Lazarus, or Western Islands. For nearly two decades thereafter nothing was done to advance the interests of Spain in the Far East, but Portuguese profits in the spice trade were tempting to both sovereign and subject, and the king set about making a new effort to share in these advantages.

The obvious base for such a trade was Mexico, and in 1559 Philip ordered Velasco to equip two vessels for discovery in the western islands, to test the chance for profits and the possibility of a return voyage across the Pacific. This order was issued just at the time when Spain was attempting to occupy the Carolina coasts, with a view, in part, to finding a northern strait leading to the Spice Islands. Thus were all these widely separated enterprises unified.

The Legazpi expedition.—To lead the expedition, Miguel López de Legazpi was chosen, with Fray Andrés de Urdaneta as chief navigator. The spiritual work was entrusted to Urdaneta and a band of Augustinians. Owing to many delays it was November, 1564, when the fleet left Navidad. In February, 1565, seven months before Menéndez reached Florida, Legazpi reached the Philippines. Three of the vessels were sent back with Urdaneta on board to discover a return route to New Spain. Instead of sailing east against wind and current, he turned northward beyond the trade belt, and entered that of the westerly winds. After a long and hard voyage he reached the American continent off the northern California coast, which he descended to Mexico. At last the Spaniards had discovered a way to return from the East safe from the Portuguese attacks.

Meanwhile Legazpi had occupied Cebú. Portuguese resistance caused a removal to Panay, but in 1571 Cebú was reoccupied and Manila founded. In the previous year Legazpi had received a commission as adelantado of the Islands, subject to the viceroy of Mexico. When Legazpi died in 1572 the conquest of the principal islands had been effected and with little bloodshed. In 1583 the Audiencia of Manila was established, subordinate to Mexico.

The Manila galleon.—In 1580 Portugal was united with Spain, and, until 1640, when Portugal regained her independence, Manila was an important center for the commerce of the combined Spanish and Portuguese colonies. A regular trade was established from Manila to Mexico and Spain, but was restricted to one or two annual galleons each way between Manila and Acapulco.

New interest in the California coast.—The development of the Philippine trade, the necessity of protecting it from other nations, continued interest in the Northern Mystery, and the opening of pearl fisheries in the Gulf of California, led to renewed exploration of the northern Pacific coasts and to renewed attempts to settle and develop California.

The regular course of the east-bound Manila galleon lay along the path marked out by Urdaneta northeastward from Manila to about latitude 42,° thence across the Pacific to the American

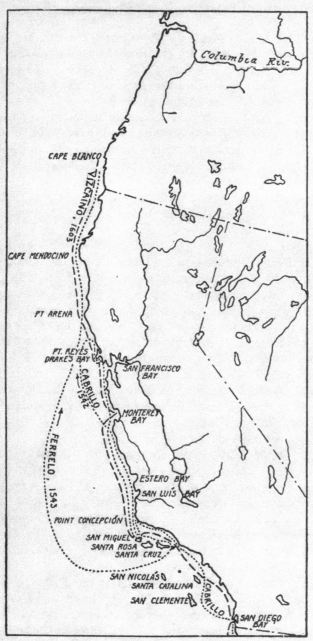

Explorations on the California Coast, 1542–1603

69

continent off Cape Mendocino, and down the coast to Acapulco. The voyage was arduous. By the time the vessels reached the American coast half of the scurvy-afflicted crew and passengers were dead, and the vessels needed repairs. Hence a port of call was gravely needed for the Manila galleons.

The Strait of Anian.—Moreover, Spanish interests in the Pacific were insecure. The Portuguese were no longer rivals, but French and English freebooters were active on the Atlantic and might venture upon the Pacific. Besides, there was the fear that the French, English, or Dutch, operating in the northern Atlantic, would discover the Strait of Anian and secure control of the direct route to the Spice Islands, just as Portugal had monopolized the African route.

Drake and Cavendish.—These fears were made realities in 1579 when Drake appeared on the California coast. In 1577 he had passed through the Straits of Magellan. Reaching the Pacific with only one vessel of the five with which he had started, he proceeded up the coast of South America, plundering as he went. In the harbour now known as Drake's Bay, just north of San Francisco, he refitted, claiming the country for England, and calling it New Albion. Drake then sailed to the East Indies, obtained a cargo of spices, crossed the Indian Ocean, rounded the Cape of Good Hope, and reached Plymouth in November, 1580. He claimed to have discovered the Strait of Anian, and this further disturbed the minds of the Spaniards. For his daring voyage he was knighted by Queen Elizabeth.

In 1586 Thomas Cavendish followed Drake's course. Reaching the point of California, he plundered the Manila galleon, the *Santa Ana*, and burned it to the water's edge. The voyages of Drake and Cavendish were soon followed by the formation of the British East India Company (1600) and by conflicts with the Spanish merchants in the Orient. In the wake of the English came the Dutch, who had passed the Straits of Magellan before the end of the sixteenth century.

Gali and Cermeño.—With the needs of the Pacific coast in view, Viceroy Moya Contreras (1584–1585) instructed Francisco de Gali to explore the northwestern coasts of America on his return from Manila in the galleon. Nothing came of Gali's orders, and Moya's successor discouraged further exploration. The second Viceroy Velasco (1590-1595), however, took up Moya's plan, and in 1595 Sebastián Rodríguez Cermeño undertook to carry out the project on his return from Manila. He was wrecked at Drake's Bay, however, and his crew made their way to Mexico in an improvised craft. The plan of reconnoitering the coast with laden Manila galleons was now given up for one of exploring in light vessels sent out from the ports of Mexico.

Vizcaíno's colony.—Royal interest in the protection of California was now combined with private interest in the pearl fisheries of the Gulf of California. Occasional expeditions had been made for this purpose since the days of Cortés and Alarcón. In 1595 Sebastián Vizcaíno, who had been engaged in the Manila trade, and, indeed, had been on the *Santa Ana* when it was captured by Cavendish, secured a contract authorizing him to gather pearls, in return for subduing and colonizing California. Leaving Acapulco late in 1596 with three vessels and a good-sized company, he established a colony at La Paz and explored some distance up the Gulf. But disaster soon followed, and early in 1597 the survivors returned to Mexico.

Vizcaíno's exploring expedition.—Vizcaíno attributed his failure to ignorance of the seasons, and proposed making another attempt at settlement and pearl fishing. While this question was being discussed, the king in 1599 ordered the outer coast of California explored again, with a view to finding a port for the Manila galleons. To conduct the expedition Vizcaíno was chosen. Leaving Acapulco in May, 1602, with three vessels, he ran all the coasts covered by Cabrillo and Ferrelo sixty years before. At Magdalena Bay, Cerros Island, San Diego Bay, and Santa Catalina Island extensive explorations were made. The capital event of the expedition, however, was the exploration of the Bay of Monterey (probably entered by Cermeño) and its designation as the desired port. One of the vessels reached Cape Blanco, but San Francisco Bay was missed, as before.

Plans to Occupy Monterey Bay.—Plans were now made for occupying the port of Monterey, but delays ensued and a new viceroy concluded that a port in the mid-Pacific was more needed than one on the California coast. Accordingly, in 1611 Vizcaíno was sent to explore certain islands called Rica de Oro and Rica de Plata, but the expedition failed.

THE FOUNDING OF NEW MEXICO

Renewed exploration of New Mexico.—The expansion of Nueva Vizcaya and renewed activities on the Pacific coast in the later sixteenth century stimulated a new advance into New Mexico. Coronado's expedition had proved disappointing, and for four decades no further explorations had been made in the region. Nevertheless, the tales of great cities had not been forgotten, and in the meantime a new line of approach to New Mexico had been opened by way of the central plateau. By 1580 mines and missions had reached Santa Bárbara, while slave hunting expeditions had descended the Conchos to the Rio Grande. Through reports given by the outlying tribes, a new interest in the Pueblo region was aroused.

Rodríguez and Espejo.—To follow up these reports, with a view to missionary work, trade, and exploration, an expedition was organized at Santa Bárbara in 1580 by Fray Augustín Rodríguez, a Franciscan lay brother, and Francisco Sánchez Chamuscado. In the next year the party of three friars and nine soldiers and traders descended the Conchos River, ascended the Rio Grande to the Pueblo region, visited the buffalo plains, Ácoma, and Zuñi, and returned, leaving two friars at Puaray, one having been killed. In the following year a rescue and trading party was led to New Mexico over the same trail by Fray Bernaldino Beltrán and Antonio de Espejo. The friars had already been slain by the natives, but before returning Espejo went to Zuñi, Moqui, and western Arizona, where he discovered mines, returning to Santa Bárbara by way of the Pecos River.

Plans to colonize New Mexico.—The expeditions of Rodríguez and Espejo aroused new zeal for northern exploration and settlement, and there were dreams now, not only of conquering New Mexico, but of going beyond to colonize Quivira and the shores of the Strait of Anian. The king ordered a contract made for the purpose, and soon there was a crowd of applicants for the honor. While these men were competing for the desired contract, Castaño de Sosa in 1590 led a colony from Nuevo León up the Pecos to the Pueblos and began their conquest, but was soon arrested and taken back. Some three years later two men named Leyva and Gutiérrez de Humaña led an unlicensed expedition from Nueva Vizcaya to New Mexico, whence Gutiérrez went to northeastern Kansas, and apparently reached the Platte River.

Oñate and the founding of New Mexico.—The contract to colonize New Mexico was finally assigned in 1595 to Juan de Oñate, son of Cristóbal, one of the founders of Zacatecas. In accordance with the ordinances of 1573 he was made governor, adelantado, and captain-general, granted extensive privileges, lands, and encomiendas, while his colonists were given the usual privileges of first settlers (*primeros pobladores*). It was February, 1598, when Oñate left northern Nueva Vizcaya with his colony. It included one hundred and thirty soldiers, some with their families, a band of Franciscans under Father Martinez, and more than seven thousand head of stock. Previous expeditions had followed the Conchos, but Oñate opened a more direct route through El Paso. Without difficulty he secured the submission of the tribes, settled his colony at San Juan, and distributed the friars among the pueblos.

Oñate's explorations.—Having established his colony, Oñate turned to exploration in the east and the west. In the fall of 1598 Vicente Zaldivar was sent to the Buffalo Plains, while the governor set out for the South Sea. At Moqui he turned back, but Marcos Farfán continued west with a party, and staked out mining claims on Bill Williams Fork. Acoma rebelled at this time and as a punishment was razed. In 1599 Zaldívar was sent to the South Sea and seems to have reached the lower Colorado. Early in 1601 Oñate, with seventy men, descended the Canadian River and crossed the Arkansas to an Indian settlement called Quivira, apparently at Wichita, Kansas. During Oñate's absence most of the colonists deserted, but they were brought back, with reinforcements. Still bent on reaching the South Sea, in 1604 Oñate descended Bill Williams Fork and the Colorado to the Gulf of California, where he got the idea that California was an island. He had reëxplored most of the ground covered by Coronado and had opened new trails. But he had lost the confidence and support of the authorities, and in 1608 resigned and was displaced by a royal governor.

Santa Fé Founded.—In 1609 Santa Fé was founded and became the new capital. This event, which occurred just a hun-

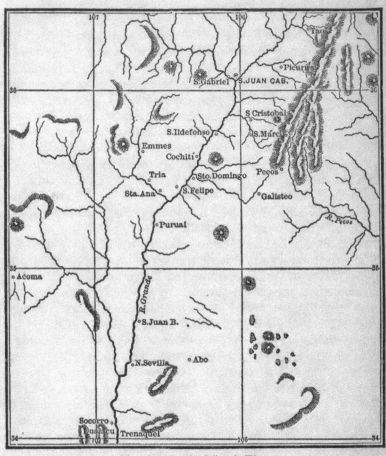

New Mexico in Oñate's Time
(From Bancroft, *Arizona and New Mexico*, p. 137)

dred years after the occupation of Darién, may be regarded as the culmination of a century of northward expansion.

SPANISH ACHIEVEMENTS IN THE SIXTEENTH CENTURY

Population and industries.—The heroic age of Spanish colonization had now passed. The surprising results achieved in the New World during the first eighty years, not counting the work of exploration, are set forth in a description of the colonies in 1574 written by López de Velasco, official geographer. At that time there were in North and South America about two hundred Spanish towns and cities, besides numerous mining camps, haciendas, and stock ranches. The Spanish population was 32,000 families, or perhaps from 160,000 to 200,000 persons. Of these about five-eighths lived in North America. In the two Americas there were 4000 encomenderos, the rest being mainly miners, merchants, ranchers, and soldiers, with their families. The population included 40,000 negro slaves, and a large element of mulattoes and mestizoes. About 1,500,000 male Indians paid tribute, representing a population of 5,000,000. In many parts occupied by Spaniards there were no encomiendas, for the Indians had died out. Mining, commerce, cattle ranching, grain and sugar raising had been established on a considerable scale.

Cities and towns.—Before the end of the sixteenth century most of the present-day state capitals and other large cities in Spanish North America had been founded. Mexico City had a population of over 2000 Spanish families (perhaps 15,000 persons), Santo Domingo, Puebla, and Guatemala 500 families each, Trinidad (in Guatemala) and Panamá 400 each, Oaxaca 350, Zacatecas 300, Toluca, Zultepec, Vera Cruz, Granada, Chiapas, and Nombre de Diós 200 each, Guadalajara and San Salvador 150 each, and many others lesser numbers.

Administrative divisions.—Spanish America was now divided into two viceroyalties, New Spain and Peru. New Spain included all of the American mainland north of Panamá, the West Indies, part of the northern coast of South America, the Islas del Poniente, and the Philippines. It comprised the four audiencias of Española, Mexico, Guatemala, and Nueva Galicia, the Audiencia of Panamá being a part of the viceroyalty of Peru. The four northern audiencia districts were subdivided into seventeen or eighteen gobiernos or provinces, corresponding closely to the modern states. The provinces were divided into *corregimientos* embracing Indian *partidos*. North America embraced twelve dioceses and the two archdioceses of Santo Domingo and Mexico.

Churches and monasteries.—Many fine churches, some of them still standing, had been built in the larger towns. The Franciscans, Dominicans, and Augustinians were well established in New Spain, and the Jesuits had just begun their work. The friars were subject to their chapters and the Jesuits to their general in Spain. The Franciscans already had four provinces in New Spain, the Dominicans and Augustinians only one each. Hundreds of monasteries had been established, especially wherever there were Indians in encomienda. The expense of erecting them was borne jointly by king, encomenderos, and Indians.

The Universities.—"Enthusiam for education characterizes the earliest establishment of the Spanish colonies in America. Wherever the priests went, a school was soon established for the instruction of the natives or a college for its clericals who were already at work as well as for those who were soon to take holy orders. From the colleges sprang the universities which, in all the Spanish dominions, were founded at a very early date for the pursuit of the 'general studies' which were at that time taught in the great peninsular universities of Alcala and Salamanca. Half a century before Jamestown was founded by the English, the University of Mexico was conferring degrees upon graduates in law and theology. Before the seventeenth century closed, no less that seven universities had been erected in Spanish America, and their graduates were accepted on an equality with those of Spanish institutions of like grade." (Priestley.)

READINGS

THE REIGN OF PHILIP II

Chapman, Charles E., *A History of Spain*, Chapter XXXIII; Gayarré, C. E. A., *Philip II of Spain;* Hume, M. A. S., *Philip II of Spain;* Hume, M. A. S., *Spain, Its Greatness and Decay;* Hume, M. A. S., *The Spanish People;* Lea, H. C., *A History of the Inquisition of Spain;* Merriman, R. B., *The Rise of the Spanish Empire;* Prescott, W. H., *History of the Reign of*

Philip the Second; Cheyney, E. P., *European Background of American History,* Chapter X.

ADVANCE INTO NORTHERN MEXICO

Bancroft, H. H., *History of Mexico,* II, chs. 22, 24, 34; *North Mexican States and Texas,* I, ch. 5; Cavo, Andrés, *Tres·Siglos de Mexico;* Coroléu, José, *America, Historia de su Colonización;* Frejes, Fr. F., *Conquista de los Estados;* Gonzáles, J. E., *Colleción de Noticias; Historia de Nuevo León;* León, A., *Historia de Nuevo León;* Mota Padilla, M., *Historia de Nueva Galicia,* ch. 23; Ortega, Fr. Joseph, *Apostólica Afanes.*

SETTLEMENT OF FLORIDA

Hamilton, P. J., *The Colonization of the South,* chs. 1-2; Lowery, Woodbury, *Spanish Settlements,* I, ch. 8, II; Shea, J. G., *The Catholic Church in Colonial Days,* pp. 100-183.

SETTLEMENT OF NEW MEXICO

Bancroft, H. H., *Arizona and New Mexico,* 74-146; Bandelier, A. D.·F., *Final Report of Investigations among the Indians of the Southwestern United States* (Papers of the Archæological Institute of America, III-IV); Benavides, *Memorial on New Mexico* (Mrs. E. E. Ayer, trans.); Bolton, H. E., ed., *Spanish Exploration in the Southwest,* 135-278; Davis, W. H. H., *Spanish Conquest in New Mexico,* 234-407; Farrand, Livingston, *The Basis of American History,* 176-187; Lummis, C. F., *Spanish Pioneers in the Southwest,* 125-143; Prince, L. B., *Historical Sketches of New Mexico,* 149-166; Twitchell, R. E., *Leading Facts of New Mexican History,* I, 7-45, 252-333; Villagrá, Gaspar de, *Historia de Nuevo Mexico.*

THE PHILIPPINES AND CALIFORNIA

Barrows, D. P., *A History of the Philippines;* Blair and Robertson, *Philippine Islands,* II, 23-330; Bolton, H. E., *Spanish Exploration in the Southwest,* 41-133; Carrasco y Guisasola, Francisco, *Documentos Referentes al Reconocimiento de las Costas de las Californias;* Hittell, T. H., *History of California,* I, 79-111; Richman, I. B., *California under Spain and Mexico,* 12-24; Robertson, J. A., "Legaspi and Philippine Island Colonization," in American Historical Association, *Rpt., 1907,* I, 145-165; Zárate, Salmerón, "Relation," in *Land of Sunshine,* XI, 336-346, XII, 39-48, 104-114, 180-187.

CHAPTER IV

THE ESTABLISHMENT OF THE FRENCH COLONIES

THE FRENCH BACKGROUND

Mediæval France and the Italian wars.—The history of Mediæval France is largely the story of the struggle of the French kings to overthrow the feudal nobility and to perfect the governmental machinery of absolutism. The process which began with the accession of Hugh Capet in 987 was practically completed by the end of the reign of Louis XI, in 1483. During the reigns of Charles VIII, Louis XII, and Francis I, the great ambition of the French monarchs was to get control of Italy, a policy which brought them into conflict with Spain. The wars were barren of results as far as conquests in Italy were concerned, but the dangers to which France was exposed united the French people into a great nation, which was destined to be the leading continental power.

The religious wars.—The Reformation spread into France, Calvinism being the form of Protestantism which there took root. Calvin's religious system had three distinguishing features: (1) the church was to be independent of any temporal power, (2) laymen and ministers were to join in the government of the church, and (3) a strict moral discipline was to be enforced. This program was distinctly democratic, and was certain to come into conflict with the absolutism of the crown. France became divided into two great parties. The Huguenots, as the French Protestants were called, were found mainly among the rich burghers of the towns and the nobles of the country districts, their chief power being in southwestern France. They were also strong in Dauphiné and Normandy. Their great leaders were Coligny and the Bourbon princes, the most distinguished of whom was Henry of Navarre. The Catholic party was headed by the Guises and Catherine de Medici. The kings during this period were mere puppets, who were used by the leaders to further their political ends.

War broke out in 1562 and continued with occasional inter-
missions until 1596. The most important events were the assassin-
ation of Francis of Guise in 1563, the ascendency of Coligny, during which he tried to unite the nation in a war against Spain,
the massacre of St. Bartholomew's in 1572, the organization of
the Catholic League headed by Henry of Guise, his assassina-
tion in 1588, and the murder of Henry III the following year,
which made the way clear for Henry of Navarre to ascend the
throne. In 1593 he accepted Catholicism. The last resistance
in France was overcome in 1596, but war with Philip II continued
two years longer. In 1598 Henry issued the Edict of Nantes,
which secured toleration to the Huguenots.

Reforms of Henry IV.—During the religious wars, the nobles
had regained some of their former power, and the ravages of war
had almost ruined the industries of the country. Henry set to
work to repair these conditions. The lesser nobles were forced
to submit and the privileges of the more powerful were purchased.
The king's great minister, Sully, carried out many of the economic
reforms. The land tax called the *taille*, which rested most heavily
upon the peasants, was more equitably distributed, and the hunting privileges of the nobles were decreased. New lines of agriculture were introduced, marshes were reclaimed, and restrictions
on the marketing of grain were removed. The king encouraged
manufactures, especially of the more expensive fabrics, glass,
and metal work. Commerce was stimulated by securing safe
transportation along the post roads, by a system of canals connecting the Seine and the Loire, and by commercial treaties with
foreign states. Attempts were also made to stimulate commerce
and colonization by the formation of mercantile companies, and
from this period date the first successful French colonies in
America.

Richelieu.—Henry IV was assassinated in 1610, and his son,
who ascended the throne as Louis XIII, was a child of nine
years. During the regency of his mother, Mary de Medici, the
nobles again became turbulent, the Huguenots revolted, and the
policy of hostility toward Spain was reversed. The regent was
under the influence of favorites who looted the treasury. Under
such conditions a strong leader was greatly needed; the man of
the hour was Richelieu. In 1624 he was placed in control of

public affairs, and for the next twenty years practically ruled France. His policy aimed to make France the first power in Europe. To accomplish this he worked at home to strengthen the power of the crown. Abroad he aimed to weaken the power of the Hapsburgs, to extend the boundaries of France, and to build up a colonial empire. ·

The chief steps by which his policy was carried out were as follows: La Rochelle, the great Huguenot stronghold, was captured and the power of the Protestants was curbed effectually; the intrigues of Mary de Medici were thwarted; an alliance was made with Sweden, and to weaken the Hapsburgs the power of France was used to assist the Protestants in Germany in the Thirty Years' War; a navy was built and important ports were fortified; to extend commerce and colonies, colonial enterprises were entrusted to exclusive corporations. During the administration of Richelieu the French hold upon eastern Canada was strengthened, settlements were made in Guiana and the West Indies, and an attempt was made to occupy Madagascar.

The Council of State.—The work of strengthening the crown at the expense of the nobility was continued. The power of the nobles was maintained by their fortified castles and by their position as governors of provinces. An edict was issued for the destruction of all but the frontier fortifications. Most of the work of administration was centered in the *conseil d'etat*, or council of state, which was the highest judicial tribunal. It also issued edicts, made peace or war, determined the amount and method of taxation, and acted as a high court of justice. In appearance this body was supreme, but in reality the power centered in the king and the chief minister, the other ministers being merely advisers. Local administration was taken from the nobles and was placed almost wholly in the hands of *intendants*, who were officers of justice, police, and finance.

Mazarin.—Richelieu died in November, 1642, and Louis XIII a few months later. Louis XIV was a child of five years and his mother, Anne of Austria, became regent. Mazarin, who was probably secretly married to her, was to rule France during the troubled minority of the king. It was a period of civil and foreign war, in which the minister found no time to devote to the development of colonies. The importance of the period lies in the fact that the great nobles were effectually quelled, that the absolutism of the crown was completely established, and that France proved herself superior to the power of Spain and the Hapsburgs. When Louis XIV took the reins of power in 1661 he was the most absolute and most powerful monarch in Europe.

Colbert.—Colonial development during the reign of Louis XIV was due mainly to Colbert, who was given charge of the finances, of the navy, and of the colonies. The finances had become deranged under Mazarin, and Colbert attacked the abuses. To stimulate commerce and manufactures, he established a protective system, furnished governmental aid to companies, and granted monopolies. The royal navy and mercantile marine were greatly increased. To develop foreign trade, corporations were granted monopolies of the commerce of the West Indies, the East Indies, Senegal, and Madagascar. Colonies were fostered by paternalistic regulations. The system of Colbert, as time proved, was founded on mistaken principles, for monopoly and overregulation stifled the growth of trade and of the colonies. Although a vast area was brought under control, the colonies never attracted a large population, or were allowed a free growth of institutions.

EARLY EXPLORATIONS AND COLONIZING EFFORTS

First French voyages.—The first Frenchmen who visited America appear to have been Norman and Breton fishermen, who engaged in fishing off the Newfoundland coast perhaps as early as 1500. Sailors from Dieppe also visited the coasts of North and South America. Vague accounts have come down to us of attempts to explore the Gulf of St. Lawrence in 1506 and 1508, and of an unsuccessful colony on Sable Island in 1518. The first expedition under the government sanction was that of the Florentine, Verrazano, sent out by Francis I in 1524. The details of the voyage are somewhat obscure. He probably explored the coast from Cape Fear to Newfoundland.

Cartier and Roberval.—The wars between Francis I and Charles V prevented the French king from giving further attention to exploration until 1534, when Cartier was sent out with two ships from St. Malo. He sighted land on the Labrador coast, passed through the straits of Belle Isle, and explored the Gulf of St. Lawrence, locating the Bay of Chaleurs, Cape Gaspé, and Anticosti Island, thence returning to France.

In 1535 he again visited America in search of a passage to China. He sailed along the northern shore of the Gulf of St. Lawrence and entered the mouth of the river, soon becoming convinced that the passage did not lead to the Far East. He stopped at the site of Quebec and later proceeded to the La Chine rapids, and to a hill which he named Montreal. He wintered at Quebec where twenty-five persons died of scurvy. The return to France was made the following summer.

Exploration was again interrupted by the wars, and it was not until 1541 that Cartier's third expedition sailed. Francis I had granted a commission to Roberval, a Picardy nobleman, as viceroy and lieutenant-general in Canada, Newfoundland, Labrador, and neighboring lands, this being the first time that the name Canada was officially used. In the king's proclamation Canada was mentioned as the extremity of Asia. The objects of the expedition were discovery, settlement, and conversion of the Indians. Cartier was appointed captain-general. He sailed in 1541, but Roberval remained in France to collect supplies and materials for defence. Cartier wasted six weeks in Newfoundland and then proceeded to Quebec, where the winter was spent in great hardship.

The colonists started to return to France, but at St. Johns, Newfoundland, they met Roberval, who ordered them to return to Quebec. Cartier, however, disobeyed, and returned to France. Roberval proceeded to Quebec, where habitations were erected and the forts of Cartier repaired. Supplies, however, ran short, and during the following winter a third of the settlers died. A mutiny threatened and Roberval checked it with great harshness. After lingering a little longer, the unfortunate remnant returned to France. In 1543 Francis I declared the Western Sea to be open to his subjects, but advantage of it was not taken, and it was over a half century before another attempt was made to colonize in the St. Lawrence Valley.

Ribaut and Laudonnière.—The next colonizing efforts were of Huguenot origin, and were made at the suggestion of Coligny.

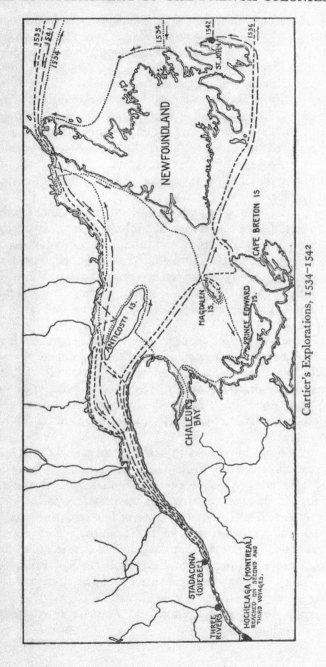

Cartier's Explorations, 1534–1542

In 1555 an attempt was made to found a colony in Brazil, but it was destroyed by the Portuguese. When Coligny developed his plan for an attack upon Spain, he determined to found a colony in the region then known as Florida. A Huguenot from Dieppe named Jean Ribaut was placed in command of the expedition, which set sail from Havre in 1562. Land was seen not far from the site of St. Augustine; they sailed northward and planted a settlement on Port Royal Sound, where thirty men were left. Ribaut explored the coast as far as the fortieth degree and returned to France. Misfortune beset the colonists, and after great suffering they built a rude vessel and succeeded in getting back to Europe.

In 1564 a large expedition was sent out under Laudonnière, which erected Fort Caroline on St. John's River. Dissensions and starvation played havoc with the colony, and when the English Captain John Hawkins offered to sell them a ship and provisions, they eagerly embraced the opportunity. When they were about to depart, Ribaut with seven vessels and six hundred soldiers hove in sight, and the idea of returning to France was abandoned.

Philip II learned of the French colony, probably from Catherine de Medici, and in 1565 sent an expedition of nineteen vessels and fifteen hundred men under Menéndez to destroy it. Ribaut's fleet was found near the mouth of the river but the larger craft escaped and Menéndez, finding the rest in a secure position, proceeded southward about fifty miles and founded St. Augustine.

Ribaut followed but failed to attack, and shortly afterwards a hurricane dispersed the fleet. Taking advantage of the misfortune, Menéndez marched overland and surprised and captured Fort Caroline, putting most of the prisoners to the sword. A little later Ribaut and his followers fell into the hands of Menéndez, and most of them were put to death. To avenge the butchery, the Chevalier de Gourgues, at his own expense, fitted out three small ships in 1567 and attacked the Spanish forts on the St. John's. They were captured and the garrisons slain. His force being too small to risk an attack on St. Augustine, De Gourgues returned to France, and Florida ceased to be a scene of French activity.

ACADIA

Colonization renewed.—The scene of the next colonization by the French was the region about the Bay of Fundy. After the religious wars, in 1598, the Marquis de la Roche landed two shiploads of colonists on Sable Island. Going in search of a site on the mainland, he encountered severe storms and returned to France. Five years later the survivors were rescued.

The fur monopoly.—In 1600 a partnership was formed between Pontgravé, a St. Malo mariner, and two Huguenot friends of Henry IV, Chauvin, a merchant of Harfleur, and Sieur de Monts, the associates being granted a fur-trading monopoly. A settlement was made at Tadoussac, on the lower St. Lawrence, but it did not prosper; two trading voyages, however, proved profitable. Shortly afterward the company was reorganized, the king making De Chastes, the governor of Dieppe, his representative. An expedition commanded by Pontgravé was sent out in 1603. Associated with him was Samuel de Champlain, who had already gained fame by a voyage to Spanish America and by his writings. A profitable trade in furs was carried on, and the St. Lawrence was explored as far as the La Chine rapids. Champlain also examined the Acadian coast as far as the Bay of Chaleurs.

Port Royal.—Upon the return of the traders, De Chastes having died, the king issued a patent to De Monts granting him viceregal powers and a trade monopoly between the fortieth and forty-sixth degrees. Settlements were to be founded and the savages were to be instructed in Christianity. In 1604 De Monts and Champlain sailed for Acadia. An unsuccessful attempt at settlement was made at St. Croix Island and later the survivors moved to Port Royal. De Monts then returned to France to defend his rights against those who objected to his patent, and Champlain busied himself with the exploration of the New England coast, on one expedition rounding Cape Cod. In 1607 it became known that De Monts's patent had been revoked, and Champlain returned to France.

Acadia, 1610–1632.—In 1610 Poutrincourt reëstablished Port Royal and soon afterward his son, Biencourt, was placed in command. The coast was surveyed as far as the Kennebec. Pontgravé had a trading post at St. John, and this Biencourt captured. In 1613 Port Royal was taken and burned by a Virginia expedition under Argall, but was soon rebuilt. In 1623 or 1624 Biencourt died and his lieutenant, Charles de la Tour, succeeded him. Before his powers could be confirmed, Acadia, in 1628, fell into English hands, but was restored in 1632.

Charnisay and La Tour.—Isaac de Rezilly was sent to receive the submission of the English, being shortly afterward succeeded by Charnisay. La Tour soon afterward received from the company of New France a grant at the mouth of the St. John's River, where he built Fort St. Jean. A civil war broke out in which La Tour finally secured aid from Boston. For a time he was successful, but Charnisay obtained help from France and La Tour was defeated. From 1645 to 1650 Charnisay was supreme in Acadia. Upon his death La Tour was made governor and lieutenant-general, and the animosities of the past were dissipated by his marriage to Charnisay's widow.

English Rivalry.—In 1654 an English fleet captured the French forts, and Acadia remained under English rule until 1667, when it was restored to France by the treaty of Breda.

THE ST. LAWRENCE VALLEY

The founding of Quebec.—In 1608 De Monts obtained a renewal of his patent for one year, and, after consulting Champlain, he decided to found a settlement at Quebec. Champlain was appointed his lieutenant with full powers, and with two vessels he arrived at Quebec on July 3. A storehouse and dwelling were built surrounded by a palisade and ditch. Of the twenty-eight men who began the settlement, only eight survived the first winter, but considerable reinforcements arrived in the spring. In the summer of 1609 Champlain accompanied a war party of Algonquins and Hurons up the Richelieu River to the lake which bears his name, where a successful attack was made upon the Iroquois. The consequences of this act were far reaching, for from that time the Iroquois confederation was hostile to the French, crippling the colony for many years.

A new company formed.—De Monts's exclusive privileges were not renewed, but he was allowed to retain his position of king's representative. Seeing no chance for profit, he withdrew from further activities in the New World. Another company was at once formed, composed of traders of Rouen and St. Malo. Champlain was retained by the new company.

Champlain's explorations.—In 1613 Champlain explored the Ottawa River to a point about one hundred miles above the modern capital of Canada. In 1615 four Recollet friars were induced to come to Quebec, this being the beginning of missionary activities in New France. The same year Champlain joined a Huron war party, passed up the Ottawa to Lake Nipissing, thence by the French River to Georgian Bay, being the first white man to find the way which eventually became the regular fur trader's route to the interior. Lake Ontario was also seen and crossed for the first time on this expedition. Fur trading was actively carried on, but because of dishonest dealings the company gradually lost influence with the Indians, a condition which also hampered the missionaries. As the Recollets met with little success, in 1625 the Jesuits were induced to send out five representatives, thus beginning the activities of that order in New France.

The Company of the Hundred Associates.—In spite of all the efforts which had been made, the financial results were trifling. So badly were affairs going that Richelieu determined to change the organization; in 1627 he established the Company of the Hundred Associates, who were to send out annually from two to three hundred settlers and a sufficient number of clergy to meet the needs. The company was to possess all lands between Florida and the Arctic Circle, and from Newfoundland as far west as it was able to take possession. With the exception of the cod and whale fisheries, the company was granted a complete monopoly of trade.

The English occupation.—Before the company could land colonists, difficulties arose between France and England, and a fleet of privateers under Captain David Kirke raided the French possessions off Gaspé, capturing eighteen vessels which were carrying colonists and supplies to Quebec; after destroying the settlements in Acadia, Kirke sailed for England. The following year he landed at Tadoussac and sent three vessels to Quebec to demand its surrender. The place capitulated and over a hundred of the inhabitants were sent to England. Upon their arrival, it was found that peace had been made. Negotiations were terminated in 1632, Canada and Acadia being restored to France.

Last years of Champlain. Nicolet.—Upon his return Champlain immediately repaired the buildings at Quebec, and established a fort at Three Rivers to protect the Hurons against the Iroquois. From time to time Champlain had heard of a great waterway in the west. Believing that it might be a route to China, in 1634 he sent Nicolet on an exploring expedition. Nicolet passed up the Ottawa, traversed Georgian Bay, and reached Sault Ste. Marie. He then explored the south shore of the upper peninsula of Michigan, and reached the southern extremity of Green Bay. From the Winnebagoes he learned of a "great water" three days' journey toward the south. After visiting the Illinois country, he returned without having reached the Mississippi. In 1635 Champlain died; there was no master mind to direct operations, and the colony languished.

The Jesuits.—The first Jesuit superior was Father Le Jeune, who in 1632 was stationed at Quebec in the residence of Notre Dame des Anges, the parent establishment of the missions of New France. Le Jeune ministered to the Algonquins of the neighborhood. In 1633 Bréboeuf headed a group of missionaries to the Huron villages at the southern end of Georgian Bay, and in 1641 a mission was founded at Sault Ste. Marie, but it was not permanent. Pestilence and the war parties of the Iroquois gradually destroyed the Hurons; the Jesuits toiled amid scenes of famine, disease, and death, several succumbing to the hardships, others suffering martyrdom. So constant were the attacks of the Iroquois, that in 1649 it was determined to establish a more sheltered mission on the Island of St. Joseph in Georgian Bay. The missions on the mainland being destroyed by the Iroquois, and the Hurons having been greatly reduced in numbers, in 1650 the Jesuits abandoned that region. Attempts to establish missions among the Iroquois also failed completely at this time. In the settlements the Jesuits were the most important social factor, until 1665 practically controlling the life of the people. At Quebec they established schools for Huron and French boys, and at their suggestion the Ursulines opened a convent. Private endowments made possible a school for girls near Quebec and a hospital at Montreal.

The French in Canada, 17th Century

The founding of Montreal.—For the purpose of founding an evangelical colony, a group of religious persons at Paris formed an association called the Association of Montreal. The island on which the city now stands was purchased, and in 1641 De Maisonneuve, with a Jesuit priest and thirty-seven laymen, sailed from La Rochelle. After taking formal possession of the island, the party wintered at Quebec, and the following spring founded the town of Montreal.

The New Company.—The Hundred Associates not having fulfilled their agreement regarding settlers, and the colony having proved a financial failure, an arrangement was made in 1645 between the company and the inhabitants acting as a corporation, henceforth known as the New Company. The old company retained its governmental rights, but the fur trade was thrown open to the New Company on condition that it would assume the expenses of civil administration, defence, and religion, that it would bring in twenty settlers annually, and would pay to the old company a thousand pounds of beaver skins every year.

Coureurs de bois.—Up to this time the fur trade had been carried on mainly at the settlements, but after the New Company was formed a larger number of men began to frequent the forests, giving rise to the type known as *coureurs de bois*. These were of two classes, those who merely traded with the Indians for peltries, and those who attached themselves to native tribes. This latter class lapsed into barbarism and became a lawless element which gave great annoyance to the officials. Later a third class of traders appeared when the governors were allowed to grant licenses to frequent the forests. Great abuses crept into the fur trade, large quantities of spirits being sold to the Indians, who were roundly cheated when intoxicated. It was the intention of the French government to restrict the trade to the settlements, but the officials usually winked at violations of the law, and some of them shared in the illicit trading. The most famous of the fur traders of this period were Radisson and Groseilliers, who, in 1658–1659 and possibly earlier, traded and explored in the country at the western end of Lake Superior.

REORGANIZATION AND THE IROQUOIS WARS

A centralist system established.—As complaints arose regarding the last governmental arrangements, the king changed the form of control, creating a council to consist of the governor, any ex-governor who might be in the country, and the superior of the Jesuits, who was later to give way to a bishop when one was appointed; these were to select for membership two inhabitants, or three if no ex-governor was in the colony. Quebec, Montreal, and Three Rivers were each to select a syndic, who could hold office for three years and could deliberate with but could not vote in the council. The centralist system, which Mazarin was perfecting in France, was thus established in Canada.

Laval.—New France had been attached to the archbishopric of Rouen, and De Queylus, a Sulpician priest at Montreal, had acted as vicar-general for the whole colony. His followers hoped that he would be created bishop, but instead, in 1659 a Jesuit, the Abbé Laval, was appointed vicar-apostolic and Bishop of Petraea *in partibus*. After a spirited contest with De Queylus, Laval was successful in establishing his supremacy, the power of the Jesuits thus being assured.

War with the Iroquois.—The following year witnessed a serious Iroquois outbreak. News arrived that twelve hundred warriors had gathered to wipe out the settlements. A young nobleman, popularly known as Dollard, conceived the quixotic scheme of intercepting a large force of Iroquois who had wintered on the Ottawa. With sixteen enlisted men and a few Hurons and Algonquins he proceeded to a palisade at the great rapids of the Ottawa, and there met the Indians. Dollard and his followers were slain to a man, but so stubborn had been their resistance that the Iroquois retired to the forests and New France was saved. A regiment was sent out to protect the colony, forts were established along the Richelieu, and two expeditions were sent into the Iroquois country, the result being that a peace was made with the Indians which lasted for several years. Later an expedition was sent to the outlet of Lake Ontario to impress the savages with the power of France.

The West India Company.—In 1663 the company of New France surrendered its rights to the king, who created a council to consist of the governor, bishop, and five councillors chosen by them jointly. The following year, at the suggestion of Colbert, he chartered a new corporation known as the West India Company, to which was given a monopoly of all the trade of New France and the west coast of Africa, with the privilege of nominating the governor of Canada. The office of intendant was also created to act as a check upon the governor. This official was to act as a legal and financial officer who was to report directly to the crown. The first intendant was Talon, who was a prominent figure for several years. The governor who was the military, political, and administrative agent of the king, the intendant, and the bishop were the real rulers of New France. Their divided authority and jealousies later led to frequent disputes, which greatly retarded the development of the colonies.

Talon.—It was Talon who first realized the possibilities of New France. To promote commerce he built a vessel which he despatched to the West Indies with a cargo of fish, staves, and lumber. He planned an overland road to Acadia and urged the occupation of the Hudson River Valley, projects, however, which were not realized. At Quebec he erected a brewery and tannery. Young women were brought from France as wives for the colonists and soldiers, and bounties were offered for the birth of children. In 1666 the total population was 3418; five years later it had increased to 6000.

Seignorial grants.—To aid in colonization and protection Talon established a type of feudalism. Along the Richelieu River as high up as Chambly and along the St. Lawrence from the neighborhood of Montreal to a point several miles below Quebec, most of the lands were portioned out. The majority of these seignorial grants were made to officers of the regiment of Carrigan, which had been stationed in Canada. Discharged soldiers were settled on the grants as tenant farmers. The seignorial holdings varied in size from half a league to six leagues on the river and extended back from half a league to two leagues. The buildings of the seigniory were the "mansion," which was usually a log house, a fort, chapel, and mill. The poverty of the proprietor, however, frequently prevented the erection of some of the buildings, the mill sometimes being lacking or serving the double duty of fort and mill; on other grants chapel, mill, and

fort were never built. In the more exposed localities the houses of
the tenants were built together in palisaded villages. On other
grants the dwellings lined the shore, forming what were called
cotes. Near Quebec Talon laid out a model seigniory and three
model villages, each village being provided with a carpenter,
mason, blacksmith, and shoemaker. But the settlers did not
profit by the example and continued to build near the rivers.
With the exception of Talon's villages, one could have seen
nearly every house in Canada by paddling a canoe up the St.
Lawrence and the Richelieu. One of the most famous seigniories
in Canada was that of the Le Moyne family.

THE WEST INDIES

The Company of St. Christopher.—In 1625 a small brigantine
commanded by Pierre d'Esnambuc and Urbain de Roissey, "the
pirate of Dieppe," sailed to the West Indies. After escaping
from a Spanish galleon near Jamaica, they proceeded to St.
Christopher, where a settlement was begun. The following year
the Company of St. Christopher was formed, and three vessels
with over five hundred men set sail from France in 1627, but
only half of them survived the voyage. Two settlements were
formed, one at each end of the island, the English having already occupied the middle. In 1628 and 1629 about five hundred more were sent out, and in the latter year ten vessels were
despatched to defend the colonists. In spite of this a Spanish
fleet broke up the settlements; the fugitives fled to St. Martin,
and after a vain attempt to settle Antigua and Montserrat,
most of them returned to St. Christopher, which had been abandoned by the Spanish. Only three hundred and fifty survived.

Santo Domingo.—A few of them went to the northern coast of
Santo Domingo, whence they carried on buccaneering enterprises against the Spaniards. After the Spanish attack the
company did little to assist, and the colony was left to its own
devices. Trade with the Dutch immediately sprang up and the
settlers began to make a profit from tobacco.

Guadeloupe, Martinique, and Tortuga.—In 1634 the Company of St. Christopher was bankrupt, and the following year it
was reorganized as the Company of the Isles of America. Guadeloupe and Martinique were immediately occupied. In 1640 the

English were expelled from Tortuga, and the island was occupied by Levasseur, who soon broke loose from the control of the company and conducted a pirate haven. Several of the smaller islands were also occupied. The French West Indies soon attracted a considerable immigration, in 1642 the population being estimated at more than seven thousand. The tobacco business not continuing profitable, sugar began to take its place as the staple product. Due mainly to the clash of authority among officials, a condition which led to anarchy, by 1648 the company was bankrupt.

Other Islands occupied.—Between 1649 and 1651 the various islands were sold to proprietors who ruled them until 1664. Between 1648 and 1656 settlements were made on St. Martin, St. Bartholomew, St. Croix, The Saints, Marie Galante, St. Lucia, and Granada, and by 1664 the French flag floated over fourteen of the Antilles. The sugar business proved to be exceedingly profitable and cultivation of the cane made slave-labor desirable. Population increased rapidly, in 1655 the whites numbering about fifteen thousand and slaves being almost as numerous. During the period of the proprietors there was little restriction on commerce, most of the carrying trade passing into the hands of the Dutch.

The Crown assumes control.—Colbert became controller-general of the finances in 1662, one of his functions being the control of the colonies. He determined to send a representative to assert the king's authority; in 1663 De Tracy was made lieutenant-general in all the French colonies and was given supreme executive and judicial powers. The following year he sailed with De La Barre who was about to establish a colony at Cayenne. De Tracy soon established the king's authority and corrected abuses in the West Indies, and then proceeded to Quebec, where he remained until 1667.

The West India Company.—In 1664 Louis chartered the great company which was granted the mainland of South America from the Orinoco to the Amazon, the island of Cayenne, the French West Indies, Newfoundland, Acadia, Canada, the rest of the mainland of North America as far south as Florida, and the African coast from Cape Verde to the Cape of Good Hope. Former proprietors were to be compensated, and with the excep-

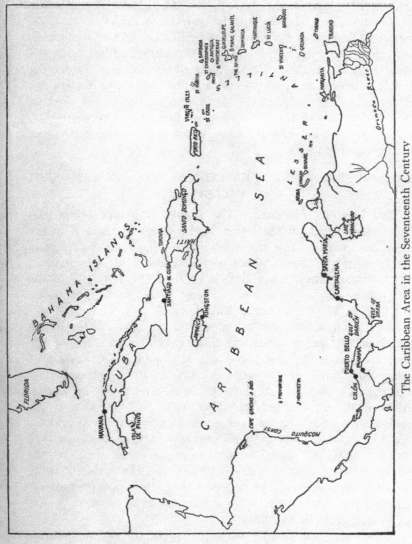

The Caribbean Area in the Seventeenth Century

tion of the fisheries of Newfoundland, the company was to have
a monopoly of trade and colonization for forty years. After
considerable opposition the company succeeded in establishing its
authority in the islands, but the war which broke out in 1666
between France, and England and Holland proved disastrous,
a French fleet which was sent to protect the Antilles being destroyed by the English. Colbert assisted the company financially,
but it failed to become a profitable undertaking and in 1674 was
dissolved. The inhabitants, however, continued to prosper,
mainly because of the increasing number of independent merchants who traded with the islands and the growing importance
of the sugar industry.

OPENING THE UPPER LAKE REGION AND THE MISSISSIPPI VALLEY

Two Lines of Approach.—The French had now established
themselves firmly in the lower St. Lawrence basin and in the
Caribbean area. From these two bases they now proceeded to
the Mississippi Valley and the northern Gulf littoral. From the
St. Lawrence they made their way over the portages to the
tributaries of the Father of Waters. From the West Indies
the Gulf of Mexico served as a highway.

Occupation of the upper lakes.—After the failure of the Huron
missions, the Jesuits extended their field of operations to the
shores of Lake Superior and Lake Michigan. The mission at
Sault Ste. Marie was revived; in 1665 La Pointe mission near
the western end of Lake Superior was established by Father
Allouez, who was succeeded by Marquette four years later. Between 1670 and 1672 St. Ignace, at Michillimackinac, and St.
Xavier on Green Bay (at De Pere) were established. In 1670
Talon despatched Saint Lusson to take possession of the Northwest; at a meeting of the tribes at Sault Ste. Marie the following
year the sovereignty of the king over that region was proclaimed.
Albanel was also sent to open communication between the St.
Lawrence and Hudson Bay.

Marquette and Joliet.—In 1672 Count Frontenac became
governor and lieutenant-general of New France. Shortly after
his arrival at Quebec, at the suggestion of Talon, he sent the
fur trader Joliet to find the Mississippi. At Michillimackinac

he met the missionary Marquette, who decided to accompany him. On May 17, 1673, they started westward; after reaching Green Bay, they followed the Fox and Wisconsin rivers to the Mississippi, which they descended to the mouth of the Arkansas, just at the time when Father Larios was founding Spanish missions near the Rio Grande. Being convinced that the Mississippi emptied into the Gulf of Mexico, and fearing that they might fall into the hands of the Spaniards, they determined to turn back. The return was by the Mississippi, the Illinois, and Chicago rivers and the western shores of Lake Michigan. Father Marquette returned to work among the Illinois, but was soon forced by illness to abandon the field. On his way north he died at the site of Ludington. His work among the Illinois was taken up by others, among them being Fathers Allouez and Hennepin.

Fort Frontenac.—While Joliet and Marquette were exploring the Mississippi, the governor was engaged in founding Fort Frontenac, on the northern shore of the outlet of Lake Ontario, near modern Kingston, his purpose being to overawe the Iroquois, and to divert their trade and allegiance from the English. With the governor was La Salle, who later became commandant of the new fort.

Frontenac's quarrels.—Shortly after Frontenac became governor the king again changed the form of government. The council was increased to seven members who held office directly from the king. Its chief function was judicial. A minor court called the *prévôté*, having original jurisdiction in civil and criminal cases, was reëstablished, appeals being taken from the *prévôté* to the council. Frontenac, who was of an imperious nature and exceedingly jealous of his authority, quarreled with the officials and clergy of Montreal, with Laval who had recently been made Bishop of Quebec, with the new intendant Duchesneau, and with the council. Regulation of the fur trade and questions of authority were the fruitful sources of disagreement. Under such conditions the colony did not advance rapidly. As Le Sueur says in his life of Frontenac, "The great trouble in Canada was that it was an overgoverned country. . . . What these people needed in the first place was freedom to seek their living in their own way, and secondly, an extremely simple form of government." The constant bickering finally exhausted the patience of the home government, and in 1682 both Frontenac and Duchesneau were recalled.

La Salle's fur trade monopoly.—During Frontenac's administration La Salle was engaged in the exploration of the Illinois country and the Mississippi. Having secured a royal patent to build forts and engage in the fur trade in the interior, La Salle, with a party which included Tonty, an Italian soldier of fortune, and the Recollet Hennepin, erected a fort at Niagara Falls and built a vessel called the *Griffon*, on which in 1679 they sailed up the lakes to Green Bay. The boat was sent back with a cargo of furs, but never reached its destination. The shores of Lake Michigan and the Illinois country were explored and Fort Crêvecœur was erected near the site of Peoria. From there Accau and Hennepin were sent to explore the upper Mississippi. La Salle then returned to Fort Frontenac, crossing lower Michigan and following Lake Erie and Lake Ontario.

Exploration of the Mississippi.—While La Salle was gone, Tonty occupied Starved Rock, later known as Fort St. Louis, but a mutiny and an Iroquois invasion forced the French to return to Green Bay, so that when La Salle returned he found the country abandoned. After a fruitless search, he heard from the Indians of Tonty's whereabouts and hastened north to meet him. Together they returned to Fort Frontenac. Nothing daunted, they again sought the Mississippi. On December 21, 1681, they were again at Fort Miami, at the mouth of the St. Joseph River. On February 6, 1682, they reached the Mississippi, and arrived at its mouth in April, when they took formal possession of the great valley, naming it Louisiana in honor of the king. By the end of September they were back at Fort Miami, and in 1683 the leader returned to Quebec.

La Salle's Colony on the Gulf.—La Salle now planned a colony at the mouth of the Mississippi River, as a means of developing the fur trade, controlling the Mississippi Valley, providing a base for commanding the Gulf, and, in case of war, for attack on the coveted mines of New Spain. France and Spain were on the verge of war, and in 1683 French buccaneers three times sacked the Spanish settlement of Apalache. La Salle's proposals were favored, therefore, by Louis XIV. In the summer of 1684 La Salle left France with a colony of some four hundred people. In the autumn he reached the West Indies, the ketch *St. François* having been captured by the Spaniards on the way. Continuing the voyage in November, La Salle missed the mouth

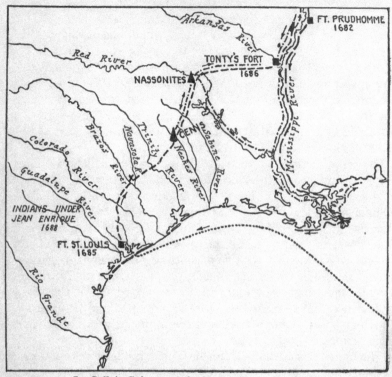

La Salle's Colony on the Texas Coast, 1684–1689

of the Mississippi and landed on the Texas coast at Matagorda Bay. Tonty descended the Mississippi to coöperate (1686), but did not find his chief. On the way he built a small post on the Arkansas.

Failure.—The expedition rapidly went to pieces. One vessel was wrecked in landing, and Beaujeu, the naval commander, returned to France with a second, and part of the men and supplies. La Salle moved his colony inland to the Garcitas River, near the head of the Lavaca Bay, where he founded Fort St. Louis, and then began a series of expeditions northeastward in the hope of finding the Mississippi River. While engaged in

exploring, the last of his vessels was wrecked. Through desertion
and sickness the colony rapidly dwindled. On his third expedition northeastward, in 1687, La Salle reached the Hasinai (Cenis)
Indians, east of the Trinity River. On his fourth expedition he
was murdered by his companions near the Brazos River. The
remainder of his party, led by Joutel, made their way to the
Arkansas post and to Canada. In the fall of 1689 Tonty, in an
effort to rescue La Salle's colonists, descended the Mississippi
River, and made his way to the Cadodacho and Hasinai villages.
Meanwhile the colony on the Gulf had been completely wiped
out by an Indian massacre which occurred early in 1689. La
Salle's occupation of Matagorda Bay later became a basis of the
claim of the United States to Texas.

Explorers in the Southwest.—The failure of La Salle's colony
did not put an end to exploration in the Southwest. Interest
in a passage to the South Sea was perennial, and no tale of
Spanish treasure was too glittering to find credence on the
French frontier. Mathieu Sagean told of a golden country of the
Accanibas, and Baron La Hontan of a Long River. The *coureurs
de bois* were ever led west and southwest in their fur trading
operations. The result was that in this western country traders
from Canada roamed far and wide at an early date. A Canadian
is known to have reached the Rio Grande overland before 1688
and by 1694 Canadian traders were among the Missouri and
Osage tribes.

The upper Mississippi—Duluth.—While La Salle was operating
in the Illinois country, others were at work in northern Wisconsin
and Minnesota. In 1678 Duluth, a cousin of Tonty, left Montreal
for the west. For several years he traded among the tribes west
of Lake Superior. Hearing in 1680 that Frenchmen were near,
he went in search of them, and found Accau and Hennepin,
who had explored the upper Mississippi. Duluth went to
France, where he secured a license to trade with the Sioux. In
1683 he returned to Wisconsin with thirty men, proceeded to
the north shore of Lake Superior, and built forts near Lake
Nipigon and Pigeon River. The highway from Brulé River
to the St. Croix became known as Duluth's Portage. In
1686 he erected a temporary fort near Detroit to bar the English
traders.

Le Sueur.—Between 1683 and 1700 Le Sueur, a prominent fur trader, operated in Minnesota and Wisconsin. In 1683 he was at St. Anthony's Falls. The Fox Indians of Wisconsin opposed the passage of the French to the Sioux and practically cut off their trade route. For this reason Le Sueur protected the Brulé-St. Croix highway. To effect this, in 1693 he built a fort at Chequamegon Bay, on the south shore of Lake Superior, and another on the Mississippi near the mouth of the St. Croix. This post became a center of commerce for the western posts. In 1697 Le Sueur was in France, where he secured permission to work copper mines near Lake Superior. In 1699 he went from France to Louisiana with Iberville. Thence, with twenty-nine men, he ascended the Mississippi to Blue River, Minnesota, and built Fort L'Huiller (1700) at Mankato, where he traded with the Sioux.

Perrot.—In 1685 Nicholas Perrot, who had been in Wisconsin as early as 1665, and had acquired great influence over the western tribes, was made "commander of the west" and sent among the Sioux. In 1686 he built Fort St. Antoine on the Mississippi near Trempealeau, Wisconsin. Other posts established by him were Fort Perrot on the west side of Lake Pepin, Fort Nicholas at Prairie du Chien, and one farther down the Mississippi near the Galena lead mines, which he discovered and worked.

The Illinois and Detroit.—In the Illinois country the French Jesuits labored from the time of Marquette, among his successors being Fathers Allouez and Hennepin. In 1699 a Sulpician mission was established at Cahokia and in 1700 the Jesuits moved down the Illinois River to Kaskaskia. A year later Detroit was founded to protect the route from Lake Erie to Lake Huron, cut off English trade with the Indians, and afford a base for the Illinois trade. Missionaries entered the region of the lower Mississippi and the lower Ohio, where Tonty and other Frenchmen maintained a considerable trade.

Traders on the Tennessee.—Because of Iroquois control of the country south of the Great Lakes and as far as the Tennessee River, the French in La Salle's time had little knowledge of the Ohio and its tributaries. At that period the Shawnee of the Tennessee and Cumberland Rivers were declining under Iroquois attacks. On the upper Tennessee lived the Cherokees. In spite of the Iroquois, however, by the end of the century several *coureurs de bois* of Canada had ascended the Ohio and Tennessee Rivers, crossed the divide, and descended the Savannah River into South Carolina, in defiance of the government, which tried to maintain a trade monopoly. Their activities brought them into rivalry with the English on the Carolina frontier.

Couture and Bellefeuille.—Among these pathfinders was Jean Couture, who had been left by Tonty at the Arkansas post. As early as 1693 he deserted the French colony and made his way overland to the English. In 1699 he was on the Savannah, where he proposed to lead the English to certain mines in the west. Returning, he led a party of English traders, sent by Governor Blake of South Carolina, up the Savannah, and down the Tennessee and Ohio, in an attempt to divert the western trade from Canada to the English. In February, 1700, they reached the Arkansas River, where they were met by Le Sueur on his way up the river to Minnesota. At the request of Iberville, the new governor of Louisiana, the government now permitted Illinois traders to sell their peltry in Louisiana, to prevent them from carrying it over the mountains to the English. In 1701 a party of Frenchmen under Bellefeuille and Soton crossed the mountains to South Carolina, and attempted to open up trade. Returning they descended the Mississippi and visited Biloxi. It was now proposed, in order to stop the road to Carolina, that posts be established on the Miami and the lower Ohio. For this purpose Juchereau de St. Denis established a post at Cairo in 1702. Through the establishment of Louisiana and the opening of trade with Canada, this danger was largely averted.

READINGS

EARLY EXPLORATIONS AND COLONIZING EFFORTS

Baird, C. W., *Huguenot Emigration;* Brevoort, J. C., *Verrazano the Navigator;* Channing, Edward, *History of the United States,* I, 90–112; De Costa, B. F., *Verrazano the Explorer;* French, B. F., *Historical Collections of Louisiana and Florida,* 117–362; Hamilton, P. J., *The Colonization of the South,* 27–41; Hart, A. B., *Contemporaries,* I, 102–112; Leacock, Stephen, *The Mariner of St. Malo;* Lescarbot, Marc, *History of New France;* Munro, W. B., *Crusaders of New France,* 11–32; Murphy, H. C., *Voyage of Verrazano;* Parkman, Francis, *The Pioneers of France in the New World,* 1–228; Shea, J. G., in

THE ESTABLISHMENT OF THE FRENCH COLONIES 103

Winsor, *Narrative and Critical History*, II, 260–283; Tracy, F. B., *Tercentenary History of Canada*, I, 20–37; Winsor, Justin, *Cartier to Frontenac*, 1–47; Biggar, H. P., *The Precursors of Jacques Cartier*.

ACADIA AND THE ST. LAWRENCE VALLEY

Biggar, H. P., *Early Trading Companies of New France;* Bourne, E. G., *Voyages and Explorations of Champlain (Trail Makers' Series);* Champlain, Samuel, *Œuvres* (Laverdière, ed.); Colby, C. W., *The Founder of New France;* Dionne, N. E., *Champlain;* Grant, W. L., *Voyages of Champlain (Original Narratives Series);* Kingsford, William, *The History of Canada*, I, 147–294; Le Sueur, W. D., *Frontenac*, 1–60; Marquis, T. G., *The Jesuit Missions;* Parkman, Francis, *Old Régime in Canada*, 3–168; *Pioneers of New France*, 324–454; *The Jesuits in North America;* Thwaites, R. G., *France in America*, 10–48; Tracy, F. B., *Tercentenary History of Canada*, I, 41–279; Winsor, Justin, *From Cartier to Frontenac*, 77–183; Munro, W. B., *Crusaders of New France*.

REORGANIZATION AND THE WEST INDIES

Chapais, Thomas, *The Great Intendant;* Haring, C. H., *The Buccaneers in the West Indies in the XVII Century;* Mims, S. L., *Colbert's West India Policy;* Munro, W. B., *The Seigneurs of Old Canada;* Parkman, Francis, *The Old Régime*, 169–330.

THE UPPER LAKES AND THE MISSISSIPPI VALLEY

Bolton, H. E., "The Location of La Salle's Colony on the Gulf of Mexico," in *Mississippi Valley Historical Review*, II, 165–182; Charlevoix, P. F. X., *Histoire Générale de la Nouvelle France* (J. G. Shea, trans.): Cox, I. J., *Journeys of La Salle (Trail Makers' Series);* Folwell, W. W., *Minnesota*, 59–65; Hamilton, P. J., *The Colonization of the South*, 187–196; Kellogg, L. P., ed., *Early Narratives of the Northwest (Original Narratives Series)*: Le Sueur, W. D., *Frontenac*, 61–169; Ogg, F. A., *The Opening of the Mississippi*, 59–163; Parish, J. C., *The Man with the Iron Hand;* Parkman, Francis, *La Salle and the Discovery of the Great West;* Phelps, Albert, *Louisiana*, 6–20; Shea, J. G., *Exploration of the Mississippi Valley;* Thwaites, R. G., *France in America*, 48–71; *Wisconsin*, 40–71; Winsor, Justin, *Cartier to Frontenac*, 183–295.

CHAPTER V

THE BEGINNINGS OF ENGLISH EXPANSION (1485-1603)

THE TUDOR PERIOD

Periods of English activities.—While the French were colonizing Canada and the West Indies, and the Spaniards were opening mines and ranches in northern Mexico, the English were founding still more vigorous settlements on the Atlantic seaboard, in the islands, and in the region of Hudson Bay.

The history of English activities in America before 1783 may be divided into four periods: (1) The Tudor epoch (1485-1603), which was a period of commercial expansion, exploration, and attempted colonization; (2) the Stuart and Cromwellian era (1603-1689), the period of colony planting; (3) the international struggle for territory (1689-1763); and (4) the struggle of a part of the English colonists for independence (1763-1783).

Henry VII.—When Henry Tudor ascended the throne of England a new era was ushered in. The continental possessions except Calais had been swept away in the Hundred Years' War. The Wars of the Roses had broken the power of the feudal barony, and the middle class Englishman had become the most important political element in the nation. The general form of the constitution had become fixed, the functions of the three branches of the government, the king and his council, parliament, and the courts, having become fairly well defined. The work of Henry Tudor was to restore the finances, to build up commerce and industry, to keep England at peace, and at the same time, by a series of marriage alliances and by adroit diplomacy to raise England to her former position as a great European power. He also built up the kingship at the expense of a subservient parliament.

The English Reformation.—During the three succeeding reigns, England played little part in exploration. While Spain was founding her vast colonial empire, the attention of Englishmen was centered on the European situation created by Charles V and on the great religious controversy, which resulted in the break with Rome and the establishment of the Anglican church.

Queen Elizabeth.—With the accession of Queen Elizabeth a new situation arose. To the Catholic powers, Elizabeth had no right to the throne of England. Philip II of Spain hoped to restore the country to the Catholic fold; his first wife was Queen Mary of England, and under his influence a short-lived Catholic reaction had been produced; if Elizabeth could now be induced to turn Catholic and marry Philip, England might be won back to the Roman church. Elizabeth, however, followed an independent course, dangling before the eyes of the Spanish ambassador the possibility of a marriage with Philip, while perfecting the organization of the Anglican church, increasing her hold upon the affections of her subjects, strengthening her treasury, army, navy, and defences, and stimulating industry and commerce. Her path was beset with additional difficulties, for the powerful Catholic party in France was intriguing to place Mary Stuart, the queen of Scotland, on the English throne. To weaken her foes, Elizabeth aided the Huguenots, assisted the Dutch in their war against Spain, and connived with English mariners to raid the Spanish Main. In 1588 the patience of Philip was exhausted, and he sought to humble the haughty queen by sending the Invincible Armada against England. A running fight occurred in the Channel and several of the galleons were sunk or driven on shore. The Armada entered the roads of Calais but a great storm shattered the fleet. Of the original one hundred and thirty vessels only one-third returned to Spain. The defeat of the Armada marks a turning point in Spanish and English history. From that time Spain was thrown on the defensive and her power on the continent gradually declined, though her colonies continued to expand. England followed up her success by taking the offensive; an era of greater commercial activity followed, and she soon entered upon her rôle of a colonizing nation.

COMMERCIAL EXPANSION

John Cabot.—The discovery of new lands in the west soon became known in England, and when the Venetian citizen, John Cabot, applied for letters patent to go on a western voyage,

Henry VII readily complied. In May, 1497, his single ship with eighteen men set sail from Bristol and crossed the north Atlantic. It is impossible to state with certainty what part of the coast was visited, but it appears to have been in the neighborhood of Cape Breton Island. The idea that Sebastian Cabot accompanied his father is generally rejected by the best authorities. The importance of the voyage lies in the fact that it was used at a later date to strengthen the English claim to a large part of North America. The following year John Cabot sailed for the new found land but never returned.

The Newfoundland fisheries.—Cabot's voyage had another important result. He had discovered a convenient trade route to the fisheries of Newfoundland, and English, French, Spanish, and Portuguese fishing vessels soon swarmed the region. English ships are thought to have traded there regularly after 1502. Expeditions are known to have been made thither in 1527 and 1536, and before 1550 fishing fleets went from southern England to Newfoundland every spring and autumn.

The Muscovy Company.—The latter half of the Tudor period witnessed the formation of great companies which reached out for foreign trade. In 1553 a group of London merchants decided to make an attempt to reach China and the East Indies by a northern route. Under the command of Willoughby and Chancellor, three ships sailed along the Norway coast and rounded the North Cape. Willoughby and the crews of two of the ships perished on the coast of Lapland, but Chancellor entered the White Sea and penetrated to Moscow, where he was promised trading privileges by Ivan the Terrible. In 1555 the merchants who were interested in the expedition were granted a royal charter, the company being familiarly known as the Muscovy Company. Annual fleets were despatched to the White and Baltic seas, warehouses were established at various points in Russia, and the agents of the company extended their activities to the Caspian Sea, to Bokhara, and to Persia. In 1580 the Turks cut them off from the region outside of European Russia. Occasional unsuccessful attempts were also made by the company to reach China by the northern route. In 1579 the Eastland Company, a rival organization, was chartered to trade in the Baltic, and developed an extensive trade in Poland.

The Levant Company.—English merchants also turned their attention to the Mediterranean to renew a trade which had formerly been of some importance. In 1581 a charter was issued to the Levant Company, which engaged in trading with the Turkish ports along the southern and eastern shores of the Mediterranean. The same year a charter was granted to the Venetian Company and in 1592 the two were combined as the Levant Company. Among those interested in the Mediterranean commerce were Sir Thomas Smythe and Sir Walter Raleigh, both of whom were important figures in the colonization of Virginia. Other groups of merchants opened trade with Morocco, and the Senegambia and Guinea coasts. In all of these enterprises Englishmen were reaching out for the trade with the East Indies, which had long been monopolized by the Portuguese. In 1581, the year in which the Levant Company was chartered, Portugal was incorporated with Spain, and hostility to that power added another incentive to reach the East.

THE ELIZABETHAN SEA-DOGS

John Hawkins.—Among those interested in the African trade was William Hawkins, who filled the important positions of mayor of Plymouth and member of parliament. He made three voyages to Guiana and Brazil. His son, John Hawkins, became one of the most famous mariners of his time. In 1562 he sailed for Africa to obtain slaves, which he disposed of in Española. In 1564-1565 he engaged in a second voyage which resulted in great profit. A third voyage in 1567-1568 ended disastrously. The Spanish government had sent a fleet to stop the traffic; but in spite of it he forced an entrance to the West Indian ports and disposed of his cargo. Being driven by a storm into the harbor of Vera Cruz, he was attacked by a Spanish fleet and but two of the English vessels escaped.

Drake and Cavendish.—Francis Drake, a nephew of John Hawkins, had accompanied him on his third expedition and had suffered the loss of his investment. He soon began a series of reprisals. In 1572 he made an unsuccessful attack on Nombre de Diós and ascended the Chagres River where he waylaid a train of mules laden with bullion. The example set by him was frequently followed by raids of English mariners in the following decade. In 1577 another fleet sailed under Drake's command. After capturing several Spanish and Portuguese vessels on the African coast, the fleet crossed the Atlantic and attempted to pass through the Straits of Magellan. Only one vessel reached the Pacific. Drake proceeded up the western coast, plundering as he went. In a harbor known as Drake's Bay, north of San Francisco Bay, he refitted, and claimed the California region for the queen, calling it New Albion. He then sailed to the East Indies where a cargo of spice was obtained. From Java, Drake crossed the Indian Ocean, rounded the Cape of Good Hope, and proceeded to England, entering the harbor of Plymouth in November, 1580, having completed the first English circumnavigation of the globe. In 1586 Thomas Cavendish followed almost the same course, plundered the Spanish commerce in the Pacific, and in 1588 completed the circumnavigation of the world. Besides Hawkins, Drake, and Cavendish a score of English mariners engaged in raiding the Spanish Main. They were assisted financially by the queen and by many of her councillors who considered the raiding of Spanish commerce good business as well as good state policy.

East Indian trade.—A party of English merchants had also succeeded in penetrating from the Syrian coast to India. The report of their journey and the voyages of Drake and Cavendish stimulated the desire to open trade with the Far East. The result was that in 1591 an expedition was fitted out which rounded the Cape of Good Hope and reached Ceylon, India, and the Malay Peninsula. Reports of the successes of the Dutch in the East Indies increased the interest of the English merchants, and in 1600 the East India Company was formed.

SEARCH FOR A NORTHWEST PASSAGE

Frobisher.—The unsuccessful attempts of the Muscovy Company to reach the East by a northeast passage led to the search for a northwestern route. The great exponent of the idea was Martin Frobisher. After vainly seeking many years for a patron who would furnish funds, in 1574 he received the support of Michael Lock, a member of the Muscovy Company, and the following year a royal license was granted to undertake the work.

In June, 1576, Frobisher sailed from England in command of three small vessels, only one of which reached America. The vessel passed along the Labrador coast, crossed the entrance of Hudson Strait, and coasted Baffin Land, entering the inlet now known as Frobisher's Bay. Upon his return to England, Frobisher took back a large stone, which an assayer claimed contained gold. In consequence the queen and many influential men subscribed liberally for another voyage. The Company of Cathay was formed which was to have a monopoly in all lands to the westward where Englishmen had not traded before. Expeditions in search of gold were sent out under Frobisher in 1577 and 1578, but the rocks which were brought back proved to be worthless.

Gilbert.—Among those interested in the search for a northwest passage was Raleigh's half-brother, Sir Humphrey Gilbert, who believed that a colony might be established on the American coast. In 1578 he obtained a six-year monopoly of discovery and settlement in America. A fleet was equipped, but being twice scattered by storms, the attempt was abandoned. In 1583 Gilbert made a second venture. Arriving at St. Johns, Newfoundland, Gilbert informed the crews of the fishing fleet of his commission, and took possession in the name of Elizabeth. On the return voyage the *Squirrel* with Gilbert and all on board was lost in a storm just north of the Azores.

Davis.—In 1584 John Davis, Walter Raleigh, and others were granted a charter to explore a route to China and to trade in lands which might be discovered. Command of an expedition was given to Davis, who sailed from Dartmouth in 1585. The southern coast of Greenland was explored and Davis Strait was crossed, but the illusive opening was not found. In 1586 and 1587 Davis sought the passage but without success.

ATTEMPTS AT COLONIZATION

Raleigh and the attempted colonization of Virginia.—England's struggle with Spain for empire did not end with an attack on her fleets and her colonies. Men soon arose who dared to dispute Spain's monopoly by planting colonies in the lands claimed by His Catholic Majesty. The leader in the enterprise was Sir

Walter Raleigh. In 1584 he received a patent similar to that of Gilbert. Two vessels were soon despatched under Amadas and Barlowe. They followed the southern route by the Canaries and the West Indies, and finally landed on Roanoke Island, taking possession of that region, which was named Virginia in honor of Elizabeth, a name which was soon applied to the country from the Spanish settlements to Newfoundland. In April of the following year Grenville commanded a second expedition which took out the first colonists, who made a settlement on Roanoke Island. In 1586 supply ships were sent out, but they found the settlement deserted. Wearied by the hard winter, the settlers had accepted an offer from Sir Francis Drake, who had been raiding in the Caribbean, to carry them back to England.

In 1587 another group of colonists including almost a hundred men, seventeen women, and several children, was sent out under Governor John White and landed at Roanoke. White returned to England, but owing to the naval war with Spain and other difficulties he was unable to go to Virginia again until 1591, when he found only deserted ruins. News of the English intrusion caused alarm on the Spanish frontier, and the governor of Florida in person led a counter expedition up the coast as far as Chesapeake Bay. To this day the fate of the Roanoke colony is a mystery, but light on the matter may yet be shed by the Spanish archives.

Raleigh's Orinoco expedition.—The discoveries of the Spaniards in Mexico and Peru spurred the Englishman to attempt to find similar lands of treasure. A story became current that in the interior of South America on the upper waters of the Amazon and the Orinoco was a great kingdom, which contained a powerful city called Manoa. It was also believed that in the interior there was a mountain of sapphire and a land ruled by female warriors called Amazons. After the failure of the Roanoke enterprise, Raleigh became interested in this land of wonders, and in 1594 sent a vessel to the Guiana coast to obtain information. The following year Raleigh himself made an exploration of the delta of the Orinoco and ascended the main stream a considerable distance. But the city of Manoa proved elusive, supplies ran short, and the expedition returned to England.

READINGS

CABOT

Bourne, E. G., *Spain in America*, 54–61; Channing, Edward, *History of the United States*, I, 33–42; Fiske, John, *Discovery of America*, II, 2–15; Markham, C. R., *Columbus*, 226–233; Olson, J. E., ed., *The Northmen, Columbus and Cabot*.

COMMERCIAL COMPANIES

Cheyney, E. P., *A History of England from the Defeat of the Armada to the Death of Elizabeth*, I, 309–348, 375–422, 433–459; Cunningham, William, *The Growth of English Industry and Commerce in Modern Times—The Mercantile System*, 214–279; Scott, W. R., *The Constitution and Finance of English, Scottish and Irish Joint-Stock Companies to 1720*, II, 3–11, 36–52, 83–89; Tilby, A. W., *The English People Overseas*, I, 38–43.

SEA ROVERS, THE NORTHWEST PASSAGE, AND RALEIGH

Buchan, J., *Sir Walter Ralegh;* Channing, Edward, *History of the United States*, I, 115–140; Cheyney, E. P., *A History of England from the Defeat of the Armada to the Death of Elizabeth*, I, 349–374, 423–459; Corbett, J. S., *Drake and the Tudor Navy; Sir Francis Drake;* Hume, M. A. S., *Sir Walter Ralegh;* Nuttall, Zelia, *New Light on Drake;* Payne, E. J., *Elizabethan Seamen;* Scott, W. R., *The Constitution and Finance of English, Scottish and Irish Joint-Stock Companies to 1720*, II, 76–82, 241–245; Tilby, A. W., *The English People Overseas*, I, 24–38; Woodward, W. H., *A Short History of the Expansion of the British Empire*, 17–63; Wood, W., *Elizabethan Sea-Dogs*.

CHAPTER VI

THE CHESAPEAKE BAY AND INSULAR COLONIES

ENGLAND UNDER THE EARLY STUARTS, 1603-1640

James I.—When James Stuart came to the throne, he had an exalted idea of the kingship, believing that he ruled by divine right. The Tudors had wielded almost absolute power, the privy council overshadowing parliament. James naturally intended to rule in a similar manner, and resented any legislative action which tended to decrease his prerogative. He also stood as a staunch supporter of the English church. His foreign policy was based upon a sincere desire for peace. With this in view he ended the war with Spain and projected a marriage between his son and a Spanish princess. In the latter part of James' reign, when the Thirty Years' War broke out, the king hoped to become the arbiter of Europe. Though he failed in this, he at least had the satisfaction of keeping his country out of war.

Charles I.—The Parliamentarians who had nursed their wrath during the reign of James, soon clashed with his successor. Charles I was a man of staunch self-righteousness, who had little of pliability and much of stubbornness in his nature. His idea of the royal prerogative was fully as exalted as that of his father. From the beginning of the reign, king and parliament clashed. When a war, which broke out with France and Spain, went badly, the unpopularity of the king increased. When he summoned parliament in 1628 to ask for supplies, he found that body unwilling to comply with his demands until he had signed the Petition of Right.

The experience which the king had with parliament determined him to rule without it, and from 1629 to 1640 he carried on a personal government. Acting through his privy council, the king ruled England. His chief difficulty was to secure sufficient revenue to carry on the government. Ancient feudal laws were resurrected and put into force. So long as no extraordinary emergency arose the king was able to carry on the government. During this period the religious controversy was also becoming acute, the tyranny of Laud, the Archbishop of Canterbury, constantly adding fuel to the fire. Puritans and Parliamentarians found a common ground of opposition. When the king attempted to force the English prayer book and church organization on the Scotch Prebysterians, war broke out. Charles found it necessary to summon parliament, whereupon he found religious and political opponents united against him.

THE COLONIAL ADMINISTRATIVE SYSTEM OF THE EARLY STUARTS

Early experiments.—During the reigns of the first two Stuarts a colonial administrative policy was developed. With James I permanent settlements began. They were regarded as dependent upon the crown rather than as an integral part of the state. The king created a Council of Virginia which was to have general control over settlements between 34° and 45° north latitude. But the council was short lived and the privy council soon became the center of the colonial system. The connecting links between the settlers and the crown were the corporations which were granted jurisdiction over more or less definite areas. Both king and parliament claimed to have jurisdiction over the colonies, but the first two Stuarts were able to keep control in their hands.

The privy council in charge.—The charters of the commercial companies could be annulled by the courts in suits brought by the crown. Such was the method followed when the charter of the Virginia Company was revoked; the work of administration then passed into the hands of the privy council. As this council was large and its duties numerous, the actual work was usually done by committees, such a committee being appointed to look after Virginia. Late in the reign of James I the crown also appointed commissioners to examine the state of the colony, and report on a form of government.

Policy of Charles I.—Under Charles I, though the commissioners continued to attend to some business, most of the work of administration devolved upon the privy council. In 1631 the commission was revived, but in 1634 it was superseded by another at whose head was Archbishop Laud. This was made up of the highest officers of church and state, and it was given jurisdiction over all dependencies. Its chief acts required the approval of the crown, and as this could only be obtained through the privy council, it was responsible to that body. A standing committee of the privy council for foreign plantations was also appointed, the membership of this committee and the commission headed by Laud being identical. Sub-committees composed of men of lower rank but who had expert knowledge of colonial affairs were also appointed to assist the higher bodies.

Special administrative bodies.—From time to time special bodies were created for aiding the development of commerce and industry. In 1622 James constituted a council of trade for investigating commerce, shipping, and industry. Charles I, in 1625, created a similar council, but it did not become very active, and soon its duties devolved upon a committee of the privy council, which investigated all phases of economic activity, the regulation of the tobacco industry of Virginia being one of the important subjects which occupied its attention.

THE FOUNDING OF VIRGINIA

Opposition of the Early Stuarts to Spain.—The settled policy of Spain was to maintain a territorial and commercial monopoly in all the lands west of the line of the treaty of Tordesillas. During the reign of Elizabeth, the mariners of England had struck at Spanish commerce and had made unsuccessful attempts at colonization; in the reigns of the first two Stuarts, serious attempts were made by Englishmen to wrest from the Spanish colossus some of his island possessions, and to occupy Guiana and portions of North America. The attitude of James I toward these enterprises depended upon the state of his negotiations with Spain. In 1604 a treaty was signed which brought the long war between the countries to an end. By the treaty the English crown surrendered the right of trade to the Indies. The English mariners snapped their fingers at the treaty and continued to visit the Indies, either running the chance of being taken as pirates, or registering their vessels under the flags of Holland or Savoy. The difficulties besetting this trade led some of the merchants to invest their capital in enterprises of colonization.

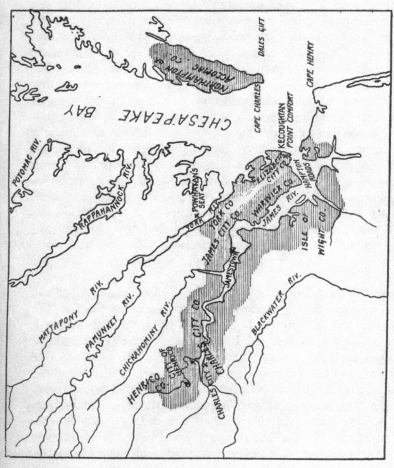

Settlements in Virginia, 1634

The charter of 1606.—Between 1602 and 1606 several voyages were made to America, the most important being that of George Weymouth, who visited the New England coast in 1604; h's favorable report greatly stimulated the desire to plant colonies. In April, 1606, a charter was drawn up which provided for two companies; one composed of men from London, familiarly known as the London Company, which was to operate between the thirty-fourth and forty-first degrees of latitude; the other made up of men from Plymouth, Bristol, and Exeter, known as the Plymouth Company, which was to plant colonies between the thirty-eighth and forty-fifth degrees. Each company was to have control of fifty miles both north and south of its first settlement, a hundred miles out to sea, and a hundred miles inland. Neither was to settle within one hundred miles of the other. Each company was to have a council of thirteen persons, and each was to have the right to mine gold, silver, and copper; the king was to receive one-fifth of all the precious metals and one-fifteenth of the copper. No import duties were to be levied for seven years. The charter also provided that the Christian religion was to be spread among the natives. Colonists who went to the New World were guaranteed all the privileges of Englishmen.

Founding of Jamestown.—In August, 1606, Henry Challons was sent ahead in the *Richard* to select a site for the London Company, but was captured off Florida by a Spanish fleet and taken a prisoner to Seville. In December, three vessels, which belonged to the Muscovy Company, the *Susan Constant*, the *Godspeed*, and the *Discovery*, sailed for Virginia under the command of Sir Christopher Newport. They followed the southern route by the Canaries and the West Indies, arriving in Chesapeake Bay in May, 1607. Of the hundred and twenty colonists who had embarked, sixteen died during the voyage. Sealed instructions had been sent for the government and management of Virginia. When opened, they disclosed the names of the members of the council, a body possessed of executive, legislative, and judicial powers, presided over by a president. A site was to be selected on an island in a navigable river, marshy or heavily wooded ground to be avoided. Contrary to instructions, the site selected was on a swampy peninsula, located near the mouth of the James River. Near the western end of the peninsula a triangular log fort was laid out. The settlement was in the district known to the Spaniards as Axacan, and not far from the site of the Jesuit mission founded in 1570. While the fortification was being built, Newport explored the James River as far as the site of Richmond. While he was gone, the Indians attacked the fort but were driven off. Besides the fortification, a church and storehouse were erected. In July Newport sailed for England, taking with him worthless specimens of rock which were believed to contain gold.

Early difficulties.—Shortly after the departure of Newport the colonists began to suffer from famine, malaria, and Indian attacks. President Wingfield husbanded the stores left by Newport, an action which angered the settlers, and he was soon deposed. John Smith was sent to secure food from the Indians, and succeeded in obtaining a considerable supply. When Newport returned in January, 1608, he found only forty survivors. During 1608 and 1609 the little settlement was barely able to hold its own. The few additional settlers who came merely offset the ravages of disease and starvation. During this period John Smith appears to have been the chief factor in keeping the colony alive. So precarious had conditions become by May, 1609, that he dispersed the colonists in groups, one being sent to live among the Indians, another to fish at Point Comfort, and a third to obtain oysters. In July a vessel commanded by Samuel Argall arrived with supplies, bringing the news that the first charter had been repealed and a new one granted.

Charter of 1609.—The lack of success in the original venture had caused those interested to make an effort to enlarge the company. The incorporators of the charter of 1609 were fifty-six of the guilds and companies of London, and six hundred and fifty-nine persons, among whom were included twenty-one peers, ninety-six knights, eleven professional men, and fifty-three captains. The new company was to have the land two hundred miles north and two hundred miles south of Point Comfort and stretching from sea to sea west and northwest, and the islands within one hundred miles of the coast. The government was vested in a council, which was given power to appoint its own officers, to make laws for the government of the colony, and to take in new stockholders. The English church was established as the religion of the colony.

The starving time.—In June, 1609, nine vessels commanded by Newport sailed from England with the new governor, Sir Thomas Gates, and about five hundred emigrants. Beset by pestilence and storms, many died on the voyage, about four hundred being landed at Jamestown in August. The vessel carrying the governor was stranded in the Bermudas, and he did not arrive at Jamestown until May, 1610. There he found the colonists in a frightful condition, dissensions among the officers, Indian attacks, disease, and starvation having brought the colony to the brink of destruction. Gates decided to give up the ill-fated attempt, and taking all the settlers on board, sailed down the James River, but met a vessel bearing the news that a new governor, Lord Delaware, had arrived at Point Comfort with supplies and a hundred and fifty emigrants. Gates immediately returned to Jamestown. Of the nine hundred persons who had been landed in Virginia during the first three years, only one hundred and fifty were alive upon the arrival of Delaware.

Spanish resistance.—Spain regarded the Jamestown colony as an intruder, and both Spaniards and Englishmen considered it as a menace to Spain's northern outposts, and to her merchant fleets, which passed close by on their homeward voyage. Dale remarked that the settlement "wyll put such a byt in our ainchent enemyes mouth as wyll curb his hautynes of monarchie." Zúñiga, Spanish ambassador to England, urged that "such a bad project should be uprooted now, while it can be done so easily."

At Jamestown fear of a Spanish attack was almost constant, and Newport sought aid in England lest the "all devouring Spaniard lay his ravenous hands" upon the infant colony. Spanish resistance had already been felt by way of vigorous diplomatic protest and through the capture of the *Richard* in 1606. In 1609 a Spanish expedition was sent to Jamestown under Captain Ecija, commander of the garrison at St. Augustine. On July 24 Ecija entered Chesapeake Bay. Concluding that the settlement was too strong to capture with one small vessel, he withdrew, but on his way down the coast he conferred with the Indian tribes, and sent a delegation of natives overland to spy upon the

English. On Ecija's return to St. Augustine another native delegation was sent to Virginia from Florida by Governor Ybarra. The success of these embassies has been inferred from the Indian massacres at Jamestown in the following winter. Two years later another Spanish expedition was sent to Jamestown. Captures were made on both sides and the episode was followed by a demand at the English settlement for reinforcements.

Zúñiga continued to urge the destruction of the colony, but Philip III temporized, allured by the hope of an English alliance and encouraged by his informants to believe that the struggling colony would fail through misery. Instead of dying out, however, as time went on Virginia waxed stronger, and soon became a base for attacks on Spanish commerce, as had been predicted. The founding of Jamestown in Axacan was the first English nibble at the Spanish mainland possessions, a process which continued for a century and a half.

Delaware's governorship.—Delaware remained in Virginia less than a year, during which period new colonists arrived, the settlement at Jamestown was rebuilt, the Indians were driven from Kecoughtan, and forts Charles and Henry were established at the mouth of the James River. An expedition was also sent to the falls in search of a gold mine, but it found none. Delaware was unable to check the ravages of disease, and during the summer a hundred and fifty died. The governor left the colony in March, 1611, but remained in office until his death in 1618, during which period the government was administered by deputy governors.

Dale's strong hand.—Sir Thomas Dale was left in charge. He was a brusque old soldier who had seen service in the Netherlands, and during his administration, the colony was governed by military law. The men were forced to work like slaves, and those who rebelled were punished with the greatest severity, several captured runaways being burned at the stake. The Indians along the James and York rivers were attacked; Pocahontas, the daughter of Powhatan, was captured, and the hostage was used to force that powerful chief to make peace. Hearing of the French occupation of Acadia, Dale sent Captain Argall to destroy the settlements.

Charter of 1612.—During the administration of Dale, a change was made in the charter, the powers of the council being considerably enlarged. The Bermudas were also placed under its jurisdiction. The rights in the islands, however, were subsequently sold to some of the members of the London Company, who obtained a charter in 1614 under the name of the Somers Island Company.

Change in the management of the company.—Sir Thomas Smythe had been the moving spirit of the company, but in spite of his efforts, the colony had proved a financial failure, and he was willing to let others carry on the enterprise. The central figure in the company after 1618 was Sir Edwin Sandys. Smythe had realized that it was necessary to change the communal form of ownership to one of landed proprietorship, and had issued instructions that fifty acres of land be assigned to every person who would transport one person to the colony. This policy was carried out by Sandys, and the "old colonists" were allowed to obtain larger tracts of land.

House of Burgesses.—In April, 1619, Sir George Yeardley assumed control as governor of Virginia. He brought out instructions by which the inhabitants of each place and plantation were to elect two burgesses, who were to meet at Jamestown in a general assembly. This first representative assembly in America met in the church at Jamestown on July 30. It was composed of the governor, councilors, and twenty-two burgesses. At the first session, the assembly sat in the two-fold capacity of law makers and court of law.

Agricultural development.—The original instructions had provided that the products of labor should belong to the community instead of to the individual, an arrangement by which the slothful profited at the expense of the industrious. During the first season, only four acres were cleared and planted. The insufficiency of the supply of grain made it necessary to depend upon the Indians for maize. In 1608 John Smith succeeded in getting forty acres of land broken, and the following year this was planted to maize. Just before the arrival of Delaware, the attempts at agriculture were abandoned, the colonists relying for subsistence on roots, herbs, nuts, berries, and fish. Delaware immediately set to work to right conditions, the hours of labor being set from six to ten in the morning, and from two to four in the afternoon.

When Dale took charge he forced the men to plant seed and assigned to each a garden. Livestock had been imported, and were allowed to roam at large in the woods. Dale erected a blockhouse on the mainland to protect them, and warned the settlers against letting stock wander. Henrico was selected as the site for another settlement and the town site of seven acres he caused to be fenced in. Other palings back of the settlement were erected and within the fenced areas corn was planted. On the south side of the river fences were built which protected a circuit of twelve miles, the enclosed land being used for a hog range. The lands of the Indians near the mouth of the Appamatox River were seized, fenced, and planted with maize.

In 1612 the cultivation of tobacco began, the first tobacco planter being John Rolfe, who had married Pocahontas. Tobacco soon became the only export, its cultivation absorbing the economic life of the colony. To make certain of the food supply, Dale commanded that no one should be permitted to plant tobacco until he had planted two acres of grain. To encourage industry, Dale allowed some of the "old colonists" to lease three acres. He also put in force a rule that every man with a family who arrived in the colony should be provided with a house free of rent, tools, and livestock, and with subsistence for himself and family for the first year. If he confined himself to the planting of grain and vegetables, he was given twelve acres of fenced land. At the time of Dale's departure in 1616 there were three hundred and fifty inhabitants settled at Henrico, Bermuda, West and Shirley Hundreds, Jamestown, Kecoughtan, and Dale's Gift.

Immigration.—In 1619 twenty negroes were brought into Virginia, the first blacks to be introduced. Up to this time there were few women in the colony, but the company succeeded in sending over several ship-loads of unmarried women. Upon arrival there was a speedy courtship, and the lucky swain gladly paid a hundred and twenty pounds of the best tobacco for the cost of transportation. In general the type of settler was excellent, but in the later years of the company convicted felons and a large number of waifs and vagabonds from the streets of Lon-

don were sent. The emigrants who had no capital were usually
indented servants, the terms of indenture varying from two to
seven years.

Growth of large estates.—In this early period began the formation of great estates. The company retained twelve thousand
acres for itself. As new officers were created lands were set
aside to support them. The treasurer, marshal, and cape merchant were each granted fifteen hundred acres, the physician
and secretary five hundred acres each. The large estates were
worked by tenants, the number on each estate being fixed by
the company. Grants of large tracts were also made to groups
of capitalists who agreed to bring out settlers.

The Indian massacre of 1622.—The reaching out for new lands
for tobacco culture resulted in encroachment upon the fields of
the Indians. Angered by this the Indians suddenly attacked
the outlying plantations, killing between three and four hundred
persons, nearly one-fourth of the entire population. The planting of the crops was interrupted and a winter of hardship followed. When the Indian maize crop was nearly ripe, the settlers
retaliated, almost exterminating the natives along the lower
courses of the James and York rivers.

Crown regulation of the tobacco industry.—To free himself
from parliamentary control and to regulate industry, James I
granted monopolies to private individuals. Royal commissioners
were appointed to inspect the tobacco and to prevent smuggling,
and planting in England was prohibited. In 1620 the London
Company petitioned the king to do away with the tobacco monopoly and as a result the London and Bermuda companies were
allowed to import fifty-five thousand pounds annually. The companies immediately attempted to ship Virginia tobacco to Holland; this led to a dispute with the privy council and the matter
was discussed in parliament, where Sandys defended the right of
free shipment. The dispute was settled by a compromise, by
which the companies agreed to ship the entire product to England, and no restriction was placed upon the amount which they
might import.

Neither side was entirely pleased with the arrangement and
in November, 1622, an agreement was reached by the Lord
Treasurer and the companies. The companies were given the

sole right for seven years to import tobacco into England and Ireland; they were to pay into the royal exchequer the net proceeds of one-third of all tobacco imported; no tobacco was to be planted in England and Ireland, and a small amount of Spanish tobacco was to be imported for three years. Like previous arrangements, this did not meet with the approval of all, and it was annulled in 1623, the companies being allowed the exclusive right to import tobacco into England and Ireland, except a small amount of Spanish tobacco, and to pay a duty of nine pence a pound.

End of the London Company.—The king had looked with scant favor upon the administration of Sandys, for popular government was not to the liking of James. Friction between the king and the company also added to the royal displeasure. James, who was personally opposed to the use of tobacco, was also trying to please the Spanish court, which made frequent protests against the Virginia enterprise. Internal dissensions also disturbed the company, a group headed by Sir Thomas Smythe being opposed to the Sandys faction. Royal commissioners were appointed to examine the condition of affairs, and as a result of their report, in 1624 the charter of the London Company was annulled, the colony passing under the direct control of the crown.

Increase of population by 1625.—When Charles I came to the throne Virginia contained about twelve hundred inhabitants, of whom nearly five hundred were servants, and about a hundred were children. They were scattered through nineteen settlements, the largest being Elizabeth City, which contained two hundred and fifty-seven inhabitants. Jamestown had thirty-three houses and a population of one hundred and seventy-five.

Population in 1635.—By 1635 the population had increased to five thousand. The country had been divided into shires, which later were called counties. The six counties along the James River contained about four thousand inhabitants; Charles River County on the York River five hundred, and Accomac County on the opposite side of the bay four hundred. By 1640 the population had increased to seven thousand five hundred.

Tobacco lands.—The most desirable lands for tobacco were the bottoms along the streams. Tobacco exhausted the soil rapidly, three years being the usual life of a field. This made it necessary for the planter to take up new lands and increased his desire for larger holdings. Land patents were issued for large tracts, usually of from one hundred to three hundred acres, although many obtained patents for a thousand acres.

Charles I and the tobacco business.—Charles was opposed to the tobacco business, but he realized that it was necessary to the colony. The king favored Virginia by reducing the duty on tobacco and excluding the Spanish leaf from England and Ireland. But in 1627, when parliament had not granted adequate supplies to the crown, he renewed the monopoly. To put it in force, a proclamation was issued which forbade the annual importation of more than fifty thousand pounds of Spanish tobacco, prohibited the growing of the plant in England and Ireland, and made London the only port of entry. As the colonists objected to the monopoly, the king issued another proclamation, which provided that no colonial tobacco should be imported without special license and should be delivered to tobacco commissioners, who were to have the sole right of disposing of the product. The price was to be fixed by agreement between the shippers and commissioners. Efforts were made to have the colony engage in the production of more substantial commodities, the planters being commanded to produce pitch, tar, potash, timber, iron, and salt, to plant vines and grain, and to search for minerals. The efforts of the king, however, were but partially successful, and tobacco remained the great staple. It had also become the medium of exchange, and though attempts were made to introduce a metallic currency, they did not succeed, in spite of the fact that the fluctuating price of the staple made financial transactions difficult.

Harvey's tobacco policy.—In 1630 Governor Harvey commenced his administration. He immediately began to encourage the planting of grain and the raising of stock. The low price of tobacco at this time assisted him, and in 1631 the colony was able to export a large quantity of grain. Efforts were also made to improve the quality of tobacco. A law of the colonial legislature of 1632 provided for five points of inspection. Storehouses were built where inspectors examined the stock and condemned the poorer qualities. The number of plants to be raised by each family was limited to two thousand, and not more than nine leaves were allowed to be taken from a plant. In 1633 the number of plants per family was reduced to fifteen hundred. English merchants trading to the colonies purchased a consiaerable amount of tobacco, which they took in exchange for other commodities, for which they charged abnormally high prices. To right this and to increase the royal revenues, in 1634 the king again renewed the monopoly. When Governor Harvey attempted to contract for the crop, an acrimonious debate ensued. This, coupled with the fact that the governor attempted to assist Lord Baltimore's colonists, caused the council illegally to depose the governor.

Continued efforts to enforce the monopoly.—The king continued to make efforts to enforce the monopoly. In 1638 he issued another proclamation, stating that it was necessary to regulate tobacco planting, to decide how much was to be imported, and to handle the product. The colony as usual objected. Owing to the troublous times in England, the proclamation was not strictly enforced and much tobacco was sold to other than government agents.

THE FOUNDING OF MARYLAND

Calvert's attempted settlement in Newfoundland.—The northern end of Chesapeake Bay was soon occupied by a rival tobacco colony, the proprietary province of Lord Baltimore. In 1609 George Calvert became a stockholder of the Virginia Company, and ten years later was made secretary of state by James I. His new office gave him an opportunity to begin an independent colony. In 1620 he bought the southeastern peninsula of Newfoundland from Sir William Vaughan, to whom it had previously been granted, and the following year sent out a few colonists. In 1623 the king granted him a charter for his colony, which was called Avalon. Two years later Calvert resigned the secretaryship. In spite of the fact that he had recently become a Catholic, he was raised to the Irish peerage with the title of Baron of Baltimore. In 1627 he visited Newfoundland with his family, but the inclemency of the climate convinced him of the undesirability of Avalon.

Application for land in Virginia.—In 1629 Baltimore applied for a grant in Virginia, to which colony he immediately proceeded.

There he met with a cold reception and shortly departed for England, where he made every effort to obtain a charter. The Virginians opposed him strongly, but in April, 1632, his suit was successful and the grant was made. George Calvert died

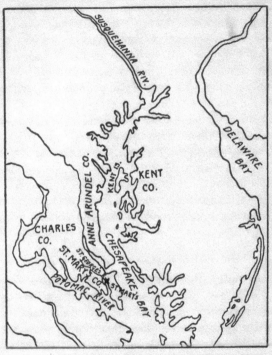

Settlements in Maryland, 1634

the same month and the charter was drawn in the name of his son Cecilius.

The charter.—The province was named Maryland in honor of Henrietta Maria, the wife of Charles I. In general it extended from the fortieth parallel to the southern bank of the Potomac River, and from the meridian which crossed the source of that river to the Atlantic; but the description of boundaries was so indefinite, because of the lack of precise geographical knowledge, that many disputes soon arose over ownership of territory.

The government of Maryland was modeled upon that of the Palatinate of Durham, a feudatory on the border of Scotland in which the bishop had almost absolute powers; but the lord proprietor of Maryland was restricted by several clauses in the charter. He was given the right to ordain, make, and enact laws, provided they were approved by the freemen of the province, or by a majority of them, or by their delegates, and were not contrary to the laws of England. Baltimore was given very large judicial powers, such as the creation of courts and the pardoning of criminals. He was also given the right to make ordinances, provided they did not deprive any person of life, limb, or property. The proprietor could collect taxes, make grants of lands, and create manors, over which the lord of the manor would have the rights of a feudal baron. The proprietor was also given control of ecclesiastical matters such as the power of appointing ministers and founding churches, which were "to be dedicated and consecrated according to the Ecclesiastical Laws of our Kingdom of England." The charter did not prohibit him from permitting the establishment of other churches, an omission which Baltimore used to assist the Catholics. The proprietor's motives, however, were not entirely religious; he no doubt desired to found an asylum for people of his own faith, but he was also a keen business man and desired to increase his worldly goods.

The first settlers.—In October, 1633, Baltimore sent two small vessels, the *Ark* and the *Dove*, to Maryland. On board there were about twenty gentlemen, most of whom were Catholics, and probably two hundred laborers, the majority of whom were Protestants. Among the influential members were the governor, Leonard Calvert, the brother of Lord Baltimore, and the two councilors who were to assist him in the government. Three Jesuit priests accompanied the expedition, which arrived at the mouth of the Potomac in March, 1634. The site for a settlement was selected nine miles up St. George's River, a small stream which flows into the north side of the Potomac near its mouth, the place being named St. Mary's. The location was favorable, for it was surrounded by fields cleared by the Indians. The tribes in the neighborhood had been at war with the Susquehannas, and were glad to sell their lands and move across the Potomac.

Trouble with Virginia.—William Claiborne had been the principal opponent of George Calvert, when he attempted to obtain the charter for Maryland. In 1631 Claiborne had established a settlement on Kent Island in Chesapeake Bay, which fell within the bounds of Maryland. In 1634 Governor Calvert informed Claiborne that he would not molest the settlement, but that the owner of Kent Island must be considered as a tenant of the proprietor. Claiborne laid the matter before the Virginia council, which decided that the Maryland charter infringed upon the rights of Virginia. A miniature war followed which was ended by a decision of the king, who ruled that the Virginia charter of 1609 had become null when the crown took over the colony in 1624, and that Kent Island belonged to Maryland.

Religious, economic, and social life.—The religious life of the colony was greatly influenced by the presence of the Jesuits. Father White and his colleagues labored incessantly to convert the Protestant colonists and to establish missions among the Indians. In 1641 the Catholics made up about one-fourth of the population but included most of the influential families. The economic life of the colony developed much like that of Virginia, although unaccompanied by the great hardships of the James River settlements. Nor did the Indians prove as troublesome, although from 1639 to 1644 an expedition was sent against them each year. Tobacco cultivation became the principal occupation. The plantations developed along the rivers and the shore of the bay, for many years extending but a few miles inland. The manors usually contained from one thousand to two thousand acres, although a few contained five thousand acres or more, the lords of the manors being granted lands in proportion to the number of colonists they provided. Many of the large grants were later divided, and small proprietors increased in number. There was practically no town life, the seat of government containing only a few houses. There were few mills and no factories. Few roads were built, the water courses and the bay affording the principal means of communication.

The government.—Cecilius Calvert never visited the colony, but he appointed all the important officers, who resided in the province. The chief of these was the governor, to whom the proprietor delegated most of his powers. He was at the head of military affairs. As chancellor he was the keeper of the seal and issued patents for land, commissions for office, and other legal documents. As chief magistrate he appointed officers for the preservation of peace and the administration of justice, and had power to issue and enforce ordinances, to establish ports, fairs and markets, to remit fines, and pardon all offenses except high treason. He could summon the legislative assembly, prepare bills for its consideration, assent to the laws, and dissolve the assembly. He also acted as chief justice. Leonard Calvert occupied the position until 1647. Assisting the governor was a council. In 1636 it contained three members, but was gradually increased in size in later years. Before this body the governor brought matters of importance, such as the creation of offices, establishment of courts, granting of pardons, levying of taxes, issuing of ordinances, and military expeditions.

The legislative assembly at first was made up of all the freemen, but as the colonists took up more distant lands, a custom of giving proxies grew up. The first assembly met in 1635, but about all that is known of it is that it attempted to initiate legislation, to which the proprietor objected. The second assembly, which met in 1638, consisted of the governor and council, freemen especially summoned by the governor, freemen present of their own will, and proxies. The governor presented a code approved by the proprietor, but it was rejected by the assembly. The same year the proprietor temporarily yielded the right of initiating legislation, authorizing the governor to consent to laws enacted by the assembly until the proprietor could examine them. In 1639 the local divisions, which were called hundreds, sent representatives. This assembly fixed its own membership, which was to be composed of councilors, persons especially summoned, and burgesses elected in hundreds. The assembly sat at times as a law court, but most of the cases were brought before the governor and his councilors, who acted as associate justices, or before the local courts.

THE BERMUDAS

The Somers Islands Company.—Almost simultaneously with the occupation of the Atlantic seaboard, the English had been establishing vigorous colonies in the islands adjacent to North America. In 1609 a Virginia supply ship commanded by Sir George Somers was wrecked on one of the Bermuda Islands.

Upon his return to England, he interested people in the islands and in 1612 the Somers Islands Company was formed, most of the stockholders being members of the Virginia Company.

Settlement and economic development of the Bermudas.—Settlers were immediately sent out and the colony prospered from the first. In 1614 it contained six hundred persons. Fortifications were built, some tobacco was shipped, and a land survey begun which was completed in 1617. By 1625 the population had increased to between two and three thousand and a larger supply of tobacco was being produced than in Virginia. As in the James River settlements, there was considerable opposition to the government monopoly of tobacco, and in 1628 a petition against it was addressed to the crown. In 1631 the privy council decreed that only a moderate amount of tobacco should be planted, and the company succeeded in getting a complete monopoly of the trade. The low price of tobacco at that time caused the colonists to devote themselves less exclusively to that business, and corn, potatoes, hogs, fowls, and fruit were produced in such quantities that the islands were able to export large amounts to the colonies on the mainland. The cedar forests also began to be utilized for ship-building. With the growth of the mainland colonies, the Bermudas became of relatively less economic importance, but they continued to be considered an important naval base.

Representative government.—The Bermudas were the second English colony to receive representative government. Besides the governor and council there was a general assembly, the first being held but a year after the establishment of the Virginia house of burgesses.

GUIANA

For a hundred years the Caribbean had been a Spanish sea. Hardy English mariners had frequently penetrated it, but always at their peril, and they had never seriously injured the Spanish colossus. To gain a foothold on its shores and to appropriate a portion of the commerce of tropical America became powerful forces in English activities.

Expeditions.—During the closing years of the reign of Elizabeth, many English ships visited the coast of Venezuela to procure salt, and after the treaty of 1604 with Spain, to obtain

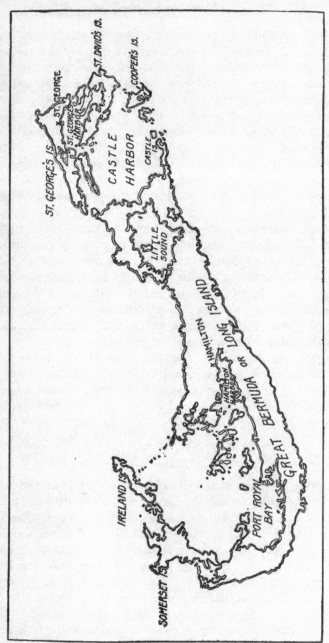

The Bermudas

tobacco. Several attempts were also made to explore and colonize Guiana. In 1604 Captain Charles Lea planted a colony on the Wyapoco, but in two years abandoned the enterprise. During 1606–1607 Sir Thomas Roe traded along the Guiana coast and explored the swamps of the Cuyuni and Wyapoco. In 1608 Robert Harcourt and two associates received a patent to lands between the Amazon and Essequibo rivers. Harcourt with ninety-seven men landed in Guiana, but after a sojourn of three years he returned to England. Part of the settlers remained and scattered among the Indians. Harcourt attempted to obtain more capital, and in 1616 another expedition was sent out but without success.

Raleigh's last attempt.—Since the first year of the reign of James I, Raleigh had been imprisoned on a charge of conspiring against the king. But in 1616 he was released, and having obtained a commission as admiral, sailed for Guiana the following year with a fleet of fourteen vessels. Attacked by the Spaniards, he lost several vessels and returned to England, where, upon complaint of the Spanish ambassador, Gondomar, he was again imprisoned and soon after executed.

North's expedition.—In 1620 an attempt was made to reorganize Raleigh's company, and Captain Roger North was sent with one hundred and twenty men to Guiana, where they joined the remnant of Harcourt's colonists. But the attempt again failed because of opposition of the Spanish ambassador.

THE LESSER ANTILLES

The English occupation.—In a great half circle at the eastern end of the Caribbean are the Lesser Antilles. After the failures on the South American coast, the English grasped these outposts of the tropics and, side by side with the French, were soon firmly established across one of the principal highways of Spanish commerce. In 1623 St. Christopher was temporarily occupied and was actually settled in 1625. The same year (1625) Sir William Courten started the first colony in Barbados. In 1627 Lord Carlisle received a grant which covered the Caribbees, and the following year the Earl of Pembroke and Montgomery also obtained rights to Trinidad, Tobago, and Barbados. In

the contest between the claimants Carlisle won. He ejected
Courten's settlers and established his own colonists. In 1628
Nevis was occupied. The following year the settlers on St.
Christopher and Nevis were evicted by the Spaniards, but upon
the retirement of the fleet the colonists returned to their plantations. In 1632 settlements were made on Antigua and Montserrat. As in the Bermudas, tobacco became the leading crop,
but later the production of sugar cane superseded it. Barbados
soon contained 6,000 inhabitants and in 1639, when Virginia
had a total population of about 7000, there were 20,000 planters in the islands governed by Carlisle. In the Lesser Antilles
the proprietary form of government prevailed for half a century.

THE PROVIDENCE ISLAND COMPANY

The Puritan leaders.—During the great struggle between king
and parliament, several of the merchant princes were on the
Puritan side. One of the most powerful of these was Robert
Rich, Lord Warwick. He had been an active member of the
Virginia and Somers Islands companies, of the Guinea and
Guiana companies, and of the Council of New England. Closely
associated with Warwick were Lord Saye and Sele, Lord Brooke,
Sir Nathaniel Rich, and John Pym. As the parliamentary con-
test increased in intensity, these leaders decided to plant a
Puritan colony in the Caribbean.

The Providence Island Company.—The site selected was on
one of the Mosquito Islands off the coast of Nicaragua. In
1629 a company was formed which was granted the greater part
of the Caribbean Sea, from Haiti to the coast of Venezuela and
to the mainland of Central America. Besides Jamaica, then in
the possession of Spain, the Caymán Islands fell within these
limits. The English fleet which was sent out in 1630 temporarily occupied Tortuga, where colonists from Nevis had recently
arrived, and the company asked that this island be included in
the patent. The request was granted, but the English were able
to hold the island only until 1635 when they were driven out by
the Spaniards. The islands along the Mosquito coast were
occupied by the company, and a project was formed to colonize
the mainland. In 1635 Providence Island was unsuccessfully

attacked by a Spanish fleet, but in 1641 the Spaniards succeeded in overcoming the colony, thus for the time ending English operations on the Central American coast.

READINGS

VIRGINIA

Becker, Carl, *The Beginnings of the American People*, pp. 65–80; Beer, G. L., *The Origins of the British Colonial System*, 78–175; Brown, Alexander, *Genesis of the United States; The First Republic in America;* Bruce, P. A., *Economic History of Virginia in the Seventeenth Century*, I, 189–330; *Institutional History of Virginia in the Seventeenth Century*, II, 229–262; Channing, Edward, *History of the United States*, I, 143–224; Doyle, J. A., *English Colonies in America*, I, 101–184; Eggleston, Edward, *The Beginners of a Nation*, 25–97; Fiske, John, *Old Virginia and her Neighbors*, I, 40–222; Hamilton, P. J., *Colonization of the South*, 55–119; MacDonald, William, *Select Charters Illustrative of American History*, 1–23; Osgood, H. L., *The American Colonies in the Seventeenth Century*, I, 23–97; Scott, W. R., *The Constitution and Finance of English, Scottish, and Irish Joint-Stock Companies to 1720*, II, 246–289; Tyler, L. G., *England in America*, 34–103; Tyler, L. G., ed., *Narratives of Early Virginia;* Wertenbaker, T. J., *Virginia under the Stuarts*, 1–84; Johnston, Mary, *Pioneers of the Old South;* Flippin, P. S., *The Royal Government in Virginia, 1624–1775*.

MARYLAND

Brown, W. H., *Maryland*, 1–50; Channing, Edward, *History of the United States*, I, 241–268; Doyle, J. A., *English Colonies in America*, I, 275–296; Eggleston, Edward, *Beginners of a Nation*, 220–257; Fiske, John, *Old Virginia and her Neighbors*, I, 255–275; Hall, C. C., ed., *Narratives of Early Maryland;* MacDonald, William, *Select Charters*, 53–59; Mereness, N. D., *Maryland as a Proprietary Province;* Osgood, H. L., *The American Colonies in the Seventeenth Century*, II, 58–79; Tyler, L. G., *England in America*, 118–132.

THE BERMUDAS AND THE CARIBBEAN

Beer, G. L., *The Origins of the British Colonial System*, 12–20; Cunningham, William, *The Growth of English Industry and Commerce in Modern Times*, I, 331–339; Lucas, C. P., *A Historical Geography of the British Colonies*, II, 5–14, 43–50; Newton, A. P., *The Colonizing Activities of the English Puritans*, 13–282; Scott, W. R., *The Constitution and Finance of English, Scottish, and Irish Joint-Stock Companies to 1720*, II, 259–299, 327–337; Tilby, A. W., *Britain in the Tropics*, 44–50.

CHAPTER VII

THE BEGINNINGS OF NEW ENGLAND

THE PURITAN MOVEMENT IN ENGLAND

The Puritans.—While the planting of colonies on the shores of Chesapeake Bay and on the Caribbean islands was in progress, other settlements were being formed in New England by English Separatists and Puritans. By the beginning of the reign of Elizabeth the Anglican church was firmly established, but it was not long before groups within the church began to show dissatisfaction. At first protests were made against some of the ceremonies and formulas of the service. After 1570 the Puritans, as they were derisively called, began to object to the episcopal form of government and to advocate the Presbyterian or Calvinistic system, which was based upon the idea of a representative form of church government. During the later years of the reign the Puritans laid more and more stress on morals. They believed that life should be sternly ascetic, that the Sabbath should be kept strictly, and that pleasures and extravagance should be suppressed.

The Independents.—Most of the Puritans had no wish to withdraw from the church, but desired to reform it. A more radical group, however, who became known as Independents, looked upon the national church as an unholy institution contrary to scripture. They wished to reëstablish the church as it was believed to be in the days of the Apostles. There were several groups of Independents or Separatists, the various groups being named after their leaders, the followers of Robert Brown being known as Brownists, those of Henry Barrow as Barrowists. They met in small groups which were called conventicles. The English church, through the Court of High Commission, proceeded with considerable severity against the Puritans, whom they attempted to make conform, but against the Separatists they showed no mercy, breaking up the conventicles, imprisoning many, and hanging some of the leaders.

James I and the Non-Conformists.—Soon after James I became king, the Puritans presented a petition asking for changes in the church. The king called the Hampton Court Conference that he might hear the views of the various parties. James soon found that many of the Puritans believed in presbyteries, a form of government with which he had had unpleasant experiences in Scotland, and he angrily ended the conference. Shortly afterward, because of the so-called "Gunpowder Plot," the king became convinced that he was personally in danger. From this time on he supported the Anglican church. Severe laws were passed against the Catholics, and the laws against Non-Conformists were enforced with greater vigor.

PLYMOUTH COLONY

Failures of the Plymouth Company.—The Plymouth Company, which received its charter in 1606, took immediate measures to occupy its territories. In that year two unsuccessful attempts were made to found colonies. The information brought back, however, so interested the company that another expedition was fitted out the following year. Colonists were landed at the mouth of the Kennebec River; but great hardships were experienced during the winter, and in the spring the discouraged settlers abandoned the enterprise.

Activity on the New England Coast, 1607-1619.—No successful settlement in New England was made until 1620, but in the meantime the coast was frequently visited. In 1613 Captain Argall attacked the French settlements at Mount Desert, Port Royal, and St. Croix. The following year John Smith explored and mapped the New England coast. In 1615 he was made Admiral of New England by the Plymouth Company and he attempted to found a colony, but it proved a failure. Several fishing and trading voyages were also made under the direction of Sir Ferdinando Gorges, an influential member of the Plymouth Company.

The Council for New England.—The failure of the company to plant a colony led Gorges and others who were still interested to petition for a new charter; on November 13, 1620, the document passed the seals incorporating the Council for New England, which was given jurisdiction over the territory from 40° to 48° north latitude.

Origin of the Pilgrims.—The first permanent settlement in New England was not the work of the Council, but of a group of Independents. Separatist congregations were located at Scrooby, Gainsborough, and Austerfield, villages in Nottinghamshire, Lincolnshire, and Yorkshire. In the Scrooby congregation were three men of unusual ability, Pastor John Robinson, Elder William Brewster, and William Bradford. To avoid persecution many Separatists had migrated to Amsterdam, and there in 1608 Robinson and his followers gathered, removing later to Leyden. From time to time a few others joined them, among the late comers being John Carver and Miles Standish. Most of the congregation found the making of a livelihood among the Dutch extremely difficult. In spite of this, some of them enrolled in the University of Leyden and Brewster set up a printing press from which appeared several theological works.

Reasons for removal from Holland.—By 1617 the leaders determined to seek new lands. Bradford in his *History of Plymouth Plantation* gives the following reasons for removal: (1) Daily life was so hard in Holland that few cared to emigrate there and in consequence the congregation did not grow; (2) many were growing old, and there was fear that the congregation would soon break up; (3) life was too hard for the children, and in addition many were slipping away, some becoming soldiers and sailors; it was also found that the morals of the young were endangered in the gay city of Leyden; (4) it was hoped to spread the gospel in remote lands. In addition, intermarriage with the Dutch had begun and it was evident that the little community would soon lose its English identity.

Removal to America.—Guiana, New Netherlands, and Virginia were discussed as possible places for settlement, the last named being the final choice. A patent was obtained from the Virginia Company, and John Carver was made governor. Seven thousand pounds were raised by Thomas Weston and other merchant adventurers to back the enterprise. A portion of the Leyden congregation sailed for England, and at Southampton met with others from London, who had determined to join them. The company, including Carver, Brewster, Bradford, and Standish, left England in the *Mayflower* and the *Speedwell*, but the latter proving unseaworthy, about twenty abandoned the enterprise. The *Mayflower* arrived at Cape Cod in November, 1620.

The Mayflower Compact.—As the region was outside of the jurisdiction of the Virginia Company, the colonists on their own initiative drew up what is known as the Mayflower Compact, by which they combined into a civil body politic, and agreed to enact such just and equitable laws as were for the general welfare of the colony. After the signing of the compact, Governor Carver was confirmed in his office. The Mayflower Compact marks the origin of the English colony based upon a social compact the basis of which was the will of the colonists rather than that of the sovereign. Of a similar nature were Rhode Island, Connecticut, New Haven, and New Hampshire in their inception, and in the latter half of the eighteenth century, when the frontiersman had crossed the mountains and freed himself from the restraints of the tidewater governments, the social compact became the basis of western state making.

Settlement at Plymouth.—Exploring parties were sent along the shores of Massachusetts Bay, and Plymouth was selected as the site for the colony, but the classic story of the landing on Plymouth Rock is now known to be only a romance. From the first settlers suffered exceedingly. Bradford describes the situation as follows: "But that which was most sadd and lamentable was, that in 2. or 3. moneths time halfe of their company dyed, espetialy in Jan: and February, being the depth of winter, and wanting houses and other comforts; being infected with the scurvie and other diseases . . . ; so as ther dyed some times 2. or 3. of a day, in the foresaid time; that of 100 and odd persons, scarce 50. remained. And of these in the time of most distres, ther was but 6. or 7. sound persons."

Indians, fur trade and maize.—The region which the Pilgrims had selected for their first settlement was almost deserted by the Indians, many of them having been swept away by a plague. At some distance to the southward lived the Wampanoags, whose chief was Massasoit. Shortly after the arrival of the Pilgrims an Indian named Squanto, who previously had been carried to Europe by one of Smith's captains, appeared in the settlement. Squanto prevailed upon Massasoit to come to Plymouth, where a treaty of peace was made which lasted for fifty years. This led to the opening of a fur trade, which became the chief source of wealth for the colony. Squanto proved to be of great service, teaching the settlers the planting of maize and instructing them in hunting and fishing. Carver died in the spring of 1621, and William Bradford was elected governor, a position which he held almost continually until 1657. In the fall the *Fortune*, poorly provisioned, arrived with thirty-five settlers, an influx which led to another winter of hardship. The boat also brought a patent from the Council for New England.

"Weston's rude fellows."—In May, 1622, sixty-seven persons arrived, having been sent out by Thomas Weston, who had obtained a grant from the Council for New England. Later they moved to Wessagusset, where they lived a turbulent life. In 1623 the Indians to the northward planned to exterminate the Wessagusset settlers, who appealed to Plymouth for aid. Captain Miles Standish led a force against the Indians, who were so severely punished that peace was established.

Expansion of Plymouth.—At first the wealth of the colony was held in a common stock. Bradford determined to assign a tract of land to each family, an experiment which greatly stimulated industry. From this time the colonists were never in danger of starvation, and in a few years they were able to pay off their debts to the English merchants. To increase the fur trade, posts were established on Buzzard's Bay, on the Kennebec River, at Penobscot, and at Machias Bay, the two latter posts, however, being soon broken up by the French. A group of traders who established themselves at Merry Mount under Thomas Morton shocked the austere people of Plymouth, who in 1628 broke up Morton's establishment. A trade was opened with the Dutch, and in 1636 a fur trading post was established on the Connecticut River. In 1624 there were one hundred and eighty settlers in the Plymouth colony, and in 1630 only three hundred; but after that the number increased rapidly, by 1642 the population being three thousand.

Government of the colony.—The first governor exercised executive and judicial powers, and the same powers were vested in Bradford and an assistant. The number of assistants was increased in 1624 to five and in 1633 to seven. The freemen composed the legislative body, which was called the General Court, one of its sessions being devoted annually to the election of officers. In 1638 a representative system was introduced, Plymouth being allowed four delegates and other towns two each. Legally every freeman could vote, but in practice the suffrage was restricted to church members. Pastors and elders were elected by the adult males of each congregation, and attendance at church meetings was vigorously enforced.

COLONIZING ACTIVITIES ON THE NEW ENGLAND COAST

Land grants and settlements.—While Plymouth was developing, the Council for New England was attempting to settle the New England coast. The region from the Bay of Fundy to Narragansett Bay was divided among twenty patentees. Captain John Mason and Sir Ferdinando Gorges procured a patent to lands between the Kennebec and Merrimac rivers; Mason received lands between Salem and the Merrimac; Sir Robert Gorges ten miles of coast lands along "the north east side of Boston Bay," and Lord Sheffield and Lord Edward Gorges extensive tracts to the south of Sir Robert Gorges's lands. Lord Warwick also received lands on Massachusetts Bay. The grantees obtained the assistance of English merchants, who, in 1623 established small settlements at Portsmouth and Dover, within the present state of New Hampshire, and at Saco Bay, Monhegan Island, and Casco Bay, within the modern state of Maine. Sir Robert Gorges made an unsuccessful attempt to plant a settlement at Weymouth, and a group of Dorchester merchants planted a settlement on Cape Ann.

Lyford, Oldham, and Morton.—In 1624 a group of colonists, including a minister named John Lyford, arrived at Plymouth. There he joined with John Oldham to get control of the government. They were banished from the colony and went to Weymouth, where they joined with Roger Conant and others, and moved to Nantasket. The following year, on the invitation of the Dorchester men, Lyford, Conant, and Oldham moved to Cape Ann. This angered the Plymouth people, who had obtained a tract on Cape Ann from Lord Sheffield. Difficulties over fishing rights soon developed, and Miles Standish was sent to the cape with a troop of soldiers. A compromise was effected, but the Plymouth men soon abandoned the enterprise. The Dorchester men found little profit in the business and in 1626 most of them departed. Oldham returned to Plymouth. Conant and three others remained, but shortly afterward removed to Naumkeag, the modern Salem. In 1625 a settlement was established a little north of Weymouth, where Thomas Morton became the leader. He established the Episcopalian service, set up a May-pole which became the scene of gaiety, and engaged in the fur trade, but Plymouth men soon broke up the settlement.

The Canada and Laconia companies.—When war broke out between England and France in 1628, Sir Ferdinando Gorges and Captain John Mason organized the Canada Company to conquer the French fur-trading colonies of Acadia and Canada, and in 1629 a fleet under Captain Kirke captured the French colonies, but in 1632 they were restored to France. The Maine proprietors also attempted to tap the fur trade of the Lake Champlain region and accordingly, in 1629, obtained a grant embracing the lake country and a thousand acres of sea coast land, the territory being known as Laconia. A governor was appointed and attempts made to penetrate the fur country in the interior, but the efforts proved abortive.

THE MASSACHUSETTS BAY COLONY

Rev. John White's association.—The Reverend John White of Dorchester interested people in Lincolnshire and London, and formed an association, which, through the assistance of Warwick, in 1628 procured a patent for lands between the parallel which passed three miles north of the source of the Merrimac to that which passed three miles south of the head of the Charles River, and from the Atlantic to the Pacific. In September, 1628, John Endicott with about fifty followers arrived at Salem.

The Massachusetts Bay Company.—Trouble for the new association was brewing in England. Members of the Gorges family attempted to interfere with the new settlement, and Morton and Oldham joined with them. The new association, however, succeeded in defeating the former patentees, and in March, 1629, a royal charter was obtained which confirmed the grant made to Endicott and his partners. The new corporation was called the

"Governor and Company of Massachusetts Bay in New England." The administration was placed in the hands of a governor, deputy governor, and eighteen assistants, who were to be elected annually by the freemen or members of the corporation. Four times a year the officers and freemen were to meet in a general court at which new freemen might be admitted to membership, subordinate officers might be appointed, and laws and ordinances enacted. On June 27, 1629, five ships with about four hundred settlers arrived at Salem.

The Cambridge agreement.—At this time Laud had begun his persecution of the Puritans and the king had started on his career of personal government. Under these circumstances the Puritan leaders looked to the New World for an asylum. John Winthrop, a wealthy gentleman of Groton in Suffolk, who had been a follower of Warwick in parliament, now became interested in the Massachusetts enterprise. Winthrop and several prominent men of Cambridge met and agreed to emigrate to New England provided the charter and government might be legally transferred to America. The company decided to transfer the government. Winthrop was made governor, and Thomas Dudley deputy governor.

The " Great Migration."—In June, 1630, eleven ships anchored at Salem and before the winter six more arrived, bringing in all over a thousand people. They found Endicott's followers in a deplorable condition. About one-fourth had died during the previous winter; many of the survivors were sick and there was a shortage of provisions. The new arrivals had brought only a limited supply and for the first year famine stalked in the land. The dreary prospect caused about a hundred of the newcomers to return immediately to England. Winthrop and most of his followers removed to Charlestown. By December two hundred had died. Believing that the inadequate water supply at Charlestown was the main cause of sickness, the settlers began to scatter, and before the new year settlements had been started at Dorchester, Boston, Watertown, Roxbury, Mystic, and Lynn.

The hardships endured by the followers of Endicott and Winthrop prevented many from coming during 1631 and 1632, but in 1633 a new wave of migration set in. Laud became archbishop in that year and began a rigorous enforcement of the laws

against nonconformists. Many ministers with their congregations in consequence migrated. By the end of 1634 there were
nearly four thousand settlers in Massachusetts. The migration
continued until the outbreak of war in 1642, by which time the
population had increased to about sixteen thousand.

The form of government.—The charter vested the government
in the governor, deputy governor, assistants, and freemen of the
company but not more than twelve of the colonists were legally
eligible to membership in the general court. Before disembarking
this little group decided that each of the assistants should exercise
the same powers as an English justice of the peace. The colony
was to be governed by the common law of England, which was
to be supplemented by biblical law. At the first general court,
held at Boston, October 19, 1630, one hundred and nine men
applied for admission as freemen of the corporation. This Winthrop and his associates hesitated to grant, but finally they agreed
to admit them, allowing them to elect assistants, but not to hold
office. It was also provided that in future no person should be
admitted as a freeman unless a member of some church within the
colony. Though Winthrop and his followers at first claimed to
be members of the Church of England, the necessities of the
frontier soon asserted themselves, and each community became
a political, economic, and a religious unit.

The New England towns.—The New England towns were based
upon the idea of group settlement and wherever New Englanders
migrated the local organization was reproduced. As Professor
Osgood says, "The settlement of a town normally began with
the laying out of a village plot and the assignment of home lots.
This to an extent determined the location of highways, of the
village common, and of some of the outlying fields. On or near
the common the church was built, and in not a few cases the site
that was chosen for this building went far toward determining
the entire lay-out of the town. The idea of a home lot was a plot
of ground for a dwelling-house and outbuildings, for a dooryard
and garden, and usually also an enclosure for feeding cattle and
raising corn."

The first settlers located wherever they pleased, but the Massachusetts general court soon took over the superintendence of
town founding and prescribed more or less definitely the bound-

aries of each town. The grants were made in tracts of thirty-six square miles or more. Within a town were many common fields

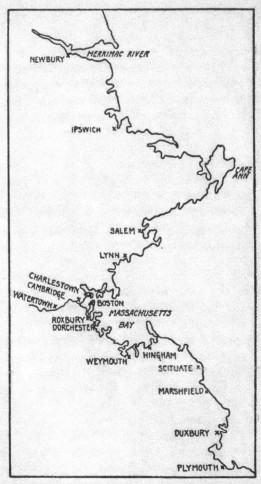

Principal Settlements in Massachusetts, 1630

which were handled by associated proprietors. The fields were surrounded by common fences and were cultivated by a joint system. The herds were also held in common. The original grantees and their legal heirs or successors made up the commoners or proprietors. Originally the town and the proprietors were approximately the same. An important function of the town meeting was in allotting land. Soon each community began to receive newcomers who were freemen but not proprietors. At first the proprietors were in control, but as the freemen increased in number frequent struggles occurred over the arrangement of town lands.

The meeting house was the center of local life. There the town meeting was held and there the people repaired on the Sabbath. In early days the military stores and equipment were usually kept in the edifice and the men attended service with arms in hand. The town constructed and took care of the meeting house and the minister was supported by taxation. One of the early acts of each town was to establish a school, the meeting house frequently being used as a school-house.

A representative system introduced.—The governor and assistants soon found their power challenged. In 1632 a tax was voted for fortifying Newtown, the modern Cambridge. The tax caused considerable grumbling, and the general court decided that, in future, the governor and assistants should be advised in matters of taxation by two delegates from each town, and that all magistrates should be elected by the entire body of freemen. In 1634 a committee of two freemen from each town demanded larger rights. The result was a representative system, each town sending representatives according to its size to meet with the general court. This system was in no sense a popular government, the franchise continuing to be restricted to a limited number of church members, the leaders of whom were distinctly aristocratic.

The struggle with Laud.—The patentees who had been deprived of their rights found a ready listener in Archbishop Laud, who disliked the Puritan commonwealth growing so lustily on the shores of Massachusetts Bay. Grounds for accusation were found in the fact that the Massachusetts magistrates expelled those who disagreed with their religious ideas. Complaints were filed with the privy council by Gorges and Mason, but a committee of the council in 1633 made a report which was favorable to the colony. In 1634 the attack was renewed, and this time with better success, for the king appointed the Commission for Foreign Plantations, headed by Laud, to take over the general supervision of all the colonies. Immediately a demand was made for the charter of the Massachusetts Bay Colony. Governor Dudley and the assistants replied that the charter could not be returned except by order of the general court, which was not in session. They immediately fortified Castle Island, Dorchester, and Charlestown.

In 1635 the coast of New England was reapportioned, Sir Ferdinando Gorges receiving the lands in Maine between the Penobscot and the Piscataqua, Mason receiving New Hampshire and northern Massachusetts as far as Cape Ann, and Lord Edward Gorges from Cape Ann to Narragansett Bay. The same year the Council for New England resigned its charter, and the king decided to seize the charter of the Massachusetts Bay Company. The pecuniary difficulties of the king, the destruction of a boat which was built by Mason and Gorges, and the death of Mason combined to help the colony. Though the charter was again demanded in 1638 by the lord commissioners, the general court refused to recognize the order, and the increasing difficulties of the king made it possible for the Massachusetts authorities to continue their independent course.

EXPANSION OF THE MASSACHUSETTS BAY COLONY

RHODE ISLAND

Roger Williams.—The power of the Massachusetts magistrates was exercised to maintain the ideal of a biblical commonwealth, whose principles were expounded by John Cotton of the Boston church. Those who did not agree were in danger. Among the dissenters was Roger Williams, a brilliant young student from Cambridge, who arrived at Boston in 1631, where he was invited to become one of the ministers. He refused to commune with those who had not broken with the English church and repaired to Salem where he was invited to become the minister, but the general court prevented his ordination. Williams soon departed for Plymouth, where he devoted much time to the study of the Indians. He concluded that the title to land belonged to the natives and that the king had no right to grant it away, a view which somewhat disturbed Brewster and Bradford.

He returned to Salem where, during the illness of Skelton, the pastor, he occasionally preached; when Skelton died, Williams became the teacher of the organization. In his sermons he argued that church and state should be separate, and denied the right of the magistrates to regulate churches. He also considered it a sin to follow the forms of the established church. When the colony was attacked by Laud, the general court ordered that a new oath of fidelity be taken. Williams objected to enforced oaths, as he thought that they obliged wicked men to perform a religious act, thus invading the freedom of the soul.

Providence plantation.—To punish Salem for harboring Williams, title to its lands on Marble Neck was refused by the general court and the town was denied the right of representation. Endicott yielded but Williams remained obdurate. In a letter to the churches he protested against the arbitrary act. Williams was summoned before the magistrates and in October, 1635, was sentenced to banishment. The sentence was not immediately enforced and at Salem he continued to be the center of a group of Separatists, who proposed to remove in the spring to the shores of Narragansett Bay. This again alarmed the magistrates, and they decided to send Williams to England. Hearing of the project, he fled from his persecutors and found refuge among the Narragansett Indians. He was warned away from the territory of Plymouth, and in June, 1636, settled at Providence, where he soon had a considerable following, this being the first settlement in Rhode Island.

Title to the land was obtained from the Indians. As the Providence people were outside of any special jurisdiction, they established a government on democratic lines. Church and state were kept separate, no one being forced to support religion. In 1640 an agreement was drawn up which served as a form of government for several years. The governing body was composed of five men called disposers, who were chosen four times in each year. They disposed of the land and managed the common stock. The freeholders retained the right to ratify or disavow, in general meetings, the acts of the disposers. There was a lack of a strong executive and judiciary. Disputes were usually settled by arbitration, but as there was no authority to enforce the settlement, disorders frequently occurred.

Anne Hutchinson.—No sooner had Williams been driven from Massachusetts Bay Colony than a second controversy shook the commonwealth. In the congregation of John Cotton was Mrs. Anne Hutchinson. She became popular by ministering to the sick, and began to hold meetings for women, where the sermons were discussed. Mrs. Hutchinson assumed the roll of teacher, discussing the questions of "a covenant of works" and "a covenant of grace." By the covenant of works she referred to the practice of the Catholic church, which considered penance, confession, and pilgrimages as means of salvation. By a covenant of grace she meant that condition of mind of Protestant Christians which found peace in the thought of the holiness of Christ. She believed that the divine spirit existed in every true Christian. John Cotton and her brother-in-law, John Wheelwright, were held up as examples of those who lived in the covenant of grace. To many of the Boston leaders it seemed as if Mrs. Hutchinson claimed to be inspired, and they feared that her teachings would endanger the authority of the church.

The Boston congregation split into two factions. In Mrs. Hutchinson's party was Governor Harry Vane. On the other side were John Winthrop and the pastor, John Wilson. Cotton attempted to remain neutral but favored the Hutchinsonian party. The question soon became a bitter political quarrel between Winthrop and Vane. At the election in 1637 Vane was defeated. Without the support of the chief executive the followers of Mrs. Hutchinson soon lost power. A synod of ministers was held at Cambridge to root out the heresies. Cotton succeeded in making his peace with the magistrates, but Wheelwright was banished, as was Mrs. Hutchinson. She was allowed to remain in the colony during the winter, but early in the spring of 1638 Winthrop ordered her to depart.

Settlements on Rhode Island.—She found a temporary asylum at Providence, but soon went to the island of Aquidneck, afterward called Rhode Island, where she joined her husband and some of her friends. The little group of nineteen settlers constituted themselves a body politic, electing William Coddington chief magistrate. Many emigrants joined the people of Portsmouth and in 1639 a new settlement was founded at Newport.

SETTLEMENTS IN THE CONNECTICUT VALLEY

Early claimants.—One of the patentees who had received lands from the Council of New England was the Earl of Warwick, whose grant covered a large part of the Connecticut Valley. In 1631 he transferred his rights to Lord Saye and Sele, Lord Brooke and others, who contemplated founding a Puritan colony, but for several years they did nothing to settle their domain. In 1633 the Dutch erected a fort where Hartford now stands, and shortly afterward men from Plymouth built a trading post ten miles farther up the river. In 1635 the English patentees, wearied with the Providence Island project, sent out settlers under John Winthrop, Jr., who erected Fort Saybrook at the mouth of the river. Scarcely were the cannon in place when a Dutch vessel appeared, but finding the English strongly posted, the Dutch made no attempt to take possession.

The migration of 1635-36.—A more important movement cáme from Massachusetts. Congregations from Watertown, Dorchester, and Cambridge, desiring better lands, migrated to the rich Connecticut Valley. The first Dorchester men arrived at Windsor in the summer of 1635. In June, 1636, the Rev. Thomas Hooker led the Cambridge people to Hartford, the rest of the Dorchester congregation joined those already at Windsor, and the people of Watertown settled at Wethersfield. By the end of 1636 eight hundred people were living in the three towns. Another congregation from Roxbury settled at Springfield.

The Pequot War.—The Pequot Indians saw with chagrin the increasing numbers of the whites. The settlers also angered them by purchasing lands from the Mohegans, and ignoring the Pequot chiefs. In 1633 the Pequots had murdered a Virginia sea-captain named Stone, and Governor Winthrop had inquired concerning the homicide. In 1634, fearing the Dutch and the Narragansetts, the Pequots had sought an alliance with Massachusetts Bay Colony. As a price of forgiveness for Stone's murder and for protection, Winthrop demanded heavy tribute. In 1636 John Oldham, who had come to collect the tribute, was murdered at Block Island. Though the Pequots were probably not guilty, Endicott led a force against them, destroying several wigwams and seizing considerable maize. Angered by the raid,

the Pequots attempted to form an alliance with the Narragansetts, but Williams prevented it, and in the ensuing war Mohegans
and Narragansetts fought on the white man's side. In the spring
of 1637 Pequots attacked Wethersfield. A general court was
immediately convened at Hartford to take measures for protection, and an expedition was sent against the Pequot fort on the
Mystic River, where the defenders were exterminated. Another
stronghold to the westward was also destroyed. A remnant of
the tribe was wiped out near New Haven by Connecticut and
Massachusetts troops and the captives were made slaves, some
being retained in New England, others being shipped to the West
Indies. The Indian menace was thus removed and the settlers
were free to push farther into the wilderness.

"The Fundamental Orders."—In 1639 Hartford, Windsor,
and Wethersfield formed a constitution, which provided that the
freemen were to hold two general meetings each year. At one
of these meetings the governor and assistants were elected, who,
with four representatives from each town, were to make up a general court with legislative and judicial powers.

New Haven.—The successful issue of the Pequot War opened
the Connecticut Valley to another important migration. This
was led by Rev. John Davenport and Theophilus Eaton, who
had come to New England to plant a colony on purely theocratic
lines. In 1638 they founded New Haven, and the following year
drew up a form of government. Citizenship was restricted to
church membership and an annual general court of freemen was
to elect a governor and assistants, who were to conduct all
governmental affairs, the only restriction on their authority being the law of Moses. Guilford, Milford, and Stamford sprang
up in the neighborhood, and each adopted a similar form of
government.

Settlement of Long Island.—English settlements also appeared
on Long Island. In 1632 Sir Edmund Plowden obtained a grant
from Charles I of Long Island and a portion of the adjoining
coasts. Three years later the Council for New England assigned
Long Island to Sir William Alexander. In 1640 settlers from
New Haven obtained a title to Long Island from Alexander's
representative and settled at Southold. Others from Massachusetts attempted a settlement opposite Manhattan, but, being

driven away by the Dutch, moved to Southampton at the eastern end of the island.

READINGS

GENERAL

Andrews, C. M., *The Fathers of New England, passim;* Becker, Carl, *The Beginnings of the American People,* 80–124.

THE PURITAN MOVEMENT AND THE PLYMOUTH COLONY

Adams, C. F., *Three Episodes of Massachusetts History,* I, 1–182; Arber, Edward, *The Story of the Pilgrim Fathers;* Bradford, William, *History of Plymouth Plantation;* Channing, Edward, *History of the United States,* I, 271–321; Cheyney, E. P., *European Background of American History,* 216–239; Dexter, Morton, *The England and Holland of the Pilgrims; The Story of the Pilgrims;* Doyle, J. A., *The Puritan Colonies,* I, 11–81; Eggleston, Edward, *The Beginners of a Nation,* 98–181; Fiske, John, *The Beginnings of New England,* 60–87; Griffis, W. E., *The Pilgrims in their Three Homes;* Neal, D., *History of the Pilgrims;* Osgood, H. L., *The American Colonies in the Seventeenth Century,* I, 98–137; Palfrey, J. G., *History of New England,* I, 101–238; Tyler, L. G., *England in America,* 148–182; Weeden, W. B., *Economic and Social History of New England,* I, 8–45; Young, Alexander, *Chronicles of the Pilgrim Fathers;* Usher, R. G., *The Pilgrims and Their History.*

MASSACHUSETTS BAY COLONY

Buffington, A. H., "New England and the Western Fur Trade, 1629–1675," in Colonial Society of Massachusetts, *Publications,* XXVIII, 160–192; Channing, Edward, *History of the United States,* I, 322–351; Doyle, J. A., *The Puritan Colonies,* I, 83–112; Eggleston, Edward, *Beginners of a Nation,* 188–215; Ellis, G. E., *The Puritan Age and Rule;* Fiske, John, *The Beginnings of New England,* 88–111; Johnson, Edward, *Wonder-Working Providence;* Newton, A. P., *The Colonizing Activities of the English Puritans;* Osgood, H. L., *The American Colonies in the Seventeenth Century,* I, 141–199, 424–467; Palfrey, J. G., *History of New England,* I, 283–405; *A Compendious History of New England,* I, 91–133; Tyler, L. G., *England in America,* 183–209; Weeden, W. B., *Economic and Social History of New England,* I, 47–164; Winthrop, John, *Journal.*

RHODE ISLAND AND THE CONNECTICUT VALLEY

Channing, Edward, *History of the United States,* I, 362–411; Doyle, J. A., *The Puritan Colonies,* I, 113–199; Eggleston, Edward, *Beginners of a Nation,* 266–346; Osgood, H. L., *The American Colonies in the Seventeenth Century,* I, 224–254, 301–370; Richman, I. B., *Rhode Island, a Study in Separatism,* 13–61; *Rhode Island, its Making and its Meaning,* 3–62; Tyler, L. G., *England in America,* 210–264; Weeden, W. B., *Early Rhode Island.*

CHAPTER VIII

THE ENGLISH COLONIES DURING THE REVOLUTIONARY PERIOD, 1640-1660

POLITICS, ADMINISTRATION, AND EXPANSION

Attitude of the colonies during the Puritan Revolution.—The personal rule of Charles I came to an end in 1641 and for eight years England was convulsed with civil war. During the struggle both Royalists and Parliamentarians claimed jurisdiction over the colonies, but neither was able to exert authority, and each colony followed its own course. The New England settlements were largely Puritan and naturally sided with parliament. In Maryland two factions formed, one Protestant, the other in favor of the Catholic proprietor. Virginia and the West Indies were almost entirely on the king's side. Incapable of rendering assistance, they attempted to maintain neutrality until the contest in England was decided.

The Bermudas and expansion in the West Indies.—In the Bermudas the colonists were divided, but the company leaders were Puritans. In 1643 the Independents seceded from the established Church, and two years later parliament granted freedom of worship in the islands. Religious feeling in the Bermudas led to a migration to a new asylum. In 1646 Captain William Sayle, who had been governor, led a colony to Segatoo, one of the Bahamas, which he now called Eleutheria, in allusion to the aim of the project. Later on Bermudans conducted extensive salt works in the Turks Islands in spite of frequent attacks by the Spaniards.

The Commonwealth, 1649-1653.—The military party, dominated by Cromwell, drove from parliament all those who hesitated to execute the king, the remnant being known as the Rump Parliament. It named a Council of State which was to carry on the executive work. The Commonwealth proceeded at once to overthrow its enemies outside of England. Rebellions in Ireland and Scotland were ruthlessly put down; the navy was greatly strengthened, and Admiral Sir George Ayscue was sent to the West Indies and Virginia to overthrow the Royalists. Friction with the Dutch had been growing for some time, due mainly to rivalry for the commerce of the East and West Indies and the growing trade of the Dutch along the Atlantic seaboard. Navigation laws were passed in 1650 and 1651 which were intended to deprive the Dutch of the trade of England and her possessions. War followed in 1652 and lasted for two years with varying success.

Colonial administration during the Commonwealth.—Colonial administration was carried on by various committees of parliament or of the Council of State. On March 2, 1650, the Council of State ordered that the entire council or any five of the members, should be a Committee for Trade and Plantations. In 1652 the Council of State appointed a standing committee of Trade, Plantations, and Foreign Affairs of which Cromwell and Vane were members. Special committees were also appointed from time to time to handle special colonial business or committees already in existence discussed matters referred to them.

Acquisition of Jamaica.—In December, 1653, Cromwell was made Lord Protector for life and in 1654 the war with the Dutch was brought to a close. To divert attention from home affairs Cromwell desired a foreign war. West Indian expansion had brought England into close contact with Spain. The aggressive acts of the latter against the Providence Island Company and the intercepting of English ships, gave a ready excuse for reprisals. Admiral Penn sailed from England on Christmas Day, 1654, in command of a large fleet to attack the Spanish. An attempt to gain a footing in Española was a complete failure, but Jamaica proved to be an easy prize and became a permanent English possession.

Colonial administration during the Protectorate.—The Council of State lost most of its powers and became simply the advisory council of Cromwell. The committee system of the council was continued. In 1655 a special committee for Jamaica was appointed, and about the same time a Committee for Foreign Plantations. The Protector also obtained the assistance of a body of officers and merchants to advise regarding colonial affairs.

NEW ENGLAND DEVELOPMENT, 1640–1660

The period from 1640 to 1660 was one of practical independence for the New England colonies. This neglect and freedom from

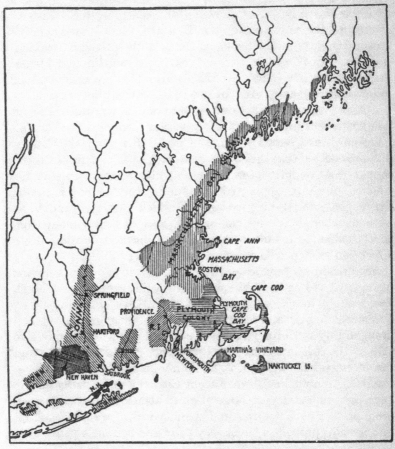

Settled areas in New England, about 1660

interference gave rise to three distinct developments: the formulation of provincial codes of law, the confederation of the colonies and of settlements within colonies, and territorial expansion.

The Massachusetts Body of Liberties.—The first of the colonial codes to be formulated was the Massachusetts Body of Liberties adopted by the general court in 1641. It provided for the protection of the private and political rights of the individual, methods of judicial procedure, rights of women, children, servants, foreigners, and strangers, the protection of animals, and the rights of the churches. Death penalties were specified, the capital crimes being the worshiping of false gods, witchcraft, blasphemy, murder, manslaughter, kidnaping, bearing false witness, and treason. Provision was also made for trial by jury. The code was amended from time to time, arson, cursing or smiting of parents, burglary, and highway robbery being added to the list of capital crimes. The Massachusetts code became the basis of the Connecticut code of 1650 and the New Haven code of 1656.

Causes of federation.—The development of self-government was fostered not only by neglect on the part of England, but also by the necessity of protection. Being hedged in on the north by the French and on the west by the Dutch, and with hostile Indian tribes encircling the English frontiers, the various groups of settlements were in danger. Massachusetts was strong enough to protect herself, but the settlements in the Connecticut Valley and on Long Island were menaced by the Dutch and Indians.

One of the fruitful causes of dispute between New England and the Dutch was the fur-trade. The choicest hunting grounds to the west were possessed by the Dutch and Swedes. To obtain a foothold on the Delaware, the upper Connecticut, and the Hudson became a settled economic policy of several of the New England colonies and was a potent factor in the formation of the New England Confederation. To exploit the Delaware River trade a company was formed at New Haven and in 1641 a settlement was made at Varkens Kill on the site of modern Salem, New Jersey, and later another post was established at the mouth of the Schuylkill, above the Dutch and Swedish forts. The Dutch, probably assisted by the Swedes, destroyed the Schuylkill fort, and the settlement at Varkens Kill did not prosper, most of the settlers dying or removing to New Haven. Massachusetts also attempted to obtain a share in the Delaware trade. In 1644 prominent merchants of Boston formed a company, but when their pinnace appeared in the Delaware, it was turned back by the Dutch, and shortly afterwards a small group of Boston traders were severely handled by the Indians.

The New England Confederation.—For several years plans for a confederation had been discussed, but the Dutch war against the Indians in 1642 and the struggle between De la Tour and D'Aulnay in Acadia brought matters to a head. At the general court which met at Boston on May 10, 1643, commissioners from Massachusetts, Plymouth, Connecticut, and New Haven signed a compact, Rhode Island and the settlements in Maine being excluded. The government of the confederation was placed in the hands of two commissioners from each of the four colonies. Internal affairs were not to be interfered with, but the confederation was to determine matters of war and foreign relations. Expenses were to be assessed on the colonies according to population. A vote of six commissioners was necessary to determine matters, the three small colonies thus being able to override Massachusetts. The confederation contained two serious defects which eventually led to its abandonment. The central government had no authority over individuals, and the equal vote of each colony violated the principle of representative government, Massachusetts having no more power then her weaker neighbors.

Work of the Confederation.—No incident occurred to require action on the part of the confederation until 1645, when the Narragansetts attacked the Mohegans. A force of three hundred men was raised by the confederation, an action which brought the Narragansetts to terms without hostilities. When a society for the propagation of the faith was incorporated in England to assist the missionary efforts of John Eliot and Thomas Mayhew, the commissioners handled the funds. When questions of boundaries and customs arose, they were settled by the commissioners. When Massachusetts assisted De la Tour against D'Aulnay, the commissioners exerted their influence to keep the colony from interfering in French affairs. In 1650 a treaty was made between Stuyvesant, the Dutch governor, and the commissioners, with the result that the Dutch retained their fort at Hartford, but were otherwise excluded from the Connecticut Valley and the eastern part of Long Island. The English were granted the right of colonization on the Delaware, but when New Haven men attempted to found a settlement, they were turned back by the Dutch and the confederation failed to take action. When hostilities broke out between the Dutch and English in 1651, the three smaller colonies desired war, but the Massachusetts general court refused, and when Cromwell's fleet appeared at Boston in 1654 on its way to attack the Dutch settlements, Massachusetts continued her opposition. Possible complications were averted by the treaty of peace. The action of Massachusetts in the relations with the Dutch so weakened the confederation that it soon ceased to be an important factor in New England history.

The Puritan movement into New Hampshire.—Massachusetts took advantage of the disturbed conditions in England to absorb the territory to the northward. In 1629 Mason had obtained a second patent for a tract extending sixty miles inland and lying between the Merrimac and Piscataqua rivers, which he named New Hampshire, and Mason and Gorges obtained title to lands between the Merrimac and Kennebec. In 1631 the two patentees and others obtained a tract of twenty thousand acres which included the Portsmouth settlement. In 1633 the English merchants who had founded Dover sold their shares in the settlement to Lord Saye and Sele, Lord Brooke, and others, a transaction which was followed by a Puritan migration. The same noblemen also obtained title to the Portsmouth settlement. During the Hutchinsonian controversy, Wheelwright and others found refuge at Dover, but shortly afterward established themselves at Exeter. Massachusetts claimed that the New Hampshire settlements fell within her boundaries, and in 1641, upon the suggestion of Lord Saye and Sele and Lord Brooke, extended her jurisdiction over Portsmouth and Dover. In 1643 Exeter also came under the protection of Massachusetts.

The incorporation of Maine with Massachusetts.—Several conflicting patents to lands in Maine were issued between 1630 and 1645. Few settlers came, the only new group of importance being the three towns of Georgiana (York), Welles, and Kittery on the Piscataqua. Massachusetts claimed that her charter entitled her to the Maine region, and in 1639 took the first step toward ownership by purchasing a tract on the Androscoggin River. When the region about Saco and Casco bays became a matter of dispute between rival patentees in 1644, the case was referred to the Massachusetts general court, but no decision was reached. When referred to the English commissioners for plantations, the Gorges estate lost most of its property, being left only the settled region near the Piscataqua. In 1647 Gorges died and the settlers were left without guidance. Two years later the three towns declared themselves a body politic. In 1651 Massachusetts asserted her claim to the Maine region, and the Royalists there found themselves powerless. The following year the Massachusetts authorities ordered the survey of the Merrimac and established civil government at York. In 1653 all the settlements in southern Maine accepted the jurisdiction of Massachusetts. The settlements about Casco Bay refused to submit until 1658, when they also acknowledged the authority of Massachusetts.

Massachusetts hopes to obtain the trade on the Hudson.— In 1657 the general court of Massachusetts declared that the fur-trade ought to be controlled by the commonwealth and in the following year a report was made which showed that fur-trading privileges at Springfield, Concord, Sudbury, Lancaster, Groton, Marlborough, and Cambridge were farmed out to various individuals. In 1659 a company was formed whose main purpose was to obtain access to the fur-trade of the upper Hudson, but it failed to carry out the project.

Connecticut.—In the Connecticut colony the period from 1640 to 1660 was one of expansion and consolidation. Southampton and East Hampton on Long Island, and on the mainland Farmington, Saybrook, New London, and Norwalk were brought under the jurisdiction of the colony.

New Haven.—In the New Haven colony the danger from the Dutch and Indians in 1643 brought about a union of the isolated units. A constitution was adopted which restricted the suffrage to church membership. Minor cases were to be judged in each town, and a governor, deputy-governor, and three associates were to judge the more important cases. No provision for trial by jury was made. The general court, consisting of the magistrates and two deputies from each of the towns, was to meet at New Haven twice a year to enact laws. In 1649 Southold on Long Island, in 1651 Bradford, and in 1656 Greenwich were added to the New Haven confederation.

Rhode Island.—Admission to the New England Confederation was denied to the Narragansett Bay settlements. Providence,

Portsmouth, and Newport had all been founded by outcasts from Massachusetts, and a fourth settlement of a similar nature was founded at Shawomet, now Warwick, in 1643 by Samuel Gorton. The danger from powerful and grasping neighbors caused Williams to seek a patent to the lands about Narragansett Bay, and on March 14, 1644, a patent was granted which allowed the inhabitants of Providence, Portsmouth, and Newport to form their own government. The Warwick settlers were asked to join the others.

In 1647 a code remarkable for its mildness was adopted, and by 1650 the government had been formed. The legislative powers were vested in a general court composed of six representatives from each town, the presiding officer of which was called a president. In executive matters he was to be aided by an assistant from each town. Provision was also made for a treasurer, sergeant, general recorder, attorney-general, and solicitor-general. The president and assistants acted as a court for important cases, which were to be tried by jury. The legislative body and the court made the circuit of the towns. The initiative and referendum were introduced, each settlement having the right to propose legislation, and acts of the general court were referred to the towns for ratification or rejection. Membership in a particular church was not made the basis of citizenship as in the other New England colonies. The disturbing element in Rhode Island at this time was Coddington. In 1651 he obtained from the Council of State a commission as governor of the islands in Narragansett Bay, but his power was short-lived, for the following year Williams obtained a revocation of the Coddington patent and in 1654 was elected president of the confederation.

VIRGINIA AND MARYLAND, 1640–1660

Virginia loyalists.—During the civil war Virginia remained loyal to the king. The large plantation owners, who were almost all members of the Established Church, were in control of the house of burgesses. The small landowners made up the minority. In this class were a few Puritans and many freemen who had formerly been indented servants. Their sympathies were on the side of parliament. Sir William Berkeley, who was appointed in 1642, was a staunch supporter of the king. His administration seems to have been tempered with justice, and he showed little of the arbitrary attitude which appeared in his later career.

Opechancanough's War.—The chief event in Berkeley's administration was the Indian war of 1644. The plantations had gradually spread up the James and Rappahannock, encroaching upon the Indian lands. The chief Opechancanough planned to massacre the whites. On April 18 the outlying settlements were attacked and five hundred people were massacred. The governor led several expeditions against the Indians, their crops and villages were destroyed and their chief became a captive. While in captivity he was foully murdered. The Indians sued for peace, and in a treaty acknowledged the rights of the white man to all the lands between the York and the James as far as the falls.

Berkeley's struggle with the Commonwealth.—When the news of the death of Charles I reached Virginia, Berkeley proclaimed Charles II as king and the assembly declared it high treason to question his right to Virginia. Parliament decided to punish the colony by blockading it. Berkeley, nowise daunted, delivered a defiant address to the assembly, which warmly supported him. The blockade proved a failure, for Dutch traders sailed unmolested into Chesapeake Bay. A group of Virginia parliamentarians visited England and demanded that Berkeley be overthrown. The Council of State responded by sending out a fleet to subdue both Barbados and Virginia. Commissioners were also sent to Virginia to persuade the colony to submit peaceably. In the spring of 1652 when the fleet appeared in the James River, it found the governor prepared for resistance. The commissioners intervened, and by offering lenient terms, bloodshed was avoided. It was agreed that the colony should "voluntarily" acknowledge the authority of the Commonwealth, that the Virginians should have as free trade as the people of England, and that taxation was to be in the hands of the house of burgesses. Neither Berkeley nor his councilors were to be compelled to take the oath of allegiance for a year, and the use of the Book of Common Prayer was permitted for a similar length of time. Berkeley retired from the governorship but remained in the colony.

Government under the commonwealth.—The burgesses and commissioners proceeded to remodel the government. The house

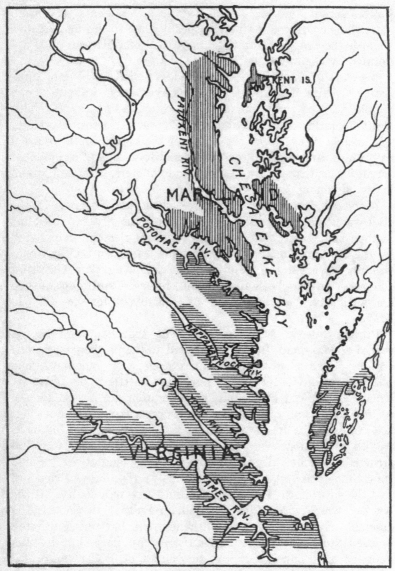

Settled Areas in Virginia and Maryland, 1660

of burgesses was made the chief governing body, with unlimited powers except the veto of the English government. It was to elect the governor and council, specify their duties and remove them if they proved unsatisfactory. All officials were also appointed by the burgesses.

A period of prosperity.—The kingless period was one of prosperity for Virginia. In 1649 the colony contained about 15,000 people; in 1666 the population was estimated at 40,000. This great migration was recruited from various classes: Cavaliers who sought refuge after the death of the king, people who fled from the horrors of civil war, prisoners who were sent as indented servants, gentlemen, tradesmen, and laborers, all found room in the abundant lands of tide-water Virginia.

Maryland during the civil war.—During the first part of the civil war, Lord Baltimore leaned toward the royalist side, but in the colony there was a strong Protestant element, augmented by this time by Puritans from Virginia. In 1645 they got control and expelled the Jesuits. The following year Governor Calvert, who had been in England, returned and reëstablished his authority, but his rule was shortlived, for he died in 1647.

Puritan rule in Maryland.—Fearing that he would be deprived of Maryland, Baltimore veered to the parliamentary side and appointed as governor William Stone, a prominent Virginia planter, and invited Virginia Puritans to settle in his territory. This was followed by a religious toleration act passed by the Maryland assembly in 1649. Baltimore's trimming, however, did not save him from trouble, for in 1650, when the Commonwealth expedition was sent out, the commissioners were instructed to reduce all the Chesapeake Bay plantations. For a time Stone was left in authority, but in 1654 he was deposed and the government was placed in the hands of a council, at the head of which was a Puritan, William Fuller. In the ensuing assembly the Royalists and Catholics were barred. Baltimore ordered Stone to recover his authority by force, but he was defeated and imprisoned by the forces of Fuller, and four of his followers executed. Baltimore appears to have ingratiated himself with Cromwell, for in 1657 he was restored to power.

READINGS

NEW ENGLAND

Channing, Edward, *History of the United States*, I, 414–420; Doyle, J. A., *The Puritan Colonies*, I, 220–319; Frothingham, Richard, *The Rise of the Republic*, 33–71; James, B. B., *The Colonization of New England*, 119–157; Mathews, L. K., *The Expansion of New England*, 31–34; Osgood, H. L., *The American Colonies in the Seventeenth Century*, I, 392–423; Palfrey, J. G., *A Compendious History of New England*, I, 247–268; Tyler, L. G., *England in America*, 266–281, 297–317.

VIRGINIA AND MARYLAND

Beer, G. L., *The Origins of the British Colonial System*, 340–424; Browne, W. H., *Maryland*, 72–104; Channing, Edward, *History of the United States*, I, 485–507; Doyle, J. A., *Virginia, Maryland, and the Carolinas*, 207–228, 314–327; Hamilton, P. J., *The Colonization of the South*, 118–122; Mereness, M. D., *Maryland as a Proprietary Province;* Osgood, H. L., *The American Colonies in the Seventeenth Century*, II, 58–87; Tyler, L. G., *England in America*, 105–117, 140–148; Wertenbaker, T. J., *Virginia under the Stuarts*, 85–114.

CHAPTER IX

THE DUTCH AND SWEDISH COLONIES

DUTCH EXPANSION

Commercial expansion of the Netherlands.—During the reign of Philip II occurred the revolt in the Netherlands. Spanish political and commercial restrictions, and the establishment of the Inquisition, united the great commercial cities, the nobles, and the common people of the northeastern provinces in a rebellion which did not cease until the Hollanders had secured virtual independence by the truce of 1609. During the struggle Dutch ships raided the Spanish and Portuguese trade routes. As early as 1577 a trade to the White Sea was begun. Soon Dutch ships were trading to Italy and the Baltic, and by 1598 they had extended their commerce to Alexandria, Tripoli on the Syrian coast, and Constantinople, to the Cape Verde Islands and the Guinea coast. The desire to reach India influenced Dutch statesmen to attempt to find a northeast passage. Between 1594 and 1597 four expeditions were sent out; they failed to find the passage but gained considerable knowledge of Nova Zembla and Spitzbergen.

East Indian trade.—For years Dutch sailors had been employed by the Portuguese and were well acquainted with the routes to India and America. In 1596 a company was organized to open a trade with the Far East; their fleet sailed around the Cape of Good Hope, stopped at Madagascar, and then proceeded to Java and the Moluccas, returning home the next year. Several companies were immediately formed, and in 1598 twenty-two vessels sailed by the Cape of Good Hope route for the East, and Olivier van Noort passed through the Straits of Magellan and circumnavigated the earth. In 1602 the States General chartered the United East India Company. Several fleets were despatched and succeeded in gaining a foothold in Ceylon and along the coasts of India, in Java, the Moluccas, and various other places. The traders met with great opposition from the Portuguese and Spaniards, but when peace was made in 1609 the Dutch were given the right of trading to Spanish ports outside of Europe, and they soon firmly established their power in the Far East where they absorbed much of Portugal's commerce.

Henry Hudson.—The East India Company hoped to find a shorter route to India and in 1609 employed an English mariner, Henry Hudson, to search for a northwest passage. Meeting with ice and storms, he headed his ship, the *Half Moon*, toward the west. Sighting land at Newfoundland, he examined the New England coast, rounded Cape Cod, and sailed to Virginia and southward. Turning north, he probably ran into Chesapeake Bay, certainly entered Delaware Bay, and then sailed northward to what is now New York harbor. The Hudson River was explored to a point above Albany and friendly relations with the Iroquois were established. The East India Company, however, was making such handsome profits in the East that the furs of New Netherlands failed to attract it.

The Cape Horn route discovered.—The Dutch were still hopeful of finding another route to India, and when Jacques le Maire quarreled with the directors of the East India Company, he planned to form a separate corporation and seek a route south of the Straits of Magellan. The people of Hoorn assisted him in fitting out two vessels which were placed under the command of William Corneliaz Schouten. On the long voyage the smaller vessel was destroyed, but Schouten with the larger one in 1616 discovered Cape Horn.

Dutch activities in the Hudson River region, 1610-1621.—The Hudson River region was visited by traders in 1610-1611, and in 1612 Dutch merchants sent Christianson and Block to Manhattan Island to engage in the fur trade. In 1613 Cornelius May was also sent over. The next year Fort Nassau, later named Fort Orange, was built near the present site of Albany. An extensive exploration of the coast was also made, Block sailing along the northern shore of Long Island, examining the lower waters of the Connecticut River, and exploring Narragansett Bay and Cape Cod. The result of these activities was the formation, in 1614, of the New Netherlands Company, which was given the monopoly of the trade between the fortieth and forty-fifth parallels. An important fur trade was rapidly developed in the Hudson Valley and exploration of the coast was continued. In 1616 Hendrickson examined Delaware Bay, and in 1620 the same region and Chesapeake Bay were visited by May. The southern extremity of New Jersey still bears the name of the Dutch explorer.

The West India Company.—One of the most enterprising Dutch merchants was William Usselincx, who had long hoped to profit by the opening of West Indian trade. The idea was opposed by the East India Company and by some of the Dutch statesmen, especially Olden Barnevelt, who feared that it would bring about new difficulties with Spain. In spite of this, Dutch vessels appeared in Guiana and the Antilles, and in 1613 settlements were attempted in Guiana at Essequibo and Berbice. In 1618 Olden Barnevelt fell from power and Usselincx immediately became active in the formation of a company. In 1621 the West India Company was chartered, receiving a monopoly of Dutch trade for twenty-four years on the coast of Africa as far as the Cape, and for America and the islands east of New Guinea. Usselincx, believing that the directors had too much power and the shareholders too little, and desiring a colonizing rather than a trading corporation, severed his connection with the company and departed for Sweden, where he interested Gustavus Adolphus in commercial enterprises.

Dutch settlements in Brazil, Guiana, and the Antilles.— Settlements were now established by the "Beggars of the Sea" all the way from Brazil to Hudson River, and there were prospects that the Caribbean Sea would become a Dutch instead of a Spanish lake. Brazil was the most important base. Bahía, taken in 1624, lost in 1625, and recaptured in 1627 by the celebrated Piet Heyn, was again lost, but by 1637 Olinda, Recife and Pernambuco had been captured in spite of determined resistance. Prince Maurice of Nassau now took possession of Brazil from Bahía to the Amazon River, and established there a Dutch state, with its capital at Mauritiópolis. In spite of liberal Dutch rule, however, and of an alliance now with Holland against Spain (1641), the Brazilians arose, and after years of heroic fighting expelled the intruders (1661). Meanwhile the Dutch had established colonies in Guiana at Berbice, Aprouage, and Pomeroon, as well as at Essequibo. In the Antilles they had settlements at Curaçao, Buen Aire, Aruba (1634), St. Eustatius, Saba (1635), and St. Martin (1638). During the same period the West India Company had established a flourishing colony on the northern mainland and called it New Netherlands.

NEW NETHERLANDS

Activities of the company.—Licenses were at once granted to several traders, who in 1622 visited the Hudson, Delaware, and Connecticut rivers and trafficked with the Indians as far east as Buzzard's Bay. Thirty families of Walloons, Protestants from Flanders, were sent over in 1623, these being the first colonists. Most of them settled on Manhattan Island, at Brooklyn, and on Staten Island. A few migrated to the vicinity of Fort Orange near Albany, and others settled near the present site of Gloucester on the Delaware, where a new fort named Nassau was erected. Other settlers soon followed; the fur trade was developed; and by 1625 the success of the colony seemed assured.

Government of the colony.—The West India Company was governed by a board of directors called the College of Nineteen; of these eight were from Amsterdam, and to them was given the control of New Netherlands. In the colony the chief officer was the director-general. To assist him was a council invested with local legislative, executive, and judicial powers, subject to the supervision and appellate jurisdiction of the Amsterdam directors. There were two minor officials, the "koopman" acting as commissary, bookkeeper, and secretary, and the "schout-fiscal" as an attorney and sheriff.

Administration of Peter Minuit.—In 1626 Peter Minuit became the director-general. One of his first acts was to secure a title to Manhattan Island by purchasing it from the Indians at the nominal price of twenty-four dollars' worth of goods. A fort, the location of which is known to-day as The Battery, was immediately constructed. Near by was built the stone counting house with a thatched roof, and thirty bark houses straggled along the east side of the river, the meager beginnings of a great metropolis. Fearing for the safety of the little groups of settlers

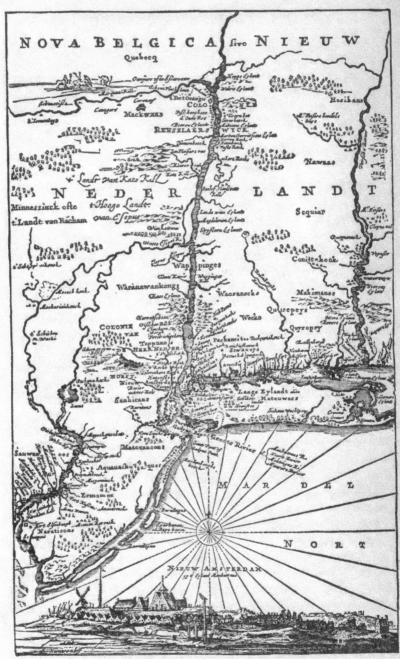

Van Der Donck's Map of New Netherland, 1656

at Fort Orange and Fort Nassau, Minuit brought them to New Amsterdam, leaving only a few soldiers and traders at Fort Orange.

Minuit's preparations for defence were not confined to fortifying the land. Conscious of foreign danger, inspired perhaps by the victories which Heyn was just now winning over Spaniards and Portuguese in the southern waters, and aided by two Belgian shipbuilders, the governor built and launched the *New Netherland*, a vessel of eight hundred tons and carrying thirty guns. The ship cost more than had been expected, and the bills were severely criticized by the West India Company.

The patroon system.—The returns from the southern raids made the small income from New Netherlands appear paltry, and the company decided to attempt an extensive colonization with a view to larger profit. A type of feudalism known as the patroon system was decided upon. The company reserved Manhattan Island, but other regions were opened to settlement. Each patroon was to receive lands four leagues along one side of a navigable river or two leagues on both sides and extending "so far into the country as the situation of the occupiers will permit," provided that within four years he settled fifty people over fifteen years of age upon his lands. Patroons were forever to "possess and enjoy all the lands lying within the aforesaid limits, together with the fruits, rights, minerals, rivers, and fountains thereof," and were to have complete control over "fishing, fowling, and grinding."

The fur trade was reserved by the company, but the patroons were allowed to trade on the coast from Newfoundland to Florida and to ship goods to neutral powers; they could also engage in fishing and the making of salt. They were to satisfy the Indians regarding land titles and were given the right to establish their own courts, from which appeal might be made to the director-general and his council. The colonists were exempt from taxation for ten years, but they could not leave the service of the patroon without his consent. The system was not intended to exclude other colonists who might come over and take up as much land as they could improve, but no colonists were to "be permitted to make any woolen, linen or cotton cloth, nor weave any other stuffs there." Patroons and colonists were "to find out ways and

means whereby they may support a Minister and Schoolmaster."
The company promised to defend the colonists and to endeavor
to supply them "with as many Blacks as they conveniently
can."

The patroons.—While the details of the charter were being
discussed, several directors took advantage of the intended system to secure large grants. Samuel Godyn and Samuel Blommaert and several associates secured practically all of what is now
Delaware and that part of the Jersey shore extending twelve
miles north from Cape May and twelve miles inland. Kiliaen van
Rensselaer obtained the lands about Fort Orange, comprising
what is now a large part of Albany and Rensselaer counties.
Michael Pauw received title to Staten Island and the region where
Jersey City is now situated. Godyn and Blommaert sent colonists to Swannendael on the present site of Lewiston, but they
were massacred by the Indians, the colonization of the grant was
abandoned, and in 1635 the company purchased the lands of the
patroons on the Delaware. In 1637 Pauw sold his holdings to the
company. The Van Rensselaer tract remained in the possession
of that family until after the American Revolution. Jealousies in
the company, due to the securing of patroonships by some of the
directors, and to the fact that the patroons attempted to obtain a
share in the fur trade, and that Minuit appeared to be working
in the interest of the great land holders, led to the recall of the
director-general.

Attempts to secure the frontiers.—The new director-general
was Wouter van Twiller. He had been a clerk in the West India
Company's warehouse at Amsterdam, and probably owed his
appointment to the fact that he was married to a niece of Van
Rensselaer. One of his first acts was to secure possession of the
Delaware. In 1633 a tract along the Schuylkill was purchased
from the Indians and a trading house was erected, the first in the
present state of Pennsylvania. In 1635 a party of Virginians
attempted to gain a foothold on the Delaware, but were expelled.
On the Connecticut the Dutch had profited by the fur trade, but
had never sent colonists to that region. In 1633 lands were purchased from the Indians, and Fort Good Hope was built at modern Hartford, but the Puritan migration soon secured the Connecticut Valley for the English.

Reforms.—Van Twiller and other officials appear to have profited by securing extensive land holdings on the islands at the mouth of the Hudson, Governor's Island deriving its name from the fact that Van Twiller owned it. Complaints began to be heard in the Amsterdam chamber and in 1637 Van Twiller was removed from office, his successor being William Kieft, who arrived in 1638. The new director-general immediately set about correcting abuses. Illicit fur trading and the sale of firearms to the Indians were prohibited. The Amsterdam chamber removed some of the trade restrictions and made easier the acquisition of land. The result was a considerable increase in the number of settlers, who came not only from the Netherlands, but from New England and Virginia as well. Restrictions on manufactures were abolished and the Dutch Reformed Church was established.

Difficulties.—Kieft's administration was beset by difficulties. In the Connecticut Valley and on Long Island the English settlements were increasing, and on the Delaware the Swedes had gained a footing. In the colony a disastrous Indian war brought devastation and ruin. The Indians on the lower Hudson and on Long Island had watched the growing settlements with alarm, an alarm which turned to resentment when they found the Iroquois supplied with firearms from Fort Orange, a privilege which was denied to them at New Amsterdam. Kieft increased the ill-feeling by demanding a contribution of corn, fur, and wampum. He also accused the Raritans of attacking fur trading vessels, and sent an expedition to punish them. In 1641 the Indians retaliated by killing several settlers.

Kieft and the twelve men.—Kieft promptly called together the settlers, who chose a committee of twelve to advise the director-general. Much to his disappointment, they counseled delay. In January, 1642, he again summoned the twelve, who consented to send an expedition against the Indians, provided Kieft should command it. At the same time they demanded that the council should contain at least five members and that the inhabitants should be allowed greater freedom of trade. To these demands Kieft assented grudgingly, and to save further embarrassment, dissolved the committee. An expedition was sent against the Indians, but it accomplished nothing.

Indian hostilities, 1643-1645.—Early in 1643 the Mohawks attacked the river Indians who sought refuge near New Amsterdam. Kieft determined to attack the fugitives, and eighty of them were massacred. The Long Island Indians were also plundered. Aroused by these acts, the Indians united and attacked the settlers. The colonists who escaped fled to Fort Amsterdam. A lull occurred in the fighting while the Indians planted their crops, but hostilities were soon renewed. Kieft again summoned the people and a committee of eight was chosen who counseled war. Settlers and servants of the company were drilled, and fifty English also enlisted. A series of expeditions were despatched against the Indians, whose villages were ruthlessly destroyed. In 1645 treaties were made with the various tribes, and the long war came to an end. One of the incidents of the war was the building of a wall across the lower end of Manhattan Island. It is from this that Wall Street takes its name.

Stuyvesant, 1647.—Both in New Amsterdam and the Netherlands Kieft was blamed for the war. The West India Company decided to remove him, and Peter Stuyvesant, the director of Curaçao, was appointed to succeed him. The first important act of Stuyvesant was to organize the council. Police regulations were made to control Sabbath-breakers, brawlers, and the sale of liquors. The court of justice was also organized, but the director-general required that his opinion be asked in all important cases, and reserved the right to preside in person when he saw fit.

Popular representation.—While Kieft was director-general, he had appealed to the people on several occasions. In answer to the public demand for representation, the council recommended to Stuyvesant that it be granted. Accordingly, the director-general ordered an election at which eighteen were chosen, from whom Stuyvesant and the council selected nine. The nine were to advise and assist, when called upon, in promoting the welfare of the province, and were to nominate their successors. The director-general retained the right to preside at meetings.

Struggle for municipal rights.—The trade restrictions of the West India Company were irksome to the people of New Amsterdam, who hoped to right conditions by obtaining a larger share in the government. After considerable trouble with Stuyvesant, the nine men submitted to the States General a remonstrance setting forth their grievances and a memorial suggesting remedies. They asked that the States General establish a citizens' government, that colonists be sent over, and that the boundaries of New Netherlands be definitely established. The Amsterdam chamber opposed the petitioners, but in 1652 it decided to make concessions. The export duty on tobacco was removed, the cost of passage to New Netherlands was reduced, and the colonists were allowed to procure negroes from Africa. A "burgher" government was allowed for New Amsterdam, the citizens being allowed a schout, two burgomasters, and five schepens, who were to form a municipal court of justice. They were not to be popularly elected, however, Stuyvesant being allowed to appoint the members. No sooner were municipal rights granted to New Amsterdam than the settlements at the western end of Long Island demanded a larger share in government. A convention was held at the capital to formulate grievances. This was brought to an end by Stuyvesant, but a little later municipal rights were granted to several of the towns.

A provincial assembly.—In 1664, during the war between England and the Dutch, so great was the alarm at New Amsterdam, that a provisional assembly was elected, composed of two delegates from each of the Dutch settlements, twenty-four representatives in all. Little was accomplished by this body, however, for shortly afterward the colony passed into English hands.

Economic development.—During the administration of Stuyvesant the material prosperity of New Netherlands steadily increased. He found New Amsterdam a town with straggling fences and crooked streets, and containing about five hundred people. Under his supervision it took on the appearance of a well-kept Dutch town. In 1656 it contained a hundred and twenty houses and a thousand people. By 1660 it had three hundred and fifty houses. By 1664 the population increased to fifteen hundred. The area of settlement in New Netherlands had gradually expanded, covering Manhattan and Staten islands, the opposite Jersey shore, the western end of Long Island, both banks of the lower Hudson, a considerable district about Ft. Orange, and scattering settlements on the Delaware. The chief source of wealth was the fur trade which was carried on largely with the Iroquois who were friendly to the Dutch and hostile to the French. In 1656 Ft. Orange alone exported thirty-five thousand beaver and otter skins, but soon afterward the trade began to decline and agriculture increased in importance. When the province passed into English hands, the population had reached ten thousand.

THE DUTCH AND THE SWEDES ON THE DELAWARE

Swedish territorial and commercial expansion.—In the first half of the seventeenth century Sweden rose to the position of a first class power. When Gustavus Adolphus ascended the throne in 1611, Sweden was at war with Denmark, Russia, and Poland. After defeating each power, the king entered the Thirty Years' War as the champion of Protestantism, his victorious career coming to an untimely end at Lützen. Until 1654 Christina was queen but the real ruler was Oxenstierna, who piloted Sweden through the closing years of the war and secured advantageous terms in the treaty of peace. From 1648 until 1654, Sweden enjoyed peace, but the frivolities of the court ruined the possibilities of greatness and the decline began. Charles X became king in 1654, and his brilliant but disastrous military ventures reduced his country to a third-rate power. At the beginning of the period of Swedish greatness, her commerce was confined to the Baltic, but when nearly all the lands on its shores had been acquired, Swedish statesmen looked forward to a wider commerce, a policy which brought them into rivalry with Holland and England. Numerous trading companies were formed, among the most important being the African and Russian companies, and the various organizations which operated on the Delaware River and in the West Indies.

Usselincx.—The attention of Sweden was drawn to the Delaware by Usselincx, the promoter of the Dutch West India Company, who had left Holland in disgust and who hoped to interest the Swedes. In 1624 he laid his plans before Gustavus Adolphus; this resulted in the granting of a charter to The South Company to establish trade "for Asia, Africa, America and Magellanica." Usselincx experienced great difficulty in raising money, and the directors ruined his schemes by diverting the capital to commercial enterprises in Sweden. In 1629 the company was reorganized and an attempt was made to trade with Spain, but this ended in disaster. Usselincx continued his endeavors, and in 1633 The New South Company was organized, but this like its predecessors came to naught.

The New Sweden Company.—The settling of the Swedes on the Delaware was directly due to the Dutchmen, Samuel Blommaert and Peter Minuit. Blommaert held out the idea that the West Indies would be a market for Swedish copper; Minuit that the Delaware region offered a place for the fur trade and colonization. Several other Dutch merchants were interested, and half of the capital of the Swedish company was furnished by Hollanders. By 1637 the company was organized and the first expedition set sail.

Fort Christina.—The two vessels arrived in the spring of 1638, lands were purchased from the Indians, fur trade opened, and a fort established on Christina Creek two miles from the Delaware. The Dutch at Ft. Nassau protested, but were too weak to oust the newcomers. In 1640 two boats arrived with settlers and goods, large tracts of land at various points on both sides of the bay and river as far as Trenton were purchased, and farms and tobacco plantations were started.

Governor Printz.—In 1642 the company was reorganized, the Swedish government taking part of the stock, the Dutch being eliminated. At the request of the Swedish council of state Johan Printz, a prominent officer in the army, became governor, a post which he filled until 1653. He erected Ft. Elfsborg and established his capital at New Gothenborg, where a fort was built. A blockhouse was also erected on the Schuylkill, other vantage points were occupied, and the Swedes soon secured the fur trade of the Delaware. From the first the weakness of the Swedish project was the lack of colonists, a few hundred being the total migration in the first ten years. In 1644 there were only one hundred and twenty men and a few women and children in the colony. During the next five years not a vessel arrived, and when Printz retired in 1653 there were only two hundred people in the colony.

End of Swedish power on the Delaware.—Stuyvesant determined to get control of the river trade. In 1651 he went to

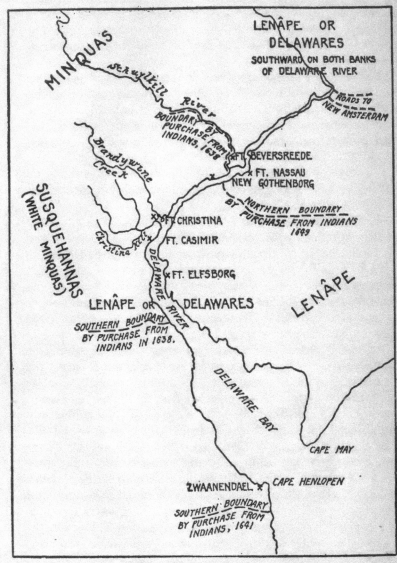

New Sweden

the Delaware with a considerable force. In spite of protests from Printz, lands were purchased from the Indians, and Ft. Casimir was built near the present site of New Castle, the other Dutch forts being abandoned. In 1653 the Swedish crown planned to help New Sweden. In the spring of 1654 about three hundred and fifty colonists were sent over under John Rising. He immediately seized Ft. Casimir. At Ft. Christina a town was laid out, new tracts were purchased from the Indians, and lands were assigned to the colonists. The action of the Swedes in seizing Ft. Casimir angered Stuyvesant, and he urged the West India Company to occupy New Sweden. In September, 1655, a Dutch fleet appeared in the Delaware, and the forts surrendered, thus ending the colony of New Sweden.

ABSORPTION OF NEW NETHERLANDS BY THE ENGLISH

Boundary treaty with New England—On the eastern frontier Stuyvesant had another difficult problem. English settlers were crowding into the Connecticut Valley and onto Long Island. In 1647 Stuyvesant informed the New England officials that the Dutch claimed all lands between the Connecticut and Delaware rivers, but the New Englanders ignored the claim. In 1650 Stuyvesant visited Hartford, where commissioners were appointed who agreed that Long Island should be divided by a line running along the western part of Oyster Bay; that on the mainland the line was "to begin at the west side of Greenwich Bay, being four miles from Stamford and so to run a northerly line twenty miles up into the country, and after as it shall be agreed by the two governments of the Dutch and New Haven; provided the said line come not within ten miles of Hudson's River;" and that the Dutch were to keep their holdings at Hartford.

The end of Dutch rule.—In 1659 Massachusetts asserted her claim to a sea to sea grant, and in 1662 the charter of Connecticut extended the bounds of the colony to the Pacific. In 1663 Stuyvesant visited Boston to attempt a settlement of existing difficulties, but to no avail, and upon his return he found that some of the Long Island settlements west of the line claimed to be under the jurisdiction of Connecticut. Dutch commissioners were sent to Hartford, but without result, and the following year Connecticut asserted her rights to the whole of Long

Island. In 1664 Charles II granted to his brother, James, the
Duke of York, the whole of Long Island and all the lands from
the Connecticut River to Delaware Bay. A fleet was despatched
to New Amsterdam, which surrendered without bloodshed, and
Dutch rule in North America came to an end three years after
it had failed in Brazil.

READINGS

THE DUTCH

Blok, P. J., *History of the People of the Netherlands*, III, 267–303; Brod-
head, J. R., *History of the State of New York*, I; Channing, Edward, *History of
the United States*, I, 438–484; Fiske, John, *The Dutch and Quaker Colonies in
America*, I; Goodwin, M. W., *Dutch and English on the Hudson;* Innes,
J. H., *New Amsterdam and its People;* Jameson, J. F., ed., *Narratives of New
Netherlands;* Janvier, T. A., *Dutch Founding of New York;* MacDonald,
William, *Select Charters*, 43–50; O'Callaghan, E. B., *History of New Nether-
lands;* Roberts, E. H., *New York*, I, 19–119; Van Loon, H. W., *The Golden
Book of the Dutch Navigators*.

THE SWEDES

Acrelius, Israel, *History of New Sweden* (Pennsylvania Historical Society,
Memoirs, XI); Holm, T. C., *Description of the Province of New Sweden*
(Pennsylvania Historical Society, *Memoirs*, VII); Johnson, Amandus, *The
Swedish Settlements on the Delaware;* Keen, G. B., in Winsor, *Narrative and
Critical History*, III, 469–495.

CHAPTER X

THE OLD ENGLISH COLONIES UNDER THE LATER STUARTS

COLONIAL POLICY AND ADMINISTRATION

The Restoration.—In 1660 Charles II was restored to the English throne and ruled until 1685, when his brother, James, the Duke of York, became king, ruling until deposed in 1688. In England the period was characterized by a reaction against Puritanism and the firm establishment of the English church. Abroad the Restoration was an era of commercial and colonial expansion. On the coasts of Asia, Africa, and America, the great trading companies were active, and powerful English nobles strove for possessions beyond the seas. To this era belong the occupation of New Netherlands, the founding of the Carolinas, the Jerseys, and Pennsylvania, and the establishment of the Hudson's Bay Fur Company. The activities of Englishmen led to clashes with rival commercial peoples, especially the Dutch, with whom two naval wars were fought in which England maintained her supremacy upon the seas. In the handling of her colonies previous to the Restoration, her efforts had been largely experimental. Under the later Stuarts colonial management was molded into a system. In private life Charles II was a man of pleasure. In his dealings with parliament he was tenacious, but when pushed to extremities, he preferred to yield rather than to "go again on his travels." In matters which affected the material prosperity of his country the king was a hard-headed man of business, warmly supporting commercial and colonial enterprises.

The Mercantilist system.—The economic theory of the time was expressed in the Mercantilist system. The welfare of the state was the main object of statesmen; this they believed required a full treasury, a large population, and extensive shipping. Specie was looked upon as the principal form of wealth; therefore exports must exceed imports so that coin would flow into the realm. In order that it might have a large amount of goods to sell, the state desired to import raw materials, which could be manufactured and exported. The ideal colony was to be a source of supply of raw materials, and was to be a market for goods of the mother country, but was not to be a manufacturing competitor. The state policy was shaped to shut out the foreigner and to build up the productivity of the colonies.

Attitude toward emigration.—The desire for a larger population in England caused statesmen to view emigration with disfavor. During the period the number going to the colonies was relatively small. The government, however, encouraged the emigration of Scotch, Irish, and Huguenots, and sent over many political prisoners, nonconformists, and criminals. Many of those who emigrated were too poor to pay for their passage and bound themselves for a period of years, a form of temporary bondage known as indenture. Many servants and children were also kidnaped and sent to the colonies. Because the colonies in the West Indies and the South mainly produced raw materials and used slave labor, thus drawing relatively less population from England, they were looked upon with the greater favor by the home government. The northern colonies produced little except fish, furs, and naval stores, which could be of use to England. The free labor system of the North was likely to drain the population of England. For these reasons the northern colonies were looked upon with scant favor.

Navigation Act of 1660.—During the Cromwellian period, parliament had asserted the right to legislate for the colonies and the restored Stuarts accepted the principle. In 1660 a new navigation act was passed which was intended to give English shipping an advantage over competitors, especially the Dutch. The act provided that goods carried to or from English possessions in America, Africa, or Asia, must be carried in English, Irish, or colonial vessels. Under penalty of forfeiture, cargoes of sugar, tobacco, indigo, and several other products could not be shipped to any ports except in England, Ireland, or some English colony.

Staple Act of 1663.—Under the navigation act of 1660 alien merchants could send foreign goods to the colonies in English ships. To obviate this the Staple Act was passed, which, with a few exceptions, such as Portuguese wines, salt, and horses, prohibited the importation into the colonies of goods which had not been loaded in England.

Plantation Duties Act of 1673.—Under the previous acts goods shipped from colony to colony escaped paying duties. In 1673 an act was passed which imposed duties on sugar, tobacco, and many other products of intercolonial trade.

Imperial defence.—The burden of defence of the empire against foreign powers fell upon England. Ships of the navy were stationed in the West Indies, Chesapeake Bay, and at Boston to protect the colonies, and suppress piracy and illegal trade. The buccaneers of the West Indies were brought under control. The Barbary pirates also were frequently attacked, and convoys for merchant vessels and fishing fleets were often furnished. Garrisons were usually stationed in Barbados, Jamaica, and St. Kitts, but on the mainland soldiers were not regularly maintained.

The fiscal system.—By the civil war parliament made good its contention that it alone had the right to levy taxes. In 1660 a general taxation act was passed by which Charles II was granted for life the income from tonnage and poundage; the former being a duty on imported wines, the latter a five per cent duty on imports and exports, whose valuation was fixed in a book of rates. To compensate the colonies somewhat for the resulting higher prices, a preferential system was introduced. By this system the valuation of the principal products of the colonies was made lower than on the same products coming from foreign countries.

MACHINERY OF GOVERNMENT

Council for Foreign Plantations.—The work of enforcing the laws devolved upon the crown and privy council. The accumulation of business and the specialized knowledge required in colonial matters made it desirable to have a body created which might handle the business in a more efficient manner. Accordingly in December, 1660, a Council for Foreign Plantations was commissioned. Members of the council were to inform themselves regarding the colonies, were to introduce a more uniform system of government, and were to see that the navigation acts were enforced.

Council of Trade.—From the English standpoint the colonies were mainly commercial enterprises. To foster commerce a Council of Trade was created. The work of the two bodies was to sift the mass of business so that matters of first importance only might come before the privy council. Lack of authority interfered with the interest of the members of the minor councils; the sessions became less and less frequent, and by 1665 both had ceased.

Council for Trade and Plantations.—Supervision of the colonies again devolved upon a committee of the privy council. In 1667 Clarendon fell and the small group known as the Cabal came into power. The following year the privy council was reorganized, four standing committees being constituted, one of which had charge of trade and plantations. The need of experts, however, continued to be felt, and in 1668 a new Council of Trade was appointed. In 1670 the Council for Plantations was also revived, and in 1672 the two councils were consolidated as the Council for Trade and Plantations. The council prepared preliminary drafts of instructions to governors, examined colonial legislation, and investigated questions which arose.

Lords of Trade.—Executive powers remained in the privy council, and this necessarily curbed the Council for Trade and Plantations, which was purely an advisory body. In 1674 the latter council was abolished, and the following year the king again committed its work to the Committee for Trade and Plantations of the privy council. This committee, known henceforth as the Lords of Trade, was a permanent body with its own clerks. William Blathwayt soon became the secretary and for twenty years he held the position. The efficiency of the body and the development of the colonial policy was due more to him than to any other person. The Lords of Trade prepared the instructions to governors, supervised the development of the colonies, examined colonial questions, and enforced the navigation laws.

The Admiralty.—After the Restoration the Duke of York was appointed Lord High Admiral of England and in 1662 his powers were extended to the colonies. Cases concerning vessels seized for violating some of the clauses of the commercial laws were tried in admiralty courts which were established in the crown colonies, deputies were appointed by the admiral to attend to the business, and ships were stationed in the colonies to seize illegal traders.

Governors and customs officials.—In the colony the chief executive officer was the governor. He was expected to enforce the trade laws, but outside of the crown colonies there was great laxity in this regard. The work of enforcing the navigation laws was usually entrusted by the governor to a clerk called the naval officer but at a later period these officials were appointed by the crown. The right of collection of the English customs was leased to certain individuals who were known as farmers of the customs. They frequently complained that the governors were remiss in enforcing the navigation laws. Accordingly, the farmers of the customs were allowed to send, at their own expense, officers who would attend to the collection of duties. The farming system was soon abandoned and commissioners of customs were appointed, who sent out collectors, usually one to each colony. To examine the collector's accounts and act as a check upon him, officials called comptrollers were placed in most of the colonies, and in 1683 a superintendent for all the colonies, called the surveyor-general of the customs, was appointed. The activities of these officials led to considerable friction with colonial governors and proprietors, who resented the interference of the customs officials.

MISRULE AND REBELLION IN VIRGINIA

Effect of the trade laws.—In 1660 Sir William Berkeley began his second administration, which proved to be as unsuccessful as his first administration had been successful. Economic distress and arbitrary misrule beset Virginia for sixteen years, culminating in a popular outbreak known as Bacon's rebellion. The navigation acts fell heavily upon the tobacco planters, who were deprived of the Dutch trade. The population at the same time rapidly increased. In 1671 the inhabitants numbered about forty thousand and nearly doubled in the next decade. The increasing population meant an increasing acreage of tobacco. The price of tobacco fell, while freight rates increased and imported goods went up in price. To alleviate the situation the assembly passed several acts to encourage new industries, but the planters held to their one great staple. Several attempts were made to limit the production of tobacco, a policy in which the Virginians asked the people of Maryland and the Albemarle district to the south to coöperate, but the efforts failed. The act of 1673 worked an added injury, for it deprived the planters of the New England market.

Wars and other misfortunes.—The wars with Holland increased the economic distress. In 1667 a Dutch fleet entered the James River, captured an English frigate, and destroyed several trading vessels. Soon afterward a hurricane destroyed hundreds of houses and ruined the crops. In the winter of 1672–1673 a disease carried off fifty thousand cattle, more than half of all the stock in Virginia. A second Dutch raid in 1673 destroyed a large part of the tobacco fleet.

Governmental abuses.—Berkeley was a firm believer in the divine right of kings, and looked with disfavor upon any interference from the people. To him it seemed fitting that, as the king's representative, he should control every branch of governmental activity. His council was entirely subservient and he gained control of the house of burgesses by controlling the county elections through dishonest officials. In 1670 the assembly limited the franchise to freeholders, thus depriving the poor of voting. In the counties the justices of the peace were appointed by the governor. They exercised judicial, executive, and legislative functions. The county courts settled the more important suits and the individual justices determined minor cases. The courts also levied the direct taxes, which were very heavy. In addition, the local church divisions were governed by vestries which were selected by the governor. These bodies levied the taxes to pay the church expenses. The whole machinery of government was thus controlled by the governor. The form of taxation aggravated the situation. Instead of a property tax, which would throw the burden upon the great landholders, the poll-tax was the usual method of raising money, the poor man thus having to pay as much as the wealthy. There was also much bad judgment displayed in the use of public funds. In a period of low prices and overproduction, the heavy expenditures proved a serious burden, and discontent gradually developed into rebellion.

Proprietary grants.—The action of the English government also alarmed the colonists. In 1660 an attempt was made to renew the old Virginia Company. Berkeley visited England to prevent it and his mission proved successful. In 1649 the king had granted the region between the Potomac and the Rappahannock rivers to several of his supporters, and after the Restoration they leased their rights to Sir Humphrey Hooke and two others. In 1669 the grant was renewed. The Virginia assembly immediately sent agents to England to obtain the annulment of the patent or to allow the colony to purchase the tract. Before a settlement was made the king in 1673 granted the whole of Virginia to the Earl of Arlington and Lord Culpeper with full proprietory rights for thirty-one years. The assembly was greatly alarmed and directed its agents to seek the annulment of this patent also. The matter was finally settled by an arrangement with the proprietors by which they agreed to relinquish the patent provided the colony paid them the quit-rents and assured them the escheated property. The agents then asked the government that they be assured that no portion of the colony would be granted in future to any proprietors and that taxation would not be imposed without the consent of the house of burgesses. Before a settlement was reached Bacon's rebellion occurred.

Indian war.—The spark that kindled the rebellion was an Indian war. The Senecas, pressing upon the Susquehannas, forced them into Maryland and Virginia, where they committed depredations in the summer of 1675. The settlers retaliated by killing several Indians. The Susquehannas joined with the native tribes and harried the frontiers. Berkeley sent Colonel John Washington in command of several hundred men to join the Marylanders against an Indian fort on the Potomac, but after several weeks of fighting the red men escaped. This was followed by renewed depredations. Early in 1676 the governor prepared a second expedition but suddenly abandoned the project. In March the assembly met and decided to wage a defensive war. Forts were to be built upon the upper waters of the rivers and heavy taxes were demanded to pay for them.

Bacon's rebellion.—The people were greatly incensed at the policy, and demanded that the assembly be dissolved and a free election held. The frontiersmen also demanded that they be allowed to go against the Indians. Both of these demands the governor stubbornly refused. A rebellion immediately broke out in Charles City County, and Nathaniel Bacon, of Henrico, a member of Berkeley's council, was induced to lead it. The governor was asked to grant Bacon a commission to proceed against the Indians. Without waiting for the governor's decision, Bacon led his men against the Pamunkeys. Bacon's act angered Berkeley, who refused the commission and ordered Bacon and his men to lay down their arms. This they refused to do and retired beyond the frontier, where they destroyed an Indian stronghold on an island in the Roanoke River. Berkeley issued a proclamation declaring Bacon's acts disloyal and rebellious. To obtain popular support he dismantled the forts, dissolved the assembly, and called an election.

Bacon was elected in Henrico County and an armed guard accompanied him to the capital. Berkeley's troops fired upon Bacon's sloop, but that night Bacon entered the town to consult with friends. He was discovered, and eventually captured and brought before the governor, who, in view of the popular clamor, became lenient, granting him a pardon and promising him a commission as general. As the commission was not forthcoming, Bacon collected several hundred men and marched upon Jamestown, which he entered without opposition, and forced Berkeley to sign the commission and to write a letter to the king justifying Bacon's acts. The assembly now passed several bills which struck at the governor's power, and repealed the act which restricted the franchise to freeholders.

The burgesses had just completed their work when news came that the Indians were again on the war-path, and Bacon hastened with his volunteers to the frontier. No sooner was he gone than the governor began to enlist troops to proceed against the popular leader. Hearing of this Bacon returned and Berkeley fled to the eastern shore of Chesapeake Bay. Bacon was now in full control of the larger part of the colony. To justify his acts he took the oath of allegiance, imposed it upon his followers, and called an election. He then organized two expeditions, one against the governor, the other against the Indians. An English ship was seized and two hundred men were sent to capture Berkeley, but the governor's followers surprised the crew and captured the leaders. Berkeley then returned to Jamestown. While these events were occurring, Bacon marched against the Indians and captured a stronghold of the Pamunkeys. He then captured Jamestown and burned it, soon afterward retiring into Gloucester County, where he was taken sick and died. In a few months the people wearied of anarchy, many of the leaders surrendered, and Berkeley was again in control.

Berkeley's revenge.—In June, 1676, Berkeley had tendered his resignation to the king. Charles decided to allow him to retain the title of governor, but to have him return to England, leaving the government to a lieutenant-governor, Colonel Jeffreys being appointed. He was assisted by two commissioners, Berry and Moryson. A general pardon for the rebels was also drawn up. Berry and Moryson arrived in the colony and found the governor intractable. Jeffreys, with about a thousand troops, arrived soon afterward, but instead of asserting his authority, he allowed Berkeley to ignore the pardon proclamation and many were hung. Knowledge of Berkeley's disobedience reached the king, who ordered him to return to England at once, but before the order arrived Berkeley had embarked. He died soon after reaching England, and Lord Culpeper was appointed governor, but he did not reach Virginia until 1680.

Culpeper and Howard.—In the meantime the commissioners investigated the causes of the rebellion, and in July, 1677, Berry and Moryson took their report to England where it was laid before the privy council. Jeffreys, who was left in control, had little authority, and the government again fell into the hands of Berkeley's friends. Culpeper arrived in 1680, but he proved to be a weak individual who spent most of his time in England and did little when in the colony. In 1684 a new governor, Lord Howard of Effingham, proceeded at once to curb the powers of the house of burgesses. The right of appealing cases from the lower courts to the assembly was denied, henceforth the governor and council being the final court of appeal. The right of the king to annul laws passed by the assembly was also asserted in spite of violent opposition. The session of 1685 proved a stormy one. An attempt was made to take the power of taxation away from the assembly. The king, who had taken over the proprietory rights of Arlington and Culpeper, demanded that the quit-rents be paid in specie instead of tobacco. This the burgesses violently opposed, but they finally compromised by agreeing to pay somewhat less than the governor had demanded. A "bill of ports" was introduced which was intended to fix the points at which ships might load and unload. Another violent struggle occurred. Finally, on recommendation of the governor, the king dissolved the assembly. Lord Howard unseated several members and appointed the clerk of the assembly. The governor also collected certain fees, an act which the burgesses claimed was an encroachment upon the power of taxation. The colony was nearing another rebellion. In 1688 the assembly drew up a statement of grievances, which they sent to the king, but by the time it reached England James II had been driven from the throne and Effingham was soon recalled.

DISCONTENT IN MARYLAND

Conditions in Maryland.—Economic conditions in Maryland were similar to those in Virginia, the navigation laws affecting the colony in a similar manner, the price of tobacco falling continually after 1660 for many years. Political discontent also manifested itself, but the religious element played a larger part in Maryland than in Virginia. No widespread rebellion occurred, however, for Baltimore's government was more temperate than that of Berkeley, the settlements were more compact, frontier dangers were less acute, and no popular leader of great ability arose to lead the malcontents.

Charles Calvert's administration.—After the turmoil of the Cromwellian period, the Restoration brought comparative security to the proprietor of Maryland, who succeeded in ingratiating himself with Charles II. In 1675 Charles Calvert succeeded to the proprietorship. Previously for several years he had personally directed the governorship and had worked conscientiously to bring about prosperity in the colony. He was less tactful than his father and was exceedingly strong-willed. He placed his relatives in the important positions, restricted the suffrage, and frequently summoned to the assembly only half of the elected delegates, thus keeping out influential opponents. In

1676, while Baltimore was in England, a few malcontents attempted an uprising, but Notley, the acting governor, overthrew and hanged two of the leaders, nipping the rebellion in the bud. The proprietor and assembly continued to have difficulties, but in the main Baltimore succeeded in maintaining his power. He also had trouble with William Penn over the northern boundary, and with the Lords of Trade over the right of collecting the customs. Baltimore's Catholic leanings naturally made him support James II. When that monarch was driven from the throne, a miniature bloodless revolution occurred in Maryland. An Association for the Defense of the Protestant Religion was formed. In July, 1689, the leaders seized St. Mary's and held a representative assembly. But to their chagrin, William and Mary restored the old colonial system, and Baltimore was soon back in power.

ROYAL INTERFERENCE IN NEW ENGLAND

Massachusetts and the king.—During the Cromwellian period the New England colonies had followed their own devices, but when Charles II came to the throne, they could not expect to pursue their independent course. To forestall trouble, Massachusetts hastened to acknowledge the king's authority, and none too soon, for numerous complaints had been lodged against her. The most forceful of these came from the Quakers. In 1655 Mary Fisher and Ann Austin, two Quaker missionaries, had landed in Barbados, the first of that sect to come to the colonies. The following year they went to Boston from which they were promptly expelled. Rhode Island proved hospitable. Those who had believed in Anne Hutchinson's "covenant of grace" found the Quaker idea of the "inner light" an acceptable doctrine. From Rhode Island Quakers frequently penetrated the neighboring colonies which took violent means to expel them. The Massachusetts persecution reached its height in 1660 when three Quakers were hanged, one of them being Mary Dyer, a former friend of Anne Hutchinson. This high-handed proceeding reached the ear of the king, who was in no amiable frame of mind toward the Puritan colonists, who were believed to be sheltering two of the regicides. He accordingly ordered the Boston authorities to send Quakers to England for trial, but

Massachusetts sent representatives to England, who succeeded in getting the king to grant the colony free hand in dealing with Quakers. Charles also confirmed the Massachusetts charter, but changed the basis of voting from church membership to a property qualification.

The Connecticut charter.—Connecticut fared well with Charles II. When the king's messengers visited the colony in search of the regicides, they were given assistance, while New Haven aided the fugitives in escaping. The results of this were soon apparent. In 1661 when Connecticut sent Governor John Winthrop to England to obtain a charter, he was graciously received and the following year the document was issued. It provided for a popularly elected governor, a deputy-governor, council, and assembly. The boundaries were described as "All that part of our Dominions . . . bounded on the East by the Narrogancett River, comonly called Narrogancett Bay . . . , and on the North by the lyne of the Massachusetts Plantation, and on the South by the Sea, and . . . from the said Narrogancett Bay on the East to the South Sea on the West parte, with the Islands thereunto adjoyneinge." The boundaries included a part of the territory of Rhode Island and the whole of New Haven, and entirely ignored the Dutch possessions in the Hudson Valley. New Haven protested violently, but in 1664, when the king granted the lands between the Connecticut and Delaware rivers to the Duke of York, the New Haven towns submitted to Connecticut rather than be annexed to New York.

The Rhode Island charter.—Fearful that Charles II might divide her territory among her neighbors, Rhode Island hastened to proclaim the king and petitioned that she be granted a charter. The Rhode Island representative protested against the inclusion of Narragansett Bay territory in Connecticut and the difficulty was adjusted by fixing the boundary at the Pawtucket River, which was renamed the Narragansett. The form of government was similar to that of Connecticut, but in Rhode Island religious freedom was established.

The royal commissioners.—In 1664, when the English government had determined upon the seizure of New Netherlands, commissioners were sent to America. Respecting New England, their duties were to settle boundary questions, to consider local disputes, and to see how the colonies might be made more profitable. The commissioners visited Boston in July, 1664, where they obtained troops and demanded the repeal of the law which restricted the franchise to church membership. After the conquest of New Netherlands, three of them returned to New England. They were well received in Connecticut and Rhode Island. Plymouth at this time was attempting to obtain a charter, and the commissioners suggested that the colony might have its lands confirmed without cost if it would receive a royal governor, an offer which was declined. In Boston their reception was stormy, the Massachusetts authorities denying that the commission had any right of jurisdiction. Nicolls, the fourth commissioner, soon arrived and the debates continued, but without result. The king rebuked Massachusetts for its lack of respect, but took no immediate steps to coerce the colony.

The frontier on the eve of King Philip's War.—In 1675 the Penobscot marked the most northern settlement. Along the coasts and in the lower valleys of the short New England streams settlements had been planted. Eastern Massachusetts and Plymouth contained numerous towns. In Rhode Island the island was fairly well-settled, but with the exception of Providence and Warwick, the mainland had attracted few. Other settlements were located near the mouth of the Thames, and in the valley of the Connecticut as far up as Northfield. The coast lands of western Connecticut had also been occupied. The total population of New England did not exceed fifty thousand. The lands beyond the fringe of settlement were occupied by powerful Indian tribes, which could muster about thirty-five hundred fighting men.

Causes of the war.—The encroachment of the frontiers on the Indian hunting ground was the primary cause of the war, but other events were contributory. By 1660 the fur trade had declined, fish and lumber having become the important exports. This trade brought in silver, and wampum ceased to be the medium of exchange. With the passing of furs and wampum, the Indian became less and less useful to the white man, who looked upon him with contempt. The christianizing of the Cape Cod Indians by the Reverend John Eliot and other missionaries was viewed sullenly by the Wampanoags, who saw in it an attempt to weaken their power. Massasoit, Sachem of the Wampanoags, died in 1662, leaving two sons, called by the whites Alexander and Philip. The sudden death of Alexander gave rise to a belief among the Indians that he had been poisoned.

The war.—In the summer of 1675, outbreaks occurred in Rhode Island, and a settler was killed. An expedition was immediately sent against the Wampanoags, but Philip succeeded in escaping with his followers. The Nipmucks attacked Deerfield, Northfield, Springfield, and Hatfield, spreading terror in the Connecticut Valley. Believing that the Narragansetts were about to enter the war, Massachusetts, Plymouth, and Connecticut joined forces, and in December attacked their stronghold. After a bloody battle they captured it and dispersed the tribe. The survivors joined the other hostiles and harried the frontiers as far north as the Maine settlements. In April, 1676, Chief Canonchet, of the Narragansetts, was captured and shot, and the following month the Indians were decisively defeated near the falls of the Connecticut. After that the Indian confederation broke up and effective resistance came to an end in August with the death of Philip. The power of the tribes was broken and the way cleared for the advancement of the frontier.

Complaints against Massachusetts.—The independent course which Massachusetts had followed in her dealings with the home government had irritated Charles and the privy council, but the fall of Clarendon and the Dutch war of 1673 had kept the king from taking action against the headstrong colony. Complaints continued to be made. The heirs of Mason and Gorges claimed that Massachusetts had usurped their rights; London merchants complained that the colony was evading the navigation acts by carrying tobacco and sugar directly to Europe from other colonies; lack of respect for the king's authority, the exercising of powers not warranted by her charter, and numerous other complaints were lodged against her.

Edward Randolph.—In 1676 the king sent Edward Randolph to Massachusetts with an order that the colony send agents to England within six months to answer the Mason and Gorges claims, an order which was tardily fulfilled. He was also empowered to collect information which might be useful to the Lords of Trade. Randolph was not well received, being looked upon as an agent of the Mason and Gorges heirs. When he complained to Governor Leverett of the violation of the navigation laws, the governor boldly asserted that parliament had no power to legislate for Massachusetts, and denied that appeals might be made to the king. Randolph returned to England convinced that a change of government was necessary.

In 1678 Randolph was appointed collector of the customs, but he did not arrive in Boston until the following year. In the meantime the Massachusetts title to New Hampshire had been examined. Randolph bore a letter from the king which commanded the colony to give up its jurisdiction over both New Hampshire and Maine. The former command Massachusetts immediately obeyed, but the latter was ignored as the agents of Massachusetts had recently purchased the Gorges title.

Annulment of the charter.—As collector of the customs Randolph's course was beset with difficulties, and his reports were filled with complaints of frequent violations of the navigation acts. In 1681 he returned to England and advised that the charter of Massachusetts be abrogated and that all the New England colonies be united under one administrative head. Randolph soon returned to the colony, but the friction continued and his complaints became more and more violent. The king and the Lords of Trade finally wearied of the strong-willed colony, legal action was taken, and in 1684 the charter was annulled.

Temporary government.—The annulment of the charter did not bring about an insurrection in Massachusetts, for the colonial leaders realized that the protection of the mother country was necessary to preserve them from being conquered by the French. While the Lords of Trade were considering a form of government, a temporary plan was put in operation. Joseph Dudley was made president, Randolph secretary, and a council was appointed, but no provision was made for a legislative assembly. To enforce the laws of trade, in 1686 an admiralty court was established.

Affairs in New Hampshire.—Since New Hampshire was separated from Massachusetts, affairs in the northern colony had been going badly. A president and council had been established, but when Randolph attempted to enforce the trade laws, he had met with difficulties. The colonists also objected to paying quit-rents to the Mason heirs. In 1682 Edward Cranfield was appointed governor and was soon at loggerheads with the people over the Mason right, and in 1685 he left the colony in disgust.

Dominion of New England.—The Lords of Trade for some time had been considering the advisability of consolidating the New England colonies in order to cut down expense, to make the enforcement of the navigation acts more effective, and to bring the colonies into a closer dependence on the crown. When James became king, the plan was put into operation. In the new form of government the central figure was a governorgeneral who was to be assisted by a council, but no provision was made for a popular assembly.

Edmund Andros.—Andros, the former governor of New York, was appointed governor-general and arrived at Boston in December, 1686. In a businesslike manner he organized his government. Boston was made the seat of power. Andros acted as commander of the army and vice-admiral, and exercised the pardoning power. With the advice and consent of the council he made laws, levied taxes, and administered justice. He also made land grants and collected quit-rents. He demanded that Plymouth, Rhode Island, and Connecticut surrender their charters. Plymouth and Rhode Island complied and their representatives were admitted to the council, but Connecticut temporized. Finally Andros visited the obdurate colony, dissolved the government, and admitted representatives to his council. The charter, however, according to Connecticut tradition, was hidden in an oak tree and never left the colony. In 1688 the Lords of Trade determined to bring all the territory from the St. Croix and the St. Lawrence to the Delaware under the supervision of Andros.

Overthrow of Andros.—The system aroused the anger of the colonists, who looked upon the governor-general as a tyrant. Mutterings of discontent grew louder and louder, and when news reached Massachusetts that James II had fled from England, the people of Boston rose in revolt, seized the fortifications and royal frigate, and imprisoned Andros and Randolph. A council was established, a convention was summoned, and the old charter government was reëstablished. Connecticut and Rhode Island also restored the charter governments.

READINGS

COLONIAL POLICY AND ADMINISTRATION

Andrews, C. M., *Colonial Self-Government*, 1–40; Beer, G. L., *The Old Colonial System*, I, 1–315; "The Commercial Policy of England toward the American Colonies," in Columbia University, *Studies in History, Economics, and Public Law*, III, Pt. 2, pp. 29–54; Channing, Edward, *History of the United States*, II, 1–13; Egerton, H. E., *A Short History of British Colonial Policy*, 66–80; MacDonald, William, *Select Charters*, 106–115, 119–120, 133–136; Osgood, H. L., *The American Colonies in the Seventeenth Century*, III, 143–241.

VIRGINIA AND MARYLAND

Andrews, C. M., *Colonial Self-Government*, 202–251; Andrews, C. M., ed., *Narratives of the Insurrections*, 11–141, 299–314; Channing, Edward, *History of the United States*, II, 80–91, 209–213; Fiske, John, *Old Virginia and her Neighbors*, II, 45–107, 131–173; Osgood, H. L., *The American Colonies in the Seventeenth Century*, III, 242–308; Wertenbaker, T. J., *Virginia under the Stuarts*, 115–259.

NEW ENGLAND

Andrews, C. M., *Colonial Self-Government*, 41–73, 252–287; Andrews, C. M., ed., *Narratives of the Insurrections*, 165–297; Andrews, C. M., *The Fathers of New England;* Channing, Edward, *History of the United States*, II, 65–79, 155–203; Doyle, J. A., *The Puritan Colonies*, II, 190–276; Ellis, G. W., and Morris, J. E., *King Philip's War;* Fiske, John, *The Beginnings of New England*, 199–278; James, B. B., *The Colonization of New England*, 213–295; Osgood, H. L., *The English Colonies in the Seventeenth Century*, III, 309–335, 378–443; Palfrey, J. G., *Compendious History of New England*, II, 1–20; *History of New England*, III, chs. 3, 7–9, 12–14.

CHAPTER XI

EXPANSION UNDER THE LATER STUARTS

NEW YORK

The period of the later Stuarts was remarkable for colonial expansion. New Netherlands was acquired, the Jerseys, Pennsylvania, and the Carolinas were founded, the Hudson's Bay Fur Company was formed, and new settlements were made in the West Indies.

Causes of the attack upon the Dutch.—In 1664 New Netherlands was seized. This was not an isolated event but was a part of a general plan to weaken Dutch power. England had three main objects: to cripple the Dutch carrying trade, to get control of the slave trade, and to obtain New Netherlands, an acquisition which would give geographical unity to the colonies on the Atlantic seaboard. The navigation acts were weapons against the carrying trade. The African Company was organized to strike at the slave trade.

The African Company.—During the first half of the seventeenth century, the Dutch had obtained a monopoly of the trade in slaves to the Spanish and Portuguese colonies in America. To break this monopoly the African Company was formed in 1660, headed by the Duke of York. During the next two years the Dutch vigorously opposed the English Company, soon convincing its officers that it must be organized on a larger scale if it would succeed. In 1663 the Company of Royal Adventurers trading to Africa was organized, being granted the coast from Sallee to the Cape of Good Hope. Vessels sent to the African coast encountered such opposition that in 1664 a squadron was sent to protect them and succeeded in capturing several Dutch forts, but Admiral DeRuyter soon recaptured them.

Seizure of New Netherlands, 1664.—At the same time England prepared to seize New Netherlands, a territory which she had always claimed. The king granted to the Duke of York the

northern part of Maine, Long Island, Martha's Vineyard, Nan-
tucket, and New Netherlands. The Duke in turn granted the
Jerseys to Carteret and Lord Berkeley. A royal commission was
despatched to America with three war vessels and several hundred men. At Boston the expedition was reinforced and then
proceeded to New Amsterdam, which surrendered without a
struggle. One member of the commission went to the Delaware
and took possession. In the Treaty of Breda (1667) the English
were given important slave trading privileges, their conquests
between the Hudson and the Delaware were confirmed, and
Lord Willoughby's colony of Surinam was ceded to the Dutch,
who had captured it in the course of the recent war.

Administration of Nicolls.—Nicolls was made governor and
his administration was conducted with tact and firmness. In
dealing with Connecticut he insisted upon the Duke's right to
Long Island. In New Netherlands several Dutch place names
were changed, New Amsterdam becoming New York, and Ft.
Orange, Albany. The right of property was not disturbed;
judicial districts were organized; and to New York City he
granted a charter which provided for a mayor, aldermen, and
sheriff, whom he appointed. Nicolls drew up a code, known as
the Duke's Laws, which was a combination of portions of the
codes of Massachusetts and New Haven, Dutch customs, and
original ideas. Religious toleration was allowed, and land-
holding was made the basis for voting. The lack of a representative assembly was a noticeable feature, which led to discord
when taxes were demanded.

Representative government demanded.—Lovelace became
governor in 1668, and during his administration of five years
friction increased, but he managed to maintain his authority.
In 1673 when war broke out between England and Holland, New
York was captured by the Dutch, but the following year it was
restored to the English. Edmund Andros was then appointed
governor. He informed the proprietor of the desire for a representative assembly, but James stubbornly refused. In 1681,
when James neglected to renew the customs duties, the merchants refused to pay them. Because of the resulting loss
of revenue Andros was ordered to England, and during his
absence the disaffection greatly increased. Thomas Dongan

was appointed governor in 1682. He was instructed to call a representative assembly to advise the governor and council regarding taxation and law making. In October, 1683, seventeen representatives met at New York and drew up a Charter of Franchises and Liberties. This was sent to the Duke, who signed it, but when he became king he rejected it.

Dongan's administration.—Dongan administered the province of New York with marked ability. He granted a new charter to New York City by which the mayor, recorder, and sheriff were appointed by the governor, and the aldermen were popularly elected. He maintained the boundaries of the province against the claims of Penn on the west and Connecticut on the east. In 1684 he made a treaty with the Iroquois, and henceforth they sided with the English in the great international struggle for trade and territory.

Leisler's rebellion.—When James II attempted to consolidate all of the northern provinces under one head New York was included. But when the king was overthrown, Jacob Leisler led a rebellion and drove out Nicholson, the royal representative. Leisler summoned a convention which gave him dictatorial powers. He maintained authority until 1691, when Henry Sloughter arrived as governor. Leisler surrendered, but was tried and hanged.

THE JERSEYS

Settlements in the Jerseys.—When the Jerseys passed into the hands of Carteret and Berkeley, there were two settled areas, one of Dutch origin about Bergen, Hoboken, and Wiehawken, the other of Dutch, Swedish, and Finnish settlements on the Delaware. When Nicolls came to New York he was not aware that part of the province had been granted to others. He immediately sought to bring in settlers; about two hundred people, descendants of New Englanders, moved from Long Island to the neighborhood of what was later known as Elizabethtown. Others, most of whom were Quakers, settled at Middletown and Shrewsbury under a special grant from Nicolls.

Government in East New Jersey.—In 1665 Philip Carteret, probably a brother of the proprietor, arrived with a governor's commission. With him were about thirty persons, most of whom were French people from the Island of Jersey. Elizabethtown was made the capital. Carteret brought with him a plan of government, which provided that the governor was to choose a council of not less than six, nor more than twelve members. The freemen were to choose twelve representatives, who were to join with the governor and council in law-making. When local divisions were established each division was to elect a representative to an assembly, which would then take the place of the twelve. The assembly could pass laws subject to certain restrictions, create local divisions, incorporate towns, erect forts, provide for a militia, wage war, naturalize foreigners, and perform many other acts. Religious liberty and property rights were carefully protected. The enforcement of laws, appointment of officers, and pardoning power were left in the hands of the governor and council.

Difficulties with New Englanders.—During 1666 many families from the Connecticut Valley migrated to East New Jersey, most of them settling on the Passaic River, Bradford and Guilford being founded. Newark was also settled. The settlers drew up a form of government copied from New Haven, which restricted the franchise to membership in the Congregational church. In April, 1668, the first assembly was called by Carteret, but the people from Middletown and Shrewsbury did not send delegates. To a session held in October these towns sent representatives, but they were not allowed to sit in the meeting. A quarrel ensued between the governor and assembly, which soon adjourned and did not convene again for seven years. In 1670, when Carteret attempted to collect quit-rents, the settlers refused to pay, and for two years the colony was in turmoil. Middletown and Shrewsbury, acting under their original patent from Nicolls, set up an independent government, but the governor refused to recognize it and was sustained by the proprietors, who, however, granted some concessions, whereupon the difficulties subsided.

The Quakers in West New Jersey.—In 1672 George Fox, the founder of the Quaker sect, crossed New Jersey and visited the Quakers in the eastern part. To this visit Penn's interest in the region may be traced. In 1674 Berkeley disposed of his share of

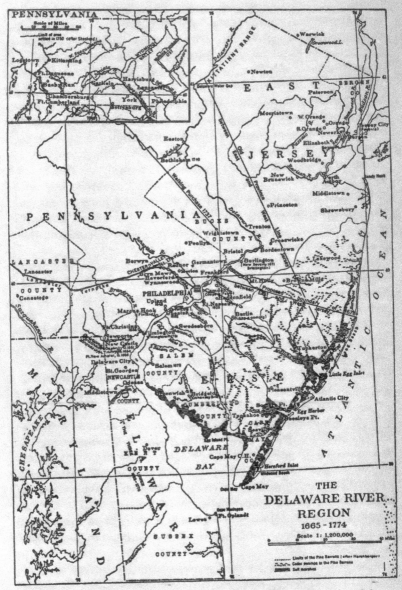

(From Fisher, *The Quaker Colonies*, in the Series, "The Chronicles of America," Yale University Press)

the colony to two Quakers, Edward Byllynge and John Fenwick, this transaction being due to a desire on the part of the Society of Friends to establish an independent colony. Byllynge and Fenwick became involved in a dispute over property rights, and William Penn was made arbiter. Penn awarded one-tenth to Fenwick, who, after considerable litigation, accepted it. Byllynge shortly afterward conveyed his holdings to Penn, Lawrie, and Lucas, who soon acquired Fenwick's interests. In 1676 Carteret and the Quaker proprietors fixed the line of demarcation between East and West New Jersey. It was to run from the "most southwardly point of the east side of Little Egg Harbor" to the point where the Delaware River crossed the forty-first parallel. The Quaker migration to West New Jersey began in 1675, when Fenwick led a group to Salem. In 1677 two hundred and thirty more settled at Burlington. During the next two years eight hundred arrived, and by 1681 nearly fourteen hundred had come to the colony. In every case title to the soil was obtained by purchase from the Indians.

Government of West New Jersey.—The original Burlington colonists brought with them a body of laws which have been described as "the broadest, sanest, and most equitable charter draughted for any body of colonists up to that time." No doubt Penn played the principal rôle in the draughting. It provided for a board of commissioners to be appointed by the proprietors and an assembly chosen by the people, which was to have full rights of making laws if they were not contrary to the charter or the laws of England. The charter provided for public trials by jury and assured the right of petition. Capital punishment was prohibited.

Trouble with the Duke of York.—After the expulsion of the Dutch in 1674, the Duke of York attempted to regain control of the Jerseys and refused to recognize the validity of Berkeley's sale to Byllynge. When Andros became governor of New York he attempted to assert the authority of James over the Jerseys, but the courts refused to uphold the claims of the Duke, and in 1680 he finally gave up the struggle.

Later history of West New Jersey.—In 1680 Byllynge obtained a title to West New Jersey from the Duke of York and the charter of 1677 was put into effect, with the exception that the executive was vested in a single person instead of in commissioners. In 1687 Byllynge died and Daniel Coxe, a London merchant, acquired his properties. Burlington was made the capital, and Coxe bent his efforts to make it a commercial center. In 1688 the colony was placed under the jurisdiction of Andros as a part of the northern administrative unit which included New York and New England, but Coxe was restored to his rights after the dethronement of James, though he soon sold out to the West New Jersey Society.

Later history of East New Jersey.—In 1682 Philip Carteret resigned, and the board of trustees who controlled the estate of Sir George Carteret sold East New Jersey to William Penn and eleven other Quakers. Shortly afterwards twelve others were taken into the company, several of whom were Scotch Presbyterians. In 1683 the twenty-four men received a deed from the Duke of York. Under these proprietors the colony prospered, and population increased rapidly. In 1688 the province came under royal jurisdiction and it was annexed to New York, but after the revolution it was restored to the proprietors.

PENNSYLVANIA

The Quaker faith.—The Reformation produced many religious sects. With the breaking down of one authoritative church and the substitution of the idea that any one might read and interpret the Bible, religious groups began forming. Among the numerous sects were the Quakers, the followers of George Fox. Seventeenth century religion was based upon the fundamental idea that the universe was dualistic, natural and supernatural. The question on which men split was how the chasm was to be bridged. Most of the Protestant sects believed that the crossing was made by a definite revelation of the word of God. Fox believed "that it was bridged by the communication of a supernatural Light given to each soul."

The coming of the Quakers.—Most of the seventeenth century religious sects, once in power, were as intolerant as the Catholics had been. The Quaker was looked upon with disfavor and persecution was his lot. In America he hoped to find an abiding place. Between 1655 and 1680 Quakers appeared in nearly all the colonies. Fox came to America in 1671 and in the course of the following year visited the Quaker communities from Barbados to Rhode Island.

Penn obtains lands on the Delaware.—The desire to obtain lands where they would be in complete control was long in the minds of the Quaker leaders. In 1680 William Penn petitioned for lands along the Delaware north of Maryland, in payment of a debt of 16,000 pounds. In spite of his faith Penn stood well at court, and on March 4, 1681, the charter of Pennsylvania was signed. The extent of the grant was defined as follows: "All that Tract or parte of land in America, with all the Islands therein conteyned, as the same is bounded on the East by Delaware River, from twelve miles distance, Northwarde of New Castle Towne unto the three and fortieth degree of Northerne Latitude if the said River doeth extend soe farre Northwards; But if the said River shall not extend soe farre Northward, then by the said River soe farr as it doth extend, and from the head of the said River the Easterne Bounds are to bee determined by a Meridian Line, to bee drawne from the head of the said River unto the said three and fortieth degree, The said lands to extend westwards, five degrees in longitude, to bee computed from the said Eastern Bounds, and the said lands to bee bounded on the North, by the beginning of the three and fortieth degree of Northern latitude, and on the South, by a Circle drawne at twelve miles, distance from New Castle Northwards, and Westwards unto the beginning of the fortieth degree of Northerne Latitude; and then by a streight Line westwards, to the Limitt of Longitude above menconed."

Both the northern and southern boundaries caused future disputes. Penn claimed as far north as the forty-third parallel, while New York insisted on the forty-second, a difference which was settled a century later in favor of New York. On the south the boundaries conflicted with the claims of Baltimore. In 1682 the question was further complicated by a grant to Penn from the Duke of York of the territory on the western shore of Delaware Bay. The difficulty was finally settled in 1760, and seven years later two surveyors, Mason and Dixon, ran the present line between Maryland and Pennsylvania at 39° 44', and erected the present boundaries of the state of Delaware.

Powers of the proprietor.—By the charter Penn was made a proprietor, having the right to make laws with the advice and consent of the freemen. The proprietor was given power to execute the laws, issue ordinances, appoint judges and magistrates, pardon criminals except in cases of treason and willful murder, erect municipalities, and grant manors. The form of government in the colony was left to the proprietor. Laws had to be sent to the privy council for approval, but if action were not taken within six months, they were valid. The king reserved the right of hearing appeals. The navigation laws were to be enforced, and if damages accrued from non-enforcement and were not settled within a year, the king had the right to take over the government of the colony until payment was made.

The founding of Philadelphia.—Penn published a prospectus of his colony which was widely circulated, and drew up a body of conditions and concessions which dealt with the division and settlement of the province and with Indian relations. In 1681 he sent to America as deputy-governor his cousin, William Markham, who received the allegiance of the settlers already within the colony. Shortly afterward the first body of colonists arrived bearing instructions to lay out a town. The site of Philadelphia was surveyed the following year, a symmetrical plan being adopted which made Penn's capital the best-arranged city in colonial America.

The " frame of government."—The government devised by Penn consisted of "the Governor and freemen of the said province, in form of a Provincial Council and General Assembly, by whom all laws shall be made, officers chosen, and publick affairs transacted." An elective council was to consist of seventy-two persons "of most note for their wisdom, virtue and ability." This body, with the governor, was to prepare and propose all bills, and together they were to share executive powers. They were to erect courts of justice, elect county officers, provide schools, and perform numerous other duties. The assembly, which was to consist at first of not more than two hundred members, was to be elected annually. Its chief business was to consider and pass upon bills prepared by the governor and council.

Penn's first sojourn in the province.—Penn arrived on the ship *Welcome* in the fall of 1682, and immediately called an election for an assembly, in this case ignoring the details of the frame of government. The first assembly annexed the territory on the western shore of Delaware Bay, naturalized foreigners, and adopted a set of laws proposed by the proprietor, which provided for liberty of conscience, a strict code of morals, and for capital punishment for treason and murder only. Penn inspected his province, watched the building of Philadelphia, and visited New York, Maryland, and West New Jersey. He also held several meetings with the Indians, entering in June, 1683, into a treaty with them which had the salutary effect of keeping Pennsylvania free from Indian war. The number of representatives provided for in the frame of government proving too large, a new frame was drawn up by which the council was reduced to eighteen and the lower house to thirty-six members.

Penn's activities in England.—In August, 1684, Penn went to England to obtain a settlement of his disputes with Baltimore and to aid the persecuted Quakers. His claim to the Delaware tract was confirmed and he secured the release from English jails of more than twelve hundred Quakers. In 1688 he also succeeded in keeping his province from being incorporated within the jurisdiction of Andros.

Friction in the colony.—The political peace for which Penn had hoped was soon disturbed. Friction over the right to initiate legislation broke out between the council and assembly. Trouble with one of the justices also occurred. Hoping to quiet affairs, Penn took away the executive powers of the council and appointed a commission of five councillors who were to compel all to do their duty. As trouble continued, he did away with the commission and appointed Captain Blackwell, a Puritan, to act for him. This choice proved unfortunate, for the Puritan could not get along with the Quakers. In despair, Penn recalled Blackwell and allowed the council to select its own executive. The council again assumed the governorship, and chose Thomas Lloyd president. Friction also existed between the settlers along the shore of Delaware Bay and those in the river settlements, a difficulty which eventually led to the separation of Delaware from Pennsylvania.

Growth of the colony.—In spite of frictions the colony prospered. When Penn acquired his province, it contained about a thousand Swedes, Finns, and Dutch, and a few Quakers. By 1685 the population had increased to more than eight thousand, made up of diverse elements; Quakers, mostly from central and southwestern England and from Wales, Mennonites from the Rhineland, Swedes, Scotch, Irish, and French. Philadelphia soon boasted a tannery, sawmill, and kiln; linen manufacture began; and the colony entered upon a prosperous intercolonial trade in flour, staves, and horses. A weekly post and a school were established, and a printing press installed. It was evident that Penn's "holy experiment" had justified itself.

THE INSULAR COLONIES

Reorganization in the Bermudas.—Complaints by the settlers against the rule of the Somers Islands Company in the Bermudas had been common since its foundation. As time went on it became composed of men who had little interest in the colony. The settlers, on the other hand, grew in numbers and independence. Under the circumstances, in the general reorganization by the later Stuarts, the company was dissolved, and in 1679 the Bermudas became a crown colony.

Reorganization in the West Indies.—Down to 1671 the English Caribbean island possessions were all included in one government within the Carlisle grant. In that year they were separated into two governments, St. Kitts, Nevis, Montserrat, Antigua, Barbuda, Anguilla and "all other the Leeward islands" to the north of French Guadeloupe were separated from Barbados and the Windward Islands, and erected into the government of the Leeward Islands, the islands to the south of Guadeloupe being formed into the government of the Windward Islands. The Leeward Islands were put under one governor-in-chief, each island being given a deputy governor, council, assembly, and courts. In 1689 the islands together were granted a general assembly, which first met in 1690.

New settlements in the West Indies.—During the period of the later Stuarts the Leeward Islands extended their influence among the smaller islands to the northwest. In 1665 a buccaneering expedition from Jamaica captured St. Eustatius and Saba. In 1666 settlers from the Bermudas settled on New Providence, one of the Bahamas, and elected a governor. Four years later six of the

Carolina proprietors secured a patent to the island but did little toward colonizing it. In 1672 Tortola was taken from the Dutch and added to the Leeward Islands.

Unrest in Barbados.—The first important movement to settle Carolina came from Barbados, the most populous of the English colonies. A spirit of unrest pervaded the island. During the Commonwealth it had been a refuge for both Cavaliers and Roundheads, and the newcomers had taken up lands without securing titles. When the Stuarts were restored, the former proprietors attempted to regain their possessions. A lively controversy ensued. The king settled it by establishing his authority in the island, but levied a tax of four and one-half per cent. on its products to be applied to satisfy in part the claims of the proprietors, an arrangement which pleased no one. The navigation acts also considerably interfered with the trade of the island which had previously been carried on largely with the Dutch. As a result many settlers were anxious to leave. Between 1643 and 1667 at least twelve hundred Barbadians went to fight or settle in Jamaica, Tobago, St. Lucia, Trinidad, Surinam, New England, Virginia, or Carolina.

THE CAROLINAS

The Carolina coast.—From the James River region to the Spanish settlements in Florida, stretched a vast territory, which, with the single exception of a settlement on the Chowan River, was unoccupied by white men when Charles II came to the throne. After Raleigh's ill-starred venture it had received little attention until 1629, when Sir Robert Heath obtained a patent to lands between 31° and 36° north latitude, but he did nothing to improve the territory. The coasts were occasionally visited by mariners, but there is no definite knowledge of any settlement until 1653, when colonists from Virginia appear to have started a settlement at Albemarle on the Chowan River. About 1660 some New Englanders inspected the Cape Fear River mouth but departed soon afterward.

The charters.—In 1660 Sir John Colleton, a prominent resident of Barbados, went to England where he became a member of the Council for Foreign Plantations. He soon interested Anthony Ashley Cooper, later known as Lord Ashley, in the Carolinas.

In 1663 a charter was granted to eight proprietors, Cooper, Clarendon, Craven, Albemarle, Carteret, Lord Berkeley, Colleton, and Sir William Berkeley. The territory granted extended from the thirty-sixth to the thirty-first parallel and from sea to sea. Over this region the proprietors were given practically the same rights as Baltimore possessed in Maryland. In 1665 a second patent was granted to the proprietors, extending the boundaries to 36° 30′ on the north and to 29° on the south.

The fundamental constitutions.—The philosopher, John Locke, drew up a constitution for the province. It provided for a high official called the palatine, and minor officials designated as admiral, chamberlain, chancellor, constable, chief justice, steward, and treasurer. The province was to be divided into counties, and each county into seigniories, baronies, and precincts. On these divisions were to be based the ranks of the nobility to be designated as land-graves, caciques, and lords of manors. An elaborate system of courts was provided; also a grand council and a parliament. This archaic feudal document is of interest mainly as a study in the political philosophy of the time, but it was of little real importance as it was totally unsuited to the needs of a frontier community. It was never put in force except in certain minor particulars, the settlers themselves soon solving their problems of government in their own way.

Beginnings of settlement.—In 1663–1664 an expedition from Barbados examined the Carolina coast, and in 1665 Sir John Yeamans conducted a group of settlers to the mouth of Cape Fear River. Yeamans soon returned to Barbados and the settlers, left to their own devices, in 1667 abandoned the settlement, most of them going to Albemarle, Virginia, and Boston. In 1669 vessels carrying ninety-two colonists sailed from England to Barbados, where Sir John Yeamans, who had been appointed governor, joined them. They then proceeded to the Bermudas, where Yeamans handed over the authority to William Sayle and abandoned the expedition. The colonists under Sayle then went to Port Royal, but finally settled on the Ashley River, where they laid out old Charles Town (1670). Political strife soon developed, owing mainly to the incompetence of the aged executive. In 1671 he died and Joseph West was chosen governor by the people.

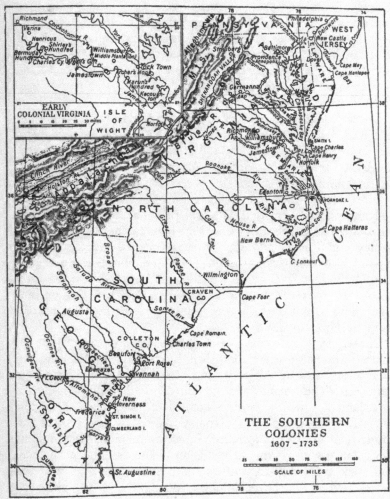

THE SOUTHERN
COLONIES
1607 – 1735

SCALE OF MILES

(From Johnston, *Pioneers of the Old South,* in the Series, "The Chronicles of
America," Yale University Press)

Plans of the proprietors.—In 1670 the proprietors obtained a grant of the Bahamas and planned to build up trade between the island and mainland settlements. They also planned to improve the Charles Town settlement and in 1671 secured settlers from Barbados. Yeamans came over and claimed the governorship, but West succeeded in keeping the office for several months. In 1672 Yeamans was again appointed governor, but he managed things so badly that in 1674 West was reappointed and remained governor for eight years.

Development of the Charles Town region.—Colonists came in considerable numbers; in 1672 there were about four hundred people in the colony, and by 1685 the population had increased to about twenty-five hundred. Among the immigrants were a hundred French Protestants, and a colony of Scots who settled at Port Royal in 1683. Other colonists came from Barbados and many from western England. In 1680 the seat of government was moved from old Charles Town to the junction of the Ashley and Cooper Rivers. After 1680 settlements began to expand into the back country. This soon brought on the inevitable Indian war, which continued intermittently for three years. In 1685 the Spaniards raided the settlements, burning many houses, and the following year destroyed the Scotch settlement at Port Royal.

Unrest at Charleston.—During West's administration the colony was not greatly disturbed by political difficulties, the proprietors making little attempt to enforce the Locke constitution. The colony was governed by a popularly elected "parliament," which chose a council of five men. The chief executive was the governor commissioned by the proprietors. From 1682 to 1689 proprietary interference increased, bringing the colony to the verge of rebellion. The colonial parliament had steadily refused to confirm the constitution. During 1682 it was revised by the proprietors, more power being placed in the hands of the people, but still the colonists refused to confirm it. This irritated the proprietors, who retaliated by introducing a new form of land tenure, which required the colonists to pay a cash quit-rent. When James II came to the throne, Governor Morton demanded that they swear allegiance to the king and accept the constitution, whereupon twelve members of the parlia-

ment refused and were excluded. The colonists also took with
ill grace the attempt to collect the customs. In 1688 the governor
and council found themselves at complete loggerheads with parliament, and legislation stopped. James Colleton, the governor,
proclaimed martial law. This led to an open rebellion, and in
1691 Colleton was expelled, but the proprietary power was soon
restored.

The Albemarle colony.—During these troublous times the
Albemarle settlement was slowly developing. The colony was
mainly recruited from Virginia, but there was also a considerable
influx of Quakers. In 1682 the Albemarle settlement contained
about twenty-five hundred inhabitants. When an attempt was
made in 1677 to collect the customs and to shut off the New
England trade, about a hundred colonists led by John Culpeper
rebelled and imprisoned Miller, who was the collector of customs
and acting governor. They also arrested the president of the
assembly and all but one of the deputies. The proprietors removed Miller from office and appointed Seth Sothell governor,
but the people soon drove him from the colony. The turbulence
did not quiet down until the appointment of Governor Ludwell,
who from 1691 resided at Charleston, Albemarle being governed
henceforth by a deputy.

WESTERN TRADE AND EXPLORATION

By now English explorers and fur traders had crossed the
Alleghanies. As early as 1648 Governor Berkeley was preparing
an expedition to the southwest, where red capped Spaniards riding "long eared beasts," came to trade with the natives. Twenty-
five years later (1673) two Virginians, James Needham and
Gabriel Arthur, reached the Cherokees on the Upper Tennessee.
To these mountain dwellers on the "western waters" the Englishmen were a novel sight, but they had long been acquainted
with the Spaniards and possessed "some sixty Spanish flint-
locks," and among them lived Spanish mulatto women. Before
the end of the century South Carolina traders had established
the "Chickasaw Trail" through the Creek and Chickasaw country, and had crossed the Mississippi. In 1699–1700 Carolinians
ascended the Savannah, descended the Tennessee, Ohio, and
Mississippi to the mouth of the Arkansas. Frontiersmen had

gone northwest as well as southwest, and before the end of the century had begun to make their way among the Indians on both sides of the upper Ohio River.

HUDSON'S BAY COMPANY

Continued search for the Northwest Passage.—Some of the same men who represented the Carolinas now extended English enterprises to the region of Hudson Bay. The English search for the Northwest Passage had not ended with the sixteenth century. Henry Hudson, who in 1609 had explored Hudson River in an attempt to find the passage, made further attempts in the following year. Finding his way in the *Discovery* through Hudson Strait, he wintered at the southern extremity of James Bay. He paid dearly for his discoveries, for he was cast adrift by mutinous followers and perished. In Hudson's wake went numerous explorers, backed by syndicates of merchants and sometimes with royal support, still seeking the passage. In 1612 Button crossed Hudson Bay and entered the mouth of Nelson River. At the same time a company was formed to seek the passage. In 1616 Bylot and Baffin discovered Baffin Bay, and in 1631 Foxe made new discoveries in Fox Channel. Denmark also entered the field of northwestern discovery and in 1619–1620 Jens Munck explored Hudson Bay, wintering at Churchill Harbor.

Radisson, Groseilliers, and Gillam.—The primary purpose of the foregoing voyages had been to find a passage to the Far East. They were followed, after an interval, by trading enterprises. The operations of the French fur traders, Radisson and Groseilliers, have been mentioned previously. Having been imprisoned and fined for illicit trading, they left Canada, went to New England, and got up an expedition to Hudson Bay to gather furs. Sailing in 1664 with Captain Zachariah Gillam, they reached Hudson Strait but not the bay. After another failure in 1665, they met Sir George Carteret whom they interested in their project. Going to England, through Carteret's influence they organized a company among whose stockholders were the Duke of York, Prince Rupert, Carteret, the Duke of Albemarle, and the Earls of Craven, Arlington, and Shaftesbury, several of whom were already influential in colonial enterprises. In 1668

the company again sent Gillam to Hudson Bay, where he built
Charles Fort on Rupert's River, and traded profitably in furs.
The part played by Radisson and Groseilliers in this enter-
prise became a basis for French claims to the Hudson Bay region.

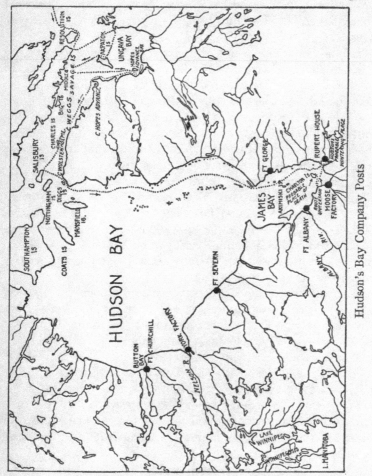

Hudson's Bay Company.—The return of Gillam to London.
in 1669 was followed by the formation of a new Company. . On
May 2, 1670, Charles II issued a royal charter to "The Governor
and Company of Adventurers of England trading into Hudson's
Bay." The Company was made absolute proprietor with a com-

plete monopoly of all trade of the Hudson Bay basin. The government was centered in a governor, deputy-governor, and committee of seven, who were empowered to make laws and were given judicial and military authority. They lost no time in establishing posts, and by 1685 there were trading houses at Albany River, Hayes Island, Rupert's River, Port Nelson, Moose River, and New Severn.

Trading Methods.—Ships were fitted out annually in London with merchandise, and brought back rich cargoes of furs. In contrast with the French traders and with the English of the Atlantic seaboard colonies, the Hudson's Bay Company did not penetrate the interior, but depended upon the natives to bring their peltry to the posts on the Bay. In the spring, therefore, after the break-up of the ice, Crees, Chipewyans, and Eskimos came down the rivers in fleets of canoes laden with furs, traded them for merchandise, and returned for another season's hunt. In London the furs were sold at auction at the Company's headquarters, where the annual fair took on the nature of a social function. Gradually the markets widened, agents being sent to establish trade with Holland, Russia, and other parts of Northern Europe. Profits were large, the dividend in 1690 being seventy-five per cent of the original stock.

French Rivalry.—The success of the English aroused the jealousy of the French traders in the St. Lawrence Valley, and there ensued a rivalry which constituted one of the important episodes of the intercolonial wars which now occurred. In the contest Radisson, who had aided in the formation of the Company, played fast and loose between the English and the French. Before the end of the century French rivalry in the interior, beyond Lake Superior, did much to shake the "H. B. C." from its exclusive, seaboard policy. By 1691 Henry Kelsey, an employe of the Company, had made an expedition to the Winnipeg district.

READINGS

NEW YORK

Andrews, C. M., *Colonial Self-Government*, 74–100, 273–287; Andrews, C. M., ed., *Narratives of the Insurrections*, 315–401; Brodhead, J. R., *History of New York*, II; Channing, Edward, *History of the United States*, II, 31–60, 203–209; Doyle, J. A., *The Middle Colonies*, 78–223; Fiske, John, *Dutch and*

Quaker Colonies, II, 1–98, 168–208; New York Historical Society, *Collections*, 1st Series, I, 307–428; Osgood, H. L., *The English Colonies in the Seventeenth Century*, II, 119–168; Winsor, Justin, *Narrative and Critical History*, III, 385–411.

THE JERSEYS AND PENNSYLVANIA

Andrews, C. M., *Colonial Self-Government*, 101–128, 162–201; Channing, Edward, *History of the United States*, II, 31–62, 94–130; Clarkson, Thomas, *Memoirs of Pennsylvania;* Doyle, J. A., *The Middle Colonies*, 287–350, 379–410; Fiske, John, *Dutch and Quaker Colonies*, II, 115–194; Fisher, Sidney, *The Quaker Colonies;* Hodgkin, Thomas, *George Fox;* Holder, C. F., *The Quakers in Great Britain and America*, 169–217; Janney, S. M., *Life of Penn;* Jones, R. M., *The Quakers in the American Colonies*, 357–371, 417–436; MacDonald, William, *Select Charters*, 139–149, 171–204; Osgood, H. L., *The English Colonies in the Seventeenth Century*, II, 169–197, 252–276; Sharpless, Isaac, *A Quaker Experiment in Government; Two Centuries of Pennsylvania History*, 17–77; Smith, Samuel, *The History of the Colony of Nova-Cæsaria or New Jersey*, 35–207; Tanner, E. P., *The Province of New Jersey*, 1–147; Whitehead, W. A., *East Jersey under the Proprietary Governments.*

THE CAROLINAS

Andrews, C. M., *Colonial Self-Government*, 129–161; Andrews, C. M., ed., *Narratives of the Insurrections*, 143–164; Ashe, S. A., *North Carolina*, I; Channing, Edward, *History of the United States*, II, 13–25; Hamilton, P. J., *Colonization of the South*, 133–135; McCrady, Edward, *The History of South Carolina under the Proprietary Government*, I, 1–209; Osgood, H. L., *The American Colonies in the Seventeenth Century*, II, 200–225; Ramsay, David, *South Carolina.*

HUDSON'S BAY COMPANY

Burpee, Laurence J., *The Search for the Western Sea*, 64–95; Bryce, George, *The Remarkable History of the Hudson's Bay Company*, 1–55; Laut, Agnes, *The Conquest of the Great Northwest*, I, 1–255; Laut, Agnes, *The Adventurers of England on Hudson Bay;* Willson, Beckles, *The Great Company*, 1–181; Winsor, J., *Narrative and Critical History*, VIII, 1–34.

WESTERN EXPLORATION

Alvord and Bidgood, *First Explorations of the Trans-Allegheny Region* . . . 1650–1674; Crane, V. W., "The Tennessee River as the Road to Carolina," in *Miss. Valley Hist. Rev.*, III, 3–18.

CHAPTER XII

THE ENGLISH MAINLAND COLONIES AT THE CLOSE OF THE SEVENTEENTH CENTURY

At the close of the Stuart period the English mainland colonies stretched along the Atlantic coast from Pemaquid to Port Royal. The settlements nestled close to the coasts, in the tide-water region, or along the lower waters of the navigable streams. The total population probably did not exceed 225,000, one-half of whom were in Massachusetts and Virginia. At the same period Barbados alone contained over 50,000 white settlers and more than 100,000 slaves.

NEW ENGLAND

Population.—New England contained some 80,000 white inhabitants. About 5,000 were in New Hampshire; Massachusetts, including the Maine and Plymouth settlements, contained about 55,000; Rhode Island probably 5,000, and Connecticut about 17,000. By far the larger part were of English stock, although there were a few Huguenots, Scotch, Irish, and Jews. The settled area extended from the Pemaquid region along the coast in an almost unbroken line to the New York border. In Maine the settled region seldom extended more than ten miles back from the coast, and between Casco and Saco bays there were large unsettled tracts. In New Hampshire the frontier line ran back from the coast fifteen to thirty miles and eastern Massachusetts was settled fifty miles inland. All of Rhode Island except some tracts in the southern part had been occupied. Portions of northeastern and northwestern Connecticut were wilderness, but in the Connecticut Valley the settlers had begun to occupy the valley lands just to the north of the Massachusetts line.

Agriculture.—The mass of the population was agricultural. The clearing of the land and the securing of a food supply were the natural pursuits of the new communities. The small farm was the prevailing type, as neither climate, crops, nor soil were suitable for the large plantation. Corn, wheat, fruits, and vegetables were the principal agricultural products, and cattle, swine, sheep, and poultry were raised for domestic use.

Furs and fish.—The forests and the sea were the principal sources of New England prosperity. In the early part of the century the fur trade was an important factor, but by the end of the century it had considerably decreased. As it declined the fishing business increased. On the Newfoundland banks the boats of the New Englanders were the most numerous. The catch of cod and mackerel was dried and salted, and became a leading export.

Lumbering and ship-building.—The uncleared back country was a continual source of profit. Logging became a regular winter pursuit. From the felled timber were produced lumber, staves, shingles, masts, and spars. The fishing business conducted close to a lumbering region led to ship-building, and almost every seacoast town engaged in the industry. Most of the boats were small, swift-sailing craft, used in the fisheries or in the coasting and West Indian trade. So well-built were they that the New Englander found a ready market in the West Indies for vessel as well as cargo.

Commerce.—Fish, furs, and lumber were the principal products which the New Englanders produced for outside consumption. Most of the carrying business was conducted by Massachusetts men, although Rhode Island also handled a considerable trade. The navigation laws were intended to keep commerce in the hands of English merchants, but in spite of them colonial vessels kept up a coast-wise trade, and shipped fish, lumber, and staves to the West Indies and Madeira. Return vessels brought wine, rum, molasses, sugar, cotton, and wool. The greater part of New England commerce was handled through Boston, although Salem and Newport were rivals. Newport traders carried on a large slave traffic from Guinea and Madagascar, but most of their cargoes were sold in the West Indies.

Manufactures.—In Massachusetts and Connecticut manufacturing for the home market developed at an early date. Grist and saw-mills, tanneries, glass and pottery works, brick yards, and salt works were commonly found in the tide-water region, and at least two iron works were in operation in Massachusetts before 1700. Every village had its cobbler and blacksmith, and the housewives did the spinning and weaving. Most of the people wore homespun, but finer fabrics were also in demand, and at an early date the manufacture of cotton and woolen goods on a more elaborate scale was undertaken in Massachusetts.

Standard of living.—Practically all New Englanders were free settlers, but a limited number of indented servants and a few hundred slaves were intermixed with the population. In the regions near the coast the standard of living had materially improved. In the larger towns the inhabitants enjoyed even a degree of luxury in dress and table, and the log huts of the first settlers had almost disappeared, frame, shingled, and even brick houses having taken their place. Most of the houses of the well-to-do had a second floor, attic, and lean-to. Every community had its meeting house, and in 1670 Boston had three places of worship. As the traveler passed into the back country, he found roads growing poorer and poorer, gradually deteriorating into mere trails. The clearings and log cabins became less and less frequent until he finally reached the wilderness, which was penetrated only by the hunter and trader. When the settlements extended a considerable distance from the coast, they were usually along a navigable stream, the indispensable means of communication in a newly settled community.

Social standards.—Daily life was simple and devoid of ostentation, but in the older communities social lines were rigidly drawn. An austere aristocracy ruled. Admitted to the inner circle were the descendants of the early leaders or of families of rank in England, Oxford and Cambridge men, and those who were selected through natural worth to fill high positions in church and state. Intelligence and piety were more potent factors than wealth in the attainment of position. Of professional men the ministers held an exalted place, exerting a powerful influence socially, religiously, and politically. There were few doctors and lawyers, the latter being looked upon as undesirable trouble makers.

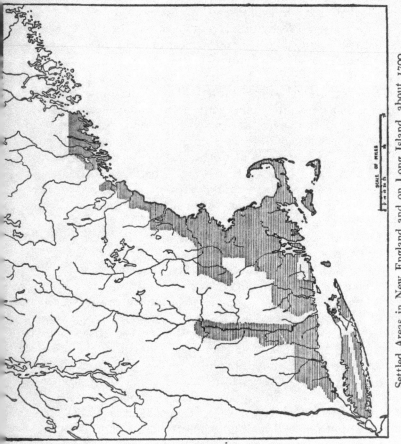

SCALE OF MILES

Settled Areas in New England and on Long Island, about 1700

Religion.—Throughout New England, except in Rhode Island, church and state were united, the Congregational church being in the ascendency. Though in 1660 Charles II commanded that the Anglican church be tolerated in Massachusetts, the authorities resisted its introduction, and not until 1686 was an Episcopalian church established in Boston. In Connecticut there were a few Presbyterians and Quakers. In Rhode Island the Baptists and Quakers were the most important element.

Superstitions.—The seventeenth century Puritan was intolerant and superstitious. Men must conform or be persecuted. Signs and portents were believed in, and strange and often filthy concoctions and ointments were administered at the suggestion of midwives or knowing housewives. Belief in witchcraft was usual both in Europe and America, and such learned men as Increase and Cotton Mather, prominent clergymen of Boston, wrote treatises to prove its truth. The Massachusetts laws recognized it as a capital offense. In 1692 occurred the famous outbreak at Salem in which nineteen innocent persons were executed.

Education.—In the English colonies New England took the lead in provision for popular education. Men who believed that the Bible was the source of authority naturally thought that every man should have sufficient intellectual training to enable him to read the word of God. In 1635 the first Latin grammar school in the English colonies was started at Boston, and several other towns soon followed the example. In 1647 Massachusetts enacted a general education law which required every town of fifty or more freeholders to appoint a teacher to instruct children to read and write. Every town of one hundred or more freeholders was required to support a Latin grammar school which would prepare students for college. Connecticut and New Haven soon followed the lead of Massachusetts. In Rhode Island and Plymouth each community was allowed to follow its own course. In Rhode Island the few schools were usually private enterprises. In Plymouth the first public school was not opened until 1671. Higher education was not neglected, Harvard being founded in 1636. In that year Massachusetts voted £400 toward the support of a college. Two years later John Harvard bequeathed his library and one-half of his estate for the erection of a college, ınd Harvard College came into existence. For many years it was devoted mainly to the training of religious leaders, and its curriculum reflected the classical viewpoint of the great English universities.

Literature.—The literature of the first century of New England was permeated with a gloomy religious viewpoint, but it was not lacking in dignity or power. It reflected the sternness of standards and purpose of the founders, who saw little of the humor, or of the lighter side of existence. The strongest of the writings were the histories, the best being the *History of Plymouth* by Governor Bradford and *The History of New England* by Governor Winthrop. Of less interest to the present day mind are the controversial religious tracts and sermons of Roger Williams and Cotton Mather, or the crude poetry of Mrs. Anne Bradstreet.

NEW YORK AND EAST NEW JERSEY

Population.—Economically and socially New York and East New Jersey were closely related. At the end of the Andros régime the population of New York was probably 18,000, and that of East New Jersey about 10,000. More than half of the New Yorkers were Dutch. The rest were mainly English, but there were some Huguenots and a few Jews. The settled area covered almost all of Long Island and the Hudson Valley to a point a few miles north of Albany. Most of the population of East New Jersey was along the coast opposite New York harbor. The English predominated, but there was a sprinkling of Dutch, Scotch, and Huguenots.

Industry in New York.—During the first decades of the Dutch occupation of the Hudson Valley the fur trade had been almost the only business, but after 1638 many settlers came who began general farming. Lumbering also developed. The general lines of industry thus begun were carried on after the English occupation. The fur trade was greatly stimulated by Dongan and it was probably the chief source of wealth in the colony. Population increased slowly. The advantageous position of New York attracted shipping, and the merchants developed a commerce with the West Indies and the Dutch possessions in the Caribbean to which were shipped bread stuffs, pease, meat, and horses.

The returning vessels brought wine, rum, molasses, and various tropical products. To England the New Yorkers shipped furs, oil, and naval supplies in return for manufactured goods.

A contemporary description of New York.—Governor Dongan

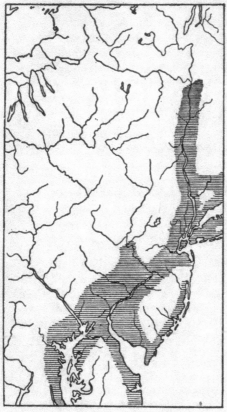

Settled Areas in the Middle Colonies about 1700

wrote concerning the province in 1687: "The principal towns within the Govermt are New York Albany & Kingston at Esopus. All the rest are country villages. The buildings in New York & Albany are generally of stone & brick. In the country the houses are mostly new built, having two or three rooms on a floor. The Dutch are great improvers of land. New York and Albany live wholly upon trade with the Indians England and the West Indies. . . . I believe for these 7 years last past, there has not come over into this province twenty English Scotch or Irish familys. But on the contrary on Long Island the people encrease soe fast that they complain for want of land and many remove from thence into the neighboring province."

Religion and education in New York.—Regarding religion Dongan wrote, "Every Town ought to have a Minister. New York has first a Chaplain belonging to the Fort of the Church of England; secondly, a Dutch Calvinist, thirdly a French Calvinist, fourthly a Dutch Lutheran—Here bee not many of the

Church of England; few Roman Catholicks; abundance of Quakers preachers men & Women especially; Singing Quakers, Ranting Quakers, Sabbatarians; anti-sabbatarians; Some Anabaptists some Independents; some Jews; in short of all sorts of opinions there are some, and the most part of none at all. . . . The most prevailing opinion is that of the Dutch Calvinists." This description applied to religious conditions in New York City, then as now a cosmopolitan place. On Long Island, where New Englanders were predominant, the Congregational church held sway, while in the Hudson Valley, where most of the settlers were Dutch, the Dutch Reformed church was in the ascendency. The Dutch had maintained elementary schools, but when the English occupied the country, most of the school-masters left, and little was done by the authorities to stimulate education. Such schools as existed were established by the local communities.

Large estates.—During the Dutch régime many large estates had been created, the most important being the patroonship of Van Rensselaer about Albany. Although the other patroons had surrendered their rights, the Dutch governors, officials, and merchants had acquired vast estates, which continued in their families after the English occupation. The English governors followed the example, and several large holdings were created, the most famous of these being the Livingston manor on the east bank of the Hudson below the Van Rensselaer tract.

Conditions in East New Jersey.—The people of East New Jersey came mainly from New England and Long Island, and they built up a miniature New England, each village being an entity surrounded by tributary farm lands. Garden truck, fish, oysters, and fruits were the principal products. The proprietors hoped to develop commerce, but the Duke of York's restrictions throttled it, and East New Jersey was forced into the position of a supply station for New York. Gawen Laurie, the deputy-governor, described conditions as follows in 1684: "There is great plenty of oysters, fish, fowl; pork is two pennies the pound, beef and venison one penny the pound, a whole fat buck for five or six shillings; Indian corn for two shillings and six pence per bushel, oats twenty pence, and barley two shillings per bushel: We have good brick earth, and stones for building at Amboy, and elsewhere: The country farm houses are built very cheap:

A carpenter, with a man's own servants, builds the house; they
have all materials for nothing, except nails, their chimnies are
of stones; they make their own ploughs and carts for the most
part, only the iron work is very dear: The poor sort set up a house
of two or three rooms themselves, after this manner; the walls
are of cloven timber, about eight or ten inches broad, like planks,
set one end to the ground, and the other nailed to the raising,
which they plaster within; they build a barn after the same
manner, and these cost not above five pounds a piece; and then
to work they go: Two or three men in one year will clear fifty
acres, in some places sixty, and in some more: They sow corn the
first year, and afterwards maintain themselves; and the increase
of corn, cows, horses, hogs and sheep comes to the landlord; . . .
the servants work not so much by a third as they do in England,
and I think feed much better; for they have beef, pork, bacon,
pudding, milk, butter and good beer and cyder for drink; when
they are out of their time, they have land for themselves, and
generally turn farmers for themselves."

Religion and education in East New Jersey.—Another letter
of the same date says: "There be people of several sorts of reli-
gions, but few very zealous; the people, being mostly New-
England men, do mostly incline to their way; and in every town
there is a meeting-house, where they worship publickly every
week: They have no publick laws in the country for maintaining
publick teachers, but the towns that have them, make way
within themselves to maintain them; we know none that have
a settled preacher, that follows no other employment, save one
town, Newark."

COLONIES ALONG DELAWARE RIVER AND BAY

Population.—The settlements along Delaware River and Bay
formed an industrial and social group. In 1700 the population numbered less than 20,000, from 12,000 to 15,000 being
in Pennsylvania which included Delaware. The interior of
West New Jersey was unoccupied, the population remaining
close to the coast. From Barnegat to Cape May the settled
area was about ten miles wide. Along the eastern shore of the
bay and river the population belt widened to twenty-five or
thirty miles. In Pennsylvania and Delaware the settled area

was continuous from the mouth of the Lehigh River to the southern boundary of Delaware. Back from the river the habitations extended for forty or fifty miles, but on the bay shore none of the settlers were more than ten or fifteen miles inland. The population of the Delaware region was composed of many nationalities. West New Jersey contained many English, but the descendants of the early Swedish and Dutch settlers were there in considerable numbers. Pennsylvania contained about 1,000 Swedes, Dutch, and Finns, the remnant of the early occupations. Penn's advertising and reputation for philanthropy brought to his colony English, Germans, Scotch, and Welsh.

Conditions in West New Jersey.—The following description of West New Jersey, written in 1698, gives an excellent picture of the colony: "In a few Years after [1675] a Ship from *London*, and another from *Hull*, sail'd thither with more People, who went higher up into the Countrey, and built there a Town, and called it *Burlington* which is now the chiefest Town in that Countrey though *Salem* is the ancientest; and a fine *Market-Town* it is, Having several Fairs kept yearly in it; likewise well furnished with good store of most Necessaries for humane Support, as *Bread*, *Beer*, *Beef*, and *Pork;* as also *Butter* and *Cheese*, of which they freight several Vessels and send them to *Barbadoes*, and other islands.

"There are very many fine *stately Brick-Houses* built [at Salem], and a *commodious Dock* for *Vessels* to come in at, and they claim equal Privilege with *Burlington* for the sake of Antiquity; tho' that is the principal Place, by reason that the late Governor *Cox*, who bought that Countrey of Edward *Billing*, encouraged and promoted that Town chiefly, in settling his *Agents* and *Deputy-governors* there, (the same Favours are continued by the *New-West-Jersey* Society, who now manage Matters there) which brings their Assemblies and chief Courts to be kept there; and by that means it is become a very famous Town, having a great many stately *Brick-Houses* in it, (as I said before) with a great *Market-House* . . . ; It hath a noble and *spacious Hall* overhead, where their *Sessions* is kept, having the Prison adjoining to it. . . .

"A Ship of Four Hundred Tuns may sail up to this *Town* in the River *Delaware;* for I my self have been on Board a Ship of that Burthen there: and several fine Ships and Vessels (besides Governour Cox's own great Ship) have been built there. . . . There are *Water-Men* who constantly Ply their Wherry Boats from that Town to the City of *Philadelphia* in *Pensilvania,* and to other places. Besides there is *Glocester-Town,* which is a very Fine and Pleasant Place, being well stor'd with Summer Fruits, as *Cherries, Mulberries,* and Strawberries whither Young People come from Philadelphia in the Wherries to eat *Strawberries* and *Cream,* within sight of which city it is sweetly Situated, being but about three Miles distant from thence."

Economic conditions in Pennsylvania.—When Penn's colonists arrived they found many farms under cultivation. Many of the new arrivals took up farming, and the lower counties became a supply region for Philadelphia. Under Penn's direction, Philadelphia soon became a trading center, and as it grew Burlington declined. Furs and food-stuffs were exchanged for manufactured articles from Europe, and for sugar and other West Indian produce. With the exception of the making of coarse cloth and cordage, there was little manufacturing. Practically all of the settlers were freemen, although slavery and indenture gradually crept in. The standard of living was higher than in most of the colonies, for Indian wars did not disturb pursuits, the lands were fertile, and the climatic conditions less rigorous than along the New England coast. Most of the early accounts tell of well-built houses, and productive gardens and orchards.

Religion and education.—In church affiliation the Delaware River country was a mixture. In West New Jersey were found Presbyterians, Baptists, Quakers, and Lutherans. In Pennsylvania there were the same denominations, but religiously and politically the Quakers were in the ascendency. In 1695 an Episcopal church was established at Philadelphia, but the Anglican church made slow progress along the Delaware. The Dutch and Swedes had established schools under the direction of the ministers. The Quakers were also keenly interested in education, and schools were immediately established. In 1682 the West New Jersey assembly granted three hundred acres for the support of a school at Burlington, and one of the first acts of the Pennsylvania assembly was intended to begin elementary education. In 1689 the Friends' Public School at Philadelphia was founded and was open to all sects. But most of the schools were founded by churches or private individuals.

THE CHESAPEAKE BAY REGION

The settled area.—The Chesapeake Bay country formed another economic unit. By the end of the Stuart régime Maryland contained about 30,000 people, Virginia nearly 60,000, and North Carolina perhaps 3,000, practically all of English extraction. From Cape Charles northward for fifty miles the peninsula was settled. Then came an uninhabited region until opposite Kent Island, where the settlements began again and extended northward to the Pennsylvania line. On the western side of the bay a population belt about twenty-five miles wide extended from the northern boundary of Maryland as far as the Potomac. On the right bank of the Potomac from a point ten miles above Alexandria to the place where the river made its great bend to the eastward the plantations covered a strip about five miles wide. From the great bend the frontier

Settled Areas in the Southern Colonies about 1700

ran almost straight south to the neighborhood of Richmond and then gradually curved to the southeast, enclosing a settled area about twenty-five miles wide on the south side of the James River.

The frontier line crossed the North Carolina boundary about forty miles from the coast and ran southwestward to the Chowan River, which with the northern shore of Albemarle Sound formed the limits of the settled region of North Carolina, then politically united but economically and socially separated from the Charleston district.

The plantations.—The Chesapeake Bay country was almost entirely devoted to agriculture. The small land holdings of the early period were rapidly disappearing and great plantations had taken their place. The average land patent in Virginia in the last decades of the century gave title to from six hundred to eight hundred acres, but many of the plantations covered from ten thousand to twenty thousand acres. So plentiful was land and so easily obtained that the planters preferred to take up new acreage rather than resort to fertilization, the result being that the plantations were widely scattered, an important factor in making each estate a social and economic unit.

Tobacco.—The great staple was tobacco. The plantations were usually located near a creek, river, or the bay shore. Each had its wharf or flatboat from which the trader could load his vessel. Most of the crop was shipped to England, and the price obtained determined the year's prosperity or depression. The large plantation owner usually dealt with some London house, which kept an open account with him, crediting his tobacco against orders for the manufactured articles and luxuries which the Virginia and Maryland gentlemen demanded.

Other industrial activity.—Some writers have held that there must have been much poverty in the plantation country because of the uncertain market for tobacco, but such statements do not take into account the fact that the plantations produced an abundance of food products. Wheat, oats, barley, and maize were grown in large quantities, the cereals usually being planted after the third crop of tobacco. At times wheat was exported. Almost every estate had its garden and orchard, and live stock was abundant, horses, cattle, and hogs usually ranging in the woods. So numerous did the hogs become that pork was an item of exportation. New England coasting vessels ran into the rivers and took on wheat, pork, and tobacco, which were exchanged for West Indian slaves, rum, and sugar. There was but little manufacturing. Cotton and woolen cloths were made for home use, and brick-making was carried on to a limited extent, but most of the manufactured articles were brought from England.

The system of labor.—The large plantations were worked either by indented servants or slaves. In 1671 Governor Berkeley estimated that there were 6,000 white servants and 2,000 slaves in Virginia. By 1683 there were about 12,000 indented servants and perhaps 3,000 slaves, and by the end of the century the slaves had probably doubled. In proportion to population the indented servants and slaves in Maryland and North Carolina were in similar ratio to the free white population.

Social position of the planter.—At the top of the social and political structure of society was the planter, his position depending largely upon his acreage. Already in Virginia and Maryland the "great-house" or manor house had made its appearance, a rather unpretentious rambling frame house with a brick chimney at either end, the splendor of which was largely due to comparison with the quarters of the slaves. Articles of luxury such as musical instruments, mirrors, brass fixtures, silverware, table linen, and damask hangings were frequently found in the houses of the wealthier planters. These were by no means typical, for pewter was far more common than silver, and in the home of recently released indented servants or small landholders there was little more than bare necessity demanded.

Religion and education.—In religion there was less uniformity than in industry. In Maryland probably three-fourths of the inhabitants belonged to various dissenting sects. Most of the great landholders were members of the Anglican church, but many were Catholics. Most of the Virginians were Episcopalians, while in North Carolina the Quakers were predominant. Popular education in the South was far below that of the North. Public sentiment was against free schools, and the few secondary educational institutions were conducted through private enterprise. The planters frequently secured educated indented servants who acted as tutors. In 1691 the Virginia legislature sent Dr. William Blair to England to secure a charter for a college and the following year he returned with it, this being the legal beginning of William and Mary College.

SOUTH CAROLINA

Population.—Economically and socially South Carolina was associated with the West Indies rather than with the mainland colonies. At the close of the seventeenth century the white population was about 5,500. Most of the inhabitants came from Barbados, but other Caribbean Islands, England, Ireland, the New England colonies, and France furnished colonists. The settled area extended from the Santee to the mouth of the Edisto, included several of the islands, and reached back from the coast about fifty miles. The social and economic center was Charleston. In the back country there were only two small towns, most of the people being located on plantations along the rivers and on the islands. The Barbadian planters had settled mainly on the Cooper River, Goose Creek, and Ashley River, and on James, John's and Edisto Islands. Four or five hundred Huguenots, most of whom had left their country because of the revocation of the Edict of Nantes, had located on the Santee, where they had received land grants aggregating over 50,000 acres, nearly half of this being the property of two individuals, the other Huguenot estates varying from 100 to 3,000 acres.

The plantations.—At the end of the century rice culture, which was destined to furnish the most important staple, was in its infancy, and a little silk and cotton were produced. The chief business of the planters was the raising of cattle and hogs, corn, and pease. The Barbadians brought in the economic system of the West Indies, which was based upon slavery, and the harsh slave code of Barbados was adopted in the colony. Accurate statistics regarding the number of slaves are inaccessible, but an apparently authentic letter of 1708 states that in that year there were 4,100 negro slaves and 1,400 Indian slaves in the colony, numbers probably in excess of those in 1700, as it was the development of the rice industry which made slaves highly profitable.

Commerce.—Charleston was the great market town. There the trader stocked for the Indian trade, which, at the close of the century was the chief source of wealth of South Carolina. Goods from Charleston are said to have penetrated a thousand miles into the interior. To the West Indies were shipped beef, pork, butter, tallow, and hides, rice and pease, lumber, staves, pitch, and tar; returning vessels brought rum, sugar, molasses, and other West Indian products. To England were shipped furs, rice, silk, and naval stores, in return for manufactured goods.

Religion and education.—The Episcopalian was the established church of the colony, and probably forty-five per cent. of the population belonged to that denomination. An equal per cent. was divided between Congregationalists and Presbyterians, and there were a few Baptists and Quakers. No public school system had been established, but many of the wealthier families employed tutors. A public library was started at Charleston in 1698, but no institution of higher learning had been established.

Society.—Already in South Carolina an aristocratic society was forming which was distinctly different from that of any other mainland colony. When the Barbadians came they brought with them the social viewpoint of the West Indian planter. As soon as the discovery was made that the swampy river bottoms were adapted to rice and indigo, slavery received a great impetus and the Barbadian social system was almost duplicated. In no other colony was such a large part of the population concentrated in a single city. In Charleston lived the merchants, and there the planter built his town house and remained with his family a portion of the year. The gathering of the wealthy classes developed a social atmosphere of gaiety which was in marked contrast to the soberness of Boston or the conservatism of Philadelphia.

READINGS

Andrews, C. M., *Colonial Self-Government*, 288–336; *Colonial Folkways;* Brodhead, J. R., *History of the State of New York*, II; Bruce, P. A., *Economic History of Virginia in the Seventeenth Century;* Burr, G. L., ed., *Narratives of the Witchcraft Cases;* Dexter, E. G., *A History of Education in the United States*, 24–71; Dexter, F. B., "Estimates of Population in the American Colonies," in American Antiquarian Society; *Proceedings*, New Series, V, pt. 1; Eggleston, E., *The Transit of Civilization;* Fiske, J., *Old Virginia and her Neighbors*, II, 174–269; McCrady, E., *South Carolina under the Proprietary Government*, I, 314–363; Mereness, N. D., *Maryland as a Proprietary Province;* Smith, S., *The History of the Colony of Nova Cæsaria, or New Jersey;* Walker, W., *A History of the Congregational Churches in the United States;* Weeden, W. B., *Economic and Social History of New England*, I; Phillips, U. B., *American Negro Slavery*, 67–84, 98–114.

EXPANSION AND INTERNATIONAL CONFLICT

CHAPTER XIII

THE SPANISH ADVANCE IN THE SEVENTEENTH CENTURY

SPAIN AND THE COLONIES IN THE SEVENTEENTH CENTURY

Decline of Spanish power in Europe.—After the reign of Philip II the power of Spain steadily declined. The long period of hostility with the Dutch and the war with Cromwell greatly weakened her power upon the sea. The continental wars sapped her military strength and France superseded her as the first power of Europe. Gradually Spain's continental possessions slipped from her. The first loss was the Protestant Netherlands. Nominally independent from 1609, their complete independence was acknowledged in 1648. By the Treaty of the Pyrenees, Roussillon became French territory, and the Spanish power in the Rhineland and Italy had been practically annulled. In 1640 Portugal threw off the Spanish yoke, and when Philip IV tried to reconquer it (1661–1665), he failed completely. With Portugal, Spain lost Brazil and the Portuguese colonies in the Far East.

Colonial expansion.—Nevertheless, the frontiers of the Spanish colonies slowly expanded, and slowly Spain extended her laws, her language, and her faith over lands and tribes more and more remote from the Mexican capital, the struggle with the natives becoming sterner at each step in advance. In the course of the seventeenth century northern Sinaloa and Sonora were colonized; permanent missionary occupation, after many failures, was effected in Lower California; southern, western, and eastern Chihuahua were settled; the new province of Coahuila was established athwart the Rio Grande, and a new and flourishing missionary district was opened in western Florida. In the course of the century the Spanish colonial frontiers began to clash with those of France and England, on the mainland now as well as in the islands, and there ensued a series of border struggles, all a part of the international conflict for the continent. To restrain the encroaching French and English, Texas was occupied temporarily and Pensacola permanently. The principal setbacks on the borders were the loss of Jamaica to England (1655), the contraction of the Florida frontier through the founding of Virginia and the Carolinas, and the temporary loss of New Mexico through the Pueblo Revolt in 1680. Thus the Spanish frontier line swung round as on a pivot, the gains in the west being partly offset by the losses in the east. Meanwhile the English, French, and Dutch occupied most of the lesser islands of the Caribbean, which had been neglected by Spain. At the same time, Spain's hold on her colonial commerce became more and more precarious through the encroachments of her national enemies.

FRONTIER ADMINISTRATION

The governors.—The old days of the *adelantados*, with unlimited powers, had passed, and the royal arm now reached the farthest outposts. The secular government of the frontier provinces was almost wholly military. A few villas or towns had their elective *cabildos*, or town councils, and a modicum of self government. The official heads of the provinces were the governors, who held office by royal appointment; *ad interim* governors might be appointed by the viceroys. Governors, like other prominent officials, frequently purchased their offices, a practice not confined at that time to Spanish America. The governor was also *capitán general* of his province, and his capital was usually at the principal presidio or garrison. In these capacities he exercised both civil and military authority. Under the governors there were usually lieutenant-governors in the sub-districts, who as a rule commanded the troops of some presidio.

The positions of governor and presidial commander were made attractive largely by the opportunity which they afforded for making money in addition to the fixed salaries. The payment of soldiers was made chiefly in supplies, purchased by the governor and commanders, and charged to the soldiers at enormous profits. Thus the post of governor or captain was almost as much that ot merchant as of soldier. Provincial administration was often corrupt with "graft," as in English and French America. Checks upon the governors were furnished through *visitas* or inspections, and through the *residencia*, or inquiry at the end of the governor's term. As a rule the *residencia* was formal, but sometimes it was a serious matter.

Central control.—All important matters of frontier administration, such as the founding of new colonies, presidios, or missions, or the making of military campaigns, were referred by the governors to the viceroy of Mexico. He in turn customarily sought the advice of the fiscal of the *real audiencia*, and of the *auditor de guerra*. In case these two functionaries disagreed, or in matters of unusual moment, a *junta de guerra y hacienda*, composed of the leading officials of the different branches of the central administration, was called. In all matters of consequence the decisions of the viceroy were made subject to royal approval, but it frequently happened that the act for which approval was asked had already been performed. In ordinary affairs of provincial administration the fiscal really controlled the government, for the viceroy usually despatched business with a laconic "as the fiscal says."

Frontier Autonomy.—The government of New Spain was highly centralized in theory, but the effects of centralization were greatly lessened by distance. Through the right of petition, which was freely exercised, the local leaders in the frontier provinces often exerted a high degree of initiative in government, and, on the other hand, through protest and delay, they frequently defeated royal orders.

THE MISSIONS

The Missionaries on the frontiers.—In extending the sway of Spain, as time went on a constantly larger part was played by the missionaries. During the early days of the conquest the natives had been largely in the hands of the *encomenderos*. But abuses arose and the encomienda system was gradually abolished. Moreover, the wild tribes of the northern frontier, unlike the Mayas and Aztecs, were considered hardly worth exploiting. This left an opening for the missionary, and to him was entrusted not only the work of conversion, but a larger and larger share of responsibility and control. Since they served the State, the missions were largely supported by the royal treasury, which was most liberal when there was some political end to be gained.

The principal missionary orders.—Under these circumstances, in the seventeenth and eighteenth centuries, on the expanding frontiers of Spanish America, missions became well-nigh universal. The work on the northern borders of New Spain was conducted largely by Franciscans, Jesuits, and Dominicans. The northeastern field fell chiefly to the Franciscans, who entered Florida, New Mexico, Nuevo Leon, Coahuila, Nuevo Santander, and Texas. To the northwest went the Jesuits, who, after withdrawing from Florida, worked especially in Sinaloa, Sonora, Chihuahua, Lower California, and Arizona. After the expulsion of the Jesuits the Dominicans and Franciscans took their places.

The missions as civilizing agencies.—The missionaries were a veritable corps of Indian agents, serving both Church and State. Their first duty was to teach the Gospel. In addition they disciplined the savage in the rudiments of civilized life. The central feature of every successful Spanish mission was the Indian pueblo, or village. If he were to be disciplined, the Indian must be kept in a definite spot where discipline could be impressed upon him. The settled Indians, such as the Pueblo Indians of New Mexico, could be instructed in their native towns, but the wandering or scattered tribes must be assembled and established in pueblos, and kept there by force if necessary. To make the Indians self-supporting as soon as possible, and to afford them the means of discipline, the missions were provided with communal lands for gardens, farms, and ranches, and with workshops in which to practice the crafts.

Defence of the frontier.—The missionaries were highly useful likewise as explorers and as diplomatic agents amongst the tribes. As defenders of the frontier they held the allegiance of the neophytes and secured their aid against savages and foreign intruders. Sometimes the mission plants were veritable fortresses.

Missions designedly temporary.—Like the presidios, or garrisons, missions were intended to be temporary. As soon as his pioneer work was finished on one frontier the missionary was expected to move on to another, his place being taken by the secular clergy and the mission lands distributed among the Indians. The result, almost without fail, was a struggle over secularization.

THE JESUITS IN SINALOA AND SONORA

The Jesuit advance up the slope.—The advance up the Pacific coast mainland was led throughout the seventeenth century by the Jesuit missionaries, supported by presidial soldiers and small citizen colonies. In 1591 the Jesuits entered Sinaloa. Beginning in the valley of the Petatlan and Mocorito rivers, their progress was gradual but steady, river by river, tribe by tribe, to the Fuerte, Mayo, Yaqui, and Sonora valleys, till by the middle of the century they had nearly reached the head of the last named stream.

Fathers Tapia and Pérez.—The first missionaries sent were Fathers Gonzalo de Tapia and Martin Pérez, who began their work among the tribes of the Petatlan and Mocorito rivers, near San Felipe, then the northern outpost of Sinaloa. From time to time they were joined by other small bands of missionaries. The natives were generally friendly at first, here as elsewhere, and were assembled in villages, baptized, and taught agriculture and crafts. Father Tapia was murdered in 1594 and was succeeded as rector by Father Pérez. By 1604 there had been 10,000 baptisms, the Jesuits had a school for boys at San Felipe, and Father Velasco had written a grammar in the native tongue. In 1600 regular missionary work was begun in Topia. What was done there is a good example of the way the Spaniards often uprooted native society by trying to improve it. Villages were transplanted at will, the chiefs replaced by alcaldes, and native priests suppressed.

Captain Hurdaide, defender of the Faith.—The year 1600 was marked also by the appointment of Captain Diego Martínez de Hurdaide, as commander of the presidio of San Felipe. By the Jesuits he was regarded as the ideal defender of the Faith, and for a quarter of a century he and his soldiers made way for and protected the missionaries in their northward advance

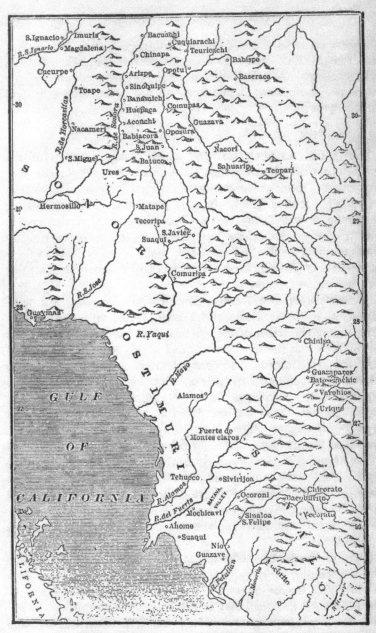

Sinaloa and Sonora in the Seventeenth Century
(From Bancroft, *North Mexican States and Texas*, I, 208)

Missions in the Fuerte valley.—The subjugation of the Suaques and Tehuecos by Hurdaide opened the way for missions in the Fuerte River valley in 1604. Among the founders was Father Pérez de Ribas, later famed as the historian. The initial success of these missions was remarkable, but it was followed by apostasy, revolts, an increase of military forces, and wars of subjugation. This, indeed, was quite the typical succession of events. Apostates fled to the Yaquis, who defeated Hurdaide in three campaigns. Having shown their mettle, in 1610 the Yaquis made peace and asked for missionaries. The Yaqui war was followed by the establishment in 1610 of the new presidio of Montesclaros near the site of the former San Juan. In spite of this new defence, the Tehuecos, led by native priests, revolted. Hurdaide went to the rescue in 1613 with forty soldiers and two thousand allies, restored order, and reëstablished the missions.

In the Mayo and Yaqui valleys.—In the same year Father Méndez and some companions advanced the mission frontier to the Mayo valley, where success was gratifying. Four years later Fathers Pérez and Pérez de Ribas founded missions among the Yaquis, where eight pueblos soon flourished. By 1621 missions had reached the Nevomes and Sahuaripas in the upper Yaqui River valley. A revolt among the Nevomes in 1622 was put down by Hurdaide. The Mayo and Yaqui valleys were now made a separate rectorate.

Several of the pioneers now left the scene. In 1620 Ribas went to Mexico as provincial; in 1625 Father Pérez died, after thirty-five years of service, and in 1626 Hurdaide was succeeded by Captain Pérea. One of the great monuments to the work of these Jesuit pioneers is Father Pérez de Ribas's history, *The Triumph of the Faith*, published in 1644.

In the Sonora valley.—By 1636 Jesuit missions were extended to Ures, in Sonora River valley, a step which was aided by the discovery of mines. Perea was made captain and *justicia mayor* of the Sonora district, called Nueva Andalucia, and established his capital at the mining town of San Juan. By 1650 mission stations had reached Cucurpe and Arispe in the upper Sonora valley. Of the northern district the new rectorate of San Francisco Xavier was now formed. In 1679 thirty missionaries in the Mayo, Yaqui, and Sonora valleys were serving about 40,000 neophytes in seventy-two pueblos.

Spanish settlements.—By the end of the seventeenth century Sinaloa had passed beyond the frontier stage. The population of pure Spanish blood numbered only six hundred families in 1678, but the half-caste Christian population was much larger, there being twelve hundred persons of Spanish or mixed blood at San Felipe alone. In Sonora the people of Spanish or mixed blood numbered about five hundred families. Mining and stock-raising were the principal and by no means inconsiderable industries in both districts.

EFFORTS TO OCCUPY LOWER CALIFORNIA

Pearl fishing and efforts to colonize.—Interest in California did not cease with Vizcaíno's failures. On the contrary, private interest in the pearl fisheries of the Gulf of California continued throughout the seventeenth century, and the government endeavored to utilize it as means of planting colonies. Numerous pearl fishing contracts were granted on condition that the beneficiaries should establish settlements. Other colonizing expeditions were fitted out at royal expense. In nearly every case missionaries were sent with the settlers to help to subdue and teach the Indians.

Iturbi's voyages.—In 1614 Thomas Cardona was granted a monopoly of pearl fishing in both the Caribbean Sea and the Gulf of California. A year later Juan de Iturbi, in Cardona's employ, made a voyage to the head of the Gulf, and like Oñate concluded that California was an island. On his return one of his vessels was captured by the Dutch freebooter Spillberg. In the following year Iturbi made another successful voyage to the Gulf, though he again lost a vessel to freebooters. The pirates in the Gulf in this century were known as the Pichilingues. Iturbi's success inspired numerous unlicensed pearl hunting voyages in the Gulf from the ports of Sinaloa, which were attended by many abuses of the natives. California came now to be commonly regarded as an island.

Later attempts.—In 1633 Francisco de Ortega, another contractor, founded a colony at La Paz, but it was short-lived. Like failures were experienced by Porter y Casante in 1648, by

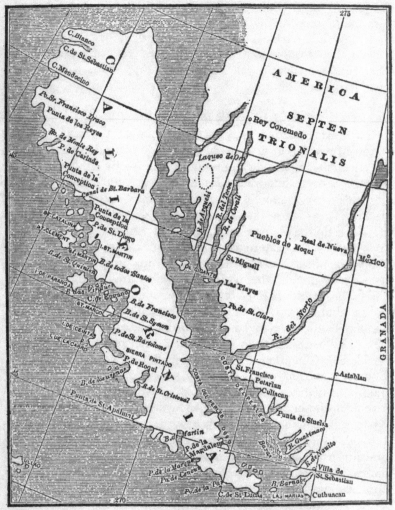

A Dutch Map Illustrating the Insular Theory of California's Geography (1624-1625). (From Bancroft, *North Mexican States and Texas*, I, 169)

Piñadero in 1664 and 1667, and by Lucenilla in 1668. The failures were due to the barrenness of the country and to the fact that colonizing was made secondary to pearl fishing. Somewhat more successful was Admiral Atondo y Antillón, with whom a contract was made in 1679, the superior of the missionaries being the Jesuit Father Kino. For two years (1683–1685) settlements were maintained at La Paz and San Bruno, explorations were made, and Kino achieved some missionary success, but in 1685 Atondo, like his predecessors, abandoned the enterprise. No other serious attempt was made until 1697, when the Jesuits took charge of California.

THE SETTLEMENT OF CHIHUAHUA

New Mexico isolated.—In the central plateau the infant colony of New Mexico, as at first established, had been a detached group of settlements, separated from Nueva Vizcaya by an uninhabited area of five or six hundred miles in breadth. But while the New Mexicans were gradually making their way into the plains of western Texas, missionaries, miners, and settlers were slowly advancing up the plateau into Chihuahua, by way of the Conchos River and by the eastern slope of the Sierra Madre.

Advance of settlement.—The Franciscans, in general, followed the eastern half of the plateau, working among the Conchos tribes; the Jesuits mainly followed the mountain slopes, among the Tarahumares. Advance of settlement was marked by the founding of the town and garrison of Parral, established in 1631–1632. By 1648 missions had been established at San Pablo, Parral, San Gerónimo, San Francisco Borja, Satevó, San Francisco de Conchos, San Pedro, Atotonilco, Mescomaha, and Mapimí. Advance was interrupted by two savage Indian wars, in the decade following 1644, in the course of which most of the missions in Chihuahua were destroyed. As soon as peace was restored, however, both orders reoccupied their abandoned establishments and founded new ones. By 1680 missionaries, miners, and settlers had reached Cusihuiriáchic, Janos, and Casas Grandes, and the last named place had for some time been the seat of an *alcaldía mayor*.

The Diocese of Guadiana.—As the frontier advanced new administrative subdivisions were carved out. The official capital of Nueva Vizcaya was still at Durango, but during the later seventeenth century the governor resided much of the time at Parral, a point near the military frontier. In 1620 the diocese of Guadiana, including Durango, Chihuahua, and New Mexico was formed out of the northern portion of that of Guadalajara.

NEW MEXICO IN THE SEVENTEENTH CENTURY

The missions.—Hopes of finding rich mines and fabulous treasures in New Mexico had failed, and for a long time after Oñate's conquest that province remained chiefly a missionary field, the only Spanish settlement being Santa Fé, founded in 1609. By 1617 eleven churches had been built and 14,000 natives baptized. Four years later the missions were organized into the *custodia* of San Pablo, under the Franciscan province of the Holy Evangel of Mexico, whence came most of the missionaries. The first custodian was Fray Alonso de Benavides, who later became bishop of Goa, in India. Besides Benavides, the best known missionary of this period was Father Gerónimo de Zárate Salmerón, who between 1618 and 1626 labored at Jémez, Cía, Sandía, and Ácoma.

New Mexico in 1630.—In 1630 Benavides made a famous report on New Mexico. The only Spanish settlement was still Santa Fé, where lived two hundred and fifty Spaniards and some seven hundred and fifty half-breeds and Indian servants. The Indians of the province who were not personal servants paid tribute of a yard of cotton cloth and two bushels of maize each year, burdens which they resented and resisted. There were now friars at work in twenty-five missions, which served ninety pueblos comprising 60,000 Indians. At each mission there were schools and workshops where the neophytes were taught reading, writing, singing, instrumental music, and manual arts.

Expeditions to the east.—The subjugation of the pueblos did not exhaust the energies of the conquerors and the friars, and they turned from time to time to exploration. To the east they were interested in Quivira, the "Seven Hills of the Aijados," and the Jumano Indians of the Colorado River. In the pursuit of these objects they heard of the "kingdom of the Texas" farther east. Missionary and trading expeditions were made to the Jumanos in 1629 and 1632. At this time (1630) Benavides proposed opening a direct route from the Gulf coast to New Mexico through the country of the Quiviras and Aijados. In 1634 Alonso de Vaca is said to have led an expedition three hundred leagues eastward to Quivira, apparently on the Arkansas. In 1650 captains Martin and Castillo visited the Jumanos and gathered pearls in the Nueces (probably the Concho) River. Four years later the viceroy, interested in the pearls, sent another expedition, under Guadalajara, to the same place. During the next thirty years small parties of private traders frequently visited

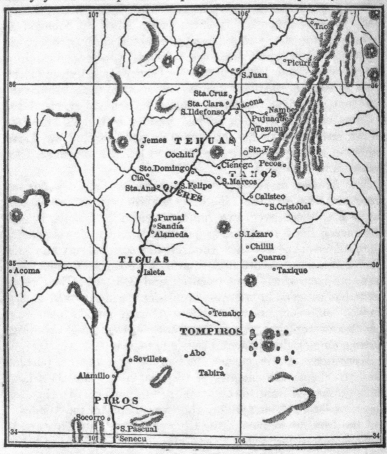

New Mexico in the Seventeenth Century
(From Bancroft, *Arizona and New Mexico*, p. 176)

the Jumanos. In this way western Texas became known to the Spaniards of New Mexico.

New Mexico in 1680.—Meanwhile the Spanish population of the province had slowly increased till in 1680 there were over 2500 settlers in the upper Rio Grande valley, mainly between

Isleta and Taos. The upper settlements were known as those of Río Arriba and the lower as those of Río Abajo. The settlers were engaged principally in farming and cattle ranching.

The beginnings of El Paso.—As a result of the northward advance from Nueva Vizcaya and of a counter movement from New Mexico, the intermediate district of El Paso was now colonized. After several unsuccessful attempts, in 1659 missionaries from New Mexico founded the mission of Guadalupe at the ford (El Paso). Before 1680 Mission San Francisco had been founded twelve leagues below, settlers had drifted in, and the place had an *alcalde mayor*. To these small beginnings there was now suddenly added the entire population of New Mexico.

The Pueblo revolt.—The Pueblo Indians, led by their native priests, had long been restless under the burden of tribute and personal service, and the suppression of their native religion. On August 9, 1680, under the leadership of Popé, a medicine man of San Juan, they revolted in unison, slew four hundred Spaniards, including twenty-one missionaries, and drove the remaining 2200 Spaniards from the Pueblo district. Under Governor Otermín and Lieutenant García the settlers retreated to El Paso. In 1681 Otermín made an attempt to reconquer the Pueblos, but it proved futile and the El Paso settlement was made permanent and attached to New Mexico. To hold the outpost a presidio was established there in 1683.

The La Junta missions and the Mendoza expedition to the Jumanos.—From El Paso missions were extended in 1683 to the La Junta district, as the junction of the Conchos and Rio Grande was called. Within a year seven churches had been built for nine tribes, living on both sides of the Rio Grande. At the same time Juan Dominguez de Mendoza and Fray Nicolás López led an expedition from El Paso to the Jumanos of central Texas, where they were to meet Tejas Indians from the east. On their return Mendoza and López went to Mexico to appeal for a new outpost of settlement among the Jumanos. This would probably have been established had not attention been called to eastern Texas through the activities of the French.

Indian uprisings.—The Pueblo revolt was followed by a general wave of Indian resistance, and the late years of the century were marked by raids all along the northern frontier, from Nuevo León to Sonora, in the course of which mines, missions, haciendas, and towns were destroyed, and travelers and merchant caravans raided. To defend the frontier, in 1685 three new presidios were established at Pasage, El Gallo, and Conchos, and two years later one was erected at Monclova. By 1690 two others were added at Casas Grandes and Janos in Chihuahua and shortly afterward (1695) another at Fronteras in Sonora. In 1690 a revolt in the Tarahumara country destroyed settlements in all directions, and was put down only by the efforts of soldiers from all the presidios from El Gallo to Janos.

Vargas and the reconquest of the Pueblos.—After expelling the Spaniards, the Pueblos, under the lead of Popé, returned to their tribal ways, and destroyed most of the signs of the hated Spanish rule. During the next decade and a half several efforts were made to reconquer the Pueblo region. Otermin was succeeded by Cruzate, and he by Reneros, who was in turn followed by Cruzate. In 1688 Cruzate led an expedition against the Queres. At Cia six hundred apostates were killed in battle and seventy captured and shot, or sold into slavery. In 1691 Diego de Vargas Zapata Luján Ponce de León was made governor especially to reconquer the Pueblos. In 1692 he led an expedition against them. As far as Sandía the towns had already been destroyed. Santa Fé he found fortified and occupied by Tanos, but they yielded without a blow, as did all of the pueblos from Pecos to Moqui. Meanwhile the friars with him baptized over two thousand native children.

A new colony.—Submission having been secured, in 1693 Vargas led a colony of eight hundred soldiers and settlers to reoccupy the pueblo region. But submission had been a hollow formality. The Tanos who held Santa Fé were evicted only after a battle, at the conclusion of which seventy warriors were shot and four hundred women and children enslaved. At the mesa of San Ildefonso, Vargas met the combined resistance of nine towns. A second siege in March, 1694, resulted in a repulse. In the course of the summer the pueblos of Cieneguilla and Jémez were defeated, and abandoned Taos was sacked and burned. A third attack on the mesa of San Ildefonso was successful. Resistance now appeared to be over, the pueblos were rebuilt, captives returned, missions reëstablished, and the Spanish régime restored. A number of the pueblos were consolidated and rebuilt on new sites. In 1695 the new Spanish villa of Santa Cruz de la Cañada was founded with seventy families on the lands of San Cristóbal and San Lázaro.

The conquest completed.—In 1696 a new revolt occurred, in which five missionaries and twenty-one other Spaniards were killed, and Vargas conducted another series of bloody campaigns, with partial success. In the following year he was succeeded by Governor Cubero, who secured the formal submission of the rest of the pueblos. The reconquest was now complete and the Spanish rule secured.

COAHUILA OCCUPIED

The Nuevo León frontier.—While there had been definite progress eastward from New Mexico during the first three-fourths of the seventeenth century, and considerable contact between that province and what is now the western half of Texas, from Nuevo León, on the natural line of advance from Mexico to Texas, progress was slow. For nearly a century the northeastern outpost on the lower Rio Grande frontier was León (Cerralvo), founded in the later sixteenth century. Temporarily a more northern outpost had been established in 1590 at Nuevo Almadén (now Monclova), but it was soon abandoned. Again in 1603 and 1644 the place was temporarily reoccupied, but without permanent success.

Zavala's rule, 1626-1664.—Hostile Indians troubled the border, and the intrusions of English, French, and Dutch colonies into the Lesser Antilles awakened fears for the safety of the western Gulf shores. In 1625 Nuevo León, therefore, was again entrusted to a *conquistador*, when a contract similar to that of Carabajal in 1579 was made with Martín de Zavala. At the same time the Florida missions were extended west to the Apalache district. For thirty-eight years Zavala controlled and governed the frontier with exemplary zeal, subduing Indians, granting *encomiendas*, operating mines, founding new towns, and opening highways to Pánuco and the interior. His most able lieutenant after 1636 was Alonso de León, one of the founders and first citizens of Cadereyta.

Looking northward.—By the middle of the seventeenth century, explorations beyond the Nuevo León frontier had been made on a small scale in all directions. That they were not more extensive was due to Indian troubles and the feebleness of the frontier settlements. To the north the Spaniards were led short distances by a desire to establish communication with Florida, by rumors of a silver deposit called Cerro de la Plata (perhaps the later San Sabá mines), and in pursuit of Indians. No doubt the Franciscan missionaries made many unrecorded visits to the outlying tribes. In 1665 Fernando de Azcué led soldiers from Saltillo and Monterey across the Rio Grande against the Cacaxtle Indians. This is the first expedition to cross the lower Rio Grande from the south of which we have any definite record.

The founding of Coahuila.—Another forward step was now taken with the founding of the new province of Coahuila, a step made necessary by Indian depredations. In 1670 Father Juan Larios, a Franciscan from Guadalajara, began missionary work on the troubled frontier. In 1673–1674, aided by other missionaries and by soldiers from Saltillo, he established two missions between the Sabinas River and the Rio Grande.* In the course of this work Fray Manuel de la Cruz visited tribes north of the Rio Grande. In 1674 Coahuila was made an *alcaldía mayor* of Nueva Vizcaya, with Antonio de Valcárcel as first *alcalde mayor*. A colony was now established at thrice abandoned Almadén and later became Monclova.

The Bosque-Lários expedition across the Rio Grande.—In 1675 Valcárcel sent Fernando del Bosque and Father Larios on a tour among the tribes north of the Rio Grande. In the following year (the very year when Bishop Calderón was in Florida) the bishop of Guadalajara visited Coahuila, and urged its further reduction, with a view to passing beyond, to the settled Tejas Indians, across the Trinity River. In 1687 a presidio was established at Monclova, and Coahuila was made a province, with Alonso de León, the younger, as first governor.

The college of the Holy Cross.—The development of Coahuila and Nuevo León was given an impetus by the coming of a new

* This was just at the time when Joliet and Marquette descended the Mississippi River.

group of Franciscan friars from the recently founded missionary college of Santa Cruz at Querétaro. Among these friars were Fathers Hidalgo, Massanet, and Olivares, all of whom figured prominently in the later development of the frontier. Beside the Querétaro friars, to the westward worked the friars of the Province of Santiago de Xalisco with its seat at Guadalajara.

FIRST ATTEMPTS IN EASTERN TEXAS

Plans to occupy the mouth of the Mississippi.—The aggressive policy of the French, English, and Dutch in the West Indies, the raids of freebooters on the Spanish settlements, the occupation of Carolina by England, and the advance of the French into the Mississippi Valley caused Spain great uneasiness for the northern Gulf Coast. As a defensive measure missions had been extended to the Apalache district at the same time that Nuevo León had been strengthened. In 1673 Joliet and Marquette descended the Mississippi to the Arkansas, and in 1682 La Salle explored it to its mouth. Four years earlier news had reached the Spanish court that Peñalosa, a discredited ex-governor of New Mexico, had proposed to attack New Spain in the name of France. Spanish officials therefore at once planned to occupy the Bay of Espíritu Santo (Mobile Bay, or perhaps the mouth of the Mississippi) and in 1695 Echagaray, an officer at St. Augustine, was ordered to explore it for the purpose.

The search for La Salle's colony.—A few months later the authorities learned with alarm that in November, 1684, La Salle had left France with a colony to occupy the same spot. Immediately several expeditions were sent out by land and sea to learn where La Salle had landed and, if necessary, to occupy the danger point. In 1686 Marcos Delgado explored west by land from Apalache to the neighborhood of Mobile Bay. In 1686–1688 five coastwise expeditions (under Barroto, Rivas, Iriarte, Pez, and Gamara) explored the Gulf between Vera Cruz and Apalache. They discovered the wrecks of La Salle's vessels at Matagorda Bay, and it was concluded that the French expedition had been destroyed.

Eastern Texas occupied.—While these coastwise voyages were being made, Alonso de León was leading expeditions from Monterey and Monclova by land. In 1686 he descended the

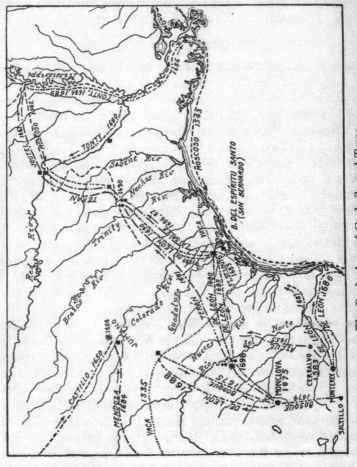

The Beginnings of Coahuila and Texas

Rio Grande to the coast. In 1687 and again in 1688 he crossed the Rio Grande, and in the latter expedition captured a stray Frenchman. Shortly afterward a party of soldiers and Indians from far distant Nueva Vizcaya crossed the Upper Rio Grande to seek out the French intruders. In 1689 De León succeeded in finding the remains of La Salle's settlement near Matagorda Bay, a few weeks after it had been destroyed by Indians. In the following year De León and Father Massanet, one of the Coahuila missionaries, led an expedition across Texas and founded two missions among the Asinai (Tejas) Indians, on Neches River. Texas was now erected into a province and Domingo de Terán made governor.

And then abandoned.—In 1691 Terán led an expedition designed to strengthen the outpost on the Neches, explore and occupy the Cadodacho country (near Texarkana) and, if time permitted, to reëxplore the coast as far as Florida. He reached the Red River but accomplished little else that was new. The Asinai Indians proved hostile, and in 1693 the missionaries withdrew. The Texas project was now abandoned for a time, and attention centered instead on western Florida, which was in danger not only from the French, but also from the English in Carolina, who were visiting the Georgia and Alabama Indians.

THE STRUGGLE IN THE WEST INDIES

Intruding colonies in the West Indies.—In the early years of the conquest Spain had occupied the larger West Indian islands,—Cuba, Española, Porto Rico, and Jamaica—but had neglected the lesser islands. They thus became a field for colonization by Spain's enemies. In the seventeenth century the subjects of Holland, France, and England began to establish settlements in the West Indies, in the heart of the Spanish sea, while England intruded in the northern mainland.

Between 1555 and 1562 the French had made unsuccessful attempts to colonize Brazil, Carolina, and Florida. Between 1585 and 1595 Raleigh had attempted to settle on Roanoke Island and in Guiana. In 1607 Jamestown was founded within Spanish dominions at Chesapeake Bay, and Spain's possessions thus delimited on the north. Between 1609 and 1612 English settlers occupied the Bermudas. Between 1609 and 1619 English, Dutch, and French all established posts in Guiana. In 1621 the Dutch West India Company was incorporated for trade and settlement. Between 1623 and 1625 both English and French settled on St. Kitts (St. Christopher). During the same period Barbados was settled by the English, and Santa Cruz by English and Dutch. By 1632 English settlements had been made at Nevis, Barbuda, Antigua, Providence Island, and Montserrat. By 1634 the Dutch had established trading stations on St. Eustatius, Tobago, and Curaçao, while in 1635 the French West India Company began the settlement of Guadeloupe, Martinique, and other Windward Islands.

Privateers.—Meanwhile French, Dutch, and English privateers swarmed the Spanish waters. Early in the century Dutch ships harassed the coasts of Chile and Peru. In 1628 Peter Heyn with thirty-one vessels pursued the Vera Cruz fleet into Matanzas River, Cuba, and captured most of a cargo worth $15,000,000. "It was an exploit which two generations of English mariners had attempted in vain." After 1633 the Dutch West India Company carried on active war against Spanish and Portuguese colonies. Within two years it sent eighty ships and nine thousand men to American waters, and its agents captured Bahia (Brazil), Pernambuco, and San Juan (Porto Rico).

English privateers in the early seventeenth century did their part. In 1642 Captain William Jackson, with a commission from the Earl of Warwick, made a raid that reminds one of Drake. With eleven hundred men he cruised the coast from Caracas to Honduras, plundering Maracaibo and Trujillo on the way. Landing at Jamaica he captured Santiago and held it for ransom.

Spanish retaliation.—The Spaniards often repaid these aggressions with good interest, and frequent raids were made on the foreign colonies. In 1629 Toledo nearly destroyed the English and French settlements on St. Kitts. Tortuga was several times assaulted. In 1635 a Spanish fleet made a five days' attack on the English colony on Providence Island but was beaten back. In 1641 Pimienta with two thousand men destroyed the forts there and captured seven hundred and seventy colonists. Ten years later a force of eight hundred men from Porto Rico destroyed the English colony on Santa Cruz Island, killing the governor and over one hundred settlers.

The English conquest of Jamaica.—Thus far the English settlements had been made chiefly on unoccupied islands. But in 1654 Cromwell sent an expedition under Venables and Penn to gain Spanish territory by conquest. They failed to take Santo Domingo but succeeded at Jamaica (1655). Twice Spain attempted to recover the island but failed (1657–1658), and in 1670 she acknowledged England's right to all her island possessions.

The Danes and Brandenburgers.—Under their absolute monarch, Frederick III, the Danes organized a West India Company, which in 1671 secured the abandoned island of St. Thomas, using it as a planting colony and a distributing center for Guinea slaves. Porto Rico and the Spanish mainland were the principal Danish markets. Even the Brandenburgers, during the latter days of the Great Elector (1685) secured a thirty-year lease of a part of the Danish island of St. Thomas, with a view to using it as a slave-trading station for supplying the Spanish colonies. But the jealousy of other European powers, especially England, prevented their securing a permanent foothold.

THE STRUGGLE WITH THE ENGLISH ON THE CAROLINA BORDER

The Georgia missions restored.—After the massacre of 1597, the Florida missions seem to have been practically abandoned for a time. But new missionaries, requested by the governor in 1601, reoccupied the abandoned sites, pushed farther up the coast, and entered the interior. The settlement of Virginia by the English was followed by remonstrance and a new wave of missionary activity. In 1612 Fray Luis de Oré came with twenty-three friars and Florida was erected into the province of Santa Elena, with the mother house at Havana. In less than two years the new missionaries had established twenty mission residences among the tribes, especially on the Guale (Georgia) coast. In 1612 was published the first of Father Pareja's numerous books in the Timuquanan language. By 1634 some thirty Franciscans were ministering to 30,000 converts in forty-four missions and mission stations. The success was parallel to that of the Franciscans in New Mexico at the same time.

The Apalachee and the Creek missions.—The simultaneous intrusion of the English, French, and Dutch into the Caribbean

waters was a new threat at Spain's Gulf possessions, and it was
followed by the advance of her outposts into western Florida.
Throughout the sixteenth century the warlike Apalachees had
resisted Spanish authority, but in 1633 successful missionary
work was begun among them by the guardian of the monastery of
St. Augustine and one companion. Within two years they had
baptized five thousand natives. In 1638 the Apalachees revolted,
but they were defeated, and the presidio of San Luís was established among them. This district now became one of the most
important missionary centers of Florida, missions being extended
to the Creeks of western Georgia.

The missions in 1647.—By 1647 St. Augustine was headquarters for fifty Franciscans, who worked among the neighboring tribes. Northward a line of ten missions extended up the
Georgia coast to Chatuache, near the Savannah River. Toward
the western interior, within a radius of one hundred and fifty
miles there were ten more, and toward the south four. In the
Apalachee district there were eight in eight large towns, with
three more on the way to St. Augustine. At these thirty-five
missions 26,000 converted Indians were served.

The Apalachee revolt.—Just now, however, the prosperous
Apalachee missions suffered a severe blow. The chiefs, refusing
to render personal service and tribute, headed a rebellion in
which several Spaniards were slain. The governor led a campaign against them, several battles were fought, and a number
of chiefs hanged. The Indians were subdued, but they were so
embittered that the Franciscans abandoned the missions.

The English in the Carolinas.—In 1653 English settlers from
Virginia began to establish themselves in North Carolina, and in
1670 the English settlement of South Carolina was begun near
Charleston. This intrusion into the old Spanish province of
Santa Elena was viewed with alarm by Spain, and, as always in
the border Spanish colonies, the foreign danger was followed by
renewed missionary activity on the threatened frontiers. Missionary work received an impetus in 1674 by the visitation of
Bishop Calderón, of Cuba, who spent eight months in a tour of
Florida. In that year and the next, five new missions were
founded, and in 1676 Father Moral took to Florida twenty-four
additional missionaries. Six or more missions were now in opera-

tion on the northern Georgia coast between Jekyl Island and the Savannah River, besides those farther south.

English incursions and the Yamassee revolt.—Hostilities with the English on the border began at once. In 1680 a force of three hundred Indians and Englishmen invaded Santa Catalina Island and expelled the garrison and mission Indians. Governor Marquez Cabrera sent soldiers to build a fort, and asked the king for Canary Island families to hold the country. The families were ordered sent (1681), but plans were changed and the Indians of the northernmost missions were moved southward. The Yamassees refused to move, joined the English, and aided them in a raid on Mission Santa Catalina (1685). In the following year Spaniards sent by Governor Marquez retaliated by sacking Carolina plantations and carrying off negro slaves. Another expedition of the same year landed at Edisto Island, burned the country residence of Governor Morton, and destroyed Stuart Town (Port Royal).

The English among the Creeks.—The English now threatened the Spaniards on another frontier. Fur traders from South Carolina had pushed south and west across Georgia and were becoming active among the Creeks of western Georgia and eastern Alabama. In 1685 Governor Marquez sent Lieutenant Matheos, commander at Apalachee, with twenty soldiers and four hundred allies to capture traders operating at Kawita, Kasihta, and Kulumi, Creek towns on the Chatahootchee and Talapoosa Rivers. The expedition failed but it was repeated, and Marquez called on the home government for help.

Plans to occupy Pensacola.—It was just at this time that La Salle formed his establishment in Texas. The combined danger from the English and the French now made it necessary to protect the northern Gulf coast. La Salle's intrusion was followed by the temporary Spanish occupation of eastern Texas in 1690, already described. At the same time (1689) the viceroy sent Andrés de Pez to Spain to urge the occupation of Pensacola Bay (Santa María de Galve). The council approved the plan and authorized the withdrawal from Texas. In 1693 Pez explored Pensacola and Mobile bays with a view to settlement. Thus, in a sense, the defence of eastern Texas was given up for the founding of Pensacola. A new French intrusion was necessary, however, to bring about the permanent occupation of either Texas or Pensacola.

READINGS

Bancroft, H. H., *Arizona and New Mexico*, 146–224; Bolton, H. E., *Spanish Exploration in the Southwest*, 279–340; "The Spanish Occupation of Texas, 1519–1690," in *Southwestern Historical Quarterly*, XVI, 1–26; Cavo, Andres, *Tres Siglos de Mexico;* Chapman, C. E., *The Founding of Spanish California*, 1–44; Clark, R. C., *The Beginnings of Texas;* Coroléu, José, *America, Historia du Colonización;* Davis, W. H. H., *Spanish Conquest in New Mexico*, 276–407; Dunn, W. E., *Spanish and French Rivalry in the Gulf Region*, 5–215; Frejes, Fr. F., *Conquista de Los Estados;* Garrison, G. P., *Texas*, 10–19; Gonzales, J. E., *Colección de Noticias; Historia de Nuevo León;* Hackett, C. W., "The Pueblo Revolt of 1680," in Texas State Historical Association, *Quarterly*, XV, 93–143; Hughes, Anne, *Beginnings of Spanish Settlement in the El Paso District;* Leon, A., *Historia de Nuevo León;* Ortega, Fr. Joseph, *Apostólicos Afanes;* Portillo, Esteban, *Apuntes para la Historia de Coahuila y Texas;* Prince, L. B., *Historical Sketches of New Mexico*, 176–220; Twitchell, R. E., *Leading Facts of New Mexico History*, I, 333–413; Villagrá, Gaspar de, *Historia de Nuevo Mexico;* Wright, I. A., *The Early History of Cuba*, ch. 17.

CHAPTER XIV

THE WARS OF THE ENGLISH AND SPANISH SUCCESSIONS

The impending conflict.—Before the close of the Stuart period, it was evident that a great international struggle was at hand. Louis XIV of France aspired to overshadow England, Austria, and Spain. The dependence of the later Stuarts upon Louis temporarily delayed the outbreak of hostilities, but when James II was driven from the English throne the contest broke forth and continued intermittently until France was humbled and England had become the foremost commercial and colonial power.

THE PRELIMINARY STRUGGLE FOR THE NORTHERN FUR COUNTRY

Sphere of French influence.—When Frontenac returned to France in 1682, the French were predominant in Acadia, in the St. Lawrence Valley, in the region of the Great Lakes, and in the Illinois country, and were extending their power into the lower valley of the Mississippi. In the West Indies they had secured a foothold. The missionary and the fur-trader had been the instruments of interior expansion, the Indian the source of wealth. To keep control of the natives and to win new tribes to church and trade was the settled policy of France. The Abenaki of Maine were between Acadia and Massachusetts and were friends of the French. To the south of Lake Ontario were the Iroquois, the friends of the English. In the upper lake region the various Algonquin tribes had long been subservient to the French. Their furs were brought to Three Rivers, Montreal, or Quebec, or were traded to the *coureurs de bois*.

The English policy.—To wrest the fur monopoly of the north from the French was one of the mainsprings of Stuart policy. The establishment of the Hudson's Bay Company posts, an alliance with the Iroquois, and the attempt to gain control of the Huron region, thus cutting off the French from the upper lakes

and the Illinois country, were the means adopted to carry out
the policy. To defeat it was the problem of the governors of
New France. A similar conflict was in process in the southwest.

La Barre and the Iroquois, 1684.—The successor of Frontenac
was La Barre. Upon arrival he found conditions deplorable. A
disastrous fire had devastated Quebec and the Iroquois were on
the warpath against the Illinois, Hurons, Ottawas, and other
"children of the French." La Barre at first temporized with the
Iroquois, but their depredations continued, fostered by Dongan,
the governor of New York. La Barre finally realized that his
policy was alienating the interior tribes and he determined upon
war. He gathered a force of Indians and French and entered the
Iroquois country where he was met by a deputation of Iroquois
chiefs. After an extended conference, instead of a war of extermination, peace was ignominiously agreed upon, in spite of
the fact that the Iroquois refused to desist from war on the
Illinois. In the meantime Duluth and other leaders had
brought five hundred warriors to Niagara, who arrived at the
rendezvous only to learn that peace had been made. With sullen
hatred in their hearts, the disappointed warriors returned to
their haunts. French influence in the region of the lakes had
suffered a severe blow.

Denonville and Dongan.—The king had determined upon the
recall of La Barre, and Denonville, "a pious colonel of dragoons,"
assumed the governorship. He at once entered into a correspondence with Dongan. Both governors lacked resources to
carry out an effective campaign; both resorted to Jesuit influence
to obtain control of the Iroquois; and both determined to build
a fort at Niagara. Denonville, in addition, planned to erect
forts at Toronto, on Lake Erie, and at Detroit, and Duluth
actually erected a stockade at the lower end of Lake Huron.
Dongan in 1685 sent eleven canoes to the upper lakes where a
successful trade was carried on. The following year a larger
flotilla was despatched, followed by an expedition which was
intended to make a treaty of trade and alliance with the lake
Indians.

French attack on the Iroquois.—Dongan, however, received
despatches from England which led him to believe that his
policy might not meet with the entire approval of his govern-

ment. He accordingly wrote a conciliatory letter to Denonville, accompanied by a present of oranges. Denonville replied, "Monsieur, I thank you for your oranges. It is a great pity that they were all rotten." His sarcasm was the more effective when it is known that eight hundred French regulars were in the colony, and that as many more were on the way. In the spring of 1687 Denonville was prepared to strike. Leaving eight hundred regulars to protect the settlements, he gathered two thousand men at Ft. Frontenac. In addition Tonty and other post commanders had raised a considerable force in the interior which captured the canoes sent by Dongan. The combined forces of French and Indians, totaling nearly three thousand, penetrated the country of the Senecas, defeated them, and burned their villages. But instead of completing the conquest of the Iroquois country, Denonville led his forces to Niagara where a fort was erected, and then returned to Montreal. The expedition served merely to set the Iroquois hive buzzing, and to increase the influence of the English.

Iroquois reprisals.—The Iroquois soon began a war of reprisal, raid after raid being made on the French settlements. Denonville's courage seemed to be paralyzed. He sent an agent to Albany to make an arrangement with Dongan, who insisted that Forts Niagara and Frontenac be abandoned. Denonville hesitated until the summer of 1688, when Big Mouth, an Onondaga chief, appeared at Montreal. An understanding was reached by which the governor agreed to abandon Niagara and restore captives, no provision being made for protection of the interior tribes. A Huron chief, the Rat, hearing of the treaty, determined that the war should continue. Ascertaining that a party of Onondagas were on their way to the French settlements to complete the peace arrangements, the Rat and his followers ambushed them. The attack had the desired effect, the Iroquois concluding that the treaty was a ruse. An ominous peace prevailed until the French believed that danger had passed. Suddenly in the summer of 1689 a force of fourteen hundred Iroquois attacked the settlements. Instead of retaliating, the frightened governor ordered the abandonment of Ft. Frontenac. This was his last important act, for he was recalled and Count Frontenac was sent to save the colony."

The Hudson Bay posts.—While these events had been taking place, in the far north another conflict was waged. No attempt

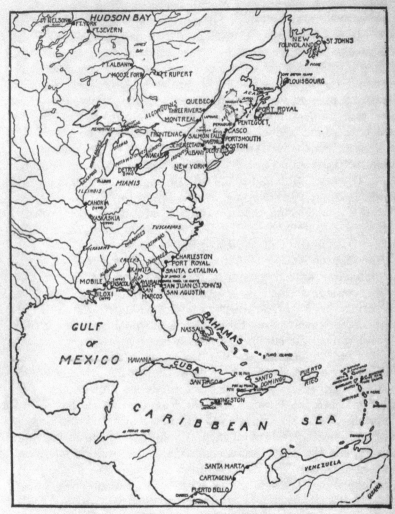

The Intercolonial Wars

was made to impede the English on Hudson Bay until 1682, when Radisson and Groseilliers, now turned French, with two vessels took possession of the English post at the mouth of the

Nelson River, but the Frenchmen soon transferred their allegiance once more to the English. La Barre was instructed to check English encroachments and to propose that neither nation establish new posts. In 1685 a Canadian company was formed to trade in the north. Denonville considered this an excuse for attacking the English. In 1686 a hundred men commanded by De Troyes, one of his lieutenants being Iberville, the future founder of Louisiana, were sent overland to make the attack. Fort Hayes, Ft. Rupert, and Ft. Albany were captured, Fort Nelson being the only post left in English hands. French ascendency for the time being was established on Hudson Bay.

THE WAR OF THE ENGLISH SUCCESSION

William's accession precipitates war.—In spite of these conditions in America, England and France at home had been at peace. It was of more importance to Louis XIV to support a Catholic king of England than to wage open war for the control of the Indian country. But with the overthrow of James II the political situation in Europe was completely changed. William of Orange ascended the throne of England, and Holland, England, several of the German states, Austria, and Spain were welded into a great coalition. Louis XIV championed the Stuart cause and the War of the English Succession was on. In America the struggle is known as King William's War; in Europe it is usually referred to as the War of the Palatinate. In the course of it the Caribbean Sea was the scene of constant conflict. The hostile zones on the mainland had been established in the struggle for the fur trade—the lands of the Abenaki, Iroquois, and upper lake tribes, and the Hudson Bay country.

THE WAR IN THE CARIBBEAN

Four years of war.—In 1689 the French inhabitants of St. Christopher rose against the English inhabitants and expelled them from the island. The French also broke up a Dutch station in Guiana. Early in 1690 England sent Commodore Wright to the West Indies. Convoying a large fleet, his squadron reached Barbados on May 11. Being reinforced by Barbadian troops he reoccupied St. Christopher, the reduction being completed July 16. A few days later St. Eustatius surrendered to the English. In 1690 Trinidad was also attacked by the French. In March, 1691, Wright attacked Guadeloupe but failed to take it or to capture the French squadron under M. Ducasse. Commodore Ralph Wrenn took command of the English fleet in January, 1692, and the following month fought an indecisive battle near Jamaica with a superior French force. In that year a great earthquake destroyed Port Royal, the English capital of Jamaica. The refugees founded Kingston which eventually superseded Port Royal as the seat of government.

Martinique, Santo Domingo, and Jamaica.—In 1693 nine vessels reinforced the West Indian fleet and the combined forces, backed by Barbadian troops, attacked Martinique, but failed to take it. In September of the following year a squadron attacked Léogane, a French town in Santo Domingo, but was repulsed. A French expedition from Santo Domingo also desolated the southeastern coast of Jamaica but at Carlisle Bay was beaten off by the colonial militia. In March, 1695, an English and Spanish fleet attacked the French settlements in Santo Domingo and succeeded in forcing the abandonment of Cape François and Port de Paix.

Cartagena and Petit Gouave.—In April, 1697, a great English fleet under Vice-Admiral John Neville rendezvoused at Barbados to forestall a rumored enterprise of the enemy. M. de Pointis had been sent with large reinforcements to assist M. Ducasse. The combined French fleet attacked Cartagena, took much booty, and eluded Neville. The English commander visited Cartagena, which he found had again been despoiled by buccaneers. He then despatched Captain Mees with nine vessels to burn Petit Gouave, a mission which he accomplished.

THE WAR ON THE CANADIAN FRONTIERS

The Maine frontier.—Andros had sent an expedition against the Abenaki and had fortified the frontier, his most northern fort being at Pemaquid, but with his fall the garrison had been reduced. During the summer of 1689 the Indians destroyed Pemaquid and killed most of the settlers in that region. Casco (Portland) was then attacked but was relieved by a counter expedition.

The French attack.—In August Frontenac was sent to assume the governorship of Canada. In New France he found despair and desolation. He decided to send out three expeditions, one from Montreal into the upper Hudson Valley, the others from Three Rivers and Quebec to raid the New England frontier. The three expeditions started about February 1, 1690. The Montreal party surprised Schenectady, where sixty persons were massacred. A party from Albany started in pursuit and succeeded in killing about twenty of the retreating French and Indians. The Three Rivers expedition attacked Salmon Falls, where thirty persons were killed and about fifty made prisoners. A relief party from Portsmouth caught up with the raiders at Wooster River, but after a spirited fight the French and Indians escaped. Being reinforced by Indians they joined the party from Quebec. The united force of four or five hundred men in May attacked the fort and blockhouses on Casco Bay, killing or capturing the garrison, massacring or carrying into captivity most of the inhabitants, and burning the settlements.

Frontenac's Indian policy.—Frontenac also sent an expedition of one hundred men to Michilimackinac to keep control of the upper lake Indians. On the way an Iroquois war party was defeated at Sand Point on the Ottawa River. The French victory and news of the successful raids on the English frontier had far-reaching effects, for they kept the Hurons and Ottawas in subjection.

The English defence.—The attack upon the English colonies was well-timed, for confusion prevailed in New England and New York. Andros had been overthrown and Leisler's rebellion was in full swing. Little help could be expected from England, for James II, with French and Irish aid, was battling to regain his throne. In May, 1690, the New England colonies sent delegates to a congress at New York to determine on a military policy. A two-fold attack was planned; a land expedition against Montreal and a naval expedition against Quebec.

The Montreal fiasco.—The expedition against Montreal was placed under Fitz-John Winthrop of Connecticut, who led his men as far as the southern end of Lake Champlain. Here smallpox broke out, disagreements with the Indians ensued, and provisions ran short. Winthrop soon discovered that a descent on

Montreal was impossible, and he ingloriously led most of his men back to Albany. Captain John Schuyler, however, with a small detachment proceeded northward and raided the village of Laprairie near Montreal.

The capture of Port Royal.—While New England delegates were at New York a preliminary expedition was sent against Acadia. Sir William Phips, a New Englander who had achieved great renown and wealth by locating a Spanish treasure ship which had been wrecked off the Bahamas, was placed in command of seven vessels. On May 11, 1690, the fleet appeared before Port Royal, which surrendered without a shot being fired. One of the vessels under Captain Alden captured a French post on the Penobscot and seized several settlements on the southern shore of Nova Scotia.

The expedition against Quebec.—In the meantime Massachusetts was preparing for her great attempt on Quebec. Thirty vessels were gathered, but the fleet was short of ammunition, due to the fact that the French had gained temporary control of the sea by defeating the English and Dutch fleets at Beachy Head. The fleet commanded by Phips sailed from Boston on August 9, 1690, but it was not until October 16 that it came in sight of Quebec. The slow progress prevented a surprise and gave Frontenac time to complete his defences. When Phips demanded that Quebec surrender, he received a haughty refusal. Phips then attempted to capture the town, but the plan was poorly executed, ammunition ran short, and reinforcements poured into the city so rapidly that the defenders soon outnumbered the English. A council of war was held, and it was decided to abandon the undertaking. A week of intermittent fighting had brought nothing but failure, which was made the more trying by the loss of several vessels on the return voyage.

Frontenac's policy in 1691.—After the attack on Quebec, the war developed into a desultory frontier conflict in which the French were usually on the offensive. The Iroquois continued to raid the French settlements, but they were soon severely chastised, when forty or fifty warriors were surrounded at Repentigny, near Montreal, and killed or captured. This event and the timely arrival of several French vessels impressed an Ottawa deputation which had come to Quebec, and the French power among the interior tribes was greatly strengthened.

Schuyler's expedition.—The English influence among the Iroquois was waning; to reassert it an expedition under Peter Schuyler was sent from Albany. It traversed Lake Champlain and the Richelieu and proceeded toward Laprairie de la Madeleine where it was attacked by a superior force. After stubborn fighting, Schuyler made an orderly retreat.

Acadia and the Abenaki.—In Acadia Phips had made the blunder of leaving no garrison; the French accordingly reoccupied it. Deeming the location of Port Royal too exposed, M. de Villebon, the lieutenant-governor of Acadia, moved his headquarters to Naxouat on the St. John's River, from which vantage point he was able to direct attacks on New England. In February, 1692, a band of Abenaki wiped out the settlement at York, and later unsuccessfully attacked Wells. Minor raids were also made on the towns of central Massachusetts. To protect the frontier Phips ordered the rebuilding of Fort Pemaquid and the erection of a fort at the falls of the Saco. Scarcely were they completed, when Iberville, in command of two French vessels, attacked Pemaquid but failed to capture it.

The Iroquois frontier.—The Iroquois continued to infest the region between the St. Lawrence and Ottawa rivers, but during 1692 and 1693 they were severely punished, and ceased to be an important factor in the war. Frontenac then determined to reopen the fur trade. He accordingly sent a detachment to Michilimackinac asking that furs be sent to Montreal. In August, 1693, a flotilla of two hundred canoes arrived and shortly afterward Tonty, with a large body of *coureurs de bois* came to discuss matters. Tonty soon returned to the Illinois country well equipped to strengthen his hold on the natives. The fortifications at Quebec were also remodeled. In 1695 Fort Frontenac was reëstablished and the following year an expedition of over two thousand men was sent against the Onondagas and Oneidas. They abandoned their villages and the French destroyed their crops. Though no battle was fought the expedition served its end, for the Iroquois were duly impressed by the power of the French.

The New England frontier.—In 1693 an English fleet from the West Indies arrived at Boston and the idea of an expedition against Quebec was revived, but there was so much sickness among the men that the plan was abandoned. During 1693 and 1694 both English and French sought to control the Abenaki, but in spite of a treaty made by Phips, the French succeeded in holding their allies. In July, 1694, the Indians attacked Durham, massacring over a hundred of the inhabitants, and a few days later killed about forty people at Groton. Two years later Iberville again appeared before Pemaquid and this time succeeded in capturing it. He then sailed to Newfoundland, captured and burned St. Johns, and plundered the settlements on the coast. The English retaliated by burning the French settlement at Beaubassin but were repulsed at Naxouat. In March, 1697, Haverhill was raided by the Indians, and in February, 1698, after the treaty of peace, they attacked Andover. In the last year of the war an attack upon Boston and New York by land and sea was determined upon and a fleet set sail from France, but the treaty of peace ended hostilities.

ACTIVITIES ON HUDSON BAY; PEACE

Operations of Iberville.—When the war opened, the French were in control of the posts about James Bay, while Fort Nelson, commanding the great interior water-ways, was in the hands of the Hudson's Bay Company. In 1689 Fort Albany was captured by the English. The following year Iberville recaptured it, but in 1692 it again passed out of French hands. In 1694 the French government determined to assist the Compagnie du Nord; Iberville, being sent to the bay with two frigates, captured Fort Nelson. Two years later it was retaken by the English. In 1697 Iberville penetrated the bay, this time with five vessels. Becoming separated from the rest of the fleet, Iberville encountered three armed vessels of the Hudson's Bay Company. After a thrilling naval battle the English were worsted, and the French once more took possession of Fort Nelson. At the end of the war the only important post left in English hands was Fort Albany.

The Peace of Ryswick.—In 1697 the war was brought to an end by the peace of Ryswick, by which Louis XIV acknowl-

edged William III as king of England. The results of the fighting
in America were ignored, the powers agreeing to restore to each
other all places taken in the war. The ownership of the Abenaki
and Iroquois lands, and of the Hudson Bay country was left
unsettled.

THE WAR OF THE SPANISH SUCCESSION

French expansion.—The peace of Ryswick was only a truce.
France took advantage of the peace to begin to establish her
power in the Mississippi Valley and to strengthen her hold upon
the Northwest. In 1699 Biloxi was founded on the Gulf and in
succeeding years France brought under control most of the
tribes of the lower Mississippi Valley. In 1701 the French
occupied Detroit to cut off the English from one of the routes
to the fur country, and strengthened their hold on the Illinois
country.*

The Spanish Succession.—Upon the death of Philip IV in
1665 the incompetent Charles II came to the throne of Spain.
Court intrigues stimulated by France and Austria, and utter
lack of statesmanship at a time when France was reaching out
in every direction, brought Spain to the lowest point in her
history. Fearing that she would pass under French control,
thereby destroying the balance of power in Europe, William III
of England sought to check French power by the so-called Second
Treaty of Partition, by which the Austrian Archduke Charles
was to inherit the crown of Spain upon the death of Charles II,
Spanish possessions in Italy were to go to the Dauphin of France,
and Spanish and Austrian possessions were never to be united.
To this arrangement France, Austria, and England agreed, but
the treaty proved to be but a scrap of paper. In 1700 Charles
II died and his will designated Philip of Anjou, a grandson of
Louis XIV, as his heir.

England determines upon war.—War was not at once declared, for the English people were slow to recognize the danger.
But when French troops occupied the border fortresses in the
Spanish Netherlands, when French edicts excluded British manufactures, when the English and Dutch trade, especially the slave

* For details see Chapter XV.

trade, was hampered in the Spanish colonies, and when Louis XIV acknowledged the son of James II as king of England, English statesmen were convinced that war was necessary. When Anne ascended the throne in 1702, war was a foregone conclusion.

War zones in America.—The war areas were even more extensive in America than in the War of the English Succession. In the South, the West Indies, and the Carolina, Florida, and Louisiana frontiers, and in the North, the New England border, Acadia, Newfoundland, and Hudson Bay were the scenes of conflict.

THE WAR IN THE WEST INDIES

An indecisive struggle.—When William III became convinced that the war was inevitable, he proposed to strike at Spanish commerce. In furtherance of this policy a squadron was sent in 1701 to the West Indies under Vice-Admiral John Benbow. In July, 1702, Benbow destroyed or captured several vessels near Port-au-Prince, and supported by troops under Major-General Hamilton, he occupied St. Christopher. The fleet in August encountered that of Ducasse off Santa Marta to the northeast of Cartagena and in a running fight which lasted several days the English were worsted. In 1703 General Codrington attacked Guadeloupe but a French reinforcement forced the English to retire. The same year a combined French and Spanish force drove the English inhabitants from New Providence and destroyed Fort Nassau, but it was soon reoccupied by the English Vice-Admiral John Graydon who had been placed in command of the West Indian fleet. Before his arrival several privateers had been destroyed near the island of Santo Domingo and descents had been made on St. Christopher and Guadeloupe. Graydon accomplished nothing and soon sailed to Newfoundland, where his operations were also fruitless.

1705–1708.—During 1705 several prizes were taken and in 1706 the French made a descent on St. Christopher. Their attack on the fort failed, but they burned and plundered several plantations. Hearing that an English fleet was expected, the French repaired to Nevis, which they occupied. The English fleet under Commodore Kerr attacked Petit Gouave but failed to capture it. In 1708 Commodore Charles Wager won an important engagement when he attacked a Spanish fleet near Cartagena. New Providence was a second time attacked by the French and Spanish, which led to the English abandonment of the island.

1711–1712.—In 1710 the Spaniards attacked the salt rakers on Turk's Island but were driven off. In 1711 Commodore James Littleton attempted to find the French fleet, which he located in the harbor of Cartagena. Finding it too strong to attack, he loafed in the neighborhood, picking up an occasional prize. Ducasse, who was convoying a fleet of Spanish galleons, succeeded in getting them out of the harbor without being observed and got them safely to Havana. A French squadron which made an attempt against Antigua was driven into St. Pierre by the English fleet, and a similar expedition against Montserrat was foiled. The following year the French nearly ruined Berbice, a Dutch settlement in Guiana.

THE WAR ON THE FLORIDA BORDER

The southern border.—On the mainland the South Carolina settlements formed the southern English frontier. The Spaniards occupied St. Augustine, contiguous territory up the Georgia coast, Pensacola, and intermediate points. To the west on the Gulf coast were the recently established French settlements. In the interior lived the Apalachees, Creeks, Cherokees, Choctaws, and Chickasaws. To control the trade of the Indians and use them as allies was the policy of English, Spanish, and French alike. The first blow fell on the Apalachee. In 1702 a force of Apalachicolas, allies of the English, destroyed the mission of Santa Fé in the Apalachee district, and a Spanish force was met at the Flint River by Englishmen and Creek allies, and driven back.

Siege of St. Augustine.—The next attack of the English was directed against St. Augustine. Hearing of their plans, Governor Zuñiga sent to Havana for reinforcements, abandoned the town of St. Augustine, and provisioned the castle. The Carolina force of about twelve hundred militia and Indians rendezvoused at Port Royal in September, 1702. Colonel Robert Daniel, conducting the land forces, destroyed the mission settlements on St. Mark's Island, captured the villages of St. Johns and St.

Marys, and plundered St. Augustine. Governor Moore conducted the fleet, and the combined forces besieged the castle. Governor Zuñiga bravely withstood the siege for fifty days, and when Spanish vessels arrived, Moore destroyed his ships, burned St. Augustine, and retreated to Carolina.

Destruction of the Apalachee Missions.—Moore was superseded as governor by Sir Nathaniel Johnson, who immediately strengthened the fortifications at and near Charleston. Moore, desiring to build up his waning reputation, persuaded Johnson to send him against the Apalachee. Setting out with a force of fifty Carolinians and a thousand Creek allies, in January, 1704, he captured the Apalachee town of Ayubale, burned the mission, and then defeated a force of Spaniards and Apalachee. The Indian villages were next destroyed; of thirteen Apalachee towns. each with its mission, only one was spared. When Moore withdrew he carried off fourteen hundred Apalachee prisoners and slaves.

Spanish expedition against Charleston.—In 1706 the French and Spaniards at Havana organized an expedition to attack Carolina. In August a frigate and four sloops, after taking on men and supplies at St. Augustine, sailed to Charleston and demanded its surrender. A small landing party was repulsed; six Carolina vessels sallied out, and after an engagement the enemy withdrew.

Indian policy of the French.—To use the Indian allies to prevent the spread of English settlement was a fundamental of French policy. Iberville, the founder of Louisiana, planned to obtain control of the great interior rivers by establishing forts, and to weld the Indians into an alliance with the French by treaties and by trade. He even contemplated moving some of the tribes to points of greater commercial vantage. He also believed that he could obtain the aid of several thousand warriors in attacking Maryland, Virginia, and Carolina. Realizing the danger, the English traders were active among the tribes. In 1708, probably at the instigation of the English, the Cherokees, Arikas, Catawbas, and Alabamas formed an alliance. Four thousand warriors descended on the French settlements, but lack of leadership destroyed the effectiveness of the attack and but little damage was done.

The Tuscarora War.—In 1711 the Tuscaroras, a North Carolina tribe, went on the warpath and massacred about two hundred settlers. Virginia and South Carolina sent aid, and in 1712 the Indians were defeated. The Tuscaroras continued their depredations and in 1713 they were almost annihilated. The remnant made their way to New York and were incorporated with the Iroquois as a sixth nation.

THE WAR ON THE CANADIAN BORDER

Newfoundland and the New England frontier.—To deprive the French of the profitable Newfoundland fisheries was the first endeavor of England in the north. Captain John Leake arrived at St. Johns in August, 1702. He cruised off Placentia Bay, making several small prizes and destroying fishing craft. Before the end of October he had captured twenty-nine sail, burned two vessels, and destroyed St. Peter's Fort. The New England frontier was harried by the French and Abenaki. In 1699 Massachusetts had made a treaty at Casco Bay with the Maine Indians, but the Jesuits soon brought them back to French allegiance. In 1703 a second peace treaty was made with them, but within two months they were on the warpath, almost wiping out the Maine settlements. In 1704 the French and Indians surprised Deerfield in the Connecticut Valley, killing about fifty and carrying off more than one hundred captives. Almost every frontier settlement was attacked. Even Reading, Sudbury, and Haverhill, within a short distance of Boston, were raided. To add to the distress French privateers did serious damage to commerce and fisheries.

Acadia.—The New Englanders retaliated with small counter raids, but succeeded in inflicting little damage. It was finally determined to strike at Acadia. An expedition was placed under Benjamin Church, a veteran of King Philip's War. French settlements on the Bay of Fundy were ravaged, but he failed to attack Port Royal. In 1707 an expedition, recruited by Massachusetts, New Hampshire, and Rhode Island, was again sent against Port Royal, but the stubborn defense discouraged the attacking force and the siege was abandoned. English vessels under Captain John Underwood raided the Newfoundland coast, destroying many settlements and fishing craft.

Plan to conquer Canada.—The conquest of Canada was urged by many of the colonial leaders, the most active of whom was Colonel Samuel Vetch, a Scotchman who had formerly seen service in the English army. In 1709 his plan was endorsed by the British government, and preparations were made to send a large force against Quebec by sea and a land expedition against Montreal. But after great efforts had been made by the New England colonies and New York, the British regulars were diverted to Portugal, and the conquest of Canada had to be abandoned.

Conquest of Acadia.—The following year a force of four thousand colonials, commanded by Francis Nicholson, aided by British men-of-war and a regiment of marines, attacked and captured Port Royal. Acadia became the British province of Nova Scotia, and the name of its capital was changed to Annapolis Royal. The following year the English again raided the French fishing stations in Newfoundland.

Failure of Walker's expedition.—In 1710 a Tory ministry came into power, its chief members being the Earl of Oxford and Viscount Bolingbroke. They were opposed to carrying on the war in Europe, believing that England's best policy lay in colonial undertakings. The conquest of Canada became the great object. As before, the attack was to be by land and sea. Under Nicholson the land force, composed mainly of colonials and eight hundred Iroquois, prepared to attack Montreal. The expedition against Quebec was entrusted to Admiral Sir Hovenden Walker and General Sir John Hill, a court favorite. Seven of Marlborough's best regiments, veterans of Oudenarde and Ramillies, were placed on transports which were convoyed by a large fleet of war vessels. The great force gathered at Boston, where it was reinforced by fifteen hundred colonials. In August, 1711, the fleet entered the St. Lawrence, but there it met disaster. Sailing too close to the northern shore, ten vessels were wrecked on the reefs and shoals of the Egg Islands. Stunned by the calamity, the faint-hearted commander gave up the enterprise. News of the disaster reached Nicholson at Lake Champlain. His force was not strong enough to accomplish the conquest alone, and the attack on Montreal was abandoned.

THE HUDSON BAY COUNTRY

The Hudson's Bay Company had been sadly crippled at the end of the War of the English Succession. Its shares fell in value and most of the original owners sold their holdings. The only post which the company held was Fort Albany, and in 1704 this was unsuccessfully attacked by a party of French and Indians. The same year an English frigate captured the principal ship of the Compagnie du Nord, causing great hardship in the French forts. The Hudson's Bay Company during the war frequently petitioned the Board of Trade for assistance, but, as they received none, they appealed directly to the queen. When the final treaty was made, the Hudson Bay country was taken into account.

THE PEACE OF UTRECHT

At the end of the war a series of agreements was drawn up by the various powers. The treaties involving America dealt both with territory and commerce. England obtained a recognition of her claims in the Hudson Bay country and the possession of Newfoundland and Acadia. The claim of the English to the Iroquois country was also admitted, and they were given St. Christopher. Commercially the agreements dealt with the fisheries and Spanish trade. The French were excluded from fishing on the Acadian coast, but were allowed to keep Cape Breton Island and were given certain fishing privileges on the Newfoundland coasts. An agreement with Spain, known as the *Asiento* or contract, gave the English the exclusive right for thirty years of bringing negroes into the Spanish possessions. The English were also allowed to send an annual merchant ship of five hundred tons burden to trade with Spanish ports.

READINGS

THE STRUGGLE FOR THE FUR COUNTRY

Bryce, George, *The Remarkable History of the Hudson's Bay Company*, 1–46; Kingsford, William, *The History of Canada*, II, 36–107; Laut, Agnes, *The Conquest of the Great Northwest*, I, 97–255; Le Sueur, W. D., *Count Frontenac*, 170–228; Lorin, Henri, *Le Comte de Frontenac*, 275–352; Parkman, Francis, *Count Frontenac and New France under Louis XIV*, 72–183; Thwaites, R. G., ed., *The Jesuit Relations*, LXII–LXIV.

THE WAR OF THE ENGLISH SUCCESSION

Bryce, George, *The Remarkable History of the Hudson's Bay Company*, 47–55; Clowes, W. L., *The Royal Navy*, II, 462–472, 492–495; Kingsford, William, *The History of Canada*, II, 198–386; Laut, A. C., *The Conquest of the Great Northwest*, I, 228–255; Le Sueur, W. D., *Count Frontenac*, 229–362; Lorin, Henri, *Le Comte de Frontenac*, 353–488; Mahan, A. T., *The Influence of Sea Power upon History, 1660–1783*, pp. 173–198; Parkman, Francis, *Count Frontenac and New France under Louis XIV*, 184–427; Willson, Beckles, *The Great Company*, 182–197.

WAR OF THE SPANISH SUCCESSION

Clowes, W. L., *The Royal Navy*, II, chs. 23–24; Greene, E. B., *Provincial America*, 136–165; Kingsford, William, *The History of Canada*, III; McCrady, Edward, *The History of Carolina under the Proprietary Government, 1670–1719*, pp. 364–548; Parkman, Francis, *A Half-Century of Conflict*, I, 1–297; Shea, J. G., *Catholic Church in Colonial Days*, 454–479; Hamilton, P. J., *Colonization of the South*, ch. 15.

CHAPTER XV

THE FRENCH IN LOUISIANA AND THE FAR NORTHWEST
(1699-1762)

THE FOUNDING OF LOUISIANA

Applicants for La Salle's grant.—During the War of the Palatinate Louis XIV showed little desire to develop La Salle's plan for a colony on the Gulf. In the interim, however, a number of individuals proposed taking up La Salle's work. In 1690 his brother, the Abbé Cavelier, strongly urged that it be continued. In 1694 Tonty asked permission to carry out the project. In 1697 De Louvigny, Captain of Marines in Canada, proposed making an expedition against the Spanish mines by way of the Río Bravo. In the same year Sieur de Argaud, at Paris, sought a grant of the territory between Florida and New Mexico, the Gulf and the Illinois River. The control of the Gulf and the checking of the Spanish advance were prominent among the arguments for all these projects.

Iberville.—But not until the treaty of Ryswick was signed did the king again take up the plan. The founding of the proposed colony was then entrusted to Iberville, a son of Charles Le Moyne, one of the great seigniors of Canada. Iberville and his brother Bienville had already distinguished themselves in their attacks upon the English on Hudson Bay. Activities were hastened by reports that the English were preparing to take possession of the mouth of the Mississippi. To forestall them, Pontchartram, the Minister of Marine, in 1698 sent an expedition to the Gulf of Mexico.

Pensacola founded by Spain.—News of Iberville's preparations reached Madrid early in 1698, and again Spain proved that in an emergency she could act. Assuming that Pensacola was the French objective, the viceroy sent Andrés de Arriola to intercept them, and in November he fortified the place.

Biloxi founded by France.—The movement was timely. Two months behind Arriola Iberville's fleet appeared before the harbor and demanded admission (January, 1699). The request being politely refused, Iberville established himself at Biloxi, after which he returned to France, leaving Bienville in command. During Iberville's absence, the coast and the lower courses of the Mississippi and Red Rivers were thoroughly explored and friendly relations with the Indian tribes promoted. Shortly afterward Iberville returned to the colony, and in 1702 the settlement was moved to Mobile Bay where the Spaniards at Pensacola could be more effectually checked, the new settlement being called St. Louis.

Alliance with the tribes.—An Indian policy was also developed. Tonty, who had found it to his advantage to divert his fur trade to Louisiana, was sent on a peace mission to the Chickasaws. This resulted in a conference of Chickasaws and Choctaws at Mobile Bay, at which the friendship and trade of those powerful tribes were assured. By alliances with the interior tribes, Iberville hoped to be able eventually to check and, if possible, annihilate the English settlements of Maryland, Virginia, and Carolina. After the conference at Mobile Bay, Iberville left the colony, and Bienville became the central figure in Louisiana.

Bienville's first administration.—The government of the colony was of a military type. At the head was the governor, who was assisted by a *commissaire* who had charge of the stores. A council with judicial powers was also established. Like Frontenac, Bienville was beset by many difficulties, quarrels with officials and clergy being frequent. The colony was threatened by an alliance of Cherokees, Choctaws, and other tribes who were instigated to hostility by the English. In 1710 a new site for St. Louis was selected, the settlement being located on the present site of Mobile, and by that name it became known.

Crozat.—The colony had not prospered, and the government desired to rid itself of the expense of the establishment. In 1712 the king therefore granted to Antoine Crozat, a wealthy merchant, a fifteen-year monopoly of trade in the vast territory from Illinois to the Gulf and from the Carolinas to New Mexico. He was also permitted to send a ship annually to the Guinea coast for negro slaves. On the other hand, Crozat agreed to

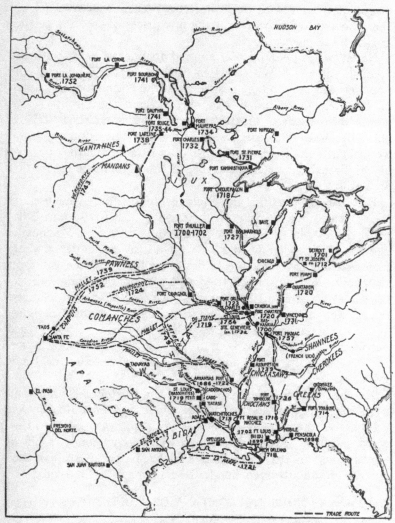

The French in Louisiana and the Far Northwest

send out two shiploads of settlers yearly. The executive powers
were vested in a council appointed by the king from nominations
made by Crozat; it consisted of a governor, intendant, and two
agents of the proprietor. The first governor was Lamothe
Cadillac, the founder of Detroit. At first a considerable number

of colonists were sent over, but the French commercial laws, the monopoly of Crozat, and the low prices offered for peltries crippled the colony.

Natchitoches.—Cadillac attempted to open a trade with the Spanish colonies. With this in view in 1713 St. Denis, the younger, was sent to take possession of the Natchitoches country on the Red River and to open an overland trade route across Texas into Mexico. A trading post was established at Natchitoches, but the commercial results of the expedition to Mexico were slight. St. Denis was arrested and the Spaniards, alarmed at the French encroachments, began the permanent occupation of Texas.

Fort Toulouse.—In 1714 Bienville built Fort Toulouse, on the Alabama River, near the junction of the Coosa and Talapoosa Rivers, in the country of the upper Creeks, Mandeville being made first commander. Fort Toulouse was a depot where furs were bought from the Indians and floated down the river to Mobile. Round about it the Jesuit missionaries worked among the Creeks. The fort became the base for the control of these tribes, and an outpost against the English of the Carolinas. When the latter settled Georgia, feeling the menace of the French outposts, they built Fort Okfuskee, on the Talapoosa River, forty miles away, and induced the Creeks to destroy the Jesuit missions.

Natchez.—Difficulties arose with the Natchez Indians; in 1716 Bienville was sent to subdue them, and Fort Rosalie was erected on the site of Natchez. Cadillac was shortly afterward recalled. Crozat had found his colony merely a bill of expense and in 1717 he surrendered his patent. At that time there were about seven hundred Frenchmen in Louisiana.

LOUISIANA UNDER THE COMPANY OF THE INDIES (1717–1731)

The Mississippi Bubble.—When Crozat surrendered his patent John Law was ushering in his era of speculation. Louisiana was taken over by the Compagnie d'Occident, which was granted complete political and commercial powers. The capital of the Company, amounting to one hundred million livres, was divided into two hundred thousand shares. In 1719 the company received, in addition, a monopoly of the trade of Africa and the Orient, and increased its capital by fifty thousand shares, thenceforth being known as the Compagnie des Indies. Law made Louisiana the center of his system, and represented the country as an earthly paradise, fabulous in mines.

New Orleans founded.—Bienville was made governor and the capital was established at New Biloxi. In 1718 New Orleans was laid out and named in honor of the regent. A garrison was established at the Natchitoches trading post, and Fort Chartres was built in the Illinois country. Feudal seignories were not extended as in Canada, but extensive tracts were granted to *concessionaires*, who agreed to bring out settlers. In a short time many tracts had been granted on Red River, on the Mississippi, and on the Yazoo. As colonists did not volunteer in sufficient numbers, emigrants were secured from hospitals and jails, or were spirited away from France. A few negro slaves had been previously introduced, but Law's company brought large numbers; the first cargo, landed in 1719, contained two hundred and fifty. With this introduction of slavery, agriculture developed rapidly.

War with Spain.—At this time a brief period of war ensued between Spain and France, due to the ambitions of Elizabeth Farnese and her advisor Alberoni. An expedition from Mobile captured Pensacola, but it was soon after retaken by the Spanish, who also attacked Mobile. Shortly afterward the French again captured Pensacola, but at the end of the war it was restored to Spain. At the same time the Spaniards were driven out of eastern Texas and an expedition under Villazur was defeated by French allies on the Platte River.

Growth of population.—In 1720 the Mississippi Bubble burst, stock in Law's numerous enterprises fell rapidly, and the great financier left France a ruined man. Though Louisiana ceased to be the center of the financial system of France, the Company continued operations with considerable success. The white population had increased to about five thousand. New Orleans had a considerable population, and in 1722 it was made the capital.

The government.—In order that the country might be better governed, it was divided into the nine judicial departments of Biloxi, Mobile, Alibamon, New Orleans, Yazoo, Natchez, Natchitoches, Arkansas, and Illinois. The negro population increased so rapidly that there was considerable fear of an uprising. To govern them, in 1724 a set of laws known as the Black Code was promulgated by the governor. The legal religion of the colony was decreed to be Catholic, and masters were to give religious instruction to slaves. Intermarriage of whites and blacks was prohibited. The slaves were forbidden to carry weapons or to gather in assemblies. Masters were bound to clothe, protect, and give subsistence to slaves, and negro families were not to be broken up by sales. Masters were also responsible for acts of their slaves. The crimes of those in bondage were punished by whipping, branding, or, in extreme cases, by death. This code was the last important act of Bienville, who shortly afterward returned to France. The central government under the company was practically the same as that of Canada in the time of Frontenac, and similar quarrels between governor and intendant ensued. Ecclesiastically Louisiana was divided roughly into three districts; the Mobile region was under the Carmelites, the Jesuits ministered to those in the Illinois country and along the lower Ohio, and the rest was under the Capuchins.

The Natchez War.—Owing to the French occupation of Natchez lands, the tribe in 1729 formed a conspiracy, which embraced the Choctaws and other tribes, for the purpose of exterminating the whites. In the first attack two hundred and fifty French at Fort Rosalie were killed, and many women and children taken into captivity. The Choctaws turned against the Natchez. An army of French and Choctaws was collected, and finally succeeded in dispersing the hostile tribe. A second expedition pursued the fugitives, and the Natchez were so severely chastised that they ceased to exist as a unit.

LOUISIANA UNDER THE ROYAL GOVERNORS

Bienville again governor.—The expense of the Natchez War convinced the directors of the company that the Louisiana project could not be made a paying investment, and in 1731 the king released them from their charter. In 1731 the Company of the Indies withdrew from Louisiana and it became a royal province. A council was organized to replace the company and Bienville was again made governor.

The Chickasaw War: Fort Tombecbé.—After the Natchez War the remnant of the tribe had fled to the Chickasaws. In 1736 Bienville made war on the latter tribe, who had not only harbored the Natchez, but were in alliance with the English and had formed a league to cut off French activities along the Mississippi, Mobile, and Tombigbee Rivers. Bienville led troops from Natchitoches, Natchez, Mobile, and New Orleans, while D'Artaguette from the Illinois coöperated. As a base of attack Fort Tombecbé was built on the Tombigbee River in the Choctaw country. The expedition against the Chickasaws ended in disaster, but Fort Tombecbé continued to be important as a base for the control of the Choctaws, who were kept hostile toward Chickasaws and English. In 1740 a second attempt was made. At Fort Assumption, on the site of Memphis, a force of thirty-six hundred was gathered. The size of the army frightened the Chickasaws, who sued for peace. The French, however, failed to secure their friendship, and they remained allies of the English.

End of Bienville's rule.—In 1743 Bienville retired from the governorship without having succeeded in making the colony a success. The white population near the Gulf had declined to thirty-two hundred and there were about two thousand slaves in the colony, while the Illinois country contained about fifteen hundred people. During the remaining twenty years of French rule in Louisiana the New Orleans region showed but slight development.

The Illinois.—The Illinois district throve especially under the Company of the Indies. At first the settlements had been governed from Canada, but because of the Fox wars and difficulties of transportation, there was little connection with Canada, and after 1717 the Illinois district was attached to Louisiana. The settlement profited by the John Law "boom" in 1719, eight hundred new colonists coming, chiefly from Canada and New Orleans. In 1720 Fort Chartres, in 1723 St. Philippe, and ten years later Prairie du Rocher, were established. Across the river St. Genevieve and St. Charles were founded. Further east, the Wabash was fortified to keep out the advancing English traders. In 1720 Ouiatanon post was established at Lafayette. This post and Fort Miami, at Fort Wayne, were attached to

Canada, while Vincennes, founded in 1731, belonged to Louisiana, as did Fort Massac founded later on the Ohio. The dividing line between the districts was Terre Haute, or the highlands. Ouiatanon was at the head of navigation on the Wabash for larger pirogues. Here peltries for Canada were reshipped in canoes. Twenty thousand skins a year were sent from Ouiatanon in the decade after 1720.

The Garden of New France.—The Illinois district became an important agricultural center, whence large shipments of grain were made to Detroit, the Ohio River posts, New Orleans, Mobile, and Europe. Negro slaves were introduced and tobacco-raising was begun. At Kaskaskia there was a Jesuit academy for white boys, and at Cahokia a Sulpician Indian school.

The Missouri lead mines.—During the rule of the Company of the Indies lead mines were opened in Missouri, where lead had been early discovered, especially on Maramec River. While governor, Cadillac had made a personal visit to inspect them. Mining was begun on an important scale by Renault, who received grants on the Missouri in 1723. He is said to have taken to these mines two hundred miners from France, and five hundred negroes from Santo Domingo. He was actively engaged in mining until 1746.

THE TRANS-MISSISSIPPI WEST

French advance into the Far West.—Meanwhile the French explorers had reached the Rocky Mountains. In or before 1703 twenty Canadians went from the Illinois country toward New Mexico to trade and learn about the mines. By 1705 Laurain had been on the Missouri and in 1708 Canadians are said to have explored that stream for three hundred or four hundred leagues. By 1712 salines were being worked in Missouri and settlers were living about them. Under the Company of the Indies exploration and trade were pushed for a time with vigor in the trans-Mississippi West, all along the border from the Gulf of Mexico to Nebraska. From Natchitoches French traders made their way among the tribes of eastern and northern Texas, and sometimes reached the Spanish settlements. In 1717 St. Denis the younger and several partners made a second trading expedition overland from Mobile via Natchitoches to San Juan Bautista on the Rio Grande. His goods being seized, he went to Mexico, where he was imprisoned, though his goods were sold with profit. His associates, who reached the border somewhat after him, made their way to Presidio del Norte, disposed of their goods, and returned to Louisiana.

La Harpe on the Red River.—While St. Denis was in Mexico, Bénard de la Harpe was sent to establish a post on the Red River above Natchitoches. He was urged to inform himself concerning the source of the Red River and the tribes near New Mexico, and to open commerce with the Spanish provinces. In 1719 he established his post among the Cadodachos. Du Rivage was sent up the Red River, and La Harpe made an expedition to the Touacaras near the mouth of the Canadian River, where he proposed to found a post as a base for trade with New Mexico, the Padoucas, and the Aricaras.

Du Tisné on the Osage and the Arkansas.—At the same time (1719) Du Tisné was on the Missouri, Osage, and Arkansas rivers. He ascended the Missouri River to the Missouri Indian village, on his way to the Pawnees, but was unable to proceed. He returned to the Illinois, and went to the Osage tribe on the Osage River. From there he continued southwest to the Pawnees on the Arkansas. He made an alliance with the Pawnees, bought Spanish horses from them, and established a French flag in their villages. He was prevented by his hosts from going to the Padouca, but he inquired about New Mexico.

La Harpe on the Gulf Coast.—In 1718 the company was ordered to occupy the Bay of St. Bernard, discovered by La Salle. In 1719 and 1720 preliminary expeditions were made, and in 1721 La Harpe himself led an expedition to a bay on the Texas coast, but he was expelled by the Indians. The bay reached by him was the Bay of the Bidayes (Galveston Bay) and not the St. Bernard of La Salle. La Harpe urged a new attempt, to keep out the Spaniards, but the company abandoned the project.

La Harpe on the Arkansas.—After returning from the Gulf coast expedition, La Harpe was sent from Mobile in December, 1721, to explore the Arkansas River, with the idea of developing Indian trade, preventing Spanish encroachment, and opening commerce with New Mexico. He ascended the Arkansas about halfway to the mouth of the Canadian River, and on his return recommended establishing posts at Little Rock, the mouth of the Canadian, and the Touacara villages.

Bourgmont on the Missouri and Kansas Rivers.—In the years immediately following the Spanish expedition under Villazur (1720), the French made active efforts to communicate with New Mexico on the one hand, and to forestall any hostile movement of the Spaniards on the other. Having heard that Spaniards were preparing to return to avenge their defeat and to occupy the Kansas River country, Bienville in 1722 ordered Boisbriant, commander at the Illinois, to anticipate the Spaniards and build a fort. The person sent was Bourgmont, who had lived among the Missouris fifteen or more years, and had been made commander on the Missouri. Late in 1723 he established Fort Orleans above the mouth of the Grand River, in modern Carroll County, Missouri. From there in 1724 he went up the river among the Otos and Iowas, and then southwest to the Padoucas in Western Kansas, taking with him Missouris, Osages, Kansas, Otos, and Iowas. He made peace between these tribes and the Padoucas, and arranged to send traders to the last named. A primary object was to open a way to New Mexico. Shortly afterward Fort Orleans was destroyed by an Indian massacre, and wars of the Foxes for several years practically closed the lower Missouri.

ADVANCE TOWARD NEW MEXICO

The western fur trade.—For a decade and a half after the Bourgmont expedition the French made no noteworthy western exploration. Meanwhile, however, the traders quietly carried on their trade among the western tribes. Important items in this trade were Indian captives, and mules stolen from the Spaniards. French traders sometimes found a ready market for goods smuggled into Spanish settlements on the northern frontier of New Spain. From New Orleans, Opeluzas, Natchitoches, Yatasi, Petit Caddo, and Cadadocho posts they worked among the tribes of eastern and northern Texas. By 1730 they had reached the lower Trinity to trade among the Orcoquiza and Bidai tribes. Further north they traded with the Asinai and Cadadochos, in the very face of the Spanish posts. By the middle of the century they were well established among the Wichita tribes of the Red River Valley, and northeastern Texas was virtually under French control. The way to western Texas and the upper Red River was barred by the hostile Apaches, but in 1753 Governor Kerlérec proposed breaking through this strong barrier.

From the Arkansas post traders worked among the Quapaws and Jumanos, and other tribes adjacent to the Arkansas River. From the Illinois, and from lesser posts among the Osages, Missouris, and Kansas, traders worked among these tribes, the Iowas, Otos, Pawnees of the Platte, and other more northern bands of Indians.

Interest in New Mexico.—French voyageurs, *chasseurs*, and traders of Louisiana and Canada continued to look with covetous eyes toward New Mexico. To the adventurer it was a land promising gold and silver and a path to the South Sea; to the merchant it offered rich profits in trade. The natural avenues of approach to this Promised Land were the Red, Arkansas, and Missouri Rivers. But there were obstacles to expeditions bound for New Mexico. One was the jealous and exclusive policy of Spain, which made the reception of such Frenchmen as might reach Santa Fé a matter of uncertainty; another was the Indian barrier which stood in the way. The Red River highway was effectually blocked by the Apaches, mortal enemies of all the tribes along the lower valley; the Arkansas and Missouri avenues were impeded by the Comanches for analogous reasons. The Apaches and Comanches opposed the passage of the trader to their foes with supplies of weapons. As the fur traders and official explorers pushed rapidly west, one of their constant aims was to open the way to New Mexico by effecting peace between the Comanche and the tribes further east, an attempt at which had been made by Du Tisné and Bourgmont at an earlier day.

The Mallet brothers.—After the cessation of the Fox wars, which had closed the lower Missouri, traders again frequented the Pawnees and Aricaras, and in 1734 one is known to have ascended the Missouri to the Mandans, from whose villages a trade route was soon opened to western Canada. In 1739 a party led by the Mallet brothers made their way, by the Missouri and Platte Rivers, across Nebraska, Kansas, and Colorado to Santa Fé. After a nine months' stay they returned, part going northeastward to the Illinois and part down the Canadian and Arkansas to New Orleans.

Fabry's attempt: Fort Cavagnolle.—The Mallet party had
succeeded in getting through the Comanche country to New
Mexico and had returned safely and with good prospects for
trade. Immediately there was renewed interest in the Spanish
border on the part of both government officials and private
adventurers. At once, in 1741 Governor Bienville sent Fabry
de la Bruyère with members of the Mallet party to open a trade
route to New Mexico up the Canadian River, and to explore
the Far West. He failed to reach New Mexico. Fort Cavagnolle was established among the Kansas, and the Arkansas
route was made safe by effecting a much-desired treaty (1746 or
1747) between the Comanches and their eastern enemies.

New expeditions to New Mexico.—The effect of this treaty
was immediate, and at once there were new expeditions to New
Mexico by deserters, traders, and official agents. In 1748 thirty-
three Frenchmen were reported among the Xicarillas. Early
in 1749 a party led by Pierre Satren reached Santa Fé by way
of the Arkansas River, conducted by Jumano and Comanche
Indians. They were kept in New Mexico to work at their trades.
Early in 1750 another party arrived by way of the Arkansas.
They were ordered sent to Sonora to prevent their return to
Illinois. In the meantime peace had been made between the
Comanches and Pawnees, and in 1751 traders reached New
Mexico by way of the Missouri. In the same year Jean Chapuis
led a party of nine from Illinois with a commission from St.
Clair, the commander of Fort Chartres. Arriving at Santa Fé
in 1752, via Platte River, he proposed a regular caravan trade
with military escort. The intruders were arrested and sent to
Mexico, where they languished in prison for many months, and
were finally sent to Spain.

The French advance through the Comanche country gives
significance to the proposal of Governor Kerlérec in 1753 to
break through the Apache barrier and open up a trade with
Nuevo Leon, Coahuila, and New Mexico. As a means of
doing so he proposed securing an alliance between the Apaches
and their eastern enemies. These intrusions of Frenchmen
into New Mexico were closely bound up in their effect on
Spanish policy, with similar infringements upon the Texas
border.

THE FAR NORTHWEST

The Fox wars.—By the end of the seventeenth century Fox hostilities had practically closed the Fox-Wisconsin trade route to the Mississippi. Hostility was increased by the massacre of many Fox Indians at Detroit in 1712. In 1715 De Lignery led a futile expedition against the tribe at Green Bay. In the following year Louvigny with eight hundred men won a partial victory at Butte des Morts, near Lake Winnebago. The European war had now closed, and the Lake Superior posts—Green Bay, La Fointe, Pigeon River, and Lake Nepigon—were reoccupied. The Fox-Wisconsin route being closed, the western trade was divided between the Lake Superior district and that of the Illinois.

The new Sioux posts.—A new movement into the Sioux country was stimulated by the long standing desire to find a route to the Pacific. In 1723 Father Charlevoix suggested finding it either by means of a line of posts through the Sioux country or by way of the Missouri and over the mountains. The former plan was adopted, and in 1727 Fort Beauharnois was built on the west bank of Lake Pepin, with Perrière in command, and with new missions in the vicinity. But, through another uprising of the Fox Indians, the post was soon abandoned. New expeditions against the Foxes and the Sauks, their allies, broke their resistance, and after 1733 the Fox-Wisconsin trade route to the Iowa and Minnesota country was again open. After 1750 the Foxes were regular allies of the French in their wars with the British.

The Vérendrye and the Post of the Western Sea.—The search for the route to the Western Sea was taken up by Gaultier de Varennes (the elder La Vérendrye), commander at Fort Nepigon, who planned a line of posts through the waterways northwest of Lake Superior. His movements were stimulated by the activities of the Hudson's Bay Company in Canada, and by those of the Spaniards in the Southwest. To pay the expenses of his scheme he was granted a monopoly of the northwestern fur trade. In the course of ten years he founded posts on Rainy Lake (St. Pierre, 1731), Lake of the Woods (St. Charles, 1731), Lake Winnipeg (Maurepas, 1732), Assiniboine River (La Reine),

and on the Saskatchewan (Fort Dauphin, 1741). In 1742 La
France had penetrated the Hudson's Bay Company territory by
crossing from Lake Winnipeg to York Factory.

From this line of posts the elder La Vérendrye turned his
attention to the upper Missouri, leading an expedition southwestward to the Mantannes in 1738. Four years later his son,
Pierre de Varennes, made another expedition to the Mantannes,
where they heard of bearded white men to the west. Setting out
southwestward, they visited the Cheyennes, Crows, Little Foxes,
and Bows. On January 1, 1743, when in the neighborhood of the
North Platte River, they saw the Rocky Mountains.

After Vérendrye died, his successor, Legardeur St. Pierre,
extended the line of posts up the Saskatchewan to the foot of
the Rockies, where in 1752 he founded Fort La Jonquiere. The
French had thus reached the Rockies by way of nearly every
important stream between the Red River and the Saskatchewan.

READINGS

Bolton, H. E., *Athanase de Mézières*, I, Introduction; *Texas in the Middle
Eighteenth Century*, 1–133; "French Intrusions into New Mexico," in *The
Pacific Ocean in History;* Dunn, W. E., *Spanish and French Rivalry in the
Gulf Region of the United States, 1678–1702: The Beginnings of Texas and
Pensacola;* Fortier, Alcée, *History of Louisiana*, I, 30–140; French, B. F.,
Historical Collections of Louisiana and Florida; Gayarré, Charles, *History of
Louisiana, French Domination;* Hamilton, P. J., *Colonial Mobile; The
Colonization of the South*, 197–275; Heinrich, Pierre, *La Louisiane sous la
compagnie des Indies, 1717–1731;* King, Grace, *New Orleans; Sieur de Bien-
ville;* King, Grace, and Ficklen, John, *History of Louisiana;* LePage du
Pratz, *Histoire de la Louisiane;* Martin, F. X., *History of Louisiana;* Ogg,
F. A., *The Opening of the Mississippi*, 169–237; Parkman, Francis, *A Half-
Century of Conflict*, I, 298–368, II, 3–44; Phelps, Albert, *Louisiana*, 20–105;
Shea, J. G., *Exploration of the Mississippi Valley; The Catholic Church in the
United States;* Thwaites, R. G., *France in America*, 72–88; Villiers du Ter-
rage, Marc de, *Les Dernières Années de la Louisiane Française*, 1–48; Winsor,
Justin, *The Mississippi Basin*, 1–217; Burpee, Lawrence, *Pathfinders of the
Great Plains*.

CHAPTER XVI

TEXAS, PIMERÍA ALTA AND THE FRANCO-SPANISH BORDER CONFLICT

The advance of the French into Louisiana and the Trans-Mississippi West stimulated a new counter movement north-eastward by the Spaniards from Chihuahua, New Mexico, and Coahuila, and there ensued on the Franco-Spanish border a contest for the control of Texas and all the plains country as far north as the Platte River—a contest much like the better-known "half-century of conflict" between the English and the French on the other border. At the same time, the Spanish frontier forged slowly northwestward into Lower California and southern Arizona. On the other hand, the Florida frontier, which in the seventeenth century had been pushed back by the English colonies of Virginia and the Carolinas, was now still further contracted by the establishment of French Louisiana and English Georgia, while in the West Indies and Honduras Spanish rule suffered a like diminution through the continued advance of the English, French, and Dutch. The *Asiento* of 1713 with Great Britain was a particularly hard blow at Spain's commercial independence, and was made worse by England's gross violation of the compact.

NORTHEASTWARD ADVANCE OF THE SPANISH FRONTIER

The Chihuahua mines.—In Nueva Vizcaya two notable forward steps north were taken in the early eighteenth century. These were the opening of the Chihuahua silver deposits and the advance down the Conchos valley. In 1703–1704 rich ores were discovered near the recently founded mission of Nombre de Diôs. The mines proved to be among the best in America, and, it has been estimated, produced silver worth from $50,000,000 to $100,000,000 in the eighteenth century. Two *reales de minas*, Chihuahua and Santa Eulalia, were established near by, and became the most thriving centers on the northern frontier. By

1763 each had a population of 5000, and the church at Chihuahua was one of the finest in the new world.

Advance down the Conchos Valley.—At the same time the frontier advanced down the fertile Conchos River Valley and across the Rio Grande into western Texas. In 1715 the abandoned missions at La Junta were reëstablished. Soon six missions were in operation and serving Indian towns on both sides of the Rio Grande. For ten years they succeeded, and then, in 1725, the Indians revolted and deserted. During the subsequent years the padres made them occasional visits, while settlement pushed down the Conchos Valley. In 1753 the La Junta missions were restored, and in 1760 were protected by the new presidio of Belén.

The New Mexico border. Moqui and Zuñi resistance.— The reconquest of the New Mexico pueblos had been effected by Vargas at the end of the seventeenth century. The Moquis and Zuñis, however, stubbornly resisted Spanish influence and harbored apostates. In 1726 and again in 1741 the Moqui district was assigned to the Jesuits of Sonora, but they accomplished little. Rivalry led to new Franciscan visits, and in 1742 the missionaries recovered more than four hundred Tigua fugitives who had fled during the great revolt of sixty years before. In 1745 the field was restored to the Franciscans, but they were unable to make permanent establishments.

Xicarrilla and Navajo missions.—In 1733 a mission was founded near Taos for the Xicarrilla Apaches who were hard pressed by the Comanches. Between 1744 and 1750 efforts were made to convert the Navajo, but without avail.

New settlements.—The population of New Mexico grew slowly but steadily. In 1706 Governor Cubero founded the new villa of Albuquerque and reëstablished La Cañada. In 1760 there were 7666 Spaniards in fourteen settlements in the upper district and 3588 about El Paso. This was a population larger than that of English Georgia at the same time. The largest towns were Albuquerque (1814), La Cañada (1515), and Santa Fé (1285). At the same time the Christian Indians in the province numbered 10,000.

Indian depredations.—New Mexico was constantly harassed by Navajos on the west, Yutas and Comanches on the north, and Apaches on the east and south. The main object of the savages was to steal stock and other property, but they often shed human blood freely. On the basis of horses and mules stolen in New Mexico, a regular trade was maintained by Indians across the country to Louisiana. The exterior tribes attacked the Pueblo Indians even more freely than the Spaniards. The Spanish soldiery, with Indian allies, often retaliated with telling effect and recovered stolen horses and mules. Captives taken were sold as slaves to the settlers or in the interior. Yet there were truces between campaigns, and by the middle of the century the Comanches and Yutas in large numbers attended the annual Taos fair, where they sold skins and captives.

Rumors of the French.—The French advance up the Missouri stimulated a counter movement of the Spaniards of the New Mexico border. Before the end of the seventeenth century wild rumors of the approaching French had reached Santa Fé. Other interests, especially Indian relations, furnished motives for northeastward expeditions early in the eighteenth century. In 1706 Juan de Urribarri was sent by Governor Cubero "to the unknown land of the plains" to ransom Christian captives from the northern tribes. He crossed the Napestle (Arkansas) River, near the present city of Pueblo, Colorado, and reached the Indian settlement of El Cuartelejo, near the Colorado-Kansas border, where he heard new reports of the French among the Pawnees.

Expeditions to the northeast and north.—The frequent campaigns against the Indians were occasions for new exploration. In 1715 Juan Paez Hurtado, with two hundred and fifty men, pursued Apaches into western Texas. During the next four years several expeditions were made northeast against Comanches and Yutas, in the course of which new reports were heard of the French, who were now pushing up all the western tributaries of the Mississippi. In 1719 a campaign against the Yutas and Comanches led Governor Valverde across the Arkansas. In 1720 occurred the disastrous Villazur expedition to the Platte described later. About 1750 Bustamente y Tagle pursued Comanches down the Arkansas nearly to the Jumanos.

Explorers in Colorado.—Explorers also entered the Utah Basin. Juan María Rivera, sent out by Governor Cachupín in search of ore, visited and named the La Plata (Silver) Mountains, and continued to the junction of the Uncompahgre River with the Gunnison (1765). In the following year Nicolás de la Fora, writing in New Mexico, stated that the Spaniards were acquainted with the country along the Cordillera de las Grullas (in western Colorado) for a hundred leagues above Santa Fé. A decade later (1779) Anza ascended the San Luís Valley, descended the Arkansas River, and returned to Santa Fé over the mountains.

THE FOUNDING OF TEXAS

The Coahuila frontier.—In 1693 eastern Texas, after a temporary occupation, had been abandoned, and the frontier fell back to Coahuila. In the course of the next decade, however, it was gradually extended until it crossed the Rio Grande. A most important factor in the work were the Querétaro friars, who ever urged the government forward. By 1698 Boca de Leones and Lampazos had become the seats of flourishing mines, missions, and ranches. Between 1699 and 1703 three missions and a presidio had been established on the Rio Grande at San Juan Bautista, below modern Eagle Pass. The site, being a great rendezvous and trading place for the tribes, was known as the "Cádiz of the interior." Near most of the missions small colonies of Spaniards and Tlascaltecans settled. These missions served many Indians from beyond the Rio Grande, and frequent expeditions were made into the outlying country.

Plans to reoccupy Texas.—During all this time the missionaries were desirous of returning to the Asinai or Texas Indians, whom they had left in 1693, and with whom they had since maintained communication. In 1706 the governor of Coahuila urged the founding of a mission on the Rio Frio as a means of securing the road to the Asinai. Three years later Fathers Olivares and Espinosa made an expedition to the Colorado River, where they hoped to meet the tribe. Father Hidalgo long made strenuous efforts to get permission to return to his former charges, and Father Olivares went to Spain to procure it. Frequent rumors of French incursions from Louisiana were discussed in government circles, but it required an actual danger to cause the government to act.

St. Denis in Mexico.—In 1714, led by two survivors of La Salle's expedition, St. Denis made his expedition across Texas to trade. At San Juan Bautista he was arrested and taken to

Mexico, where it was realized by the officials that a real menace had arisen. In a council of war held on August 22, 1715, it was decided to reoccupy Texas with missions, a garrison, and a small colony. Domingo Ramón, a frontier officer, was put in charge of the expedition, and the missionary field was assigned to the two Franciscan colleges *de Propaganda Fide* of Querétaro and Zacatecas. Of the missions of the former, Father Espinosa, later known as the historian, was made president; of the latter the president appointed was the still more renowned Father Antonio Margil.

Eastern Texas reoccupied.—In February, 1716, the expedition left Saltillo, and in April it crossed the Rio Grande at San Juan Bautista. In the party were nine friars, twenty-five soldiers, six women, and enough other persons to make a total of sixty-five. They drove with them more than 1000 head of cattle and goats, and an outfit for missions, farms, and a presidio. A direct northeast route was followed, through San Pedro Springs, where the city of San Antonio later grew up. By the Asinai Indians they were given a warm welcome, and four missions were at once founded near the Neches and Angelina Rivers. Near the latter stream the presidio of Dolores was established. At the same time an attempt was made to establish a mission on the Red River among the Cadodachos, but it was frustrated by the Indians, who were under French influence.

A new base needed.—Eastern Texas had been reoccupied, but the outposts there were weak and isolated. The French were trading among the surrounding tribes; St. Denis was known to be planning another commercial expedition to Mexico; and it was rumored that a large French colony was to be established at the mouth of the Mississippi. This prediction was verified by the founding of New Orleans in 1718. On the other hand, Father Olivares urged advancing from the Rio Grande to the San Antonio. These motives to action coincided with a more aggressive Spanish policy toward the French since the death of Louis XIV, a policy exemplified by the new viceroy Linares.

San Antonio founded.—In a *junta de guerra* held December 2, 1716, it was therefore decided to establish posts on the San Antonio and among the Cadodachos, while Ramón was to destroy the French establishments at Natchitoches. The new enterprise

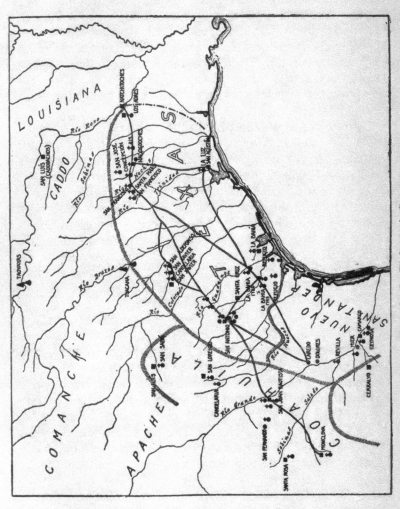

Texas in the Eighteenth Century

was entrusted to Martin de Alarcón, who was made governor of
Texas and, before setting out, of Coahuila. While the expedition
was preparing, St. Denis reached the Rio Grande (April, 1717),
where his goods were confiscated. Going to Mexico, he was
there imprisoned. Meanwhile Ramón had reconnoitered Natchitoches, and on his return early in 1717 two new missions were
founded among the Ays and Adaes, the latter being within seven
leagues of Natchitoches, and thenceforth a vital spot in the
history of international frontiers.

Early in 1718 Alarcón left Coahuila with a colony of sixty-two
persons, besides the neophytes of mission San Francisco Solano,
who were to be transferred to the new site on the San Antonio
River. Arrived there, a mission, presidio, and town were founded,
the beginnings of the modern city of San Antonio. In the east
Alarcón accomplished little more than to displease the missionaries and to protest against La Harpe's new French establishment among the Cadodachos.

WAR WITH FRANCE

Attack on Pensacola and Texas.—In January, 1719, as a result of European complications, France declared war on Spain.
The war extended at once to the colonies, where a border contest
ensued at various points all the way from Pensacola to the Platte
River. In the course of the summer Pensacola was captured
by the French of Mobile, recaptured by the Spaniards, and
again taken by Bienville and Serigney. In June, Blondel, commander at Natchitoches, invaded eastern Texas, whence the Spanish missionaries and garrison retreated to San Antonio without a
struggle. For two years thereafter the region was left unoccupied
by Spain. While waiting at San Antonio Father Margil in 1720
founded there a new mission called San José, which later was
called the finest in New Spain.

Spanish plans to fortify the Platte River.—In the course of
the campaigns against the Indians to the northeast of New
Mexico, constantly more disturbing reports had been heard of
the French, who were now making their way up all the western
tributaries of the Mississippi. In 1719 Governor Valverde pursued Yutas and Comanches across the Napestle (Arkansas) and
heard that the French had settled on the Jesus María (North

Platte) River. New significance was attached to these reports because of the outbreak of war between France and Spain a short time before. Valverde warned the viceroy of the danger; wild rumors spread through the northern provinces; and measures for defence were taken. In 1720, while plans were being made to recover Texas, the viceroy ordered counter alliances made with the tribes northeast of New Mexico, a Spanish colony planted at El Cuartelejo, in eastern Colorado, and a presidio established on the Jesus María River, that is, in Nebraska or Wyoming.

Destruction of the Villazur Expedition.—Although a truce had already been declared between France and Spain, Governor Valverde, perhaps in ignorance of this fact, sent Pedro de Villazur in June, 1720, at the head of one hundred and ten men to reconnoiter the French. Passing through El Cuartelejo, in August he reached the Jesus María. Not finding the French, he set out to return, but on the San Lorenzo (South Platte), in northern Colorado, he was killed and his expedition cut to pieces by Indians using French weapons. There are indications that tribes living as far north as Lake Winnebago in Wisconsin took part in the attack, a fact which illustrates the wide-reaching influence of these international contests. The Spaniards charged the massacre to the French, and there was a new panic on the frontier. But peace had been restored between France and Spain, and, in spite of appeals from New Mexico, the plans for advancing to El Cuartelejo and the Platte were dropped.

The Aguayo Expedition.—An offer to assist in the reconquest of Texas was made by the Marquis of Aguayo, governor and the most prominent figure of Coahuila. Abetted by Father Hidalgo, he had been interested in a new attempt to discover Gran Quivira, and the Texas crisis seemed to give him an opening. His offer was accepted, and before the end of 1720 he had raised, partly at his own expense, eight companies of cavalry, comprising over five hundred men and five thousand horses. By his instructions he was expected to reoccupy and strengthen the abandoned posts and occupy Cadadachos, on the Red River, and Bahía del Espíritu Santo on the Gulf.

Eastern Texas reoccupied.—The Marquis left Monclova in November, 1720, shortly after Villazur's defeat on the Platte.

From the Rio Grande in January, 1721, he sent Captain Ramón with forty soldiers to take possession of Bahía del Espíritu Santo, to which a supply ship was sent from Vera Cruz. This was shortly before La Harpe attempted to reoccupy the place for the French. Because of swollen streams, Aguayo made a wide detour to the north, crossing the Brazos near Waco. Peace had been declared in Europe, and at the Neches he was met by St. Denis, who agreed to permit an unresisted reoccupation of the abandoned posts. It was learned here that St. Denis had recently assembled Indian allies with a view to seizing Bahía del Espíritu Santo and San Antonio, in coöperation, no doubt, with La Harpe.

Proceeding east, between August and November Aguayo reestablished the six abandoned missions and the presidio of Dolores, and added a presidio at Los Adaes, facing Natchitoches, and garrisoned it with one hundred men. To this last act Bienville made vigorous protest. On the return to San Antonio the weather was so severe that of five thousand horses only fifty were left when Aguayo arrived in January, 1722. After establishing there another mission and rebuilding the presidio, he took forty additional men to La Bahía, and erected a presidio on the site of La Salle's fort. Having thus completed his work, he returned to Monclova.

Texas won for Spain.—Aguayo's expedition fixed the hold of Spain on Texas. He left ten missions where there had been but seven, two hundred and sixty-eight soldiers instead of sixty or seventy, and four presidios instead of two, two of them being at strategic points. Since 1718 Texas and Coahuila had been under the same governor, but now Texas was made independent, with its capital at Los Adaes (now Robeline, Louisiana) where it remained for half a century. The Medina River now became the western boundary of Texas. In 1726 the La Bahía establishment was moved to the lower Guadalupe River.

THE EXPANSION OF TEXAS

Rivera's inspection of the frontiers.—In the years 1724–1728 a general inspection of the frontier defences of New Spain was made by Pedro de Rivera, ex-governor of the province of Tlascala. His remarkable journey of 3082 leagues began at the City of Mexico on November 21, 1724, and ended there on June 9, 1728. The northern line of military outposts at this time ran from Fronteras through Janos, El Paso, Santa Fé, Conchos, Monclova, San Juan Bautista, Cerralvo, San Antonio, Bahía del Espíritu Santo, Dolores, and Los Adaes. On the whole Rivera found the presidios in fair condition, but encountered many abuses. His reforms in the main were in the direction of retrenchment. This was particularly true regarding Texas, and in 1729 the post on the Angelina was suppressed and the forces of others reduced.

San Antonio strengthened.—Rivera's policy of retrenchment was strongly opposed by the missionaries; among the Indians of eastern Texas they had had little success, and when the garrison of Dolores was withdrawn the Querétaran friars moved their three missions to San Antonio, where they were reëstablished in 1731 and where their ruins still stand. In the same year a colony of Canary Islanders was established beside the presidio and missions, and formed into the Villa of San Fernando. There were now at San Antonio five missions, a presidio, and a municipality. Texas was now definitely formed in outline; Spain had maintained her claim as against France, and had established three centers of occupation, Los Adaes, Bahía del Espíritu Santo, and San Antonio.

The Apache Wars.—For a decade and a half after the founding of the Villa of San Fernando the province of Texas underwent little expansion. From the beginning of San Antonio its inhabitants were subjected to raids by the Eastern Apaches, who also infested the highways. To check their outrages occasional campaigns were made into their country by the soldiery, supported by contingents of mission Indians. Notable among the forays were those of Captain Flores (1723), Governor Bustillo (1732), Captain Jose Urrutia (1739), and his son Captain Thoribio Urrutia (1745). These expeditions served not only to punish the enemy and recover stolen horses and mules, but to capture slaves as well, and to make known the northwestern frontier. In the course of them the Spaniards learned of mineral deposits in the Llano River country.

The work of the missionaries.—In spite of Apache hostilities, the missionaries on the San Antonio and the Guadalupe made some progress. The leading figures of the period were Fathers Santa Ana and Dolores y Viana, presidents. No new missions were founded in the fifteen years' interval, but the friars improved their buildings and farms, and sought new neophytes in regions constantly more remote from the mission centers. At the mission of San Antonio de Valero alone no less than forty bands or tribes were represented by the baptisms between 1731 and 1745.

The Tonkawa missions.—During the next fifteen years the frontiers of Texas were expanded in all directions. Between 1745 and 1749 Fathers Viana and Santa Ana founded three missions on the San Xavier (San Gabriel) River, in the Tonkawa country, and in 1751 a presidio was established there. But quarrels ensued, the location proved unsuitable, and the missions were abandoned, efforts now being transferred to the Apache country.

The Apache missions.—Under pressure from the southward moving Comanches, the Lipan-Apaches had ceased their hostilities and asked for missions. Minerals had been found near the Llano River, and communciation with New Mexico was desired. Accordingly, with the aid of a munificent gift by Don Pedro de Terreros, in 1757 a great plan for reducing the Apaches by means of missions was launched. A presidio and mission had scarcely been founded on the San Sabá, however, when the mission was destroyed by the Comanches and their allies (1758). In the following year Colonel Parrilla, with a force of some six hundred men, raised in various parts of northern New Spain, set out to punish the offenders. At the fortified village of the Taovayas, on the Red River, where French influence was predominant, he was routed and driven back. The Apache mission was now transferred to the Upper Nueces, and for several years the San Sabá post sustained incessant war with the northern tribes.

Nuevo Santander.—Wars with England and Indian hostilities now made imperative the colonization of the Gulf coast between the San Antonio River and Tampico—the eastern portion of Nuevo León—and in 1746 the district was erected into a new colony called Nuevo Santander. Colonel José de Escandón, a distinguished officer of Querétaro, was put in charge of the enterprise, and the missionary work was entrusted to the Zacatecan friars. Within the next three years the entire region was explored by Escandón and his lieutenants and a number of colonies were planned. In 1749 Escandón led a colony of more than three thousand people from Querétaro, and in a short time established them in more than twenty settlements, most of which persist to-day. North of the Rio Grande the principal ones were Laredo and Dolores, but ranching soon spread as far as the Nueces River. The post and mission of La Bahía were now moved to the lower San Antonio River and a new mission for the Karankawa (Rosario) was established near by. Though legally in Nuevo Santander, this district was administered as a part of Texas, and by 1775 the Texas-Nuevo Santander boundary was officially moved west to the Nueces.

THE FRANCO–SPANISH BORDER

The Texas-Louisiana boundary question.—The proximity of Los Adaes and Natchitoches had furnished numerous grounds for irritation between Texas and Louisiana. French traders engaged in contraband trade, and the international boundary was uncertain. In 1735, when Natchitoches was moved from the island in the Red River to the west bank of the stream, a quarrel ensued. After several years of bickering, the Arroyo Hondo was tentatively adopted as the international boundary in that region.

Meanwhile French traders had invaded the coast tribes and monopolized the Indian trade of northern Texas. In 1750 the military strength of Louisiana was considerably augmented, and it was reported in Mexico that the new arrivals were for the western Louisiana frontier. These conditions again brought forward the quiescent boundary question, which was inconclusively discussed in Spanish circles for several years. While the higher authorities debated, residents on the frontier generally agreed on the Arroyo Hondo. In 1754 the King of Spain declared that "boundaries between the Spaniards and the French in that region have never been a subject of treaty nor is it best at present that they should be."

The New Mexico border.—By this time renewed French intrusions into New Mexico were becoming alarming. The return of the Mallet party (1739) and the peace between the Comanches and their eastern enemies (ca. 1746) were followed by the arrival in New Mexico of trading parties from Canada and Louisiana under Fébre, Chapuis, and others. A more vigorous policy was now adopted and the recent comers were arrested and sent to Spain. The intrusion into New Mexico found an echo in far western Sonora, where in 1751 the French advance was given by a prominent official as a reason for Spanish haste to occupy the Colorado of the West.

The lower Trinity fortified.—The more stringent policy toward intruders was extended to Texas, where a new outpost was established to ward off French aggression. In the fall of 1754 traders on the lower Trinity were arrested and sent to Mexico, and in 1756-1757 the region was defended by a presidio (San Agustín) and a mission east of the stream among the Orcoquiza Indians. Thus another point on the Texas-Louisiana frontier was occupied and defended by Spain. The site was disputed by Governor Kérlerec, of Louisiana, who proposed a joint boundary commission. The offer was rejected and the viceroy of Mexico, on the contrary, proposed a Spanish post on the Mississippi "to protect the boundaries." With his proposal he sent to Spain a map showing Texas as extending to the Mississippi. Thus the region in dispute extended from the Trinity to the Mississippi, at least.

PIMERÍA ALTA

The Jesuits.—The occupation of Texas was contemporaneous with the advance into Pimería Alta (northern Sonora and southern Arizona) and Lower California. The work of the indefatigable Jesuits on the northern frontier of New Spain is admirably illustrated by that of Father Kino and his companions in this region.

Kino.—After the failure of Atondo's enterprise in California in 1685, Father Eusebio Kino entered northern Sonora, arriving in March, 1687, just at the time of La Salle's death in Texas. Mission Dolores, founded by him in the upper Sonora Valley, became his headquarters for twenty-four years of exploration, ranching, and missionary work among the upper Pimas, between the Altar and Gila Rivers.

Explorations in Arizona.—In the Altar Valley Kino and his companions founded a number of missions, which were destroyed during the revolt in 1695 and then rebuilt. In 1691, accompanied by Father Salvatierra, who later went to California, Kino descended the Santa Cruz River to the village of Tumacácori. Three years later, by the same route, he reached the Casa Grande on the Gila. In 1697, with a military escort from Fronteras (Corodéguachi), he again went to the Casa Grande, this time by way of the San Pedro River. In the following year he was again on the Gila, whence he returned across the Papaguería (the country of the Pápagos) by way of Sonóita, Caborca, and the Altar Valley. In 1699 he went to the Gila by way of Sonóita and the Gila Range, and then ascended the Gila.

A land route to California.—The current view still was that California was an island, but during the last journey Kino returned to the peninsular theory. If this were true, he reasoned, it would be possible to find a land route over which to send supplies to Salvatierra's struggling missions just established in Lower California. To test his views he made several more journeys, crossing the lower Colorado in 1701 and reaching its mouth in 1702. He was now convinced that California was a peninsula. In 1705 was published his map of Pimería Alta, setting forth this view.

Missions and ranches in Arizona.—Meanwhile Kino and his companions had pushed the missionary frontier to the Gila and the Colorado. Kino's exploring tours were also itinerant missions, in the course of which he baptized and taught in numerous villages. During his career in Pimería Alta he alone baptized 4000 Indians. In 1700 he founded the mission of San Xavier del Bac, and within the next two years those of Guebavi and Tumacácori, all in the valley of the Santa Cruz River, and within the present Arizona. To support his missions, near them he established flourishing stock ranches, thus making the beginnings of stock raising in at least twenty places still existing in northern Sonora and southern Arizona.

Decline of the missions.—The power of Spain was now at its lowest ebb, funds were scarce, and Kino's last days were to him a time of stagnation and disappointment. To a certain ex-

Father Kino's Map of Pimería Alta
(Bancroft, *Arizona and New Mexico*, p. 360)

tent royal support was transferred for the time being to the missions in Lower California. After Kino's death in 1711 stagnation became decline, few new missionaries were sent, and northern tours became infrequent or ceased altogether. Officials and frontier leaders often planned to advance the frontier of settlement to the Colorado River, but other interests interfered.

Revival after 1732.—A visit by the bishop of Durango in 1725, the military inspection of that frontier by Rivera in 1726, and a royal decree of 1728 gave new life to the moribund missions. New missionaries arrived in 1732, the northern missions were reoccupied, and journeys to the Gila were renewed after 1736 by Fathers Keller and Sedelmayr.

The Arizonac mines.—Interest in the northern frontier was accentuated at this time by a temporary mining excitement at Arizonac in the upper Altar Valley, where in 1736 silver nuggets of astonishing size were discovered. There was a "rush" to the place, and considerable wealth was found, but in 1741 the surface veins were exhausted and the camp was abandoned. The mining incident furnished an occasion for new plans to advance to the Gila. But Indian troubles in Sinaloa and Sonora interfered. These troubles, on the other hand, served to advance the military frontier by the founding of two presidios at Pitiqui (Hermosillo) and Terrenate in 1741.

Keller and Sedelmayr.—After much discussion, in 1741 the Moqui district was assigned to the Jesuits, who now tried to reach that region. In 1743 Keller crossed the Gila, but was driven back by the Apaches. In 1744 Sedelmayr ascended the Colorado to Bill Williams Fork. In the following year the Moquis were again assigned to the Franciscans.

Plans to occupy the Gila and Colorado.—Sedelmayr now turned his attention to exploring the lower Gila and Colorado Rivers, and his Order, particularly Father Escobar, the provincial, urged the occupation of these valleys, both as a means of support for Lower California, and as a base for advance to Moqui and Alta California. In 1748 Father Consag of California explored the Gulf to its head in the interest of this plan. Royal interest was aroused also by the entry of the French of Louisiana into New Mexico and the need of protecting California. In 1744 and 1747, therefore, the king approved advancing to the

Gila. Five years later, especially because of emphatic reports of the French advance toward the Pacific Ocean, the king seriously considered occupying the Bay of Monterey.

The Pima Revolt.—The new viceroy, Revillagigedo, was occupied with founding Nuevo Santander and other absorbing tasks, while new Indian wars in Sonora made advance impossible. In 1750 a war of extermination, led by Governor Diego Parrilla, was begun on the Seris and lasted several years. In 1751 a revolt occurred among the northern Pimas. At Caborca and Sonóita the missionaries were slain, over one hundred settlers were killed on the Arizona border, and missions and ranches were abandoned. The uprising was suppressed by Parrilla without great difficulty; most of the missions were reoccupied; and for greater security two new presidios were founded, at Altar, near Caborca, and at Tubac near San Xavier del Bac. Thus, each uprising helped to advance the military frontier.

Continued obstacles to advance.—For twenty years more the question of advance to the Colorado was subordinate to that of good order and settled conditions in Sonora, necessary preliminaries to advance. The Pima War was followed by a bitter quarrel between Governor Parrilla and the Jesuits. The Seris made constant trouble, and when attacked retreated safely to Cerro Prieto. Apache wars on the northern border were even more severe, and many settlements in Sonora and Nueva Vizcaya were destroyed by them. Nevertheless, within the protection of the presidios several small Spanish settlements grew up, as at Terrenate, Guebavi, Santa Bárbara, Buenavista, Tubac, Saric, Altar, and San Ignacio. The Jesuits continued to appeal, and others, pointing out the danger from advancing Russians, English, and French, urged the settlement of Alta California. But Spain was occupied elsewhere.

The northwestern frontier in 1763.—Sinaloa and Sonora had been detached from Nueva Vizcaya in 1734, when the province of Sinaloa was erected. Both were still within the diocese of Durango. By 1763 Sinaloa and Ostimuri (southern Sonora) had ceased to be frontier regions. Most of the missions had been secularized, the Indians had become assimilated, and there was a considerable white population. In Sinaloa there were six towns with white and mixed populations ranging from 1000 to

3500 each. In Ostimuri, the part of Sonora south of Yaqui River, there were five towns with populations ranging from 300 to 3400. In the Sonora Valley there was a string of mining towns and small Spanish settlements extending as far north as Fronteras. In Pimería Alta there were eight missions and several Spanish settlements, the latter aggregating, with the garrisons, nearly 1500 persons. In all of the frontier settlements there was a large element of mulattoes and mestizoes.

THE JESUITS IN LOWER CALIFORNIA

California assigned to the Jesuits.—While Kino and his successors were struggling to advance the frontiers of Pimería Alta, another band of Jesuits founded missions and opened trails nearly the whole length of the Peninsula of Lower California, and made explorations northward with a view to meeting the mainland group at the Colorado River. After repeated failures to occupy the Peninsula, the government of Spain turned it over to the Jesuits, with full military and civil authority, as in Paraguay. The missions depended at first mainly on private alms, and in a short time $47,000 were subscribed. This was the beginning of the famous Pious Fund of California.

Salvatierra and his companions.—In 1697 Juan Maria Salvatierra, who had been a missionary in Sinaloa, entered the Peninsula with a handful of soldiers, and began work at Loreto, opposite Guaymas, which became the supply base. Missionary work was attended by unusual difficulties, because of the sterility of the country. More than once the abandonment of California was prevented only by the aid of Father Kino, who drove cattle hundreds of miles to Guaymas and shipped them across the Gulf. Transportation was difficult, and many precious cargoes were wrecked. By the time of Salvatierra's death in 1717 he, Picolo, Juan de Ugarte, and their companions had planted five missions in the middle region of the Peninsula, and had made extensive explorations, north, south, and across California to the Pacific. In 1701 Salvatierra had explored with Kino in quest of a land route from Sonora. In 1721 Father Ugarte in the same interest explored the Gulf to its head.

Development in the South.—Salvatierra's death was followed by more liberal royal aid and private alms, and by more rapid mission extension, particularly in the South. The importance of this step was enhanced by making San Bernabé a stopping place for the Manila galleon. By 1732 Fathers Guillen, Tamaral, and Taraval had explored the west coast as far as Cedros Island. A widespread Indian rebellion in 1734, attended by the martyrdom of Fathers Carranco and Tamaral, caused the founding of the presidio of San José del Cabo, which protected the Cape, but by 1748 Indian disturbances had greatly reduced the southern missions.

The Jesuits, fearful of interference in their work, as a rule opposed Spanish settlements, presidios, and the development of industries in the Peninsula. In 1716, 1719, 1723, and later, the government urged the founding of forts and colonies on the western coast, with a view to protecting and advancing the frontier, but the Jesuits usually objected, and the settlements were not founded. The Indian revolt, war with England in 1739, Anson's raid on the coast in 1742, and the westward advance of the French toward the Pacific Coast, increased the anxiety, and in 1744 new orders were given looking to the defence of the Peninsula, but nothing came of them.

By 1750 the exclusive policy of the Jesuits had given way to some extent, pearl fishing was again permitted, private trading vessels came from time to time, and the Manila galleon stopped regularly at San José. Mines were opened in the South, and around them a small Spanish and mixed breed population grew up, La Paz becoming the principal center.

Missions in the North.—The conditions which had stimulated efforts to advance to the Gila by the mainland after 1744, had a corresponding effect on California development. Sterile California needed overland communication with a mainland base. It was with this need in view that in 1746 the Jesuit provincial, Escobar, sent Father Consag to reëxplore the Gulf, whose head he reached shortly before Sedelmayr descended the Colorado to the same point.

The Colorado-Gila base was not supplied, but with new private gifts and royal aid, the Jesuits on the Peninsula pushed northward. Santa Gertrudis (1752), San Francisco Borja (1762), and Santa María (1767) were the last Jesuit foundations, while Father Link's land journey to the head of the Gulf in 1766 was the final step in Jesuit explorations.

READINGS

TEXAS

Arricivita, *Crónica Serafica y Apostólica*, 321–442; Bancroft, H. H., *North Mexican States and Texas*, I, 391–406, 609–617; Bolton, H. E., *Athanase De Mézières*, I, 1–66; "The Native Tribes about the East Texas Missions," in Tex. State Hist. Assoc., *Quarterly*, XI, 249–276; "The Location of La Salle's Colony on the Gulf of Mexico," in *The Mississippi Valley Historical Review*, II, 165–182; Bolton, H. E., ed., *Spanish Exploration in the Southwest*, 281–422; Bonilla, Antonio, in Tex. State Hist. Assoc., *Quarterly*, VIII, 1–78; Buckley, E., "The Aguayo Expedition into Texas and Louisiana, 1721–1722," in Tex. State Hist. Assoc., *Quarterly*, XV, 1–65; Clark, R. C., *The Beginnings of Texas;* Cox, I. J., "The Early Settlers of San Fernando," in Tex. State Hist. Assoc., *Quarterly*, V, 142–161; "The Louisiana-Texas Frontier," in Tex. State Hist. Assoc., *Quarterly*, X, 1–76; "The Southwestern Boundary of Texas," in Tex. State Hist. Assoc., *Quarterly*, VI, 81–103; DeLeón, A., "Itinerary," in Tex. State Hist. Assoc., *Quarterly*, VIII, 199–224; *Historia de Nuevo León*, 310–348; Dunn, W. E., "Apache Relations in Texas, 1718–1750," in Tex. State Hist. Assoc., *Quarterly*, XIV, 198–274; "The Apache Mission on the San Saba," in *Southwestern Historical Quarterly*, XVIII, 379–415; Espinosa, Isidro, *Chrónica*, 1–10, 41–158, 206–227; Garrison, G. P., *Texas*, 20–96; Manzanet, in Tex. State Hist. Assoc., *Quarterly*, III, 252–312; Parkman, Francis, *La Salle and the Discovery of the Great West*, chs. 20–29.

PIMERÍA ALTA

Alegre, Xavier, *Historia de la Compañia de Jesus*, III; Bancroft, H. H., *Arizona and New Mexico*, 344–407; *History of the North Mexican States*, I, 237–274, 548–580, 660–691; Bolton, H. E., *Kino's Historical Memoir of Pimería Alta*, especially Vol. I, 27–65; Bolton, H. E., ed., *Spanish Exploration in the Southwest*, 425–463; Chapman, C. E., *The Founding of Spanish California*, 1–67; Ortega, José, *Apostólicos Afanes*, libros II–III; Richman, I. B., *California under Spain and Mexico*, 42–61.

LOWER CALIFORNIA

Alegre, Xavier, *Historia de la Compañia de Jesus*, III, 91–309; Bancroft, H. H., *History of the North Mexican States*, I, 276–304, 407–466, 476–491; Bolton, H. E., *Kino's Historical Memoir*, consult Index under "California," "Picolo," and "Salvatierra"; Engelhardt, Fr. Zephyrin, *Missions and Missionaries of California*, I, 61–600; Hittell, T. H., *History of California*, I, 148–308; North, A. W., *Mother of California*, 1–78; Richman, I. B., *California under Spain and Mexico*, 1–41; Venegas, Migual, *Natural and Civil History of California*, I, 215–455, II, 1–213.

CHAPTER XVII

THE ENGLISH ADVANCE INTO THE PIEDMONT, 1715-1750

THE WESTWARD MOVEMENT

The colonization of North America by the English was not complete with the founding of the seaboard settlements, but continued in a series of steps westward. At each step American society has returned to simple frontier conditions, under which it has been free to try out new experiments in democracy. Each stage of advance has made its special contribution to our institutions.

In a broad way these steps in the westward movement have corresponded with great physiographic areas. The seventeenth century had witnessed the occupation of the Tidewater region, between the coast and the Fall Line. Within that area there had been established two types of society which now projected themselves westward. The New England type was democratic, corporate, theocratic, and industrial, and here the township became the unit of local government. The Southern type, based on a plantation system, staple crops, and dependent labor, was aristocratic, individualistic, and expansive. Here the county became the unit of local government. Intermediate between these types was the society of the middle Tidewater. In spite of these special characteristics, due chiefly to American environment, Tidewater society at the end of the century was still largely European in thought and feeling.

The first half of the eighteenth century witnessed the movement of settlement into the next great physiographic region, the Piedmont, or the area lying between the Fall Line and the Appalachian Mountains. Here, under frontier conditions, was formed a society farther removed from that of Europe, and further modified by American conditions.

This westward movement was the resultant of numerous factors. To the frontier people were attracted by cheap land and unlimited opportunity. From the Tidewater settlements emigrants were driven by increase of population, scarcity of good land, and class conflicts. The less prosperous everywhere, and in the South indented servants who had served their time, were glad to begin life anew on the frontier. Prosperous planters whose estates had been exhausted by tobacco sought the Piedmont, and left their former lands to become "old fields." Speculation in frontier lands became a passion, and while John Law floated his Mississippi Bubble in Louisiana, New England deacons and Virginia aristocrats alike built hopes of fortune on tracts purchased for a song on the border. The movement to the frontier was stimulated in some cases by intercolonial and international rivalry; thus the settlement of Georgia was at once a philanthropic experiment and a defensive movement against Spain. Of larger consequence than the emigrants from the Tidewater settlements were the new arrivals from Europe, who came in tens of thousands, attracted by cheap land and opportunity or driven by economic, political, or religious unrest.

Trails to the Piedmont had been opened by furtraders, who, even in the seventeenth century, had made their way into the wilderness in all directions; by official explorers, like Governor Spotswood; and by the Southern cattlemen who had established "cowpens" at long distances beyond the frontiers of settlement. The Indian barrier was removed at the turn of the century by a series of frontier wars, which either evicted the natives or broke their resistance. Of these the chief examples are King Philip's War in New England, the Susquehannah War in Virginia, the Tuscarora War in North Carolina, and the Yamassee War in South Carolina. The process of expansion, however, involved further struggles with the Indians, and border conflicts with French neighbors on the north and Spanish neighbors on the south.

Under these influences the migration took place and by the middle of the century a continuous back-country settlement had been formed, all the way from Maine to Georgia. New England industries were coastwise, the Piedmont was rough and stony, and expansion was consequently slow. But the open spaces were nearly all filled in, to the northern boundary of Massachusetts, while long spurs of settlement were pushed up the rivers into Vermont, New Hampshire, and Maine, where French rivalry

Mainland Regions occupied by the English, 1700–1760

was encountered. In New York settlement was retarded by the practice of land leasing instead of sales, a relic of the patroon system. Nevertheless a narrow ribbon of settlement pushed up the Mohawk from Albany nearly to Oneida Lake, while the lower Hudson River settlements widened out toward Pennsylvania and into New Jersey.

Into the Southern Piedmont the movement was a double one. Some newcomers and many old settlers crossed the Tidewater and pushed over the Fall Line. But for the Germans, Swiss, and Scotch-Irish, Philadelphia was the chief port of entry and the main distributing point. Thence some pushed up the Delaware into New Jersey and northeastern Pennsylvania; others west into the valleys east of the Kittatiny Range. Those who followed, finding the lands occupied, and meeting here the mountain barrier to the westward march, moved south across the Susquehannah and up the Shenandoah Valley, whence they turned eastward into the Piedmont of Virginia, North Carolina, South Carolina, and even of Georgia. The Scotch-Irish in general kept nearest the outward frontier and became *par excellence* the Indian fighters.

DEFENSE OF THE NORTHERN FRONTIER

English policy.—After the War of the Spanish Succession the English government was keenly alive to the necessity of defending the colonial frontiers. Although the period has been characterized as one of "salutary neglect" on the part of the home government, nevertheless the frontier defences were greatly strengthened. Soon after the signing of the Treaty of Utrecht, the English government became aware of French activities in Louisiana, and advice was sought from several colonial governors as to the best means of checking French and Spanish advance. A policy of defence was soon developed. It included the erection of forts, exploration of the mountain passes, alliances with Indian tribes, development of trade, reorganization of the incompetent proprietary government of the Carolinas, the establishment of the buffer colony of Georgia, and the encouragement of the settlement of the back country by the Germans and Scotch-Irish.

Acadia and the Maine border.—A strange apathy regarding

Acadia was shown by the English government. A small garrison was maintained at Annapolis, but the Acadians continued loyal to the French, and French priests and officials from Cape Breton Island and Canada continued to exert influence over them. The Maine border was strongly held. English settlers again appeared on the lower Kennebec and forts were erected at Augusta and at the falls of the Androscoggin. Somewhat later Ft. Richmond was built on the Kennebec. English activity alarmed the Abenaki and the French soon influenced them to go on the warpath. From 1720 to 1725 a border war continued, but after much bloodshed on both sides the Indians sought peace.

The New York border.—On the New York border, efforts of the French to bring the Iroquois into alliance aroused the English and in 1727 Governor Burnet erected a fort at Oswego. Owing to petty strife between New Hampshire and Massachusetts, and between New York and New Jersey, funds were not provided for a fortification on Lake Champlain, an oversight which gave the French an opportunity to erect a fort at Crown Point.

Pennsylvania and Virginia.—In 1716 Governor Spotswood of Virginia led an expedition to the Blue Ridge and entered the Shenandoah Valley. In his subsequent report he advised the making of settlements on Lake Erie and the securing of the mountain passes. The proposals were not carried out, but soon the back country was settled by Germans and Scotch-Irish, who formed a stronger barrier of defence than walls and palisades.

REORGANIZATION OF THE CAROLINAS

Separation of the Carolinas.—Economically the Carolinas had been drifting apart. Between the Albemarle and Cape Fear districts lay a primeval wilderness two hundred miles in width. The northern district was devoted to the production of naval stores and tobacco, the southern more to rice culture. Politically the governments had been practically separate almost from the beginning, the governor being located at Charleston and a deputy governor being appointed for the north. In 1713 the proprietors appointed Charles Eden as governor of North Carolina, and from this time the two provinces were practically separate.

The Yamassee War.—Between the South Carolina and Spanish settlements lived the Yamassee Indians. In the War of the
Spanish Succession they had remained faithful to the English,
but by 1715 they were won over by the St. Augustine officials.
The French at Mobile were also working on the Creeks and
Cherokees, and a confederation was formed whose object was
the destruction of the South Carolina settlements. The war
began on April 15, 1715, the Yamassee beginning the attack
without the assistance of their allies, and the plantations and
settlements were assailed all along the border. Martial law
was immediately proclaimed in the province, volunteers were
organized, and calls for assistance were sent to North Carolina,
Virginia, New England, and England, the two former respond-
ing with men and ammunition. Several bloody engagements
were fought which turned in favor of the Carolinians. The
Yamassees received reinforcements and renewed their incursions,
but Governor Craven showed such a superior force that the
Indians fled beyond the Edisto and were subsequently driven
far back into the interior.

Overthrow of the proprietors.—The responsibility of defence
against Indians and pirates who infested the coast devolved upon
the settlers, the proprietors showing little ability to assist. The
assembly now took matters in its own hands and changed the
method of elections, so that many large landholders were practically disfranchised. The acts were not approved by the proprietors and the slumbering discontent in the province soon
approached rebellion. The situation was made worse by the
refusal of the proprietors to allow the distribution of the Yamassee lands, and by an order that tracts be set aside for themselves.
Rumors spread that another Spanish invasion threatened and
Governor Johnson sought means of meeting it, but when he asked
advice as to how funds might be raised, he was informed that
the duty which had been imposed after the Yamassee War was
still in force and that other legislation was unnecessary. The
colonists answered the governor's call to arms but soon showed
that they were against him. When Johnson refused to act in
the name of the king instead of the proprietors, he was set aside.
The proprietary government had been in ill favor with the English government for some time. Its incompetence in the Yam-

assee War had convinced the Board of Trade that a change was necessary, and it upheld the popular movement. In 1729 an act of parliament established royal governments in both North and South Carolina.

THE FOUNDING OF GEORGIA

The debatable land.—In the great triangle formed by the Carolinas, Florida, and southeastern Louisiana, English, Spanish, and French came into close proximity. The international boundaries had never been satisfactorily defined and each power strove to acquire control of the powerful Indian tribes of the interior, thereby gaining territory and trade. To protect the border and to aid the Charleston traders, in 1716 the Carolinians established a fort on the Savannah River, and from 1721 to 1727 maintained Ft. King George on the Altamaha. In 1730 Sir Alexander Cuming was sent on a mission to the Cherokees, on which he succeeded in obtaining an acknowledgment of English supremacy, considerably strengthening the English position.

Azilia.—The need of a buffer colony on the southern border was long realized by English statesmen. In 1717 a project was launched which gave promise of fulfillment. Sir Robert Montgomery secured from the Carolina proprietors a grant of the lands between the Savannah and Altamaha Rivers which was called the Margravate of Azilia. Plans for its settlement were drawn up and an attempt made to obtain colonists, but Sir Robert failed to attract settlers and the grant lapsed.

Oglethorpe.—It remained for James Oglethorpe to carry out the project. Oglethorpe had seen considerable military service, and for thirty years was a member of the House of Commons, in the latter capacity advocating an aggressive policy against Spain. Possessed of broadly humanitarian sympathies, he became interested in ameliorating the conditions of imprisoned debtors. He conceived the idea of planting a barrier colony on the southern frontier, which would serve the two-fold purpose of protecting Carolina against Spanish and Indian attacks, and of offering a place of refuge for the debtor class. In 1732 he secured a charter conveying to himself and a group of interested persons the land between the Savannah and Altamaha Rivers and extending westward from their head waters to the sea.

The government.—The government was of the proprietary type, but the proprietors were not to receive any profits individually; financial reports and legislation were to be submitted to the crown for approval. The proprietorship was limited to twenty-one years, after which the province was to become a royal colony. Religious liberty was guaranteed to all but Catholics; provision was made to prevent large land holdings; slavery was prohibited, a restriction which was subsequently removed; the importation of rum was forbidden, as was trade with the Indians without a license.

Savannah.—In the autumn of 1732 about one hundred men, women, and children were sent to America, arriving at Charleston in January, 1733. A treaty was made with the Creeks who surrendered most of their coast lands and the town of Savannah was immediately laid out. The colony was soon strengthened by German and Scotch immigration. In 1737 a fort was established at Augusta and a town grew up which soon developed an important trade with the Cherokees.

Measures of defence.—The Scotch were settled near the mouth of the Altamaha. In 1736 Ft. Frederica was established on St. Simon's Island at the mouth of the river, and military posts were built between the Altamaha and the St. John's Rivers. This encroachment aroused the ire of the Spanish government, which demanded Oglethorpe's recall, but instead, while in Europe, he was given permission to raise a regiment of troops for the protection of Georgia, and upon his return he visited the Creeks, with whom he renewed the former alliance.

THE GERMAN AND SWISS MIGRATION

In 1690 the population of the English colonies on the continent of North America was only two hundred thousand; fifty years later it had increased to a million, and by 1760 another half million had been added. In part this was due to natural increase, but a large population came from the influx of Europeans other than English, the two principal immigrant peoples being the Germans and the Scotch-Irish.

The German migration.—The causes of the German migration are to be found in the disturbed condition of Germany. Religious persecution, political oppression, and economic distress caused by wars and bad seasons, each played its part in the movement. Most of the immigrants came from southwestern Germany, especially from the Palatinate, Württemberg, and Baden, and from Switzerland. The first period of migration, dating from 1683 to 1710, was characterized by a small movement of per-

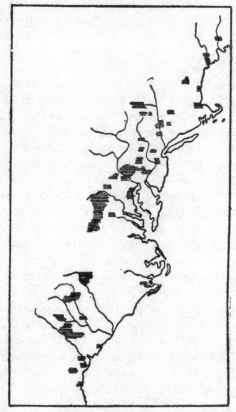

Principal Areas of German Settlement before 1763

secuted sects; but after 1710 an ever-increasing migration took place in which the religious, political, and economic causes blended.

The early migration to Pennsylvania.—The first German settlement in the English colonies may be traced directly to William Penn's visit to the Rhineland in 1677. A group of pietists from Frankfort-on-the-Main purchased fifteen thousand acres of Penn's land and in 1683 sent over a young lawyer, Francis Daniel Pastorius, as advance agent, who became the recognized leader of the Pennsylvania Germans. He was soon followed by a considerable number of emigrants. More land was purchased and the settlement of Germantown begun. In 1684 a group of Labadists settled on the Bohemian River in the present state of Delaware. Every year a few people joined the original group at Germantown. The most important addition was in 1694 when forty Rosicrucians under John Kelpius settled on the banks of the Wissahickon.

The migration to New York.—Not until 1710 did the great flood of migration begin. In 1707 a portion of the Palatinate was devastated. The following year sixty-one homeless people led by Joshua von Kockerthal made their way to London. The Board of Trade sent them to New York, where Governor Lovelace gave them lands on the Hudson, where they began the town of Newburg. Religious persecution, political oppression, the devastation of Württemberg and a part of the Palatinate, and a hard winter caused a great exodus in 1709. In May of that year the Germans began to arrive in London, and by October the numbers had swelled to thirteen thousand. About thirty-five hundred were sent to the colonies. Six hundred and fifty were settled at Newbern near the mouth of the Neuse River in North Carolina, and about three thousand were sent to New York, where Governor Hunter hoped to settle them on lands where tar and pitch could be produced. The story goes that in London the Palatines had met a delegation of Indian chiefs who had promised them lands on the Schoharie, a branch of the Mohawk. Instead of being sent there, however, many were placed on lands along both sides of the Hudson near Saugerties. The colony on the west side was called West Camp, and contained about six hundred people. The East Camp, which was located on the manor of Robert Livingston, received nearly twelve hundred; it was here that difficulties occurred. The attempts to produce tar and pitch failed, and the colonists demanded that they be moved to the Schoharie. After much bickering with the governor, in 1712 and 1713 many of the people from East Camp moved to the Schoharie; but their troubles did not end, for the question of land title brought them into disputes with certain landowners from Albany. Some of the Palatines moved again, many taking up lands in the Mohawk Valley between Ft. Hunter and Frankfort, while others in 1723 and 1727 migrated to Pennsylvania, settling in Berks County.

The later Pennsylvania migration.—The harsh treatment in New York and the kind reception of Germans in Pennsylvania made the Quaker colony a favorite place for their coming. Between 1710 and 1727 from fifteen to twenty thousand entered Pennsylvania and settled in Lancaster, Berks, and Montgomery counties. Between 1727 and 1740 the arrivals numbered about fifty-seven thousand, and between 1741 and 1756 about twenty thousand. Many of the newcomers settled in Philadelphia, and neighboring counties, but the desire for cheap land carried a large number into the fertile valleys of the Susquehanna, Lehigh, and Shenandoah. In the words of Professor Faust, "They . . . pushed northward and westward to Lehigh, Northampton, and Monroe counties, and to Lebanon and Dauphin; reaching the Susquehanna they crossed and settled the counties of York, Cumberland, and Adams, then following the slopes of the mountains they went southward through Maryland into Virginia, ascending the Shenandoah Valley and settling it from Harpers Ferry to Lexington, Virginia. Using this main avenue for their progress, they settled in North Carolina and Virginia and later in Kentucky and Tennessee. Pennsylvania, therefore, was the distributing center for the German immigrations, whence German settlers spread over all the neighboring provinces."

New Jersey.—As early as 1707 several members of the German Reformed Church appear to have settled in Morris County, and later spread into Somerset, Bergen, and Essex counties. Later groups, mainly of Lutherans or German Reformed, settled in Hunterdon, Somerset, Morris, Sussex, and Warren counties, and there were scattered settlements elsewhere.

Maryland.—A few Germans came to Maryland before 1730, but with the founding of Baltimore in that year a considerable German migration began, enterprising Germans from Pennsylvania finding the new town a place for their capital and energy. At about the same time the Germans were settling in western Maryland. In 1729 Germans from Pennsylvania settled about ten miles north of the modern town of Frederick, and soon many German settlements dotted Frederick and neighboring counties.

Virginia.—The first Germans in Virginia were skilled iron-workers from Westphalia, brought in by Governor Spotswood to operate his iron works which were located on the Piedmont Plateau at Germanna, in modern Orange County. The settlers at Germanna afterward migrated to Germantown near the Rappahannock and to Madison County. A far more important movement was the migration into the Shenandoah Valley. The northern part was settled almost entirely by Germans, but in the southern part they formed only a small part of the population. The first of the settlers came from Lancaster County, Pennsylvania, in 1726 or 1727, settling near Elkton. They were soon followed by others, among them Joist Hite at the head of sixteen families from York, Pennsylvania, who settled at the site of Winchester. In 1734 Robert Harper founded Harper's Ferry. The most remote settlements were located in the Alleghanies within the present state of West Virginia; one on Patterson's Creek, another on the south branch of the Potomac, and a third on the New River, which with the Greenbrier forms the Great Kanawha. Thus the frontier had already reached the "Western Waters."

North Carolina.—As already noted, the first migration of Germans into North Carolina was connected with the Palatine movement of 1710; the lands of Baron Graffenried on which they settled being at the confluence of the Neuse and Trent Rivers. In the following year the Tuscaroras went on the war-path; about sixty of the newcomers were slain and their settlement destroyed. The Tuscaroras eventually were incorporated with the Iroquois Confederation and the settlers took advantage of the removal to occupy their lands, soon spreading over a large part of what is now Craven County. About 1745, Germans from Pennsylvania began to arrive in the western part of North Carolina, taking up lands along the Yadkin River. Not until 1750 did the immigrants become numerous. By the time of the Revolution there were important German settlements in Stokes, Forsyth, Guilford, Davidson, Rowan, and Cabarrus counties.

South Carolina.—In South Carolina the first German colonists settled in or near Charleston. In 1732 a settlement was made in Beaufort County and German villages soon dotted both sides of the Edisto and Congaree Rivers in Orangeburg and Lexington counties and spread out toward the Georgia boundary, Baden, Württemberg, Switzerland, and discontents from Maine furnishing most of the South Carolina Germans.

Swiss migration to Carolina and Pennsylvania.—With the exception of Graffenried's project, no large enterprise for bringing Swiss settlers to America was launched until 1725, when Jean Purry of Neufchatel began to advertise for Swiss Protestants to found a colony in Carolina. In 1732 Purry succeeded in establishing Purrysburgh, which soon had several hundred inhabitants. Crop failures in Switzerland coupled with heavy taxation and a dislike for foreign military service caused a large number to migrate between 1730 and 1750. Although accurate statistics are lacking, recent investigation shows that during the eighteenth century probably twenty-five thousand Swiss emigrated to Pennsylvania and the Carolinas.

Georgia.—In 1731 thirty thousand Protestants of Salzburg were exiled. Some of them made their way to England and eventually became settlers in the newly-constituted colony of Georgia. The first ones arrived at Savannah in 1734 and moved to lands on the Savannah River about forty miles from its mouth, naming their settlement Ebenezer. Others soon followed. Oglethorpe wished some of them to settle about the fort on St. Simon Island, but they objected to bearing arms and were allowed to go to Ebenezer. Others, who had no religious scruples regarding war, were settled at Frederica. The settlers from Ebenezer soon moved down the river eight miles to New Ebenezer, across the river from Purrysburgh. By 1741 over twelve hundred Germans had come to Georgia.

New England and Nova Scotia.—A small number of Germans made their way to New England. The head of the movement was Samuel Waldo, who became interested in lands on the shores of Broad Bay in Maine. In 1740 forty families from Brunswick and Saxony founded Waldoborough. In 1749–1750 Massachusetts made an effort to increase German immigration by setting aside lands for their use. One of these districts was near Fort

Massachusetts in modern Franklin County and extended beyond into what is now Vermont. Three years later the first German settlers entered the region. In 1751 Joseph Crellius brought over twenty or thirty families who founded Frankfort, subsequently called Dresden, on the Kennebec River. It has been estimated that fifteen hundred Germans entered New England in 1752–1753, but many of them moved subsequently to South Carolina. Another group settled at Braintree near Boston, but by 1760 they had all moved to the Maine settlements. During 1750–1753 occurred a considerable German migration to Nova Scotia, sixteen hundred settling in Lunenburg County. In the latter year the English Government checked the movement, which was deflected to New England, and the settlements at Broad Bay and on the Kennebec were considerably enlarged.

THE SCOTCH–IRISH

Causes of the Scotch-Irish migration.—Of equal importance with the German migration was that of the Scotch-Irish from Ulster. The causes of the migration to America were both religious and economic. The Presbyterianism of the Scotch found scant favor with the English authorities. The efforts to enforce uniformity, and the various religious laws of the reign of Charles II and Anne were especially obnoxious to Presbyterians. Though few migrated because of them, they left a feeling of injury, which, coupled with industrial hardships, brought about the great migration to America. English restrictive legislation was also an important factor. Laws prohibiting the importation into England of Irish stock and dairy products, acts excluding Irish vessels from American trade and prohibiting direct importation to Ireland from the colonies, and the act of 1699 prohibiting the exportation of Irish wool worked great hardships on the people of Ulster. The enforced payment of tithes to support the Episcopalian clergy touched both the purse and the conscience of the Scotch-Irish. But more important than any of these was the tenant system. In 1714–1718 many of the original leases expired and the landlords doubled or trebled the rents. This is the chief explanation of the great acceleration of the movement to America which began in 1714. No doubt the natural business instinct of the Scotch

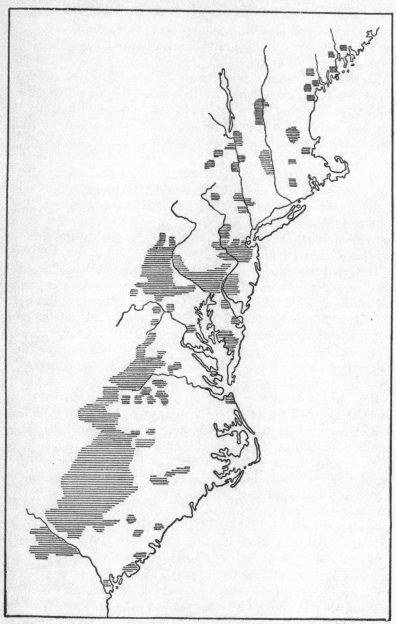

The Areas Largely Populated by Scotch-Irish before 1763

323

people, and occasional crop failures, such as the potato famine in 1725, 1740–1741, also hastened many who otherwise might have lingered in Ulster.

Seventeenth century migration.—In 1612 the Rev. George Keith, a Scotchman, went to Bermuda, the first dissenting minister in the English colonies. In 1652 Cromwell sent about two hundred and fifty Scotch prisoners to New England. Before 1669 a considerable number of Scotch and Scotch-Irish settled on the eastern shore of Chesapeake Bay and by 1680 some Scotch Presbyterians were located near Norfolk. In 1683 Scottish colonists landed at Port Royal and Charleston, and others founded Stuartstown. In 1684 and 1685, many Scotch dissenters sought refuge in East New Jersey, the beginning of a movement which eventually made New Jersey one of the strongholds of Presbyterianism.

The great migration.—During the early years of the eighteenth century a few Scotch-Irish made their way to America, but not until after the close of the War of the Spanish Succession did the movement assume large proportions. The tide of immigration which set in brought the Scotch-Irish to every colony. Many of them found homes in the tide-water lands among the older settlements, where vast areas were still thinly settled, but a larger number sought the frontier.

New England.—Between 1714 and 1720 fifty-four vessels brought Scotch-Irish immigrants to Boston. The large influx of foreigners began to alarm the authorities. When over five hundred arrived at Boston in the summer of 1718, a shortage of provisions threatened. To place the immigrants on a self-supporting basis was highly desirable. In addition the more remote settlements needed protection. The plan was accordingly adopted of sending the Scotch-Irish to the frontier. About fifty miles from Boston was the post of Worcester containing about two hundred people. Soon its population was doubled by Scotch-Irish. Others came and Worcester became the distributing point for interior settlement. In 1731 Pelham was started thirty miles to the westward, and two years later Colerain, twenty miles farther in the wilderness, was formed. In 1741 Warren and Blandford were incorporated. From western Massachusetts the settlers turned northward, following the Connecticut Valley, forming settlements in Windsor, Orange, and Caledonia counties in Vermont and in Grafton County in New Hampshire.

While Worcester was being settled, other immigrants sought lands in Maine. Thirty families were landed at Falmouth on Casco Bay, another group settled on the Kennebec near its mouth, and by 1720 several hundred families had settled on the Kennebec or the Androscoggin, but soon afterward Indian troubles caused a large part of them to move to New Hampshire cr Pennsylvania. In 1719 Nutfield on the site of modern Manchester was founded. When the town was incorporated in 1722 its name was changed to Londonderry. It became the distributing point for Scotch-Irish in that region; from there Rockingham, Hillsboro, and Merrimack counties in New Hampshire were settled. Emigration spread over into Vermont, joining that from Worcester, and pushed on to the north and west. Still other Scotch-Irish settlements were formed later in Maine. A hundred and fifty families from Nova Scotia in 1729 settled at Pemaquid and Samuel Waldo induced a few to settle on the St. George at Warren. Connecticut and Rhode Island also received an infusion of Scotch-Irish blood but in a much less degree than the northern frontier.

New York.—About 1718 large numbers of Scotch-Irish came to New York, most of them settling in Orange and Ulster counties. In 1738 John Lindesay and three associates obtained an extensive land grant in Cherry Valley in modern Otsego County. Many settlers were induced to come from Londonderry, New Hampshire, and from Scotland and Ulster, but the exposed position prevented a great influx in succeeding years.

Pennsylvania.—As in the German movement, in the Scotch-Irish migration the largest number came to Pennsylvania. The earliest comers appear to have settled on either side of the Pennsylvania-Maryland line in the Susquehanna Valley. The exact date of their arrival is uncertain, but a church had been organized as early as 1708. About 1720 the immigrants began working up the Delaware River, settling in Bucks County and spreading over into Northampton County. Another stream of immigrants passed up the Susquehanna Valley, settling along the creek bottoms on the east side of the river, their chief centers being in Chester, Lancaster, and Dauphin counties in Pennsylvania, and in Cecil County, Maryland. Before 1730 the settlers pushed over into Cumberland County, Pennsylvania, which gave them access to the valleys of the interior. They spread into Franklin, Adams, and York counties and the later movement carried them southward into the great valleys.

The Southern Piedmont.—By 1735 or earlier, the Scotch-Irish began moving into the Shenandoah Valley. Some of them remained in Maryland and the most eastern counties of what is now West Virginia, but most of them moved into Virginia, taking up the lands west of the Blue Ridge Mountains. Many went through the passes and made their homes in the Piedmont region to the east of the Blue Ridge. The movement was greatly stimulated by the fact that several large land grants were made to various Pennsylvanians and Virginians, who encouraged the settlement of their lands. The early records of the Scotch-Irish in the southern Piedmont give us little exact data, but between 1740 and 1760 scattered settlements were made along the frontier from Virginia to Florida. In North Carolina the lands between the Yadkin and Catawba Rivers were settled. By 1750 the vanguard appeared in the western part of South Carolina, and a few years later in the upland country of Georgia.

SIGNIFICANCE OF THE SETTLEMENT OF THE PIEDMONT

By the middle of the century results of great significance had come about. All the way from New England to Georgia a back country society had been formed, with characteristics in many ways distinct from that of the Tidewater settlements. A large portion of the settlers, particularly south of New York, were of non-English stock, and had brought with them diverse notions; but, under the influence of frontier environment, they had been moulded, together with the English stock, into a more or less homogeneous mass. In the main the settlers were persons of slender means, and lived hard, frontier lives. They tilled small farms with their own hands, and indentured servitude and slave-holding were consequently unimportant. Society, on the whole, was democratic, individualistic, tolerant, and self-reliant. In spite of this homogeneity of the frontier, the original traits of the settlers persisted, and can still be found in the Pennsylvania

"Dutch" or in the Scotch Presbyterians of the Southern Piedmont.

Being distinct in character and interests, the Piedmont and Tidewater clashed at many points, and thus arose "sectional" contests between the East and the West, a feature which has marked American development down to the present. The simple back country constituted a debtor society, in need of an expanding credit; the coast was more aristocratic and more capitalistic. The East attempted to dominate politics, legislation, and administration. The West resisted, and before the Revolution contests arose in nearly every colony. In many instances the back country won; its victories are reflected in the provisions for religious toleration and in the democratic tendencies of the new state constitutions formed during and after the Revolution.

There were other important consequences from the settlement of the back country. In spite of divergent interests, there were bonds of union between the East and the West. The new settlements furnished a market for eastern goods and provided commodities in exchange, and thus lessened the dependence of the coast upon Europe. Attended by Indian wars and border hostilities with French and Spanish neighbors, the westward movement had created a fighting frontier. At the same time, by bringing the international frontiers into conflict, it had prepared the way for the final struggle between France and England in America.

It was the southern Piedmont which furnished leaders for the southwestward movement in the succeeding generations. Says Turner: "Among this moving mass, as it passed along the Valley into the Piedmont, in the middle of the eighteenth century, were Daniel Boone, John Sevier, James Robertson, and the ancestors of John C. Calhoun, Abraham Lincoln, Jefferson Davis, Stonewall Jackson, James K. Polk, Sam Houston, and Davy Crockett; while the father of Andrew Jackson came to the Piedmont at the same time from the coast. Recalling that Thomas Jefferson's home was in this frontier, at the edge of the Blue Ridge, we perceive that these names represent the militant expansive movement in American life. They foretell the settlement across the Alleghanies in Kentucky and Tennessee; the Louisiana Purchase, the Lewis and Clark's transcontinental exploration; the conquest of the Gulf Plains in the War of 1812–15; the annexation of Texas; the acquisition of California and the Spanish Southwest. They represent, too, frontier democracy in its two aspects personified in Andrew Jackson and Abraham Lincoln. It was a democracy responsive to leadership, susceptible to waves of emotion, of a 'high religious voltage'—quick and direct in action."

READINGS

DEFENCE OF THE FRONTIERS

Channing, Edward, *History of the United States*, II, 341–365; Dickerson, O. M., *American Colonial Government*, 326–332; Fiske, John, *Old Virginia and her Neighbors*, II, 383–389; Greene, E. B., *Provincial America*, 181–184, 249–262; Hamilton, P. J., *The Colonization of the South*, 291–308; Jones, C. C., *The History of Georgia*, I, 67–313; Kingsford, William, *The History of Canada*, III, 121–201; McCrady, Edward, *A History of South Carolina*, I, 531–680; Parkman, Francis, *A Half-Century of Conflict*, I, 183–271, II, 53–56; McCain, J. R., *Georgia as a Proprietary Province*.

THE GERMAN AND SWISS MIGRATION

Bernheim, G. D., *German Settlements in North and South Carolina;* Bittinger, L. F., *The Germans in Colonial Times*, 11–183; Cobb, S. H.. *The Story of the Palatines;* Faust, A. B., *The German Element in the United States*, I, 30–262; "Swiss Emigration to the American Colonies in the Eighteenth Century," in *The American Historical Review*, XXII, 21–44; Jones, C. C., *The History of Georgia*, I, 163–173, 208–214; Kuhns, O., *The German and Swiss Settlements of Colonial Pennsylvania*, 1–192; Wayland, J. W., *The German Element of the Shenandoah Valley of Virginia*.

THE SCOTCH-IRISH

Campbell, Douglas, *The Puritan in Holland, England, and America*, II, 469–485; Ford, H. J., *The Scotch-Irish in America*, 1–290; Hanna, C. A., *The Scotch-Irish*, II, 6–126; Turner, F. J., "The Old West," in Wis. Hist. Soc., *Proceedings, 1908*.

CHAPTER XVIII

ENGLISH COLONIAL SOCIETY IN THE MIDDLE EIGHTEENTH CENTURY

GENERAL FEATURES

Population and settled area.—By 1760 the population of the English continental colonies was probably 1,650,000; of these the New England colonies contained about a half-million, the middle group about four hundred and fifty thousand, and south of the Mason-Dixon line there were about seven hundred thousand. Nearly half of the inhabitants were in Massachusetts, Pennsylvania and Virginia. The bulk of the population still clung to the coastal regions, but the rivers had pointed the way to the interior; many of the valleys were occupied for a considerable distance, and the Germans and Scotch-Irish had penetrated the great valleys of the central and southern Appalachians. Practically the whole of Massachusetts, Rhode Island, and Connecticut had been occupied; to the northward extended three narrow lines of settlement, one along the New Hampshire and Maine coast as far as the Penobscot and extending fifty miles up the Kennebec, another reaching up the Merrimac for sixty miles into central New Hampshire, and a third following the Connecticut for fifty miles above the northern Massachusetts line. Long Island was almost entirely settled, as was the Hudson Valley to a point a little above Albany, and the lower Mohawk Valley had been settled. New Jersey, except in the central part and a small section of the eastern coast, was occupied. Eastern Pennsylvania, the lower valley of the Susquehanna, and adjacent valleys were peopled, as was the western shore of Delaware Bay. Maryland and Virginia were settled up to the mountains and had overflowed into the valleys of the Blue Ridge. In North Carolina the settlements extended back for a hundred and fifty miles or more from the coast and as far south as the valley of the Cape Fear River. In the back country of North and South Carolina and Georgia the valleys were occupied and the population had flowed over onto the eastern slopes of the Appalachians. The coast lands of South Carolina and Georgia as far as the Altamaha, and the lowlands along the Pedee, Santee, and Savannah Rivers were occupied for a hundred miles from the coast.

The older settled areas were below the Fall Line. There the industrial and social life was less in a state of flux than along the ever-advancing frontier. The economic tendencies in the coast country were already fixed and showed little change until machinery and transporation worked an industrial revolution early in the nineteenth century. The social life was also comparatively stable and was so to remain until the Revolutionary War.

Manufacturing and mining.—During the colonial period manufacturing made little progress, due mainly to the abundance of cheap land and English restrictions. The colonists depended mainly upon England for manufactured goods. Nevertheless, manufacturing made some headway, especially in the North, where agricultural pursuits brought less profit than in the South. The coarser fabrics, linen, hats, and shoes were produced for the local markets. Mining was also beginning, iron mines having been developed in New England, Pennsylvania, Maryland, and Virginia, and at least one copper mine was worked in New Jersey. Ironworks were established in the neighborhood of the mines and supplied many of the local needs. In 1750 an act was passed by parliament which allowed colonial pig-iron to be imported into England and bar-iron to enter the port of London. The manufacture of rum was an important northern industry.

NEW ENGLAND INDUSTRY

Farming.—During the colonial period the great mass of the people were engaged in agriculture. In New England, where soil and climate were less favorable than in the South, the small farm with diversified crops was the prevailing type. The supply of labor was limited and wages relatively high. Under such conditions, the farmer, his sons, and the "hired man" worked the place, and by dint of industry made a living. The New England farmer was more nearly self-sufficient than any other class, a condition which no doubt increased his feeling of independence. The products of the farm were usually adequate for local needs but furnished practically nothing for exportation.

Lumbering and ship-building.—The New England forests continued to be a source of wealth. Lumber was produced in large quantities and ship-building was carried on extensively in the coast and river towns, the craft being of a somewhat larger type than formerly, vessels of five hundred tons burden frequently leaving the ways. The English navy and merchant marine obtained large quantities of masts and spars from New England.

The fisheries.—The importance of the fisheries increased greatly after the War of the Spanish Succession. From the Newfoundland banks were derived the chief products for foreign trade. Almost every coast town had its fishing fleet, Gloucester alone boasting nearly a hundred vessels. The cod was the most important catch, but as the century progressed whaling became a more and more important industry.

Commerce.—With the West Indies the New Englanders carried on an extensive trade, lumber, fish, and rum being exchanged for sugar, molasses, and other tropical products. Rum was also an important factor in the slave trade, which was carried on mainly by the Rhode Islanders, who exchanged the products of the distilleries for negroes on the Guinea Coast and in the West Indies. These in turn were traded to the southern colonies for tobacco, rice, indigo, and naval stores. From the profits of southern commerce and from fish, lumber, and naval stores, the New Englanders were able to puchase English textiles, hardware, glass, and other manufactured articles. The chief port was Boston which contained about twenty thousand inhabitants.

THE MIDDLE COLONIES

Intensive farming was at its best in the middle colonies, which were the great producers of provisions. Live stock, cereals, fruit, and vegetables were raised in large quantities, the animal products and grain furnishing the chief products for exportation. Lumber and furs were also important items of commerce.

New York.—An observant English traveler who visited New York in 1760, gives the following excellent description of the colony: "The province in its cultivated state affords grain of

all sorts, cattle, hogs, and great variety of English fruits. . . .
The people . . . export chiefly grain, flour, pork, skins, furs,
pig-iron, lumber, and staves. . . . They make a small quantity
of cloth, some linen, hats, shoes, and other articles of wearing
apparel. They make glass also, and wampum; refine sugars,
which they import from the West Indies; and distil considerable
quantities of rum." He also noted that the New Yorkers were
engaged in ship-building. The Indian traffic was mainly carried
on through Albany. The foreign and coastwise trade was concentrated at New York, a city with a population of sixteen
or seventeen thousand.

New Jersey.—New Jersey was fortunate in having an historian who has left us an excellent account of the province.
Samuel Smith's history gives the following description: "Almost
the whole extent of the province adjoining on the atlantick, is
barrens, or nearly approaching it; yet there are scattering settlements all along the coast, the people subsisting in great part by
raising cattle in the bog undrained meadows and marshes, and
selling them to graziers, and cutting down the cedars. . . . Another means of subsistence along the coast, is the plenty of fish
and oysters, these are carried to New-York and Philadelphia
markets. . . . The lands in general, (perhaps something better
than two thirds of the whole) are good, and bear wheat, barley,
or anything else suitable to the climate, to perfection. As the
province has very little foreign trade on bottoms of its own, the
produce of all kinds for sale, goes chiefly to New-York and
Philadelphia; much of it is there purchased for markets abroad;
but some consumed among themselves."

Pennsylvania and Delaware.—Agriculture was the mainstay
of the people of Pennsylvania and Delaware. The thrifty
Quakers, Germans, Scotch-Irish, and Swedes who formed the
bulk of the population, produced large quantities of grain and
live-stock. The surplus was brought to Philadelphia, a well-
built city of nearly twenty thousand inhabitants. Peter Kalm
has left the following picture of its industrial life: "Several
ships are annually built of American oak in the docks. . . . The
town carries on a great trade both with the inhabitants of the
country and to other parts of the world, especially to the West
Indies, South America, and the Antilles; to England, Ireland,

Portugal, and to several English colonies in North America. Yet none but English ships are allowed to come into this port. Philadelphia reaps the greatest profits from its trade to the West Indies: for thither the inhabitants ship almost every day a quantity of flour, butter, flesh, and other victuals, timber, plank, and the like. In return they receive either sugar, molasses, rum, indigo, mahogany, and other goods, or ready money. . . . They send both West India goods and their own products to England; the latter are all sorts of woods, especially walnut, and oak planks for ships; ships ready built, iron, hides, and tar. . . . Ready money is likewise sent over to England; from whence in return they get all sorts of goods there manufactured, viz: fine and coarse cloth, linen, iron ware, and other wrought metals, and East India goods; for it is to be observed, that England supplies Philadelphia with almost all stuffs and manufactured goods which are wanted here. A great quantity of linseed goes annually to Ireland, together with many of the ships which are built here. Portugal gets wheat, flour, and maize which is not ground. Spain sometimes takes some corn. But all the money which is got in these several countries, must immediately be sent to England, in payment for the goods which are got from thence, and yet those sums are not sufficient to pay all the debts."

THE SOUTHERN COLONIES

The tobacco colonies.—Maryland, Virginia, and the northeastern part of North Carolina continued to be devoted largely to the raising of tobacco. Except on the frontiers the small farms had disappeared, having been absorbed by great landholdings. Many of the plantations covered thousands of acres, but probably not more than a tenth of the land was under cultivation. The tobacco crop was extremely exhaustive to the soil, and when the land had been cropped until its productivity decreased, wheat or corn were usually planted, or it was turned into pasturage. The tangled thicket soon sprang up and in the wilderness ranged cattle and hogs. The breeding of horses was attended to with care, for horse-racing and fox-hunting were favorite diversions among the planters, but the cattle and hogs were of inferior quality. The great article of commerce was tobacco, but grain, pork, and lumber were also exported. From

the Madeiras the planters received wines and from the West
Indies rum, sugar, molasses, and slaves. Most of the manufactured articles came directly from England. In spite of the considerable trade, no large towns had sprung up, the plantation
continuing to be the economic and social unit of the tobacco
colonies.

The industries of North Carolina were more diversified than
those of the other southern colonies as is shown by the following
statement from Edmund Burke's *Account of the European
Settlements in America:* "Exported from all the ports of North
Carolina in 1753:

Tar..........................	61,528 barrels
Pitch.........................	12,055 ditto
Turpentine....................	10,429 ditto
Staves........................	762,330 no.
Shingles......................	2,500,000 no.
Lumber.......................	2,000,647 feet
Corn.........................	61,580 bushels
Peas, about...................	10,000 ditto.
Pork & Beef..................	3,300 barrels
Tobacco, about...............	100 hogsheads
Tanned lea[ther] about.........	1,000 hundred weight
Deer skins, in all ways, about....	30,000

"Besides a very considerable quantity of wheat, rice, bread,
potatoes, bees-wax, tallow, candles, bacon, hog's lard, some
cotton, and a vast deal of squared timber of walnut and cedar,
and hoops and headings of all sorts. Of late they raise indigo,
but in what quantity I cannot determine, for it is all exported
from South Carolina. They raise likewise much more tobacco
than I have mentioned, but this, as it is produced on the frontiers
of Virginia, so it is exported from thence. They export too no
inconsiderable quantity of beaver, racoon, otter, fox, minx, and
wild cat skins, and in every ship a good deal of live cattle, besides
what they vend in Virginia."

The rice country.—The great staple of South Carolina was
rice, which was grown upon the marshy lands. A limited amount
was also produced in North Carolina and Georgia. The unhealthfulness of the rice fields, coupled with the large profits from the
business, were factors which made negro slavery seem desirable.
In 1733 the whites in South Carolina numbered about seven

thousand, in 1748 about twenty-five thousand, and in 1765 about forty thousand, but this increase was due largely to the great migration to the back country. Between 1753 and 1773 it is estimated that about forty-three thousand slaves were brought into the province.

Indigo.—In 1741 or 1742 Miss Elizabeth Lucas, the daughter of the governor of Antigua, planted some indigo seed on the Lucas plantation near Charleston. From this beginning the indigo business rapidly developed. In 1747 the colony produced 134,118 pounds; in 1754 over 200,000 pounds were exported, and shortly before the Revolution over 1,000,000 pounds were shipped annually.

Commerce.—Charleston was the commercial center. Its white population was about five thousand in 1760 and it contained about an equal number of negroes. In the summer and autumn the population increased, as the planters' families stayed in the metropolis to escape the unhealthfulness of the back country. Hundreds of vessels were engaged in the South Carolina trade, the products being shipped to the northern colonies and to the West Indies, to Holland, Portugal, the Mediterranean, and England. From the profits the planters purchased the necessities and luxuries of English manufacture, the wines of Portugal and Madeira, and the rum, sugar, molasses, and slaves of the West Indies.

Georgia.—In 1760 Georgia contained about six thousand whites and thirty-five hundred negroes. Industry was diversified, as is shown by a report of Governor Wright of 1766 which says: "Our whole time and strength . . . is applied in planting rice, corn, peas, and a small quantity of wheat and rye, and in making pitch, tar, and turpentine, and in making shingles and staves, and sawing lumber and scantling, and boards of every kind, and in raising stocks of cattle, mules and hogs. . . ." In addition there was considerable fur trade, for which Augusta was the center.

LABOR SYSTEMS

Free labor.—The preponderance of agriculture and the abundance of cheap land made a continual demand for laborers. The climatic and soil conditions determined the labor system of each area. In the north the small farm was usually tilled by the owner and his sons, aided by hired help especially during harvest time. The men of a neighborhood frequently combined to do important pieces of work, such as clearing land, house-building, haying, harvesting, and corn-husking.

Indented servants.—The great plantations of the south demanded large forces of laborers, and there the bond servants and slaves formed the important elements of the laboring classes. The indented servants were of two classes, voluntary and involuntary. The voluntary servants were those who, for transportation and maintenance, willingly bound themselves to a master for a term of years. In the seventeenth century the usual term had been seven years, but in the eighteenth the demand for labor was so strong that the limit was usually four years. At the end of the term of service the servant either worked for hire or "took up" land. Many moved to the frontier where they soon became prosperous farmers.

The involuntary bond servants were paupers, disorderly persons, and criminals. The harsh penal laws of England at that time recognized three hundred capital crimes. Imprisonment for debt and for political offenses swelled the numbers in confinement. To relieve the situation parliamentary acts were passed which allowed the commutation of the death penalty to a service of fourteen years in the colonies, and seven years in place of branding and whipping. We have no data for exact numbers of indented servants, but a careful student of industrial life in the colonies has estimated that they probably constituted one-half of all English immigrants, the middle colonies, Maryland, and Virginia, receiving the larger numbers.

Slavery.—In the seventeenth century negro slavery was of minor importance in the mainland colonies, but as the plantation system developed slaves became an ever-increasing element. In the New England colonies and Pennsylvania they were used principally as house servants. In New York and New Jersey they formed from eight to ten per cent. of the population. It has been estimated that in 1760 there were four hundred thousand slaves south of Pennsylvania. In Maryland they constituted about thirty per cent. of the population, probably forty per cent. in Virginia, and sixty per cent. in South Carolina.

FEATURES OF SOCIETY

Near the coast.—Colonial society in the older settled regions was aristocratic rather than democratic. This was due mainly to English customs and traditions, to an increasing wealth and corresponding raising of the standard of living, to the strength of the religious institutions, and to the colonial system, which provided for a considerable body of officials. In New England the ruling classes were the clergy and the selectmen, who occupied the important places both in the church and in political life; the official class, at the head of whom was the governor; and a third group, the merchants, who usually were not admitted to the governor's circle, and who were apt to voice their social disapprobation in their influence upon legislation. In New York and eastern New Jersey the great landholders and the official group controlled politics and society. In western New Jersey and Pennsylvania the Quakers were politically, socially, and commercially the preponderant element. In the South the plantation owners formed an aristocracy whose social lines were drawn with distinctness.

The frontier.—In contrast to the tide-water country, frontier society was distinctly individualistic and democratic. The Scotch-Irish and Germans had flocked to the mountain country. There they had built their cabins, made their clearings in the forest, and lived a life free from the conventions of the longer settled communities. Hunting, fur-trading, lumbering, and cattle raising were their chief pursuits. The danger from Indian attack was a constant menace, and personal bravery and resourcefulness were strongly marked characteristics. With it all they were a religious people, the Presbyterians and Pietists being predominant.

The Anglican church.—The religious lines marked out in the seventeenth century were followed in the eighteenth with one notable exception, namely, the growth of the Anglican church. This was due mainly in the first instance to the efforts of the Bishop of London who sent commissaries to America, the first being James Blair who was sent to Virginia in 1689, and the second Thomas Bray, who in 1695 was sent to inquire into the state of the colonial church. The result of Bray's inquiry was

the founding in 1701 of the Society for Propagating the Gospel.
At the time of its foundation nearly all of the Episcopal churches
were in Virginia and Maryland. In 1759 Thomas Sherlock, the
Bishop of London, reported that, "at least one half of the Plantations are of the established Church. . . . This is the case of
S° Carolina, N° Carolina, Virginia, Maryland, Jamaica, Barbadoes, Antegoa, Nevis, and the rest of the Caribbee Islands.
On the other side—Pennsylvania is in the hands and under the
governmt of the Quakers, and New England and the adjoining
Colonies are in the hands of the Independents. But in some of
them are great numbers of Churchmen."

The Great Awakening.—The eighteenth century witnessed a
great change in the New England churches. After a hundred
years the early enthusiasm of the Puritan church had subsided,
and though its doctrine had changed but slightly, a marked
change in emphasis had taken place. Conversion was still considered a divine work, but the belief had become current that
the soul could be put in touch with the spirit of God by prayer,
scriptural study, regular church attendance, participation in the
Lord's Supper, a moral life, and having been born of parents who
belonged to the church, by "owning the covenant." Against
these views Jonathan Edwards rebelled. In 1734 at Northampton, Edwards preached a series of sermons in which he
defended the doctrine of justification by faith alone. He
pleaded for immediate repentance and denied that good deeds
would lead to salvation. The religious revival, started at Northampton, soon spread throughout Connecticut, and reverberated
in Boston. At the height of the movement George Whitefield,
the friend of the Wesleys, after preaching in Georgia and South
Carolina, in 1740 visited New England where thousands were
converted. By 1744 the movement had somewhat spent itself,
and when Whitefield arrived at Boston for a second preaching
tour he found that a reaction had set in. The followers of Edwards and Whitefield had come to be known as the "New Light"
party, while the reactionaries formed the "Old Light" party.
Two generations later this led to the separation of the Congregational body into the "Orthodox" and "Unitarian" groups.

Colleges.—Religion played a large part in eighteenth century
education. William and Mary College, founded in Virginia in

1691 under Anglican influence, was the only institution of advanced learning in the South. Yale, founded in 1701 under strong clerical influence, became the seat of orthodox Calvinism. Harvard also came on apace, in 1721 and 1727 establishing professorships in divinity and natural philosophy. Through the influence of Presbyterian ministers, in 1746 the College of New Jersey was granted a charter. King's College, now Columbia University, founded in New York in 1754, was made possible by the efforts of Dean Berkeley. In 1755, largely through the instrumentality of Benjamin Franklin, the first college was founded in Pennsylvania, the institution being freer from religious influence than any other colonial college.

BARBADOS, THE LEEWARD ISLES, AND JAMAICA

West Indian planters.—In the British West Indies, the production of sugar profoundly influenced social and economic conditions. The West Indian planter with his vast estate worked by slaves had crowded out the small landholder. He represented the capitalistic class, belonged to the Anglican church, and held views similar to those of the rural aristocracy of the mother country. It has been customary for historians to paint a roseate picture of life on the West India plantations, and no doubt there were many pretentious homes and many of the planters were possessed of great wealth. But it is a striking fact that a large percentage of the owners spent much of their time in England where their reckless living gave a false impression of West Indian prosperity. Slavery fostered industrial waste, and coupled with a tropical climate, produced a manner of life which undermined character; drinking, gambling, immorality, and sloth were common vices. Earthquakes and hurricanes frequently devastated the islands, the numerous wars destroyed shipping and cargoes, and slave insurrections were a constant terror. Churches, schools, and newspapers were sadly inadequate. Codrington College in Barbados, the only notable school in the islands, had but fifty students. Children of the planters were frequently sent to England to be educated, but they there acquired a point of view which made plantation life distasteful and tended to swell the large group of absentee landlords.

Barbados and the Leeward Isles.—During the seventeenth century most of the British sugar came from Barbados and the Leeward Isles, but lack of fertilization and slave labor had brought about deterioration on the estates, and during the eighteenth century both population and productivity were on the decline. In 1762 the white population of Barbados was about 18,000 and the blacks numbered 70,000. In 1736 the island produced 22,769 hogsheads of sugar, while during 1740–1748 the average annual production was 13,948 hogsheads. In 1744, Antigua, St. Christopher, Nevis, and Montserrat contained a total of about 11,000 whites and 60,000 slaves. As the lands became less productive, the planters attempted to make up the loss by increasing the number of slaves, a method which probably aggravated the condition.

Jamaica.—In the eighteenth century, Jamaica was the West Indian frontier. There could be found large tracts of unoccupied land suitable for sugar culture. In spite of this the population increased slowly; this was mainly due to slave insurrections which were frequent until 1739, to the fact that there was a constant migration of small landholders from the British West Indies, and to a depressed sugar market. The Island of Jamaica contained 3,840,000 acres; in 1754, 1620 planters had under cultivation 1,671,569 acres. The demand for slaves was keener than in any other British sugar island. During 1702–1775 it has been estimated that the planters purchased about 5,000 negroes a year from the slave traders.

A contemporary description of Jamaica.—Leslie described the island customs in 1740 as follows: "The Gentlemens Houses are generally built low, of one Story, consisting of five or six handsome Apartments, beautifully lined and floored with mahogany, which looks exceeding gay; they have generally a Piazza to which you ascend by several Steps, and serves for a Screen against the Heat. . . . The Negroes have nothing but a Parcel of poor miserable Huts built of Reeds, any of which can scarce contain upwards of two or three.

"The common Dress here is none of the most becoming, the Heat makes many clothes intolerable, and therefore the Men generally wear only Thread Stockings, Linen Drawers, and Vest, a Handkerchief tied around their Head, and a hat above.

. . . The negroes go mostly naked, except those who attend Gentlemen. . . . The Laidies are as gay as any in *Europe*, dress as richly, and appear with as good a Grace. . . . Learning is here at the lowest Ebb; there is no publick School in the whole Island, neither do they seem fond of the Thing. . . . The Office of a Teacher is looked upon as contemptible, and no Gentlemen keeps Company with one of that Character; to read, write, and cast up Accounts is all the Education they desire, and even these are but scurvily taught. . . . The Gentlemen, whose Fortunes can allow, send their children to *Great Britain*. . . . The Laidies read some, dance a great deal, coquet much, dress for Admirers, and at last, for the most Part, run away with the most insignificant of their humble Servants. Their Education consists entirely in acquiring these little Arts."

Emigration.—There was a constant migration of small landholders from the British West Indies to the French and Dutch islands, to Guiana and to the North American colonies. Several acts were passed whose object was to increase the number of colonists, but they had little effect, for the small landowners could not compete with the great slave proprietors. The colonists with small capital preferred to start where lands were cheaper and where social lines were not so tightly drawn.

Illicit trade.—The largest market for northern goods was found in the West Indies. Here was a field which required the products of the temperate zone. As Pitman observes, "Its demands upon Northern lumbermen, stock-raisers, and farmers, furnish a powerful incentive for the clearing and settlement of the continent." In spite of legal restrictions the Yankee skipper plied his trade. The planters of the sugar islands believed that the Molasses Act would restore their prosperity, but they soon found that natural economic laws were stronger than parliamentary enactments and that the northern sea-captain smuggled as of old. A considerable inter-island trade which ignored nationality was also carried on. St. Eustatius and the Virgin Isles became important smuggler havens, and even when war was in progress, the British Americans did not hesitate to supply their enemies with provisions and lumber in exchange for sugar, rum, and molasses.

READINGS

THE CONTINENTAL COLONIES

Bassett, J. S., ed., *The Writings of Colonel William Byrd of Westover in Virginia, Esqr.;* Bogart, E. L., *The Economic History of the United States,* 53–104; Burke, Edmund, *An Account of the European Settlements in America,* II, 145–273; Burnaby, Andrew, *Travels through the Middle Settlements in North America;* Callender, G. S., *Selections from the Economic History of the United States,* 6–84; Clark, V. S., *History of Manufactures in the United States, 1607–1860,* 73–214; Cross, A. L., *The Anglican Episcopate and the American Colonies;* Dexter, F. B , "Estimates of Population," in Am. Antiquarian Society, *Proceedings, 1887;* Fiske, John, *Old Virginia and her Neighbors,* II, 174–369; Greene, E. B., *Provincial America,* 270–342; Hart, A. B., *Contemporaries,* II, 224–311; Johnson, E. R., and others, *History of Domestic and Foreign Commerce of the United States,* I, 84–121; Kalm, Peter, *Travels in North America,* in Pinkerton, *Travels,* XIII, 374–700; McCrady, Edward, *The History of South Carolina under the Royal Government, 1719–1776,* pp. 376–540; Smith, Samuel, *The History of the Colony of Nova Caesaria, or New Jersey,* 419–509; Weeden, W. B., *Economic and Social History of New England,* II, 449–713; Andrews, C. M., *Colonial Folkways;* Phillips, U. B., *American Negro Slavery,* 67–114.

THE WEST INDIES

Edwards, Bryan, *History of the West Indies;* Gardner, W. J., *History of Jamaica;* Long, Edward, *History of Jamaica;* Pitman, Frank W., *The Development of the British West Indies, 1700–1763;* Phillips, U. B., *American Negro Slavery,* 46–66.

CHAPTER XIX

THE ENGLISH COLONIAL SYSTEM (1689-1763)

Before 1689 English colonial administration had been largely a personal matter with the king. Royal control had been exercised through the Privy Council assisted by advisory committees, boards and commissioners, after 1674 the most important of these bodies being the Lords of Trade. Between 1689 and 1714 colonial administration underwent fundamental changes both in theory and organization. By the end of the reign of Anne it had become largely departmental and official rather than personal, and Parliament had begun to take a somewhat larger hand in running affairs than during the former period. The Board of Trade, a body independent of the Privy Council, replaced the Lords of Trade in 1696 and for a time was the chief agency in the direction of colonial affairs. It lacked executive authority but conducted routine business and gathered information on which the Privy Council, Parliament, and the departments of the treasury, admiralty, and war acted. Under the Hanoverians the Secretary of State for the Southern Department became the colonial minister and the Board of Trade lost much of its importance. In America the principal agents of imperial control were the royal governors, judges, customs officials, and naval and military officers.

THE FIRST REORGANIZATION OF WILLIAM III

The system as William found it.—When William III ascended the throne, the later Stuart colonial system had not been perfected. It had been characterized by the principles that the authority of the crown should be strengthened at the expense of the colonial legislatures, that commerce should be regulated by the imperial administration, and that larger governmental units should take the place of the multiplicity of colonies. The colonial governments had gradually evolved toward a common type, composed of governor and council representing the crown

343

or proprietor, and a legislature in which the council acted as an upper house while the lower elective house represented the interests of the colony.

Committee on trade and plantations.—William III at first adopted the machinery of colonial administration as he found it, continuing the committee of the privy council on trade and plantations, but he appointed new members, including leading ministers from both the Whig and Tory parties. The navigation laws were continued in force, and Edward Randolph was retained as surveyor general of the customs.

Governmental changes in New England.—In the colonies several changes were introduced, the most striking being in New England. The idea of a consolidated New England was abandoned. The charters of Rhode Island and Connecticut were restored, and New Hampshire was established as a royal province. In 1691 Massachusetts, Plymouth, Maine, and Acadia were consolidated into the Province of Massachusetts Bay, but the immediate reconquest of Acadia by the French made the new charter inoperative in that region.

Massachusetts charter of 1691.—The form of government established in the Province of Massachusetts Bay was a compromise between the old independent form of earlier days and the type of the royal colony. The charter provided for a governor, deputy-governor, and secretary, to be appointed by the crown; a council of twenty-eight; and a lower house composed of freeholders, elected by the people. The general court composed of the governor, council, and lower house, was given the power, after the last Wednesday in May, 1693, of selecting annually the members of the council, at least eighteen of whom were to be from the old colony of Massachusetts, four from New Plymouth, and three from Maine. Legislation which met the approval of the governor was sent to the king in council, who within three years of the passage of the act, could disallow or nullify the colonial legislation. Laws not disallowed within three years remained in force.

New York.—The Leisler rebellion in New York complicated the problem of reorganization. Instead of Leisler being countenanced, New York, shorn of New Jersey, was again made a royal colony, with a government composed of governor, council, and elected assembly. Governor Henry Sloughter arrived on March 19, 1691, and the first assembly met on April 9. It promptly repealed the Duke's Laws, and voted that the revenues be made payable to the receiver-general, a crown appointee, and that issuance of funds be made by the governor's warrant, an action which made the governor for the time being independent and paved the way for future disputes. Sloughter died in July, 1691, and in August, 1692, Colonel Benjamin Fletcher arrived to assume the governorship, Richard Ingoldesby, an appointee of the council, having acted as governor in the interim.

Virginia.—In Virginia the revolution was effected without violence. Lord Howard of Effingham continued in the governorship but remained in England, Sir Francis Nicholson, who had been deposed in New York, being sent out as governor in 1690. Though he resisted the calling of an assembly, popular clamor forced his hand. A new capital city called Williamsburg was immediately laid out.

The Jerseys.—No settled policy regarding the proprietary governments was followed by William. Instead of attempting to readjust them after some formulated plan, each colony was dealt with as an individual unit with its own problem. In the Jerseys William restored the proprietors. Little authority was exercised by them, however, until 1692, when Andrew Hamilton was sent out as governor of both East and West New Jersey, a distinct step toward consolidation into a single province.

Pennsylvania.—The marked favor with which James II looked upon Penn placed the Pennsylvania proprietor under William's suspicion. Charges of misgovernment on the part of Penn's appointees, bickerings in the colony between the upper and lower counties, controversies among the Quakers, claims of religious intolerance, and the set attitude of the Quakers against war, made an accumulation of troubles for the proprietor. In 1692 he was deprived of his government, Benjamin Fletcher being sent over as governor. Fletcher introduced the royal colony type of government, selecting a council and summoning an elective assembly from both the upper and lower counties. When Fletcher demanded appropriations to assist in the war, the assembly proved factious, claiming that the governor was violating the chartered rights of the colony. Fletcher was unable to overcome the constitutional objections and withdrew to New York, sending a deputy to the colony to represent him. Penn in the meantime had been pressing his claims, and having succeeded in convincing the king of his loyalty, in 1694 was restored to his rights.

Maryland.—The Catholicism of Baltimore placed him under the ban of the government, in spite of the fact that he hastened to proclaim the new sovereigns. A rebellion against the proprietor gave ample excuse for the crown to take over the government of the colony. Baltimore was left in possession of his territorial rights, retaining the quit-rents, ownership of vacant lands, and his share of the customs, but the government was taken from him. In 1692 Sir Lionel Copley came over as royal governor, a council was selected from the anti-Baltimore party, and an assembly was convened. The assembly established the Episcopal church and divided the counties into parishes. Copley died in 1693, and for a brief period Sir Edmund Andros was governor, but Francis Nicholson soon succeeded him, and transferred the capital from St. Mary's to Annapolis.

The Carolinas.—The proprietors of the Carolinas fared better. Though there was much opposition to them in the colonies, they succeeded in ingratiating themselves with William and were left in undisturbed possession. In 1691 the Charleston and Albermarle districts were united under a single government, Philip Ludwell, who in 1689 had been appointed governor of the district north and east of Cape Fear, being made governor of the whole of Carolina.

WILLIAM'S SECOND REORGANIZATION

The Board of Trade.—As the war progressed, the enforcement of the navigation laws became more and more difficult; piracy and smuggling increased, and the Dutch obtained a larger part of the carrying trade than formerly. The complaints of English merchants were voiced in the House of Commons, where an insistent minority demanded a reorganization of the machinery of colonial administration and a revision of the navigation laws. William was opposed to the creation of a new board by parliament, considering that such action would be an encroachment upon the prerogative of the crown. The parliamentary bill was dropped, and in May, 1696, the king organized the Board of Commissioners for Trade and Plantations. Instead of being a committee of the privy council, the new board was an independent organization. It was composed of nominal and real members. The nominal members were the chief officers of state who seldom attended meetings. The working members of the board were eight non-ministerial paid officials, among those first commissioned being John Locke and William Blathwayt, the efficient secretary of the old committee.

The board had general supervision of colonial trade and government, gathered information, and reported on colonial affairs to the king or to parliament. Instructions to royal governors were draughted by them and they made nominations in cases of vacancy in the colonial service. They examined colonial legislation with a view to its confirmation or disallowance, listened to complaints, examined the accounts of the colonial treasuries, and attended to many minor matters. The board was in reality a clearing house for colonial administration; it examined, reported, and recommended, but it could not execute. During the reigns of William and Anne, its recommendations carried great weight, but its importance gradually declined as the cabinet system developed.

The secretaries of state.—Of William's ministers, those to whom colonial affairs were usually entrusted were the two secretaries of state, one or the other attending to the work. Governors usually corresponded directly with the secretaries. Questions which involved foreign countries, questions of defence, Indian outbreaks, and violations of the navigation acts were usually handled by the secretaries without being referred to the Board of Trade.

The privy council.—The privy council continued to be the executive center of the system. Recommendations which were read before it were usually referred to a committee of the whole, and upon the decision of this committee the council acted. As Dickerson says, "The whole machinery . . . for colonial administration included a Board of Trade to investigate, gather facts, and make recommendations; a committee of the Privy Council to act as a board of review and a court of appeals, both administrative and legal; and the privy council, meeting with the king, before which all final actions of importance were registered."

The Board of Trade and other departments of government.— The commissioners of the customs worked in close touch with the Board of Trade. The bodies were mutually helpful in collecting information. The admiralty and the treasury were also necessarily in close touch with the Board of Trade as was the Bishop of London. Many members of the Board of Trade occupied seats in parliament and prepared bills which affected the colonies. The board members also furnished information to parliament concerning trade and colonial matters.

Evasion of the trade laws.—The earlier navigation laws had not been thoroughly enforced. Most of the customs officials and some of the governors exerted themselves to enforce the laws, and several ships were fitted out to stop illicit traffic, but many of the officials were negligent, and several of them no doubt profited by non-enforcement of the laws. When arrests were made convictions proved difficult, for the juries were in sympathy with the law-breakers. In 1693 a Scotch commercial company was organized with the object of trading to India and Africa. This alarmed the English East India and the Royal African companies. The complaints of the customs officials and individual merchants, when reinforced by these powerful corporations, resulted in the passage of "An Act for preventing Frauds and regulating abuses in the Plantation Trade," a law familiarly known as the Navigation Act of 1696.

Navigation Act of 1696.—The act provided that after March 25, 1698, no goods should be imported into or exported from any English colony in Asia, Africa, or America, or be carried from or to any colony, or England, Wales, or Berwick-upon-Tweed, except in ships built by English subjects and navigated by English masters, with three-fourths of the crews English subjects. Exception was made of prizes condemned in the admiralty courts, and, for three years, of ships which were under contract to deliver supplies to the English navy. All ships engaged in colonial trade were made subject to the same rules of search and the same penalties for violations as prevailed in England. No vessel was allowed to engage in colonial trade until one or more of the owners had registered the vessel and taken a prescribed oath.

The Lord Treasurer, Commissioners of the Navy, and Commissioners of the Customs were allowed to appoint customs officers for any place which they saw fit. Forfeiture of vessel and cargo was the penalty for breach of the law, one-third of the proceeds to go to the crown, one-third to the governor of the colony, and one-third to the informant who brought the suit. Governors or commanders-in-chief of the colonies were required to take oath to enforce the acts of trade, under penalty of a fine of a thousand pounds and removal from office. Naval officers in the customs service were required to give ample security to the Commissioners of the Customs in England. In order to secure convictions, the act provided that in cases arising under the navigation laws, only natives of England, Ireland, or persons born in the English colonies could serve on juries. Those having land grants were forbidden to dispose of any lands to foreigners without an order in council, and the crown reserved the right to approve the nomination of governors in the proprietary colonies. Any colonial act at variance with the navigation laws was declared null and void.

Woolen Act of 1698.—The frequent interruptions of trade during the War of the English Succession caused the New Englanders to manufacture many woolen goods. In order to retain a monopoly for English manufacturers, in 1698 an act was passed forbidding the colonists to ship wool or woolen products from one colony to another.

Admiralty courts.—The Navigation Act of 1696 presupposed the establishment of admiralty courts in the colonies. The continental colonies were soon organized into two admiralty districts, New England, New York, and after 1702 New Jersey comprising the northern, and the rest the southern district. At a later period the districts were subdivided. In these courts there were no juries, a fact which made the admiralty courts exceedingly unpopular.

The Piracy Act.—Piracy had long existed, especially in the West Indies, and though stringent measures were taken to suppress it, the black flag still floated over many a pirate craft. Madagascar became a favorite haven, and from its harbors went forth the sea rovers to prey upon the East and West Indiamen. In many ports of the American colonies they were able to dispose of their booty, while officials closed their eyes or shared in the profits. Of the pirates of the period, the best known is Captain Kidd, about whose name has clustered much of fable and romance. The Navigation Act of 1696 made smuggling more difficult, and out and out piracy increased greatly after the passage of the act. To protect the merchant ships and make the navigation laws more effective, in 1700 an act was passed which provided that piracy and other felonies committed on the high seas might be tried in special colonial courts created by the crown.

The " Charter of Privileges " and the formation of Delaware.— Near the close of the reign of William III the government of Pennsylvania was changed. In 1701 in the hope of quieting dissension in Pennsylvania, Penn consented to the "Charter of Privileges," which was passed by the council and assembly. The proprietor continued to appoint the governor and councillors, but the assembly was henceforth composed of four representatives from each county who were elected by the freemen. The assembly was allowed to elect its own officers and to initiate legislation. Delaware was allowed to have its own assembly but remained under the jurisdiction of the proprietor.

New Jersey.—The policy of bringing all the colonies to a common type was evidenced by various attempts to send governors to the chartered and proprietary colonies, but in the end the attempts were abandoned. Various bills were introduced in parliament to make all the colonies royal, but they failed except in the case of New Jersey. The position of the proprietors in East and West New Jersey had always been precarious, and in 1702 they surrendered their rights to the crown. The two colonies were consolidated into the single colony of New Jersey, the royal type of government being established, Governor Cornbury of New York being commissioned as the first royal executive.

THE COLONIAL SYSTEM DURING THE REIGN OF ANNE

Cabinet development.—During the reign of Anne the cabinet system was gradually evolving. The privy council continued as the legal advisory body of the crown, but a small group of ministers, the forerunner of the modern cabinet, was in control

Colonial affairs were placed definitely in the hands of the secretary of state for the southern department. The Board of Trade continued, but as the cabinet system developed, it became less important, the secretary of state for the southern department and parliament gradually encroaching upon the activities of the board. The union with Scotland in 1707 profoundly affected the commercial system, for after the union the Scots were no longer excluded from colonial commerce.

Commercial legislation.—In 1705 another important act of trade was passed which added rice, molasses, and various naval stores to the list of enumerated articles which must be shipped to England. To offset these new restrictions, bounties were to be given on naval stores produced in the colonies and shipped to England, and in 1707 colonial seamen were exempted from impressment in the royal navy. During the reign of William III the Bank of England was established and the financial system was completely renovated. No definite money system had been established in the colonies; Spanish coins were in common use, but they had no fixed value, a condition which greatly hampered commerce. In 1707 parliament passed an act which imposed penalties for taking foreign coins at a rate above the legal ratio. The colonial post-office was also reorganized. Before 1689 each colony had regulated its postal offices. In 1692 a patent for twenty-one years was issued to Thomas Neale to establish colonial post-offices; Neale's deputy, Andrew Hamilton of New Jersey, obtained the support of several of the colonial governments in establishing postal rates, but the arrangements were lacking in uniformity. In 1710 parliament passed an act reorganizing the post-office of the entire realm. In the colonies a post-office was to be established in New York and at other convenient points in each of the colonies on the continent and in each of the Leeward Isles.

Disallowance and appeals.—During the reigns of William III and Anne the crown was constantly seeking to harmonize the colonial and home governments, both in legislation and administration. The chief crown instrument for achieving harmony was the right of royal disallowance of colonial legislation. By 1692 it had been established in the royal provinces and in Pennsylvania. In 1702 it was extended to New Jersey, and at

various times during the reign of Anne laws of chartered colonies
were disallowed, although such action was of doubtful legality.
The unity of the English court system was maintained by insist-
ence that cases involving individuals in the colonies might be
appealed to the privy council. When the colonies attempted to
restrict the right, colonial legislation was disallowed.

Causes of friction.—The constitutional development in England which followed the Revolution of 1688 was reflected in the
colonies, where each lower house was a miniature house of commons representing the will of the enfranchised people, while the
governors and proprietors were considered as representatives of
the royal will. Struggles between the governor and assembly
occurred in almost every colony, the most common causes of
quarrel being the control of elections and of the purse, and
appointments.

Control of elections and the purse.—In several of the colonies
the popular control of elections was maintained either by specific statements in the charters or by legislative enactment. In
Virginia the burgesses in 1692 declared themselves the sole
judges of the qualifications of their members. The Massachusetts charter provided for annual elections, and the same right
was given to Pennsylvania in 1701. Legislative acts in the
Carolinas secured biennial elections. The most potent factor
in limiting the power of governors was the control of taxation
by the lower house. That money raised by direct taxation
should be disbursed by the representatives of the people was a
growing idea. The assemblies frequently fixed salaries, refused
to provide for fixed civil lists, specified how much should be
drawn and spent, and limited grants for governors to annual
appropriations. Massachusetts was the most insistent on her
rights, but each of the colonies in one way or another sought to
curb the executive.

Appointments.—The appointment of administrative officers
by the assemblies became more and more frequent. The theory
that the representatives of the people should control taxation
and disbursements naturally led to the assertion of the right to
appoint financial officers, and by 1715 in most of the colonies
the treasurer was appointed by the assembly. The colonies
also maintained agents in England who guarded their interests.

THE COLONIAL SYSTEM UNDER THE WHIGS

Whig ascendency.—The peaceful establishment of George I on the English throne marked the downfall of the Tory party. To keep England at peace and at the same time to maintain the balance of power in Europe was the difficult task which the Whig statesmen performed, in the main successfully. To build up English industry and commerce on mercantilist principles was the basis of the Whig economic system.

Establishment of the Cabinet system.—The statesmen who had placed a Hanoverian on the throne did not propose to surrender the powers of government. The king, ignorant of English speech and English politics, soon learned that a Whig-made king was also a Whig-ruled king. During the two previous reigns a small group of men within the privy council had invariably directed affairs of state. This group had gradually come to represent the majority in parliament, an arrangement which became a definitely established principle, the ministerial group forming the cabinet. From 1714 to 1721 no one man dominated, but the financial crisis, brought about by the bursting of the South Sea Bubble, gave the great financier, Robert Walpole, his opportunity. As First Lord of the Treasury and Chancellor of the Exchequer, for twenty years he maintained his leadership, the first of the prime ministers.

The Secretary of State for the Southern Department. —In the evolution of the cabinet system the machinery of colonial government also changed. Under the Whig régime the Board of Trade, which, since 1696 had been the chief instrument of colonial control, soon became of secondary importance, the Secretary of State for the Southern Department being recognized as the responsible head of the colonial system. Until 1724 no one held the office long enough to develop a colonial policy, but in that year the Duke of Newcastle was appointed to the position, which he held for twenty-four years. Newcastle is generally regarded as an inefficient administrator, a politician who found the colonial system a convenient place to reward supporters. In his hands was the power of appointment of colonial governors and other important officials; many of them proved to be excellent officials, but others were corrupt or incapable. Jealous of his authority and fearful of entrusting power to others, Newcastle attempted to attend to the mass of colonial business, with the result that it was frequently neglected.

The Board of Trade.—The Board of Trade necessarily lost in power. When the Whigs came in office, they made a clean sweep of the board. The new members were usually friends of the ministers or indigent members of the house of commons, most of whom were ignorant of colonial affairs. The board became mainly an information bureau. At a later period, when Newcastle became prime minister, it regained some of its former prestige under the able leadership of Halifax.

The privy council.—During the reign of Anne the deliberative work of the privy council had been transacted largely by a committee, the council formally approving business settled in committee. This became the uniform rule under George I. Petitions, complaints, and memorials were usually referred to the Board of Trade for investigation and report, and then considered by a committee, of which the Secretary of State for the Southern Department was invariably a member. Colonial laws were also referred to the board for examination, while appeals were usually handled by a committee of the council. The crown continued to disallow colonial legislation, but exercised the right less frequently under the first two Georges than under William and Anne.

Attitude toward colonial governments.—As compared with earlier periods, little was done to reorganize colonial governments. Though plans for doing away with the charters of Rhode Island and Connecticut were frequently discussed, no action was taken, but in the proprietary colonies changes occurred. In Maryland the Baltimore family was restored to power, and in Pennsylvania the Penn family was confirmed in its rights. In the Carolinas the colonists had grown weary of proprietary neglect in defending the colonies against the Indians, Spanish, and French. Revolutionary movements occurred which resulted in the overthrow of proprietary power and in the complete separation of North and South Carolina, a government of the royal type being established in each colony.

Trade laws.—During the Walpole period the mercantilist economic theories were still the basis of trade regulation. The colonies continued to be looked upon as a base of supply for raw material. Their industrial and commerical activities were not to interfere with those of English manufacturers and shippers. To prevent smuggling, to provide for the treasury, and at the same time foster the resources of the colonies, were the difficult tasks of Walpole and his colleagues.

Naval stores.—The wars of William and Anne had caused a great demand for naval stores, and their production in the colonies had been encouraged. During that period England had drawn her greatest supply from the Baltic countries. But the defeat of Sweden in her wars with Russia meant a decline of English influence in the Baltic, and England turned to the colonies for her ship supplies. In 1721 a new bounty act was accordingly passed to encourage the colonial supply, and the best hemp from the colonies was allowed to come into England free of duty. Eight years later the bounties on pitch, turpentine, and tar were somewhat lessened, the encouragement still being sufficient to give the producers a decided advantage over their competitors, the Carolinas being the principal gainers in the business. In 1731 the drawback on unwrought hemp exported from England to the colonies was removed, an act which also appears to have favored the colonial trade. The production of hemp, however, did not flourish in America as did that of other naval stores. In 1721 copper was placed upon the enumerated list, but every effort to include iron was defeated until 1750. In line with the policy of stimulating the production of naval stores was a provision that timber from the colonies could be imported into England duty free, the result being that New England became the source of supply for masts both in the navy and the mercantile marine.

Furs and hats.—The fur business in the Atlantic seaboard colonies had steadily declined, and the government wished to build it up. To accomplish this beaver and other peltry were placed on the enumerated list, but the duties payable in England were materially decreased. Much of the beaver was used in the colonies in the manufacture of hats. As this was an important English industry, in 1732 an act was passed which stopped the exportation of hats from the colonies and restricted their manufacture.

Rice.—The rice industry had been introduced in Carolina about 1688, and found an important market in Portugal and Spain. Rice being placed on the enumerated list in the reign of Anne, the colonies soon lost the market. To rectify this, in 1730 Carolina was allowed to send rice direct to countries south of Cape Finisterre. Five years later Georgia, and somewhat later the West Indies, were allowed the same privilege. American rice immediately regained its place in the trade of southern Europe and also found a market in Holland and Germany.

The Molasses Act.—The great staple of the West Indies was sugar. In its production the English Islands had surpassed the French colonies, a condition which was due to the restrictive measures of the French government. But in 1717 France adopted a liberal policy toward her colonies and the production of sugar increased to such an extent that the English sugar-producing islands experienced a financial depression. The thrifty colonial traders from the mainland, especially from New England, took advantage of the low price of French and Dutch sugar, molasses, and rum. To bolster up the West Indian planters and to prevent the trade with foreign colonies, in 1733 the Molasses Act was passed, imposing prohibitory duties on molasses, sugar, and rum imported into the continental colonies from other than English possessions. But in spite of the act the trade continued, and but little effort was made to enforce the law.

Constitutional principles.—During the period from 1714 to 1740 the constitutional rights of the people in the colonies were defined more clearly than before. In 1720 the principle was established that the common law applied to the colonies as well as to England, but the question of whether English statute law extended to the colonies was not satisfactorily settled. The writ of habeas corpus was usually granted under the common law. Progress was also made toward gaining the freedom of the press. After a struggle in Massachusetts in 1721 the right of the governor to censor books was abridged. In 1735 Zenger, a New York publisher, was tried for libel. The court held that it should decide the libellous nature of the statements made, and that the jury should determine the fact of publication. Zenger's lawyer argued that the jury must decide on whether or not the publication was libellous. On this ground he won his suit, thereby greatly strengthening the power of the press.

Increasing power of assemblies.—English colonial policy does not appear to have aroused serious opposition. Each colony had its political parties, but no question arose which welded together any group of colonies, or of classes in various colonies. As in the earlier period there were frequent quarrels between the assemblies and the governors, control of finance being the most usual cause of friction. The governors demanded fixed salaries, while the assemblies insisted on making temporary grants. The assemblies also ignored the necessity of the governor's warrant in drawing money, and insisted that the councils should not amend money bills. In these controversies the governors were usually bested, and by the close of the Walpole régime, the principle was well defined that the assemblies should control the purse.

Paper money.—Closely allied to the question of control of taxation and the governor's salary was that regarding the issuance of paper money. A shortage of coin was usual, and the issuance of paper money was the remedy by which the assemblies and banks attempted to provide a medium of exchange. In general the governors opposed such issues as financially unsound, but their actions were frequently misunderstood and were considered tyrannous.

Friction between colonies.—The difficulties between the executives and the assemblies might have developed into a general opposition to English control had it not been for the quarrels between colonies over boundaries and trade laws. Boundaries were based upon charters, which in many cases were conflicting and almost every colony had chronic disputes with its neighbors. The trade laws of one colony frequently discriminated against its neighbors, the natural result being retaliatory legislation. The English government was often called in as umpire, but its decisions seldom met with the approval of both parties.

READINGS

Andrews, C. M., *The Colonial Period*, 128–154; Beer, G. L., "The Commercial Policy of England toward the American Colonies," in Columbia University, *Studies in History, Economics, and Public Law*, III, No. 2;

358   THE COLONIZATION OF NORTH AMERICA

Bingham, H., "Early History of the Scots Darien Company," in *The Scottish Historical Review*, January, April, July, 1906; Briscoe, N. A., "The Economic Policy of Robert Walpole," in Columbia University, *Studies in History, Economics, and Public Law*, XXVII, No. 1; Channing, Edward, *History of the United States*, II, 217–281; Dickerson, O. M., *American Colonial Government, 1697–1765;* Egerton, H. E., *A Short History of British Colonial Policy*, 114–152; Greene, E. B., *Provincial America*, 166–207; *The Provincial Governor in the English Colonies of North America;* Root, W. T., *The Relations of Pennsylvania with the British Government, 1696–1765;* Pitman, Frank W., *The Development of the British West Indies, 1700–1763,* pp. 127–333.

CHAPTER XX

A QUARTER-CENTURY OF CONFLICT: THE EXPULSION OF THE FRENCH

SPAIN AND THE POWERS, 1715-1739

Spanish dynastic ambitions.—From 1715 to 1739 the relations of England and Spain were frequently strained, due to the clashing of commercial and colonial interests, or to the ambitions of Spanish rulers. Philip V hoped to become the king of France. His second wife, Elizabeth Farnese, was ambitious to secure territories in Italy for her sons, the elder, Don Carlos, being destined to play an important part in Italian and Spanish history. The Spanish minister, Alberoni, devoted himself to building up Spanish influence in Italy.

The Triple and Quadruple Alliances.—Her Italian policy brought Spain into discord with the Emperor Charles VI, as the House of Austria hoped to remain the dominant factor in Italy. In 1717 Austrian acts in the Milanese provoked hostilities. Spanish forces immediately occupied Sardinia and the following year Sicily. The same year an alliance had been made between England, France, and Holland, and in 1718 Austria joined the alliance. Austrian troops were sent to Italy, a Spanish fleet was defeated by the English Admiral Byng, and in 1719 a French army crossed the Spanish frontier. Spain was brought to terms and Alberoni was dismissed. But before definite terms could be arranged, France opened negotiations with Spain and French influence was greatly strengthened. The war between Spain and France extended to their North American colonies, with important consequences, as has been set forth in an earlier chapter.

Spanish-Austrian alliance.—From 1721 to 1724 Elizabeth Farnese depended on the French alliance to attain her ends. But France made no effort to dislodge the English from Gibraltar, and Spanish merchants complained of English smugglers in the colonies. Furthermore, Don Carlos had not been established in Italy. To bring about the desired ends, in 1725 an alliance between Spain and Austria was formed. This was made possible by the ambitions of the Emperor Charles VI, who had been unable to obtain the adhesion of England, Holland, and France to the Pragmatic Sanction. He also hoped to secure a part of the Oriental trade by the formation of the Ostend East India Company, an enterprise which ran counter to English, Dutch, and French interests. Spain immediately demanded from England the cession of Gibraltar. The reply was the formation of the League of Hanover between England, France, and Prussia, the last named power, however, soon deserting its allies. Hostilities began in 1726 when an English fleet blockaded Puerto Bello and in 1727 the Spanish besieged Gibraltar. Austria was unprepared for war. Powerful parties in England and France did not favor it, and a considerable faction in Spain opposed the Austrian alliance. In consequence a peace was patched up. The operations of the Ostend Company were suspended for seven years, and the siege of Gibraltar was abandoned.

The treaty of Seville.—Abandoned by Austria, Elizabeth Farnese turned to England and Holland. A treaty was made which provided that the privileges of the Ostend Company be revoked, that England's former rights of trade in the Spanish colonies be renewed, that Spain abandon her claims to Minorca and Gibraltar, and that the succession of Don Carlos to the Italian duchies be guaranteed. The Austrian emperor was furious, but was pacified by a recognition of the Pragmatic Sanction on the part of England and Holland. In 1731 Don Carlos became Duke of Parma and Piacenza and was assured the succession to Tuscany.

French and Spanish alliance.—Walpole was not inclined to strengthen Spanish influence in Italy, so the shifty queen abandoned England and brought about an alliance with France. This was made possible by commercial difficulties in the colonies, and by the fact that French and English colonial interests were approaching a collision. The alliance of France and Spain was not disclosed, however, until 1739. In 1733 the War of the Polish Succession broke out; in the struggle England remained neutral, but France and Spain took an active part against Austria. At the end of the war Naples and Sicily were united under the rule of Don Carlos and the great ambition of Elizabeth Farnese was attained.

Commercial relations of Spain and England, 1715–1739.—By the treaty of Utrecht England had gained the right to supply the Spanish colonies with slaves and to send an annual cargo of five hundred tons to Spanish ports. English merchants were not satisfied with this paltry trade, and smuggling increased. Spanish coast guard ships seized many of the English traders, who received rough handling by the Spanish officials. During 1738 and 1739 public opinion in England became more and more inflamed against Spain. A paper presented to parliament in 1738 showed that in recent years fifty-two vessels had been plundered by the Spaniards, and that British seamen had been harshly treated. The most famous case was that of Thomas Jenkins, who declared that a coast guard captain had captured him, cut off his ears, and insolently remarked, "Carry this home to the King, your master, whom, if he were present, I would serve in like fashion." Attempts to settle difficulties by diplomacy failed, and by the summer of 1739 it became evident that war was at hand. On July 10 George II issued a proclamation authorizing reprisals and letters of marque against Spanish commerce. England declared war on October 23, and Spain on November 28.

THE WAR OF JENKINS' EAR

Puerto Bello, Cartagena, and Chagres.—As soon as war appeared inevitable, orders were despatched to Jamaica to make reprisals and Admiral Edward Vernon, in command of nine war vessels, was sent to the West Indies. Hearing that the Spanish galleons would rendezvous at Cartagena and then sail to Puerto Bello, where bullion was waiting to be exchanged for merchandise, Vernon determined to attack Puerto Bello. On November 22, 1739, the place was captured and the fortifications demolished. On March 6 and 7, 1740, Cartagena was bombarded, and a part of the fleet then attacked and captured Chagres.

The Georgia frontier.—While these events were taking place, Oglethorpe was taking measures to strengthen the Georgia frontier. Hearing that the Spanish and French were tampering with the Indians, he visited Kawita, the principal Lower Creek village, where a conference was held with chieftains of many tribes, who acknowledged the sovereignty of George II. Upon his return to Augusta, Oglethorpe was visited by Chickasaw and Cherokee chiefs, who made complaint against the traders, but he succeeded in appeasing them. By these conferences the frontier was made safe from Indian depredations in the coming war. As soon as Oglethorpe received information that a state of war existed, he recruited his forces and sent runners to the Indian villages asking for a thousand warriors to coöperate against the Spaniards. Fortifications were strengthened and vessels patrolled the coast. In November, 1739, word came that the settlement on Amelia Island had been attacked. In retaliation the Spaniards were driven from their outposts on the St. John's. On January 1, 1740, Oglethorpe proceeded against Fort Picolata on the St. John's River, surprised and captured it, and shortly afterward Fort San Francisco de Papa, only twenty-one miles from St. Augustine, was reduced but later abandoned.

Attack on St. Augustine.—Oglethorpe determined to make an attempt to capture St. Augustine. He repaired to Charleston, where he succeeded in getting the assembly to pass an act to contribute five hundred men and a schooner. The mouth of the St. John's River was to be the rendezvous for the Carolina and Georgia troops. The Indians were asked to send forces to Frederica. Oglethorpe also obtained the coöperation of nine small vessels of the British fleet. Without waiting for a complete concentration of his forces, he entered Florida in May, 1740, and soon captured the Spanish outposts. He then concentrated his forces and moved against St. Augustine. Oglethorpe expected to capture it by a combined sea and land attack, but the fleet failed to coöperate and a siege had to be instituted. The city was closely invested until June 14, when a sortie succeeded in recapturing one of the outposts. A ship of war which had been guarding the Matanzas River was withdrawn and the Spaniards took advantage of the opportunity to land reinforcements and supplies from Havana. After a consultation between the naval and military commanders, Oglethorpe decided to give up the undertaking.

Spanish and English preparations.—The Spaniards, alarmed by English activities, in July, 1740, sent out a large squadron under Admiral Don Rodrigo de Torres. France was persuaded to proclaim her close alliance with Spain and she made known her decision not to allow England to make conquests or new settlements in the West Indies, but the death of the Emperor Charles VI determined her to stay out of the war for the time being. When news of Torres' fleet reached England, twenty large vessels, several frigates and small craft, and many transports carrying nine thousand troops were sent to the West Indies, where they arrived in December. "A fleet such as had never before been assembled in the waters of the New World was now at the disposal of the British commander." Commodore George Anson was also despatched around Cape Horn to the Pacific to prey upon Spanish commerce.

English failures.—In March, 1740, the English fleet anchored before Cartagena. From March 9 to April 11 the city was besieged, but lack of harmony between the commanders of the land and sea forces, and general mismanagement coupled with sickness among the besiegers, contributed to one of the most striking failures in English naval history. After destroying the works which had been taken, the expedition sailed for Jamaica and shortly afterward eleven of the heavier vessels and five frigates were withdrawn from the West Indian station. The English ministry also hoped to conquer Cuba, but an attack on Santiago failed as dismally as that on Cartagena. In 1742 the capture of Panama by an overland expedition from Puerto Bello was planned, but after again occupying Puerto Bello the scheme was found to be impossible of attainment. The only success of the year was the occupation of Roatan Island off Honduras Bay. In October Vernon returned to England, leaving Oglethorpe in command of the West Indian station. An expedition along the Venezuelan coast failed as completely as other English ventures on the Spanish main.

The Georgia frontier, 1742-1743.—The failures of the English made it possible for the Spanish to assume the offensive, and forces estimated at about five thousand, besides a large fleet, were collected at St. Augustine for an attack upon Georgia. The Spanish attack was launched against the fortifications on

St. Simon Island, but the spirited defence disheartened the invaders and they soon withdrew to St. Augustine. In March of the following year Oglethorpe retaliated by a descent on Florida and drove the Spanish within their defences at St. Augustine, but being too weak to attack the city, withdrew again to Georgia.

THE WAR OF THE AUSTRIAN SUCCESSION

France enters the war.—The European situation had developed along lines by 1743 which brought France into an offensive alliance with Spain. In 1740 the Emperor Charles VI died and his daughter Maria Theresa became Archduchess of Austria and Queen of Hungary and Bohemia. Portions of her domains were coveted by Prussia and France. Prussia seized Silesia; this was followed by a French attack, and the War of the Austrian Succession was on. England and Holland feared that France might annex the Austrian Netherlands. France found a ready ally in Spain, and the conflict which had been waged between England and Spain since 1739, by 1743 had developed into a great European war.

French attack on Acadia.—Events in Europe and the Mediterranean were far more important in bringing the struggle to a conclusion than those in America, but it is beyond the scope of this work to deal with them. During the peace the French had fortified Louisbourg on Cape Breton Island, making it one of the strongest fortifications in America. The governor of Cape Breton decided to attempt to regain Acadia and sent out an expedition which captured Canso. After destroying the town the French proceeded to Annapolis. The place was saved, however, by the vigilance of the Massachusetts authorities, Governor Shirley and the assembly having despatched a body of volunteers, who arrived before the enemy.

Capture of Louisbourg.—Governor Shirley then proposed to the assembly the quixotic scheme of capturing Louisbourg. Nearly four thousand volunteers from Connecticut, New Hampshire, and Massachusetts were assembled and placed under the command of William Pepperel of Kittery, Maine. Each of the New England colonies furnished war vessels and transports, and Commodore Peter Warren was sent from the West Indies with several ships of war. In April, 1745, the great flotilla appeared before Louisbourg and the place was soon invested by land and sea. After one of the most remarkable sieges in American history, in which the untrained colonials acquitted themselves with bravery and efficiency, on June 28 the place surrendered.

Border warfare, 1746-1748.—The success at Louisbourg encouraged the colonists to attempt the conquest of Canada. All of the colonies as far south as Virginia furnished men, and the Duke of Newcastle promised a large force of regulars. But the English troops were diverted to Europe and the plan came to naught. The failure of the projected conquest spurred the French colonists to attack the outlying settlements; from Acadia to the New York border, bands of French and Indians harried the frontier. Grand Pré and Fort Massachusetts were captured but were soon reoccupied. Until the close of the war, the New England borders were harassed by frequent raids. The New York and Pennsylvania frontiers were protected, mainly through the influence of the Indian agent, William Johnson, who kept the Mohawks friendly, and the Pennsylvania interpreter Conrad Weiser, whose policy of favoring the Iroquois land claims in Pennsylvania at the expense of the Delawares held the powerful New York confederation on the English side.

French and English naval activity, 1745-1746.—In March, 1745, a large French fleet under DeCaylus was sent to the West Indies. As soon as the English ministry heard of this, Vice-Admiral William Rowley was sent out with large reinforcements. Though De Caylus's fleet was not engaged, on October 31 Rowley fell in with another squadron of war vessels and supply ships, and captured or destroyed thirty out of forty sail. In 1746 France made an attempt to regain Cape Breton and Acadia. Under D'Anville a fleet of eleven large war vessels, several frigates and small craft, and transports carrying thirty-five hundred troops, arrived off the Acadian coast but the fleet was shattered by a storm, and the enterprise was abandoned.

Decisive battles off Cape Finisterre.—In 1747 another French fleet was sent out to recapture Cape Breton, but an English fleet under Anson and Warren intercepted it off Cape Finisterre and nearly every French vessel was captured. Later in the year France despatched a fleet to the West Indies convoying over two hundred merchantmen, but near the scene of the former battle a second great engagement occurred in which the English were again victorious. These two great victories completed the destruction of the French fighting navy.

Knowles's attack on the Spanish, 1748.—Early in 1748 Rear-Admiral Charles Knowles attacked and captured Port Louis on the southern shore of Española. In April he bombarded Santiago de Cuba. In September an engagement with a Spanish fleet took place off Havana, but he succeeded in capturing only one vessel.

The Peace of Aix-la-Chapelle.—The long war was drawing to an end, neither side having attained unqualified success. In the Peace of Aix-la-Chapelle, signed in October, 1748, all conquests were restored. The peace was but a truce. Both England and France realized it and both put forth efforts to strengthen and extend their colonial possessions.

THE APPROACH OF ANOTHER CONFLICT

Acadia.—Acadia, the upper valley of the Ohio, and the Cherokee country were debatable territories. To insure English possession of Acadia, Lord Halifax, the president of the Board of Trade, insisted upon the strengthening of the peninsula of Nova Scotia. In 1749 twenty-five hundred emigrants were sent over and the city of Halifax was founded. Three years later the English population had increased to four thousand. Edward Cornwallis was installed as governor, and the usual form of crown colony government established. Fort Lawrence was erected on the isthmus. Since many of the Acadians had failed to be neutral in the last war, Cornwallis asked that they again take the oath of allegiance, a request which was refused, and three or four thousand emigrated rather than swear allegiance. The policy of France regarding Acadia was to restrict its boundaries to the peninsula of Nova Scotia, to incite the Indians to make depredations, and to keep the Acadians loyal to the French king. Fort Beauséjour on the isthmus was converted into a formidable fortress and Louisbourg was greatly strengthened.

English activities on the Ohio.—Victories on the sea in the recent war had made it possible for English merchants to undersell their French rivals. From Albany and Oswego officials and traders worked in unison to keep the friendship of the Iroquois. From his estate on the Mohawk, William Johnson, a nephew of Admiral Warren, exerted great influence over the neighboring tribes, an influence which was to increase as the years went by. To the southward the frontiersmen grasped the opportunity for profit, and soon the Ohio country was frequented by many traders from Virginia and Pennsylvania. They penetrated to the Indian villages as far as the Mississippi and even into the country beyond. The principal trading centers were Picka- willany in the Miami confederacy, Logstown on the Ohio, and Venango on the Alleghany. Settlers also began to cross the mountains; in 1748 Virginia frontiersmen made a settlement at Draper's Meadow on the Greenbrier River.

The Ohio Company.—In 1744, at a council held at Lancaster, Pennsylvania, the Iroquois granted to the English the control of the country north of the upper Ohio. By subsequent agree- ments title was obtained to lands south of the river. In 1749 definite action was taken to occupy the territory. The project was launched by Virginia, partly to check the western preten- sions of Pennsylvania. A charter was granted conveying a half-million acres on the upper Ohio to a group of Virginia and English gentlemen, among the stockholders being several of Washington's relatives. The grantees agreed to build a fort on the Ohio and within seven years to settle a hundred families on their lands. In the same year the Loyal Company secured a grant of 800,000 acres in the West. In 1750 Christopher Gist, a well-known fur trader, was sent by the Ohio Company to explore as far as the Falls of the Ohio, the site of modern Louis- ville. During 1750–1751 he traversed portions of what are now Ohio, Kentucky, West Virginia, Maryland, and Pennsylvania. His favorable report stimulated activity; a trading house was built at Wills' Creek where Cumberland, Maryland, now stands, and a trail was blazed to the junction of Redstone Creek and the Monongahela, the primitive beginning of the Cumberland Pike. A few Virginians immediately settled at the western terminal of the trail.

The French frontier strengthened.—In general the Iroquois had been faithful to the English, but the French continued their efforts to gain the support of the powerful confederation. An

Iroquois mission was established near Montreal, and in 1748 Father Piquet founded the mission of La Presentation at modern Ogdensburg. To divert trade from Oswego, in 1749 Fort Rouillé was built where Toronto now flourishes. A new post was established at the Niagara portage, Detroit was strengthened, and a garrison stationed at Sault Ste. Marie. The Marquis de la Galissonière, the governor of Canada, saw the danger of the English occupation of the Ohio country. In 1749 he despatched a force under Céloron de Bienville to take possession. The expedition passed from Lake Erie to Chautauqua Lake and proceeded southward to the Alleghany, where the work of taking formal possession began. The procedure was to proclaim French sovereignty, to nail to a tree a sheet of tin bearing the arms of France, and to bury at the foot of the tree a leaden plate which stated that the land along the Ohio and its tributaries belonged to the King of France. Many Indian villages in the Ohio Valley were visited and several plates buried, but wherever Céloron went he found evidences that the tribes were friendly to the English. At the Great Miami the last plate was buried, and the party proceeded to the French post on the Maumee and then returned to Canada.

French occupation of the upper Ohio.—In May, 1749, the Marquis de la Jonquiére was appointed governor general. He was instructed to get rid of Oswego by inciting the Iroquois to attack it. Jonquiére found his government permeated with dishonesty, the intendant Bigot having used his official position to fatten the purses of himself and friends. The governor was powerless to occupy the Ohio country, having neither soldiers nor money sufficient for the enterprise. When he ordered Céloron to attack Pickawillany, that officer refused because of disaffection among the neighboring Indians. But help came from an unexpected quarter. A young French trader from Green Bay named Charles Langlade gathered two hundred and fifty Ottawas and Ojibways and destroyed the Miami village. Jonquiére died in 1752; his successor, the Marquis Duquesne, proved to be of sterner stuff. In 1753 he sent an expedition of fifteen hundred men to occupy the Ohio country. Fort Presq'Isle was erected and a road was cut to French Creek, where Fort LeBoeuf was built The French planned to build another fort at the forks of the Ohio, but sickness and the lateness of the season interrupted their operations.

Washington's mission, 1753.—Dinwiddie, the lieutenant-governor of Virginia, realized the import of the French advance. He warned the home government which authorized him to demand the departure of the enemy, and in case of refusal, to drive them out by force. He at once sent an embassy to protest. The bearer of the message was George Washington, a surveyor who had barely reached the age of twenty-one. Guided by Christopher Gist, he proceeded to the forks of the Ohio, then to Logstown where parleys were held with the Indians, and later to Venango. Washington was civilly received but was told that the French intended to keep possession of the Ohio. He then proceeded to Fort LeBoeuf, where he was told that Dinwiddie's letter would be sent to Duquesne and that in the meantime the commander would remain at his post. It was evident that force must be employed if the Ohio country was to become English territory.

The southern frontier.—The back country of the Carolinas and Georgia was the land of the hunters, cowboys, and Indian traders. The headquarters of the Georgia traders was Augusta, while those of South Carolina had a place of deposit at the residence of Peter St. Julien near Dorchester. From there the caravans followed the Congaree trail or that which led to the Chickasaw. French agents were continually working among the interior tribes and in 1753 a war broke out between the Creeks and Cherokees. Governor Glen of South Carolina called the Indians to conferences and finally succeeded in maintaining peace for the time being. The governor then visited the lower Cherokee and purchased a tract of land on which Fort Prince George was built, one hundred and seventy miles above Augusta on the Savannah River.

THE FRENCH AND INDIAN WAR

Virginia prepares to attack the French.—When Dinwiddie heard the French reply, he prepared for war. From the house of burgesses he demanded men and money, and messengers were sent to the Catawbas, Cherokees, Chickasaws, and the Iroquois of the Ohio Valley asking them to join in a war against the French.

Dinwiddie also appealed to the governors of Pennsylvania, North and South Carolina, Maryland, and New Jersey for men and he asked the governors of New York and Massachusetts to make a demonstration against Canada to distract forces from the Ohio. The replies proved disappointing. The only outside troops which immediately came were a company of regulars from South Carolina sent by royal order. Two companies of regulars from New York arrived too late to be of service.

Washington's first campaign.—Three hundred provincial troops were raised in Virginia and placed under Joshua Frye, with Washington second in command. A few backwoodsmen were sent forward in February, 1754, to build a fort at the forks of the Ohio, but were captured by a body of French and Indians. The prisoners were released and brought back the news of their mishap. The French demolished the fortification and built a stronger one which they named Fort Duquesne. Washington pushed on toward the west with a portion of the troops and by the middle of May reached the Great Meadows. Hearing that a party of French were scouting in the neighborhood, Washington, with forty men surprised them, captured twenty-two, and killed ten.

The death of Frye gave Washington the command. Realizing the imminence of an attack, he constructed a rude fortification at Great Meadows, which he called Fort Necessity, and here the rest of the Virginia troops and the regulars from South Carolina were concentrated. From Ft. Duquesne a force variously estimated at from five hundred to seven hundred men under Coulon de Villiers, was despatched to attack Washington's forces, now reduced to about three hundred and fifty effectives. The fortifications proved to be badly constructed and poorly located, and ammunition ran short. In a few hours fifty or sixty men had fallen, and when Villiers proposed terms of surrender it was evident that they must be accepted. "Not an English flag now waved beyond the Alleghanies," and the red warriors of the West and even many of the Iroquois flocked to the standards of France.

Apathy of the colonial legislatures.—Even Washington's defeat did not greatly arouse the colonial assemblies. After much delay Virginia voted twenty thousand pounds, Pennsylvania a paltry five hundred pounds for presents to the Indians, New York five thousand pounds, Maryland six thousand. In Massachusetts Governor Shirley used a rumor that the French were seizing places in the back country to obtain a large grant. He also sent eight hundred men to build two forts on the Kennebec. The southern colonies appear to have taken no action.

The Albany convention.—The encroachments of the French showed the necessity of adopting some plan of defence. In June, 1754, representatives from New York, Pennsylvania, Maryland, and the New England colonies met at Albany. The Indian chiefs stated their grievances and were sent away soothed but hardly satisfied. The representatives then took up the subject of defence. A plan of union, chiefly the work of Franklin, was proposed, but when it was submitted to the colonies they unanimously rejected it. The Board of Trade then formulated a plan of union for military purposes only, but events were occurring which made it necessary to take immediate action. The plan was laid aside, and the board suggested the appointment of a commander-in-chief over all the forces in America, a suggestion which was eventually put into effect.

Preparations for war.—In Europe, England and France were nominally at peace. At the head of the English ministry was the Duke of Newcastle, who maintained his control of a parliamentary majority by corruption rather than by statesmanship. Fortunately for England, she had a fleet which was far more numerous than that of her opponent. The strength of France lay in her army which was nearly ten times as strong as that of her rival. Major-General Edward Braddock, a former governor of Gibraltar, stubborn, irascible, and little given to taking advice, was sent to Virginia with two regiments, which embarked at Cork in January, 1755. As soon as the French heard of this, eighteen men-of-war with three thousand soldiers were sent to Canada, followed shortly by nine more war vessels. The English immediately sent twelve vessels under Admiral Boscawen in pursuit, followed shortly by seven more, but only two of the French vessels were captured.

The council of governors.—Braddock summoned the governors for a consultation and they met in April, 1755, at Alexandria in Virginia. Those who responded were the governors of Virginia,

North Carolina, Pennsylvania, Maryland, New York, and Massachusetts. William Johnson was also at Alexandria but was not in the council. A four-fold attack was planned. Braddock was to attack Fort Duquesne; Shirley was to strike at Niagara; Johnson to attack Crown Point; and Lieutenant-Colonel Monckton was to proceed against Beauséjour.

Braddock's campaign.—After great difficulty in obtaining wagons and supplies, Braddock moved toward the frontier. In May his forces, composed of about two thousand men, were gathered at Fort Cumberland. At Little Meadows, thirty miles from Fort Cumberland, Braddock left the heavy baggage and marched on, though slowly, to attack Fort Duquesne. On July 9 when the forces were about seven miles from the fort they began to march along a rough path through the forest. As the English advanced forces were crossing a ravine they were attacked by the French and Indians, who spread out on either side and fought from behind trees, while the English regulars wheeled into line and returned the fire. The bravery and discipline of the English regulars proved of little avail against the invisible enemy and they soon broke and fled. Braddock hastened up with the second division, but the troops retreating from the front threw them into hopeless confusion. Braddock realized that his force was in danger of annihilation and ordered a retreat. As he fell back he received a mortal wound. Washington, left in command, extricated the troops as best he could and once more led back the sorry remnant of a defeated force.

The harrying of the frontiers.—With the defeat of Braddock, the frontiers of Pennsylvania, Maryland, and Virginia were left almost defenceless. Washington could muster barely fifteen hundred men to protect a mountainous frontier nearly four hundred miles long. No assistance was offered by Pennsylvania, whose Quaker representatives, religiously opposed to war, quarreled with the governor over raising money for defence, in every revenue bill asserting the right to tax the lands of the proprietor, a course in which the governor was unable to acquiese. The deadlock between governor and assembly continued for months, while Indian war bands killed hundreds of settlers. The back country of Virginia was also a scene of massacre and rapine. Under Washington's supervision a plan of defence was devised.

THE
WESTERN FRONTIER
1763
Bradstreet's Route
Boquet's Route
SCALE OF MILES
0 50 100 150 200
Longitude West from Greenwich
CHIPPEWA
MENOMINEE
SAUK AND FOX
Ft. Edward Augustus
WINNEBAGO
Arbre Croche
Michillimackinac
OTTAWA
CHIPPEWA
Lake Michigan
Lake Huron
Georgian Bay
SAGINAW CHIPPEWA
OTTAWA
Lake Ontario
Ft. Oswego
Ft. Stanwix
Ft. Niagara
Devil's Hole
SENECA
IROQUOIS
WYANDOT
L. St. Clair
Detroit
POTAWATOMI
Lake Erie
BRADSTREET
Ft. Presq'Isle
Ft. Le Boeuf
Ft. Venango
Ft. St. Joseph
Maumee
Ft. Sandusky
Kuskuskie
DELAWARES
BOUQUET
Ft. Pitt
Ft. Ligonier
Battle of Bushy Run
Ft. Bedford
Ft. Necessity
Ft. Cumberland
Ft. Miami
Ft. Ouiatanon
ILLINOIS
Illinois R.
KICKAPOO AND MASCOUTIN
Wabash R.
MUSKINGUM
Chillicothe
SHAWNEE
MIAMI
Vincennes
Missouri R.
Cahokia
Ft. Chartres
Ste. Genevieve
Kaskaskia
Kentucky R.
Kanawha
ALLEGHANY MTS.
Beverly Manor
Staunton
Draper's Meadows
Ft. Chiswell
CHEROKEE
Cumberland R.
Tennessee R.
Holston
Ft. Dobbs
Ft. Loudon
Chota
C. Fear R.
Mississippi R.
CHICKASAW
CATAWBA
Santee
Savannah R.
Ft. Augusta
Charleston
Coosa
Chattahoochee R.
Altamaha R.
Flint R.
CHOCTAW
Tombigbee
Alabama R.
CREEK
Savannah
Natchez or Ft. Panmure
Natchitoches
Manchac or Ft. Bute
Mobile
Ft. Charlotte
Pensacola
SEMINOLE
New Orleans
GULF OF MEXICO
St. Augustine
ATLANTIC OCEAN
90°
85°
80°
45°
40°
35°
30°

(From Thwaites, *France in America*, opposite p. 256 [Harpers])

Blockhouses were built at advantageous points along the frontier, the most important being Fort Ligonier near the Alleghany
River, Fort Chiswell in the Shenandoah Valley, Fort Bird on
the Holston River, and Fort Loudoun on the Little Tennessee.
Fort Cumberland protected the upper Potomac.

Operations in Acadia.—While the war was going badly on
the western frontier Nova Scotia was the scene of victory. In
June Monckton with two thousand colonials landed at Fort
Lawrence and soon captured Fort Beauséjour. Fort Gaspereau
and a fortification at the mouth of the St. John were also occupied. Then followed one of those tragic dramas of war, the
removal of the Acadians. They had constantly been in sympathy with France and many of them had broken their neutrality
in the recent conflict. When they were again asked to take the
oath of allegiance they stubbornly refused. Fearing their defection in case the French attempted to reconquer the peninsula,
their deportation was ordered. Over six thousand were sent
away, many being placed in the mainland English colonies;
others went to Louisiana and the West Indies, and still others
to Canada and France. One shipload of the unfortunates landed
in Texas and fell into the hands of the Spaniards.

The Crown Point campaign.—For the advance against Crown
Point about three thousand men from the New England colonies
and New York were brought together at Albany under William
Johnson. It was not until August that they encamped at the
southern end of Lake George. The slowness of Johnson's movements had given the French ample time for preparation. Baron
Dieskau with thirty-four hundred men had been sent to Crown
Point. He now moved southward with a part of his force to a
point almost east of the English camp. In the first engagement
Dieskau scored a success. He then rashly attacked the English
camp, but his forces suffered heavily, were finally routed, and the
commander captured. After the battle Johnson, who was
wounded, decided not to attempt to capture Crown Point.

The Niagara campaign.—Governor Shirley undertook the reduction of Niagara. With two regiments of colonials and five hundred New Jersey men he advanced to Oswego. But there Shirley
found himself checkmated, for the French had sent fourteen
hundred men to Fort Frontenac and had brought twelve hun-

dred from Fort Duquesne to Niagara. If Shirley attacked, he would be in danger of forces from Fort Frontenac cutting his line of communications. After a summer of inactivity he left a garrison of seven hundred men at Oswego and abandoned the campaign.

The diplomatic revolution.—In 1756 the old alignment of England and Austria against Prussia, France, and Spain changed. Since the War of the Austrian Succession, Maria Theresa had bided her time, until she could recover Silesia. With the aid of her great minister, Kaunitz, she succeeded in forming new alliances, France, Russia, Austria, and some of the minor German states uniting against Frederick the Great. To protect Hanover, the hereditary possession of George II, England made an alliance with Prussia, and thus became a participant in the Seven Years' War. Although a state of war with France had existed in India and America, neither power had made a declaration of war. But there was no longer need for subterfuge; England declared war on May 18, 1756, and France on June 9.

French preparations.—Already France had despatched to America the Marquis de Montcalm to take command of the forces, with the Chevalier de Levis as second in command. Almost from the first Montcalm was beset with difficulties. Vaudreuil, who had taken Duquesne's place as governor-general, was a colonial, jealous of any official from France, a man lacking in decision, desirous of appearing as the mainspring of success, but ever ready to blame failure upon others. The Intendant Bigot was entirely venal, a man of low morality, who feathered his nest regardless of the public danger. Montcalm's command contained three thousand French regulars in Canada and eleven hundred at Louisbourg, two thousand trained colonials, and about fifteen thousand militia. The Indian allies furnished varying numbers.

English preparations.—Upon his return from Oswego Shirley planned a new offensive, which included attacks upon Ft. Duquesne, the Lake Ontario and Lake Champlain defences, and the settlements above Quebec. This was approved by a war council at Albany, but the colonies refused to embark in such an extensive scheme and the attack on Ft. Duquesne and Quebec had to be abandoned. John Winslow was commissioned to lead the troops against Ticonderoga and Crown Point, and

Shirley proposed to command against the Ontario strongholds. But before the plan could be executed Shirley was superseded by Colonel Daniel Webb, who in turn was followed by General James Abercromby, with the understanding that Loudoun was soon to take command.

The fall of Oswego.—While the colonial forces were slowly preparing to take the offensive, Montcalm struck at Oswego. A three days' siege made the forts untenable and the place surrendered on August 14, 1756, sixteen hundred prisoners being taken. Montcalm then returned to Ticonderoga, where his garrison of five thousand men defied Loudoun, who dared not attack him. The year had been one of dismal disasters for the English: Oswego fallen, the Ticonderoga attack abandoned, the frontiers from Maine to South Carolina harried by Indian war, Minorca captured by the French, and Calcutta fallen to Surajah Dowlah.

Pitt becomes the moving spirit.—Newcastle's mismanagement raised a popular outcry and in November, 1756, he resigned. The Duke of Devonshire became Prime Minister, but Pitt was the strong man of the new cabinet. He was not in the king's favor, however, and, by April, 1757, was forced out of office. In July a new ministry was formed. "To Newcastle was given the name of Prime Minister, to Pitt the reality. With the control of foreign affairs as Principal Secretary of State he was also to have control of the war." He saw that England's opportunity was on the seas and in the colonies.

Louisbourg and Ft. William Henry.—At the advice of Loudoun an attack on Louisbourg had been planned. A part of the troops were withdrawn from the northern frontier and in June eleven or twelve thousand men were gathered at Halifax, where they were joined by a squadron under Vice-Admiral Holburne. The news that Louisbourg had been heavily reinforced alarmed Loudoun and he returned to New York. Holburne cruised off Louisbourg, hoping to attack the French, but his fleet was shattered by a storm. Loudoun had left an insufficient force to defend the Lake George region. Montcalm, ever on the alert to take advantage of the blunders of the enemy, descended from Ticonderoga and attacked Fort William Henry at the southern end of the lake. After a three days' bombardment the English force of about two thousand surrendered. On the continent the

British had failed dismally. An attempt to capture Rochefort had been unsuccessful and the Duke of Cumberland had conducted an inglorious campaign in Germany. The only great British successes of the year were in India where Calcutta and Chandernagore were captured and the battle of Plassey was won.

Preparations and plans, 1758.—By 1758 Pitt, ably seconded by Admiral Anson, had brought the army and navy to a high standard. A squadron was sent to watch Brest, flying squadrons attacked several French ports, a fleet was maintained in the Mediterranean to prevent the fleet at Toulon from getting into the Atlantic, and small squadrons were sent to India, to the African coast, and the West Indies. The army was raised to a hundred thousand. In America Loudoun was superseded by Abercromby, Major-General Amherst was sent over, and twenty thousand provincial troops were put in the field. A three-fold offensive was planned. Forbes with about seven thousand men was to attack Fort Duquesne; Abercromby and Howe with fifteen thousand men were to clear the French from Lake Champlain, and Amherst with twelve thousand regulars aided by a powerful fleet under Admiral Boscawen was to attack Louisbourg.

Capture of Louisbourg.—Boscawen and Amherst rendezvoused at Halifax and on June 1, 1758, over a hundred and fifty vessels appeared before Louisbourg. Gradually the English forces encompassed the fortress. The French sunk several war vessels in the harbor mouth to prevent the entrance of the English fleet, but in the course of the bombardment three of the remaining French vessels caught fire and two others were destroyed by a night attack. The defences were battered down one by one and on July 26 Ducour, the French commander, offered to capitulate and six thousand prisoners of war passed into English hands.

Abercromby's defeat.—While the English were besieging Louisbourg, Abercromby led his army of fifteen thousand against Ticonderoga. Montcalm was in command of the French fortress, which was garrisoned by less than four thousand men. The English army crossed Lake George on a great flotilla, and on July 6 was within four miles of Ticonderoga. Abercromby foolishly thought that the fortifications could be rushed with the bayonet and on July 8 the attempt was made. The French fire mowed down the charging ranks with frightful slaughter. A desultory fight continued, followed by a second charge which also failed, and Abercromby, after losing nearly two thousand men, decided to retreat. In October Amherst took command of the forces which were encamped at the southern end of Lake George, but the season was too far advanced to attempt another great offensive in that region until spring.

Forts Frontenac and Duquesne.—The French forces on Lake Ontario had been weakened by withdrawals. Taking advantage of this, in August Lieutenant-Colonel Bradstreet led twenty-five hundred men against Fort Frontenac. The feeble garrison of one hundred soon surrendered, and the fort and ships in the harbor were destroyed. Lake Ontario was now in the hands of the English, and French control on the upper Ohio was weakening. General Forbes gathered a force of six or seven thousand men and advanced toward Fort Duquesne. Upon the approach of the English in November, the French destroyed the fortifications and scattered to the various western posts which they still possessed.

Kerlérec and the southern Indians.—That the English did not carry the war into the Southwest was due in no small part to the Indian policy of Kerlérec, the governor of Louisiana. The Creeks and Choctaws were traditionally favorable to the French, but their loyalty was always strained by the superior quality of English goods. Kerlérec made annual visits to Mobile to distribute presents, and prevented the Choctaws from threatened defection. Through his influence, in 1755 and again in 1757 the Creeks expelled Englishmen sent to establish posts among them, and murdered English traders. In 1757 Fort Massac was built on the Ohio to prevent an English expedition descending that stream or the Cumberland. At the same time the Shawnees returned to French allegiance.

The Cherokee War.—For three years Kerlérec intrigued with the Cherokees and succeeded in winning them over. He soon incited them to attack the settlements and many depredations occurred. In October, 1759, Governor Lyttleton of South Carolina, after a show of force, patched up a truce, but shortly afterward the Cherokees surrounded Fort Prince George and killed the commander and two others. The garrison then massacred Indian hostages within the fort, and immediately the southern frontier was ablaze with war. Hostilities assumed such proportions that it was necessary, early in 1760, for Amherst to send twelve hundred men to assist the colony. An expedition under Colonel Montgomery destroyed many Cherokee villages, but Montgomery's orders did not allow him to remain long in the colony, and in August he departed for New York. The Cherokees then captured Fort Loudoun. In 1761 an expedition of twenty-six hundred Highlanders and colonials under Colonel Grant was sent against the Indians. The heart of the Cherokee country was penetrated and the Indians were forced to sue for peace.

Operations in the West Indies.—Late in 1758 British reinforcements were sent to the West Indies to attempt the capture of the French island possessions, twenty-five vessels being gathered under Commodore John Moore. In January an attempt was made to take Martinique, but the French force of ten thousand regulars and militia prevented the occupation. During the following months Guadeloupe, Marie Galante, the Saintes, La Désirade, and Petit Terre surrendered to the English.

The campaigns of 1759.—Four expeditions against the French in North America were planned for 1759; one under Prideaux against Niagara, a second under Stanwix against settlements on Lake Erie, and a third under Amherst against Ticonderoga and Crown Point. The fourth under Vice-Admiral Saunders and Major-General Wolfe was directed against Quebec.

Niagara captured.—Prideaux arrived before Niagara in July. In the attack the general was accidentally killed and Sir William Johnson took command. He defeated a relieving force and the fort surrendered. The fall of Niagara made it unnecessary for Stanwix to proceed, and he devoted his energies to the building of Fort Pitt, on the site of modern Pittsburgh.

The fall of Quebec.—While Amherst was slowly moving toward Lake Champlain, the more important operations were proceeding against Quebec. The rendezvous was at Louisbourg. There were gathered nine thousand troops, thirty-nine men-of-war, ten auxiliaries, twenty-six transports, and a hundred and sixty-two other craft, manned by eighteen thousand men. In June the vast armament sailed up the St. Lawrence to attack the strongest fortification on the continent. For the defence of the city Montcalm was able to muster an army of seventeen thousand, four thousand of whom were French regulars. The city occupies a promontory which juts into the St. Lawrence. Behind it are the Plains of Abraham, a plateau with almost perpendicular cliffs. To the eastward flows the River St. Charles. Between the St. Charles and the Montmorency stretched the fortified French camp. The only weak place in the defence was Point Levis across the river. This Montcalm had wished to fortify but had been overruled by Vaudreuil.

On June 26 the fleet approached the city and Point Levis was immediately occupied. Then began a series of attacks upon the French positions below the city, but every assault was repulsed and frequently with heavy loss. It became evident that the French encampment could not be taken and the plan of attack was changed. The fleet, which formed a screen for land operations on the southern shore, had gradually succeeded in getting several vessels above the city, intercepting supplies and reinforcements. At a council of war an attack above the city was determined upon. Wolfe withdrew his forces from the Montmorency and they were transferred to a point above the town. This movement was covered by the movement of the ships, which continually passed up and down the river as if to make a landing. On September 12 Saunders bombarded the French camp below the city. Montcalm, completely deceived, hurried reinforcements to that quarter. Before dawn of September 13 Wolfe landed his first detachment at the foot of the cliffs two miles above the city. Up the steep side clambered a small party, who overcame the guard at the top. By sunrise forty-five hundred men had mounted to the Plains of Abraham. Montcalm made a desperate effort to regain the position but the battle went in favor of the English. Both Wolfe and Montcalm were killed. On September 17 the British troops entered Quebec, the key to the St. Lawrence.

Important naval operations.—Elsewhere the English were equally successful. In 1758 Sénégal and Gorée on the African coast had been captured, and in 1759 on the coast of India a French fleet was bested and abandoned the East Indian waters. Rodney destroyed a French fleet at Havre, Boscawen in August completely defeated the French Mediterranean fleet, and Hawke in November annihilated the channel fleet in a great battle near Quiberon Bay.

The French fail to recapture Quebec.—Although Quebec had fallen the French still had a formidable force in the field. The troops were withdrawn from Lake Champlain and new levies were raised. By April, 1760, Levis had gathered an army of eleven thousand men and he proceeded boldly to attempt the recapture of Quebec. A hard winter had greatly reduced the effectiveness of the English garrison and General Murray was able to meet the French with only three thousand men. On April 18 occurred the second battle on the Plains of Abraham. The artillery saved the English and the attack failed. An English fleet soon blocked the St. Lawrence and the possibility of aid from France was at an end.

The capture of Montreal.—The last important Canadian stronghold was Montreal, and here Vaudreuil and Levis made their final stand. Three English armies were sent against the place. Murray ascended the St. Lawrence, Haviland advanced from Lake Champlain, and Amherst with eleven thousand men proceeded from Lake Ontario down the St. Lawrence. The French, weakened by desertions and discouraged by defeats, offered little resistance; on September 8 articles of capitulation were signed and the struggle for New France was practically ended. Forts Miami, Detroit, Mackinac, and St. Joseph soon surrendered; of the mainland colonies Louisiana alone remained in the possession of France and this also she was destined to lose.

George III becomes king.—The year 1760 also saw the breaking of French power in India. Colonel Eyre Coote decisively defeated Count Lally at the battle of Wandewash and the next year Pondicherry was captured, putting an effectual end to French influence in the Carnatic. When English success was at its height George III ascended the throne of England. He opposed the war of conquest which Pitt was waging, desiring to break the power of the Whig oligarchy which long had dominated English politics. In 1761 Pitt resigned but the king was unable to bring the struggle to an immediate close, for Charles III of Spain renewed the family compact with France, and Spain entered the war.

Operations in the West Indies and the Philippines.—Against the new antagonist England's sea power was overwhelmingly superior. In 1761 Rodney was sent to take command in the West Indies. He found Dominica already in English hands. Rodney immediately ordered the blockade of Martinique and in February, 1762, the island was surrendered. Shortly afterward Granada, the Grenadines, and St. Lucia were occupied. Admiral Pocock was sent out with reinforcements, and a great fleet of fifty-three war vessels, besides transports and other craft, with an army of fifteen thousand proceeded against Havana. In June the place was invested by land and sea. On July 30 Moro Castle was carried by storm, and on August 13 the city surrendered. Nine ships of the line and loot to the value of £3,000,000 fell into English hands. The extinguishment of French power in India made it possible to turn attention to the Philippines, and a squadron under Draper was sent against Manila. The place was feebly garrisoned and quickly surrendered, the capitulation taking place on October 5.

The Peace of Paris.—France, Spain, and England were ready for peace. At the decisive moment Russia had turned to the side of Prussia, and Austria was unable to continue the war alone. France made overtures to England for peace, and on November 3, 1762, the preliminaries were signed. The definitive treaty between England, France, and Spain was signed at Paris on February 10, 1763. France surrendered to England Canada, St. John's, Cape Breton, and all that part of Louisiana which was east of the Mississippi except the Island of Orleans. France retained certain fishing rights on the Newfoundland banks and was given the islands of St. Pierre and Miquelon. She also obtained Martinique, Guadeloupe, Marie Galante, and St. Lucia. Belle Isle and Gorée were restored to France, but England kept Sénégal. Minorca was restored to England. In Asia English conquests were restored to France but no fortifications were to be erected by her in Bengal. The preliminary agreements had arranged matters with Spain. In exchange for Havana, Florida was ceded to England. Manila was eventually restored to Spain as the news of the capture did not arrive until the preliminaries had been signed. Louisiana had been an expensive province, and Louis XV gladly surrendered all the territory west of the

Mississippi and the Isle of Orleans to Spain as a compensation for the losses of his ally. France was virtually eliminated from America. England and Spain stood out as the world's great colonizing powers.

READINGS

THE WARS OF JENKINS' EAR AND THE AUSTRIAN SUCCESSION

Armstrong, E., *Elizabeth Farnese;* Clowes, W. L., *The Royal Navy*, III, 50–138, 263–289; Jones, C. C., *The History of Georgia*, I, 314–369; Mahan, A. T., *The Influence of Sea-Power upon History, 1660–1783*, pp. 254–279; McCrady, E., *The History of South Carolina under the Royal Government, 1719–1776*, pp. 187–229; Parkman, F., *A Half-Century of Conflict*, II, 33–256; Thwaites, R. G., *France in America*, 105–123; Walton, J. S., *Conrad Weiser and the Indian Policy of Colonial Pennsylvania*, 9–121; Wood, W., *The Great Fortress;* Shea, J. G., *Catholic Church in Colonial Days*, 470–479.

FRENCH AND INDIAN WAR

Beer, G. L., *British Colonial Policy, 1754-1765*, pp. 6–77; Casgrain, R. R., *Wolfe and Montcalm;* Channing, Edward, *A History of the United States*, II, 550–599; Clowes, W. L., *The Royal Navy*, III, 138–255; Kingsford, W., *The History of Canada*, III, 387–568, IV.; Lucas, C. P., *A Historical Geography of the British Colonies*, V, 216–328; McCrady, Edward, *The History of South Carolina under the Royal Government, 1719–1776*, pp. 329–352; Mahan, A. T., *The Influence of Sea-Power upon History, 1660–1783*, pp. 281–329; Parkman, Francis, *Montcalm and Wolfe;* Short, A., and Doughty, A. G., *Canada and its Provinces*, I, 231–312; Smith, P. H., *Acadia, a lost Chapter in American History*, 145–249; Stone, W. L., *The Life and Times of Sir William Johnson*, I, 327–555, II, 1–213; Thwaites, R. G., *France in America*, 143–280; Villiers du Terrage, Marc de, *Les Dernières Années de la Louisiane Française*, 48–108; Walton, J. S., *Conrad Weiser and the Indian Policy of Colonial Pennsylvania*, 121–381; Wood, W., *The Passing of New France; The Winning of Canada;* Corbett, J. S., *England in the Seven Years' War;* Wrong, G. M., *The Conquest of New France.*

CHAPTER XXI

THE RUSSIAN ADVANCE: THE OCCUPATION OF ALTA CALIFORNIA AND LOUISIANA BY SPAIN

READJUSTMENT IN SPANISH NORTH AMERICA

Effect of the Seven Years' War.—The outcome of the Seven Years' War caused several readjustments in Spanish North America. It left Spain in a position where she must restore her colonial power or sink to the rank of a third rate nation. Renewed war with England was regarded as inevitable. Florida was lost, and was poorly compensated for, it was thought, by western Louisiana. The French barrier having been removed, Spain's hold on Louisiana and the Pacific Slope was threatened by the English, advancing both through Canada and from the thirteen colonies. On the Pacific Slope the Russians seemed even more threatening than the English. Added to all this, northern New Spain was overrun by increasingly hostile tribes. Poor and unprepared though she was, therefore, Spain was forced to get ready for another war with England, occupy Louisiana and Alta California, strengthen the frontier defences of New Spain against the Indians, and explore or reëxplore the northern interior.

The Reforms of Charles III.—All these demands could be met only by the most heroic measures; and these were applied by the energetic Charles III. This king, a Bourbon, had come to the throne in 1759, after a long and forceful reign as King of Naples. By the time of his accession, Spain had already profited much by the Bourbon reforms which from time to time had been instituted since the opening of the century, but the national revenue was still small, commerce stagnant, the army and navy weak, and colonial administration corrupt. Now came the new demands entailed by the outcome of the great war. To make the program of defence possible, it was necessary to provide revenue. This could be done only by increasing commerce and reforming the fiscal administration of the colonies.

384

Commercial reforms.—Commercial reforms were outlined in a series of decrees enacted between 1764 and 1778. The ends at which they aimed are indicated by the deliberations of the *junta* held in 1765. This body condemned especially the monopoly enjoyed by Cadiz, delays due to the flota system, the export duties on Spanish goods, restrictions upon intercolonial commerce, the smuggling habit, and the English monopoly of the slave carrying trade.

Reforms of José de Gálvez.—To carry out the reforms in New Spain King Charles sent José de Gálvez, who, as *visitador general*, was entrusted with a complete overhauling of the administration. The special function of Gálvez was to increase the revenues from New Spain. The amount collected had been limited by crude fiscal methods and by corrupt officials. Gálvez laid a heavy hand upon "graft," and devised new sources of revenue. Conspicuous among the latter was the tobacco industry, which he made a royal monopoly.

Explorations on the Gulf coast.—One of the first steps toward readjustment of the frontier to the new situation was a series of explorations looking to the defence of the northern coast of the Gulf of Mexico against rumored dangers from the English, now in possession of Florida. To this end, in 1766 Colonel Escandón and Colonel Parrilla explored the Nuevo Santander and Texas coasts between Tampico and Matagorda Bay.

Rubí's tour.—To inspect and report on the northern outposts of New Spain, the Marqués de Rubí was commissioned. Leaving Mexico in March, 1766, he passed through the frontier establishments from Sonora to the borders of Louisiana. He found the whole northern frontier infested with warlike tribes, especially the Apaches and Comanches, who committed depredations all the way from the Gila to central Texas. Rubí recommended rearranging the northern posts so as to form a cordon of fifteen, extending from Altar in Sonora to La Bahía in Texas. Regarding Texas he recommended that the Comanche harassed district of San Sabá and all of the establishments on the Louisiana border be abandoned, and that a war of extermination be made against the Eastern Apaches, relying for the purpose on the aid of their enemies. In 1772 most of the Rubí recommendations were adopted in the form of a "New Regulation of Presidios." To Hugo O'Conor, as *comandante inspector*, fell the task of arranging the line of presidios.

Expulsion of the Jesuits.—For reasons which need not be discussed here, in 1767 the king of Spain expelled the Jesuits from all of the Spanish dominions. This caused a general shifting of the missionary forces, the places of the Jesuits in the northeastern provinces being taken by the Franciscans. The temporalities were at first put in the hands of soldier commissioners, but were soon turned over to the Franciscan missionaries. To Pimería Alta were sent Franciscans from the College of the Holy Cross of Querétaro. To Lower California went members of the College of San Fernando of Mexico, the president being Junípero Serra, already distinguished for work in Sierra Gorda.

Gálvez in Lower California.—In 1768 the visitor, Gálvez, was called to California and Sonora. In California he restored the temporalities to the missionaries, consolidated the Indian pueblos, and tried to stimulate Spanish colonization and mining, but without great success. It was while on the Peninsula, too, that he organized the expedition to occupy Alta California.

Gálvez in Sonora.—To end the Indian disturbance which for many years had been menacing Sinaloa and Sonora, Gálvez sent Colonel Domingo Elizondo at the head of eleven hundred men. The war began in 1768. After a year of futile campaigns, chiefly against Cerro Prieto, the hiding place of the enemy, Gálvez himself took command for a time, with little better results. Elizondo was restored to the command, and for another year the war continued. By dint of guerrilla warfare, presents, and coaxing, by the middle of 1771 the rebels were pacified and settled in towns.

The Provincias Internas.—Prominent among the plans of Gálvez were the establishment of the intendant system in New Spain, the erection of the northern provinces into an independent commandancy general, and the establishment there of one or more bishoprics. The project of a separate government for part or all of the northern provinces had often been considered. It was felt that the viceroy was overworked, and too far from the frontier to understand its needs. The demand was sectional, based on regional interests. In 1760 a separate viceroyalty had been proposed, but Gálvez favored a military commandancy general. In 1776, after he became Minister of the Indies, his ideas were put into effect. Nueva Vizcaya, Sinaloa, Sonora, the Californias, Coahuila, New Mexico, and Texas were put under the military and political government of a *comandante general* of the Interior Provinces, directly responsible to the king and practically independent of the viceroy, the Audiencia of Guadalajara retaining its judicial authority. Chihuahua became the capital, except for a short time when Arispe was the seat of government (1780–1782). The first *comandante general* (1776–1783) was Teodoro de Croix, brother of Viceroy Croix, and himself later viceroy of Peru. By writers on California history, with attention fixed on the West, he has been regarded as incompetent.

New dioceses in the North.—In 1777 the Diocese of Linares was created to embrace the northeastern provinces of Coahuila, Nuevo León, Nuevo Santander, and Texas. Two years later was formed the Diocese of Sonora, to include Sinaloa, Sonora, and the two Californias.

The intendancies.—The primary purpose of the intendancies was to provide for the fiscal administration. A French institution, the system had been established in Spain in 1749 with satisfactory results. In 1764 the intendancy of Havana was established, likewise with good results. In 1768 the system was tentatively established in Sonora. At that time Gálvez favored eleven intendancies, dependent on the viceroy as superintendent general of revenues. The plan was not put into general operation until 1786, when Gálvez was Minister of the Indies.

The captaincy-general of Havana.—Up to the middle of the eighteenth century the audiencia and captaincy-general of Santo Domingo comprised all of the West Indies and Venezuela. Though nominally within the district, Florida was a separate captaincy-general, dependent directly on the Council of the Indies for judicial and military affairs. In other respects it was subject to the Viceroy of Mexico. As a result of the English war, in 1764 Havana was made the seat of an independent captaincy-general and of an intendancy. In 1795 the Audiencia of Santo Domingo was moved to Havana.

THE RUSSIAN MENACE

The Russian advance.—Spain had long been uneasy about upper California because of the activities of the English, Dutch, and French. Now the advance of the Russians seemed more threatening, and caused the long contemplated step to be taken. In the seventeenth century the Russians had crossed Siberia and opened up trade with China. In the early eighteenth century large portions of northern Asia were conquered by Russia in the interest of the east-moving fur traders. Before he died Peter the Great set on foot the project of sending an expedition to seek the northern passage from the Pacific to the Atlantic by going east. In pursuance of this task Vitus Bering made his stupendous expeditions into the Pacific (1725–28, 1733–41), in the second of which he discovered Bering Strait, coasted the American mainland, and made known the possibilities of profit in the fur trade.

Fur trade on the Aleutian Islands.—Bering's voyage was followed by a rush of fur traders to the Aleutian Islands. Companies were formed, vessels built at the port of Okhotsk, and posts established within a few years on Bering, Unalaska, Kadiak, and other islands, for a distance of nearly a thousand miles. The principal market for furs was China. The fur trade was attended by wanton slaughter of animals and harsh treatment of natives, who sometimes rebelled, as at Unalaska in 1761.

Decision of Spain to occupy Alta California.—Though Russian activities were as yet confined largely to the Aleutian Islands, the Spanish government feared that they would be extended down the coast. Moreover, there was a growing friendship between Russia and England, Spain's chief enemy. But these dangers, like others discussed during three centuries, might have resulted in nothing but correspondence had there not been on the northern frontier of New Spain a man of action, clothed with full authority to act. This man was the visitor-general, José de Gálvez. On January 23, 1768, Grimaldi, royal minister, sent the viceroy orders to resist any aggressions of the Russians that might arise. This order, which coincided with the views of the visitor and the viceroy, reached Gálvez while on his way to California.

THE FOUNDING OF ALTA CALIFORNIA

The Portolá expedition.—While settling affairs in the Peninsula Gálvez organized the expedition. It was designed to establish garrisons at San Diego and Monterey, and to plant missions, under their protection, to convert and subdue the natives. The command was entrusted to Governor Portolá, and the missionary work to Father Junípero Serra, president of the California missions. The enterprise was carried out in 1769 by joint land and sea expeditions. The *San Carlos* under Captain Vicente Vila and the *San Antonio* under Captain Juan Pérez conducted a portion of the party, while the rest marched overland from Lower California, under Captain Rivera and Governor Portolá.

San Diego founded.—By the end of June all but one vessel had arrived at the Bay of San Diego. While Vila, Serra, and some fifty soldiers remained to found a mission and presidio there, Portolá led others to occupy the port of Monterey. Following the coast and the Salinas Valley, he reached Monterey Bay, but failed to recognize it. Continuing up the coast he discovered the present San Francisco Bay and then returned to San Diego.

Monterey founded.—At San Diego affairs had gone badly. Many persons had died, provisions were scarce, and Portolá decided to abandon the enterprise. Persuaded by Serra, he deferred the day of departure, and new supplies came. Another expedition to Monterey was successful, and the presidio and mission of San Carlos were founded there in 1770.

Plans for expansion.—At last the long talked of ports of San Diego and Monterey had been occupied. But the newly found port of San Francisco, further north, needed protection, the large Indian population called for more missions, settlers were lacking, and permanent naval and land bases were necessary. One by one these matters were considered and adjusted. To assist in the plans for expansion Serra went to Mexico in 1772 and made many recommendations. The temporary naval base at San Blas was made permanent, and thereafter played an important part in the development of California. The new foundations were assured support from the Pious Fund, and in 1771 and 1772 three new missions were founded—San Antonio,

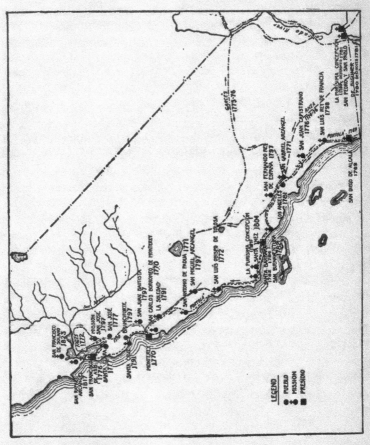

Alta California Settlements

San Gabriel, and San Luis Obispo. In 1772 California was divided, the peninsula being assigned to the Dominicans. Politically the two Californias were continued under one governor, with his residence at Loreto, Fages being replaced as commander in the north by Rivera y Moncada.

A land route to California.—The next step was the opening of a land route from Arizona to California, and was the work especially of two frontier leaders. When the Franciscans in 1768 took the place of the Jesuits in Pimería Alta, Father Francisco Garcés was sent to San Xavier del Bac, the northern outpost. He at once began to make visits to the Gila, and in 1771 alone he crossed the Yuma Desert from Sonóita, and the California Desert to the foot of the western Sierras. Encouraged by these discoveries, Captain Anza of Tubac offered to open a land route to Monterey. The plan was approved by the viceroy, and in 1774 Anza, with Garcés as guide and with twenty soldiers, made the expedition, with great hardships but with notable success.

San Francisco founded.—The opening of the land route from Sonora facilitated the occupation of the port of San Francisco. Plans for its occupation had been discussed ever since its discovery by Portolá. Meanwhile the region had been throughly explored from Monterey as a base. In December, 1774, Anza was ordered to lead a soldier colony from Sonora to occupy the port, and plans were made for a mission. Enlisting some two hundred and fifty persons, Anza assembled them at Tubac, and in October set out for California. Descending the Santa Cruz and Gila Rivers to the Colorado, thence he followed his former trail to Monterey, where he arrived in March, 1776. Aided by Father Font, he reëxplored the Bay region, selected sites for a presidio and mission, and returned to Sonora. In September the presidio and in October the mission of San Francisco were founded.

A route from New Mexico.—The Sonora base for California was not altogether satisfactory and some thought that New Mexico would serve better. Among the latter was Father Garcés, and by a most remarkable exploration he put his views to the test. He accompanied Anza's second expedition to the Gila-Colorado junction, but from there set out to explore a new route.

Ascending the Colorado to the Mojave tribe, near Needles he turned west and crossed the Mojave Desert. It was his plan to go straight to San Luis Obispo, but his guides refused, and he threaded Cajón Pass to Mission San Gabriel. From there he continued through Téjon Pass into the San Joaquin Valley, descended it to the Tulare region, emerged through an eastern pass, probably the Tehachapi, and recrossed the desert to the Mojaves. Thence he continued east to the Moquis, reaching Oraibe on July 2. Here he was given a cold reception, so he turned back to the Yumas.

Exploration by Escalante and Domínguez.—Shortly after Garcés returned, a party set out from Santa Fé to attempt reaching Monterey by a more northern route. The party consisted of Fathers Domínguez and Escalante, Captain Bernardo de Miera y Pacheco, and nine soldiers. Leaving Santa Fé on July 29, 1776, they went northward into Colorado, followed the western line across the San Juan, Dolores, Grand and Colorado Rivers, turned westward to Utah Lake and south past Sevier Lake. In October, concluding that it was too late to attempt to cross the Sierras, they returned eastward to Moqui, Zuñi, and Santa Fé. Thus had another great feat of exploration resulted from the attempt to find land connection with California.

Spanish Pueblos.—California still lacked the civil element to make it complete in outline, and this was now provided. In 1777 Governor Neve moved his capital from Loreto to Monterey, where he received orders from the viceroy to take steps toward founding colonies of settlers, as a means toward making the province self-supporting. Neve therefore proceeded to establish two Spanish pueblos.

San José.—With fourteen families from Monterey and San Francisco, in 1777 Lieutenant Moraga founded the Pueblo of San José in the Santa Clara Valley, near the head of San Francisco Bay, and near by the mission of Santa Clara was founded. The pueblo was established according to the general laws of the Indies. Five years later titles were issued to those settlers who had fulfilled their contracts.

Los Angeles.—The second pueblo was located beside Mission San Gabriel, in the southern part of the province. To procure colonists Rivera y Moncada was sent in 1779 to Sinaloa and

Sonora. Recruiting fourteen families, Rivera sent them over-land by way of Loreto and the Peninsula. Rivera himself, with forty-two soldiers, went with nearly a thousand head of horses and mules over the Anza route by way of the Gila junction, where he and part of his men were massacred. The settlers reached their destination, and in September, 1781, the Pueblo de los Angeles was founded, with eleven families comprising forty-six persons.

Plans for a new outpost.—The old question of advancing the Sonora frontier northward to provide missions for the Pimas and Yumas, and a halfway station on the road to California, had been much discussed ever since Anza's exploration in 1774. Opinions varied as to the best location, one proposing the Gila-Colorado junction, another the middle Gila, another the Colorado above the Yumas, and another even the Moqui country.

Mission-Pueblos at Yuma.—But the weight of opinion was with the Gila-Colorado junction. The chief advocate of this location was the Yuma chief Ollyquotquiebe. In 1776 he went with Anza to Mexico City to ask for a mission and a presidio, made submission for his tribe, and was baptized as Salvador Palma. In the following year the king ordered the petition granted. Delays ensued and Palma became impatient. In 1779 Fathers Garcés and Díaz were sent, with a small garrison, to Palma's village. Their slender outfit of presents and supplies was disappointing, and the Yumas were dissatisfied. In the following year, at Croix's order, two missions were founded west of the Colorado, at the junction, but not of the usual type. Instead of a presidio, ten families were settled near each mission to serve as a protection to the missionaries and an example to the neophytes, who were to live among the settlers instead of in an Indian pueblo.

The massacre.—Trouble soon ensued, and in July, 1781, while Rivera y Moncada was on his way to found Los Angeles, the Yumas, led by Palma, massacred Father Garcés, his three companions, Rivera and his men, and most of the settlers. The women and children were spared. The experience at the Yuma missions is a pointed commentary on the need of soldiers to control mission Indians, and on the wisdom of the usual Spanish custom of separating the neophytes from the settlers. For his part in the plan Croix has been severely critized, but it must be remembered that at the time he needed every soldier available for the Apache wars, and that the Yumas had much vaunted their friendship.

The Yumas punished.—Learning of the massacre, in September, 1781, Croix sent Pedro Fages to the scene with one hundred and ten men from Pitic and Altar. In the course of two journeys he ransomed some seventy-five captives. In the following year Captain Romeu, of Sonora, made a campaign against the Yumas, killed or captured nearly two hundred, and recovered over one thousand horses. But the massacre put an end for the time being to the long series of efforts to establish the Yuma outpost, and practically closed the Anza route to California.

The Santa Barbara Channel occupied.—From the first Father Serra had been anxious to found a group of missions among the numerous Indians along the Santa Barbara Channel, but there had been a lack of funds and soldiers. The reduction of these tribes was important also from a military standpoint, because they held a strategic position on the coast and on the road to the north. With the coming of more soldiers in 1781 the desired step was taken, and in 1782 Mission San Buenaventura and the presidio of Santa Barbara, and in 1786 Mission Santa Barbara were founded.

With the occupation of this district California was complete in outline. There were four presidios, each occupying a strategic position and protecting a group of missions. In the succeeding years new missions were planted in the interior valleys, till the total reached twenty-one. They became marvellously prosperous, converting and giving industrial training to thousands of Indians, and acquiring great wealth in farms and herds. In 1784 Father Serra, the master spirit of the missions, died.

NORTHERN EXPLORATIONS

English and Russian activities.—Continued rumors of Russian and English activities had by now led to a new series of explorations which gave Spain claim to the Pacific Coast for nearly a thousand miles beyond the points reached by Cabrillo and Vizcaino. In 1773 came rumors that an English expedition was about to attempt to pass through the Northern Strait to Cali-

fornia, and that Russia was planning an expedition from Kamt-
chatka to the American coast.

Pérez.—Accordingly, in 1774 Viceroy Bucarely sent Juan
Pérez north in the *Santiago* with orders to take formal possession
of the country as far as 60°. Sailing from San Blas, and taking
on Fathers Crespi and Peña at Monterey as diarists, Pérez sailed
to 55°, exploring Nootka Sound on the way.

Heçeta and Bodega.—Pérez having failed to reach 60°, another expedition was sent from San Blas in 1775 in two vessels,
under Heçeta and Bodega y Quadra. Heçeta reached 49°, discovering Trinidad Bay and the mouth of the Columbia River on
the way (1776). Bodega, in his thirty-six foot schooner, reached
58°, and on the way discovered Bodega Bay.

Arteaga and Bodega.—No Russians had been found, but
news had come of the preparations being made by the English
captain, James Cook, for a voyage to the northwest coast in
search of the strait. Accordingly, another expedition was ordered
by the King of Spain to explore to 70°. Through delays it was
1779 before Arteaga and Bodega, in the *Favorita* and the *Princesa*,
left San Blas. Meanwhile Cook had made his famous voyage
to Nootka Sound. Arteaga's expedition reached 60°, where it
was forced to return because of scurvy among the crews.

LOUISIANA UNDER SPAIN, 1762–1783

The cession.—On October 9, 1762, Louis XV offered western
Louisiana, with New Orleans, to Charles III, king of Spain,
both as a compensation for the loss of Florida, and to put an
end to the constant Franco-Spanish friction over contraband
trade. Charles at first rejected the gift, but reconsidered, and
the treaty of cession was signed on November 3, the day of the
signature of the preliminaries of the peace with England.

The state of the province.—With Spain's small means and
great responsibilities, the gift was not very tempting, and Spain
was not eager to take possession of it. The ceded district embraced New Orleans and the western watershed of the Mississippi
River. The principal settlements lay along the Mississippi and
Missouri, as far as the Kansas post, and along the lower Red
River, as far as the Cadadacho post. The bulk of the population
lay between Pointe Coupée and New Orleans, where there were

over 7000 persons, of whom nearly two-thirds were colored.
Other settlements in the lower district were La Balize, Attakapa,
Opelousas, Avoyelle, and Natchitoches. On the way to the Missouri district were the post opposite Natchez and the Arkansas
settlement. Near or on the Missouri were St. Charles and Ste.
Genevieve. Farther in the interior were slender trading posts,
such as St. Louis among the Cadadacho, a post on the Osage,
and Ft. Cavagnolle, near the mouth of the Kansas River. The
total population of the province ceded to Spain was estimated
at from 8250 to 11,500, over half of whom were colored.

Industries.—Rice, indigo, tobacco, and grain were cultivated in small quantities, but there was little stock raising. For
horses, mules, and cattle dependence was placed upon trade
with the Indians and the Spaniards of the West, much of which
trade was contraband. The principal industries of the province
were the fur trade and commerce with Illinois. The paper money
issued during the recent war, of which there was nearly a million
unredeemed, had depreciated to 25 per cent. of its face value.

Dissatisfaction with the transfer.—It was not till September,
1764, that the cession was known in New Orleans. The news
caused consternation and protest. Some of the inhabitants
of Illinois, left under English rule, moved across the Mississippi
River to La Clede's recently founded fur-trading post of St.
Louis. When, in 1765, the British took possession of Fort Chartres, Captain St. Ange, in charge of the latter place, moved with
his garrison to St. Louis, where he continued to rule until Spanish
possession was taken. Some French settlers from the more
southern districts moved across the Mississippi or to New
Orleans. There the feeling was intense. In January, 1765, the
inhabitants held a meeting and sent a delegate, Jean Milhet, to
France to remonstrate, but without avail, for after months of
waiting he failed even to get an audience with the king.

Ulloa expelled.—At last, in March, 1766, Don Antonio de
Ulloa arrived at La Balize as Spanish governor. The choice
was not a happy one, for although a distinguished scientist and
naval officer, Ulloa had an unpleasant and inflexible personality
which made him unpopular. In July he reached New Orleans,
with ninety soldiers. But the French militia refused to serve
him, and Aubry was left in command. Bickerings and dissatis-

taction followed. The colonists demanded the redemption of the depreciated paper money at face value; the recently arrived Acadians, who had become indentured servants, made constant complaint, until at last redeemed by Ulloa.

Ulloa did not confine his efforts to New Orleans, but established Spanish garrisons at several interior posts and issued ordinances regarding the Indian trade. In the spring of 1766, with Aubry, he visited the settlements between New Orleans and Natchitoches, and sent an officer to report on the best means of defending the upper posts against the English. In 1767 he sent Captain Francisco Rui to establish posts on the lower Missouri at St. Charles and Bellefontaine.

The prohibition of trade with France, promulgated in October, 1768, caused a veritable insurrection in New Orleans, and Ulloa was expelled from the province. His departure was followed by a removal of the Spanish garrisons from the Missouri and elsewhere in the interior, and there was an interregnum of several months, during which Aubry governed.

O'Reilly.—Charles III now sent a man made of sterner stuff. He was Alexandro O'Reilly, an officer who had served with distinction in Europe, had reorganized the defences of Havana after the recent war, and was now recalled to cope with the situation in Louisiana. With 4500 regulars he reached Balize in July, 1769. There was renewed excitement. Some talked of independence and others of joining the English colonies; but Aubry counselled against resistance and the disturbance subsided.

His coup d'état.—King Charles had demanded nothing more severe than the sending of the leaders of the opposition to France, but O'Reilly was not so mild. By a ruse he arrested a number of prominent citizens, executed five and imprisoned others. For this violent deed he has become known as "The Bloody O'Reilly." If the government of Charles III had been imbued with a full sense of its responsibility, it would never have left unpunished such a violation of the fundamental rules of justice.

The Spanish régime installed.—For thirty-four years Louisiana remained under Spanish rule, and during that time it prospered as never before. O'Reilly governed for a year or more with great vigor, not as governor, but as special commissioner to establish Spanish authority. Possession was taken of the interior posts, and by the end of 1770 the Spanish flag had been raised at Ste. Genevieve, the last place to haul down the French emblem. Having accomplished his coup d'état, O'Reilly was conciliatory, and appointed numerous old French officers, like Villiers and De Mézières, to important positions. After authority had been established, the military force was reduced to 1200 men. Spanish law was installed, although the French Black Code was retained. New Orleans was given a cabildo with direct appeal to the Council of the Indies instead of to the Audiencia of Santo Domingo. Louisiana was put under a governor, the first incumbent being Luis de Unzaga y Amezaga. Each of the principal subdistricts was put under a lieutenant-governor, Pedro Piernas going to St. Louis, Villiers to the Arkansas Post (now Fort Carlos III), and Athanase De Mézières at Natchitoches. Until 1771 Louisiana was an independent *gobierno* directly dependent on the Council of the Indies. In 1771 it was attached for military purposes to the captaincy-general of Havana, and for judicial matters to the Audiencia of Santo Domingo. In 1795 it was attached to the Audiencia of Havana. After 1783 West Florida and Louisiana were put under one governor. Later the province was divided into Upper and Lower Louisiana.

Unzaga and Gálvez.—Unzaga ruled till 1776, and proved popular, particularly since he shut his eyes to English smuggling in the lower Mississippi River. Unzaga's successor, Bernardo de Gálvez, nephew of the visitor, son of the viceroy, and himself a viceroy later, was a remarkable man. He too, was popular; he married a French wife, and stimulated tobacco raising by pledging himself to buy each year eight hundred pounds of tobacco.

Encouragement of commerce.—Trade regulations, as promulgated by Ulloa in 1766, restricted all trade to Spanish vessels, and certain specified Spanish ports. Under these conditions English smugglers very soon monopolized the trade of the lower Mississippi, and made their way among the tribes of the Gulf coast. This contraband Unzaga tacitly permitted for the good of the colony. In 1776 an agreement was made with France by which Louisiana was permitted to trade with the French West Indies, under the supervision of two French commissioners resident in New Orleans. Gálvez now promptly seized eleven English vessels and the commerce of the colony passed largely into

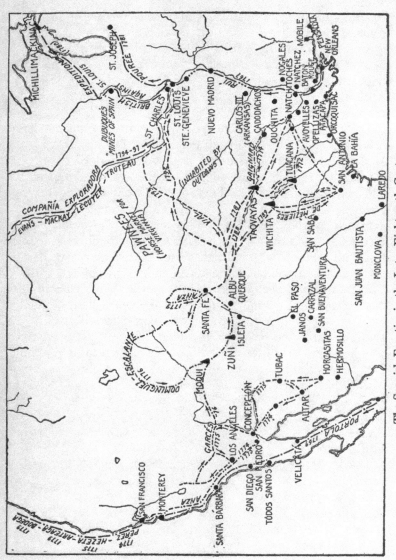

The Spanish Frontier in the Later Eighteenth Century

the hands of the French. In 1778 the produce of the colony was
admitted to any of the ports of France or the United States, and
to any of the ports of Spain to which the commerce of any of the
colonies was admitted. The exportation of furs was encouraged
by exemption from duty for a period of ten years. English trade
in Louisiana was now completely ruined. Under Spanish rule
population grew steadily and by 1803 had reached about 50,000.
After the American Revolution efforts were made to counter-
colonize against the American advance.

The English danger.—The principal military problems of the
new government were to keep the English out and to keep the
Indians quiet. Already English traders were entering the tribes
west of the Mississippi, ascending the Missouri and the Arkansas,
and reaching the borders of Texas overland, or ascending its rivers
from the Gulf of Mexico. Trade in Pawnee and Spanish horses
extended to the English seaboard colonies, Governor Patrick
Henry being among the purchasers of thoroughbred Spanish
stock. To keep out the English, defence was concentrated on
the Mississippi and efforts made to control the Indian tribes.

Eastern Texas abandoned.—On the other hand, since Louisiana belonged to Spain, the defences of eastern Texas, and the
weak missions which they protected, were now withdrawn. At
the same time the few settlers, some five hundred in number,
who lived on the border, were evicted and taken to San Antonio.
But they demurred, sent their Creole leader Gil Ybarbo to
Mexico to represent them, and were allowed in 1774 to settle on
the Trinity River. Five years later, taking advantage of a flood
and Indian raids, and led by Ybarbo, they moved to Nacog-
doches (1779), and from there scattered eastward toward their
former homes.

The fur trade continued.—Louisiana was Spain's first colony
previously occupied by Europeans, and in it many departures
were made from her traditional system. As a means of controlling
the Indians of Louisiana, Spain utilized the corps of French
traders already among the tribes, instead of attempting to use
the mission as a means of control, as was being done at the same
time in California. A regular system of licensed traders was
installed, vagabonds and unlicensed persons were driven from
the tribes, presents were annually distributed, and medals of

merit were given to friendly chiefs. St. Louis, the Arkansas post, and Natchitoches became important centers for the fur trade and for distributing presents. To St Louis tribes went to receive presents from the Illinois country, the upper Mississippi, and the upper Missouri. To remove them from English influence, tribes were induced to cross the Mississippi to settle.

De Mézières.—One of the most difficult problems which confronted Spain was the control of the Red River tribes, which had been friendly to the French but hostile to the Spaniards. It was now necessary to win them over to Spanish allegiance. This was accomplished by Athanase de Mézières, lieutenant-governor at Natchitoches. He installed French traders, drove out vagabonds, expelled English intruders, called in the hostile Red River tribes to make treaties, and himself made a series of notable tours among them. In 1770 he held a great council at the Cadodacho post, where the Cadodacho chief Tin-hi-ou-en was mediator. Two years later he made an expedition through the Asinai, Tonkawa, and Wichita tribes, reaching the upper Brazos River, and going thence to San Antonio. His excellent report first made northern Texas well known to Spanish officials.

Croix's plans for a war on the Apaches.—It was in 1776 that the northern provinces of New Spain were put under a *comandante general* with his capital at Chihuahua. The first comandante, Teodoro de Croix, arrived at the frontier in 1777. As his first great task he set about checking Indian hostilities, particularly those of the Apaches on the Texas-Coahuila frontier. The essence of his plan was to unite the Red River and the eastern Texas tribes (the Nations of the North) and *chasseurs* from Louisiana, commanded by Gálvez, with the soldiery of the Interior Provinces, commanded by Croix, in a joint war of extermination against the eastern Apaches.

Set aside by the American Revolution.—To consider the matter Croix held a council of war at San Antonio in January, 1778. The arrangement of details with the Indians was left to De Mézières. In 1778 he made a tour of the upper Red River, and in the following year again visited the Texas tribes. Spain soon afterward entered the American war, Gálvez was unable to leave Louisiana, and the conduct of the Apache War was left for the time being to Juan de Ugalde, governor of Coahuila.

Communication with Santa Fé and the Upper Missouri.—
The explorations of De Mézières were soon followed by the opening of routes from Santa Fé to San Antonio, Natchitoches, and
St. Louis. In this work the chief pathfinder was Pedro Vial.
Just as the American Pike in his southwestern exploration (1807)
was preceded by Vial and his associates, so Lewis and Clark, in
their ascent of the Missouri River (1804), were anticipated by
the agents of Clamorgan's fur trading and exploring company,
who operated from St. Louis to the country of the Mandans
(1794-1797).

READINGS

REFORMS OF CHARLES III AND GÁLVEZ

Addison, Joseph, *Charles the Third of Spain;* Altamira y Crevea, Rafael,
Historia de España, IV; Chapman, C. E., *The Founding of Spanish California,* ch. IV; Danvila y Collado, Manuel, *Reinado de Carlos III;* Desdevises
du Desert, Gaston, *L'Espagne de l'Ancien Régime;* Ferrer del Rio, Antonio,
Historia del Reinado de Carlos III; Hume, M. A. S., *Spain: Its Greatness and
Decay;* Priestley, H. I., *José de Gálvez, Visitor-General of New Spain;* Rousseau, François, *Règne de Charles III d'Espagne, 1759-1788;* Scelle, G., *La
Traite Négriere aux Indes de Castille;* Viollet, A., *Historie des Bourbons
d'Espagne.*

CALIFORNIA

Academy of Pacific Coast History, *Publications,* I–III; Bancroft, H. H.,
History of California, I, 110–480; Chapman, C. E., *The Founding of Spanish
California;* Eldredge, Z. S., *The Beginnings of San Francisco,* I, 31–170;
Engelhardt, Fr. Zephyrin, *Missions and Missionaries of California,* I, 289–
385; II, 3–414; Hittell, T. H., *History of California,* I, 300–429; 441–452;
509–540; Norton, H. K., *Story of California,* 1–103; Palou, Fr. Francisco,
Relación Histórica de la Vida [de] . . . Serra; Richman, I. B., *California
under Spain and Mexico,* 32–158.

LOUISIANA

Bolton, Herbert E., *Athanase de Mézières and the Louisiana-Texas
Frontier,* I, 66–122; Gayarré, C., *History of Louisiana,* III, 1–617; Hamilton,
P. J., *The Colonization of the South,* 423–445; 447–456; Houck, L., *The
Spanish Régime in Missouri,* I–II; Mason, E. C., "The March of the Span-
iards across Illinois," in *Magazine of American History,* XV, 457–470;
Robertson, J. A., *Louisiana under the rule of Spain, France, and the United
States;* Shepherd, W. R., "The Cession of Louisiana to Spain," in *The
Political Science Quarterly,* XIX, 439–458; Teggart, F. J., "Capture of
St. Joseph, Michigan, by the Spaniards in 1781," in *The Missouri Historical
Review,* V, 214–228; Thwaites, R. G., *France in America,* 281–295.

CHAPTER XXII

THE NEW BRITISH POSSESSIONS

PROVISIONS FOR DEFENCE, GOVERNMENT, AND THE FUR TRADE

Amherst's plan for defence.—While the Spaniards were occupying western Louisiana the British were organizing the country ceded by France and Spain east of the Mississippi, in Canada, and in the West Indies. In 1763 the Secretary of War asked General Amherst, commander-in-chief in America, for a plan of defence of the British possessions. In response he drew up a "Plan of Forts and Garrisons prepared for the security of North America" which reveals England's outlook upon her newly·acquired territory. It provided for ten regiments of approximately seven hundred and fifty men each. The stated purposes were: (1) to keep the king's new subjects in Canada and Louisiana "in due subjection," (2) to keep the old provinces "in a state of Constitutional Dependence upon Great Britain," (3) to command the respect of the Indians, (4) to prevent encroachments of the French or Spaniards, (5) and to protect the colonies in case of war. The regiments were to be distributed in posts along the St. Lawrence, about the Great Lakes, in the Illinois country, along the lower Mississippi, and in Nova Scotia, South Carolina, Georgia, and the Floridas.

Purposes regarding the West.—Regarding the interior posts the particular aims expressed were to keep open the navigation of the St. Lawrence and the Great Lakes, maintain communication between Canada and the Gulf of Mexico, hold the western tribes in check, and guard against French or Spanish intrusion. A post at St. Augustine was especially desirable as a defence against Spain, and Pensacola and Mobile would command the commerce of the Gulf as well as the tribes of the Alabama Basin. The lower Mississippi posts were essential to control the Chickasaws. A post at Crown Point was not only needed to maintain a winter highway to Canada, but might also be useful to suppress disaffection in the maritime colonies, "who already begin to entertain some extraordinary Opinions, concerning their Relations to and Dependence upon the Mother Country."

The Proclamation of 1763.—In October, 1763, the king issued a proclamation creating, within the newly acquired territory, four distinct provinces, Quebec, East Florida, West Florida, and Grenada, and providing a form of government for them. Quebec comprised the Valley of the St. Lawrence from the western end of Anticosti Island to the 45th parallel and Lake Nipissing. Labrador, Anticosti, and the Magdalen Islands were attached to Newfoundland. St. Johns, Cape Breton, and the lesser adjacent islands were attached to Nova Scotia.

East Florida extended to Appalachicola River, and was bounded on the north by St. Mary's River and a line from the head of that stream to the junction of the Chattahoochee and Flint Rivers. The district between St. Mary's and Altamaha Rivers, formerly in dispute between Spain and England, was attached to Georgia. West Florida was the district south of latitude 31° and between the Appalachicola River and the Isle of Orleans. The Island of Grenada, the Grenadines, St. Vincent's, and Tobago were erected into the Government of Grenada.

Crown colonies created.—These new jurisdictions were made crown colonies. For each a governor was to be appointed, with power to call assemblies, "in such Manner and Form as is used and directed in the Colonies and Provinces in America which are under our immediate Government." Until such assemblies should meet, the governors, with their executive councils, were empowered to erect courts, having appeals to the privy council.

The Indian reservation.—For the time being all British possessions on the continent not included in the foregoing jurisdictions, or within the Territory of Hudson Bay, and all lands west or north of the streams flowing into the Atlantic Ocean, were reserved as crown lands for the use of the Indians. No colony might grant lands within this Indian reservation, and settlers were requested to move out. The considerable French settlements in the reserve were ignored.

Until 1755 the English government had managed its Indian affairs through the different colonies, but the results were far

from satisfactory. In that year the government assumed political control over the Indians, creating a southern and a northern
department, and appointing a superintendent for each. In 1761

The New British Possessions, 1763-1783

the purchase of Indian lands was taken out of the hands of the
colonies.

Regulation of Indian trade.—The acquisition of extensive
territories in 1763 called for new trade regulations. The proclamation had created an Indian reserve and opened trade to all

duly licensed subjects. In the following year Lord Hillsborough
drew up a general plan for the management of Indians and the
fur trade. It safeguarded the rights of the Hudson's Bay Company and provided for the continuation of the two superintendents, with three deputies for the northern and two for the southern
district. In the North all trade must be conducted at regularly
established posts, and in the South at the Indian towns. All
traders must be licensed, must trade at schedule prices, and
must have no dealings with Indians except at the prescribed
places. By 1768 the plan had proved too expensive, and the
management of the fur trade was restored to the individual
colonies.

THE OCCUPATION OF THE FLORIDAS

The West Florida posts.—On August 6, 1763, Colonel Prevost
took possession of Pensacola, which became the capital of West
Florida. Shortly afterwards Mobile was occupied by Major
Robert Farmar. The French troops there withdrew to New
Orleans, as did some of the people, but most of the latter
remained. Fort Tombecbé, renamed Fort York, was given a
garrison of thirty men, for the express purpose of keeping the
Choctaws hostile to the Chickasaws, but was abandoned in 1768.
The French among the Choctaws moved across the Mississippi
into Spanish territory, but continued to trade with the
tribe.

The boundary and the river forts.—In 1764 the northern boundary of West Florida was moved north to 32° 28' to take in the
Natchez settlements, and to make room for the land speculators
who were seeking land grants on the lower Mississippi. A garrison was placed at Natchez (Fort Panmure). In connection
with efforts to keep the Mississippi open and to establish navigation through the Iberville River, Fort Bute was built near the
latter stream in 1766. These Mississippi posts were designed
also to prevent French and Spanish smuggling among the Choctaws. But there was English smuggling likewise, and to stop it
Spanish posts were later built on the other bank of the river.
In 1769 the troops of most of the English posts were withdrawn
to St. Augustine, but there was a protest at once. Pensacola
drew up a memorial, and immigrants recently arrived at the

Mississippi demanded protection. O'Reilly had just come to New Orleans, and it was feared that he might have designs on West Florida. In 1770, therefore, most of the troops were restored, and a new garrison was established at Manchac.

Indian agents and fur magnates.—The possession of West Florida proved an important asset to Great Britain in the control of the southwestern Indians, especially during the Revolution. John Stuart, Superintendent for the Southern Department, made his headquarters at Pensacola, but Mobile was the real center of control for the whole Southwest. Subagents convened at Mobile a great congress of all the tribes and effected an alliance with them, and soon afterward the Indian lands about Mobile were ceded to the English. The military authorities encouraged inter-tribal dissensions, and the Creeks and Choctaws were frequently at war, in which the Chickasaws sometimes joined. According to the general system, the fur trade of the Southwest was opened to all traders having a government license and a proper bond. The fur magnates at Mobile were the house of Swanson and McGillivray, who by 1777 had a branch house at Fort Bute, which conducted trade with the Illinois. At Pensacola Panton, Leslie, and Company, the largest business house, became an important factor in the trade and in the management of the tribes.

Politics and government.—West Florida was accorded a governor, council, and assembly. Governor George Johnstone arrived at Pensacola in October, 1764, but the first assembly was not elected until 1766. Mobile, Pensacola, and Campbell Town were electoral precincts at first, and after 1778 Natchez and Manchac were represented. The brief political experiences of the province were as interesting as those of the older colonies in early days. The governor and assembly frequently quarreled. In 1772 Governor Chester prorogued that body and for six years got along without it. More harmful than these quarrels were the factional disputes between the civil and military officials.

Development of West Florida.—When England took possession, Pensacola consisted of some forty thatched huts and small barracks, all enclosed within a palisade, but it was rebuilt, and practically dates from British rule. Mobile remained largely French, and was reduced in size by the emigration to New Orleans. British rule gave impetus to Mobile's commerce, and by 1776 the port was paying £4000 a year to the London custom house alone.

Immigration.—Efforts were made also to secure immigrants for West Florida. In 1763 the Board of Trade put an advertisement regarding land grants in the *London Gazette*, and in 1764 Governor Johnstone issued a circular to attract settlers. In 1765 or 1766 a colony from North Carolina went by sea and settled about Natchez and Baton Rouge. Speculators obtained large grants of land about Natchez as early as 1767, among them being Daniel Clark, later a great figure at New Orleans. Before the Revolution numerous settlers arrived from England, the West Indies, and most of the mainland colonies, including New England. Most of them settled on the Mississippi River between Manchac and Natchez. In 1772 three hundred persons from Virginia and the Carolinas are said to have been established on the lower Mississippi, and three or four hundred families were expected that summer. As a result, the Mississippi posts were repaired and civil government established. In 1775 a considerable immigration from New England was led by General Lyman. About the same time Colonel Putnam led a company from New England to the Yazoo district. In 1777, according to the botanist Bartram, more than half of the population of Mobile were people who had come from the northern colonies and Great Britain.

During the Revolution West Florida was a refuge for Loyalists. In November, 1776, Mathew Phelps led a colony of New Englanders to the lower Mississippi. Highland soldiers defeated in North Carolina that year took refuge in the province. Loyalists from Georgia and South Carolina settled on the Tombigbee River and Mobile Bay, and others from the same colonies settled on the Tensaws Bayou.

East Florida under British rule.—In East Florida, St. Augustine became the capital and the chief military post. St. Marks on the Gulf was occupied for military purposes and the posts of Matanzas, Picolata, and Mosquito were also maintained for a time. The military of both East and West Florida were under the general command at Pensacola. James Grant was made first governor. In East Florida there was no assembly till 1781. Difficulties between military and civil authorities prevailed as in West Florida.

At the time of the British occupation, St. Augustine was a small Spanish town with adobe houses and narrow streets. Under British rule East Florida prospered. Harbors were improved, and highways were constructed, one being built from St. Mary's River to St. Augustine. In 1766 some forty families went from the Bermudas to Mosquito Inlet to engage in shipbuilding. In the following year Dr. Turnbull brought fifteen hundred indentured colonists from the Mediterranean region and settled them at New Smyrna. In 1776 the indentures were cancelled and the settlers moved to St. Augustine, where their descendants still live. During the Revolution East Florida, like West Florida, became a Mecca for southern Loyalists.

MILITARY OCCUPATION OF THE ILLINOIS COUNTRY

Plans to occupy the Illinois country.—By the end of 1761 British troops had taken possession of all the lake posts from Niagara to Green Bay, besides Venango, Miamis, and Ouiatanon further south. In July, 1763, orders were sent by the Governor of Louisiana for the evacuation of the Illinois posts, and boats were prepared at Fort Pitt for sending four hundred English troops to relieve the French garrisons. But the conspiracy of Pontiac delayed the complete transfer of this region for nearly three years.

The conspiracy of Pontiac.—Early in the war the tribes north of the Ohio had ravaged the Virginia and Pennsylvania frontiers, but after 1758 they had been quiet, although they did not like the English. They feared eviction from their lands, English traders had proved arrogant and dishonest, and General Amherst was attempting a policy of economy in presents, in spite of the criticism of the better informed Indian agents. Pontiac, head chief of the Ottawas, organized a general revolt, embracing the Algonquins, some of the tribes of the lower Mississippi, and some of the Iroquois. By a simultaneous assault in May, 1763, all but three northwestern posts—Detroit, Fort Pitt, and Niagara —fell almost without a blow. At Presq'Isle, Le Boeuf, Venango,

Mackinac, Sandusky, St. Josephs, and Ouiatanon, there were massacres, and the garrison fled from Green Bay.

Failure of the Loftus expedition.—It being impracticable now to send troops to the Illinois country by way of the Ohio, this was attempted by an expedition up the Mississippi. Major Loftus was sent from Mobile with three hundred and fifty men to occupy Fort Massac, Kaskaskia, and Fort Chartres. In February, 1764, he left New Orleans, but when two hundred and forty miles up the river, at Rocher á Davion, he was attacked by Tunica Indians, whereupon he abandoned the expedition and returned to Mobile.

Peace.—While Colonel Bradstreet reoccupied the Lakes, General Gage, Amherst's successor, resorted to conciliation, and a series of peace embassies were sent to the Illinois country from Mobile and from the northern garrisons. The submission of the Ohio tribes, failure of hopes for aid from New Orleans, and news of the transfer of western Louisiana to Spain, led Pontiac to negotiate at Ouiatanon in 1765 with George Croghan. At Detroit Croghan secured peace with all the western tribes. Thomas Stirling then descended the Ohio with a detachment and in October occupied Fort Chartres. "Thus, after nearly three years of fighting and negotiating, British forces were in possession of the last of the French posts in the West."

Establishment of government.—In accordance with the Treaty of Paris a proclamation of General Gage guaranteed the inhabitants the free exercise of the Catholic religion. Settlers were allowed to sell their lands and emigrate, or to become British subjects on taking the oath of allegiance. The inhabitants of Kaskaskia and other places asked and received an extension of the time for decision to March, 1766. Many of them emigrated to St. Louis and Ste. Genevieve, or to New Orleans. The Proclamation of 1763 made no provision for civil government in the Indian reserve, and local administration was left to the military authorities and Indian agents. The French people were dissatisfied, and many misunderstandings arose between them and the English settlers and officers. By 1770 the complaint took the form of a demand for civil government, which was provided in 1774 by the Quebec Act.

LAND SPECULATION AND PLANS FOR WESTERN COLONIES

Western schemes.—Before the French and Indian War grants had been made by the British government of lands beyond the Alleghanies, and settlement on the back lands had been favored as a means of opposing the French and of extending British trade. During the war the frontiers of settlement were contracted, but, in anticipation of victory, new grants were sought and new schemes proposed. Not only were lands desired, but prominent men proposed new colonial governments west of the mountains. Nearly all of the proposals involved territory in the Ohio Valley. After the Albany Congress of 1754 Franklin urged the formation of two barrier colonies in the West. In 1756 Thomas Pownall, ex-governor of New Jersey, made a similar proposal. About the same time Samuel Hazard of Philadelphia promoted the formation of a Presbyterian colony to embrace most of the Ohio Valley and extending across the Mississippi. In 1757 the Greenbrier Company secured 100,000 acres of land on the western waters.

The victory over the French stimulated new speculative and colonizing schemes for the West both in England and America. In June, 1763, the Mississippi Company was formed, composed of prominent Virginians, including Colonel George Washington and Richard Henry Lee. A memorial to the king was drawn asking for 2,500,000 acres on both sides of the lower Ohio, quit rent free for twelve years, and protection by royal forts, on condition of settling two hundred families. Late in 1763 a pamphlet published in Edinborough, Scotland, proposed a colony named Charlotiana, to include the country between the Wabash, Ohio, Mississippi, and the Great Lakes. About the same time Charles Lee proposed a colony on the Illinois and another on the Ohio.

Effect of the Proclamation.—The Proclamation of 1763 closing the Trans-Alleghany country to settlement seems to have checked for a time the schemes for speculation. The Proclamation contained an implied promise that the boundary would be revised, while it was well known that influential politicians in England favored the opening of the West. New schemes for western lands, therefore, were not long suppressed. In 1766 William Franklin, governor of New Jersey, launched a plan for two colonies, one at Detroit, the other on the lower Ohio. Through the aid of Benjamin Franklin, father of the governor, the Ohio country was favored by the Board of Trade, but in 1768 the plan dropped from sight. Meanwhile many other land companies were formed.

A policy of expansion adopted.—The policy of the ministry regarding the West was vacillating, and more so, no doubt, because of the pressure of conflicting interests. But in 1768 the ministry decided on a definite plan for western settlement, the principle being that expansion should be gradual and under control of imperial agents, who should purchase land from the Indians as needed. Johnson and Stuart, Indian superintendents, had already made tentative arrangements for revising the proclamation line. In 1765 the Six Nations ceded their claims to lands between the Ohio and the Tennessee. Stuart, by a series of treaties, secured a line from the southern boundary of Virginia to the St. Mary's River, Florida, thence along the tidewater line to the Appalachicola River. West of that point the line was not completed, but important cessions were made along the Mobile coast. In 1768 the former lines were ratified, and Stuart, in two treaties with the Cherokees and Creeks (October, November, 1768), secured the extension of the line to the mouth of the Kanawha River on the north and to the Choctaw River on the south. At Fort Stanwix in 1768 the Iroquois ratified essentially their cession of 1765. The lines did not correspond, since the Iroquois cession included Western Tennessee and Kentucky, which were not within the other cessions. Meanwhile the southern line was modified by the treaty of Lochaber by running it west along the southern boundary of Virginia to the Holston River, thence direct to the mouth of the Kanawha. The purpose of the change was to take in the recently formed Watauga settlement.

Vandalia.—Having extinguished the Indian titles, it was now possible to found a new colony back of Pennsylvania and Virginia, and such a project was put on foot. Samuel Wharton of Philadelphia formed a company for the purpose of purchasing part of the lands. The company included some of the leading men in England and America, among them being Benjamin Franklin and Thomas Walpole. Official aid was enlisted by

including two members of the ministry. In 1769 the purchase
was made, and, in spite of Lord Hillsborough's opposition, by
1775 the project of a new and separate province named Vandalia
had been approved by king and council. The outbreak of the
Revolution set the plan aside. Had it been carried out it would
have cut Virginia off from her back lands. The Quebec Act of
1774 operated in the same direction, by attaching the Northwest
to Quebec. Virginia therefore resisted. Governor Dunmore opposed the Vandalia colony, made grants of land both within and
beyond it, and joined a company which purchased Indian lands
north of the Ohio.

TRANS-ALLEGHANY SETTLEMENT

Western settlements before 1763.—But it was the backwoodsmen, and not the corporations, who opened the Trans-Alleghany
country. Before the war a few settlements had been made on
the western waters, In 1748 Draper's Meadows, on the Greenbrier, in West Virginia, were settled. Between 1750 and 1752
a settlement was made by the Ohio Company at Redstone on
the Monongahela. By 1758 several small settlements had been
made on the Holston, Watauga, and Cheat Rivers. But during
the war these western settlements were abandoned, and the
frontier pushed eastward a hundred miles or more.

The westward movement after the war.—The French and In-
dian War was scarcely over when the westward movement began
again, regardless of proclamations or the deliberations of the
Board of Trade. In 1760 Daniel Boone, from the Yadkin in
North Carolina, "cilled a bar" on the Watauga River. Between
1761 and 1765 Wallen annually led hunters to the west. In 1765
Croghan surveyed the Ohio River, and the next year James
Smith and others explored the Tennessee. In 1767 Finley was
in Kentucky, and Stoner, Harrod, and Lindsay were at French
Lick (the site of Nashville). In 1767 and 1770 Boone was
"prospecting" for Judge Richard Henderson, a land speculator
of North Carolina. At the same time Mansker led a party down
the Cumberland and on to Natchez. By this time others had
wandered far beyond the Mississippi and were causing the Spanish officials anxiety.

The hunters, traders, and prospectors were followed by surveyors and settlers. The chief participants in the movement were from the middle region and the South: Pennsylvania, Maryland, Virginia, and North Carolina. Prominent among the pioneers on the western waters were the Scotch-Irish who had settled the back country of the older colonies and stood waiting at the western passes.

The Appalachian barrier.—To reach the Mississippi Valley the frontiersman was forced to pass the Appalachian barrier, extending from Maine to Georgia. The easiest pass through it, by way of the Hudson and Mohawk Rivers, was impeded by the Six Nations who stood between the western frontier of settlement and the vacant lands beyond. Farther south the barrier was traversed by a series of interlocking rivers, flowing in opposite directions, whose valleys afforded trails. The Susquehannah led to the Alleghany, the Potomac to the Monongahela, the James and Roanoke to the Great Kanawha, the Great Pedee, the Yadkin, and Catawba to the head waters of the Tennessee. A series of longitudinal valleys on the eastern front of the southern Appalachians gave access from Virginia and North Carolina to the upper Tennessee, from whose valley an easy pass was found to Kentucky by way of Cumberland Gap.

The Indian barrier.—The Iroquois Confederacy, though friendly, was a retarding force to the northern stream of emigration. The Algonquin tribes north of the Ohio had been friendly with the French, and after the French and Indian War they favored the French traders rather than those from the seaboard colonies. At the southern end of the Appalachians westward expansion was retarded by the strong confederacies of the Cherokees, Creeks, Choctaws, and Chickasaws. The region between the Ohio and the Tennessee was the "dark and bloody ground" between the northern and southern tribes, but permanently inhabited by neither. It was this region which was opened to settlement by the Indian cessions between 1768 and 1770. The cessions were followed immediately by a movement of settlers into the area.

THE SETTLEMENT OF EASTERN TENNESSEE

The North Carolina Regulators.—The movement across the mountains was stimulated by a popular upheaval in the back country of North Carolina. Shortly before 1740 the Scotch-Irish and German migration reached North Carolina and by 1765 the lands along the headwaters of the Yadkin, Haw, Neuse, Tar, Catawba, and Deep Rivers had been occupied. Many English and Welsh also had settled in the same region. Between the Piedmont and the coastal plain was a sparsely settled country of pine forests. "Cut off . . . from the men of the east, the men of the 'back country' felt no more sympathy for the former than they received from them." The coast country controlled the legislature and the courts. The men of the West complained that they were forced to pay excessive taxes, that the sheriffs were dishonest, and fees extortionate. An additional grievance was the scarcity of money. During 1765–1767 the frontiersmen began to organize and from 1767 to 1771 the back country was in a state of rebellion. Lawyers were seized and whipped, and the Hillsboro court was broken up. In 1771 the Regulators were defeated by Governor Tryon's troops in the battle of the Alamance and the rebellion soon subsided. During those troubled years many had sought new homes in the western valleys.

The Watauga settlement.—Permanent settlement was made in eastern Tennessee in 1769. In that year a band of pioneers moved down the valley from Virginia and settled on the Watauga River, a branch of the Tennessee, thinking that they were still in Virginia. A short time afterward they were joined by settlers from North Carolina, within whose bounds the colony proved to be. Two able leaders soon emerged. James Robertson, a backwoodsman and a "mighty hunter," went to Watauga in 1770 and took thither a colony of sixteen North Carolina families in 1771. A year later arrived John Sevier, a Virginian of Huguenot extraction. Like Robertson, he was an able Indian fighter and a leader of men.

The Watauga Association.—Finding themselves outside of Virginia and beyond the reach and protection of the North Carolina administration, the settlers, like the Pilgrim Fathers in a similar situation, reverted to the social compact—familiar to Scotch-Irish Presbyterians and to back-country North Carolinians who had "regulated" horse stealing—and formed a government for themselves. In 1772 a convention of the settlers created

an independent government called the Watauga Association.
It had a written constitution, vesting the administration in an
executive committee of five, two of whom were Sevier and Robertson. This committee exercised most of the powers of sovereignty,
making treaties, administering justice, granting lands, and
making war on the Indians. In 1776 the Watauga Association, realizing the need of help, petitioned the Council of North
Carolina to extend its government over the new settlements,
and in 1777 they were organized as Washington County.

THE BEGINNINGS OF KENTUCKY

The surveyors and first settlers.—Settlement had also begun
in what is now Kentucky. Ahead of the settlers went the prospectors and surveyors, who descended the Ohio and the Kanawha
to select and survey lands. In 1770 and 1772 George Washington explored lands in what is now northeastern Kentucky. In
1773 the McAfees led a party of surveyors down the Ohio,
crossed Kentucky, and returned over the Cumberland Mountains.
In the following year several parties of surveyors and land hunters
were sent by Virginia officials to lay out bounty lands for soldiers.
Others went without official sanction. One party was led by
John Floyd from Fincastle County, Virginia, who descended
the Kanawha and Ohio to the Falls, crossed Kentucky, and
returned by Cumberland Gap. During his expedition he surveyed lands for George Washington, Patrick Henry, and others.
Attempts at settlement had already been made. In 1773 Daniel
Boone led a colony from North Carolina toward Kentucky,
but was driven back by Indians. The next year Harrod, of
Virginia, founded a settlement in Kentucky called Harrodsburg,
but it was broken up by Indians, whose hostilities drove out all
settlers and land hunters.

Indian ravages.—The border war which now occurred was
the culmination of a long series of troubles between the frontiersmen of Pennsylvania and Virginia, and the Indians of the Ohio
Valley. The Delawares had been pushed over the Pennsylvania
Mountains to the Muskingum and Tuscarawas Rivers. Among
them settled the Moravian missionaries, who formed them 'nto
Christian towns and kept them peaceful when others were hos-

tile. The Shawanee had been pushed north to the Scioto River, whence they marauded the Virginia border. Behind them were the hostile tribes who had taken part in Pontiac's War. Through 1773 an Indian uprising was threatening, and preparations were made in the westernmost settlements of Virginia. Early in 1774 many settlers fled from the Holston and Clinch Valleys. Minor outrages being committed along the Ohio, alarm spread, and in April there was a retreat across the Monongahela, which was crossed by more than a thousand refugees in a single day.

Lord Dunmore's War.—Governor Dunmore now prepared for war, which, there is some ground for thinking, he helped to bring on as a means of strengthening Virginia's claims to the Northwest. To warn the surveyors and settlers Colonel Preston, lieutenant-sheriff and surveyor of Fincastle County, Virginia, sent Boone and Stoner through Kentucky. They went as far as the Falls of the Ohio, and saved most of the men on the frontier. The governor organized a campaign, himself leading the Virginia regulars down the Ohio, while the frontier levies were led by Colonel Andrew Lewis. They were to meet at the mouth of the Great Kanawha. When Lewis reached that point he was attacked before the arrival of Dunmore by the Indians under Chief Cornstalk, whom he defeated. Thereupon the Indians sued for peace with Dunmore, who had entered their country north of the Ohio. In the following October a treaty was made at Fort Pitt which kept the northern Indians quiet during the first two years of the Revolution and made it possible to settle Kentucky.

Henderson and Transylvania.—Harrodsburg was now refounded by Virginians (1775) who constituted the majority of the settlers. Henderson, the North Carolina land speculator, formed a land company, called the Transylvania Company. To improve his title in 1775 he made a treaty with the Overhill Cherokees paying them £10,000 for their claims to lands along and between the Cumberland and the Kentucky. Boone, with a party of thirty men, was sent ahead to clear a road for Henderson's colony from the Holston River to the Kentucky (1775). It became the famous highway known as the Wilderness Road. Henderson followed with his colony, founded Boonesborough, built a fort, and opened a land office, naming his colony

Transylvania. He attempted to set up in the wilderness a modi-fied proprietary régime. Having established his colony, he called a convention; the delegates made laws which Henderson ap-proved, and a compact was formed between the delegates and proprietors defining the irrespective rights. The proprietors re-tained control by reserving to themselves the veto power.

Transylvania absorbed by Virginia.—Henderson's procedure was regarded as illegal, and he was denounced by the governors of both Virginia and North Carolina. When the Revolution broke out the proprietors sent a delegate to the Continental Congress and appealed to that body for protection, but, largely through Virginia's influence, the delegation was rejected. The Virginia settlers in Kentucky, led by Harrod, opposed Hender-son's claim to lands, appealed to Virginia, and sent George Rogers Clark to the assembly. Virginia asserted sovereignty over Kentucky, and stormy times continued till 1777, when Kentucky with her present boundaries was organized as Ken-tucky County, Virginia.

THE UPPER OHIO AND MIDDLE TENNESSEE

Westsylvania.—While Henderson was founding Transylvania another region west of the mountains was being settled and was struggling for independent statehood. Emigrants from Penn-sylvania, Maryland, Virginia, and other states had crossed the mountains and settled on the tributaries of the upper Ohio in what are now western Pennsylvania, West Virginia, and eastern Ohio. By the middle of 1776 there were said to be 25,000 families on the tributaries of the Ohio above the Scioto River. But the land which they occupied was in dispute be-tween Virginia and Pennsylvania, and the Indiana and Van-dalia Companies, and the settlers took up the struggle, quarreling over land titles and jurisdiction. The disorders prevented ef-fective organization against the Indians. Shortly after the Declaration of Independence the settlers memorialized Congress, asking independent statehood as a "sister colony and fourteenth province of the American confederacy," under the name of Westsylvania, whose boundaries they described, but the request was not granted.

The Cumberland settlement.—Robertson was the type of frontiersmen desirous to be ever on the move. In 1779 he prospected at French Lick, returned to Watauga, raised a colony, and in the fall led it forth. The women and children were conducted by Donelson down the Tennessee and up the Cumberland, while Robertson, guided by Mansker, led the men overland. Nashborough, now Nashville, was founded at the Cumberland Bend, and other stations were occupied along the river. In 1780 a convention formed an "Association" much like that of Watauga, but after three years of independence the district became Davidson County, North Carolina.

THE PROVINCE OF QUEBEC

The French people.—At the time of the conquest the Canadian people numbered about 65,000 living in the St. Lawrence Valley, with several thousand scattered among the western posts. The settlers were in the main a frugal, industrious, unlettered, religious people. They were of two distinct classes, the gentry and the peasant tenants. After the war there was a considerable emigration to France of the official, noble, and commercial classes, leaving chiefly cultivators of the soil and fur traders. By 1775 the population had grown to perhaps 90,000, chiefly through natural increase of the French. By 1784 the population was 113,000.

The British settlers.—The conquest left in the province and attracted to it later a small body of British settlers, but by 1775 they did not number more than five or six hundred. Most of them lived in the towns of Quebec and Montreal, and engaged in business, especially in the fur trade, many as agents for English houses, others being independent merchants. When Hillsborough restored seignorial tenure, many of them acquired seigniories, though they continued to live by trade.

Military rule.—British rule in Canada began with the capitulation of Montreal in September, 1760. General Amherst was made governor-general, with lieutenant-governors at Quebec, Montreal, and Three Rivers. From that time to the enforcement of the Proclamation of 1763 Canada was under military rule. But French law and customs were followed in the main, and there was little discontent.

Civil government established.—Civil government was established in August, 1764. The governor was assisted by an executive council composed of the lieutenant-governor, chief justice, and eight citizens. The government provided by the Proclamation of 1763 was unsuited to a population almost wholly French, professing the Catholic religion, and living under laws and customs of their own. The Proclamation provided for an assembly, but none was held in Quebec because the French people would not take the test oath, and the British settlers were too few in numbers to warrant an assembly representing them alone. Uncertainty existed regarding tithes and the future status of the Catholic Church. The Proclamation contemplated the establishment of British law, but practice was uncertain. The French inhabitants were not politically ambitious, but the British were aggressive in their demands for an assembly and the uniform establishment of English law.

The Quebec Act.—Under these circumstances a change of system was deemed necessary. It was provided by the Quebec Act of 1774, the first parliamentary legislation for Canada. The act maintained the privileges of the Catholic clergy, tithes from Catholic subjects being continued. French civil procedure was established, with some exceptions, but English criminal procedure was enforced. Provision was made for an appointive executive council with powers to make ordinances for the province, but no provision was made for a provincial assembly.

Boundaries extended.—The population of the Illinois country was similar to that of Quebec. The French *habitants* there had been demanding civil government, and it had been complained by the Montreal traders that the prosperity of Canada had been impaired by cutting off the western posts. Therefore the boundaries of Quebec were extended to include the region between the Ohio River and the Upper Mississippi. By the Proclamation of 1763 Labrador east of River St. John's, Anticosti, and the Magdalens, had been attached to Newfoundland. Labrador now began to develop commerce with the interior and the North and with Newfoundland. Opposition to the fishing admirals of Newfoundland caused these three districts to be annexed to Quebec in 1774.

Not intended as a blow at liberty.—The Quebec Act was regarded in the other colonies as a blow at popular liberties and as an encroachment upon colonies whose chartered boundaries extended into the Northwest. It was in fact an administrative act intended primarily as a means of providing for the interests of the great body of the inhabitants, the French. The attachment of the Ohio country to Quebec, however, checked the natural spread of settlement from the seaboard colonies, and the act, on the other hand, prevented the assimilation of the French people by the English in Canada.

The Loyalists in Canada.—During the American Revolution a considerable number of Loyalists crossed into Canada and settled at the border posts. Many others joined the British army against the Americans. At the close of the war some of the border counties of New York were almost depopulated. In 1783 there were in the Montreal district seventeen hundred Loyalists at seventeen posts, not counting enlisted men. Of those who migrated after the revolution the greater number at first settled in Nova Scotia. By the end of 1784 the number there exceeded 28,000 and caused the forming of the new province of New Brunswick. Over three thousand went to Cape Breton Island, and three times that number to the interior of Canada. Thirteen hundred settled at Kingston and formed the nucleus of Upper Canada, which was separated from Lower Canada in 1791. More important than this, the Revolution determined the course of Canadian history. In order not to be absorbed by the United States, Canada was forced into unswerving loyalty to the British Empire.

THE NORTHERN FUR TRADERS

Supervision of the fur trade.—The fur trade of Quebec under the new régime was supervised according to the principles of the Proclamation of 1763. The most fundamental fact was that the French monopolistic system was discontinued, except at certain "King's posts" in the lower St. Lawrence Valley. The trade was open to any duly licensed subject, superintendents were established at the posts, local courts were erected in the interior, and settlement limited to the immediate neighborhood of the posts in order not to drive away the fur bearing animals.

The French traders ruined.—The conquest had destroyed the French fur trading organization. Under the mercantile system then in vogue, supplies and markets had now to be sought in England. The French merchants were ruined, and the entire trade of the Great Lake region was thrown into the hands of the British traders. The French *coureurs de bois*, however, remained in the country, and, in the employ of the British, continued to be the backbone of the fur gathering business in the interior.

The rush to the interior.—As early as 1761 British traders of Montreal began to enter the field left vacant by the French. Pontiac's War caused a suspension of their activities, and during it British traders were plundered and murdered. By 1765, however, there was a new rush to the interior, though it was 1771 before they could safely trade in the most remote posts on the Saskatchewan. In the meantime the Indians had learned to take their furs to the posts on Hudson Bay or down the Mississippi.

Extent of operations.—The American Revolution destroyed the western fur trade of the seaboard colonies and threw the commerce of the entire Northwest into the hands of the Quebec and Montreal traders. By the close of the war they were conducting operations on both sides of the Great Lakes, in the Illinois country, beyond the upper Mississippi, on the Winnipeg, Saskatchewan, Churchill, and Athabasca Rivers, to the neighborhood of Great Slave Lake. They traded on the Assiniboine, and may have reached the Missouri by that route.

Management of the trade.—During and after the Revolution the value of the furs annually sent from Montreal and Quebec to London was probably $1,000,000. The trade centered mainly in Montreal. In London great mercantile establishments throve by the commerce. At Montreal other great houses were founded. Detroit and Michillimackinac were interior supply posts, where branch houses or lesser merchants conducted business. Wintering partners and clerks went with the fleets of batteaux into the far interior, but most of the common hands or *engagés* were French and half-breed *coureurs de bois*, just as in the case of the Spanish fur trade in Louisiana. The entire business was conducted on the credit system.

The fur magnates.—Many of the fur magnates were Scotchmen. Among the Montreal merchants of importance in this period were Alexander Henry, Benjamin and Joseph Frobisher, James Finlay, and Peter Pond. Henry was one of the earliest in the West. Finlay is said to have been among the first on the Saskatchewan River. The Frobishers were leading traders on the Saskatchewan and Churchill. Pond was probably the pioneer on the Athabasca, having wintered there in 1778–1789.

The Northwest Company formed.—The free access of all licensed traders to the interior resulted in reckless competition in regions remote from the military posts. Acts of violence were committed and Indians were involved in the contest. Besides the grave disadvantages of competition, there were obvious advantages of combination. In 1779, therefore, nine enterprises were consolidated for one year. The success caused the arrangement to be repeated, and finally in 1783-1784 the Northwest Company was organized and became permanent. This company soon monopolized the larger part of the Montreal trade, and became the great rival of the Hudson's Bay Company.

Advance of Hudson's Bay Company.—After the Peace of Utrecht the Hudson's Bay Company had returned to an era of prosperity. Urged on by French competition, by 1700 expeditions inland had been made by Kelsey (1691) and Sanford, and Henley House had been built a hundred and fifty miles inland from Fort Albany; and by 1720 other minor inland expeditions had been made by Macklish and Stewart, but in the main the Company had held to the shores of the Bay. Instead of sending employees inland, as did the French, reliance was placed on furs brought by the Indians to the posts, all of which were close to the Bay. The monopoly enjoyed was a cause of jealousy among British merchants, and critics arose, notably Arthur Dobbs, who charged that the Company had failed in its obligation to seek the northwest passage and explore the interior. Coerced by criticism, between 1719 and 1737 the Company made some explorations, but little was accomplished.

Hearne's explorations.—After 1763 criticism of the Company was reinforced by the rise of the Montreal trade, and new explorations northwestward were undertaken. After two unsuccessful attempts in 1769 and 1770 to reach the Coppermine River overland, in December, 1770, Samuel Hearne set out from Fort Prince of Wales to seek "a North-West Passage, copper-mines, or any other thing that may be serviceable to the British nation in general, or the Hudson's Bay Company in particular." Going west, then north, on July 18, 1771, Hearne reached the mouth of the Coppermine River near latitude 68°, where he took formal possession of the Arctic Ocean for the Company. Returning by way of Lake Athabasca, which he discovered and crossed, he reached his fort on June 30, 1772.

Rival posts in the interior.—Hearne's explorations were indicative of a new policy. Coerced by the aggressive Montreal traders, the Company now pushed into the interior in a struggle for the mastery. Side by side the two companies placed rival forts on all the important streams from the Hudson Bay to the Rockies and from the Red River of the North to Great Slave Lake.

READINGS

Alden, G. H., *New Governments west of the Alleghanies before 1780;* Alvord, C. W., "Virginia and the West: An Interpretation," in *The Mississippi Valley Historical Review,* III, 19–38; *The Critical Period, 1763–1765; The Mississippi Valley in British Politics;* Alvord, C. W., and Carter, C. E., editors, *The New Régime, 1765–1767;* Bassett, J. S., "The Regulators of North Carolina," in American Hist. Assoc., *Annual Report, 1894,* pp. 141–212; Bourinot, J. G., *Canada under British Rule, 1760–1905* (G. W. Wrong revision), chs. 2–3; Bryce, George, *The Remarkable History of the Hudson's Bay Company,* chs. 8–13; Carter, C. E., *Great Britain and the Illinois Country, 1763–1774;* "The Beginnings of British West Florida," in *The Mississippi Valley Historical Review,* IV, 314–341; Coffin, Victor, *The Quebec Act;* Hamilton, P. J., *Colonial Mobile,* chs. 23–31; *The Colonization of the South,* chs. 20–21; Henderson, A., "Richard Henderson and the Occupation of Kentucky, 1775," in *The Mississippi Valley Historical Review,* I, 341–363; Hinsdale, B. A., *The Old Northwest,* ch. 8; Howard, G. E., *Preliminaries of the Revolution, 1763–1775,* ch. 13; Roosevelt, Theodore, *The Winning of the West,* I–II; Siebert, W. H., "The Loyalists in West Florida and the Natchez District," in *The Mississippi Valley Historical Review,* II, 465–483; Stevens, W. E., "The Organization of the British Fur Trade, 1760–1800," in *The Mississippi Valley Historical Review,* III, 172–202; Thwaites, R. G., *Daniel Boone;* Thwaites, R. G., and Kellogg, L. P., editors, *Documentary History of Dunmore's War, 1774,* Introduction; Turner, F. J., "Western State-Making in the Revolutionary Era," in *American Historical Review,* I, 70–87, 251–269; Wallace, S., *The United Empire Loyalists;* Winsor, Justin, *The Westward Movement,* 38–100; Wood, W., *The Father of British Canada;* Davidson, G. C., *The North West Company.*

THE REVOLT OF THE ENGLISH COLONIES

CHAPTER XXIII

THE CONTROVERSY OF THE ENGLISH COLONIES WITH THE HOME GOVERNMENT

THE BACKGROUND OF THE CONTEST

Nature of the causes.—While British statesmen were working out a system of government for the newly acquired domains, in the empire forces of disintegration were at work which brought on the American Revolution. The causes of that convulsion cannot be traced to a group of events or laws. Through a long period social, political, and economic forces were at work which gradually brought thirteen of the mainland colonies into open rebellion. Because this opposition is more evident after the French and Indian War, and because the economic is the most obvious phase of the struggle, historians have sometimes concluded that the laws passed by parliament between 1763 and 1776 were the cause of the Revolution. The policy pursued by the British government no doubt hastened it, but alone does not account for it.

A mixed population.—For more than a century the colonies had been receiving new elements which were producing a society in many respects different from that of England. America had been the recipient of many of the radicals, the down-trodden, and the discontented from the mother country. The acquisition of New Netherlands had brought under British control a considerable number of Dutch, Swedes, and Finns. The Huguenot migration which followed the revocation of the Edict of Nantes had added another element. The German and Scotch-Irish influxes had brought in thousands. Welsh, Scotch, Irish, and Jews were also to be found in the colonies. America, then as now, was a melting pot of the nations.

Lack of American nationality.—Influenced largely by climatic and physiographic conditions, distinct industrial systems had developed. In the northern colonies the small farm prevailed, in the South the plantation system. The North produced the seamen, fishermen, and merchants, while few of the southerners were seafarers. The frontier with its foreign elements, its scattered settlements, and freedom from restraint had produced a society which differed from the tide-water region. The fur-trader, the cattleman, the lumberman, and the small farmer were distinctly different in speech, dress, habits, and point of view from the Boston merchant, the Philadelphia Quaker, or the Virginia planter. Separatist tendencies were stronger than those of coalescence. A Virginian was a Virginian and not an American. There was little in common between the New Englander and the southern planter, or between the people of the Hudson Valley and the Quakers.

Class distinctions.—In individual colonies society was continually growing in complexity. Though the great mass of the population continued to be rural, town life was becoming an important factor. Members of an aristocracy, of which the governor was usually the central social figure, were inclined to rear their heads above their fellows. The merchants and lawyers, ever increasing in numbers, found themselves outside the social pale of the official aristocracy, a source of silent mortification which was a real force in producing radicals.

Evolution of English society.—English as well as American society had also undergone a rapid evolution. Puritan England had passed away; the Stuarts, the Hanoverians, and foreign conquests had transformed the viewpoint of the Englishman. Little was there in common between John Milton and Horace Walpole, or between a Cromwell and a Newcastle. The sudden greatness that had come through the Seven Years' War well-nigh turned the heads of Englishmen. To acquire wealth, to wield power, and to live gaily seemed to be the ideals of the upper class Englishman of the reign of George III. The colonial who still considered the mother country as the traditional England of Magna Carta, the Puritan Revolution, and the Bill of Rights, had as little understanding of a Townshend as had a Townshend a comprehension of the colonial.

The assemblies control the purse.—The governmental institutions of the colonies had gradually evolved toward a common type, whose constituent parts were the governor, council, and assembly, the governor and council, except in Connecticut and Rhode Island, representing imperial or proprietary authority, and the assembly the will of the colonial inhabitants. The power of the assemblies to control the purse had been steadily growing, until the colonies considered the principle established both by precedent and by inherent rights guaranteed by the English constitution. By controlling the budgets and the salaries of the governors, the assemblies held the whip hand over the executives.

English and colonial ideas of representation.—The meaning of the term representation differed in England and the colonies. To the Englishman parliament represented the British Empire and legislated for the whole of it, allowing the colonies to handle local matters within their chartered rights. Parliament was regarded as representing the three estates or classes of society, rather than individuals. The idea that every Englishman was represented by a man in whose selection he had had a voice had not become a part of the English political system. Members of parliament were frequently chosen in rotten boroughs. A few thousand men at most chose the entire parliamentary body. The king's ministers, selected from the party which could command a majority in the House of Commons, directed public policy and enforced their will upon a subservient commons. In America the suffrage was usually restricted by a property or church qualification, but every member of an assembly actually represented a colonial community and a known constituency. When the colonial orator declared for no taxation without representation, he was talking in the terms of a system that had grown up in America, but which England did not begin to adopt until the Reform Bill of 1832.

The causes of the development of nationalism.—French political philosophers and observant travelers had predicted that the removal of French power from America would cause the colonies to seek independence. Franklin ridiculed the idea, for he believed that colonial jealousies were too strong to allow united action, a view which was also held by Pitt. After the French and Indian War the English government, by enforcing and extending the colonial system, quickened public opinion, overthrew separatist tendencies, and brought many of the colonists to think and act together in opposition to English policy. When this was attained, a national consciousness had come into existence which gradually developed into open rebellion.

Illicit traffic during the French and Indian War.—Since the reign of Anne England had not enforced the trade laws strictly. The Molasses Act of 1733 had been practically a dead letter from the date of its passage and the other navigation acts had been frequently violated. Smuggling was winked at by governors and customs officials, who in many cases profited from the traffic. During the French and Indian War the colonies traded extensively with the French West Indies. This was especially galling to England, whose chief weapon against France was control of the seas. Though the colonies in 1756 were forbidden to trade with the French, the colonial skippers evaded the command by shipping goods to the Dutch ports of Curaçoa and St. Eustatius, or to the French West Indies. In 1757 parliament forbade the exportation of food stuffs from the colonies to foreign ports, but the colonials continued to make shipments to the French or Dutch colonies and to bring back cargoes of molasses, sugar, and rum. To stop Dutch trade with the French colonies, Dutch merchant vessels were seized. As the English navy gradually isolated or captured the French West Indies, the colonials found a new method of circumventing the regulations by shipping to Monte Cristi, a Spanish port in Española near the French boundary. A commerce of less importance but of similar nature was also maintained with Florida and Louisiana. In 1760, when the English navy had gained the upper hand, the illicit commerce diminished but did not entirely cease. When Spain entered the war a considerable increase occurred. The naval and military authorities did all in their power to end the traffic with the enemy, for they considered that its continuance meant a prolongation of the war.

Writs of assistance.—To prevent smuggling English officials resorted to the issuance of writs of assistance. These were general search warrants which enabled the holder to search any house, ship, or other property where smuggled goods might be stored. The writs naturally aroused great opposition among the merchants, who claimed that they were illegal. In 1761 when the Boston customs officers applied for the writs, the merchants objected to them. When the merchants' cause was presented before the Massachusetts Supreme Court, James Otis argued that the writs, being general, were illegal and struck at the liberty of the individual. "No acts of parliament can establish such a writ. . . . An act against the constitution is void." The courts upheld the legality of the writs but Otis's speech did much to arouse and formulate public opinion.

The Parson's Cause.—In Virginia Patrick Henry performed a similar function in formulating public opinion. The speech which made him the leader of the Virginia radicals was delivered in connection with a suit brought by one of the Virginia clergy. Tobacco was the medium of exchange in the Old Dominion and ministers were paid annually 17,000 pounds of tobacco. In 1755 and 1758, the burgesses passed acts which allowed debts to be redeemed at two pence for each pound of tobacco. This worked a hardship upon the ministers, who naturally desired the benefit of the high price of tobacco to compensate them for the hard years when prices were low. The acts were disallowed by the crown in 1759, and the ministers attempted to recover their losses. In a suit brought in 1763 by Reverend James Maury, Patrick Henry appeared for the vestry. Realizing the weakness of his legal position, Henry resolved to carry the jury by an emotional attack upon the king's prerogative. He argued that the act of 1758 was a law of general utility consistent with the original compact between ruler and ruled, upon which government was based, and that the king, by disallowing this salutary act, became a tyrant and forfeited his right to the obedience of his subjects.

REFORMS OF THE GRENVILLE MINISTRY

Economy and reform.—At the end of the French and Indian War, England was burdened with a staggering debt. To build up the resources of the empire, increase the revenues, and protect the dominions were the objects of the ministers of George III. In this program the colonies were expected to play their part. The Bute Ministry planned to enforce the navigation acts, to tax the colonies directly, and to use the colonial revenue to support an army in America. The powers of the admiralty courts were immediately enlarged and commanders of war vessels were authorized to act as customs officials. Soon after Grenville came into office (April, 1763), he ordered customs collectors who were lingering in England to proceed at once to their colonial stations and he instructed the governors to enforce the trade laws rigidly.

Trade encouragement during 1764-1765.—To encourage commerce several important provisions were made during 1764 and 1765. To stimulate the fur business the old duties were abolished and an import duty of only one pence a skin and an export duty of seven pence were levied. To stimulate hemp and flax production bounties were paid on those products shipped from the colonies to England. The bounty on indigo was somewhat reduced but was still sufficient to protect the planters. The duties on whale fins were repealed to the great benefit of Massachusetts. The rice business was stimulated by allowing Georgia and the Carolinas to ship without restrictions to the southward.

The Sugar Act.—Grenville's beneficial measures were more than offset by the Sugar, Colonial Currency, Stamp, and Quartering Acts. The Sugar Act "was a comprehensive measure, whose openly expressed aim was, in the first place to raise a colonial revenue, and in the second to reform the old colonial system both in its administrative and in its economic features." The act confirmed and modified the Molasses Act of 1733. The duty on sugar shipped to the British colonies was raised but that on molasses was lowered. To injure the French island trade, the importation of foreign rum or spirits and commerce with Miquelon and St. Pierre were forbidden. Oriental and French textiles, Portuguese and Spanish wines, and coffee, if brought directly to the British colonies, were taxed heavily, but if shipped from England the duty was low. To protect South Carolina a duty was imposed upon foreign indigo shipped to the colonies. With a few exceptions no drawbacks were henceforth to be allowed, and revenues derived from the Sugar Act were to be paid into the royal exchequer. They were to be kept separate from other moneys and were to be used only for the protection of the British colonies in America.

Stringent regulations were provided for the enforcement of

the Sugar Act and other navigation laws. At the option of the informer or prosecutor, penalties for breach of the trade laws might be recovered in any court of record in the district where the offence was committed or in any admiralty court in America. The accused was required to give security for costs if he lost his suit, but if he won his case, he was not entitled to costs if the judge certified that the grounds of action seemed probable. Furthermore in the Molasses Act which was now confirmed, the burden of proof was placed upon the owner or claimant.

Every shipmaster was required to give a bond to land only enumerated goods at European ports north of Cape Finisterre and to possess a certificate from the customs collector at the point of loading. West Indian goods not properly certified were to be treated as foreign goods. Vessels cleared from British ports must contain only goods loaded in Great Britain: This, however, did not apply to salt and Irish linen. Breaches of these regulations subjected the law breaker to severe penalties.

Regulation of Colonial Currency.—Another important measure was the Colonial Currency Act. Lack of specie had compelled the issuance of colonial paper money, and though Massachusetts had retired such issues in 1749, most of the colonies were still suffering from depreciated and unstable currency. To protect the English merchant, parliament passed the Colonial Currency Act which prevented colonists from paying their debts to the home country in depreciated currency and stopped the issues of unsound money. The act caused a shortage of the medium of exchange at the time that the colonists were deprived of the West Indian commerce which had supplied them with specie to settle balances in London. The act produced embittered feeling which paved the way for greater opposition.

Colonial protests.—When it became known in the colonies that the Ministry intended to enforce a more rigid policy which included the levying of internal taxes by parliamentary enactment, vigorous protests were made. Memorials, resolutions, and addresses poured in upon the king, lords, commons, and Board of Trade, and numerous pamphlets appeared which presented the economic and constitutional viewpoint of the colonists.

The Massachusetts protest.—The Boston town meeting urged the assembly to use its influence to protect the rights of the colonies and in its instructions to the Boston representatives the principles were stated that there should be no taxation without representation and that colonials were entitled to full rights of Englishmen. It was also suggested that other injured colonies should be asked to coöperate in seeking redress. A committee of the assembly presented a memorial drafted by Otis which contained the additional principle that parliament had no right to alter the constitution. The memorial was sent to the Massachusetts agent in England with instructions to urge the repeal of the Sugar Act and to protest against the proposed Stamp Act. A committee of correspondence headed by Otis was authorized to inform the other colonies of the action of Massachusetts and to seek their coöperation. As the action had been taken by the assembly without the consent of the council, the governor was soon petitioned to call the general court. He complied and a petition was drawn which temperately protested.

The Rhode Island protest.—Before the Sugar Act was passed a remonstrance was prepared in Rhode Island, which was to be presented to the Board of Trade if three other colonial agents would coöperate. Committees of correspondence were also formed in various towns. After the passage of the act the committee of correspondence of which Governor Hopkins was a member sent out a circular letter protesting against the Sugar Act and the proposed Stamp Act. In November, 1764, the assembly sent a petition to the king in which the principle was stated that an essential privilege of Englishmen was that they should be governed by laws made by their own consent.

Connecticut protest.—In Connecticut Governor Fitch, at the suggestion of the assembly, prepared an address to parliament which protested against the proposed Stamp Act or any other bill for internal taxes. This and the governor's book of *Reasons Why the British Colonies in America should not be Charged with Internal Taxes by Authority of Parliament* were sent.

New York protest.—In March, 1764, the New York merchants presented to the council a memorial against the renewal of the Molasses Act. In October the assembly appointed a committee of correspondence and sent statements of grievances to the king and the lords, and a petition to the commons. In the petition the significant statement was made that the loss of colonial rights was likely to shake the power of Great Britain.

Pennsylvania's protest.—The Pennsylvania assembly considered that parliament had no right to tax the colony. Jackson, the colonial agent, was instructed to remonstrate against the proposed Stamp Act and to endeavor to secure the repeal or modification of the Sugar Act. Franklin was sent over to assist Jackson.

Maryland and Virginia.—In Maryland the governor prevented the meeting of the assembly, but the Virginia council and burgesses prepared an address to the king, a memorial to the lords, and a remonstrance to the commons. The Virginians claimed the rights and privileges that their ancestors had had in England and laid down the fundamental principle of no taxation without representation.

The Carolinas.—North Carolina protested strongly and in South Carolina the assembly appointed a committee which instructed the colonial agent to complain of the laws of trade. The instructions also declared that a Stamp Act would violate the inherent right of every British subject to be taxed only by his own consent or by his representatives. The governor prorogued the assembly before a vote could be taken upon the committee's action, but the instructions, nevertheless, were sent.

The Stamp Act.—In spite of colonial protests Grenville pursued his policy, the appeals of the colonies being rejected under the rule that petitions against money bills should not be received, and in March, 1765, parliament passed the Stamp Act. By its provisions stamps were to be placed on commercial and legal documents, pamphlets, newspapers, almanacs, playing cards, and dice. The enforcement of the act was placed under the management of English commissioners who were empowered to appoint persons to attend in every court or public office in the colonies to see that the law was enforced. For infringements of the law there were heavy penalties which might be collected through the admiralty courts if the informer or prosecutor so elected. Certain cases of forging and counterfeiting were punishable by death. The revenue derived from the Stamp Act was to be paid into the exchequer to be used for colonial defence.

Quartering Act.—The ministry intended to establish an army of 10,000 men in the colonies and the annual Mutiny Act of 1765 authorized the sending of such troops as might be deemed necessary. This was followed by the Quartering Act. As "*the publick houses and barracks, in his Majesty's dominions in America, may not be sufficient to supply quarters for such forces: and whereas it is expedient and necessary that carriages and other conveniences, upon the march of troops . . . should be supplied for that purpose,*" it was enacted that, if colonial barracks were insufficient, officers and troops were to be quartered in public hostelries. If more room were needed, vacant buildings were to be rented. Troops were to be supplied with fire, candles, vinegar, salt, bedding, cooking utensils, and small quantities of beer, cider, or rum. Persons giving houses for troops and furnishing supplies were to be reimbursed by the province. The colonies were to furnish conveyances at rates fixed by the act, but if the expense exceeded the rate, the province had to make up the deficit.

Colonial opposition.—To the colonies the Stamp Act, the Quartering Act, and the extension of admiralty jurisdiction were unconstitutional. Trials in the admiralty courts had always been looked upon with disfavor, as they violated the right of trial by jury. The new regulation allowing alleged violators of the trade laws to be taken to Halifax for trial was looked upon as a dangerous innovation. The Quartering Act was viewed as a violation of the constitutional principle that troops were not to be quartered upon the people. The provisions of the law were especially aggravating to New York which, because of the strategic position of the colony, would have to bear an undue part in the support and transportation of troops. But the Stamp Act aroused the greatest furor. All of the elements of discontent united against an act which encroached upon the right of the assemblies to control taxation. Indirect taxation was not looked upon as taxation. To the colonial economists the navigation acts were merely trade regulations and the right of parliament to regulate commerce was fully recognized. But a direct tax imposed by parliament to support an obnoxious soldiery set in motion the forces of discontent and produced a unity of opposition which surprised the ministers of George III.

The Virginia Resolutions.—Virginia took the lead in opposition. On May 29, 1765, the burgesses resolved themselves into a committee of the whole to consider the steps necessary to be taken in consequence of the Stamp Act. Patrick Henry, the "rustic and clownish youth of the terrible tongue," introduced a series of resolutions which boldly challenged the British government. The preamble stated that, as the House of Commons had raised the question of how far the general assembly had power to enact laws for laying taxes and imposing duties payable by the people of Virginia, the House of Burgesses, to settle and ascertain the same to all future time, resolved: (1) that the first adventurers and settlers of Virginia brought with them and transmitted to their posterity and to other English subjects who had come to live in the colony all the rights of the people of Great Britain; (2) that these were granted to them by two charters of James I; (3) that taxation of the people by themselves or by their representatives was a distinguishing characteristic of British freedom without which the ancient constitution could not exist; (4) that the people of Virginia had uninterruptedly enjoyed the right of being governed by their own assembly in matters of taxes and internal police, a right which had never been forfeited and had been constantly recognized by the kings and people of Great Britain. (5) Therefore it was resolved that the general assembly had the sole right and power to lay taxes and impositions upon the inhabitants of Virginia, and that every attempt to vest such power in any other person or persons had a tendency to destroy British as well as American freedom; (6) that the inhabitants of Virginia were not bound by any law or ordinance designed to impose any tax upon them other than those imposed by the general assembly; (7) and that any person who maintained that Virginians were bound to obey such laws not imposed by the assembly should be deemed an enemy of the colony.

The resolutions precipitated an acrimonious debate in which the democratic members of the western counties supported Henry against the aristocratic leaders. The committee of the whole appears to have adopted the resolutions, but on the following day the burgesses rejected the preamble and the last two resolutions, the other five being passed by a slender majority.

Henry then left the assembly and the following morning the conservatives expunged from the record the fifth resolution. The manuscript of the entire series, except the third resolution which was omitted by error, was already on its way to the other colonies and was widely published. "Beyond question the Virginia resolves mark an important crisis in the impending revolution."

Resistance and violence.—In June the Massachusetts general court, at the suggestion of Otis, sent a circular letter to the other colonial assemblies asking them to send delegates to meet at New York in the following October to consider the danger from the Stamp Act. Before the delegates met fierce opposition appeared in nearly every colony. Remonstrances came from towns, counties, and assemblies. Newspapers and pamphlets inveighed against the act, and non-importation agreements were made in many localities. Associations called "Sons of Liberty" sprang up. At first they worked secretly, but they soon announced their committees of correspondence which worked to unify the opposition.

In Boston occurred riots of greater violence than in any other place. On August 14 the stamp distributor's effigy was hung on the "Liberty Tree," and after other demonstrations, that night a mob demolished a building which it was believed the collector was erecting for an office. On August 26 the houses of two of the customs officials were sacked and the house of Chief Justice Hutchinson was pillaged and destroyed. At Newport the stamp distributor and a sympathizer found it necessary to seek safety on a British man-of-war. Scenes of violence occurred in the other colonies and the stamp distributors resigned with more haste than dignity.

REPEAL OF THE STAMP ACT

The Stamp Act Congress.—The Stamp Act Congress met at New York on October 7, 1765. Nine colonies were represented, Virginia, North Carolina, Georgia, and New Hampshire failing to send delegates. Prominent among those in attendance were John Dickinson of Pennsylvania, John Rutledge and Christopher Gadsden of South Carolina, and James Otis of Massachusetts.

On October 19 a declaration of rights and grievances, originally drafted by Dickinson, was adopted. In the declaration the argument was presented that the colonies were entitled to the inherent rights and liberties of native-born Englishmen, one of which was that no taxes were to be imposed upon them except by their own consent or by their representatives. The colonists were not and from their local circumstances could not be represented in the House of Commons, their only representatives being those in the colonies who alone had the constitutional right to impose taxes upon them. All supplies to the crown being free gifts of the people, it was unreasonable and inconsistent with the principles and spirit of the British constitution for the people of Great Britain to grant to the king the property of the colonists. Trial by jury was an inherent right of every British subject in the colonies, but the Stamp Act and other laws, by extending the jurisdiction of the admiralty courts, had a tendency to subvert the rights and liberties of the colonists. The duties imposed by recent acts of parliament would be burdensome and grievous, and from the scarcity of specie the payment of them would be impracticable. The recent restrictions would make it impossible to purchase the manufactures of Great Britain. The right to petition the king or either house of parliament was also asserted. By an address to the king and by applications to both houses of parliament, they endeavored to procure the repeal of the Stamp Act, of clauses in recent acts which increased admiralty jurisdiction, and of recent acts placing restrictions on American commerce.

Repeal of the Stamp Act.—In July, 1765, Grenville fell from power, but not because of opposition to the Stamp Act. The Marquis of Rockingham, a man of moderate ability, was selected to form the new cabinet. The question of the repeal of the Stamp Act came up in parliament early in 1766. During the debate in the commons on February 13, Franklin, then agent for Pennsylvania and Massachusetts, was questioned regarding the colonial attitude, and he made it clear that the Stamp Act could not be enforced. The American cause was strengthened by the powerful support of Pitt and by the protests of English merchants and manufacturers who were losing trade through colonial boycotts. After a momentous debate, the act was repealed.

The Declaratory Act.—Although parliament had given ground it did not surrender, for in the Declaratory Act of March 18, 1766, it asserted its right to tax the colonies. The act declared that the colonies were subordinate unto and dependent upon the crown and parliament, and that the king by and with the consent of parliament had full power and authority to make laws to bind the colonies in all cases. All resolutions, votes, orders, and proceedings in the colonies denying the power and authority of parliament to make laws imposing taxes and regulations were declared null and void.

Other legislation.—The Quartering Act was then renewed, but with certain changes to make it more effective. The imposts on textiles which had previously been collected in America were henceforth to be collected at the point of exportation. The duty on molasses was changed from three pence a gallon on the foreign product to one penny a gallon on all molasses brought to the continental colonies.

Colonial rejoicing.—The Declaratory and other acts attracted little attention in America, where there was great rejoicing over the repeal of the Stamp Act. The constitutional principles for which the colonists had contended had in no wise been conceded, but to the colonist his point seemed won. He was soon to be rudely awakened.

THE TOWNSHEND ACTS

Townshend.—In July, 1766, Rockingham fell from power and the Pitt-Grafton Ministry was formed. Unfortunately for the colonies, Pitt was in ill-health and took little part in shaping policies. The strong man of the cabinet was Charles Townshend. He was fully in sympathy with Grenville's ideas, and was responsible for a new series of irritating acts.

Suspension of the New York assembly.—Trouble had arisen in New York over the enforcement of the Quartering Act. In June, 1766, in reply to Governor Moore's request that provision be made for the expected troops, the assembly excused itself from compliance but intimated that about £4000 then in the treasury might be used. Later the assembly passed an act making provision for one year for a thousand men and one company of artillery. When a request was made for full compliance with the Quartering Act, the assembly refused. On December 19 it was prorogued, and on June 15, 1767, was suspended by act of parliament.

Colonial customs commissioners.—Another act provided for a board of commissioners of customs to be established in America. The preamble stated that, as the colonial customs officials had found it inconvenient to apply to the commissioners in England for directions when difficulties arose, and as colonial shippers were greatly delayed in carrying on business, commissioners were to be stationed in America. Five commissioners were appointed with headquarters at Boston.

Revenue acts.—A new revenue act was passed "for making a more certain and adequate provision for defraying the charge of the administration of justice and the support of civil government, in such provinces where it shall be found necessary, and toward further defraying the expenses of defending, protecting, and securing" the dominions in America. Duties were imposed upon glass, red and white lead, painter's colors, tea, and paper. Drawbacks were allowed on coffee and cocoanuts, but chinaware was no longer subject to drawback. Writs of assistance were declared legal. By another act a drawback for five years was granted on tea reëxported from England to Ireland or the colonies.

Dickinson's " Farmer's Letters."—The Townshend Acts were received with alarm throughout the colonies. "Awed by the suddenness and magnitude of the peril, the colonial leaders acted with circumspection and rare self-control." The most powerful statement of the colonial viewpoint came from John Dickinson whose "Farmer's Letters" were read throughout the colonies, were published in London, translated into French, "and were read by everybody in the two capitals of civilization who read anything more serious than a playbill." Dickinson recognized the vagueness of the constitutional relations of the colonies to the mother country. He urged that a spirit of compromise should prevail and that no abstract theory of sovereignty should be pushed to its logical conclusions. He admitted that parliament possessed legal authority to regulate the trade of the empire, but the recent attempts to raise a revenue he considered a most dangerous innovation. "Great Britain claims and exercises the right to prohibit manufactures in America. Once admit that she may lay duties upon her exportations to us, for the purpose of levying money on us only, she then will have nothing to do but to lay those duties on the articles which she prohibits us to manufacture, and the tragedy of American liberty is finished."

"I would persuade the people of these Colonies . . . to exert themselves in the most firm, but the most peaceable manner, for obtaining relief. If an inveterate resolution is formed to annihilate the liberties of the governed, English history affords examples of resistance by force."

"Let us consider ourselves as . . . freemen, . . . *firmly bound together* by the *same rights, interests,* and *dangers.* . . . What have these colonies to *ask,* while they continue free; Or what have they to *dread,* but insidious attempts to subvert their freedom? . . . They form *one* political body, of which *each colony* is a *member.*"

The Massachusetts protest.—In Massachusetts the Townshend Acts were received by a public which was already irritated by the untactful course of Governor Bernard. Soon after the repeal of the Stamp Act he had negatived the election of Otis as speaker of the assembly, and when that body retaliated by refusing to reëlect certain members of the council, the governor had refused to accept six members elected by the popular party. Difficulties had also arisen when the governor demanded compensation for those who had suffered by the Stamp Act riots and when he demanded compliance with the Quartering Act.

The first protest of Massachusetts against the Townshend Acts was on October 28, 1767, when the Boston town-meeting renewed the non-importation agreement. The General Court convened on December 30 and shortly afterward the acts were read in the assembly and referred to a committee for consideration. The committee drafted a letter to the colonial agent which reviewed the arguments against taxation and protested against the Townshend Acts. A petition to the king and letters to members of the ministry were also prepared. A circular letter to the assemblies in the other colonies, drawn by Samuel Adams, was adopted on February 11, 1768.

The circular letter stated that it seemed necessary that the representatives of the several assemblies should act in harmony "upon so delicate a point" as the recent imposition of duties and taxes. The argument regarding taxation without representation was restated, and objection was made to the payment of the salaries of governors and judges by the crown, to the large powers of appointment given to the commissioners of the customs, and to the Quartering Act. Denial was made that independence was in the minds of the Massachusetts representatives and the letter closed with an expression of confidence in the king. Several of the colonies sent sympathetic replies and Virginia issued a circular letter to the other colonies calling upon them to unite with Massachusetts in her petition for redress.

Hillsborough's reply.—When the Massachusetts protests reached England, they came before a ministry which was prejudiced by letters from royal officials in America. Lord Hillsborough, who had recently been appointed to the newly created position of colonial secretary, laid the Massachusetts protests before the cabinet. On April 21 he sent letters to all the colonial governors, with the exception of Bernard, ordering them to ignore the Massachusetts circular letter. If the assemblies took notice of it, they were to prorogue or dissolve them. Bernard was commanded to require the Massachusetts assembly to rescind its action and to declare its disapprobation of its recent action. The Massachustts assembly refused and the other assemblies commended its course.

The customs officials defied.—Acts of violence soon occurred. The warship *Romney* was anchored in Boston harbor and the captain angered the people by impressing seamen, one of whom was rescued. On the same day the sloop *Liberty*, owned by John Hancock, arrived with a cargo of Madeira wine. The customs collector was locked up by the crew while the cargo was landed and a false entry made. The *Liberty* was seized and moored under the guns of the *Romney*. A riot then occurred; the houses of two of the customs officials were damaged and a boat belonging to the controller was burned. The officials fled to the *Romney* and later took refuge in Castle William. The Boston town-meeting requested the removal of the war vessel, but the governor refused on the ground that such action would be beyond his jurisdiction. At Newport a revenue cutter was burned and at Providence a coat of tar and feathers was administered to a customs official.

Action of the Boston town-meeting and the Massachusetts convention.—Before the occurrence of these riotous acts, the ministry had determined to send troops to Boston. When this became known, the town-meeting assembled in Faneuil Hall and resolved that the inhabitants defend their rights, and they were called upon to provide themselves with arms. When the governor refused to summon the assembly, the selectmen called a convention of delegates from the Massachusetts towns. Ninety-six towns responded. The governor refused to recognize the convention, but it remained in session for six days and did not adjourn until a statement of grievances had been formulated. On September 28, 1768, the day of adjournment, two regiments arrived at Boston.

Prisoners accused of treason to be tried in England.—The rebellious acts of Massachusetts were condemned by parliament which also advised the enforcement of the statute of Henry VIII which allowed the government to bring to England for trial persons accused of treason committed outside of the kingdom. This aroused a storm of protest. In Virginia the burgesses adopted resolutions which asserted that the right of taxation was vested in the House of Burgesses, that petitioning the sovereign was an undoubted privilege of the colony, and that it was lawful and expedient to procure the concurrence of other colonies "in dutiful addresses, praying the royal interposition in favour of the violated rights of America;" that trials for treason or for any felony or crime committed in the colony should be held in the courts of that colony, and that the sending of suspected persons beyond the sea for trial was derogatory of the right of trial by a jury of the vicinage and deprived the accused of summoning witnesses. The resolutions were sent to the other assemblies. When the governor dissolved the burgesses, the members met in a private house and drew up a non-importation agreement. Other assemblies approved the Virginia resolutions and non-importation agreements were signed throughout the colonies.

Departure of Bernard.—Massachusetts continued to be the center of unrest. The unpopularity of Governor Bernard increased when it became known that he was collecting evidence against Samuel Adams. The public ire grew more intense when some of the governor's letters to the Ministry were published. The council drew up charges against him and the assembly petitioned for his recall. In July, 1770, he voluntarily departed, leaving Hutchinson in charge.

The Boston " Massacre."—The troops remained in Boston where they were heartily detested. Difficulties between soldiers and townspeople became more and more frequent and in March, 1770, there was a serious collision. On the fifth a sentinel at the custom house was pelted with snow balls, and when he called for aid the guard came to his assistance. A soldier was knocked down, shots were fired by the guard, and several citizens were killed or wounded. Preston, the commanding officer of the guard, surrendered to the civil authorities, and the privates were placed under arrest. The selectmen demanded the withdrawal of the troops to Castle William and Hutchinson hesitatingly complied. When the soldiers were brought to trial, they were defended by John Adams and Josiah Quincy, who obtained acquittal for all but two who were lightly sentenced.

BEGINNING OF ORGANIZED RESISTANCE

Partial repeal of the Townshend Acts.—The Townshend Acts had proved a complete failure. Exports from England to America had dropped from £2,378,000 in 1768 to £1,634,000 in 1769. The customs were yielding little revenue while the colonial military establishment had become extremely expensive. In addition the colonies had been brought close to rebellion. Lord North, who became Prime Minister on January 31, 1770, hoped to end the commotions in America which had been so injurious to English merchants and manufacturers. He accordingly obtained a repeal of the duties on paints, glass, and paper, but at the suggestion of the king, the tea tax was retained in order to maintain the principle that parliament had the right to tax the colonies. The economic result of the repeal was immediately evident, for in 1770 the English exports to America reached nearly two million pounds sterling and during the next year more than doubled.

Arbitrary attitude of the governors.—The public, however, was kept in a state of agitation by the arbitrary acts of the governors who reflected the royal will. In Georgia the governor vetoed the assembly's choice for speaker, provoking a controversy which ended in the dissolution of the assembly. In South Carolina the governor was in frequent quarrels with the assembly, first over the salaries of the judges, then regarding the veto of an appropriation bill, and finally over convening the assembly at Beaufort instead of at Charleston. Virginia was irritated by the royal instructions which forbade the governor to assent to any law which would prohibit or obstruct the importation of slaves. In Maryland the governor by proclamation revived a law regulating fees which had expired by limitation, an action which was looked upon as an assertion of the right to levy taxes.

In Massachusetts the General Court, which was to have met at Boston in January, 1770, was called to meet at Cambridge on March 15. The assembly objected to the change of time and place and demanded a copy of Hutchinson's instructions, but he refused to comply. The assembly would do no business while thus constrained to hold its sessions away from Boston, and declared that the people and their representatives had a right to withstand "the abusive exercise" of the crown's prerogative. Under protest the assembly finally proceeded to business, but another difficulty immediately arose when the colonial troops were removed from Castle William which was then garrisoned by the regulars. In July, 1771, Hutchinson, who had recently been appointed governor, vetoed a bill which provided for the salaries of the crown officials, an action which called forth a protest from the assembly which held that royal instructions were thus given the force of law. The following year the assembly was informed that henceforth the salaries of the governor and judges would be paid by the crown.

The Gaspee affair.—In Rhode Island an event occurred in 1772 which had far-reaching influence. The numerous inlets and islands of Narragansett Bay made smuggling easy, and revenue vessels, though constantly on the alert, experienced great difficulty in detecting the illicit traders. The revenue boats *St. Johns* and *Liberty* were destroyed by men from Newport and the customs officials were annoyed by suits to recover vessels and cargoes which they had seized; Admiral Montagu accordingly ordered that seized vessels be sent to Boston. To Rhode Islanders Dudington, the commander of the *Gaspee*, was especially obnoxious. According to Trevelyan, "He stopped and searched vessels without adequate pretext, seized goods illegally, and fired at the market boats as they entered Newport harbour. He treated the farmers on the islands much as the Saracens in the Middle Ages treated the coast population of Italy, cutting down their trees for fuel, and taking their sheep when his crew ran short of meat." The injured parties made their voices heard, and the case was laid before the Admiral, who approved the conduct of his subordinate officer, and announced that, " as sure as any people from Newport attempted to rescue a vessel, he would hang them as pirates." On June 9 the *Gaspee* ran aground seven miles below Providence and during the night the vessel was boarded, Dudington was wounded, he and his crew were put on shore, and the vessel was burned. The act of violence aroused the British government and orders were sent to the governor of Rhode Island, the admiralty judge at Boston, and the chief justices of Massachusetts, New Jersey, and New York to act as a commission of inquiry. The commission held sessions in January and May, 1773, but failed to obtain any evidence.

Local committees of correspondence.—The arbitrary acts of the crown officials, the extension of the royal prerogative, and the *Gaspee* affair made possible the organization of the radical elements in the colonies. In Massachusetts opposition centered in Samuel Adams, "the man of the town meeting," who put forth pamphlet after pamphlet which struck at the encroachments upon colonial rights. "While he restated the old argument against the right of parliament to tax, he closely examined the foundations of the claim of the ministers to govern by royal instructions. He had grasped the idea that the king, lords, and commons, as well as the colonies, were subject to the authority and bound by the limitations of constitutional law." In the assembly, in the town meeting, through the press, on the street, among the sailors, fishermen, and ropemakers, he advocated the necessity of union. During the contest over the salaries of the crown officials, Adams seized the opportunity to put his ideas into tangible form. On November 2, 1772, in the Boston town meeting he moved that a committee of twenty-one be appointed to state the rights of the colonists, particularly of Massachusetts, and to communicate and publish the same to the Massachusetts towns and to the world as the sense of Boston "with the infringements and violations thereof that have been or . . . may be, made; also requesting of each town a free communication of their sentiments on this subject." By January, 1773, more than eighty towns in Massachusetts had committees.

"The Boston committee of correspondence has been likened to a political party manager. It provided for regular meetings, consulted with similar bodies in the vicinity, stimulated the spread of committees in surrounding towns, kept up a correspondence with them, prepared political matter for the press, circulated it in newspapers and broadsides, matured political measures, created and guided public sentiment—in short, heated the popular temper to the boiling point of revolution and then drew from it the authority to act."

Standing committees of correspondence.—Aroused by the *Gaspee* inquiry, the Virginia burgesses on March 12, 1773, adopted resolutions which provided for a standing committee of correspondence and inquiry whose business was "to obtain the most early and authentic intelligence of all such acts and reso lutions of the British Parliament, or proceedings of Administration, as may relate to or affect the British colonies in America, and to keep up and maintain a correspondence and communication with our sister colonies, respecting these important considerations; and the result of such their proceedings, from time to time, to lay before this House." The committee was also instructed to obtain information regarding "the principles and authority on which was constituted a court of inquiry, said to have been lately held in Rhode Island, with powers to transmit persons accused of offences committed in America to places beyond the seas to be tried." The speaker was instructed to transmit to the speakers of the different assemblies of the British colonies on the continent copies of the resolutions, that they might lay them before their assemblies and request them to appoint a person or persons to communicate from time to time with the committee of the burgesses.

The Virginia suggestion was first acted upon by the Rhode Island assembly, which on May 15 informed Virginia of the appointment of a committee of correspondence. Before the close of the month the assemblies of Connecticut, New Hampshire, and Massachusetts had appointed similar committees. The South Carolina assembly acted in July, Georgia in September, Maryland and Delaware in October, and North Carolina in December. The New York assembly appointed its committee on January 20, 1774, and New Jersey on February 8. The Pennsylvania assembly dissolved without taking action.

The committees did not prove to be active agents, because (1) "there was little or nothing for them to do;" (2) they "were chosen from members of the assembly, all of whom were desirous of going home when the assembly adjourned "; (3) "the assembly committees were extremely cautious about acting on their own authority." "However, the choice of such committees was not entirely without result. The popular assembly in each colony received preliminary testing. Constitutional questions were raised and discussed, and arguments disseminated. . . . More important still had been the demonstration that a body could be created which might continue to act in successful opposition to the crown when the royal governors dissolved or prorogued the assemblies."

THE TEA CONTROVERSY

Attempted relief of the East India Company.—During this period George III and his ministers took the fatal step of attempting to force tea upon the colonies. The colonists had refrained from using tea which paid a duty and had supplied themselves with smuggled tea from France, Sweden, and Holland. At this time the East India Company was on the verge of bankruptcy, a condition due in part to the loss of American customers. In the company's warehouses a vast amount of tea had accumulated. As a measure of relief the directors of the company advised the repeal of the tea duty, but "a course which went direct to the point was not of a nature to find favor with George the Third and his Ministers." Instead they allowed the company a drawback of the entire tea duty in England, but the tea was to be subject to the three penny tax payable in the colonies.

The tea arrives.—George III was soon to learn that he could not force tea down colonial throats. Late in 1773 several tea-laden ships arrived at American ports. In Charleston the agents of the company resigned, and when the duty was not paid, the collector seized the tea and stored it in a damp cellar. In Philadelphia a public meeting resolved that the duty on tea was illegal and persons who assisted in its being landed were declared public enemies. Under pressure of public opinion the consignees resigned and the captain of the tea vessel wisely decided not to unload his cargo. "When New York learned that the tea-ships allotted to it had been driven by a gale off the coast, men scanned the horizon, like the garrison of Londonderry watching for the English fleet in Lough Foyle, in their fear lest fate should rob them of their opportunity of proving themselves not inferior in mettle to the Bostonians."

The Boston Tea Party.—The Massachusetts people had recently been greatly irritated by certain private letters of Hutchinson, Oliver, and Paxton. The letters had been obtained in England by Franklin and had been sent under the seal of secrecy to some of the Massachusetts leaders who, however, published them. Before the excitement subsided three tea-laden vessels arrived at Boston. Hutchinson refused to allow the ships to leave until regularly cleared and this could not be done until the entire cargo had been unloaded. A mass meeting held in the Old South Church resolved that the tea should not be landed, and when the governor ordered the dispersal of the meeting, the bearer of the proclamation met with insult. Neighboring towns agreed to assist Boston, with force if necessary, and a guard watched the vessels to see that none of the tea was landed. On December 17 the cargo would be seized by the collector for non-payment of duty. On the evening of December 16, fifty or sixty men disguised as Indians boarded the tea ships, rifled the chests, and threw the contents into the bay.

The course of Massachusetts.—The British government was being sorely tried by Massachusetts. On January 29, 1774, a petition of the general court for the removal of Hutchinson and Oliver came before the Privy Council Committee for Foreign Plantations. The petition was pronounced a seditious document. Franklin was summoned before the committee, was charged with intercepting letters, and was dismissed from the deputy post-master-generalship. Soon after the Boston Tea Party, the assembly voted to impeach Justice Oliver for accepting a salary from the crown. In retaliation Hutchinson dissolved the assembly and soon left the colony.

LORD NORTH'S COERCIVE POLICY

The intolerable acts.—The revolutionary acts which were taking place in America, especially those in Massachusetts, caused deep concern in England. Pitt and Burke favored conciliation as the only means of preserving the empire, but the king insisted upon repression. The ministry speedily adopted a legislative program to punish Massachusetts, and parliament legalized the ministerial policy by passing the so-called intolerable acts.

Boston Port Act.—The first of these acts closed the port of Boston from June 1, 1774, until such time as "it shall be made to appear to his Majesty, in his privy council, that peace and obedience to the laws shall be so far restored in the said town of *Boston*, that the trade of *Great Britain* may safely be carried on there, and his Majesty's customs duly collected." The king was not to open the port until the inhabitants of Boston had given full satisfaction to the East India Company and to the revenue officers and others who had suffered by the recent outbreaks.

Massachusetts Government Act.—By the "regulating act" the people of Massachusetts were deprived of most of their chartered rights. After July 1, 1774, the council was to be appointed by the king instead of by the assembly. The governor was to appoint and remove, without the consent of the council, all judges of the inferior courts, the attorney general, provosts, marshals, and other officers belonging to the council or courts of justice. Sheriffs were also appointed by the governor but could not be removed without the consent of the council. The chief justice and judges of the superior court were to be appointed by the governor, but were to hold their commissions during the king's pleasure, and they could not be removed unless by order of the crown. Grand and petit juries were to be summoned by the sheriffs instead of being chosen in town meetings. Except for elections, town meetings were to be called only by consent of the governor and discussion was to be limited to subjects stated in the leave. The people were still allowed to elect the assembly.

Administration of Justice Act.—The third act provided, "That if any inquisition or indictment shall be found, or if any appeal shall be sued or preferred against any person, for murther, or other capital offence, in the province of the *Massachusett's Bay*, and it shall appear, by information given upon oath to the governor . . , that the fact was committed by the person against whom such inquisition or indictment shall be found, or against whom such appeal shall be sued or preferred . . . , either in the execution of his duty as a magistrate, for the suppression of riots, or in the support of the laws of revenue, or in acting in his duty as an officer of revenue, or in acting under the direction and order of any magistrate, for the suppression of riots, or for the carrying into effect the laws of revenue, or in aiding and assisting in any of the cases aforesaid; and if it shall also appear, to the satisfaction of the said governor . . . that an indifferent trial cannot be had within the said province, in that case, it shall and may be lawful for the governor . . . to direct, with the advice and consent of the council, that the inquisition, indictment, or appeal, shall be tried in some other of his Majesty's colonies, or in *Great Britain*." The act also made it possible to transport witnesses to the scene of the trial.

Quartering Act, June 2, 1774.—The fourth law was entitled "An act for the better providing suitable quarters for officers and soldiers in his Majesty's service in North America." It provided that, if any officers or soldiers should be without quarters for twenty-four hours after a proper demand had been made, the governor might order that "uninhabited houses, outhouses, barns, or other buildings" be made fit for quarters. The law was to remain in force until March 24, 1776. Though the act was general in its terms, in reality it was intended "to facilitate the establishment of a temporary military government in Massachusetts." Of ominous import was the appointment of General Gage as governor of Massachusetts.

The Quebec Act.—The Quebec Act which extended the province of Quebec to the Ohio River also aroused the anger of

Massachusetts, New York, Connecticut, and Virginia, as it deprived those colonies of large tracts of western lands which they claimed under their ancient charters. It was not intended as a coercive act, but was so considered in the colonies.

THE FIRST CONTINENTAL CONGRESS

Call for a congress.—On May 10 a copy of the Port Act was received in Boston. On the twelfth the committee of correspondence met with eight neighboring committees and recommended non-intercourse with Great Britain. The other colonies were asked to follow the same course. While this was taking place the four additional regiments which Gage had called for began to arrive and on June 1, 1774, the port was blocked by men-of-war. Boston began to receive money and supplies from other towns and colonies, and a new impetus was given to the formation of committees of correspondence. Committees in New York and Philadelphia recommended the appointment of delegates to a general congress. The Virginia burgesses resolved to set aside June 1 as a day of fasting and prayer. The governor dissolved the house, but the burgesses assembled on May 27 at the Raleigh Tavern and adopted a resolution calling for a congress. Copies of the resolution were sent to the other assemblies.

On June 17 the Massachusetts assembly resolved, "That a meeting of committees from several colonies . . . is highly expedient and necessary, to consult upon the present state of the colonies, and the miseries to which they are and must be reduced by the operation of certain acts of Parliament respecting America, and to deliberate and determine upon wise and proper measures, to be by them recommended to all the colonies, for the recovery and establishment of their just rights and liberties, civil and religious, and the restoration of union and harmony between Great Britain and the colonies, most ardently desired by all good men: Therefore, resolved, that the Hon. James Bowdoin, Esq., the Hon. Thomas Cushing, Esq., Mr. Samuel Adams and Robert Treat Paine, Esqrs., be . . . appointed a committee . . . to meet with such committees or delegates from the other colonies as have been or may be appointed, either by their respective houses of burgesses or representatives, or by convention, or by the committees of correspondence appointed by the respective

houses of assembly, in the city of Philadelphia, or any other
place that shall be judged most suitable by the committee, on
the 1st day of September next; and that the speaker of the house
be directed, in a letter to the speakers of the house of burgesses
or representatives in the several colonies, to inform them of the
substance of these resolves."

Meeting of the First Continental Congress.—Every colony
but Georgia responded to the call. In September over fifty
delegates assembled in Carpenters' Hall at Philadelphia. Among
them were John and Samuel Adams of Massachusetts, John
Dickinson of Pennsylvania, Richard Henry Lee, Patrick Henry
and George Washington of Virginia, Roger Sherman of Connecticut, John Jay of New York, and Edward and John Rutledge of South Carolina. "The congress of 1774 was not thought
of by the people as a congress in the modern legislative sense.
It was rather a convention of ambassadors of subordinate, but
distinct communities which had found it needful to take counsel
of one another regarding a crisis in their common relations to
the parent state, in order, if possible, to adopt some common
plan of action. It was essentially an advisory or consultative
body. In another aspect it may be regarded as the completion
of the revolutionary party organization of which the basis was
laid in the committees of correspondence."

The Suffolk Resolves approved.—The delegates were soon
divided into well-defined groups; the radicals led by Samuel
Adams wanted resistance, the conservatives headed by Joseph
Galloway favored compromise. The radicals succeeded in getting Congress to approve the resolves recently drawn up in the
Suffolk County convention in Massachusetts. The resolves declared that no obedience to the recent acts of parliament was
due from Massachusetts, advised that no money be turned into
the treasury by the tax-collectors until the restoration of the
constitution, denounced as enemies the king's councillors who
had not resigned, and threatened armed resistance. Congress
published these resolves with its resolutions commending the
course of Boston.

A plan of union.—The conservatives favored a plan of union
proposed by Galloway, which provided for a crown appointed
president-general and a council of deputies chosen every three

years by the legislatures. The acts of the council were to be subject to parliamentary veto and acts of parliament relating to the colonies might be vetoed by the council. The plan was defeated by a narrow margin.

The Declaration and Resolves.—On September 7 a committee of two from each colony had been appointed to draw up a statement of the rights of the colonies, instances of their violation, and means of restoring them. Agreement on the committee's report was reached on October 14. The declaration of grievances thus adopted complained that parliament had imposed taxes upon them and under various pretences, but in fact for the purpose of raising revenue, had established a board of commissioners with unconstitutional powers, and had extended the jurisdiction of the admiralty courts, not only for collecting duties, but for trial of causes arising merely within the body of a county. Complaint was also made that judges had been made dependent on the crown for salaries, that standing armies had been kept in times of peace, and that the removal to distant places for trial of prisoners charged with treason and certain other crimes had been legalized. The intolerable acts were described as "impolitic, unjust, and cruel, as well as unconstitutional." Other complaints were the dissolution of assemblies when they attempted to deliberate on grievances, and treating with contempt petitions for redress.

Congress accordingly resolved that the inhabitants of the English colonies in North America were "entitled to life, liberty and property: and they had never ceded to any foreign power whatever, a right to dispose of either without their consent;" that they were entitled to the same rights as their ancestors; "that the foundation of English liberty, and of all free government, is a right in the people to participate in their legislative council: and as the English colonies are not represented . . . in the British parliament, they are entitled to a free and exclusive power of legislation in their several provincial legislatures, where their right of representation can alone be preserved, in all cases of taxation and internal policy, subject only to the negative of their sovereign." For the mutual interests of both countries they consented to parliamentary regulation of external commerce. The right of trial by their peers of the vicinage, rights confirmed by royal charters and secured by provincial codes, and the right of assembly and petition were asserted. Keeping of a standing army in time of peace without the consent of the legislature of the colony where the army was kept was declared illegal. The exercise of legislative power by a crown appointed council was declared "unconstitutional, dangerous and destructive to the freedom of American legislation."

"All and each of which the . . . deputies, in behalf of themselves, and their constituents, do claim, demand, and insist on, as their indubitable rights and liberties; which cannot be legally taken from them, altered or abridged by any power whatever, without their own consent, by their representatives in their several provincial legislatures."

The acts passed by parliament since 1763 to which they were opposed were then enumerated. "To these grievous acts and measures, Americans cannot submit, but in hopes their fellow subjects in Great-Britain will, on a revision of them, restore us to that state, in which both countries found happiness and prosperity, we have for the present, only resolved to pursue the following peaceable measures: 1. To enter into a non-importation, non-consumption, and non-exportation agreement or association. 2. To prepare an address to the people of Great-Britain, and a memorial to the inhabitants of British America: and 3. To prepare a loyal address to his majesty, agreeable to resolutions already entered into."

Non-importation, non-consumption, and non-exportation.—By commercial restrictions the delegates hoped to force the British government to change its policy. On September 22 Congress voted to request colonial merchants and others not to place orders for British goods and to delay or suspend orders already sent until Congress could make known its policy. Five days later it resolved that from December 1 there should be no importation of goods from Great Britain or Ireland, or of British or Irish make, and that such goods be neither used nor purchased. On September 30 it was resolved that exportation to Great Britain, Ireland, and the British West Indies ought to cease after September 10, 1775, unless grievances were redressed, and a committee was appointed to formulate a plan for the enforcement of non-importation, non-consumption, and non-exportation.

The Association.—On October 20 the delegates adopted the "Association" which provided that after December 1 British or Irish goods, East India tea, molasses, syrups, paneles, coffee, and pimento from the British plantations or from Dominica, wines from Madeira or the Western Islands, and foreign indigo should not be imported into British America. It was agreed that slaves should not be imported or purchased after December 1, and slave traders were not to be allowed to rent vessels or purchase goods. Non-exportation was not to be put into force until September 10, 1775, but if redress had not been obtained by that time, American goods would be cut off from Great Britain, Ireland, or the West Indies. Rice, however, might be exported to Europe. Congress agreed to encourage frugality, economy, and industry, to promote agriculture, the arts, and manufactures, especially of wool, and to discourage extravagance and dissipation. Merchants and manufacturers were not to raise prices. A committee in each county, city, and town was to observe the conduct of persons, and if violations of the Association were discovered, the truth was to be published in the newspapers. If any colony did not accede to the Association, intercourse with that colony was to be cut off.

Attempts to obtain coöperation of other Colonies.—Congress also made an effort to obtain the coöperation of neighboring colonies by an address to the people of Quebec and by letters to the inhabitants of St. Johns, Nova Scotia, Georgia, and East and West Florida. A memorial to the people of British America, an address to the people of Great Britain, and a petition to the king were also prepared. May 10, 1775, was set as the date for the assembly of another congress, and on October 26 the First Continental Congress dissolved.

North's conciliatory resolution.—In January, 1775, parliament began consideration of the petition to the king and other papers relating to America. Chatham moved the withdrawal of the troops from Boston but the motion was defeated. On February 1 he presented a plan of conciliation based upon mutual concessions, but this was also rejected. On February 20 Lord North undertook the unexpected rôle of conciliator by a resolution which was considered in committee of the whole and passed by the commons a week later. The resolution provided "that when the Governour, Council, and Assembly, or General Court, of any . . . colonies in *America*, shall propose to make provision . . . for contributing their proportion to the common defence, (such proportion to be raised under the authority of the General Court, or General Assembly, of such Province or Colony, and disposable by Parliament,) and shall engage to make provision also for the support of the Civil Government, and the Administration of Justice, in such Province or Colony, it will be proper, if such proposal shall be approved by his Majesty and . . . Parliament . . . to forbear, in respect of such Province or Colony, to levy any Duty, Tax, or Assessment, or to impose any farther Duty, Tax, or Assessment, except only such Duties as it may be expedient to continue to levy or to impose for the regulation of commerce; the nett produce of the Duties last mentioned to be carried to the account of such Province or Colony respectively."

The Restraining Act.—The effect of North's resolution was nullified by the Restraining Act, which, in spite of Burke's powerful speech on conciliation, became law on March 13. This act confined the commerce of the New England colonies to Great Britain, Ireland, and the British West Indies, and prohibited the New Englanders from fishing in the northern fisheries, until "the trade and commerce of his Majesty's subjects may be carried on without interruption." In April the act was extended to New Jersey, Pennsylvania, Delaware, Maryland, Virginia, and South Carolina. The British government thus closed the door of conciliation and made the American Revolution inevitable.

READINGS

Adams, J., *Works*, II, 337–517; Adams, S., *Writing*, II–III; Becker, C. L., *Beginnings of the American People*, 202–253; Beer, G. L., *British Colonial Policy, 1754–1765*, 72–315; Bigelow, J., *The Life of Benjamin Franklin*, II, 7–337; Channing, E., *A History of the United States*, III, 29–154; Dickinson, J., *Writings*, in Historical Society of Pennsylvania, *Memoirs*, XIV, 307–406; Doyle, J. A., "The Quarrel with Great Britain, 1761–1776," in *Cambridge Modern History*, VII, 148–208; Fisher, S. G., *The Struggle for American Independence*, I, 1–300; Frothingham, Richard, *The Rise of the Republic*, 158–455; Henry, W. W., *Patrick Henry*, I, 24–357; Howard, G. E., *Preliminaries of the Revolution;* Hutchinson, P. O., *The Diary and Letters of his Excellency Thomas Hutchinson*, I; Johnson, E. R., *History of Domestic and*

Foreign Commerce of the United States, I, 84–121; *Journals of the Continental Congress*, I (Worthington C. Ford, ed.); Lecky, W. E. H., *History of England in the Eighteenth Century*, III, 290–460; Lincoln, C. H., *The Revolutionary Movement in Pennsylvania, 1760–1776;* Macdonald, William, *Select Charters*, 272–396; Trevelyan, G. O., *The American Revolution*, Part I, 1–253; Tyler, M. C., *Literary History of the American Revolution*, I; *Patrick Henry*, 32–134; Van Tyne, C. H., *The American Revolution*, 3–24; Becker, C. L., *The Eve of the Revolution;* Eckenrode, H. J., *The Revolution in Virginia;* Schlesinger, A. M., *The Colonial Merchants and the American Revolution, 1763–1776*.

CHAPTER XXIV

FROM LEXINGTON TO INDEPENDENCE

THE OPENING OF HOSTILITIES

Enforcement of the Association.—The Association adopted by the Continental Congress was approved throughout the colonies. In county and town meetings, in assemblies, provincial congresses, or special conventions, the patriot party expressed its approval. Though the New York assembly refused to sanction the proceedings of Congress, the committee of correspondence and many counties chose inspection committees. In Georgia the patriots had a difficult time, but when the provincial congress assembled at Savannah in March, 1775, forty-five of the deputies ratified the Association and local inspection committees were formed.

Military preparations.—Throughout the colonies military preparations were in progress. In October, 1774, Charles Lee wrote from Philadelphia to an English nobleman, "Virginia, Rhode Island and Carolina are forming corps. Massachusetts Bay has long had a sufficient number instructed to become instructive of the rest. Even this Quakering province is following the example." In December the provincial convention of Maryland recommended that all males between the ages of sixteen and fifty should form themselves into military companies. Delaware made provision for the arming and drilling of militia. Connecticut ordered the towns to double their military supplies, and Rhode Islanders seized forty-four cannon from the Newport batteries.

Whigs, neutrals, and Tories.—In spite of the military ardor thus displayed, public opinion was by no means a unit. In general the people were divided into three groups, patriots, neutrals, and Loyalists. Among the patriots, or Whigs as they were called, was a small group of ultra-radicals who favored

independence. A great majority of the Whigs stood for strenuous opposition to British policy but not for independence.
The neutrals in the main presented three shades of opinion:
those with patriot sympathies but who were still wavering, those
who were indifferent or were religiously opposed to violence,
and those who had Loyalist leanings but had not made a definite
decision. The third great group was composed of Loyalists or
Tories. These were not all of like mind, one portion being openly
in favor of the king but not ready to take up arms, the rest being
openly belligerent. As the Revolution progressed shadings within
groups gradually disappeared, wavering neutrals linked themselves with patriots or Loyalists, and sections became distinctly
Whig or Tory.

Even before the adoption of the Association, ill feeling showed
itself. As Howard says, "Tarring and featherings was becoming
the order of the day. . . . Loyalists were bitterly stigmatized
as Tories and traitors, and the cause of liberty was sullied by
acts of intolerance and persecution." Channing says, "The
story of tarring and featherings, riotings and burnings becomes
monotonous, almost as much so as the reading of the papers
that poured forth from counties, towns, conventions, meetings,
congresses, and private individuals."

Revolution in Massachusetts.—The people of Massachusetts
refused to submit to the Regulating Act. The "mandamus"
councillors were threatened with violence and either declined
the appointment or resigned, and the courts were unable to sit.
On September 1, 1774, Gage sent soldiers to seize some powder
stored near Boston and a rumor spread that the war ships had
fired on Boston. The militia began to gather from neighboring
counties, and Israel Putnam summoned the Connecticut militia
to march to the assistance of Boston.

Gage refused to allow the meeting of the assembly called for
October 5, but most of the representatives met at Salem where
they declared themselves a provincial congress. A few days
later the congress moved to Concord and then to Cambridge.
It appointed a committee of safety which was empowered to call
out the militia, and other committees attended to the collecting
of stores and general defence. After the gathering of the second
provincial congress on February 1, 1775, the committee of

safety under the leadership of John Hancock and Joseph Warren
was authorized to distribute arms.

Lexington.—On April 18 the watchful patriots discovered
that British troops were preparing for an expedition, and William
Dawes and Paul Revere were sent to spread the alarm. Soon

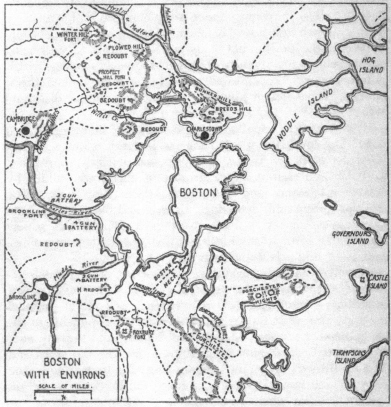

(Based on map in G. O. Trevelyan, *The American Revolution*, Part I, at end)

after dawn of April 19 the British troops approached Lexington
where they found sixty or seventy minutemen under arms.
When they did not obey the order to lay down their arms and
disperse, a shot was fired, followed by a volley which killed
eight and wounded ten of the colonials. The regulars went on
to Concord where another encounter occurred at the old North
Bridge where the British had stationed a guard. After destroy-

ing some stores, the troops started back toward Boston. By this time the militia had gathered, and the incensed farmers and villagers from behind trees, rocks, and fences poured in a deadly fire which did not slacken until the soldiers were relieved at Lexington by troops under Lord Percy. When the march was resumed the battle began again, nor did it cease until the weary soldiers reached Charlestown.

Boston besieged.—The news of Lexington started thousands of New England volunteers toward Boston. John Stark led the New Hampshire men; Israel Putnam left his plow in the furrow to lead the Connecticut volunteers; and Nathanael Greene headed the Rhode Islanders. The volunteer forces in a few weeks were reinforced by large bodies of colonial troops. The Massachusetts congress voted to raise thirteen thousand six hundred men, and it called upon the other New England colonies to bring the army up to thirty thousand. The Rhode Island assembly voted to raise fifteen hundred men, and Connecticut six thousand, two-thirds of whom were to be sent to the aid of Boston. Gage, who had been reinforced with troops under Howe, Clinton, and Burgoyne, found his army of six or seven thousand veterans shut up in Boston by an undisciplined and poorly organized force, which, however, outnumbered him three or four to one.

Bunker Hill.—The city was open to attack from Dorchester Heights and the Charlestown hills. To forestall the British, the colonials decided to occupy Bunker Hill. On the night of June 16 Colonel William Prescott was sent to fortify the position. For reasons which are not entirely clear, he led his men to Breed's Hill where a redoubt was constructed. When dawn disclosed the fortification, the warships and batteries opened fire. Prescott asked for reinforcements and small detachments came to his assistance. A British council of war was called. Clinton suggested the seizure of the causeway on Charlestown neck, a movement which would have cut off the colonial force from the mainland. But Gage and Howe, underestimating the fighting ability of their opponents, foolishly insisted upon a frontal attack. Twice the British were repulsed with staggering losses, but during the third charge the colonials exhausted their ammunition and were forced to retreat, first to Bunker Hill and then back to their own lines. Though the colonials technically had suffered a defeat, great was the rejoicing over the battle, for colonial troops had proven their prowess against the British regulars and had taken a toll of two for one.

Ticonderoga and Crown Point.—While the troops were gathering about Boston, it occurred to Benedict Arnold that Ticonderoga would be an easy prize. He submitted his ideas to Warren and the committee of safety, who authorized him to proceed with not over four hundred men to reduce the fort. On the way to Boston Arnold had divulged his thoughts to certain Connecticut friends who immediately organized an expedition with the same object. Ethan Allen and others from the Hampshire grants had also conceived the idea of capturing the fortress and were on the march when joined by Arnold, who had gone forward ahead of his troops. Immediately the question of rank arose and after considerable discussion Allen and Arnold agreed to command jointly for the time being.

On May 10 Ticonderoga surrendered without a struggle and this was followed by an easy conquest of Crown Point and Ft. George. By this time Allen completely ignored his colleague, but the arrival of about a hundred of Arnold's men gave him his opportunity. Having captured a British schooner Arnold decided to make a raid on St. Johns. The town was easily captured and a British sloop fell into the hands of the audacious colonial. The operations supplied the Whig army with much needed artillery and stores, and it opened the way for operations in Canada.

Rebellion in Virginia.—Virginia at the same time was in a state of rebellion. The second revolutionary convention assembled at Richmond in March, 1775, and Patrick Henry boldly sounded the call to arms. The governor, Lord Dunmore, in alarm ordered the removal of the gunpowder from the magazine at Williamsburg and soon several thousand armed men made ready to march on the capital. When some of the leaders hesitated, Henry placed himself at the head of an armed band and marched toward Williamsburg. The governor discreetly agreed to pay for the powder, but two days later (May 6, 1775) issued a proclamation charging the people "not to aid, abet, or give countenance to the said Patrick Henry, or any other persons concerned in such unwarrantable combinations." In May a legal assembly was called but the members appeared in arms, and an attempted conciliation failed when it became known that a trap was prepared to kill any one who tampered with the magazine. Fearful of the mob, the governor fled to a war vessel.

The Mecklenburg Resolves.—The news of Lexington aroused every colony. South Carolina immediately raised two regiments. In North Carolina some of the frontiersmen held a meeting at Charlotte, Mecklenburg County, and passed resolutions that crown commissions in the colonies were null and void, and that colonial constitutions were suspended. They also made governmental regulations until Congress could provide laws for them. The original resolutions were destroyed and afterward were reproduced from memory in the form of the so-called "Mecklenburg Declaration of Independence" of May 20. Reliable historians now reject the authenticity of this document, but the original resolves were undoubtedly genuine.

THE SECOND CONTINENTAL CONGRESS

The delegates.—The Second Continental Congress assembled at Philadelphia on May 10, 1775, all but Georgia and Rhode Island being represented. On May 13 Lyman Hall, representing St. John's parish, Georgia, arrived, but not until July 20 was notice received that Georgia had acceded to the Association and appointed delegates. Stephen Hopkins, the first Rhode Island delegate to appear, arrived May 18. Peyton Randolph of Virginia was elected president, but he found it necessary to leave Congress on May 24, and John Hancock was chosen president. Most of the delegates had been in the first Congress; among the new members was Benjamin Franklin, who had recently returned from England; Thomas Jefferson was elected to represent Virginia in the place of Peyton Randolph.

Nature of the work of Congress.—The conservative Whigs were still in the majority. They favored another petition to the king, but the state of war was recognized by all and Congress shouldered the responsibility of directing the Revolution as a defensive war. The early activities of Congress were devoted mainly to the raising, organizing, and equipping of the armies,

to building and equipping a fleet, to perfecting the organization
of the Revolution, to protecting the frontiers and obtaining alliances with the Indians, to enforcing the Association, to justifying
the Revolution and seeking aid outside of the thirteen colonies,
and to seeking redress from the British crown.

Military preparations.—Congress worked strenuously to raise
troops and to obtain munitions and other stores. Efforts were
made to stimulate recruiting, to perfect the organization of the
militia, and to hasten the assembling of forces. The manufacture
of cannon, guns, and gunpowder was encouraged and attempts
were made to increase the supplies of lead, nitre, and salt. Congress recommended to the various assemblies and conventions
that they provide sufficient stores of ammunition for their
colonies and that they devise means for furnishing with arms
such effective men as were too poor to buy them.

Organization of the army.—The armies already in the field
were recognized by Congress. On June 14 a committee was
appointed to draft rules for the army and on the following day
Washington was appointed to command the continental forces.
Arrangements were soon made for the appointment of four
major-generals, eight brigadier-generals, and minor officers.
The first major-generals were Artemus Ward, Charles Lee,
Philip Schuyler, and Israel Putnam, Schuyler being placed in
command of the New York department. Rules and regulations
for the army were also adopted and provision was made for the
establishment of a hospital.

Organization of the navy.—For the protection of the coasts
Congress at first depended upon the efforts of individual colonies,
recommending that they make provision, by armed vessels or
otherwise, for the protection of their harbors and navigation
on their coasts. Colonial vessels were utilized to capture British
transports, but it soon became evident that a navy under congressional control would be more effective. During October,
1775, Congress decided to fit out four vessels and on November
28 adopted rules for the regulation of the navy. On December
13 provision was made for the building of thirteen war craft
and on the twenty-second officers were appointed. Ezek Hopkins
was made commander-in-chief of the fleet; the captains were
Dudley Saltonstall, Abraham Whipple, Nicholas Biddle, and

John B. Hopkins. Among the first-lieutenants was John Paul Jones.

Prizes and privateers.—On November 25 Congress adopted regulations regarding prizes, and advised the legislative bodies to erect admiralty courts or to give to the local courts admiralty jurisdiction. It also provided "That in all cases an appeal shall be allowed to Congress, or such person or persons as they shall appoint for the trials of appeals." In March, 1776, Congress resolved "That the inhabitants of these colonies be permitted to fit out armed vessels to cruize on the enemies of these United Colonies." In April Congress adopted a form of commission and instructions to commanders of privateers, and decided to issue letters of marque and reprisal.

First steps in financing the Revolution.—The financing of the Revolution was one of the most difficult tasks confronting Congress. The first step in raising money was taken on June 3, 1775, when a committee was appointed to borrow £6,000 to purchase gunpowder. A committee was also appointed to bring in an estimate of money necessary to be raised. On June 22 Congress resolved to emit $2,000,000 in bills of credit and pledged the "confederated colonies" for their redemption. Once embarked upon the perilous course of paper finance, issue followed issue in rapid succession. At first the promissory notes passed readily, but they soon began to depreciate and eventually became worthless. Nevertheless they carried the Revolution through its most trying years.

Establishment of a post office.—The need of "speedy and secure conveyance of intelligence from one end of the Continent to the other" was recognized and a committee was appointed to consider the establishment of posts. On July 26 the post office was established, Benjamin Franklin being elected Postmaster General. He was authorized to establish "a line of posts . . . from Falmouth in New England to Savannah in Georgia, with as many cross posts as he shall think fit."

An Indian policy adopted.—Control of the Indians was vital for the safety of the frontier. It was felt that if the British ministry should induce the tribes to commit hostile acts, the colonies would be justified in entering into alliances with Indian nations. It was hoped that the Iroquois might be kept neutral.

"Talks" were prepared, goods to be used as presents were purchased, and money was provided. The frontier was laid off into three departments which were placed under commissioners. The Six Nations and tribes to the north of them were in the northern department; tribes between the Iroquois and the Cherokee were in the middle department; and the Cherokee and Indians south of them were in the southern department.

Enforcement of the Association.—Congress continued the policy of trade restriction. On May 17 it resolved that exports to Quebec, Nova Scotia, the Island of St. Johns, Newfoundland, Georgia except St. John's parish, and to East and West Florida, must cease, and that supplies must not be furnished to the British fisheries. After Georgia appointed delegates, the colony was admitted to the Association. On June 2 Congress resolved that no bill of exchange, draught, or order of any British officer should be honored, and that no money, provisions, or other necessaries be furnished the British army or navy.

On June 26 Congress resolved that, as attempts were being made to divide the people of North Carolina and defeat the Association, it was recommended to that colony to associate for the defence of American liberty and to organize the militia, Congress offering to provide pay for a thousand men in the colony. On July 4 a resolution was adopted that the restraining acts were "unconstitutional, oppressive, and cruel," and that commercial opposition should be made to them.

As doubts had arisen with respect to the true spirit and construction of the Association, on August 1 Congress defined it as follows: "Under the prohibition . . . to export to, or import from, the Islands of Great Britain and Ireland, this Congress intends to comprise all exportation to, and importation from, the islands of Jersey, Guernsey, Sark, Alderney, and Mann, and every European island and settlement within the British dominions: and that under the denomination of the West Indies, this Congress means to comprehend all the West India islands, British and foreign, to whatever state, power, or prince belonging, or by whomsoever governed, and also the Summer islands, Bahama Islands, Berbicia and Surinam on the Main, and every island and settlement within the latitude of the southern line of Georgia and the Equator."

The necessity of obtaining supplies forced Congress to make special provisions for the importation of munitions of war. On July 15, 1775, a resolution was adopted that "every vessel importing Gun powder, Salt petre, Sulphur, provided they bring with the sulphur four times as much salt petre, brass field pieces, or good muskets fitted with Bayonets, within nine Months from the date of this resolution, shall be permitted to load and export the produce of these colonies, to the value of such powder and stores aforesd, the non-exportation agreement notwithstanding." On November 2 Congress adopted a resolution to close the ports until March 1, but from time to time special provisions were made for the exportation and importation of goods. The delegates frequently discussed the question of opening the ports, as shown by John Adams's *Autobiography* which says: "This measure . . . labored exceedingly, because it was considered as a bold step to independence. Indeed, I urged it expressly with that view, and as connected with the institution of government in all the States, and a declaration of national independence." On April 6, 1776, the ports were opened to world commerce except trade with Great Britain and her possessions.

Letter to the people of Canada.—The congressional leaders hoped to strengthen their resistance by obtaining the coöperation of the Canadians. A letter "to the oppressed inhabitants of Canada" was approved on May 29. Congress condoled with them "on the arrival of that day, in the course of which, the sun could not shine on a single freeman in all your extensive dominion. . . . By the introduction of your present form of government, or rather present form of tyranny, you and your wives and your children are made slaves. . . . We are informed you have already been called upon to waste your lives in a contest with us. Should you, by complying in this instance, assent to your new establishment [the Quebec Act], and a war break out with France, your wealth and your sons may be sent to perish in expeditions against their islands in the West Indies. We yet entertain hopes of your uniting with us in the defence of our common liberty."

Attempts to influence public opinion in the British Empire.— Congress hoped by appeals to the inhabitants of the British Isles to arouse public opinion, thereby bringing pressure to bear upon a Ministry and subservient parliament which had shown themselves to be irresponsible and tyrannous. Addresses to the people of Great Britain and Ireland were accordingly prepared. A letter to the Lord Mayor, aldermen, and liveries of London was drawn up expressing thanks "for the virtuous and unsolicited resentment you have shown to the violated rights of a free people." A letter of friendship was sent to the assembly of Jamaica and a communication regarding commerce was sent to Bermuda.

Statement to the army.—On July 6 Congress approved a declaration setting forth the causes and necessity of taking up arms, which was to be published by Washington upon his arrival at Boston. The declaration presented the usual arguments regarding constitutional rights and gave an account of the progress of events. That independence was desired was denied in the following words: "We have not raised armies with ambitious designs of separating from Great Britain, and establishing independent states. We fight not for glory or for conquest. . . . In our own native land, in defence of the freedom that is our birth right, . . . and for the protection of our property . . . we have taken up arms."

Petition to the king.—The radicals believed that a war of independence could not be avoided, but the conservatives restrained them, hoping that the force of public opinion, a bold show of resistance, and commercial restrictions would change the ministerial policy. Another direct appeal to the king was decided upon and on May 29 resolutions were adopted, "that with a sincere design of contributing by all the means in our power, not incompatible with just regard for the undoubted rights and true interests of these colonies, to the promotion of this most desirable reconciliation, an humble and dutiful petition be presented to his Majesty." The petition, signed on July 8, was couched in respectful terms as the following quotation shows: "We . . . beseech your Majesty, that your royal authority and influence may be graciously interposed to procure us relief from our afflicting fears and jealousies, occasioned by the system before mentioned, and to settle peace through every part of your dominions, with all humility submitting to your Majesty's wise consideration whether it may not be expedient for facilitating those important purposes, that your Majesty be pleased to direct some mode, by which the united applications of your faithful colonists to the throne, in pursuance of their common councils, may be improved into a happy and permanent reconciliation; and that, in the mean time, measures may be taken for preventing the further destruction of the lives of your Majesty's subjects; and that such statutes as more immediately distress any of your Majesty's colonies may be repealed."

Reply to Lord North.—As several of the colonies were desirous of knowing the congressional attitude toward Lord North's conciliatory resolution, on July 31 Congress adopted a formal report which closed with the following statement: "When the world reflects how inadequate to justice are these vaunted terms; when it attends to the rapid and bold succession of injuries, which have been aimed at these colonies, when it reviews the pacific and respectful expostulations, which . . . were the sole arms we opposed to them; when it observes that our complaints were either not heard at all, or were answered with new and accumulated injury, . . . when it considers the great armaments with which they have invaded us, and the circumstances of cruelty with which they have commenced and prosecuted hostilities; when these things we say, are laid together and attentively considered, can the world be deceived into an opinion that we are unreasonable, or can it hesitate to believe with us, that nothing but our own exertions may defeat the ministerial sentence of death or abject submission."

Stubborn attitude of the government.—George III and his ministers had gained no wisdom from the rebellious attitude in America. The petition, which had been entrusted to Richard Penn, reached London on August 14, but not until a week later did Lord Dartmouth, the secretary for the colonies, consent to look at a copy of the document and not until September was it presented to the king. On August 23 George III published a proclamation which declared the Americans rebels, and after his examination of the petition, the king saw no reason for revising it. At the next session of parliament acts were passed which prohibited trade with the thirteen colonies, ordered the seizure and confiscation of ships engaged in trade with them, and permitted British commanders to impress sailors from seized vessels.

The German mercenaries.—A reorganization of the cabinet had forced the amiable Dartmouth out of the colonial office, his successor being Lord George Germaine. Lord Rochford was made secretary of state for the southern department, and Lord Suffolk was retained in the northern department to which office fell the business with Germany. The British army was sadly in need of recruits. In Scotland the men of Argyllshire and Inverness-shire readily entered the army for colonial service, but in Ireland and England the people showed little enthusiasm for a war which was intended to subdue their freedom-loving brethren over the seas. To raise the necessary troops the king turned to the continent. An attempt to obtain the use of the Scotch troops which had long been in Dutch service failed and Catherine II refused to furnish Russian infantry, but in Germany British overtures met with better success. The Landgrave of Hesse-Cassel, the Duke of Brunswick, and some other needy princes were willing to sell the services of their subjects for British gold. During the war over thirty thousand mercenaries were hired in Germany for service in America. In the words of Lecky, "The conduct of England in hiring German mercenaries to subdue the essentially English population beyond the Atlantic, made reconciliation hopeless, and the Declaration of Independence inevitable."

PROGRESS OF THE WAR

Burning of Falmouth.—Events were also taking place in America which were convincing the public that the war for independence must be fought to the bitter end. In October, 1775, four British war vessels sailed into the harbor of Falmouth, now known as Portland, and set fire to the town. Three-fourths of the dwellings were destroyed and a thousand unoffending people were made homeless.

The Canadian campaign.—The efforts of Congress to enlist the Canadians in the colonial cause did not meet with success and the invasion of Canada was determined upon. Two forces were sent northward. One under Richard Montgomery was to proceed by the Lake Champlain route, seize Montreal, and then march to Quebec. The other under Benedict Arnold was to go up the Kennebec and down the Chaudière, and join the other force. Montgomery captured Montreal and then made a juncture with Arnold. On December 31 an attack was made on Quebec, but Montgomery was killed, Arnold was wounded, and the forces were repulsed. But in spite of terrible sufferings in his army, Arnold kept Quebec in a state of blockade the rest of the winter.

Siege of Boston.—When Washington arrived at Cambridge, he found a disorganized army which was short of food, ammunition, and uniforms, and without hospital service. Fortunately the British did not take advantage of the situation, and gradually the commander brought order out of chaos. By March, 1776, Washington was prepared to make an offensive move. Taking advantage of the fact that the British had not fortified Dorchester Heights, on the night of March 4 colonial troops seized the position which commanded Boston. On the seventeenth the British army, accompanied by about a thousand Loyalists, sailed for Halifax.

Fighting in Virginia and North Carolina.—While Washington was besieging Boston, Lord Dunmore was making reprisals along the Virginia rivers. After the defeat of some of his Loyalist supporters at Great Bridge, the governor caused the burning of Norfolk on January 1, 1776. North Carolina was also torn by civil war. Governor Martin had been driven from the colony, and from the refuge of a war vessel commissioned Donald McDonald to collect an army of Loyalists in the central and western counties. He also appealed to Sir Henry Clinton for aid. With a force of sixteen hundred men McDonald marched toward the coast, but on February 27, 1776, he was met by patriot forces at Moore's Creek and his Loyalist army was practically annihilated. When Clinton's fleet appeared off the coast, ten thousand North Carolina militia were ready to meet him. Clinton lingered for a time off Cape Fear and then sailed to Charleston where he hoped to arouse the Loyalists of the coasts and the German settlers of the interior.

Defence of Charleston.—Edward Rutledge with six thousand militia prepared to defend the city. Colonel Moultrie, with his forces back of rude fortifications on Sullivan's Island, made

ready to defend the harbor. On June 28 the fleet attacked.
Most of the British shot buried themselves in the palmetto logs
and banks of sand from behind which Moultrie's men poured a
fire which wrought havoc on the crowded decks. An attempt
to make a landing proved a failure and Charleston was saved.

THE LOYALISTS

The people not united.—Up to 1774 the majority of Americans were not united in opposition to British policy, but acts of
violence and retaliation, the meeting of Congress, and the organization of revolutionary committees, brought about a rapid
crystallization of public opinion. Loyalty to Great Britain was
the normal state. The Whigs were the nullifiers and eventually
the secessionists. That they were able to perfect an organization
and carry on a successful rebellion has obscured the fact that
they were in reality but an active minority. The masses were
indifferent or were loyal supporters of Great Britain. It is impossible to estimate accurately the number of Loyalists; they
varied with localities and fluctuated with the fortunes of war.
Some historians estimate them as a third of the population,
others as one-half.

The Tory element in the colonies.—The great Loyalist stronghold was New York. There the moderate Tories had controlled
the situation for several years. They had favored the assembling
of the First Continental Congress, but when that body adopted
the Association, they opposed it. After the battle of Lexington
the Whigs grew in power and succeeded in setting up a provincial congress. But several counties remained Loyalist, and
until the occupation of New York City by British troops a
state of civil war existed in the province. After that event the
British lines furnished a refuge for Tories from all the colonies.

Next to New York Pennsylvania contained the largest Tory
element. There the Quakers, the proprietary interests, and a
large German population combined to oppose the Whig movement. In New Jersey, Maryland, and Delaware, the Tory element was so numerous that only with the greatest difficulty did
the Whigs obtain the support of those colonies for independence.
In New England the Loyalists were not powerful. In Massachusetts, New Hampshire, and Rhode Island they formed an

insignificant part of the population, but in the region which afterward became the state of Vermont and in Connecticut they were numerous enough to be a menace.

In the South, Virginia was dominated by the Whigs. The impolitic acts of Lord Dunmore had alienated all but a small element of the population. The Scotch merchants of Norfolk and many planters had supported the governor, but his reprisals on the coast, his proclamation offering freedom to negroes and indented servants who would enlist, and the burning of Norfolk destroyed the Tory power in the province. North Carolina which had recently been torn by the War of the Regulators was probably about equally divided, and in South Carolina and Georgia the farmers and cattlemen of the interior were usually Loyalists; but the British naval demonstrations and the defeat of Tory bands did much to win converts to the Whig cause in the three southern colonies.

A classification of the Loyalists.—The Loyalists, or Tories as they were called in derision, have been classified by Professor Van Tyne as the office holders whose incomes depended upon the existing régime; those whose friends were among the official class or who depended upon that class for preferment; the majority of the Anglican clergy; the conservative people of all classes, especially the wealthy merchants, the aristocracy of culture, of dignified professions and callings, and of hereditary wealth, and those who held office by virtue of wise selection; the king worshipers who were moved by theory of government rather than by concrete facts; the legality Tories who believed that parliament had a constitutional right to tax the colonies; the religious Tories whose dictum was fear God and honor the king; and the factional Tories who were influenced by family feuds and political animosities.

The religious division.—The religious factor was one of the most important causes of division. An Anglican bishopric for the colonies had long been contemplated and the dissenting churches believed that the ministry was about to urge its establishment. In New England where the Congregational church was in the ascendency and in those sections where the Presbyterians and Baptists were powerful, the establishment of an episcopate was especially feared. Already the Anglican church numbered three hundred parishes in America. Throughout the colonies it was the church of the official class and in the South it was the church of the aristocracy. The southern Episcopalians were divided on the paramount political questions, but in New York the religious and political parties coincided. New York politics for many years had been factional, the De Lanceys who were Episcopalians being leaders in invariable opposition to the Livingstons who were Presbyterians. Both in New York and Connecticut those of the Episcopal faith were almost invariably Loyalists.

The Tory argument.—The Tories believed in no taxation without representation, but they differed with the Whigs in their interpretation of the word representation. The Tories accepted the English meaning which was based upon the idea that a man enjoyed representation not by the fact that he had voted for a member of parliament but by his belonging to one of the three great estates of the nation, each estate being represented in parliament. They admitted that this was an imperfect type of representation, but it was the ancient constitutional type. They believed that the relationship of the colonies to the mother country should be defined more clearly, but they did not believe that the Whigs had a right to demand a fundamental change in the constitution of the British Empire.

Moses Coit Tyler has pointed out that the other Tory arguments were based upon questions of expediency. (1) Was it expedient to reject the taxing power of parliament? (2) Was separation from the empire expedient? The Whigs argued that parliamentary taxes might become confiscatory. The Tories replied that parliament recognized the principle that all parts of the empire should be taxed equitably and justly, and that a powerful minority, which counted among its members Fox and Burke, were bent upon protecting the colonies. The Tories could see no reason for separation. They pointed out that until the beginning of 1776 the Whigs had consistently disavowed the idea of independence. Why then this sudden change? The Tories believed that concessions were about to be made which would make separation unnecessary and undesirable.

Persecution of the Loyalists.—After Lexington the Loyalists became intolerable to the Whigs. They must show their alle giance to the patriot cause or suffer the consequences. The favorite method of persecution was tarring and feathering, but riding the Tory on the liberty pole or ducking occurred frequently. Under the direction of the revolutionary committees freedom of speech was suppressed and the liberty of the press was destroyed. Any one who opposed the Association was considered an enemy; he must agree or be persecuted. When the Loyalists attempted to form counter associations, they were met with stern methods of repression. Whig clergymen held conferences in Loyalist communities to try to convert them, and obdurate places were visited by armed bands. When the Tories attempted to arm, their leaders were seized.

Congress attempts to control the Loyalists.—The Loyalists were lacking in organization, and when the governors were driven from the colonies, they lost their natural leaders. When calls for aid came from the deposed officials, many Tories formed bands and attempted to coöperate with the British forces. So serious was the situation that Congress, as early as October, 1775, recommended to the revolutionary governments that they arrest every person who might endanger the colonies or "the liberties of America." On December 30 a congressional committee reported that the Tories of Tryon County, New York, had collected arms and munitions, and that several Loyalists had enlisted in British service. Orders were issued to General Schuyler to seize the stores, disarm the Tories, and apprehend their leaders.

Congress extends the olive branch.—Congress hoped to win over a large part of the Loyalists and on January 2, 1776, it passed a pacific resolution which stated that as certain honest, well-meaning, but uniformed people had been deceived by ministerial agents, it recommended to the various committees and friends of American liberty to treat such persons with kindness and attention, to view their errors as proceeding from want of information, to explain to them the true nature of the controversy, and to try to convince them of the justice of the American cause. The colonial governments were instructed to frustrate the machinations of enemies and restrain wicked practices. It was the opinion of Congress that the more dangerous ones should be placed in custody, and to accomplish this the local authorities were given the right to call to their aid the con-tinental troops.

The Queen's County Tories.—Immediately afterward Congress learned that the Tories of Queen's County, New York, were especially troublesome. Congress accordingly decided that they should be put outside of the protection of the United Colonies, that all trade and intercourse with them should cease, and that none of them should be allowed to travel or reside outside of that county without a certificate from the revolutionary government of New York. Violators of this provision were to be imprisoned for three months and lawyers were forbidden to try causes for them. Troops were sent into the county.

Disarming of the Loyalists.—A congressional committee which had under consideration the defence of New York, on March 14 advised the disarming of the Loyalists on Staten Island. Congress immediately ordered that eight thousand men be sent to the defence of New York and recommendation was made to all the colonies to disarm all persons "notoriously disaffected to the cause of America," or who refused to associate to defend, by arms, the United Colonies. The confiscated arms were to be used in arming troops.

THE DECLARATION OF INDEPENDENCE

The colonies advised to form temporary governments.—Up to the beginning of 1776 the Whigs disavowed the purpose or desire for independence. But in spite of the view of the conservatives, Congress had been forced to assume the direction of the war and had been called upon to advise several of the colonies regarding the course to be pursued in organizing their governments. In answer to an inquiry from Massachusetts, Congress replied that no obedience was due to the parliamentary act altering the charter, and that the governor and lieutenant-governor were to be considered absent and the offices vacant. As there was no council, the provincial convention was advised to write letters to the inhabitants of the places which were entitled to representation in the assembly, requesting them to choose representatives; and when the assembly was chosen, it was to elect councillors, "which assembly and council should exercise the powers of Government, until a Governor, of his Majesty's appointment, will consent to govern the colony according to its charter." New Hampshire was advised to call a full and free representation of the people who might establish such a form of temporary government as would "produce the happiness of the people and most effectually secure peace and good order in the province" during the dispute with Great Britain. Similar advice was given to South Carolina and Virginia.

Paine's " Common Sense."—The attitude of the British government, the events on the Canadian frontier and about Boston, and the burning of Falmouth and Norfolk, fanned the flames of rebellion to a white heat. When Tom Paine issued his pamphlet *Common Sense,* "the first open and unqualified argument in championship of the doctrine of American Independence," he found a receptive audience. The pamphlet held up to scorn the idea of kingship, argued that the security and happiness of the British people were due to their character and not to their constitution, asserted that the British colonial system was based upon English self-interest, and that only injuries and disadvantages would result from continued allegiance to Great Britain. Reconciliation, Paine argued, would result in the ruin of America, because England, ruled by self-interest, would still be the governing power, because any arrangement which might be obtained would be a temporary expedient, and because nothing but independence would keep the peace of the American continent. From every point of view, independence, he declared, was necessary. "The period of debate is closed. Arms, as the last resort, must decide the contest. . . . By referring the matter from argument to arms, a new era for politics is struck; a new method of thinking hath arisen. All plans, proposals, and so forth, prior to the nineteenth of April . . . are like the almanacs of last year." The pamphlet met with immediate success. It was read throughout the colonies and convinced thousands that independence was necessary.

The independence movement in the three southern colonies.— Early in 1776 three southern colonies took definite steps toward independence. In February a small revolutionary group in Savannah instructed delegates to agree to any measure for the general good which might be adopted by Congress. In March South Carolina gave similar instructions, and on April 12 the provincial congress of North Carolina instructed its delegates to concur with representatives from other colonies in declaring independence. In spite of the action of South Carolina, the colony was probably unconvinced of the necessity of separation from Great Britain until the Charleston hostilities.

Congress advises the colonies to suppress the authority of Great Britain.—On May 10 Congress recommended to the various assemblies and conventions that where no sufficient government had been established, such governments as would best conduce to the happiness and safety of the people and of America in general should be established. Five days later Congress adopted a preamble to this resolution which contained the significant statement that the exercise of every kind of authority under the British crown should be suppressed and all the powers of government exerted under the authority of the people of the colonies.

The German mercenaries.—On May 21 Congress received copies of the treaties which Great Britain had made with the Duke of Brunswick, the Landgrave of Hesse-Cassel, and the Count of Anhalt-Zerbst, by which they agreed to furnish about seventeen thousand troops to be used against the rebellious colonies. These treaties were immediately published and were a potent force in bringing some of the wavering colonies to instruct their delegates for independence.

Lee's Resolution.—In Virginia a convention was called to form a new government, and on May 15 the Virginia delegates in Congress were instructed to propose independence. Accordingly on June 7 Richard Henry Lee moved in Congress "That these United Colonies are, and of right ought to be, free and independent States, that they are absolved from all allegiance to the British Crown, and that all political connection between them and the State of Great Britain is, and ought to be, totally dissolved. That it is expedient forthwith to take the most effectual measures for forming foreign alliances. That a plan of confederation be prepared and transmitted to the respective Colonies for their consideration and approbation."

The debate on the resolution.—A declaration of independence at that time was opposed by James Wilson, Robert R. Livingston, John Dickinson, Edward Rutledge, and others. They declared that they were friends of the measure but thought that it should be postponed until the people demanded it. The middle colonies, they thought, "were not yet ripe for bidding adieu to British connection, but . . . were fast ripening." They argued that a declaration which was not unanimous would cause foreign powers either to refuse to make alliances with the colonies or to insist upon hard terms. It was believed that a successful termination of the New York campaign would make alliances possible on excellent terms.

John Adams, Lee, Wythe, and others argued for an immediate declaration. They saw no reason for waiting for every colony to express itself. They argued that a declaration of independence alone could bring about desired alliances. Without it the colonies would never know whether or not aid could be obtained from France or Spain. It was pointed out that the New York campaign might not be successful and that an alliance ought to be made while affairs bore a hopeful aspect. If an alliance were made at once with France, she might assist in cutting off British supplies and might divert enemy forces by an attack on the British West Indies. It was also pointed out that an immediate alliance would assist the people, who were in need of clothing and money.

Committees appointed.—It was decided to get the consent of the colonies before issuing the declaration, but a committee composed of Thomas Jefferson, John Adams, Benjamin Franklin, Roger Sherman, and Robert R. Livingston was appointed to prepare the document. Congress also decided to appoint committees to formulate a plan of confederation and to draft a form of treaties.

New England takes formal action.—The New England colonies had favored independence for some time. They now took formal action. In May Rhode Island instructed its delegates to agree to any acts which would hold the colonies together. In June Massachusetts, Connecticut, and New Hampshire instructed their delegates to support Lee's resolution.

The independence movement in the middle colonies.—The middle colonies still stood out and Congress made great efforts to induce them to give their support. After a hard struggle with Governor William Franklin, on June 22 the provincial congress of New Jersey authorized its delegates to agree to independence. Pennsylvania had been held back by the Quakers, Germans, and proprietary interests. When the conservative assembly refused to sanction independence, a vast crowd assembled in Philadelphia and voiced its displeasure. The Loyalists were terrorized and a patriot convention was formed which agreed to favor independence. Delaware formed a new government but failed to instruct its delegates regarding independence. In Maryland the provisional government induced Governor Eden to leave the colony and a special convention called by the council of safety gave the delegates the desired instructions. New York failed to express itself in favor of the great measure.

The Declaration of Independence.—On July 1 Lee's motion was debated in Congress, John Adams speaking for an immediate declaration of independence and Dickinson for delay. When the debate closed, nine states voted in the affirmative. Pennsylvania and South Carolina opposed immediate action; the Delaware vote was a tie, and the New York delegates were excused from voting. The final vote was postponed until the next day. The arrival of Rodney of Delaware gave the vote of that state for the Declaration. Dickinson and Morris did not appear and the other delegates from Pennsylvania voted in the affirmative. The South Carolina delegates, influenced by news that a great British fleet was off New York, took matters in their own hands and voted for independence. New York alone stood out.

The congressional committee had entrusted the preparation of the Declaration to Thomas Jefferson. After it had undergone the fire of criticism, on the evening of July 4 the document was approved by twelve states. On the following day copies signed by President Hancock and Secretary Thomson were sent to the various assemblies. The other signatures were added later. Although the New York delegates had not voted for the Declaration, on July 9 the New York provincial congress approved it, completing the long chain of states which stretched along the Atlantic seaboard from Nova Scotia to East Florida.

Contents of the Declaration.—This immortal document begins by setting forth certain "self-evident truths" concerning the rights of mankind and the nature of government. Then follow in nearly thirty paragraphs a list of charges against King George III, and a review of the efforts of the colonies to obtain redress. The last paragraph declares, in the resounding words of Lee's Resolution, "That these United Colonies are, and of right ought to be Free and Independent States; that they are absolved from all allegiance to the British Crown, and that all political connection between them and the State of Great Britain, is and ought to be totally dissolved." A new nation had been born.

READINGS

MILITARY EVENTS AND THE CONTINENTAL CONGRESS

Bolton, C. K., *The Private Soldier under Washington;* Channing, Edward, *History of the United States,* III, 155–206; Fiske, John, *The American Revolution,* I, 100–197; Greene, F. V., *The Revolutionary War,* 1–27; *Journals of the Continental Congress* (Worthington C. Ford, ed.), II–VI; Lecky, W. E. H., *History of England in the Eighteenth Century,* III, 461–500; Smith, J. H., *Our Struggle for the Fourteenth Colony,* I, 107–165; Trevelyan, G. O., *The American Revolution,* I, 254–390; Van Tyne, C. H., *The American Revolution,* 24–49; Winsor, Justin, *Narrative and Critical History,* VI, 1–274; Adams, C. F., *Studies Military and Diplomatic, 1775–1865,* pp. 1–21.

THE LOYALISTS

Flick, A. C., *Loyalism in New York* (Columbia University, *Studies in History,* etc., XIV, No. 1.); Tyler, M. C., "The Party of the Loyalists in the American Revolution," in *The American Historical Review,* I, 24–45; Van Tyne, C. H., *The Loyalists in the American Revolution;* Wallace, S., *The United Empire Loyalists.*

THE DECLARATION OF INDEPENDENCE

Friedenwald, H., *The Declaration of Independence;* Hazelton, J. H., *The Declaration of Independence;* Trevelyan, G. O., *The American Revolution,* II, 133–171; Van Tyne, C. H., *The American Revolution,* 50–101; Becker, C. L., *The Eve of the Revolution,* 200–256.

CHAPTER XXV

THE STRUGGLE FOR THE MIDDLE STATES

THE CONTEST FOR NEW YORK

Preparations to defend New York.—After the evacuation of Boston it was realized that New York would be a probable point of attack and great exertions were made to put it in a state of defence. Washington arrived on April 13, 1776; his troops, delayed by bad roads, came straggling in, and new levies began to arrive, the army being gradually augmented until it numbered about twenty thousand men. But the effective fighting force was several thousand less, for disease was ever present. Furthermore the raw recruits were poorly trained and equipped, and there were not enough artillerymen to man the batteries. The only cavalrymen who appeared were a small force from Connecticut and these, for reasons best known to himself, Washington did not retain in service. The defences were strengthened by works at Paulus Hook on the Jersey shore, and others on Governor's Island and at Red Hook on Long Island. Eleven redoubts were erected on Manhattan Island along the battery and up to a point opposite Hell Gate, and the hamlet of Brooklyn was fortified with seven redoubts. Obstructions were placed in the Hudson and a second line of defence was established at Forts Washington and Lee. Many historians point out that New York should have been abandoned, for Washington's army was too small to cope with the British, the Tories were certain to keep the enemy informed of the movements, the defences were not powerful enough to control the water approaches, and an active enemy could run by the defenses and land troops in the rear of the American army. To make the situation worse, the line of hills on Long Island, known as Brooklyn Heights, commanded New York. To occupy them it was necessary to divide the army, and in case of defeat, the defenders would be separated by a difficult channel from the main army on Manhattan Island.

As Trevelyan observes, Washington "placed, and kept, his troops in a position where they were certain to be defeated, and where, when defeated, they would most probably be surrounded and destroyed."

The British plan.—The British government hoped to anni-hilate the armies and cut off New England from the other col-onies. By occupying New York and sending converging armies, one from the north, the other up the Hudson, the government believed that it could accomplish its purpose. Large reinforce-ments were sent to Quebec, and during July and August, 1776, British forces were concentrated on Staten Island and a great fleet assembled. The first forces to arrive at New York were those under General Howe which he brought from Halifax. Large reinforcements under Admiral Lord Howe and forces under Clinton and Cornwallis augmented the army until it numbered about thirty thousand men.

An attempt at conciliation.—Lord Howe hoped that peace could be made, and soon after his arrival, he addressed a letter to "George Washington, Esquire," but the epistle, which failed to recognize the position of the commander-in-chief, was returned. A personal envoy from Lord Howe also met with a rebuff. The British admiral had prepared a circular letter to several of the royal governors setting forth his authority as commissioner and stating the conciliatory terms sanctioned by the cabinet. These contained a mere promise of pardon to those who returned to allegiance and assisted in the restoration of tranquillity. In fact John Adams was marked out for a halter, but this was not divulged. The letters fell into the hands of Congress which ordered that they be published "that the good people of these United States may be informed of what nature are the com-missioners, and what the terms, with the expectation of which, the insidious court of Britain has endeavoured to amuse and disarm them. . . ."

Battle of Long Island.—General Howe finally decided to attack the American position on Long Island. On the twenty-second and twenty-third of August twenty thousand troops and forty cannon were disembarked at Gravesend Bay, six or seven miles south of Brooklyn, but not until the evening of the twenty-sixth did the British advance. Washington had been misin-

formed as to the size of the landing force and had stationed only
nine thousand men on Long Island. These were under General
Nathanael Greene, but stricken by illness, he was forced to
retire from the command on August 23, and Sullivan who succeeded him was superseded by Putnam on the twenty-fifth.
Washington spent the twenty-sixth on the island and super-
intended the disposition of the forces.

The chief line of defence was the densely wooded Brooklyn
Heights which were crossed by several roads. One ran up from
Gravesend near the coast; four miles to the eastward two wagon
roads from Flatbush penetrated the heights; three miles farther
east a highway ran from the village of Jamaica. About five
thousand men were sent to defend the Gravesend and Flatbush
roads but Jamaica Pass was neglected. The British frontal
attacks met with stubborn resistance from the forces of Stirling and Sullivan, but their valor was useless for a large British
force pushed along the Jamaica road and got in the rear of the
American positions. A portion of the army succeeded in getting
back to the Brooklyn intrenchments, but Sullivan and Stirling
with about eleven hundred men were captured and several hundred were killed.

The withdrawal from Brooklyn.—Howe, who remembered
the disastrous frontal attack at Bunker Hill, decided not to
attack the Brooklyn defences until supported by the fleet, which
was held back by an adverse wind. His caution saved the
American army. Washington saw that Brooklyn was untenable
and he secretly planned to evacuate it. A brave show of force
was made by bringing over three regiments and by keeping up a
fusillade while water craft were being collected. Favored by a
subsidence of the storm and by a fog, during the night of the
twenty-ninth the entire army was successfully withdrawn.

Harlem.—After the battle of Long Island the British commissioners made overtures to Congress and a committee composed of Franklin, Edward Rutledge, and John Adams went to
Staten Island for a conference, but it failed completely. There
was nothing to do but to fight it out. That Manhattan Island
should have been abandoned immediately after the defeat at
Brooklyn Heights has been maintained by strategists, but Congress hesitated to evacuate New York City and Washington

does not appear to have insisted upon a withdrawal. As Tre-velyan observes, "It is equally difficult to explain satisfactorily why Howe was so long about landing . . . , and why Washington was so slow in evacuating the city." On September 10 Hancock informed Washington that Congress did not desire to have him hold the city longer than he thought proper. Washington immediately acted. The removal of stores was hastened and most of the troops were withdrawn to Harlem Heights about halfway up the island, but Putnam was left in the city with some infantry and artillery, and five brigades were posted at points along the eastern shore. Not until September 13 did the British begin the movement for the occupation of Manhattan Island. On that day and the next several war vessels moved up into the East River and at eleven o'clock on the morning of the fifteenth British forces landed at Kip's Bay. There the American troops disgraced themselves by slight resistance followed by a confused flight. Howe neglected to follow up his initial success; had he done so he could have cut off the garrison of New York, but his procrastination allowed Putnam's force to rejoin the main army. Not until four in the afternoon did the British commence "a stately progress northward" and not until the next morning did they attack the American position. This time Washington's troops behaved well and the British were checked.

White Plains.—For four weeks the British army remained in front of the American position at Harlem. Howe finally decided upon his plan of campaign; leaving a force to protect New York City, on October 12 he moved his main army to the Westchester Peninsula with the object of getting on the flank and rear of the American army, and cutting off its supplies from the east; war ships were sent up the Hudson to cut off a retreat into New Jersey. After his landing on the peninsula Howe's movements were very slow and it was not until October 25 that he took up a position a few miles south of White Plains. The dilatory movement had given Washington the opportunity of moving his army to the mainland, and when Howe finally arrived near White Plains, he found the American army blocking his advance.   .

The British commander had just been heavily reinforced and his overwhelming army should have made short work of Wash-

ington's forces, but again Howe failed to win a decisive victory.
On October 28 he ordered a general engagement and the first

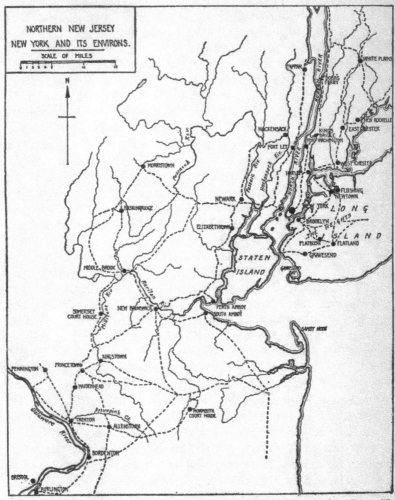

(Based on map in G. O. Trevelyan, *The American Revolution*, Part II,
Vol. I, at end)

assault drove in the American outposts. A mile to the west
of the main position was Chatterton's Hill which was held by
fourteen hundred men. Against this hill Howe sent eight regi-

ments. Five which advanced for a frontal attack were checked
and the defenders only retired when outflanked by the other
three. A general engagement did not develop and on October
31 Washington retired to a line of heights somewhat back of
his former position.

The withdrawal from Quebec.—While Washington's army
rested at White Plains, heartening news came from the north;
and especially good news it was, for during the summer the
reports from the Canadian border had been filled with stories
of defeat and distress. Congress had made great efforts to
reinforce the army before Quebec, but on May 1 when General
Thomas arrived to take command, he had found less than two
thousand men assembled and half of them were in the hospitals.
Within a week the first British reinforcements arrived and Carleton took the offensive. Thomas was forced to fall back to Sorel
and the Americans were driven from their camp near Montreal.

The army falls back to Crown Point.—On June 5 General
John Sullivan arrived at Sorel with three thousand troops. As
Thomas had died of the smallpox Sullivan took command. He
determined to attack Three Rivers but the surprise failed and
his troops were routed. On June 14 an English fleet carrying
Carleton's army came up the river. Sullivan immediately broke
up his camp and retired to Crown Point, where for the time
being he was out of reach of the enemy, for Carleton's vessels
were of too deep draft to navigate the Sorel River. But disease
proved to be more dangerous than the British, for smallpox and
dysentery carried off the men by hundreds.

Ticonderoga becomes the base.—General Philip Schuyler was
in command of the northern department with headquarters at
Albany and General Horatio Gates was now in charge at Crown
Point. In July Gates withdrew most of the depleted force to
Ticonderoga. Large numbers of troops were sent north so that
by August the garrison numbered thirty-five hundred. Arnold
equipped a fleet of small vessels which he hoped would delay
if it would not check the British advance.

Valcour Island.—During the summer Carleton's shipyard at
St. Johns was busy building the fleet which would give him
control of Lake Champlain. On October 4 Carleton advanced
with an army of twelve thousand men. Arnold started with

his fleet manned by only five hundred men to harass the advance. He ran into the narrow channel between Valcour Island and the western shore and there on October 11 encountered the light advance craft of the British fleet. For five hours he held his own. During the night he withdrew his shattered boats to an island twelve miles to the south where he attempted to repair the damage. On October 13 when the fog lifted, it disclosed the British fleet. Arnold immediately sent off his best vessels and with his crippled ships stayed to fight. One vessel struck its colors but Arnold ran his flag ship and four gondolas into a creek and burned them. He then hastened to Ticonderoga where he displayed tremendous energy in strengthening the fortifications. The spirited fight on the lake, the strength of the American position, and the lateness of the season convinced Carleton that it was useless to continue the operations. On November 3 he evacuated Crown Point and began the withdrawal to Canada. Washington was thus relieved from the danger of an enemy from the north.

Tactical movements.—Before he was aware of Carleton's withdrawal, Howe had determined to force Washington's army into the open. He sent a force of Hessians to occupy the northern end of Manhattan Island and on November 5 moved his main army to Dobb's Ferry on the Hudson, from which vantage point he could strike at Fort Washington, advance toward Albany, or threaten Philadelphia. Washington's position was endangered and the situation was made doubly precarious by the fact that his army was being depleted by desertions and by the termination of enlistments. To counteract the British movement he sent one corps to Hackensac in New Jersey, and Heath's division was stationed at Peekskill to protect the Hudson. Charles Lee was left at White Plains with about seven thousand men subject to future orders.

Forts Washington and Lee.—The British moved next against Forts Washington and Lee, which, garrisoned by about five thousand men, were under the supervision of General Greene. They ought to have been abandoned, but Washington unfortunately left the decision to his subordinate who believed that they could be held. On November 16 overwhelming forces advanced against Fort Washington which was obliged to surrender. Cornwallis secretly sent six thousand troops across the Hudson and on November 20 advanced against Fort Lee. He all but surprised it and Greene, with the greatest difficulty, succeeded only in saving the garrison.

THE NEW JERSEY CAMPAIGN

Retreat to the Raritan.—The fall of the forts had added greatly to the difficulty of the situation, for Washington's army was in danger of being enveloped. To avert disaster he determined to retreat into New Jersey. He accordingly crossed the Passaic and moved to Newark. The forces under Lee were ordered to join the retreating army, but that vain and conceited officer, who had visions of becoming commander-in-chief as soon as Washington was eliminated, refused to obey orders. On November 28 Washington marched out of Newark and as his rear guard left the town the advanced guard of the British entered it. The American army pushed on to New Brunswick where it found a temporary haven behind the Raritan. On December 1 Cornwallis's troops reached the river, but there he was halted by an order from Howe not to advance until he arrived with reinforcements.

Expedition against Rhode Island.—A week later Howe came up with a single brigade. Instead of concentrating his troops to crush the remnant of Washington's army, the British commander decided to send two divisions to conquer Rhode Island. They easily occupied the island but it was a fruitless venture for "several thousand Royal troops were thenceforward locked up in a sea-girt strip of land no larger than the estate of many an English Lord-Lieutenant."

Retreat across the Delaware.—Washington's army was constantly reduced by desertion and sickness, and the New Jersey people failed to rally to his assistance. It has been estimated that not a hundred men enlisted during the retreat across the state. The people of New Jersey paid dearly for their indifference, for during the winter they were constantly subjected to indignities from the Hessians who were billeted upon them. Among the atrocious acts was the pillaging of Princeton College. Taking advantage of British inactivity, Washington prepared to retire beyond the Delaware, from New Brunswick having ordered the collection of boats for many miles along the river front.   Covering his retreat with fourteen hundred of his best troops under Stirling, the army and stores were landed on the Pennsylvania shore.   When the British troops arrived on the eastern bank, they were forced to halt, for not a boat was available and the short-sighted Howe had failed to provide his army with pontoons.

To the British commander the campaign was over and he prepared to go into winter quarters, fancying that the rebellion was practically crushed and that the spring campaign would be a mere parade.   The Whig cause appeared to be lost and gloomy forebodings and grumblings of discontent took the place of declamation and heroics.   On December 10 Congress resolved to defend Philadelphia but two days later it adjourned and hied away to Baltimore.   Washington's lack of authority had frequently hampered his military operations, but this difficulty was now removed, for before adjournment Congress resolved, that until otherwise ordered, Washington was to have full power to direct operations.

Washington's army reinforced.—The dispirited army which crossed the Delaware was soon strongly reinforced.   After many days of inaction, General Lee had left his camp at White Plains with the intention, as he grandiloquently put it, of reconquering New Jersey.   After the retreat of Carleton, Schuyler had sent seven battalions under Sullivan to assist Washington, but Lee succeeded in getting control of four of them.   On December 13 he was captured at a tavern at Baskingridge.   As soon as Sullivan heard of it, he started the troops for the Delaware and on the twentieth of December joined Washington.   Four other battalions from Schuyler's army arrived shortly afterward and General Mifflin brought in a goodly body of Pennsylvania militia. Before Christmas the army numbered eight thousand.

Position of the Hessians.—To the east of the Delaware was a Hessian division under Colonel Von Donop, Colonel Rall being stationed at Trenton with three regiments.   Rall had taken no measures to strengthen a naturally weak position; highways converged to the north of the village and artillery stationed at the junction could sweep the streets.   Scouting parties and spies informed Washington that Rall's troops were scattered through the town and that the place was practically without defences.

Trenton.—Washington determined to strike. With the greatest secrecy he perfected his plans. One body of troops under Cadwalader was to attack Von Donop's position at Bordentown and Ewing with a thousand men was to strike at troops stationed on Assumpink Creek, while Washington with Greene and Sullivan in command of twenty-four hundred men and eighteen cannon were to advance against Trenton from the north. During a furious tempest on Christmas night Washington succeeded in crossing the Delaware, but Ewing failed to get over and Cadwalader crossed too late to coöperate. At four in the morning Washington's troops began the weary march toward Trenton. While the valiant army was toiling over the frozen roads, the Hessians were sleeping off the effects of their Christmas wassail. At 8:15 the American forces drove in the Hessian outposts. Aroused from his bed Rall tried to make a stand, but the streets were raked with round shot and the sharpshooters fired relentlessly into the huddled Hessians, several hundred of whom fled across the Assumpink Creek bridge and escaped to Bordentown. Rall tried to rally his men but fell mortally wounded. When Sullivan cut off the retreat to the south and Greene ordered up his reserves, resistance ended. Nine hundred prisoners, a thousand muskets, six field pieces, and a large quantity of stores fell into the hands of the successful commander. But not in terms of men and guns should the battle of Trenton be judged. Its importance lies in the fact that Washington had won a clean cut victory when the Whig cause was tottering and by that victory had raised the drooping spirits of a despairing nation.

Movements of the armies.—When the news of Trenton reached New York, it roused the British from their fancied security. Lord Cornwallis at the head of eight thousand men proceeded by forced marches toward the west. Washington had determined to hold a position east of the Delaware, and on December 30 he again crossed the river and by January 2, 1777, had assembled five thousand men and forty pieces of artillery just below Trenton. As Cornwallis approached the American position, he realized the costliness of a frontal attack, and decided that as soon as his forces assembled he would attempt a flanking movement from Allentown.

Princeton, January 3, 1777.—Washington saw the danger and decided on a daring plan. On the night of January 2 all was activity in the American camp. Sentinels challenged, infantry moved about in the light of the camp fires, and the sound of pick and shovel was plainly audible to the British. But in the darkness to the rear another kind of activity was in progress. Cannon, stores, and baggage were being silently moved to Bordentown and Burlington, and at one in the morning the bulk of the army began a stealthy march which at daybreak brought them out within a mile and a half of Princeton. Three of Cornwallis's regiments had remained there during the night and were now under way. Suddenly the first of these troops under Colonel Mawhood found themselves confronted by the American advance guard. The British charged bravely, scoring an initial success, but Washington's presence in front of his lines steadied the troops and they soon forced a retreat. Sullivan then led the advance against the two remaining regiments, which were driven through and beyond Princeton, leaving three hundred prisoners in Washington's hands. The roar of the guns brought the unwelcome tidings to Cornwallis that the American army had escaped, had cut across his rear, and had defeated three of his crack regiments.

Morristown.—Five miles beyond Princeton Washington turned to the north and soon established his army in a powerful position at Morristown where they remained in security the rest of the winter. Howe made no attempt to dislodge his opponent, but concentrated ten thousand troops in camps at New Brunswick and Perth Amboy. The Jersey people had been cured of their Toryism; supplies poured into the American camp, while the British experienced the greatest difficulty in securing fuel and food, and by March 1 were reduced to a ration of salt provisions and "ammunition bread." When Washington reached Morristown he had about four thousand men and during the winter his army did not increase, but he made the most of the opportunity to drill his men and perfect his organization. Throughout the country men were drilling for the spring campaign, powder mills were being built, and lead mines were being opened. The greatest shortage was in muskets, but fortunately these were obtained from France.

Middlebrook.—In May, 1777, everything was in readiness and Washington led his army to a powerful position at Middlebrook, only a few miles from the British camp at New Brunswick. On June 13 Howe transferred large forces to the southern bank of the Raritan, but he failed to draw Washington from his point of vantage and on the nineteenth he began the withdrawal of his army to Staten Island, having had the satisfaction only of a rear guard action with Stirling's division.

THE STRUGGLE WITH BURGOYNE

British plans for 1777.—Howe's plan for the campaign of 1777 called for fifteen thousand more troops. With this addition he believed that he could crush Washington and conquer Pennsylvania, New Jersey, and New York. The subjugation of the southern colonies would then be attempted, followed by operations in New England. But Lord Germaine thought otherwise. Ignoring the general in the field, he planned to send a force under St. Leger down the Mohawk Valley, a second army under Burgoyne to penetrate New York by the Lake Champlain route, while Howe was to proceed up the Hudson Valley. The three armies were to meet at Albany. The plan looked good on paper, but it failed to take into account the long distances to be traversed and the difficulties of transportation on the frontier. When Germaine planned the campaign, he should have sent precise orders to Howe, but this he failed to do, and on May 18 he even wrote acquiescing in the proposed expedition against Philadelphia and expressing the hope that the business might be concluded in season so that Howe could coöperate with Burgoyne.

Ticonderoga and Ft. Independence.—On June 15, 1777, General Schuyler learned that Burgoyne's army was in motion and that St. Leger was concentrating forces on the upper Mohawk. The American army was in a sorry plight for smallpox and dysentery were still the bane of the northern department. Congress had done much to destroy efficiency by temporarily removing Schuyler. At a time when all should have been working in harmony, Gates was intriguing with members of Congress to overthrow his superior. The advance part of the army was at Ticonderoga. Across the narrow bay Fort Independence had been erected and a bridge connected the fortifications, which were commanded by General St. Clair who had only twenty-five hundred men to man works which demanded ten thousand defenders.

Burgoyne captures the forts.—Late in June Burgoyne's flotilla carrying about eight thousand soldiers reached Crown Point.

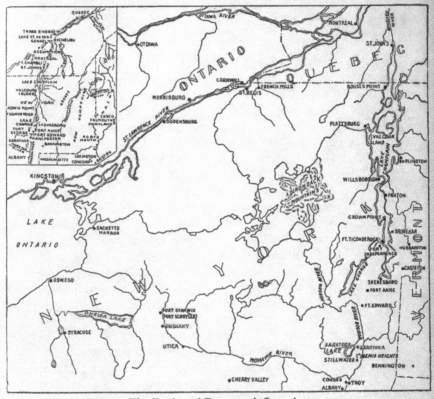

The Region of Burgoyne's Invasion
(The large map is based on E. G. Foster's *Historical Chart;* the inset is from Trevelyan, *The American Revolution*, Part II, Vol. I)

His engineers soon discovered the fundamental weaknesses of the American position. Mt. Hope dominated the passage to Lake George and Sugar Hill towered above the forts. On July 2 the former position was occupied by the British and on July 5 St. Clair saw Sugar Hill bristling with cannon. He realized that the forts were untenable and on the night of July 6 he loaded his stores and light artillery on barges and sent them under convoy to Skenesborough. The main body of troops under St. Clair attempted to reach the same place by a circuitous route which led through Hubbardtown.

The disastrous retreat.—Burgoyne's vessels broke through the impediments and pursued the American flotilla. They encountered it at anchor in South Bay and short work they made of it. The Americans destroyed the stores and buildings on the shore before they retreated. General Fraser had been sent in pursuit of St. Clair's forces and at Hubbardtown he fell in with the American rear guard and defeated it. St. Clair succeeded in getting his troops to Ft. Edward where he joined Schuyler. Only three thousand men barred the way to Albany.

The withdrawal to Stillwater.—Schuyler sent out calls for help to New England, to New York, and to Washington. While waiting for reinforcements he destroyed the standing crops, drove off the stock, and broke up the roads. Having despoiled the country, he abandoned Fort Edward and withdrew to Stillwater on the west bank of the Hudson. It was not long before reinforcements began pouring in. Although his army was inferior to that of Howe, Washington sent on Morgan's riflemen and he ordered Putnam to send two brigades. General Lincoln was sent to organize the New England militia and Benedict Arnold was called from Connecticut to help Schuyler.

Bennington.—Burgoyne reached the head of Lake Champlain on July 10, but from that point his progress was exceedingly slow, the twenty miles to Ft. Edwards being traversed in as many days. Schuyler's work of devastation had been complete and the British commissariat suffered accordingly. To replenish his depleted stores, Burgoyne embarked upon a rash enterprise. At Bennington large quantities of stores had been collected and a Tory named Philip Skene suggested that they would be an easy prize. Burgoyne followed Skene's advice and sent Colonel Baum with five or six hundred troops to make the capture. Near Bennington John Stark was in command of two brigades of New England troops and at Manchester were the remnants of regiments which had retreated from Hubbardtown. On August 15 Baum came in touch with Stark's forces, but he hesitated to attack and proceeded to intrench. The New England troops gradually encircled the position, and when they attacked on the afternoooon of the sixteenth, they killed, wounded, or captured nearly the entire force. While the Americans were engaged in plundering the camp, they were suddenly attacked by another force of six hundred under Breymann, sent by Burgoyne at Baum's request. Things were going badly for Stark's men when Seth Warner with forces from Manchester arrived. After a sharp contest Breymann's troops were driven from the field with a loss of a third of the rank and file. The day's fighting had deprived the invaders of a considerable force which they could not afford to lose in the face of an army which was increasing daily.

Oriskany.—While Burgoyne was advancing, St. Leger was invading the Mohawk Valley. On August 3 his army of British regulars, Hessians, Canadians, Tories, and Indians invested Ft. Stanwix. Colonel Herkimer gathered the Tryon County militia and went to the relief of the fort, but at Oriskany, which was only six miles from the fort, he was surprised. In the desperate battle the losses were higher in proportion to men engaged than in any other battle of the war. Herkimer was killed and so badly cut up were the militia that the expedition was unable to proceed.

Ft. Stanwix relieved.—Schuyler realized the danger of a flank attack from the Mohawk Valley. St. Leger must be checked. Schuyler called for a volunteer to lead a relief expedition. Arnold offered his services and at the head of eight hundred men advanced up the valley. As he proceeded his force was continually increased by recruits. As he approached Ft. Stanwix, Arnold succeeded in creating the impression that his army was of overwhelming numbers. The Senecas were the first to desert St. Leger and the Tories soon made off to the woods. Abandoned by his allies, St. Leger retreated, leaving behind stores, tents, and artillery. The battle of Bennington and the retirement from the Mohawk Valley sealed the fate of Burgoyne.

Gates supersedes Schuyler.—By the middle of August Schuyler had the satisfaction of being in command of a force which outnumbered Burgoyne's army. But on August 19 Horatio Gates arrived at Albany with a commission to take command. Gates was a man of little ability, but of an unscrupulous, intriguing,

and ambitious nature. He had spent many months at the seat
of government influencing members of Congress, a task made
easy by the fact that the New England delegates disliked Schuyler. With victory already assured, Gates came forward to reap
the honors. Burgoyne was in a sorry plight. His line of communication was in danger of being cut and his force had been
reduced to about six thousand effectives. In vain he looked for
despatches from Howe, but though he had sent ten messengers,
an ominous silence was his only answer. Two courses were
open to him; an ignominious retreat or an advance that at best
was but a forlorn hope. Fortunately for the American cause he
chose the latter.

First battle of Bemis's Heights, September 19.—On September 13 the British army crossed the Hudson on a bridge of boats
and encamped at Saratoga. Six miles to the south was a table
land called Bemis's Heights which the Americans had fortified.
Between the heights and the river stretched a pasture five hundred yards in width. It was a position easily defended provided
Gates extended his left wing. This he failed to do and Burgoyne,
quick to see the opportunity for a turning movement, disposed
his forces in such a manner that while Philips in command of the
British left and Burgoyne in the center engaged the American
army, General Fraser on the right could encircle the heights.
Arnold saw the danger and besought Gates to let him attack
the British right. Gates finally consented and Arnold immediately flung his men against Fraser's position. A confused fight
occurred in the tangled underbrush, and though Morgan's riflemen got out of hand, the effect of the attack was to stop Fraser's
advance. Having been reinforced, Arnold threw his troops
against the British center at Freeman's Farm. A very hot
engagement ensued and victory would probably have resulted
had Gates engaged Philips, but the American commander failed
to attack and the British left came to the assistance of the hard-
pressed center. At nightfall Arnold fell back a short distance,
but he had saved the American army and had inflicted such
great injury that Burgoyne was unable to continue the battle
the next day.

Clinton fails to coöperate.—The British commander fortified
his position and there his army remained inactive for more than

a fortnight. The situation was daily becoming more critical, for Lincoln had succeeded in cutting the line of communication with Canada. A belated despatch had reached Burgoyne informing him of Howe's expedition against Philadelphia. He also received information which led him to believe that Clinton expected to clear the Hudson and come to his relief. Early in October Clinton captured three forts on the lower Hudson, but instead of following up his success, he returned to New York and left the northern army to its fate.

Second battle of Bemis's Heights.—The situation in the American camp was far from harmonious. Gates had not mentioned Arnold's division in his official report of the recent battle. This slight was followed by studied insults and cowardly persecution. The protests of the regimental officers caused Arnold to postpone his resignation, but Gates deprived him of his command and elevated Lincoln. On October 7 Burgoyne again prepared to attack the American lines. His initial assault was repulsed and Fraser was mortally wounded. Soon after the fighting began Arnold put himself at the head of his old troops and broke the British center. The British right wing was also forced back, but Gates did nothing to follow up the advantage. Arnold seized the opportunity and assaulted Freeman's Farm. There he was repulsed but he turned his troops against a redoubt on the right and carried it by assault. The redoubtable general, however, was severely wounded, his thigh bone being shattered, but his generalship had won the battle which broke the British army.

Burgoyne's surrender.—The day after the battle Gates pushed forward his left wing, a movement which threatened to pen Burgoyne between the Hudson and a hostile army. The British commander should have sunk his heavy guns in the river and beaten a hasty retreat, but instead he attempted to save his stores and artillery. He fell back eight miles and took a position on the north bank of Fishkill Creek near Saratoga. Gates threw a force across the Hudson which prevented a crossing, troops were posted on the flank of the British Camp and the main army was drawn up on the south bank of Fishkill Creek. The British were trapped and Burgoyne at last realized that the game was up. On October 13 he called a council of war at which it was decided to negotiate terms. Gates demanded an unconditional surrender, but Burgoyne refused and the next day Gates, who appears neither to have been able to win a battle or to make the most of a fortunate situation created by the bravery and skill of another, agreed that Burgoyne should surrender with the honors of war and that his army should be given free passage to Great Britain upon the condition that they would not serve in North America during the war. Congress, to its shame, did not carry out the agreement and the troops were kept as prisoners in America.

THE CONTEST FOR PHILADELPHIA

Howe moves on Philadelphia.—While the northern army was struggling with Burgoyne, another great contest was taking place in Pennsylvania. Germaine had not given Howe definite orders to coöperate with Burgoyne and, in fact, had approved the proposed expedition against Philadelphia. After the retirement from before Middlebrook, Howe's movements were a mystery to Washington. In July he learned that the British fleet was being prepared for a voyage, but whether the enemy would sail up the Hudson, or strike at Boston, Philadelphia, or Charleston, he could not tell. To forestall an advance northward Washington moved his army toward the New York highlands. On July 31 he heard that the British fleet had appeared in Delaware Bay. Immediately the American army was started for Philadelphia, but before the city was reached the astonishing news came that the fleet had disappeared. Washington immediately went into camp twenty miles north of Philadelphia to await developments. Two weeks later the British fleet sailed into Chesapeake Bay and on August 25 the army, which numbered seventeen thousand, began to disembark at the Head of Elk at the northern end of the bay.

Battle of the Brandywine.—As soon as Washington heard of the British landing, he started his army southward. On August 24 eleven thousand men paraded through the spacious streets of Philadelphia and on September 9 the army was posted on the north bank of the Brandywine. The main road to Philadelphia crossed the stream at Chad's Ford and here Wayne's division was stationed. Below the ford the steep banks were defended by a small force of militia. Above Wayne were Greene's well-drilled brigades, and the right was held by Sullivan. On September 10 Howe concentrated his army at the Kennet Square meeting house, where he divided it into two columns. At four the next morning Cornwallis in command of one column started for the upper fords of the Brandywine; by making this wide detour it was hoped that he could get in the rear of the American right wing. An hour later General von Knyphausen in command of the other column advanced toward Chad's Ford. He drove a small group of skirmishers across the stream, arranged his army as if for an assault, and opened with his artillery. Washington spent the morning in uncertainty, but at length Sullivan sent word that Cornwallis's troops were getting in his rear. Washington immediately ordered him to throw his entire force across the path of the enemy, but the movement was not carried out with precision and soon the wings of Sullivan's force were routed. Stirling, who held the center, made a gallant defence, but with both flanks exposed, he was forced to retire. When Von Knyphausen heard the firing, he advanced across Chad's Ford, and carried Wayne's intrenchments. Washington had ordered Greene to go to Sullivan's assistance. His men covered four miles in about forty minutes and then came into action against Cornwallis's victorious troops. For an hour the battle raged with great intensity, and as darkness set in, Greene drew off his men. His stubborn fight had saved the army, which was brought together at Chester.

Paoli.—Washington moved his army thirty-five miles up the Schuylkill and the British encamped south of the river near Valley Forge. To harass the rear of Howe's army Washington sent Wayne's division across the Schuylkill. At 1 A. M. on September 21 this force was surprised near the Paoli Tavern. The British fell upon the American camp with sword and bayonet, and before the grim work was over Wayne had lost more than three hundred men.

The British in Philadelphia.—On September 23 the British army crossed the Schuylkill and began to advance toward Philadelphia. When the news reached the city a Whig exodus began, probably a third of the population taking their departure. Congress removed the prisoners, archives, and most of the

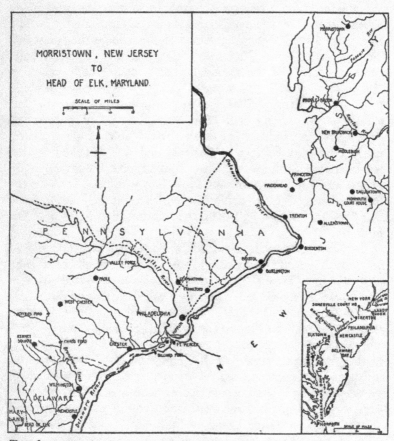

(Based on map in G. O. Trevelyan, *The American Revolution*, Part. III, op. p. 492)

stores; upon Washington it conferred dictatorial powers for sixty days in the vicinity, and then adjourned to Lancaster and later to York. On September 25 Howe entered the capital.

Germantown.—Within a week Washington was ready to try to retake the city. The approach from the northwest lay through Germantown. In the outskirts Howe had stationed a strong force of infantry. Near the center of the village the fine brick mansion of Benjamin Chew, the Chief Justice of Pennsylvania, formed the pivot of the second line of defence which was commanded by Colonel Musgrave. A mile to the rear lay the bulk of the British army. Washington planned to advance in four columns. Armstrong with the Pennsylvania militia on the right was to get in the rear of the British left. Sullivan commanded the next column to the east and was followed by the reserve under Stirling. A third column was commanded by Greene, and the Maryland and New Jersey militia, forming the fourth column, were to strike the British right. Save for a few shots fired by Armstrong's men, the militia failed to get into the fighting.

The dawn of October 4 broke in a dense fog, which destroyed the possibility of coöperation and led to much confusion. Sullivan's men arrived first and soon drove the British from their advanced position. Then followed an attack which centered at Chew's house where Musgrave and his men had taken refuge. The sound of the firing attracted some of Greene's men who joined in the attack. The brick walls proved too strong for the American three-pounders, and most of the forces of Sullivan and Greene passed on to attack the next line where five brigades of royal troops were drawn up along a narrow lane. The American units became separated, Greene having advanced a considerable distance ahead of Sullivan's troops. Suddenly Sullivan's force broke and fled in an unaccountable panic. This placed Greene in great jeopardy, for his flank was exposed and British reinforcements were approaching, but he coolly saved his men and guns. So heavy were the British losses that no serious attempt was made to follow the retreating army which was able to get away with all its artillery.

Opening the Delaware.—Philadelphia was firmly held by the British but the Delaware was still closed. At Billingsport a fort had been built and an obstruction had been thrown across the river. Another obstruction blocked the passage below Mud Island, on which stood Fort Mifflin and opposite on the Jersey shore was Ft. Mercer. A flotilla of small craft patrolled the Delaware. On October 4 part of Lord Howe's fleet anchored in the river and two days later the obstruction at Billingsport was removed. On October 22 Colonel von Donop attempted to capture Ft. Mercer but he met with a bloody repulse. After this defeat the British proceeded with more caution in the reduction of Ft. Mifflin. Shore batteries were constructed which bombarded Mud Island for days. On November 15 two battleships navigated the difficult channel and soon battered the walls of the fort to pieces. At nightfall the garrison abandoned the fortress. Four days later Ft. Mercer was evacuated when an overwhelming force advanced against it, and on November 21 most of the American vessels were set on fire by their crews. Communication with New York was thus opened and Howe prepared to settle down in Philadelphia for the winter.

Valley Forge.—In marked contrast to the comfort of the British camp was the condition of the American army. Washington had chosen Valley Forge for his winter quarters and there a fortified camp was constructed and rude cabins erected to house the men. The camp soon became a charnel house, for Congress failed to supply the necessary food and clothing, and sickness inevitably resulted. For days the men were without meat and existed on dough baked in the embers. "Fire-cake" and water became the ration for breakfast, dinner, and supper. Blankets were lacking and the men were soon barefooted and in tatters. On Christmas day the winter broke with great severity and soon the hospitals, which were mere hovels unsupplied with beds, were crowded with the dying.

The Conway Cabal.—The anguish of Washington was intensified by an intrigue which threatened to deprive him of his command. This centered about Gates and an Irish soldier of fortune named Conway who had been sent over from France by Silas Deane. In November, 1777, Congress had vested the management of military affairs in a Board of War. Gates was made president of the board and Conway was appointed inspector general of the army. They were supported by the New England delegates in Congress and by those who opposed the Fabian policy of Washington. Fortunately the intrigues of Conway and Gates to displace Washington became known to the public and so great was the popularity of the commander-in-chief that Congress dared not remove him.

READINGS

Channing, Edward, *History of the United States*, III, 210–273; Fisher, S. G., *The Struggle for American Independence*, I, 490–574, II, 1–174; Fiske, John, *The American Revolution*, I, 198–344, II, 25–81, 110–115; Greene, F. V., *The Revolutionary War*, 28–131; Hildreth, Richard, *History of the United States of America*, III, 140–162, 186–237; Lecky, W. E. H., *History of England in the Eighteenth Century*, IV, 1–41, 55–98; Smith, J. H., *Our Struggle for the Fourteenth Colony*, I, 193–606, II; Trevelyan, G. O., *The American Revolution*, II, 172–349, III, 1–147, IV, 111–319; Van Tyne, C. H., *The American Revolution*, 102–135, 157–174, 227–247; Winsor, Justin, *Narrative and Critical History*, VI, 275–447; Adams, C. F., *Studies Military and Diplomatic, 1775–1865*, pp. 22–173.

CHAPTER XXVI

THE WAR AS AN INTERNATIONAL CONTEST

THE FRENCH ALLIANCE

The French motives.—On February 6, 1778, France entered into an alliance with the United States. That event changed the war from a struggle between England and her former colonies to an international contest in which Spain and Holland were soon engaged. The motives of France in entering the contest have been variously ascribed to revenge for the loss of her possessions and the desire to regain them, to the intellectual movement in France, to the desire to build up French commerce at the expense of England, and to the fear that Great Britain would adjust the difficulties with the colonies and unite with them in an attack upon the French West Indies. Professor Corwin, who has recently examined the question, concludes that these explanations are not adequate. He contends that the basic principle of French diplomacy was the maintenance of leadership in Europe, and that in return for this commanding position, France was willing to forego the extension of her dominion. In the Seven Years' War French prestige had been destroyed; to rebuild it was the object of her statesmen.

The policy of Vergennes.—In 1774 Louis XVI became king. No better intentioned ruler ever mounted a throne but his weak will and vacillating course led to his undoing. For two years Turgot was the reigning influence at the council board. He installed a system of economy and reform, which, had it been adhered to, would probably have saved France from the throes of her great revolution. Turgot's plans ran counter to the policy of Vergennes, the foreign minister, who desired to see his country take its place in the sun as the dictator of European politics. The attainment of Vergennes's policy was based upon three main ideas: the preservation of peace on the continent by a close alliance with Austria; a renewal of the Family Compact with Spain; and the humbling of England. The last was to be accomplished by the building up of the French navy, by secretly aiding the colonies, and when the time seemed auspicious, by entering into an alliance with them, an alliance in which Vergennes hoped that Spain would join. To win over the latter power and to overcome the aversion of Louis XVI to aiding rebellious subjects were the immediate problems of Vergennes.

Vergennes wins over the king.—A secret agent, Bonvouloir, was sent to America to ascertain the condition of the colonies. His first report, which reached Paris in March, 1776, gave a favorable statement of the military situation. Vergennes immediately attempted to convince the king that secret aid should be given the colonies. He argued that the prolongation of the struggle would be advantageous to France and Spain as it would weaken both contestants, and he pointed out that England would probably attack the French West Indies as soon as the present war was over. Aided by Beaumarchais, the author of *Le Mariage de Figaro*, Vergennes countered the advice of Turgot and won over the king to his plan.

Deane and Beaumarchais.—The secret committee on foreign correspondence of the Continental Congress in March, 1776, sent Silas Deane to Paris. His presence became known to Lord Stormont, the British ambassador, who demanded his deportation, but France refused and continually aided him in securing supplies. The French government also loaned the colonies a million livres and obtained a similar amount for them from Spain. When news of the Declaration of Independence reached Paris, Vergennes urged that France and Spain enter the war, but Washington's defeats around New York held back both countries. France continued to aid the colonies, the business being transacted by Beaumarchais through the fictitious house of Hortalez et Cie. Beaumarchais also drew heavily upon his private fortune to assist the colonies.

Franklin.—The delay of France in making an open alliance caused Congress to appoint a commission composed of Silas Deane, Arthur Lee, and Benjamin Franklin. Of all colonials Franklin was the best known in Europe. As a scientist, philosopher, wit, and statesman, his name was familiar to all classes in the French capital. His unpretentious dress, unaffected manners, and simplicity of life made him seem to Parisians the impersonation of the natural man of Rousseau's philosophy. On the street, at the theater, in the salon, Franklin was the center of interest. Artists made busts of him and jewelers exhibited his countenance on medallions, watches, and snuff-boxes. Franklin soon discovered that he could not hurry matters; he quietly bided his time, never losing an opportunity to win supporters to the American cause. Even the court became enthusiastic, and Marie Antoinette, with little understanding or prophetic vision, applauded the republicans of America.

The American proposals.—In January, 1777, the commissioners presented their views to Vergennes. They proposed that France and Spain furnish the United States eight ships of the line, twenty or thirty thousand stand of arms, and a large quantity of cannon and ammunition. Congress in return offered the two nations a commercial treaty and a guarantee of their possessions in the West Indies. Vergennes was unable to comply but he advanced two hundred and fifty thousand livres as the first instalment of a secret loan of two millions. In February the commissioners suggested that, if France and Spain became involved in war because of a treaty with the United States, the states would not conclude a separate peace. In March they proposed a triple alliance between France, Spain, and the United States. The bait for Spain was the conquest of Portugal, and the war was to continue until England was expelled from North America and the West Indies.

The attitude of Spain.—The American proposals included both France and Spain, and in the latter country the commissioners met with a stumbling block. Spain at first showed a friendly attitude. Through the firm of Josef Gardoqui and Sons supplies were secretly furnished to the United States, but when Arthur Lee attempted to go to Madrid, he was turned back by the Spanish authorities, who preferred to work in secret. In February, 1777, the Count de Florida Blanca became minister of foreign affairs. To Florida Blanca Spain's interests must take precedence over those of France in determining Spanish policy. Difficulties with Portugal had been adjusted, and Florida Blanca could see no advantage in an immediate war with Great Britain. He was willing to keep the contest in America going until both parties were exhausted. Then Spain and France might enter the war, Spain to get the Floridas and France to obtain Canada. But as to the recognition of American independence, king and minister were unalterably opposed.

Lafayette.—Of no little importance in bringing France and the United States together was the coming of the young nobleman Lafayette to America. Fired by the Declaration of Independence, he determined to enlist in the American cause. In April, 1777, Lafayette with the Baron de Kalb and several other officers sailed for America. They reached Philadelphia on July 27 but Congress gave them a chilly reception. Nothing daunted, Lafayette proudly announced that he asked nothing but the opportunity of serving as a volunteer. Congress was deeply impressed by his unselfish attitude and promptly made him a Major-General. Washington received him gladly, took him into his military family and through the long war, with the exception of a period when he was promoting American interests in France, he served as a trusted officer of the commander-in-chief.

The French alliance.—During the summer of 1777 the American question was held in abeyance at Paris but Burgoyne's surrender stirred Vergennes to action. He appears to have feared that Great Britain was about to effect a reconciliation with the United States. To prevent it he believed that France must openly espouse the American cause. One more effort was made to draw Spain into the alliance, but the reply proved unfavorable. On January 7, 1778, at a French royal council meeting the final decision was made and on February 6 treaties of commerce and alliance were signed. The latter agreement was described as a defensive alliance to maintain effectually the liberty, sovereignty, and independence of the United States, as well in matters of government as in commerce.

Lord North attempts conciliation.—When news of Burgoyne's surrender reached London, hope of subduing the rebellion by force was temporarily abandoned and Lord North was empowered to try his hand at conciliation. On February 17, 1778, the Prime Minister presented his plan to the Commons. He proposed (1) the repeal of the tea duty, (2) the passage of an act removing apprehension regarding parliamentary taxation of the colonies, (3) opening the port of Boston, (4) restoration of the Massachusetts charter, (5) opening the fisheries, (6) restoration of commerce, and (7) full pardon to those engaged in rebellion. (8) Prisoners charged with treason were not to be brought over the sea for trial, and (9) no bill for changing a colonial constitution was to be introduced in parliament except at the request of the colony involved. (10) Regulation of colonial courts was to follow colonial opinion, and (11) officials were to be elected by popular vote subject, however, to the approval of the king. (12) The royal treasury was to assist in the withdrawal of colonial currency, and (13) a promise was given that the question of colonial representation in parliament would be considered.

The Carlisle Commission.—A royal commission was to visit America to settle points in dispute. Headed by the Earl of Carlisle, the commission proceeded to Philadelphia but it was soon discovered that nothing could be accomplished. General Howe had been recalled and Clinton, who was placed in command, was under orders to evacuate Philadelphia. The alliance with France was already known in America and nothing short of a recognition of independence would satisfy the Whig leaders.

Change in British plans.—The French alliance brought about a complete change in British plans. Henceforth garrisons were to be kept in New York, Newport, Canada, and the Floridas, and hostilities on the mainland were to be devoted to the destruction of coastwise trade and coast towns, and to the harassing of the frontiers by Indian raids. Attacks in force were to be made on the French possessions in the West Indies.

Evacuation of Philadelphia and the battle of Monmouth.—In pursuance of this plan in May, 1778, the British prepared to evacuate Philadelphia. General Howe returned to England and Clinton took command. Most of the stores, some of the troops, and about three thousand Loyalists were placed on transports, and the main army on June 18 started on its march across New Jersey. Washington succeeded in getting in touch with the British army ten days later at Monmouth. Clinton's forces were stretched out to such an extent that it was difficult to bring them into action. Washington sent Lee to attack, but after a slight demonstration, the poltroon ordered a retreat. Lee's cowardice gave the British time to form and a bloody battle followed which ended only with nightfall. In the darkness the British army broke camp and when morning dawned it was beyond the reach of Washington.

The coming of D'Estaing.—On April 15 Admiral D'Estaing sailed from Toulon in command of twelve ships of the line and five frigates which carried four thousand infantry. The voyage was pursued in a leisurely fashion which gave Lord Howe time to get his transports out of the Delaware and concentrate the fleet at New York. It also made it possible for a reinforcement under Commodore Byron to arrive in American waters. Not until July 8 was D'Estaing's fleet within the Delaware capes. After landing Gérard, the French minister, the admiral proceeded to New York. Though the French fleet was superior to the British, D'Estaing failed to attack.

The failure at Newport.—Instead he entered into a plan with Washington to take Newport which was garrisoned by five or six thousand British troops. Sullivan, with about a thousand continental soldiers and several thousand militia, was to coöperate with the French fleet. The opening was auspicious. The war vessels ran by the batteries and anchored in the inner waters. The British commander to prevent capture destroyed several frigates and small craft. On August 9 Sullivan moved nine thousand troops to the island. The same day Howe's fleet appeared at the entrance of Narragansett Bay and D'Estaing, carrying his infantry with him, sailed out to meet the enemy. Before the fleets could engage a terrific storm arose which scattered the vessels. Howe finally regained New York and D'Estaing sailed to Boston for repairs, leaving Sullivan unsupported and in a precarious position. When word came that Clinton was sending large reinforcements, Sullivan abandoned the siege.

D'Estaing in the West Indies.—D'Estaing lingered at Boston ten weeks and then sailed for the West Indies. Before his arrival a French force from Martinique had captured Dominica. The English retaliated by capturing St. Lucia, and when D'Estaing attempted to relieve it, he was repulsed. On June 18, 1779, the French occupied St. Vincent and on July 2 Grenada. On July 6 Byron attacked the French fleet off Grenada, but D'Estaing had the better of the fighting although he failed to follow up his victory. After attempting the relief of Savannah, the French commander despatched part of his fleet to the West Indies and then sailed for Europe.

Stony Point and the evacuation of Newport.—After the Newport failure Washington drew a cordon about New York and strengthened the line of the Hudson. On May 31, 1779, Clinton seized the fortifications at Stony Point and Verplanck's Point, but on July 16 General Wayne carried the works at Stony Point. Clinton also sent raiding parties to the Chesapeake and along the Connecticut coast, but in October he ordered the evacuation of Newport and concentrated his forces at New York.

The second French expedition.—Washington still hoped for effective help from the French fleet in the West Indies, but his hopes were blasted early in 1780 by the arrival in the islands of British naval reinforcements under Admiral Rodney, who during April and May fought three indecisive actions with the French fleet. Largely through the influence of Lafayette France was induced to send a large force to America in 1780. In July a fleet of seven vessels convoying six thousand men commanded by Rochambeau arrived at Newport. The second division, however, was blockaded at Brest and was unable to sail. Washington's hopes mounted high but they were soon dashed again, for Clinton, who had just returned to New York after the capture of Charleston, was able to send a considerable armament to blockade the French at Newport, and there they remained for months to come.

Arnold's treason.—During the long contest Washington had often been disappointed by the incompetence of his subordinates, but Nathanael Greene and Benedict Arnold had seldom been found wanting. The former was soon to win fame as the conqueror of the South; the other chose a path which made his name despised. Arnold had not been justly treated by Congress, although he had the absolute confidence of Washington. Brooding over his wrongs and convinced that the country would welcome the reëstablishment of the king's authority, he determined to play the part of a General Monk. While in command of Philadelphia, he entered into a treasonable correspondence with Clinton. He then asked for the command of the great fortress at West Point. This was readily given to him and there he perfected his plans to deliver this key position of the Hudson to the British. Clinton sent Major André to communicate with Arnold, but upon his return on September 23, 1780, André was captured and on his person were found papers which disclosed the plot. André was condemned and hung as a spy, but Arnold made good his escape to the British lines.

THE WAR IN THE WEST

Competition for the support of the Indians.—The westward movement across the mountains was almost simultaneous with the outbreak of the Revolution, and the western settlements were soon drawn into the current. The frontiersmen held back the Indian allies of the British, and by settlement and conquest secured large areas of the back country. At the opening of the war both British and Americans made great efforts to secure the support of the Indians, but in the main the tribes favored the British who did not encroach upon their lands and whose posts on the frontiers were centers for the distribution of presents and for the work of the traders. During the war British agents were kept at work among the tribes, distributing presents and weapons, and often leading the Indian raids.

The Cherokee War.—In the summer of 1776 the Cherokee went on the warpath. From their villages in the southern Alleghanies they were in a position to raid the frontier settlements of Georgia, the Carolinas, Virginia, and Tennessee. The Cherokee towns were in three groups. The upper towns inhabited by the Overhill Cherokee were along the mountain streams that ran into the Tennessee. The lower towns were in the foothills of the back country of Georgia and South Carolina. In the mountainous region between were the middle towns. During June and July Cherokee war parties, at times assisted by Creeks and Tories, fell upon the Georgia and Carolina frontiers and upon the Watauga settlements. The Georgia invaders were met by Colonel Samuel Jack at the head of two hundred rangers who drove them back and destroyed one or two of the lower towns. In North Carolina the Indians came down the Catawba and drove the settlers into the blockhouses. General Griffith Rutherford raised the frontier levies and chased the Indians back to their villages. In South Carolina the Cherokees from the lower and middle towns, aided by Tories and led by the British agent, Cameron, descended upon the settlements. Colonel Andrew Williamson collected eleven hundred militia, defeated the invaders, and by the middle of August destroyed the lower towns. In July seven hundred Overhill Cherokee raided the Watauga settlements. One party under Chief Dragging Canoe attacked the settlers about Eaton's Station, but the frontiersmen sallied forth and defeated the Indians at Island Flats. For three weeks Fort Watauga was invested by another band, but so stubborn was the defence conducted by Robertson and Sevier that the Indians abandoned the siege. The Carolinians and Virginians determined to carry the war into the enemy's country. In September Rutherford and Williamson completely destroyed the valley towns of the Cherokee; and in October Colonel William Christian led the Virginia troops into the Overhill country, destroyed the principal village, and brought the warriors to terms.

Indian raids in the Northwest, 1776-1778.—In the Northwest the memory of the Battle of the Kanawha kept the Indians quiet for a time while the diplomats struggled for mastery. Colonel George Morgan was made congressional agent at Fort Pitt, while Hamilton at Detroit was the most active British agent on that frontier. In the fall of 1776 Hamilton sent raiding parties along the border. During 1777 the frontiers of Pennsylvania, Virginia, and Kentucky were kept in a state of terror. Colonel Morgan urged an expedition against Detroit, and when his advice was rejected, he resigned. Governor Patrick Henry sent Virginia militia to relieve Kentucky and Congress sent General Hand to defend the upper Ohio. Hand and his successor, McIntosh, had little success, for the raids continued and by the end of 1778 Kentucky was nearly depopulated.

Willing's raids.—In 1777 James Willing, a former resident of Natchez, obtained permission from Congress to make an expedition down the Mississippi to secure the neutrality of the Tories in the Southwest. Descending the Ohio from Pittsburg, his expedition became a raid on the Loyalist plantations along the Mississippi. Far from having the desired effect, the raid drove the inhabitants into active resistance. In May Willing led a second expedition down the Mississippi but he failed to win over

the inhabitants.   The Chickasaw and Choctaw went over to
the British side.   The Southwest had thus definitely taken its
stand against the United States.

Clark conquers the Northwest.—To Virginia fell the task of
conquering the Northwest.   The chief actor in the enterprise
was George Rogers Clark, who, though only twenty-six, had
already played a prominent part in Kentucky.   With one hundred and seventy-five frontiersmen, mainly Virginians, in June,
1778, Clark descended the Ohio to Fort Massac, crossed Illinois,
and in July took Kaskaskia, Prairie du Rocher, St. Philippe, and
Cahokia, and French sympathizers secured the submission of
Vincennes.   Hamilton at once organized a force at Detroit to
retake the lost posts.   In December he occupied Vincennes without difficulty, but was unable to proceed farther.   In February,
1779, after a difficult march over flooded prairies, Clark captured
Hamilton and his force.   In December, 1778 the Virginia legislature erected the territory north of the Ohio into the county of
Illinois, John Todd being made civil and Clark military head.
Clark planned the capture of Detroit, but was unable to get the
necessary aid.   Instead, in 1780 he founded Fort Jefferson on
the Mississippi near the mouth of the Ohio and it soon became
the center of a settled area.

Depredations of the Iroquois and Tories.—On the New York
frontier Burgoyne's invasion had aroused the Iroquois and even
after his defeat the Six Nations, except the Tuscaroras, Oneidas,
and part of the Mohawks, adhered to the British.   Many Tory
refugees settled among the Indians and incited them to go on
the warpath.   In July, 1778, a force of Tories and Iroquois,
mainly Senecas, descended into the Wyoming Valley and laid
it waste, killing and capturing many of the inhabitants.   Continental troops presently reoccupied the valley and in October the
Indian town of Unadilla.   The Indians and Tories retaliated by
a descent on Cherry Valley.   The depredations continued in
1779.   Troops sent out from Ft. Stanwix destroyed the Onondaga
villages.   The Indians then assailed the Schoharie Valley and
the western settlements in Ulster County, and spread destruction
about Pittsburg.

Expeditions sent into the Iroquois country.—So extensive
were the depredations that Congress decided to send an over-

whelming force into the Iroquois country.   Three brigades from Washington's army were assembled at Wyoming under Sullivan. While he was waiting for a New York brigade to join him, Chief Brant and his warriors burned Minisink and ambushed the militia who went in pursuit.   Sullivan at the head of five thousand men passed up the Chemung branch of the Susquehanna, defeated a strong force of Indians and Tories on the site of modern Elmira, and then burned eighteen Indian villages and destroyed the crops.   Sullivan, however, failed to attack Niagara which was a British stronghold.   Another expedition from Pittsburg ascended the Alleghany and destroyed the Indian villages along the river.   These operations scattered the Indians and Tories but did not destroy them, and frequent depredations occurred on the New York and Pennsylvania frontiers during the remainder of the war.

SPAIN IN THE WAR [1]

Spain enters the war.—When Spain became a factor in the war in 1779, a new element entered the contest in the West. During 1778 Vergennes did not relax his efforts to induce Spain to become a belligerent.   But Carlos III and Florida Blanca had no intention of risking a war with Great Britain unless they were well paid for their assistance.   Not until they were certain that France would assist in the recovery of Gibraltar and the Floridas did they consent to make war.   On another point the king was insistent; he refused to recognize the independence of the United States.   The secret convention of Aranjuez between France and Spain was signed on April 12, 1779, and in June Spain definitely entered the war.

Gálvez on the lower Mississippi.—Orders were given at once to seize the British posts on the Mississippi.   With a hastily built fleet, Bernardo de Gálvez, the Governor of Louisiana, ascended the Mississippi at the head of fifteen hundred men. On September 7 he took Fort Bute at Manchac, and then proceeded to Baton Rouge which he captured, the capitulation including Fort Panmure at Natchez.   Meanwhile Grandpré had taken two small British outposts and a fleet had captured eight British vessels on Lake Pontchartrain.

[1] See map on page 400.

British attack on St. Louis.—As soon as war was declared, the British planned to capture New Orleans. An expedition from the north was to descend the Mississippi, attack St. Louis, reconquer the Illinois country, and meet General Campbell at Natchez with a force from Pensacola. The campaign against St. Louis was directed by Sinclair, commander at Mackinac. Emmanuel Hesse, a trader, was sent to assemble a force of Indians at the Fox-Wisconsin portage. In March, 1780, seven hundred and fifty men left Mackinac and joined Hesse at Prairie du Chien. To coöperate Charles Langlade was sent with Indians via Chicago, while Captain Bird, despatched from Detroit, was to raid Kentucky. None of the plans succeeded. Leyba, the commander at St. Louis, was forewarned and was aided by George Rogers Clark. On May 26 the British attacked St. Louis but were repulsed and forced to withdraw. Bird's expedition also miscarried, and Campbell's movement was frustrated by Gálvez.

The Spanish expedition against St. Joseph.—Sinclair at once planned a second expedition for the spring of 1781. Learning of the project, Cruzat, the new commander at St. Louis prepared a counter stroke. He despatched parties up the Mississippi and to Peoria, and sent sixty-five men under Purée to destroy the stores at St. Joseph. On February 12 the post was taken in a surprise attack and the stores destroyed.

Capture of Mobile and Pensacola.—Meanwhile more important events had been taking place on the Gulf of Mexico. In February, 1780, Gálvez sailed from New Orleans with two thousand men to capture Fort Charlotte at Mobile, and on March 14 the place capitulated. Going to Cuba for reinforcements, after losing one fleet in a hurricane, in February, 1781, he sailed with fourteen hundred men to attack Pensacola. After a siege of nearly two months, General Campbell with more than eight hundred men surrendered. A simultaneous French and Spanish attack on Jamaica was next planned, and Gálvez sailed for Santo Domingo to command the Spanish forces, but the campaign was made unnecessary by the ending of the war. Spain had played an important part. She had defeated the British attempt to gain control of the Mississippi, had enabled Clark to maintain his hold on the Northwest, and had recovered Mobile and Pensacola.

THE WAR ON THE SEA AND THE DUTCH ALLIANCE

Washington's fleets.—From the beginning of the war American vessels were an important factor. They captured supply ships and transports, harassed commerce, captured many small war vessels, and protected trading vessels. At the opening of hostilities Washington turned to New England to supply him with vessels, and during the siege of Boston he sent out ten armed craft which made several important captures of arms and supplies. When operations were transferred to New York, he also engaged several vessels which rendered good service.

Congress provides a navy.—Largely through the influence of the Rhode Island delegates, Congress was convinced that a navy should be provided, and by January, 1776, ten vessels had been purchased and the building of thirteen others authorized. Before the end of the war over forty vessels were added to the high seas fleet in addition to minor craft on Lake Champlain.

First cruise of the fleet.—In February, 1776, Esek Hopkins, who had been appointed commander-in-chief of the navy, put to sea with a fleet of eight vessels. He cruised to the West Indies, captured New Providence, and sailed away with eighty-eight cannon, fifteen mortars, and a large quantity of stores. The fleet sailed to Long Island and off the eastern end it captured two small vessels, but on April 6 it allowed the *Glasgow* to escape.

Nature of the operations during 1776-1777.—By the end of 1776 the navy had been increased to twenty-five vessels. During the year it was constantly engaged in commerce destroying, and in capturing transports and small war craft. The operations were confined mainly to American and West Indian waters, although before the end of the year the *Reprisal*, which carried Franklin to France, had captured several vessels in European waters. During 1777 the congressional vessels, privateers, and state cruisers captured four hundred and sixty-seven vessels, many being taken near the British Isles. The depredations caused great alarm in England and the West Indies; merchants were often deterred from shipping goods, insurance rates and prices rose, and the demands for escorts became insistent.

Privateers.—The swift sailing craft of the Yankee skippers made ideal blockade runners and commerce destroyers, and hundreds of them put to sea. During the war Massachusetts commissioned nine hundred and ninety-eight. While the greater number of these vessels put out from New England, other states gave many commissions, Maryland alone commissioning two hundred and fifty. It is estimated that during the war the privateers captured or destroyed six hundred vessels with cargoes valued at $18,000,000, besides making several important captures of troops and supplies.

State navies.—With the exception of New Jersey and Delaware, the states had navies, the largest being those of Massachusetts, Connecticut, Pennsylvania, Maryland, Virginia, and South Carolina. At times these operated independently, sometimes in conjunction with privateers, and at other times as adjuncts of the regular navy. They were used chiefly to protect the trade in home waters and for coast defence.

The Penobscot expedition.—The most pretentious operation undertaken by a state navy was the attempt to capture Penobscot in 1779. The British had established a naval base near the mouth of the Penobscot River and Massachusetts determined to break it up. Fifteen hundred men were loaded on privateers and transports, and were convoyed by the *Warren*, the *Diligent*, and the *Providence*. The expedition arrived off the Penobscot late in July, but before it could take the fort, a larger British fleet appeared (August 13). The privateers and transports scattered, but the three war vessels were forced to run up the river where their crews destroyed them.

The navy during 1778-1779.—During 1778 the British navy succeeded in greatly decreasing the depredations of American vessels. By the close of the year the national navy was reduced to fourteen. But in 1779 the fleet was somewhat rehabilitated by the securing of several French vessels.

The Bonhomme Richard and the Serapis.—In 1779 the most famous sea-fight of the Revolution occurred. John Paul Jones was given command of an old French East Indiaman which was refitted with forty-two guns and renamed the *Bonhomme Richard*.

In August the French frigate *Alliance* and three small vessels accompanied the *Bonhomme Richard* on a cruise along the west coast of Ireland, northern Scotland, and the eastern coast of England, several prizes being taken. On September 23 off Flamborough Head Jones sighted a large merchant fleet convoyed by the forty-four gun frigate *Serapis* and the smaller *Countess of Scarborough*. The *Bonhomme Richard* engaged the *Serapis* in one of the most thrilling of naval battles. For three and a half hours the frigates fought at close range, much of the time being lashed together. Although Jones's vessel was in a sinking condition, he refused to surrender. When the English captain had lost more than a third of his crew, he pulled down his flag. The *Pallas* captured the *Countess of Scarborough*. Jones placed his crew on board the *Serapis*, and the squadron soon after arrived at the Dutch port of Texel.

Decline of the navy.—When Charleston surrendered in 1780, four ships fell into British hands and only six vessels were left in the American navy. At the same time parliament voted to increase the naval service. The American coast was closely blockaded, and though cruisers occasionally got through, the navy ceased to be an important factor in the war.

The league of armed neutrals.—As the war progressed England's exercise of the right of search on the high seas provoked the neutral powers. At that time international law recognized a belligerent's right to seize enemy's goods, but not the vessel in which they were being carried. England acted within the law, but her seizures worked great hardship upon neutrals. Largely through the influence of Frederick the Great, who had not forgiven England for abandoning him in the Seven Years' War, Catherine II of Russia was induced to champion the cause of the neutral states. On February 26, 1780, she addressed a message to the neutral courts which asserted, (1) that neutral vessels should be allowed to navigate freely even upon the coasts of powers at war; (2) that, with the exception of contraband, goods belonging to the subjects of belligerents should be free in neutral ships; (3) that naval stores and provisions of neutrals should not be considered contraband; (4) that a port must be effectively guarded to constitute a blockade; and (5) that the above principles should be considered as rules in determining

520 THE COLONIZATION OF NORTH AMERICA

the legality of prizes. Denmark and Sweden promptly entered into an agreement with Russia mutually to protect their commerce, by force if necessary, the arrangement being known as the League of Armed Neutrality. The principles proclaimed by the Czarina were approved by France and Spain. The Netherlands joined the league in November, 1780; Prussia came in in May, 1781, and the Empire in October. Even Portugal, the ancient ally of England, and Turkey became parties to the league.

Attitude of the Netherlands.—At the opening of the American Revolution there were two parties in The Netherlands; the English party headed by the stadtholder, William V, and the Anti-Orange party which had strong French leanings. The strength of the Anti-Orange party lay chiefly in Holland and in the large cities, especially in Amsterdam where the great merchants were powerful. The Dutch people watched the contest between the United States and Great Britain with a filial interest, looking upon it as a counterpart of their own struggle for independence, but policy forced the government to remain neutral.

St. Eustatius.—The Dutch merchants saw an opportunity for immense profits in supplying the United States with war materials. The Dutch island of St. Eustatius in the West Indies became the center for a vast trade in contraband goods. The island became a veritable storehouse for the goods of all nations and here the American skippers brought tobacco and indigo, or gave promissory notes or continental currency in exchange for munitions of war. Great Britain complained of the trade and succeeded in getting the States General to prohibit the export of arms and munitions except by special permission from the Dutch admiralty, but nevertheless the traffic went merrily on. When British war vessels began to patrol the waters about the island and search vessels for contraband, it aroused the ire of the Dutch merchants.

The Scotch brigade and the Jones incident.—Two incidents added greatly to the ill-feeling which was growing rapidly between the two countries. The British government asked for the loan of the Scotch brigade, a body of troops which had been in Dutch service for many years. The government gave a suave answer. It was willing to loan the soldiers, but not for service outside of Europe. As George III wanted the troops for American service, the answer was practically a refusal. Another incident which increased the irritation was the sojourn of John Paul Jones at Texel. For over two months he remained on Dutch soil, while the government quibbled over its rights to order his departure.

British seizures.—During 1778 British seizures of Dutch vessels increased and the demands of the merchants for convoys became more and more insistent. France took advantage of the situation to bring The Netherlands to her side. Special commercial privileges in France had been granted to several of the Dutch cities. France now decided to force the Dutch government to take a more decided stand toward England by cutting off the special privileges to all the Dutch cities except Amsterdam. This led to a demand for an immediate adjustment with France and for convoys to protect Dutch vessels against British seizures. A climax was reached on December 31, 1779, when an encounter occurred between the convoys of a Dutch fleet and British war vessels. The result was soon evident, for The Netherlands began to build a large fleet.

The secret agreement.—The United States maintained secret agents in The Netherlands throughout the war. For several years they made unsuccessful attempts to obtain a loan, but the authorities of Amsterdam finally communicated to C. W. F. Dumas, the United States representative, that they desired to conclude a treaty provided Congress would not enter into engagements with Great Britain which might prove harmful to Dutch interests. Jean de Neufville, a prominent Amsterdam merchant, at the suggestion of Van Berckel, the pensionary of Amsterdam, visited Aix-la-Chapelle in 1778, where he met William Lee, an American representative to Germany and Austria; together they formulated the draft of a treaty which, however, was not to be considered until after the recognition of American independence by Great Britain. The agreement had no legal force, for Amsterdam could not enter into a treaty without the consent of the other provinces.

The declaration of war.—In 1780 Henry Laurens sailed for The Hague for the purpose of negotiating a loan and making a treaty with The Netherlands. On September 3 he was captured off Newfoundland. Among his papers was a copy of the secret compact drawn by Neufville and Lee. The British government demanded from the States General a disavowal of the action of Amsterdam and the punishment of Van Berckel. The States General finally disavowed the act but declared its incompetence to punish Van Berckel. On November 20, in the midst of the controversy, the States General decided to join the league of armed neutrals. When this became known at London, the British minister was ordered home, and on December 20 George III issued a manifesto which was a virtual declaration of war.

READINGS

THE FRENCH AND SPANISH ALLIANCES

Corwin, E. S., *French Policy and the American Alliance of 1778*, pp. 1–216; Hale, E. E., *Franklin in France;* Lecky, W. E. H., *History of England in the Eighteenth Century*, IV, 42–54, 99–129, 166–185; Perkins, J. B., *France in the American Revolution;* Phillips, P. C., *The West in the Diplomacy of the American Revolution;* Trescot, W. H., *Diplomacy of the American Revolution;* Trevelyan, G. O., *The American Revolution*, Part III, 387–476; Van Tyne, C. H., *The American Revolution*, 203–226; Wharton, F., *The Revolutionary Diplomatic Correspondence of the United States*, I.

THE WEST IN THE REVOLUTION

Alvord, C. W., "Virginia and the West," in *Mississippi Valley Historical Review*, III, 19–38; Alvord, C. W., ed., *Kaskaskia Records, 1778–1790*, Introduction; Gayarré, C., *History of Louisiana, the Spanish Domination*, ch. 3; Hamilton, P. J., *Colonial Mobile*, ch. 31; Hamilton, P. J., *The Colonization of the South*, ch. 23; James, J. A., ed., *George Rogers Clark Papers, 1771–1781*, Introduction; Roosevelt, Theodore, *The Winning of the West*, I, 272–327, II, 1–213; Teggart, F. J., "The Capture of St. Joseph, Michigan, by the Spaniards in 1781," in *Missouri Historical Review*, V, 214–228; Thwaites, R. G., and Kellogg, L. P., editors, *Frontier Defense on the Upper Ohio, 1778*, Introduction and maps; *The Revolution on the Upper Ohio, 1775–1777*, Introduction and maps; Van Tyne, C. H., *The American Revolution*, 269–288; Winsor, Justin, *The Westward Movement*, 101–187; Esarey, L., *A History of Indiana*, I, 47–91; McElroy, R. M., *Kentucky in the Nation's History*, 62–113.

THE NAVY, ARMED NEUTRALITY, AND DUTCH INTERVENTION

Clowes, W. L., *The Royal Navy*, III, 353–538; Edler, F., *The Dutch Republic and the American Revolution* (Johns Hopkins University, *Studies in History and Political Science*, XXIX, 187–424); Jameson, J. F., "St. Eustatius in the American Revolution," in *The American Historical Review*, VIII, 683–708; Maclay, E. S., *A History of American Privateers*, 43–222; *A History of the United States Navy*, I, 34–151; Paullin, C. O., *The Navy of the American Revolution;* Trevelyan, G. O., *George the Third and Charles Fox*, II, 36–72; Van Loon, H. W., *The Fall of the Dutch Republic*, 174–287; Van Tyne, C. H., *The American Revolution*, 309–319.

CHAPTER XXVII

THE CLOSING YEARS OF THE REVOLUTION

THE WAR IN THE SOUTH

Conquest of Georgia.—When France became the ally of the United States, British statesmen realized that the conquest of New England and the middle states was impossible, but they still hoped to conquer the South. From East Florida the British forces could strike at Georgia, and in November, 1778, the operations began. Thirty-five hundred men were sent south from New York, and General Prevost with two thousand soldiers advanced from Florida. On December 29 British forces captured Savannah and shortly afterward occupied Augusta. Within six weeks Georgia was under British control.

Reconquest fails.—General Lincoln, who had been placed in command in the South, determined to reconquer Georgia. He sent Ashe with fifteen hundred men to recapture Augusta, but the force was surprised and defeated. When Lincoln moved against Augusta, Prevost advanced against Charleston. The manœuvre succeeded and Lincoln was forced to hasten back to assist in the defence of the city. Prevost, his purpose accomplished, slowly retired to Savannah. Numerous letters were sent to the French admiral asking him to coöperate against the British. In September, 1779, D'Estaing sailed for Savannah; Lincoln advanced to assist him, and the city was besieged. On October 9 an attempt was made to carry the works by assault, but the allies were repulsed with a loss of over eight hundred men. Lincoln wished to continue the siege but D'Estaing refused. Despatching a portion of his fleet to the West Indies, with the rest he sailed for France, and Lincoln withdrew to Charleston.

Capture of Charleston.—With Georgia secure, Clinton determined to make another attempt to capture Charleston. He sailed from New York with over eight thousand men, and twelve hundred were brought from Savannah. On February 11, 1780, the troops from New York were landed thirty miles south of Charleston and they soon advanced to the Ashley River. Lincoln should have abandoned the city but instead he foolishly determined to defend it. Gradually Clinton drew his lines about the city. On April 13 Tarleton defeated the American cavalry which had kept the lines of communication open, and when British reinforcements arrived from New York the investment was completed. Soon the garrison and inhabitants were almost starving. On May 6 Tarleton dispersed the mounted militia at the crossing of the Santee River; on the following day Fort Moultrie surrendered, and the situation became hopeless. On May 12 Lincoln signed articles of capitulation; over five thousand men, nearly four hundred pieces of artillery, and vast quantities of military stores fell into British hands.

Completion of the conquest of South Carolina.—After the fall of Charleston, Clinton sent out three expeditions; one northward under Tarleton against Buford's regiment which was advancing from Virginia, another toward Augusta, and a third toward Camden. Buford started to retreat but Tarleton overtook him at the Waxhaws and almost annihilated his force. The other expeditions met with little resistance and Clinton, believing that the conquest of South Carolina was complete, sailed for New York with a portion of the army, leaving Cornwallis in command of about eight thousand men.

Gathering of a new army.—Several weeks before the fall of Charleston, Washington had sent DeKalb southward with Maryland and Delaware regiments and these were reinforced by militia as they advanced. South of the Virginia line they passed through a barren country, shortage of supplies and poor roads making their progress very slow. At the Deep River they encamped and there they were joined by Gates who had been appointed by Congress to the command of the southern department. Gates pressed on toward Camden, receiving local reinforcements as he advanced.

Camden.—A British force had collected at Camden and Cornwallis hastened from Charleston to take command. Gates decided to attempt a surprise attack on the British force at Camden, thirteen miles away. Cornwallis contemplated a similar movement against Gates and the two armies left their encampments about the same hour on the night of August 15. At daybreak they met, but the militia proved to be no match for the British soldiers and fled almost without firing a shot. The regulars

The War in the South
(Based on E. G. Foster, *Illustrative Historical Chart*)

stood firm for a time, but when DeKalb fell mortally wounded and Tarleton's cavalry swept along their flank and rear, the line gave way and the retreat turned into a rout. Gates fled from the field and such was his haste that three days later he was at Hillsborough, nearly two hundred miles away. Shortly afterward Tarleton surprised and dispersed Sumter's band, and resistance seemed completely broken.

Partisan warfare.—British arms had defeated the American armies, but the people of South Carolina were not conquered. The merciless raids of Tarleton's cavalry and Ferguson's Loyalists kept the spirit of resistance alive. Marion, Sumter, and Shelby gathered bands of patriots, who from swamp and forest pounced down on isolated detachments, captured the escorts of supply trains, intercepted messengers, and broke up companies of Loyalists. Between July and December, 1780, twenty-seven battles or skirmishes were fought on Carolina soil.

King's Mountain—Next to Tarleton, Major Ferguson was probably the most hated and most feared of Cornwallis's officers. His camp at Ninety-Six became a center of Loyalist recruiting, and his band of partisans grew to a thousand strong. They lived on the country, and the property of no man was safe. Ferguson boasted that if the frontiersmen from over the Alleghanies troubled him, he would cross the mountains, lay waste their valleys, and hang their leaders. On September 20, 1780, the borderers under the leadership of Colonel William Campbell, Sevier, and Shelby gathered at Sycamore Shoals on the Watauga River and started across the mountains. Ferguson heard of their coming and decided to teach the frontiersmen a lesson. He pitched his camp on the crest of King's Mountain, a position which would have been impregnable had his opponents been drilled in the tactics of European battlefields. But the Watauga men had been schooled in Indian warfare. Three times they charged up the steep mountain sides. After an hour of hot fighting the resistance began to weaken, and when Ferguson was killed, his troops threw down their arms and asked for quarter. The victory of the mountaineers is justly looked upon as the turning point in the war in the South, for it gave new life to the waning cause in the Carolinas.

Greene in command.—The difficult task of reconquering the South was assigned to General Nathanael Greene. On December 2 he arrived at Charlotte where Gates handed over to him a poorly disciplined and half-starved force of about two thousand men. With this insignificant army and aided by local militia and the partisan bands, Greene was confronted with the task of reconquering a province which was occupied by a skillful general whose veteran army outnumbered him four to one. His plan of campaign was matured with rare judgment. He proposed to use a mobile force of about two thousand men to keep Cornwallis busy, while Marion and Sumter harassed the enemy, prevented foraging, and broke up convoys.

The Cowpens.—Early in January, 1781, the main British army was at Winnsborough. Hoping to divide it, Greene sent Morgan with about a thousand men to threaten Augusta and Ninety-Six. The rest of the American army was stationed at Cheraw, sixty miles east of Winnsborough. When Cornwallis heard of Morgan's raid, he sent Tarleton in pursuit with eleven hundred men. Tarleton came in touch with Morgan at The Cowpens. The battle at first was stoutly contested, but Colonel Washington's cavalry turned the scale and Tarleton's force was almost annihilated.

Greene's retreat.—Morgan had accomplished his purpose and immediately started to rejoin the main army. When Greene heard of the victory, he realized that Cornwallis would retaliate, and a pitched battle with the larger British army meant disaster. Furthermore reinforcements were on their way from Virginia and Maryland. Greene's decision was a vital one. He determined to fall back to make a juncture with Morgan and to draw Cornwallis away from his base into a hostile and difficult country. Turning over the command of the main army to Huger with orders to march northward with all speed, Greene rode nearly a hundred and fifty miles in a pouring rain and joined Morgan in his bivouac on the Catawba. He had judged Cornwallis rightly. The British general divested his army of all unnecessary baggage and pressed forward, but in spite of his efforts, the American army escaped him. From river to river Greene retreated while Huger fell back rapidly, the two lines gradually converging until on February 8 they united at Guilford. From there the retreat was continued across the Dan into Virginia. The Fabian policy had succeeded, for Cornwallis had been drawn over two hundred miles from his base and had gotten in such a position that, even if he won a battle, a victory would be barren.

Guilford.—Cornwallis was running short of supplies and he could not with safety continue the pursuit. He decided to fall back to Hillsborough. Greene, whose army had been considerably reinforced, decided to follow the retiring British. When Cornwallis learned that the American army was advancing, he

determined to risk a battle. On March 15 the armies met at
Guilford. Greene posted his force of about forty-five hundred
men in three lines, while the British army was stretched out in
one long row without supporting reserves, a disposition made
necessary by the fact that it numbered only twenty-two hundred
and fifty men. When the British charged, the Carolina militia-
men who occupied the front line gave way and fled from the field.
The Virginia militia who held the second line stood their ground
more firmly, but when their right flank was enveloped, they too
retreated. The hard fighting came when the British met the continental troops of the third line. Twice the British regulars were
repulsed, and had Greene followed up the success, he might have
won a victory. But he had no intention of risking the destruction of his army. When the British advanced for a final assault,
Greene decided to fall back. Covering his retreat with the first
Virginia regiment, he retired from the field. He had lost the
battle, but the result was as valuable as a victory.

Cornwallis retreats to Wilmington.—Cornwallis had lost
nearly thirty per cent. of his fighting force; he was almost without
supplies, and his foragers were being picked off by the Carolina
guerrillas. His hospital service was deplorable. Leaving seventy
of his most sorely wounded men to the tender mercies of General
Greene, Cornwallis loaded the rest of his wounded on carts, and
started on the long journey to Wilmington, the nearest base of
supplies.

The reconquest of South Carolina and Georgia.—Greene followed Cornwallis only as far as the Deep River and then turned
to reconquer South Carolina. In this work he was ably assisted
by Marion, Sumter, Pickens, and Lee, who during April, May,
and June captured several of the outlying British posts, the
most important being Augusta, which evacuated on June 5.
On April 25 Greene encountered Lord Rawdon's force near
Camden. The British won the battle, but again they possessed
a barren field, for so heavy were their losses that they retreated
to Charleston. Greene next invested Ninety-Six. When he
heard that Rawdon was marching to its relief, he attempted to
carry it by storm. The assault failed and Greene gave up the
siege. Lord Rawdon was unable to maintain his army away from
his base. He accordingly ordered the evacuation of Ninety-Six

and returned to Charleston. Soon afterward he sailed for England, leaving Stewart in command. The last important engagement occurred on September 8 at Eutaw Springs. The American army was again defeated, but Greene as usual gathered the fruits of victory, for Stewart, who had lost forty per cent. of his effectives, moved back to Charleston. In a campaign of eleven months Greene had lost every pitched battle, but the interior of the Carolinas and Georgia had been cleared of the enemy, who retained only Savannah, Charleston, and Wilmington.

THE YORKTOWN CAMPAIGN

Arnold and Cornwallis in Virginia.—When Benedict Arnold joined the British, he was rewarded with a brigadier-general's commission and sent to Virginia to cut off Greene's retreat if Cornwallis succeeded in driving that astute commander out of the Carolinas. Arnold marched up the James River and burned Richmond, but when the Virginia militia gathered in large numbers, he retreated to Portsmouth, where Lafayette, who had been sent to command in Virginia, held him in check. In the spring of 1781 Cornwallis transferred his forces to Petersburg, and Arnold was sent to Connecticut to conduct a campaign of rapine. Reinforcements were sent from New York and with an army of over seven thousand men Cornwallis began the conquest of Virginia, but he received no Loyalist support and he failed to crush the forces of Lafayette. After several weeks of ineffectual campaigning, he retired to Yorktown where he established himself behind strong fortifications.

Rodney and De Grasse in the West Indies.—The safety of Cornwallis's army depended upon the control of the sea. Since the beginning of the war the British had kept the sea lanes open. Time and again the fleet had enabled them to win victories or to extricate themselves from dangerous positions. Washington realized this and the burden of his letters to Franklin was the necessity of naval superiority. Vergennes made every effort to equip an overwhelming fleet and in March, 1781, a great armament under De Grasse sailed for the West Indies. And none too soon did they arrive, for Rodney was carrying all before him. In January he had been reinforced by eight ships of the line under Hood and on February 3 the British fleet captured St.

Eustatius. This was followed by the seizure of St. Martin and Saba. On April 28 De Grasse arrived at Martinique and on the following day he fought an indecisive action with Hood. An attempt on St. Lucia failed but soon afterward he captured Tobago. He then repaired to Martinique where he received despatches from Washington which determined him to sail for the Chesapeake.

Washington's plans.—When the news reached Washington that De Grasse had left France, he conferred with Rochambeau. Together they drew up a despatch to the French admiral in which they gave him his choice of coöperating with the land forces against New York or of sailing to the Chesapeake. When De Grasse received the despatch, he determined to strike at Cornwallis. On August 14 Washington received his reply and he immediately formulated a masterly plan of action. He decided to move Rochambeau's force and a portion of the continental army to Virginia, leaving General Heath with several New England regiments at West Point. Letters were written with the express intention that they should be intercepted by the British. These and the sudden activity of American engineers in constructing extensive works near Sandy Hook convinced Clinton that he had better sit tight behind his defences.

De Grasse and Graves.—On August 30 De Grasse arrived in the Chesapeake and on September 5 a fleet of nineteen British vessels under Admiral Graves appeared off Cape Henry. The fleets engaged and Graves's fleet was so badly crippled that it was forced to return to New York. Unmolested, a fleet of transports from Rhode Island carrying supplies and siege guns, and convoyed by eight war vessels, sailed into the Chesapeake. At the crucial moment the British had lost control of the seas.

The assembling of the army.—On August 20 the allied army began the passage of the Hudson, but not until they were near Philadelphia were the officers informed of their destination. At the Head of Elk Washington learned that De Grasse had arrived and that he had brought three thousand French infantry from the West Indies. After the allied army reached Williamsburg, it was reinforced by the troops under Lafayette, by the West Indian contingent, and by thirty-five hundred Virginia militia. With an army of sixteen thousand men and the greatest fleet

that had ever assembled in American waters, Washington was
in a position to win an overwhelming victory.

Yorktown.—The siege of Yorktown began on September 28.
Earthworks were thrown up within six hundred yards of the
British lines and on October 9 a terrific bombardment began.
Five days later two outlying works were carried by storm and
at short range the allied artillery did fearful execution. On the
sixteenth a British counter-attack failed and on the following
day an attempt to escape across the river was frustrated. When
this failed the British commander knew that his fate was sealed.
On October 19 Cornwallis surrendered and seven thousand
soldiers became prisoners of war.

The last struggle in the West Indies.—Yorktown was the
last important event on the mainland, but the fighting continued
in the West Indies. On January 11, 1782, De Grasse captured
St. Christopher and on the twentieth took Nevis. After receiving reinforcements, he planned the conquest of Jamaica, but the
arrival of twelve ships from England so strengthened the British
fleet that the project was not carried out. On April 12 Rodney
defeated De Grasse in a final engagement off Dominica, an
event which profoundly influenced the peace negotiations.

THE TREATY OF PEACE

Western Questions.—The conquests of George Rogers Clark,
the entrance of Spain into the war, and the operations of Gálvez
turned the attention of congressional leaders to peace terms.
Would Spain be willing to grant the United States free navigation of the Mississippi? How much territory in the Southwest
would Spain demand? Would France support Spanish preten-
sions? Such were the questions which disturbed American
statesmen. To advance the interests of the United States, on
October 4, 1779, Congress appointed John Adams peace commissioner and John Jay representative at Madrid.

Adams and Vergennes.—Adams arrived at Paris in February,
1780. He surprised Vergennes by disclosing powers to conclude
treaties of peace and commerce with Great Britain. The protests and arguments of the French minister finally convinced
Adams that he had better wait until he received new instructions

from Congress, but he offended Vergennes by charging that France was purposely not exerting herself to the utmost. Vergennes distrusted Adams, for he thought that he represented the New England viewpoint which, Vergennes had been led to believe, was friendly to Great Britain. He informed Adams that in the future he would deal with Franklin.

Congressional instructions of June 15, 1781.—La Luzerne, the French representative at Philadelphia, made great efforts to have Adams curbed and to prevent a premature negotiation with Great Britain. In this he was assisted by the low state of affairs in the fall and winter of 1780. Congress finally decided to place the negotiations in the hands of a commission composed of Franklin, Jefferson, Jay, Adams, and Henry Laurens. Jefferson did not leave the United States and Laurens, who was captured by the British. did not arrive at Paris in time to take an important part in the negotiations. The instructions of the commissioners gave them considerable liberty of action, but they were to undertake nothing without the knowledge of the French ministers and were ultimately to be governed by their advice and opinion.

Jay in Spain.—In the meantime Jay had been having a difficult time in Spain. He was not officially received, and though granted occasional interviews by Florida Blanca, he was unable to make any progress toward the formulation of a treaty. When he was called to Paris in the summer of 1782 to take part in the peace negotiations, he had no illusions concerning the objects of Spain, objects which he seems to have believed were seconded by France.

The changed situation in 1782.—The commissioners were in a far stronger position than their instructions of 1781 implied. Yorktown had proved that American independence was assured, and Rodney's recent victory had weakened France at a time when her apparent support of Spain was liable to become troublesome. The situation in England had also changed. Lord North had fallen from power and at the head of the new ministry was Rockingham. Shelburne held the portfolio for the home and colonial departments and Fox was secretary of state for foreign affairs. This ministry held together from March until July, 1782, when Rockingham died. Fox, who had been unable to agree with Shelburne regarding the handling of American affairs, resigned, and Shelburne became Prime Minister.

Opening of negotiations with Great Britain.—On July 9, when Adams was at The Hague and before Jay had arrived, Franklin opened the negotiation with Oswald, the British agent, by presenting the basis of a treaty by which Great Britain was asked to acknowledge the independence of the United States, to settle boundaries and confine Canada within the bounds which maintained before the passage of the Quebec Act, and to acknowledge the right of Americans to fish on the Newfoundland banks and elsewhere.

Jay's suspicions of Vergennes.—The first hitch in the negotiations occurred when it was found that Oswald was instructed to conclude a peace or truce with the "colonies or plantations." On August 10 Jay and Franklin conferred with Vergennes about Oswald's commission. Jay contended that independence should be acknowledged by Great Britain before a treaty was negotiated, but Vergennes thought that this was of little consequence. When the question of conflicting Spanish and American claims was brought up, Vergennes became reticent, but his principal secretary, Rayneval, said that he thought the United States claimed too much. On September 7 Rayneval presented a memorial which proposed that the lands west of the mountains be divided into three Indian territories; lands north of the Ohio to be under the protection of Great Britain; south of the river the territory to be divided so that Spain would control the southwestern portion and the United States the northeastern part. On September 9 Jay learned that Rayneval had left secretly for England. Jay became thoroughly alarmed, for he believed that if the United States would not yield territory to Spain, Vergennes was ready to force his views by negotiating with England. Whether or not Jay was right in his suspicions has been a much argued question. No matter what the ultimate answer may be, the views of Jay became the determining factor in the course pursued by the American commissioners. Without consulting Franklin, Jay prevailed upon Benjamin Vaughan to visit Shelburne with the object of counteracting Rayneval's supposed mission and to let Shelburne know that the American commissioners were not to be bound by French views. A satisfactory commission was immediately issued to Oswald and negotiations proceeded with seriousness.

Proposal of October 8, 1782.—In October the American commissioners submitted proposals to Oswald. This preliminary draught provided that the independence of the United States be recognized by Great Britain and that the boundaries were to be as follows: "The said States are bounded north by a line drawn from the northwest angle of Nova Scotia, along the highlands which divide those rivers which empty themselves into the river St. Lawrence, from those which fall into the Atlantic Ocean, to the northernmost head of Connecticut River; thence down along the middle of that river to the 45th degree of north latitude, and thence due west in the latitude 45 degrees north from the equator, to the northwesternmost side of the river St. Lawrence . . . ; thence straight to the south end of the Lake Nipissing, and thence straight to the source of the river Mississippi; west by a line to be drawn along the middle of the river Mississippi, from its source to where the said line shall intersect the 31st degree of north latitude; south by a line to be drawn due east from the termination of the line last mentioned, in the latitude of 31 degrees north of the equator, to the middle of the river Apalachicola or Catahouchi; thence along the middle thereof to its junction with the Flint River; thence straight to the head of St. Mary's River; thence down along the middle of St. Mary's River to the Atlantic Ocean, and east by a line to be drawn along the middle of St. John's River from its source to its mouth in the bay of Fundy. . . ." The subjects of Great Britain and the United States were to enjoy the use of the fisheries, common commercial privileges, and the free navigation of the Mississippi. No provision was made for compensation to Loyalists, or for the collection by English merchants of debts in America.

Proposals of November 5.—The preliminary proposal was unsatisfactory to Shelburne. He accordingly sent Henry Strachey, an under official, to assist Oswald in making other arrangements. About this time Adams also arrived from The Hague. The negotiations proceeded without serious complications and in November a second draught was ready. In several important particulars it differed from the previous document. The Maine boundary on the east was to be a line drawn through the middle of the St. Croix River to its source, and thence directly north to the highlands which divide the rivers of the Atlantic from those which empty into the St. Lawrence; the line was to follow those highlands to the northwesternmost head of the Connecticut River, thence down that river to the forty-fifth parallel, and then straight west until it struck the Mississippi. British creditors were to "meet with no lawful impediment to recovering the full value or sterling amount of such *bona fide* debts as were contracted before the year 1775," but compensation to Loyalists was studiously omitted. A secret article was added to the effect, that if at the end of the war Great Britain should be, or should be put, in possession of West Florida, the boundary separating that province from the United States should be "a line drawn from the mouth of the river Yazoo, . . . due east to the river Apalachicola, and thence along the middle of that river to its junction with the Flint River, etc."

British proposal of November 25.—The failure to provide for the Loyalists caused the English government to submit other propositions which differed in two important particulars from the previous proposals. The northern boundary was changed west of the point where the Connecticut River crossed the forty-fifth parallel. From that point it was to follow the present international boundary to the Lake of the Woods, and from the northwestern point of that lake was to run due west to the Mississippi. The southern boundary was to leave the Mississippi at "the northernmost part of the 31st degree of north latitude," then "to be drawn due east . . . in the latitude of 31 degrees north of the equator to the middle of the river Apalachicola," and from there it was to follow the line of the proposal of October 8. Articles were also inserted which provided that restitution should be made of all estates, rights, and properties in America which had been confiscated during the war, that no one was to suffer in life or person, or be deprived of property on account of the part which he had taken in the war, that imprisoned Loyalists were to be set at liberty and pending prosecutions dropped. The right of Americans in the use of the fisheries were somewhat abridged.

Provisional articles of November 30. —The British proposals were satisfactory to the American commissioners except those regarding the Loyalists and the fisheries. After considerable discussion an agreement was reached and provisional articles were signed. The people of the United States were given unrestricted fishing privileges "on the Grand Bank and on all the other banks of Newfoundland," in the Gulf of St. Lawrence, and elsewhere, and the right of curing fish along the unsettled bays, harbors, and creeks of Nova Scotia, and on the shores of the Magdalen Islands and Labrador. The idea of indemnity for Loyalists was not incorporated, the articles merely pledging that Congress would make recommendations to the state legislatures that there should be no more confiscations or prosecutions, and that claimants of confiscated lands be allowed to use legal means of recovering them and might go at liberty for one year without personal risk. The articles also provided that the treaty should not be concluded until terms of peace had been agreed upon between France and Great Britain. The action of the American commissioners in arriving at an agreement without consulting the French ministers was not pleasing to Vergennes, but Franklin adroitly pacified him. It is probable that Vergennes did not have a deep feeling of resentment, for he soon obtained a loan of six million livres for the United States.

Preliminary agreements between England, France, and Spain. —Preliminary articles between England, France, and Spain were drawn in January, 1783. Spain failed to obtain Gibraltar, but received Minorca and the Floridas. France received no territory on the mainland of North America. French fishermen were granted important rights in the Newfoundland fisheries, and Great Britain gave to France Dunkirk, St. Lucia and Tobago, Senegal, and Gorée, and certain recent conquests, and guarantees of commercial privileges in India. France restored to Great Britain Grenada, the Grenadines, St. Vincent, Dominica, St. Christopher, Nevis, and Montserrat, and territory on the Gambia River.

Final agreements.—On September 3, 1783, all the definitive treaties were signed, the treaty between the United States and Great Britain being the same as the provisional articles of November 30. In the treaty the boundaries of the United States were apparently defined with exactness, but the statement of the Maine and northwestern boundaries proved to be ambiguous and became the subject of future disputes with Great Britain, the southern boundary agreement led to future difficulties with Spain, as did the question of the navigation of the Mississippi. The treaty was, however, a great triumph for American diplomacy. The United States had emerged from the contest as an independent power, with a vast domain stretching from the Mississippi to the Atlantic, and from the Great Lakes to the Floridas.

The dispersion of the Loyalists.—During the war many Loyalists had fled to England, to Canada, to the West Indies, or to Florida. A still larger number had taken refuge behind the British lines, or had joined the British Army. After the treaty, as persecutions continued, the British government arranged for the transportation of all who wished to leave the United States, offered them homes in the other British colonies, granted half pay to the officers after their regiments were reduced, and appointed a commission to provide compensation for losses. Many thousands of Loyalists left the country. Of these the more influential went to England. About two hundred families went to the West Indies. The larger number migrated to Canada, where, as "United Empire Loyalists," they laid the foundation of British Canada.

READINGS

THE WAR IN THE SOUTH AND THE YORKTOWN CAMPAIGN

Fisher, S. G., *The Struggle for American Independence*, II, 228–535; Greene, F. V., *The Revolutionary War*, 180–281; Lecky, W. E. H., *History of England in the Eighteenth Century*, IV, 130–165, 199–220; McCrady, Edward, *History of South Carolina in the Revolution*, 1780–1783; Trevelyan, G. O., *George the Third and Charles Fox*, II, 94–172.

THE TREATY OF PEACE

Channing, Edward, *History of the United States*, III, 346–373; Corwin, E. S., *French Policy and the American Alliance*, 217–377; Fiske, John, *The Critical Period*, 1–49; Lecky, W. E. H., *History of England in the Eighteenth Century*, IV, 255–322; McLaughlin, A. C., *The Confederation and the Constitution*, 3–34; Wharton, Francis, *The Revolutionary Diplomatic Correspondence of the United States*, V–VI; Winsor, Justin, *The Westward Movement*, 203–224.

CHAPTER XXVIII

GOVERNMENTAL DEVELOPMENT DURING THE REVOLUTION

The Association a step toward sovereignty.—The First Continental Congress was called to deliberate and determine upon measures to recover rights and liberties of which the colonies had been deprived and to restore harmony with Great Britain. Although the Congress was consultative in nature, it completed the revolutionary organization and made unity of action possible. The adoption of the Association was a fundamental step toward sovereignty. It could only be interpreted to mean that the colonies intended to enforce their will upon the mother country. Furthermore, Congress provided means to enforce the Association within colonies. While the petitions and addresses which were sent forth were couched in respectful terms, the tone of the declaration and resolves was distinctly revolutionary, and when considered in connection with the Association, it becomes evident that the iron hand of a sovereign power was even then visible through the mists of revolution.

THE SECOND CONTINENTAL CONGRESS

Nature of Congress.—The Second Continental Congress which convened at Philadelphia on May 10, 1775, was a purely revolutionary body, a "creature of emergency." In its inception it was in no sense a sovereign body, but was rather a great central committee, representing the revolutionary elements in the various colonies, which assumed the supreme directing power until 1781. The colonies had displayed no regularity in the method of selecting the delegates. The two New Hampshire delegates were chosen by a convention of deputies who had been appointed by various towns. The five delegates of Massachusetts were chosen by the provincial congress. The Rhode Island assembly chose two delegates, and the Connecticut house of representatives five. In New York twelve delegates were selected

by a provincial convention. The five delegates from New Jersey
were chosen by the assembly, as were the nine from Pennsylvania
and the three from Delaware. In Maryland a meeting of deputies
chose seven delegates, three or more of whom might represent
the colony. In Virginia a convention of delegates selected seven.
In North Carolina a convention chose three delegates who were
approved by the assembly, and in South Carolina the assembly
appointed five. Georgia at first was represented by a delegate
from a single parish.

Original powers of the delegates.—The delegates were not
empowered to perform sovereign acts, but were considered as a
central revolutionary committee, which was to take such measures as would be best calculated to recover and establish American rights and liberties, restore harmony between Great Britain
and her colonies, and advance the best interests of the colonies.
As the revolutionary movement spread and acts of violence
occurred, necessity forced Congress to perform many acts which
were not contemplated in the original instructions of the delegates; but from first to last it was lacking in sovereign powers
and was always the creature of the states.

Causes of the weakness of Congress.—The fundamental cause
of the weakness of Congress was its lack of legal powers. When
executive acts were necessary, the delegates were never certain
that their joint action would be upheld by the states. Congress
had no power to enforce its will, or to coerce an unruly state.
Another source of weakness was the constantly changing per-
sonnel of Congress, the numbers varying from twenty-four to a
hundred. Many of the strongest members were sent on foreign
missions, leaving important work to be done by men who had
had little experience in public affairs. Sectional jealousy frequently interfered with concerted action; the small states feared
the larger ones; states holding no western lands were suspicious
of those with such possessions; and theological differences made
it difficult for New Englanders to work with delegates from the
middle and southern states. In 1777 when Vermont was asking
to be admitted as a state, New England and New York found
their interests to be conflicting, as both claimed jurisdiction
over the Green Mountain country. Some of the members stooped
to petty acts for self-aggrandizement, breeding suspicion in the

minds of many. Congress was housed at Philadelphia in the
state house, which was poorly arranged for a body whose business was mainly conducted by committees. Military necessity
twice forced Congress to hasten from the city, the first time in
December, 1776, when it fled to Baltimore, the second time after
the battle of the Brandywine, when it became an exile, first at
Lancaster and later at York.

Nature of the business of Congress.—Dr. Albion W. Small
has classified the business of Congress under the following heads:
(1) To dispose of sundry applications in behalf of individuals;
(2) to consider requests for advice and aid to individual colonies;
(3) to act as the mouthpiece of the patriotic party; (4) to serve
as an organ of communication between the collective colonies
and other communities or individuals; (5) to devise peace plans
and measures for the general good; (6) to devise offensive and
defensive measures to be urged upon the individual colonies;
(7) to raise, organize, and regulate a continental army, and assume general direction of military affairs.

Organization of Congress and conduct of business.—When
Peyton Randolph found it necessary to leave Congress, the delegates chose John Hancock president and Charles Thomson secretary, the latter serving until 1781. Most of the work was carried
on by committees. When a vote was taken in Congress, the
members did not cast their ballots as individuals, but each
state delegation cast a solid affirmative or negative vote. Usually
committees met in the morning from 7 to 10, Congress from 10
A. M. to 4 or 5 P. M., and committees from 6 to 10 P. M. The
president's duties were manifold, for in addition to acting as presiding officer, he carried on correspondence with the commander-
in-chief, with state governors, and with local committees.

Early acts of Congress.—In spite of the conservatives who
at first were in the majority and who desired to hold in check
the revolutionary forces, circumstances forced Congress to exercise executive authority long before the Declaration of Independence. In June, 1775, Congress ordered the raising and organizing of an army, authorized a loan for the purchase of gunpowder,
and issued $2,000,000 in bills of credit. In September provision
was made for the fitting out of a navy, and steps were taken to
open relations with foreign powers, to supervise the frontiers,

and to establish a post-office. In the chaos which resulted from the overthrow of the chartered governments, several of the state revolutionary bodies appealed to Congress for advice. In answer to the Massachusetts appeal, Congress advised that, as no obedience was due to parliament and as the crown officials were absent, the provincial congress was to summon the representatives to an assembly which was to choose a council, and together the two bodies were to govern until difficulties were adjusted with the crown. Similar advice was given to New Hampshire, South Carolina, and Virginia. The various colonies were also advised to erect prize courts. In March, 1776, it advised the colonies to disarm the Loyalists, and soon afterward authorized the fitting out of privateers and opened the ports to all countries not subject to Great Britain. In May it urged all colonies which had not yet formed state governments to do so and declared that British authority should be suppressed. On July 4, 1776, it adopted the Declaration of Independence.

Judicial functions.—With the increase of privateering, prize courts became necessary, and in November, 1775, Congress advised the colonies to erect courts in which cases of capture might be tried by jury and appeals made to Congress. During 1776 the custom was followed of appointing a congressional committee to hear each appeal, but in January, 1777, a standing committee of five was appointed to hear all appeals. The increasing business and the need of legally trained men made it apparent that the committee system could not long handle the prize cases, and in January, 1780, a permanent court of appeals was established, which may be looked upon as a forerunner of the supreme court.

Military affairs.—When hostilities began, Congress acted on the theory that the colonies were loyal to the king, but were opposing Gage's ministerial army. Events soon forced it to take measures of defence, committees being appointed in May, 1775, to consider how military stores might be procured. On June 15 Washington was chosen commander-in-chief and on the following day a committee was appointed to draw up his commission and instructions. Congress also selected four major-generals, eight brigadier-generals, a quartermaster-general and commissary-general. Later a clothier-general was appointed.

At first military affairs were handled by congressional committees, but in January, 1776, a committee was appointed to consider the establishment of a war office. Five months later Congress adopted the committee's plan which provided for a Board of War and Ordnance to consist of five members of Congress and a secretary. In 1777 this congressional board was done away with and a new board, consisting of persons who were not members of Congress, was created, Gates being placed at its head. Congress also appointed an inspector-general, Thomas Conway being the first incumbent, being followed by Steuben. The system of supplying the army was found to be deficient and to rectify matters the commissary department was reorganized in 1777 and again in 1778. Congress continued to keep in touch with the army by sending special committees to examine actual conditions.

Naval affairs.—To handle maritime affairs a naval committee was appointed whose "active life lasted from October, 1775, until January, 1776, during which time it laid the foundation of the navy." On December 14, 1775, a marine committee, composed of one member from each colony, was chosen to take charge of the building and fitting out of vessels, and this committee soon assumed direction of naval affairs. Agents to superintend the work of construction were employed, and on the recommendation of the committee, Congress appointed prize agents. In November, 1776, a board of three naval experts was created to execute business under the direction of the maritime committee and a similar board was appointed in April, 1777, to handle affairs in New England alone. The marine committee continued until October, 1779. By that time it became evident that a more efficient system was needed and Congress appointed a Board of Admiralty consisting of three commissioners and two members of Congress. The board remained in charge of naval affairs until the governmental reorganization of 1781.

Foreign affairs.—To direct diplomacy was one of the difficult functions of a Congress whose members were but little versed in the intricacies of foreign courts. In the fall of 1775 a "secret committee on foreign correspondence" was chosen. In March, 1776, Silas Deane was sent to France, and in September of the same year a commission to handle American interests in

Europe, composed of Franklin, Jefferson, and Deane, was appointed. Jefferson, however, remained in America and Arthur Lee was substituted. To obtain financial aid had been the chief object up to the Declaration of Independence, but after that Congress and its agents directed their energies not only to the securing of funds, but to obtain recognition by France and Spain, and to make military and commercial alliances. In 1777 the secret committee was changed to the "committee on foreign affairs," an organization which conducted the foreign policy up to 1781.

FINANCIAL AFFAIRS

Fiscal machinery.—The most difficult problem which Congress had to solve was the raising of sufficient funds to carry on the Revolution. To handle the public moneys and devise means for raising revenue, fiscal machinery gradually came into existence. In 1775 two treasurers were appointed to receive and disburse public funds. Soon a committee of claims of thirteen members was appointed, and in February, 1776, a standing committee of five known as the Treasury Board, which supervised financial officials and attended to the emission of instruments of credit. This board, under which was an auditor-general at the head of the office of accounts, was the germ of the later treasury. In 1778 the book-keeping system was remodeled and a comptroller, auditor, treasurer, and two chambers of accounts were provided. In 1779 the old treasury board was set aside and in its place a commission of five was appointed, of which three were not congressional delegates.

Bills of credit.—Congress had three principal means of raising money: by issuance of bills of credit, by requisitions upon the states, and by domestic and foreign loans. In addition there was a considerable income from prizes and captures. The need of raising money drove Congress to the doubtful expedient of issuing large quantities of paper money unbacked by bullion or specie but based upon the credit of the states. Between June, 1775, and November, 1779, Congress authorized the issuance of $241,552,780 in denominations varying from one-sixth of a dollar to sixty-five dollars. In addition the states issued over

$200,000,000 in paper money. Such large amounts of unbacked paper could lead to but one result, a steadily increasing depreciation. At first the people took the continental money with little protest, but as issue followed issue in rapid succession, depreciation set in, and by January, 1779, the ratio of currency to specie was eight to one, by June twenty to one, and by the end of that year forty to one. In May, 1781, it ceased to pass as currency. Financiers have found it difficult to estimate the specie value of the various issues, but a careful economist has calculated that it was worth between $37,000,000 and $41,000,000.

Requisitions upon the states.—As military demands became more and more insistent, Congress found it necessary to make requisitions upon the states. The demands were met in a niggardly manner; between November, 1777, and February, 1781, the moneys received, figured in specie value, amounted to only $2,737,000. In 1780 Congress was driven to demanding specific supplies, such as corn, meat, and hay.

Domestic loans.—With the exception of a small loan for the purchase of gunpowder, Congress did not authorize a domestic loan until October, 1776, when it voted to borrow $5,000,000 at four per cent. and to establish state loan offices. Subsequent loans were at six per cent. After money from foreign loans began to come in in September, 1777, interest on the domestic debt was paid, enabling Congress to borrow more freely than before. From October, 1776, to September, 1777, only $3,787,000 was obtained from the states, and during the rest of the war $63,289,000 in paper was subscribed.

Foreign loans.—Most of the foreign financial aid came from France. In the years before France formally recognized the independence of the American states, large sums were loaned to Congress. In May, 1776, Vergennes secured a loan of a million livres from the French treasury and also obtained a small loan from Spain. Through the fictitious company of "Hortalez et Cie" in Paris organized by Beaumarchais, and the Spanish firm of Josef Gardoqui and Sons, large quantities of clothing, military stores, and considerable sums of money were placed at the disposal of the revolutionary agents. During 1777-1780 Congress borrowed from France $1,633,500.

STATE GOVERNMENTS DURING THE REVOLUTION

Organization of state governments.—As resistance to British authority intensified during 1775, the colonies took steps to organize for resistance. The colonial governors were forced to leave and the committees of safety assumed temporary executive functions. In most of the colonies revolutionary conventions were called which took over the legislative power until it became apparent that the difficulties with Great Britain could not be settled. As it grew more and more evident that the war was to be fought for independence, the conventions took steps to organize state governments. Several of them asked advice concerning such action from the Continental Congress, and that body finally advised all the colonies to proceed on the assumption that they no longer owed allegiance to the crown. The constitutional convention introduced a new principle in the theory of the state. Up to this time governmental authority had rested in England. Henceforth the powers of sovereignty were to emanate from the will of the people, the constitutional convention being the embodiment of the sovereign will.

Type of state governments.—In the formation of governments the states were guided by experience in colonial statecraft. The new constitutions disclosed the influence of the struggle with Great Britain, the framers seeking to protect the commonwealths from the possibility of encroachment of the executive at the expense of the legislative departments. The influence of the political philosophy which insisted that the separation of the departments of government was the safeguard of popular rights was also apparent in the new constitutions. Although they displayed a marked divergence on minor points, in general a common type of government prevailed. In most of the states the legislative department was in two parts, a lower and an upper house; the lower, usually elected for a year, represented the people at large, and the upper, serving for longer periods, represented the wealthier classes. In all but one state a property qualification was required for voters and representatives, and in most cases the property qualification was higher for members of the upper chamber. There was no uniformity in designation, the lower chamber being variously called the house of representatives, house of commons, or assembly; the upper house was usually called the legislative council, but in Virginia it was known as the senate, a designation afterward commonly adopted. The executive was usually weak, being vested either in a governor with limited power or in a small group. So well adapted to the needs of a state were the colonial charters of Connecticut and Rhode Island, that they continued to use their charters as constitutions for many years, merely substituting the authority of the people for that of the king.

Variations from type.—Several of the state constitutions contained unusual features. In Pennsylvania the radical convention in 1776 framed a constitution which provided for a legislature of one chamber and an executive council which could not veto an act of the assembly. Every seven years a council of censors was to be chosen by the voters to see that the constitution had not been violated. By a two-thirds vote the censors could summon a convention to amend the constitution. Georgia also set up a unicameral legislature. The Virginia constitution of 1776 contained a declaration of independence. It also provided that all bills must originate in the lower house and that money bills could not be amended by the senate. A privy council of eight members was chosen by a joint ballot of both houses. This body and the two houses selected the governor. The South Carolina constitution of 1778 provided for the election of the upper house by the people and the governor was deprived of the veto power. By the New York constitution of 1778, the governor was elected by the people, but he had neither appointive nor veto power, those functions being exercised respectively by a council of appointments chosen from the senate by the assembly, and by a council of revision composed of the governor, chancellor, and two or more judges of the supreme court. Objections raised by the council of revision could be defeated by a two-thirds vote of both houses. The first constitution of Massachusetts provided for a legislature of two houses, the upper chamber acting as a multiple executive. In 1780 a new constitution was accepted by the people. This provided that the governor be given military powers and the appointment of judges. He was to be advised by a council of nine elected from the senate by both houses.

Selection of the judiciary.—Divergences appeared in the methods of selecting judges. In Connecticut and Rhode Island they were appointed annually by the assemblies. In Georgia the chief justice was appointed by the assembly, but the people elected the county judges annually; in New Jersey, Delaware, and Pennsylvania the assemblies chose the judges for seven years; in Massachusetts, New York, and Maryland the governor and council appointed the judges who held office during good behavior; in other states the legislatures appointed them for varying terms.

The courts.—The states established superior tribunals which were authorized to review and correct decisions of inferior courts. In Georgia the county courts, when presided over by the chief-justice, acted as a final court of appeal. In New Jersey the governor and council constituted the highest appellate tribunal. In Virginia the constitution provided for a court of appeals which passed upon the constitutionality of laws and heard appeals. In Maryland and South Carolina the appellate courts were composed of the presiding officers of the district courts. In the other colonies the supreme court fulfilled the same function. The colonial system of county courts to try the smaller civil cases, and courts of session, composed of justices of the peace, for trial of petty criminal cases were retained.

English law the basis of American jurisprudence.—The English common-law forms of writs and legal process were continued with all their technicalities, a usage which has been one of the stumbling blocks in the attempts to simplify legal methods in the United States. "Either by the constitutions or by legislative enactments, English common law, and all those English statutes hitherto recognized and acted upon in the colonies respectively, were made the basis of state jurisprudence. The force of law was also continued to all existing colonial statutes until repealed or altered, except in South Carolina, where a particular enumeration and reënactment was made of the colonial statutes intended to be recognized."

The revolutionary state of Vermont.—In the Green Mountain region a new state was in the making. There New York claimed jurisdiction but her authority had never been established and in April, 1775, the inhabitants of the mountain country held a convention, eventually drew up a constitution, and asked Congress to recognize Vermont as a state. New York succeeded in defeating the movement in Congress, but the Vermonters, nothin; daunted, proceeded to organize their government. The new revolutionary state soon became embroiled in disputes with New Hampshire and Massachusetts. These and the continued opposition of New York caused Congress to delay recognition, and Vermont was not formally admitted to the union until 1791, but to all intents and purposes it was a sovereign state from 1775.

Attempts at Western State-Making.—In the course of the Revolution, likewise, the settlements beyond the Alleghanies were trying experiments in state-making. The Watauga Association in eastern Tennessee, the Transylvania government in Kentucky, and the Nashborough Association are all examples. These western communities reverted to the compact theory of government, and their experiences illustrate the democratic tendencies of the frontier. As yet, however, the communities were too weak to succeed in the midst of conflicting elements and each reverted for a time to the subordinate position of a county of the older state.

THE ARTICLES OF CONFEDERATION

The confederation movement.—When danger from without threatened, a union of the colonies as a device of safety had often been suggested, but separatist tendencies had always proved too strong for the federationists. Franklin had been a friend of the idea of union, in 1754 having penned the Albany plan. In July, 1775, when it became apparent that the colonies were facing a great war, he proposed a league of friendship whose affairs should be conducted by a general congress in which each colony should have representation according to its population. Franklin's plan was not adopted, but it focused attention upon the growing need of a confederation. The Continental Congress was a revolutionary body which had no power save the sufferance of states which were themselves revolutionary. Whether or not those states were to retain sovereign powers depended entirely on the outcome of the struggle. To insure a successful issue, it was believed that a more perfect organ than the Continental Congress should be devised to conduct the Revolution.

Work of the confederation committee.—When Lee's independence resolution was introduced in the Continental Congress on June 7, 1776, it was accompanied by a motion to appoint a committee to draw up articles of confederation. On June 12 a committee composed of one delegate from each colony was chosen, among the members being John Dickinson, Samuel Adams, Roger Sherman, and Edward Rutledge. On July 12 the committee reported a plan of confederation, drawn mainly by Dickinson, which provided that each state should have a single vote in a central congress, and that an affirmative vote of nine states should be necessary to pass any measure.

Adoption of the articles.—Stress of business, military events which forced the hasty departure of Congress from Philadelphia on several occasions, and divergence of views prevented speedy action. On two ideas only was there agreement. The delegates were convinced that the English imperial system was wrong in its theory of taxation; whatever the form of the central government might be, it must not take from the states the power of taxation. They were also agreed that the executive power of the central government must be weak. The debates turned upon three main questions, taxation, representation, and congressional power to settle boundary disputes. Dickinson's plan proposed that taxation should be apportioned among the states according to population; this aroused the opposition of the Southerners, who objected to the slaves being counted as population. Franklin objected to Dickinson's proposal of one vote per state on the ground that it was an inequitable arrangement. In reply it was argued that the confederation was a league of friendship to be formed for a specific purpose and in consequence each state ought to have equal power. In regard to congressional power to settle boundary disputes, a difference arose between those states which possessed western lands and those which did not. Not until November, 1777, did Congress give the articles a favorable vote and on June 26, 1778, a form of ratification was adopted. Delegates from the New England states, New York, Pennsylvania, Virginia, and South Carolina signed the articles on July 9, North Carolina on July 21, Georgia on July 24, and New Jersey on November 26, 1778; Delaware on May 5, 1779, and Maryland not until March 1, 1781. In consequence of the tardy action of Maryland, the Continental Congress continued to conduct the war almost to its conclusion.

The more important provisions of the articles.—The preamble stated that the delegates had agreed "to certain articles of Confederation and perpetual union." Article I named the confederacy "The United States of America." Article II said, "Each State retains its sovereignty, freedom and independence, and every power, jurisdiction and right, which is not by this confederation expressly delegated to the United States, in Congress assembled." Article III stated the purpose of the entrance of the states into a league of friendship as follows: "for their common defence, the security of their liberties, and their mutual and general welfare." Article IV declared that the free inhabitants of each state should be "entitled to all privileges and immunities of free citizens in the several States" and provided for the extradition of criminals. It also stated that, "Full faith and credit shall be given in each of these States to the records, acts and judicial proceedings of the courts and magistrates of every other State."

Article V provided that delegates should "be annually appointed in such manner as the legislature of each State shall direct," and that Congress should convene annually on the first Monday in November. No state was to be represented in Congress by less than two nor more than seven members, and in determining questions, each state should have one vote.

Article VI dealt mainly with prohibitions upon the states. Without the consent of Congress, no state was to enter into treaties, confederation, or alliance with foreign courts, nor was any state to lay imposts or duties which might interfere with any stipulations in treaties entered into between the United States and foreign powers. Such naval and military forces were to be maintained by the states in time of peace as Congress might deem necessary, and no state was to engage in war without the consent of Congress unless actually invaded or in danger of Indian attack.

Article VIII provided that expenses incurred for common defence or for the general welfare, when allowed by Congress, should be defrayed out of a common treasury, to "be supplied by the several states, in proportion to the value of all land within each state, granted to or surveyed for any person, as such land and the buildings and improvements thereon shall be estimated according to such mode as the United States in Congress assembled, shall from time to time direct and appoint."

Article IX dealt with the congressional powers. Congress was given the exclusive power (1) of determining peace or war except in the cases mentioned in Article VI, (2) of sending and receiving ambassadors, (3) of entering into treaties and alliances, provided such agreements did not interfere with the rights of the states to lay such imposts and duties on foreign goods as they were subjected to by foreigners, or prohibit exportation or importation, (4) of establishing rules for deciding prize cases, (5) of granting letters of marque and reprisal in time of peace, (6) of establishing admiralty courts, and (7) of settling disputes between two or more states, an elaborate procedure in such cases being prescribed.

Congress was also given the exclusive power (8) of regulating the alloy and value of coin struck by its authority or by that of a state, (9) of fixing the standard of weights and measures, (10) of regulating affairs with Indians not members of states provided state rights were not infringed, (11) of establishing and regulating post offices and postage, (12) of appointing military officers except regimental officers, (13) of appointing naval officers, and (14) of making rules and regulations for the army and navy.

Other powers of Congress were (15) "to appoint a committee, to sit in the recess of Congress, to be denominated 'a Committee of the States,' and to consist of one delegate from each State; and to appoint such other committees and civil officers as may be necessary for managing the general affairs of the United States under direction . . .," (16) to ascertain the necessary sums of money to be raised for the service of the United States, and to appropriate and apply the same for defraying the public expenses, (17) to borrow money or emit bills on the credit of the United States, (18) to build and equip a navy, and (19) "to agree upon the number of land forces, and to make requisition from each state for its quota, in proportion to the number of white inhabitants in each state." With the exception of a vote upon adjournment, all measures required the assent of nine states. No period of adjournment was to be longer than six months.

Article X provided that the committee of the states should be authorized to execute the delegated powers of Congress during recesses. Article XII stated that bills of credit, loans, and debts should be considered as a charge against the United States and for whose payment the United States and the public faith were pledged. Article XIII provided that every state should abide by the acts of Congress, that the union should be perpetual, and that no alteration should be made in the articles by Congress unless afterwards confirmed by the legislatures of every state.

Fundamental weaknesses of the articles.—Admirable as this document was in many respects, it contained weaknesses which were certain to make the union temporary rather than perpetual. It failed to give the central government sufficient power. The articles were distinctly the instrument of a confederation of sovereign states, and not the constitution of a federal state. Congress was not given the power to raise money or to regulate commerce. It could not compel the states to pay the national debts, to live up to treaties, or to raise armies. The articles provided for no distinct executive department, but this was remedied in part by congressional acts. With the exception of the fourth, fifth, and seventh provisions of Article IX, judicial matters were left to the states. The required vote of nine state to pass measures necessarily hindered the passage of needed regulations. The requirement that every state legislature must give its consent before an amendment could be passed made it well-nigh impossible to change the instrument.

GOVERNMENTAL REORGANIZATION

Organization of executive departments.—The failure of the congressional committee system to perform executive functions had grown more apparent as the war progressed, and in the closing days of the Second Continental Congress measures were taken to concentrate the executive departmental work under individual heads. During January and February, 1781, the Continental Congress created four new offices: superintendent of finance, secretary at war, secretary of marine, and secretary of foreign affairs, a foreshadowing of the later cabinet. The policy thus inaugurated was continued under the new Congress which held its first sitting on March 2, 1781.

The work of Robert Morris.—The failure of the bills of credit, the insufficiency of state support, and the weakness of foreign credit had made it evident that the financial system must be reorganized; accordingly the treasury commission was abolished and finances were placed in the hands of Robert Morris, a successful merchant of Philadelphia who had rendered valuable assistance as a member of the Pennsylvania assembly and of Congress. Morris realized that retrenchment and economy must be his watchwords. In the words of Dewey, he endeavored "to collect the requisitions from the States, to create a national revenue and impost, and place the revenue on a specie basis. . . ." He also sought to establish foreign credit and to found a United States bank. At every turn he was handicapped by local prejudice, petty bickerings over taxation, and the lack of power of the central government.

Foreign loans and requisitions upon states.—The adoption of the Articles of Confederation immediately strengthened foreign credit, for during 1781–1783 loans of $4,719,000 were obtained from France, $174,017 from Spain, and $1,304,000 from the bankers of Holland. The loans from Spain and Holland, however, probably would not have been obtained had it not been for the entry of those powers into the war. Requisitions upon states during the same period yielded $3,058,000 in specie value, but the proposals of Morris to institute a land tax, poll tax, excise, and tariff came to naught.

The Bank of North America.—In 1780 Congress had tried to establish a financial institution called the Bank of Pennsylvania, but it had been of little service. Morris planned a sounder institution to be known as the Bank of North America with a capitalization of not over $10,000,000. Only $70,000 was raised by private subscription and the government set aside $200,000 in specie which had recently arrived from France. From this bank during 1782–1783 the government borrowed on short term loans $1,272,842 As Congress repaid the bank before other creditors, a small working balance was maintained on which the government could draw for immediate needs.

War and navy departments.—Owing to factional quarrels, it was not until January, 1782, that General Benjamin Lincoln was made secretary at war. No one was appointed for the department of marine, and the work was turned over to the already overburdened superintendent of finance. The office of agent of marine was created, and this Morris held from September, 1781, until November, 1784.

Department of foreign affairs.—The first secretary of foreign affairs was Robert R. Livingston of New York, a former member of the committee which formulated the Declaration of Independence and famous later as minister to France at the time of the Louisiana purchase. He held office from August, 1781, to June, 1783, being succeeded in 1784 by John Jay. The department as conducted under Livingston consisted of the secretary, two assistant secretaries, and a clerk.

Conclusion.—Thus during the stress of war national and state governments had come into existence. Necessity had forced the people to act and though the leaders at times groped blindly and took many a false step, the political capacity of the American people had asserted itself and triumphed. They profited by their experiences and showed themselves ready to cast aside useless institutions and try new ones which gave fair promise of success. A government of the people, for the people, and by the people had come into existence which challenged the doctrine that the sovereign ruled by right divine.

READINGS

Bolles, A. S., *Financial History of the United States, 1774–1789;* Bullock, C. J., *Finances of the United States from 1775 to 1789;* Channing, Edward, *History of the United States*, III, 431–462; Dewey, D. R., *Financial History of the United States*, 33–56; Foster, J. W., *A Century of American Diplomacy*, 1–40; Guggenheim, J. C., "The Development of the Executive Departments, 1775–1789," in J. Franklin Jameson, *Essays in the Constitutional History of the United States in the Formative Period, 1775–1789;* Hatch, L. C., *Administration of the American Revolutionary Army;* Hildreth, Richard, *The History of the United States of America*, III, 374–410; Learned, H. B., *The President's Cabinet*, 47–63; McLaughlin, A. C., *The Confederation and the Constitution*, 35–70; Paullin, C. O., *The Navy of the American Revolution*, 31–251; Small, A. W., "The Beginnings of American Nationality," in Johns Hopkins University, *Studies in History and Political Science*, 8th Series, Parts I and II; Sumner, W. G., *The Financier and Finances of the American Revolution;* Van Tyne, C. H., *The American Revolution*, 175–202; Hunt, G., *The Department of State*, 1–37.

INDEX

Abenaki Indians, 257, 266; war of, 313.

Abercromby, General James, in French and Indian War, 376, 377, 378.

Acadia, colonization, 85-86; captured by England, restored to France, 86, 87; during War of Spanish Succession, English expeditions against, 271; conquest of, 272; attacked by French during War of Austrian Succession, 364, 365; French policy in, 366; during French and Indian War, 374.

Acapulco, Mexico, commercial port, 86.

Acatic, Nueva Galicia, in the Mixton War, 40.

Accau, explorer in Minnesota with Father Hennepin, 100.

Ácoma, New Mexico pueblo, 46, 72, 73.

Adams, John, defence of British soldiers, 443; in First Continental Congress, 452; argues for Declaration of Independence, 479; member of committee for drafting the Declaration, 479; diplomacy in France and Holland, 532-533; peace negotiations, 533-538.

Adams, Samuel, circular letter, 440-441; trouble with Governor Bernard, 443; the man of the town meeting, 445-446; in First Continental Congress, 451; on committee to draft Articles of Confederation, 550.

Adelantados, 54-55.

Administration of Justice Act, 450.

Admiralty, English, 182-183; courts, 349.

Africa, early ideas concerning, 1-2; Ptolemy's conception of, 1-2; trade with desired, 5; exploration of west coast, 5; Prester, John, 5; Sénégal and Gorée captured by English, 380; Sénégal given to British by Peace of Paris, 382.

African Company, formed to break Dutch monopoly, 196.

Agriculture, in Spanish colonies, 21, 75; in French Canada, 92, 93; in French West Indies, 94-95; in New England, 216-217, 330-331; in the Middle English colonies, 120, 122, 124, 128, 332; in the South, 333-335; in the British West Indies, 339-341; in Bermudas, 130, in Dutch colonies, 169, 170, 171, 173.

Aguas Calientes, 58, 59; mines of, 58.

Aguayo, Marquis of, expedition to Texas, 296-297.

Aguilar, Marcos de, governor in Mexico, 48.

Aijado Indians, 243.

Ailly, Pierre d', author of *Imago Mundi*, 2, 7.

Aix-la-Chapelle, Peace of, 366.

Alabama Indians, 251, 270.

Alabama River, 62.

Alamance, battle of the, 415.

Alarcón, Hernando de, explores Colorado River, 45.

Alarcón, Martín de, governor of Texas, and of Coahuila, 294-295.

Albany, 332.

Albany Congress, 371, 411.

Albemarle, Duke of. *See* Monk.

Albermarle district, settlement, 207; population, 211; Culpeper rebellion, 211.

Alberoni, 279, 359.

Albórnoz, royal *contador* of New Spain, 48.

Albuquerque, New Mexico, founding of, 290.

Alburquerque, Portuguese viceroy in India, 24.

Alacalá, University of, 76.

Alcaldes, 14, 34, 55.

Alcaldía Mayor, administrative district, 59.

Aleutian Islands, Russian fur trade, 388.

Alexander, Pillars of, 1.

factor in trans-Atlantic navigation, 8; natives of as colonists in Florida and Texas, 255, 298.

Cancer, Fray Luís, expedition to Florida, 61.

Cano, Francisco del, explorer in Coahuila, 59.

Cape Ann, settlement, 140.

Cape Blanco, California, 5, 71.

Cape Bojador, 2.

Cape Bréton Island, 273, 365–383; siege and defence of Louisbourg, 364–365.

Cape Fear, 26.

Cape Fear River, Ayllón at, 41.

Cape Finisterre, battles off, 365.

Cape Gaspé, 82, 87.

Cape of Good Hope, discovery of, 5; trade route to Far East, 5.

Cape Horn, discovery of, 165.

Cape Mendocino, California on route of Manila galleon, 70.

Cape Nun, early voyages to, 3–4.

Cape St. Vincent, 4.

Cape Verde, reached by Portuguese, 5.

Cape Verde Islands, discovery of, 5.

Capuchins, in Louisiana, 280.

Carabajal, Luís de, governor of Kingdom of New León, 60; expeditions and colonies, 60–61; arrest and condemnation, 61.

Caria, Island of, 25.

Caribs, enslaved, 23; De León's war against, 40.

Cárdenas, discovers Grand Canyon, 45.

Cardona, Thomas, monopoly of pearl fishing, 240.

Caribbean Sea. See West Indies, Lesser Antilles, and individual islands.

Carleton, General Sir Guy, 487, 488.

Carlisle Commission, 509.

Carlisle, Lord, receives grant in the Caribbean, 132.

Carlos III, attitude toward American Revolution, 515.

Carmelites, in Louisiana, 280.

Carolinas, Gordillo and Quexos in Chicora, 26; Ayllón's colony of San Miguel in, 40–41; De Soto in North Carolina Piedmont, 42; attempt of De Luna and Villafañe at Santa Elena (Port Royal), 61–62; Ribaut's

Huguenot colony at Port Royal, 62; 84; Spanish post at Santa Elena, 64; exploration of Pardo and Boyano, 64; missions at Santa Elena and Orista, 64–65; Menéndez's expeditions up coast, 65; traders in, 102; Carolina traders cross the Alleghanies, 102; grant to Sir Robert Heath, 207; settlement of Albemarle district, 207; charters of 1663 and 1665, 207–208; the proprietors, 208; Locke's constitution, 208; settlements, 208, 254; effect on Spanish frontier policy, 254; development of the colony, 210; unrest at Charleston, 210–211; the Albemarle region, 211; Culpeper's rebellion, 211; under William III, 346; separation, 313; Yamassee War, 314; overthrow of proprietors, 314–315. See also Albemarle District, North Carolina, South Carolina.

Carpenters' Hall, 452.

Carpini, John de Plano, author of *Book of the Tartars*, 3.

Carrero, Alonso, explorer in Central America, 32.

Cartagena, despoiled in War of English Succession, 262; bombarded and besieged in War of Jenkins' Ear, 361, 363.

Carteret, Sir George, grant in the Jerseys, 198; obtains East New Jersey, 198–199; Carolina proprietor, 208; interest in Hudson's Bay Company, 213.

Carteret, Philip, governor of East New Jersey, 198–199.

Cartier, Jacques, in the St. Lawrence, 81–82; map showing explorations, 83.

Carver, Governor John, goes to Leyden, 137; removal to Plymouth, 137; confirmed as governor, 138; death, 139.

Casa de Contratación, 19; duties and organization, 19; subordinate to Council of Indies, 20.

Casas Grandes (Nueva Vizcaya), 56, 242.

Casco Bay settlement, 140; submits to Massachusetts, 158; attacks on, 262, 263.

INDEX

East Indies, commerce of, 70.

Eastland Company, 106.

East New Jersey, population, 221; social conditions, 223–224; religion, 224; education, 224. *See* New Jersey.

Eaton, Theophilus, a founder of New Haven, 150.

Eaton's Station, 513.

Echagaray, ordered to explore Bay of Espíritu Santo, 249.

Ecija, expedition from Florida to Virginia, 1609, 118–119.

Edict of Nantes, 79.

Edisto Island, ravaged by Spaniards, 1686, 255.

Education, in New Spain, 50, 53; colleges and universities, 76; in New England, 220–221; in New York, 222–223; in East New Jersey, 224; in Chesapeake Bay region, 229; in South Carolina, 231; in English colonies in the eighteenth century, 338–339.

Edwards, Jonathan, 338.

Elcano, completes Magellan's voyage round the world, 25.

Eleutheria Island, settled, 152.

Eliot, John, missionary to Indians, 156.

Elizabethtown, New Jersey, 199.

Elizabeth, Queen of England, policy, 105; English expansion during reign, 107–111.

El Paso district, beginnings of, 245; attached to New Mexico, 245.

Emigration. *See* Immigration and Population.

Encomiendas, origin of, 22; granting of in conquests, 31, 34, 40, 55; upheld by Cortés, 47–48; *New Laws* concerning, 50; cessation of, in West Indies, 67; in New Spain, 55, 75.

Endicott, John, founds Salem, 141.

England, the Tudor Period, 104–105; under the early Stuarts, 112–113; the Puritan movement, 135–136; the Restoration, 179; the mercantilist system, 179; the Triple Alliance, 359; in the War of Jenkins's Ear, 361–364; in the War of the Austrian Succession, 364–366; in the Seven Years' War, 369–383; new possessions

after 1763, 403–424; controversy with American colonies, 425–555.

English colonies in North America, general history: beginning of English expansion, 1485–1603, 104–110; the Tudor period, 104–105; commercial expansion, 105–107; the Cabots, 105; Newfoundland fisheries, 106; Muscovy and Levant companies, 106; Elizabethan sea-dogs, 107–108; search for a Northwest passage, 108–109; attempts to colonize Virginia and Guiana, 109–110; the colonies under the early Stuarts, 112–113; colonial administration, 113; the founding of Virginia, 114–125; the founding of Maryland, 125–129; the Bermudas, 129; Guiana, 130; the Lesser Antilles, 132; Providence Island Company, 133; the beginnings of New England, 135–150; the Puritan movement, 135–136; Plymouth colony, 136–141; attempts on New England coast, 141–142; Massachusetts Bay Colony, 142–146; Rhode Island and Connecticut, 146–151; the English colonies during the revolutionary period, 152–163; the old colonies under the later Stuarts, 179–195; colonial policy and administration, 179–181; machinery of government, 181–183; expansion under the later Stuarts, 196–214; New York, 196–198; the Jerseys, 198–202; Pennsylvania, 202–206; expansion in the islands, 206–207; the Carolinas, 207–211; Western trade and exploration, 211; Hudson's Bay Company, 212–214; English Mainland colonies at end of 17th century described—society, industry, education, religion, population, 216–232; the struggle with the French for the fur country, 257–261; the War of the English Succession, 261–267; the War of the Spanish Succession, 267–273; the English in the Piedmont, 309–328; the Westward Movement, 309–311; defense of the northern frontier, 311–312; reorganization of the Carolinas, 312–315; Georgia, the buffer colony, 315–316;

409; conspiracy of Pontiac, 409–410; the Loftus expedition, 410; establishment of English government, 410; Quebec Act, 411; character of population, 420; conquered by G. R. Clark, 514.

Imago Mundi, possible influence on Columbus, 2, 7.

Immigration and population, Spanish colonies, 21, 75; Sinaloa and Sonora, 240, 305–306; Chihuahua, 289; New Mexico, 73, 243, 244, 290; California, 391–393; French Canada, 93, 94; Quebec, 419; Loyalists in Canada, 421, 538; French West Indies, 93, 94; Louisiana, 279, 395–396; the Illinois country, 281; Bermudas, 130; Lesser Antilles, 133, 340, 341; Barbados, 216, 340, 341; English mainland colonies, about 1700, 216; Virginia, 121, 227; Maryland, 127, 128, 227; New England, 138, 143, 216, 217; New Jersey, 200–201, 221; New York, 221; Pennsylvania and Delaware, 206, 224; the Carolinas, 208, 230; West Florida, 407–408; Ohio Valley, 413–419; German and Swiss migration, 316–322; Scotch, Irish, 322–326; English colonies in middle 18th century, 329–330; on the eve of the Revolution, 425–426; dispersion of the Loyalists, 538; New Netherlands, 167; New Sweden, 175.

Indé, Mexico, mines of, 56.

Indented servants, 122, 229, 336, 409.

Independents, 135, 137. *See* Pilgrims.

India, visited by the Polos, 3; travelers' tales regarding, 3; discovery of new route to, 5; Portuguese empire in, 24; British administration of, 34; during the French and Indian War. *See* French and Indian War; Events of the War in India.

Indian Ocean, Ptolemy's conception of, 1.

Indiana Company, 418.

Indians, in Spanish colonies, so-named by Columbus, 10; Spanish policy in West Indies, 22–23; rebellion in 1495, 22; slavery 23, 31, 37, 56, 60–61, 72, 75; Maya and Nahua

civilization, 26–28; native caciques used in conquest, 39; Mixton War, 40; Pueblo civilization in New Mexico, 46; *New Laws* concerning, 50, 53; native alcaldes, 55; Tlascaltecans as colonists, 59–60; decline in West Indies, 67; rebellion at Acoma, 73; schools for, 76; missions as frontier defense, 236; Yaqui wars, 239; Pueblo revolt in New Mexico, 245; wars on North Mexican frontier, 245–246, 248; in Eastern Texas, 251; Apalachee revolt, 254; Yamassee revolt, 255; Moqui and Zuñi resistance, 290; Navajo, Yuta, and Comanche depredations in New Mexico, 290–291; captives sold as slaves, 291; the Jumanos, 243, 244, 285, 291; destroy Villazur's party, 296; Apache wars in Texas, 298–299; the Tonkawa missions, 299; Pima revolt in Arizona, 305; Yuma massacre, 393–394; Spanish policy in Louisiana, 400–401; war on Apaches, 401; hostilities in New Netherlands, 171–172; in French colonies; Huron and Iroquois wars, 88, 91, 258–259, 265; Anglo-French rivalry for northern tribes, 257–259; Abenaki wars, 262–265; Frontenac's policy, 263; competition for southern Indians, 269; 270, 276; Natchez war on French, 278, 280; the Chickasaw War, 281; French among Western tribes (Asinais, Orcoquisas, Cadodachos, Bidayes, Touacaras, Wichitas, Osages, Missouris, Pawnees, Otos, Iowas, Kansas, Mandans), 282–284; Winnebagoes, 296; Apache-Comanche barrier to French advance, 285, 286; Fox Wars, 287; Sioux posts, 287; Vérendrye among Mantannes, Cheyennes, Crows, Little Foxes, Bows, 288; in English colonies: early attacks in Virginia, 117–119, 122; relations with Pilgrims, 138–139; land title theory of Roger Williams, 147; Williams and the Narragansetts, 147; Pequot War, 159–160; English missionary work among, 156; Opechancanough's War, 185; the Susquehanna War, 185–186; King

248. *See* New Mexico, Nuevo León, Coahuila, Texas.

Rivas, explorer of Gulf of Mexico, 249.

Rivera y Moncada, with Portolá in California, 389.

Rivera, Juan María, explores in Colorado, 291–292.

Rivera, Pedro de, inspects frontier of New Spain, 297, 298, 304.

Rich, Sir Nathaniel, interest in the Caribbean, 133.

Rich, Robert, Lord Warwick, interest in colonization, 133; land grants in New England, 140, 149; assists Reverend John White, 141.

Rising, John, governor of New Sweden, 177.

Roanoke, lost colony of, 110.

Roanoke Island, 66, 251.

Robertson, James, pioneer in Tennessee, 415, 416, 419; defense of Watauga, 513.

Roberval, French colonizer, 82; commissioned viceroy and lieutenant-general of Canada, 82.

Robinson, Rev. John, at Scrooby, 137.

Rochambeau, Comte de, 511.

Rockingham Ministry, 437–438.

Rocky Mountains, 282.

Rodney, Admiral, in the West Indies, 382, 511, 530–531; defeats de Grasse, 532.

Rodrigo del Río de Losa, expedition to open mines of Nueva Vizcaya, 56; cattle ranches of, 58.

Rodríguez, Fray Agustín, expedition to New Mexico, 72.

Roe, Sir Thomas, expedition to Guiana, 132.

Rolfe, John, 121.

Rosicrucians, 318.

Roxbury settled, 142.

Royal council, Spanish, 14; divided into three councils, justice, state, and finance, 14.

Rowley, William, English vice-admiral, 365.

Rubí, Marqués de, inspects outposts of New Spain, 385–386.

Ruí, Captain Francisco, in Missouri, 397.

Rubruquis, William de, sent to court of Great Khan, 3.

Rump Parliament, 152.

Rupert, Prince, interest in Hudson's Bay Company, 213.

Russia, 3, 375, 382, 384; expansion across Siberia, 388; expeditions of Bering on Pacific, 388; fur traders on Aleutian Islands, 388; rumors of activities of, 394.

Rutherford, Gen. Griffith, 512–513.

Rutledge, Edward, member of the First Continental Congress, 452; defense of Charleston, 471; on committee to draw up Articles of Confederation, 550.

Rutledge, John, member of the Stamp Act Congress, 436; member of the First Continental Congress, 452.

Saavedra, Alvaro de, expedition across the Pacific, 42, 46.

Saavedra, Hernando, in Honduras, 38.

Saba Island, settled by Dutch, 167; captured by English, 206, 531.

Sable Island, 81, 85.

Saco Bay, settlement, 140.

Sagres, on Cape St. Vincent, 4.

St. Augustine, Florida, founding, 62; Franciscan monastery at, 65; siege of, in War of the Spanish Succession, 269–270; attacks on, in War of Jenkins' Ear, 362, 364; under English rule, 403, 408, 409.

St. Bartholomew's, massacre of, 79.

St. Christopher Island, settled by French, 93, 94, 252; by English, 132, 133, 252; in the Leeward Isles government, 206; in wars, 261, 268; social conditions, 340; captured by De Grasse, 532; restored to Great Britain, 537.

St. Clair, Gen. Arthur, in Burgoyne campaign, 494–495.

St. Croix Island, French settlement of, 85.

St. Denis, Louis Juchereau de, founds Natchitoches, 278; expeditions to Mexico, 278, 282–283, 293; imprisonment, 283, 295; raises French expedition, 297.

St. Eustatius Island, settled by the

CPSIA information can be obtained
at www.ICGtesting.com
Printed in the USA
BVHW070206201219
567205BV00002B/313/P

9 789353 709396